D1807997

JOSÉ LUIS SERT

1901 1983

josep m. rovira

Electaarchitecture

Translation
Leonora Saavedra

Cover
Tassinari/Vetta

Graphics coordinator
Dario Tagliabue

Layout
Lucia Vigo

Coordinating editor
Giovanna Crespi

Editor
Gabriella Cursoli

Technical coordinators
Paolo Verri
Mario Farè

Abbreviations
AJFM: the Jaume Freixa Archives of the Joan Miró Foundation.

PLWC: The Paul Lester Wiener Collection, BX 55. Division of Special Collections and University Archives, University of Oregon Library System, Eugene, Oregon.

SGA: Sigfried Giedion Archives, ETH, Zurich.

FLC: Fondation Le Corbusier, Paris.

SC: Sert Collection, Cambridge, Massachussetts.

This book owes its existence to the involvement of Francesco Dal Co, who entrusted me with its writing. Without his unfailing support and constant encouragement, it would have been impossible to undertake the task.
Juanjo Lahuerta and Antonio Pizza periodically subjected the text to a rigorous analysis of great critical acumen.
Julio Garnica took care of the bibliography, and Marga Bescós, Albert Fuster and Andrés Gonzalez established unified criteria to redesign the projects that give consistency to the text. Adelina Casanovas and Daniel Rovira were responsible for the iconographic research.
I am deeply grateful for the collaboration and involvement of all the library curators and archivists who enormously facilitated my work by generously allowing me to consult material and by offering their suggestions: Jaume Freixa, one of Sert's collaborators, who has looked after the valuable documents of the Fundació Miró in Barcelona; David Ferrer, Andreu Carrascal and Marta Fernández de la Reguera of the historical archives of the Col.legi d'Arquitectes de Catalunya; Thérèse Schweizen, Bruno Mauer and Daniel Weis of the Sigfried Giedion Archives of the E.T.H. of Zurich; Evelyne Tréhine of the Fondation Le Corbusier; Mary Daniels, curator of the Sert Collection of Cambridge, Massachussetts; and Vicky Jones, curator of the Paul Lester Wiener Collection of Eugene, Oregon.
The research was partly financed with funds from the Ministerio de Educación y Ciencia, which granted me a scholarship to develop a research project within the Programa Sectorial de Promoción del Conocimiento.
The book is dedicated to two very important people in my life: Manfredo Tafuri, from whom I have learned much, and Mercé Navarro, she knows why.

Distributed by Phaidon Press
ISBN 1-904313-21-3

www.phaidon.com

© 2000 by Electa, Milano
Elemond Editori Associati
All Rights Reserved

www.electaweb.it

First published in English 2003
© 2003 by Electa Architecture
Mondadori Electa spa, Milano
All Rights Reserved

Printed in China

Contents

WALTER GROPIUS
ARCHITECT F.A.I.A.
FOURTY-SIX BRATTLE STREET
CAMBRIDGE, MASSACHUSETTS

May 1969

To José Luis Sert.

Dear Sert:

I salute you as my friend of fourty years.

As the far-sighted organizer of CIAM who was able to keep the
zealous celebrities of its membership in line for fruitful pioneer work.

As a cultural leader of broad international scope, befriended
by the best architects, painters and sculptors, a champion
of collaboration between the arts.

As an avant-gardist demanding and teaching the integration
of our whole environment.

As a great architect.

Prototypes of your own creative work grace Europe, the Middle East
and South America, and you have greatly enriched the skyline along
the Charles River for Harvard- and Boston University.

You have united the Mediterranean spirit with the New World,
giving the age-old patio idea of the dwelling a new meaning.

In all your activities you have kept a truly human concern
predominant.

I am looking forward to your future creation with high expectations.

Yours,

Walter Gropius

1. In the functional city

Barcelona, from 1901 to 1930

In register 209, number 6458 of the Barcelona Registry Office, it is stated that José Luís Sert López was born on 138 Carrer Bruc at 11.00 pm on 1 July 1901, son of Francisco Sert Badía, Count of Sert, and of Genara López Díaz de Quijano.[1] He was the second son of the couple, who had married on 25 April 1893 in the parish of Saint Peter, Barcelona.

From the files of the Superior School of Architecture of Barcelona we know that Sert obtained his high school degree on 29 November 1919, and that he concluded his architectural studies on 10 August 1929 with an unremarkable college report consisting mainly of 'average' grades, with the exception of a 'very good' in the History of the Visual Arts, another in Construction during his first year, and an 'excellent' in Urban Layout.

The above information draws our attention to three aspects: the high social class from which Sert came, his first contacts with architecture, due both to the years spent studying in the School and to his own interests, and the circumstances of the period in which he went from being a student to becoming a professional architect.

Francisco Sert had received his title of Count in 1903 after executing a tapestry bearing the image of the King and Queen, which the Royal House had commissioned from Comercial Sert,[2] his family-owned factory. Based in Taradell, a small town in the district of the Plana de Vic within the province of Barcelona, it manufactured rugs and tapestries. The penchant of Catalan industrial manufacturers for noble titles, and the Crown's largesse in handing them out, are well known: between 1872 and 1932 the ranks of the nobility were swelled by 548 additional titles.

Genara López was the niece of Antonio López, Marquis of Comillas, the head of a considerable economic empire,[3] which en-

Apartment building on Carrer Muntaner, Barcelona, 1929.

Genara López Díaz de Quijano.

Francisco, José Luis and Antonio Sert.

Ramón Casas,
oil painting
of José Luis Sert.

joyed great social standing in Barcelona. In 1905, the Sert family moved to the Avenida del Doctor Andreu in the upper-class part of the city, into a detached family house of great dimensions and dubious style designed and built by the architect José María Sagnier.[4] José Luís was to spend most of his childhood there, educated by private tutors and English nannies, this being the language most often spoken under that roof.

Once high school had ended and Sert had passed the endless exams in mathematics, ornamentation, line and figure drawing that were compulsory for all aspiring architects of that era, in 1922 he began his further architectural studies. These came to an end, though without the achievement of any remarkable grades, in 1929. On 29 July Sert presented his end-of-course project and on 10 August received his Bachelor's Degree in Architecture. However, it

is important to note that in the academic year of 1927–28 he had only one course left to do in order to finish his studies. So what occupied him during the following year, from September 1928 to June 1929? The importance of this question will be revealed in due course.

Sert's mediocre grades attest to his lack of interest in the education he was receiving at the School of Architecture, which at the time of his student days was directed by the architect Francisco de Paula Nebot.[5] Nebot was a representative of the official *Noucentista* architecture, which in those years was celebrating both its greatest urban conquest and its swan song with the inauguration of the International Exhibition on 19 May 1929.[6] However, it was not the director as such who constituted a problem, but rather the common denominator that existed between his thoughts and ideas on architecture and those of the professors working under him. In effect, Professors Bona, Florensa, Domènech Roura and Azúa, all of whom may have taught Sert, represented variations on the same theme. This was a classicism that formed the ideological framework for the programmes, urban strategies and technological advances necessary for solving the problems faced by the industrial metropolis in modern times for its urban masses. In a later chapter of this book we will investigate how classicism as an ideology came into being.

However, it was not only this type of classicism that was present at the School. Other antiquated multi-style schools of thought were accommodated, and they were akin to an even more outdated modernism, incarnated by the dynasty of the Bassegodas or by characters such as Monguió, Darder or Monraba. In that Babel where Viollet and Owen Jones were quoted alongside Palladio and Bramante, and where Brunelleschi was valued as highly as Bernini, where Greece, Rome and the Renaissance were placed together under the general heading of classicism, it was on the one hand impossible to conceive a new architecture, and on the other a difficult feat to escape the excessive historicism that pervaded the classes.

Thus it is not surprising that one of Sert's first known architectural drawings, his contribution to a scale plan for which he drew the

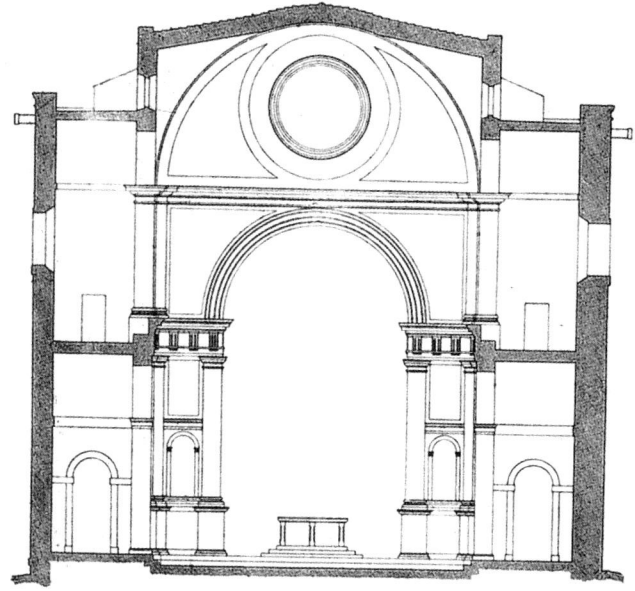

Transversal section of the Church of Sant Andreu de la Selva del Camp.

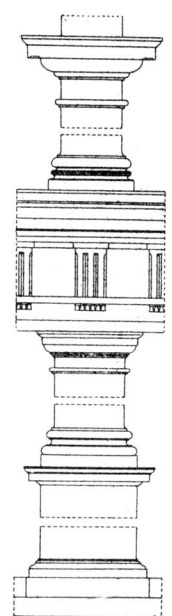

Church of Sant Andreu de la Selva del Camp, Doric order.

front elevations, was for the Church of San Andrés de la Selva de Camp by the architect Pere Blay, which Sert visited on a trip with his fellow students in 1927.[7]

However, an architecture conceived simply on the basis of style must have seemed, to the eyes of a student concerned with other matters, totally lacking in interest. It had become clear to Sert halfway through his studies that learning was a process that did not occur in classrooms. To put it even more bluntly, in class one learned on a daily basis what *not* to do. This was especially true for Sert, who was interested in issues concerning the avant-garde architecture taking place in Europe at the time. The echoes of this were reaching Barcelona through the chronicles sent by Rafael Benet from Paris in 1925, regarding his visit to the 'Exposition Internationale des Arts Décoratifs et Industriels Modernes', which were published in the pages of the local newspaper *La Veu de Catalunya*.[8]

In these articles, Benet described the artistic movements, works of art, objects and pavilions on show in the exhibition, choosing to remark on those that had dispensed with an excess of historicist ornamentation: 'Cubism has found its application: in decoration it is already an official art, well accepted by everyone. The exhibition is a triumph of Cubism as an applied art.'[9] In his chronicle of 2 August, Benet spoke of the pavilion of L'Esprit Nouveau in the following terms: 'The work of the

architects Le Corbuçier [*sic*] and Pierre Jeanneret; a type of housing of exclusively industrial construction, systematically employing "standard" elements. Another object of this pavilion is the study of these principles of "standardization" in their urban and inter-urban generalization. Everything about L'Esprit Nouveau is food for thought. It is not surprising that this pavilion of the Cours-la-Reine passed unperceived in the first few days because it is hidden away in the space left between two naves of the Grand Palais.'

We do not know if this was the first time the young Sert had heard of the man who was to become the most influential of his mentors and one of his best friends,[10] but if his memory is correct,[11] after travelling to Paris in 1926, he had already bought and was reading (along with other colleagues who championed the cause of new architecture), three books by Le Corbusier: *Vers une Architecture*, *Urbanisme*, and probably *Almanach d'architecture moderne* or *L'art décoratif d'aujourd'hui*. The gateway to the modern was thus opened up for Sert by this first contact with Le Corbusier's books. Nor do we know the tenor of the conversations between Sert and his friends, or whether they completely understood what they were reading and looking at in these books, but perhaps at the time what they most longed for was a breath of fresh air that was neither present in the classrooms nor in the city streets,[12] although it could occasionally be spotted in a

Le Corbusier and A. Ozenfant, Pavilion of L'Esprit Nouveau, Paris, 1925.

Cover of the *Almanach d'Architecture Moderne*, Paris, 1925.

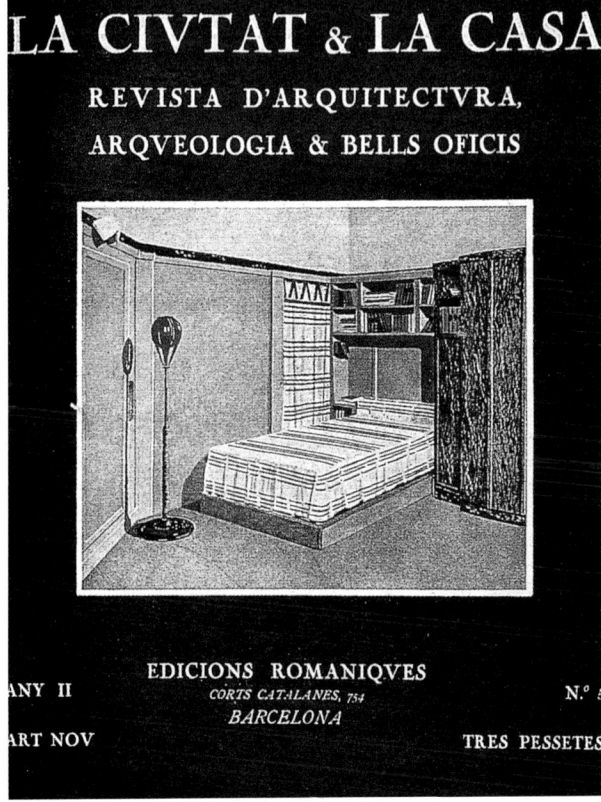

Cover of *La Ciutat i La Casa*, no. 5.

few chronicles in the daily press or in specialist publications.

We again find a reference to Le Corbusier's work in the sixth issue of the magazine edited by Benet, *La Ciutat i la Casa*, which came out in 1926, the same year in which Sert believed he travelled to Paris (leading us to speculate as to whether this trip took place after he had read the publication). The text was accompanied by pictures taken from *Vers une architecture*, particularly those showing the houses of Auteuil and the interior of the Ozenfant studio. It is also interesting to note that the content of the text had taken on a sermonizing tone: 'We have the obligation of bringing into our work the content of modernity. I'm not interested in reproducing the Greeks or the Middle Ages, because that is impossible. I'm interested in applying to our time and our land all the eternal lessons present in history … Let us try, then, to face the New Spirit.'[13] Thus, in 1926, the need for transplanting as far as possible what was modern in Paris to Barcelona was already seen as an obligation by those who wished to propose a different architecture from what could be observed in the city streets.

It is not enough to simply speak of images or sermons, however. Benet was keen to present Le Corbusier and his written work as a site to visit, which would allow access to this necessary change. The journalist presented a clear summary of modern architecture – rejection of ornaments and historicism, standardization, proportions, American grain elevators, pure forms, transatlantics, aeroplanes, steamships, etc. – to the public of a Barcelona not yet interested in it. We can get a clear idea of the situation regarding the interest of architects when we read: 'Le Corbusier has written a series of articles collected in three volumes and which have been widely read and commented on in our circle: *Vers une Architecture*, *Urbanisme* and *L'art décoratif d'aujourd'hui*.' If this assertion is true, what Sert later maintained should perhaps be questioned: by speaking of the three books written by the Swiss architect, which were present in the private libraries of some Catalan architects of the period,[14] perhaps Benet was suggesting that it was not necessary to go to Paris to form an impression of Le Corbusier's works. In the same text, moreover, Benet mentions other architects such as Mies van der Rohe, Walter Gropius, André Lurçat, Hans Poelzig, Auguste Perret, Konstantin Melnikov and Ludwig Hilberseimer. The fact that these architects and their work crop up in the text gives us an idea of the vast scale of this movement, which was so scarcely spoken about in Barcelona and so systematically ignored in one of the places where it was most needed: in the classrooms of the School of Architecture.

Shortly afterwards, in the seventh issue of *La Ciutat i la Casa* of 1927,[15] Benet published an abridged version of a widely encompassing commentary on the exhibition of the Werkbund of Stuttgart, which had first appeared in *La Veu de Catalunya*. Here, Benet mentioned that he had found out about the exhibition thanks to two magazines, *Moderne Bauformen* and *Cahiers d'Art*, which demonstrates that these magazines were readily available in Barcelona. Benet felt no hesitation in declaring the exhibition to be 'the most important one held in the last years', where one could see family dwellings 'that incorporate the most advanced principles applied to construction both from the technical and the artistic points of view, principles that should likewise be applied with the same rigour in urban planning dealing with interiors'. We do not know from where he deduced the similarities between the urban conception – an unimportant garden city with a formal hierarchy whose suspect visual effects were little to the liking of many avant-garde architects – and the technical or artistic aspects of the buildings, but for the moment we can leave the question to rest. After listing all the architects participating in the competition, Benet pointed out the difference between the majority of these and Le Corbusier, the only one whom he considered capable of offering a 'mathematical lyricism' that set him apart from the 'excessively engineered' forms of the Dutch and Germans, the sole exception being the dwellings of Stam.

At any rate, these initial contacts with Le Corbusier's work were determining factors in Sert's approach to new architecture. It was now a matter of taking the next step: making the personal acquaintance of the architect of Le Chaux-des-Fonds, although the occasion for this did not arise immediately. Meanwhile, Sert

Le Corbusier with García Mercadal on a visit to the Escorial monastery in May 1928. (FLC, photoL1 (2) 10–6).

was on the way to finish his studies, ever more aloof from what was happening at the school, and probably with his eyes turned to any architectural novelty that could be sighted from Spain. This would explain how on 15 May 1928, when Le Corbusier was returning from a trip to Madrid,[16] he was asked by Sert to make a stopover in Barcelona. The Swiss architect recalled the moment: 'It was in 1928, when the open competition was being held for the Palace of the League of Nations of Geneva; I had been called to make a dissertation on architecture in the University of Madrid (which shortly afterwards was published as a book entitled *Une maison – Un palais*). I received a telegram in Madrid signed by José Luis Sert (whom I did not yet know) asking me to take the express train Madrid-Port Bou so I could be in the Barcelona station at 10 o'clock at night and, without losing a minute, be taken somewhere in the city to give a lecture. At the railway station in Barcelona I was met by five or six young men, all short but full of energy and fire.'[17]

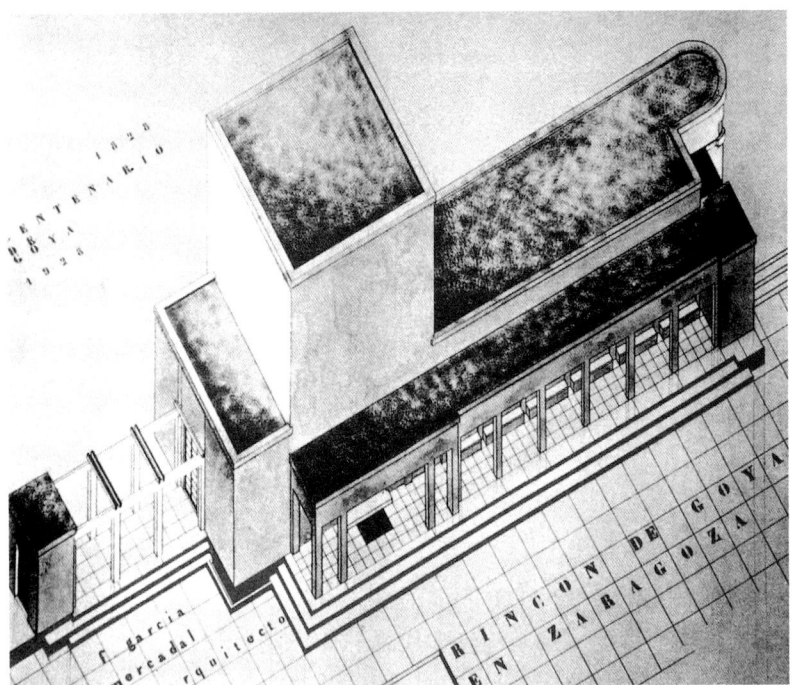

García Mercadal, museum dedicated to Goya, Zaragoza, 1926–28.

In Sert's memory, tinged with certain time lapses and imprecisions, the events were as follows: 'It was on the 27th, I believe, when Le Corbusier came as a guest speaker to the Club Fémina, if I recall the name, or a club where conferences were held, something like a lyceum club, where rich people gathered to hear conferences … At any rate, the most renowned speakers from Paris and elsewhere would come, and we were able to invite Le Corbusier.'[18]

Le Corbusier's remark about 'short stature' was perhaps partly due to the slight frame of Fernando García Mercadal,[19] who was one of the most fervent champions of new architecture, introducing it in Spain by means of the lectures he organized at the Students' Residence. Amongst the guest speakers, besides Le Corbusier, he invited architects such as Walter Gropius, Erich Mendelshon and Theo van Doesburg. He also wrote in the magazine *Arquitectura*, published in Madrid, and edited a supplement that was published in 1928 in the *Gaceta Literaria*, although he soon became tired of this activity.

The construction in Zaragoza from 1926 to 1928 of a museum dedicated to the painter Francisco Goya, and in Madrid of a petrol station in the Calle Alberto Aguilera, in 1927, by the architect Casto Fernández Shaw[20] must have seemed to Sert sure signs that new archi-

tecture, light-years ahead of what was still being taught by his professors at the School, was starting to take root in Spain. This feeling was corroborated by García Mercadal's personal acquaintance with modern European architects, which undoubtedly explains his presence at the first CIAM (International Congress of Modern Architecture), held in La Sarranz between 26 and 28 June 1928, as well as his appointment as the Spanish delegate for future congresses.[21]

Aside from being the year of Le Corbusier's visit to Madrid and Barcelona, 1928 was to be crucial in the penetration of this new architecture through other means; these should be mentioned since Sert was aware of them, even though they were somewhat removed from his immediate surroundings. In July the 'Exhibition of Basque Artists' was inaugurated in San Sebastian, 'in whose Architecture division there are projects presented by Aizpurua, Labayen, Vallejo and Zabalo, who have recently received their degrees'.[22] In September, the article 'Arquitectura racionalista' was published by the magazine *Novedades* in the Basque country, and in it they depicted works by José Manuel Aizpurua and Joaquin Labayen, a photomontage of the Weissenhof and a picture of the Bauhaus building.

In Catalonia, things were running a similar course. In the first issue of *La Gaseta de les Arts*, Benet was once again focusing on new architecture, this time embodied by the Myrurgia

Participants of the CIAM held in La Sarraz, 1928.

Antoni Puig Gairalt, Myrurgia factory, 1928.

factory building of Antoni Puig Gairalt, and by the project Hotel on a Beach, which in 1928 Sert and fellow student Josep Torres, in collaboration with Joan Baptista Subirana, exhibited in the offices of the Associació d'Arquitectes. Benet placed an eloquent subtitle beneath the announcement of the project presented by the three architects: 'Hommage to Le Corbusier', and congratulated himself on having had his sermon heard and answered: 'It has not taken me long to find out the names of the young architects who wish for renovation. We first learned of the contribution made by the architects Jaume Mestres and Lluís Girona … Later, A. Puig Gairalt … and finally the young architectural students Josep Torres and Josep Lluís Sert have sent out a clear message with their projects and model of a hotel on a beach,

José Luis Sert and Josep Torres, Hotel on a Beach, 1928.

with which they have participated in the Associació d'Arquitectes de Catalunya's open competition.'[23]

Carried out in collaboration with two of his best friends, it was Sert's first project. Even though he was still a student, it shows his desire to appropriate the new European language: horizontal windows in a pure volume, a free facade with an asymmetrical solution, a flat roof, a double-height lobby, etc., are all present in the model presented for competition.

An interesting question that is linked to Sert's circumstances at the time is, what did Le Corbusier speak about in Barcelona and what were the consequences of his speeches? Two anonymous articles published in *La Veu de Catalunya*[24] give us some clue as to their content. According to the unknown journalist, in the first conference, presented by Ramón Puig Gairalt, Le Corbusier focused on two fundamental aspects: revealing the mechanisms of access to what was new, and detailing the aesthetic parameters of this novelty; that is to say, the five famous points that the Swiss architect had laid out in 1927.[25]

The first aspect can be summarized as follows: 'Architecture … has to submit itself to three inevitable requirements. In the first place, that of science; architectural science springs from the technique of architecture itself … In the second place come the requirements of art … Thirdly, it is necessary that there be a feeling, a live creed, a conception of the world, an attitude when faced with the existence and needs of an epoch.' Among the technical requirements, Le Corbusier extolled the advantages of iron and of reinforced concrete; the requirements of art were identified as pure form and regular, simple shapes. The third requirement was left without comment, either because he did not offer more information or because the journalist simply forgot to take note of it. However, feelings, creeds, the conception of the world and an attitude towards it are ideas that can have been hardly dealt with in depth in the short time for which his speech lasted. At any rate, his intentions seem clear: to explain his own intellectual development, which we find described in the pages of *L'Esprit Nouveau*, backed up by the few construction works already carried out,

Cover of *Une maison – Un palais* by Le Corbusier, 1928.

and to reveal his aesthetic beliefs in search of followers who would share with him the same conception of architecture. Nevertheless, in the prologue to his speech he stated: 'I am not attempting … that you take my word for it; I ask that you use the same free will and the same critical spirit that I used when confronting my teachers.'

The second conference, which was announced as a 'lecture', bore the title 'Architecture and Structure', although it was in fact an elaboration of a subject that Le Corbusier had long been mulling over as a result of failing to win the Palace of the League of Nations open competition, and which bore fruits in his book *Une maison – Un palais*, published the same year. The house was no longer the radical 'machine for living in' of the early years, but had become 'a place in which to satisfy superior needs'. His mechanist radicality had lost force after its rejection in Geneva,[26] while analogies with nature recalled classical architectural theory and the imperious call for harmony and geometry that would lead to the sense of order that had been proclaimed necessary so long ago and which architecture had been forced to evoke in a victorious France. This was an order that had led Le Corbusier to prefer Renaissance to Gothic architecture, and to evoke, once again, the Parthenon as an eternal model 'where everything is pure, made up of energy, of geometrical precision.' Following this, he spent some time showing Sert and other students images of his proposal for the competition in Geneva, which the journalist defined as 'a marvel of logic, of rationality and good taste'.

The message seemed clear: new technique, new formulas. At the same time, it appeared to be possible to maintain the lyrical dimension of architecture within this proposal. However, despite a reference to the need for taking sides, to be in step with the times so as to build the necessary new architecture, not only was this image of modernity not dealt with in the first conference, but even worse, by the second it had totally disappeared, leaving the public in a state of ignorance about what it was actually about. The young Catalans had to do with a frustrated Le Corbusier who had not yet got over his failure in Geneva and who was desperately attempting to rethink some of his initial, radical approaches. As a result, they were compelled to listen to him taking up certain architectures that they detested – perhaps because they did not understand them – as models to inspire the creation of a house that could now be conceived as a palace (a type of building that the renowned speaker had scorned in previous writings),[27] with which, moreover, he intended to recover symbolic dimensions.

This was probably too much for them. Here was a modern architect gesticulating in front of the blackboard about order, palaces, the Renaissance, harmony, and meanwhile leaving aside the essentials on which he had based the discourse that had brought him fame: the analogy of the machine, which could weld time and the new architecture. The journalist of *La Veu de Catalunya* reports 'that, even though he is still so young, Le Corbusier says he already finds himself holding opinions contrary not only to those held by academists, but also by

Le Corbusier at approximately twenty years.

certain extremists, especially very young architects influenced by Russian Constructive tendencies, who consider him some kind of *pompier*!' The apparent message, therefore, was that there was no contradiction or confrontation between the new architecture and tradition. Thus, it must have seemed to the young Sert that the much-vaunted changes could take place without excessive confrontation with potential detractors, be they academic or part of the refined circle to which he belonged: it was a matter of image, where everything appeared to be different so that it could stay the same.

Apart from the opinions of the Swiss architect gathered in the pages of *La Publicitat* by Màrius Gifreda (which will be analyzed later), an article by the architect Ramón Sastre reporting in a significant manner on Le Corbusier's declarations was especially noteworthy.[28] After praising his model behaviour, Sastre went on to say: 'The brief stay of the great French architect Le Corbusier in Barcelona has been, for many of our professionals, a trumpet sounding in the dark, awakening consciences to the great responsibility of a spiritual nature inherent in this superior art, of tremendous importance to people's lives.' Sastre stressed what he saw as the excessive influence exerted by mechanistic ideas in the formulation of the latter's architecture: 'We do not believe that architecture has to be subjected to the mechanical revolution of industry. Perhaps Le Corbusier the engineer dominates Le Corbusier the architect, but that in our opinion does not merit any praise.' However, he later acknowledged the Swiss architect's capacity to understand architecture as 'an art of volumes', a topic emphasized by Le Corbusier in *L'Esprit Nouveau*,[29] claiming that it was time for these volumes to abandon every reference to a past anchored in historicist ornament, so that young architects 'may not be misled into the grave error of considering architecture to be simply a drawing skill' and 'may insist on denouncing the paltriness of imitation, which consists of hanging styles onto facades', so as to achieve 'the proclamation of structure, the sole directive of the work'. These words, understood within the context of a Barcelona that was putting the finishing touches to its International Exhibition, had a far-reaching collective dimension.

Sastre also advocated some aspects of Le Corbusier's idea of the city – judging from his examples, one gathers he had consulted the pages of *Urbanisme*. After criticizing the Barcelona in which he lived – 'Thanks to distasteful individualist ostentation and academic presumption, egged on by a housing development that is primitive and lacking in elegance, the main impression one gets from our modern city is that of something extremely grotesque' – Sastre maintained that in a modern city both circulation and free space were a priority. It therefore follows that he backed up Le Corbusier's proposal to raze Paris to the ground. To Sert – a student living in a city that hesitated to solve its gravest urban problems and yet was squandering energy and funds on the International Exhibition at Montjuïc – the fact that someone should make such a proposal, which he had read in his copy of *Urbanisme*, must have seemed like a breath of fresh air.

That others from different circles, including those opposed to his ideas, had heard of Le Corbusier's visit in Barcelona, can be gathered from Josep Farran Mayoral's article in *La Veu de Catalunya*, published on the day of his arrival. Juan José Lahuerta has fittingly analyzed this article,[30] demonstrating how the official culture, which was promoting the *Noucentista* city, nevertheless welcomed the creator of La Chaux-de-Fonds, not only without tension, but even going so far as to claim him as a fellow-believer. This was due to Le Corbusier's concealment of the most shocking elements of his thinking and his reduction of it to its most general aspects: 'Thus, Farran has no problem in writing for the conservative readers of *La Veu de Catalunya* that Le Corbusier "has been a source of very pure satisfaction for those who have for many years defended ideas similar to his". And in effect, was it not true that he had once again "extolled simple forms, the subtle art of relation and proportion, of serene and joyous structures, and of number and harmony"?' Thus, in the Barcelona of 1928, Le Corbusier was seen as a kindred spirit by everyone: both by those who wished to invest their antiquated project with some fragments of modernity, and by those who saw in official architecture a cadaver that must be buried without remorse.

The following year was an intense one, seeing many events that would speed the apprenticeship of our architect. Apart from finishing his studies, he was pursuing some other activities that should be mentioned. A main objective seems to be the consolidation of his relationship with Le Corbusier, as manifested in a

José Luis Sert in the studio at rue de Sèvres, Paris, 1929.

letter written to him in faulty French on 17 April 1929: 'Since my arrival, all my time has been taken up by the preparation of the exhibition of our little Group. In effect, we have had to set up our scale models within a very short time; this has been more complicated and difficult than I had foreseen when I left Paris. Luckily our efforts have not been in vain, and our exhibition has been a greater success than I expected, especially among young people. As you can see, your lectures last year have borne their fruit; they have been much spoken of during the exhibition. However, I must inform you that the hostility of our 'Academy' has not waned; not one professor deigned to come and visit us.'[31] He ended the letter by sending greetings to Pierre Jeanneret and 'all my comrades in the studio'.

It now becomes clear what had occupied Sert during that period of academic inactivity: learning at the worktable of Le Corbusier's studio and visiting his constructions. What we cannot pinpoint is when this activity began. Although it seems probable that Sert was already working in rue de Sèvres in the first days of 1929, the information we have at our disposal refers to a later period. Nevertheless, the Fondation Le Corbusier houses a notebook called 'Cahier Noir', in which the assistants wrote down the work they were carrying out and the dates on which they executed it. Here we find that Sert was working on a section of the sixth and seventh floors of the Draeger building on 14 June 1929. We again find him working on the facade of the same building on the 20th, and we hear no more until 7 October 1929, when he drew another section for

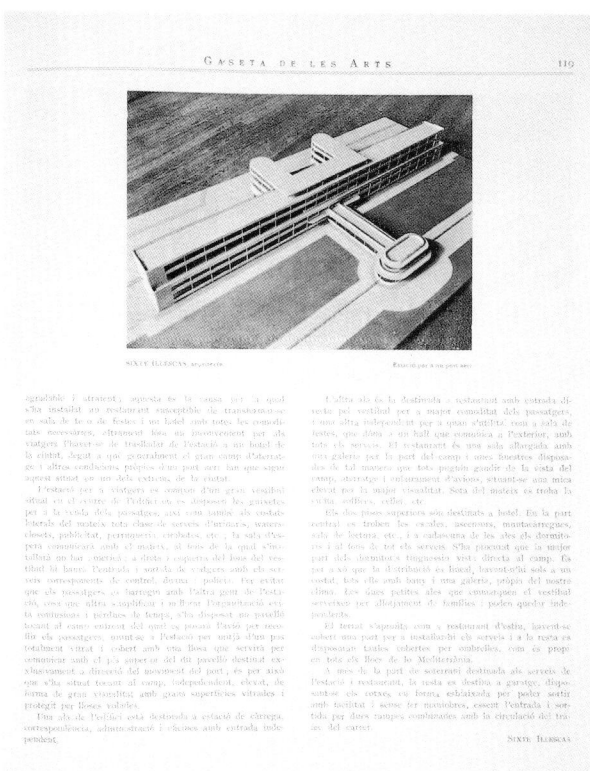

Sixte Illescas, project for an airport presented at the 'New Architecture' exhibition, 1929.

'Type MS/E'. It is possible that he spent the month of June in Paris, going back to Barcelona in July to present what was called the Convalidation Project.

As we know from the above letter, Sert organized an exhibition on which we have some information, including the small brochure and the press articles. Under the title 'New Architecture', it was held in Barcelona, in the Galeries Dalmau of 62 Passeig de Gràcia, from 13 to 27 April 1929. It presented an ensemble of plans and models far removed from the aesthetics present in the city streets. On the threshold of the International Exhibition in-

Armengou and Perales, project for a sports centre, presented at the 'New Architecture' exhibition, 1929.

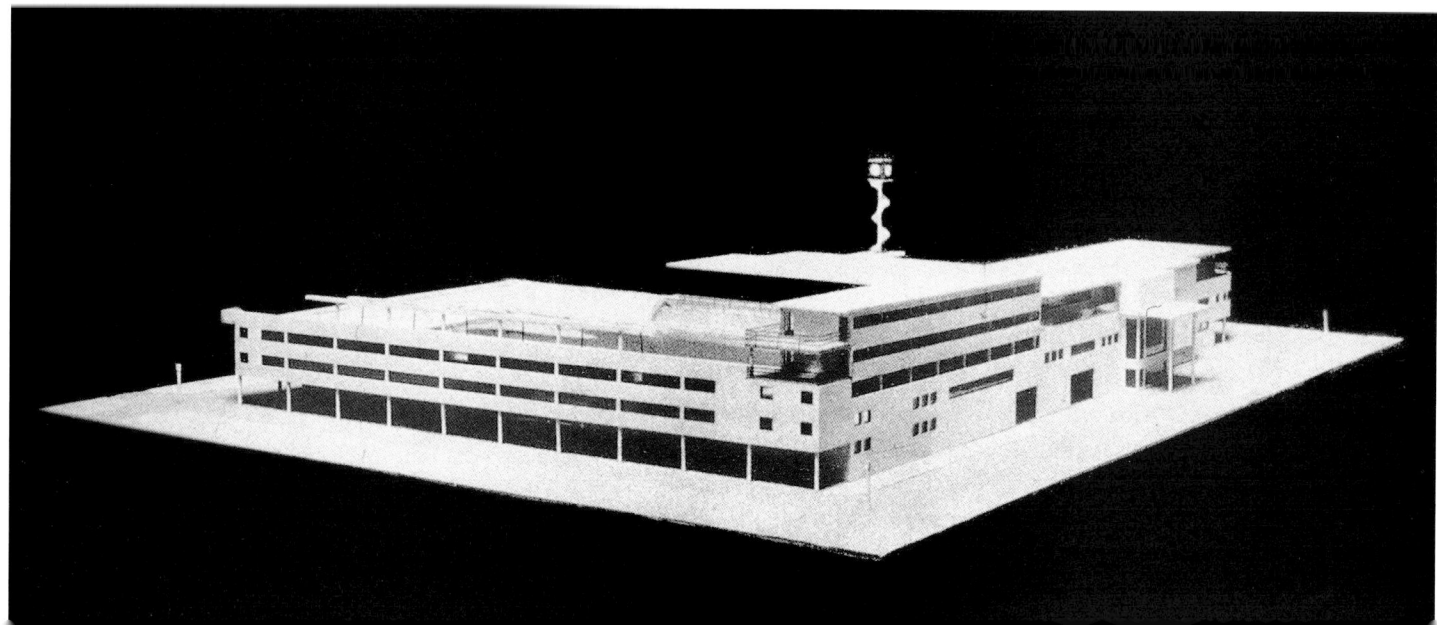

auguration, this show offered presentations of Antoni Puig Gairalt's Myrurgia Factory, a bull-ring by Churruca Fábregas and Rodríguez Arias, a clinic by Alzamora and Percourt, an indoor sports centre by Armengou and Perales, Sixte Illescas' airport, and a Summer Resort Town by Sert, Torres and Subirana. All that was shown under the unequivocal heading: 'New Architecture', in marked contrast to what would be shown shortly afterwards on Montjuïc.

The heading 'New Architecture' had long since been used to identify and proclaim a distinct, different architecture as new (and would continue to be used for some years, through a considerable historiographic process), even though the meaning of the word was not yet clear. In fact, between 1923 and 1930, many authors had used this label for elements of the architecture that was being built during the second half of the 1920s in Europe. It was a Europe that aspired to create a world possessing a 'new spirit', to quote the title of the magazine published by Le Corbusier and Ozenfant. In 1923, the Dutch architect J.J.P. Oud was already attempting to establish differences between the 'modern' and the 'new',[32] while two years later, the seventh issue of *Bauhasbücher*, edited by Walter Gropius and Lázló Moholy-Nagy, was titled: 'Neue Arbeiten der Bauhauswerkstätten'. In 1926 Rudolf Steiner published the book *Wegen zu einem neuen Baustil*, and the renowned Hannes Meyer wrote a fundamental article called 'Die Neue Welt' for the magazine *Das Werk*.[33]

In 1927, in the September issue of *Moderne Bauformen*, Ludwig Hilberseimer published another important text in which, once again, the word 'new' was chosen to focus on a specific type of architecture: *Internationale neue Baukunst*. Here we read: 'The character of the new architecture is determined by the way in which it carries out its process of design. It must not rely on its external decorativeness, but rather on a spiritual fusion of all its elements. Thus, the aesthetic element is no longer by itself the decisive end, as is the case with the facade of the architecture, which ignores the built organism, but rather it is incorporated into the ensemble like the rest of the elements … new architecture strives for balance among all of its elements … From now on, the important problems related to new architecture should not pertain to style but rather to its construction. Thus, the congruence of the external presence of this new international architecture becomes understandable.'[34] A year later, Hugo Häring published in the same magazine the article 'Neues Bauen in Deutschland', from which we can extract: 'In Germany today it is no longer necessary to defend new architecture's right to exist. After all, everybody knows that the new movement is not just a question of vogue but that it comes from something very deeply rooted … new architecture is no longer in opposition, it is on the road to becoming official.' However, when it came to explaining in formal terms what the new architecture was actually about, Häring offered vaguely: 'Nevertheless, the question remains: is this the form it should have? This is something that should be open to discussion. Its form could perhaps be another.'[35]

We are thus faced by a succession of publications, all with the adjective 'new' in their titles as if this were the only characteristic of their contents. Ernst May's magazine, published by Englert and Schlosser in Frankfurt and launched in October 1926 (and which Sert and company would copy when deciding on the format and typesetting for their *A.C.* magazine),[36] was christened *Das Neue Frankfurt*. In 1927, Curt Behrendet published *Der Sieg des Neuen Baustils*, on whose cover he reproduced a picture of the 1927 Stuttgart exhibition. Some time later, in 1930, the first three issues of a collection titled *Neues Bauen in Der Welt* came out. Joseph Ganter was in charge of the editing and El Lissitsky designed the covers of these issues entirely dedicated to the architecture being carried out in Russia, America and France.

Many more examples of this inflationary use of the word 'new' could be cited, including the response of H.R. Hitchcock, who – while in the United States in 1929 – was already expressing in the opening lines of *Modern Architecture: Romanticism and Integration* his stupor when faced with this vogue of labelling everything as new: '"New Dimensions", "New Ways of Living", "New Ways of Building", "Towards a New Architecture", "The New

Cover of *Das neue Frankfurt,* no. 1.

Cover of *A.C.,* no. 1.

Style Victorious" … A dozen books have proclaimed in the last years a new architecture.' In Barcelona, this debate took place in semi-private channels, and we also find it in *Diàlegs sobre l'arquitectura*, a book by N.M. Rubió i Tudurí, published in 1927. Through a dialogue happening in a barber's shop, he discusses the arrival of a different architecture that was called 'new' or 'modern', without being much concerned with pointing out the distinctions.

If this new art was being talked about in 1926 in Barcelona, as had earlier been the case elsewhere in Europe, it is not surprising that these young student architects chose the title they did for their exhibition. Nevertheless, what exactly were the intentions of those fiery young men when they enlisted this manner of speaking about the new forms of architecture? It is obvious that they could not attribute to themselves the role of pioneers, given the European reality of 1929 and given that their gesture in referring to 'new architecture' could not by any means be a surprise or a revelation. Nor could the 'new' be something that explodes and disappears almost simultaneously, something needed and consumed, an ephemeral condition according to the simple and conventional meaning of the term.[37] What Sert and his friends were trying to do by exhibiting these different architectures under the sign of novelty was to announce their determination to make a place for themselves, breaking into the slumbering, antiquated aesthetic consciousness of a city in search of public legitimization, offering something at the other extreme to what could be seen on Montjuïc. In this sense, 'new' can be interpreted as a profound hope to be reborn, as a promise to transform a reality that is becoming unbearable. This explains why the participants in the exhibition insisted on what was not academic, did not garnish itself with ornaments, nor had to do with the historic styles of architecture, and instead emphasized new forms, new materials and elements of construction. Naturally, we are faced with a paradox: what is new can't remain so for a long period of time, especially if one is referring to forms that have been in circulation for the last six years through books and magazines on the continent.

'New' is that which is beheld for the very first time, and this is what Sert was attempting to do – offering the passerby something different in Barcelona's showcase from what he could see on Montjuïc. Joan Sacs seems to have sensed this when he wrote a summary of the exhibition: 'As a reaction against the free-handed and dominating ornamentalism of which our architects have made use until today, we consider this present manifestation of austerity, and even of poverty and monotony, to be very positive.'[38] This was the only praise

Cover of *L'Esprit Nouveau*, no. 18.

spirit has influenced Architecture everywhere, allowing it to take full advantage of the modern technique of construction, thus creating dwellings that satisfy present needs.' Thus 'new' has suddenly become a synonym for technological advances, while dwellings and 'present needs' are thrust to the fore without prior discussion of what is meant by these terms. Technique and social needs seem to go hand in hand in this professed new architecture. We have gone very rapidly from form (previously referred to as 'style') being the only component of architecture, to other considerations.

Let us proceed, however. This new architecture 'is universal, as is the car, as is the present-day individual', and therefore answers to standard needs. It should therefore be built as a car is built, because it is aimed at the modern man who has the same needs the world over. The declarations made in Le Corbusier's articles in *L'Esprit Nouveau* were still revealing themselves as the foundation stones for the young Catalan architects' manifesto. But even if all men have the same needs in every part of the world, one cannot maintain that the geographical conditions are universal, and Sert realized that even though an elongated window facilitated the viewing of what was outside it, the intensity of light in his country made certain measures of protection necessary such as balconies or shutters on windows.[40]

they received amidst a barrage of criticism that included pointing out an excessive dependence on Le Corbusier and showing a mistrust of the false display of reinforced concrete. Sert and his friends had nevertheless started to practice the strategies used by the avant-garde in broadcasting their message: an exhibition in a gallery located in one of the most central streets of the city, as well as the publication of a manifesto within an illustrated catalogue.[39] The interest shown by the press helped to establish bridges of communication between what the avant-garde produced and what wider sectors of the public were to receive.

The heading of the catalogue is unequivocal, directly referring us to its source: 'A grand epoch is inaugurated. A new spirit exists. Programme of *L'Esprit Nouveau*, no. 1, October 1920.' Thus the 'new' was presented as a legacy that had come out into the open in Barcelona almost nine years after its original appearance elsewhere. Despite this fact, its authors still insisted that it *was* new and that its novelty had changed architecture: 'This new

Barcelona World's Fair, 1929.

It seems clear that the new architecture was presented from the viewpoint of universal technical conditions, which would solve universal problems when adapted to the conditions of each place. In the project for a Summer Resort Town in the Levante by Sert, Torres and Subirana, far too many proposals were applied. We can, however, observe some areas with protecting cantilevers over the horizontal windows, a fact that suggests the advantages of using reinforced concrete since it allowed the construction of a freestanding facade. In this proposal we can also see a compositional system typical of the mechanisms inherited from the Beaux Art composition that Le Corbusier had been employing for some time, most obviously in the Laroche House, in one of the first drawings of the Stein House, and in the project for the Palace of the League of Nations. Moreover, one can perceive a composition based on two orthogonal axes, at the end of which are located the representative buildings of the project: the hotels, spas and casinos. From a front and side view, the spectator can follow two itineraries, both going along the socle formed by the semi-detached buildings (which are separated from each other by a large empty space topped by a spectacular gable-end) and which have elongated windows as well as a porch on the ground floor. The construction reflected new social needs or

Sert, Torres and Subirana, project for A Summer Resort Town in Levante, 1929.

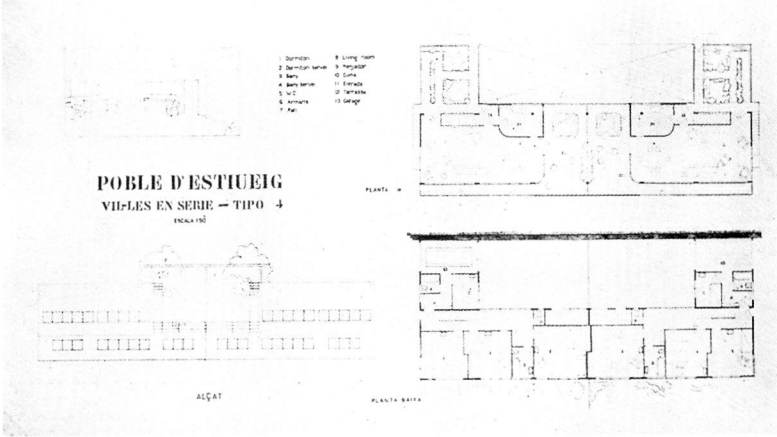

Sert, Torres and Subirana, project for A Summer Resort Town in Levante, 1929.

desires, such as the possibility of contact with nature, or spending weekends relaxing at the seaside. In Barcelona the city beaches were polluted at the time, and this resulted in people having to go further afield, causing traffic jams on the roads and overcrowding on passenger trains heading for the coast.

But the plans devised by Sert and Torres did not offer a solution to this problem. What they suggest above all is a design geared to the needs of the bourgeois classes, similar to what was already being carried out in some summer vacation spots near Sitges (whose general outline underlay the basis of Sert's proposal). What had not been taken into consideration was the logical and massive target constituted by the working classes, the group most directly affected by exhausting work in the factories and most in need of a peaceful place to relax at the weekend, instead of a summer resort to which this group in all likelihood would not have access. Between 1928 and 1929, due to both their social upbringing and their need for withdrawal from an oppressive cultural milieu, Sert and Torres were too busy learning a new language to bother understanding its relationship with possible new users.

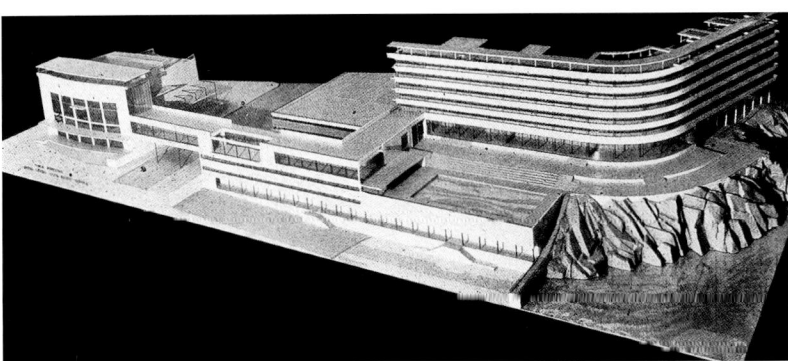

One of the last points of the manifesto helps to confirm this: 'In this new architecture, new problems necessarily give way to new rational forms created by a healthy frame of mind that is capable of giving up academic and stylistic prejudices.' They were blurting out too many words and too jumbled a set of concepts to be able to confront the common enemy, the Academy, which for many years had been taking over all the official posts in Catalonia. Thus, for the time being, the issue willingly remained within the boundaries of the academic discussion.

Sert was frantically active in these months. He went back to Paris, then returned again to Barcelona, where he finished his studies, and then in July 1929 was back in the French capital. Here, he took on the first real commission of his life, drawing up a project for the tenement house that his mother commissioned him to build on Carrer Rosselló, Barcelona. A variation of the same project, but with no relevant modifications, also appeared in December of the same year.[41]

Sert returned to Paris in October while the paperwork to obtain the licence for construction was under way, and continued working in the rue de Sèvres studio. Significantly, from the 24th to the 27th of this month, the second CIAM meeting was held in Frankfurt, and Le Corbusier did not attend because he was not in Europe.[42] Sert declared in several interviews that he had attended this meeting, although we have no documentary proof of this; we certainly know that he did not participate in the panels presented there.[43] The speech prepared by Le Corbusier was read by his cousin Pierre Jenneret. The Congress was run by the European architects who represented the *Neue Sachlichkeit*, and it became evident that what was at stake at the time was the need for studying, debating and offering solutions to the problem of mass housing.

In December of that year, Sert finished the plans for an apartment building in Carrer Muntaner, also commissioned by his mother, and these were submitted for licence to the City Hall of Barcelona on 16 December. 1929 had been an intense year in Sert's trajectory, as it had been for Spain as a whole, which was preparing for imminent political changes that

Cover of the official publication of the CIAM held in Frankfurt, 1929.

would bear a decisive influence on the events of that period.[44] On 11 December, as a consequence of the failure of Primo de Rivera's dictatorship 'to suppress the manifestations of the renewed activity of political parties, which openly call on their followers to achieve the immediate reactivation of political life',[45] a newspaper published the Esquerra Republicana's declarations, stating that the time had arrived for left-wing forces to abandon their passive attitude, grouping themselves together to create a new party. At the beginning of January 1930, several 'points of agreement' were postulated and approved by the federalists of Barcelona and by Acció Republicana Catalana, and these were published by *La Nau* on 14 December. These points specified the conditions of change from a political, social and moral point of view.[46] Special emphasis was placed on individual and collective freedom; a Republic as the chosen governmental system; the transformation of property and labour rights based on justice, human dignity and equality; liberal lay education; the separation of Church and State, and the acknowledgement of a Catalan identity.

This amounted to no more than a declara-

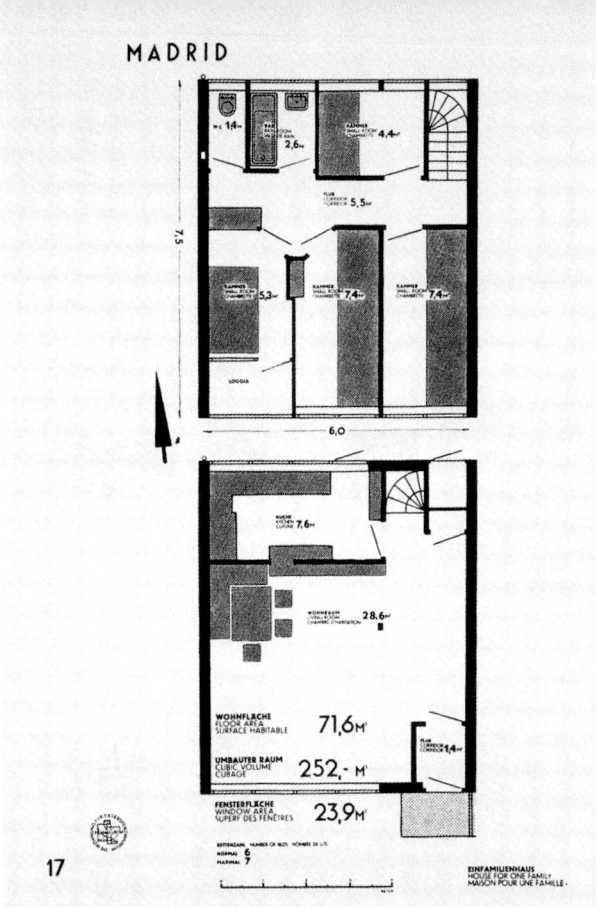

MADRID

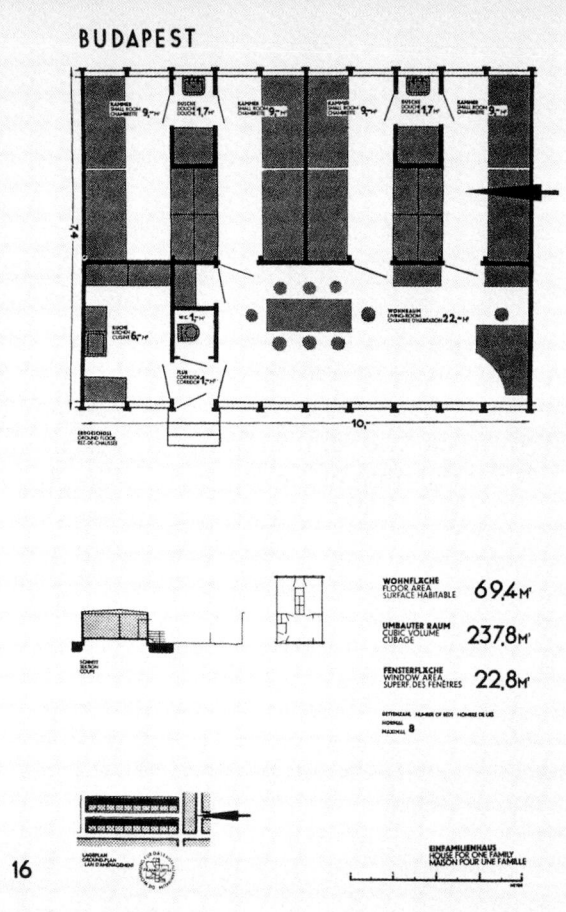

BUDAPEST

CIAM 2,
Frankfurt,
minimal housing.

CIAM 2,
Frankfurt,
exhibition hall.

tion of good intentions, but it was nevertheless symptomatic of the fact that things were about to change: on 26 January 1930 the dictator resigned after meeting with his generals. Five days later, General Dámaso Berenguer, member of the King's Military Board, was delegated 'to resolve the insoluble problem of achieving a return to the institutional regime'. The programme developed to carry out this objective initially involved granting an ample amnesty and the dissolution of the City Coun-

cil and Commissions. It also entailed a cessation of censorship and a reinstitution of the right of assembly, all of which facilitated the reorganization of political parties. While Berenguer's project was almost impossible to put into practice, that of the Republican parties (which were slowly starting to establish themselves) was clear: they meant to substitute the monarchic regime with a Republican democracy.

At the beginning of the 1930s it became necessary to create a left-wing Catalan party, open to the problems of its time, Socialist or working-class, capable of reaching agreement with a Spanish left-wing that would respect the political and geographical framework of Catalonia. In March, the *Manifest de l'Intel-ligència Republicana*, written by Rafael Campalans i Puig, and espoused by anarcho-syndicalists, was signed. Thus, in Catalonia the possibilities of a new organization necessarily implied thinking along the lines of a Republican political system, either federalist or autonomous, which would have its own Statutes, as was announced on 26 June by the General Assembly of Acció Catalana. The project of these Statutes, in which Catalonia's individuality was acknowledged, was specified through a written programme in San Sebastian on 17 August.[47]

By mid-October 1930, in an atmosphere of unruliness and strikes, Alcalá Zamora y Maura headed a Provisional Government calling for insurrection, a proclamation that sprang up in Jaca and that ended in December as a dismal failure: the ringleaders were shot down, and the rest imprisoned.

We know that Sert was again working in Le Corbusier's studio until February 1930, but we do not know for how long he remained in rue de Sèvres. Once he had finished his first two apartment-building projects in Barcelona, and while awaiting the licences for construction to be granted, he continued with his training. These licenses took a long time to arrive: the one corresponding to the Carrer Muntaner building, for example, was still held back on 7 June by the Comisión de Ornato of the City Hall, and Sert did not obtain approval until 28 August, so that the final permit only came into force during the last months of 1930.[48]

Sert wished to complete his training, and as we shall see, received a crucial impulse to do so at the end of 1930. By 24 April, however, there are already signs that he had reached a certain theoretical maturity in his contribution to the questionnaire 'What do you think of modern architecture?', which was published in the 65th issue of *Mirador* magazine, edited by Màrius Gifreda, and to which many Catalan architects had already responded. 'It is the only one that can fully satisfy the (spiritual and material) needs of an individual today', said Sert, 'by making use of constructive elements generally employed in many countries in Europe and America ... Doing away with the loadbearing wall considerably lightens the construction ... The horizontal window fulfils better than any other its double function of lighting and vision ... The results of this new technique are new forms of an airiness that it was impossible to attain until today.' The new technique of construction, he continued, possessed unequivocal characteristics: it helped to develop the individual's capacities, and introduced new aesthetics in keeping with the machine age. Moreover, it had roots in a visual tradition that Sert cites as the airy architectures represented in the frescoes of Pompeii or in Giotto's paintings. Sert compared the simplicity of these to the pretentious cladding with artificial stone that abounded in so many buildings all over the world, hiding and bearing no relation to the architectural skeleton. For Sert, modern architecture had the obligation of recovering this identity through form and structure.

From a parallel point of view, we should take into account the discredit suffered by the avant-garde (which surfaced during that period of unrest) as it reduced its declarations to purely aesthetic manifestos, even transforming its notion of what an intellectual should be and the ideal function of his work. In response to the end of the dictatorship and the new possibility of change, it seemed necessary to move away from the ivory tower of the avant-garde to face the need for commitment.

Manuel Azaña's statement in the manifesto *The Spain of the Future* of December 1930 may enlighten us on the issue. He encouraged all social classes, in a union of cultural and work forces, to join together and contribute to the urgent renovation of Spain after the dictatorship. 'We are sure that, to join their forces with ours, they will open the doors of workshops, factories, offices, universities', he declared.[49] This call took root in the university, where the majority of students had been defending the need for refreshing ideas of change since 1929, back in Sert's student days.

On 23 March 1930, two trains from Madrid carrying fifty Castilian intellectuals of heterogeneous ideals, who had been invited to Barcelona, arrived in the city. A reception for them was held in the Ateneu and there was a celebration in their honour at the Montjuïc Palace and at the Ritz Hotel. Gregorio Marañón's speech spelt out the necessary role of intellectuals in the formation of a new political reality far removed from the dictatorship: 'With our effort and with that of the investigation carried out by the scientists among us, with the work of artists, with the social activity of politicians, with the constant work of writers and professors, we all, united under the same civic faith, desire a unique and diverse Spain, federated and modern.'[50] José Ortega y Gasset also made his views clear when he an-

José Ortega y Gasset.

(even though it had come somewhat late) in discrediting the monarchy for its inability to pull itself out of the mire of the 'Berenguer mistake'. The article, after criticizing the dictatorial regime of Primo de Rivera for functioning 'without law or responsibility, without norms either established or even known', and acknowledging a slight improvement under Berenguer's mandate, stated: 'The monarchy has done nothing more than speculate on Spanish vices, and its policy has been to take advantage of them exclusively for its own benefit.' According to Ortega, the regime had simply attempted once again 'to get by', which was a mistake that led Ortega to conclude: 'And since it is undoubtedly an error, it is up to us, and not to the regime itself; we, the rank and file of the people, ordinary folks with no revolutionary tendencies, who must say to our fellow citizens: Spaniards, your state does not exist! Rebuild it! *Delenda est monarchia.*'

This pact, and the presence of intellectuals interested in contributing to the process of change, took on an extended and unavoidable role: decreeing the end of the avant-garde, which was interpreted at the time, as it is witnessed by various texts, as the will to unite literature and politics and seek a compromise.

This shift is best explained in the book *El nuevo romanticismo*, which was published in 1930 by José Díaz Fernández, a founder and previous editor of the magazine *Nueva España*, dedicated to the 'fight against dictatorship and the monarchy'.[53] The book outlined a new generation: those born at the beginning of the twentieth century, who not only had to suffer the war in Morocco but had also lived through the repercussions of the First World War and the Russian Revolution at a time in which machines had provided the technical development necessary for the Industrial Revolution, which in Spain took the form of the International Exhibition of 1929. Tensions in the colonial world and the start of the race towards modernization acted as protagonists, along with other events such as the radical social transformation of Russia. One had to be conscious of this experience, which was considered akin in spirit to the internationalist ideology that impregnated the European panorama during the 1920s: 'The Russian Revolution,

nounced the intention of 'calling an assembly, in which the most prepared and capable Spaniards would participate, to deliberate on the cardinal and pragmatic problems of public Spanish life so as to finally co-ordinate the plan for a new National State.'[51] We see a glimmering here of the desire for a federal and modern Spain, constructed by intellectuals, who now considered themselves – due to their preparation and capability and in the absence of a political class – called upon to become the cornerstones of this process.

Just before Azaña's contribution to the December manifesto, on 4 June 1930, an article by Francisco Grandmontagne was published in *La Prensa*: 'During the six or so years for which the dictatorship lasted, thousands of youths have finished their university studies. Almost all are Republican, as is the great majority of the middle class … Among professors there is also a great Republican majority. The intellectual element, writers and journalists, almost without exception, is averse to monarchy.'[52]

Ortega himself, a champion of liberalism whose writings Sert habitually read, published an article on the 15 November 1930 in *El Sol*, which was considered by many to be decisive

EXPOSICION DE PROYECTOS DE NUEVA ARQUITEC-TURA 1930

Con objeto de fomentar e interesar al pú-blico en los problemas de la nueva arqui-tectura, pensamos organizar en San Se-bastián durante los meses de Agosto y Septiembre una exposición de proyectos de nueva arquitectura.

Más que nada creemos debe interesar la solución de problemas vitales, tales como habitación mínima y media, escuelas, etc.; proyectos de no tanta transcendencia, casas de verano, restaurants, albergues, clubs de sport, golf, tennis, etc.; interiores. Esto como base.

Se admiten también otros proyectos de más importancia: hospitales, teatros ofi-cinas. El objeto principal es interesar al público en la nueva arquitectura.

Contamos con tu colaboración, pues la idea sobre esta arquitectura que quere-mos implantar redunda para el fin que nos proponemos.

Con objeto de organizarla con tiempo su-ficiente te rogamos mandes tu adhesión, indicando los temas, para 1.º de Abril y los proyectos para 1.º de Agosto, siendo conve-niente, si es posible el envío de maquetas. La exposición tendrá lugar en el Gran Ca-sino o Gran Kursaal.

Manifesto of the exhibition in the Casino Viejo, San Sebastian, 1930.

which simply seeks to organize life, transform-ing not the state but rather its morals, produces true avant-garde literature … The radical changes that the world has undergone in the last years have alienated the principles of the human soul in conflicts that vastly differ from those that used to stimulate the pens of writ-ers. One of these is testing the interior resis-tance of a man today, when he is asked to commit himself before history to the task of building a new way of life on his own. To do so, a new romanticism is needed. The real van-guard will be the one that adjusts its new forms of expression to the new restless way of thinking. Let us salute the new romanticism of man and machine, which will make an art for life, not a life for art.'[54]

Using the vanguard's discoveries to a differ-ent end came to be seen as necessary in the process of getting rid of old structures while building future ones. Thus, the new generation of intellectuals, which some have named the 'Generation of '29',[55] took on a task or oblig-ation concerning the construction of an alter-native system. They put their art, their tech-niques and their training at the service of change conceived as radical by Díaz Fernandez

because it was necessarily oriented towards a social art that actively accompanied structural change: 'The work imposed on those of us who are thirty years old and employed in in-tellectual tasks is that of joining organizations that act parallel to revolutionary working-class movements, so as to prepare for the advent of the new civilization.'

At this time Sert was twenty-nine years old and understood the future as a matter of trans-forming one's self and of transforming things. Perhaps because of this he decided to put an end to the first stage of his training and to set off on his journey into the new reality. In Sep-tember 1930, while his first two apartment buildings were being erected in Barcelona, and the initial construction of the casa Duclós[56] was taking place in Seville, he participated in an exhibition of painting and architecture held in the Casino Viejo de San Sebastián, where he presented the Hotel on a Beach, which he had shown in 1928, the Summer Resort Town ex-hibited at the Galeries Dalmau, and his two apartment buildings on Carrer Rosselló and Carrer Muntaner.[57] Shortly afterwards, on 25 and 26 October, he attended the foundation of GATPAC[58] in Zaragoza, where he was one of the initial writers, along with Subiño, of the text that declared the principles of the group.[59] Signed by nine architects headed by Sert, it re-calls the attitude of the intellectuals who wished to contribute to the transformation of

GATCPAC Statutes.

estatuts i reglaments del grup d'ar-quitectes i tècnics catalans per al progrés de l'arquitectura contem-porània.

g.a.t.c.p.a.c.

constitució i objecte del gatcpac.

a. 1º el **gatcpac,** amb residència a bar-celona és una de les agrupacions que constitueixen el grup espanyol d'arquitectes i tècnics per al progrés de l'arquitectura contemporània (**g.a.t.e.p.a.c.**) que té la repre-sentació del «comité international pour la réalisation des problèmes architecturaux contemporains» (**c.i.r.p.a.c.**)

a. 2º els fins de la **gatcpac** són: a) reunir els arquitectes, enginyers i industrials del ram de la cons-trucció i a tot altre individu que pels seus estudis o aficions demostri interès per l'arquitectura contem-porània, per fomentar i divulgar aquesta arquitectura i les indústries que amb ella es relacionen.

3

their country in those uncertain days: 'With the object of contributing to our country and to the progress of the new universal orientation of architecture, and with the object of studying and solving the problems that may arise when adapting them to our environment, an association of architects and technicians from all branches of construction and furniture-making has gathered together … firmly believing that this orientation is based on solid and fundamental principles springing from our times and our present social organization, giving architecture the meaning it should have, we are willing to work for this ideal through all possible means.' Thus, the idea was to propose a substantial shift in the role that architecture had played up until now; what had in the past been the rhetoric of power was now being offered as updated modern European knowledge, whose desire was to help in solving the remaining problems. Thus an organization came into being that not only had its own offices, publicly located on one of the most central streets of Barcelona, but was also working on the creation of a vehicle of dissemination: 'As an effective means of propaganda, a magazine will soon come out as the official organ of the group.'

Apart from the foundation of this group (which presented its statutes on 28 November 1930)[60] and the creation of their own offices,[61] the interventionist strategies conceived by Sert

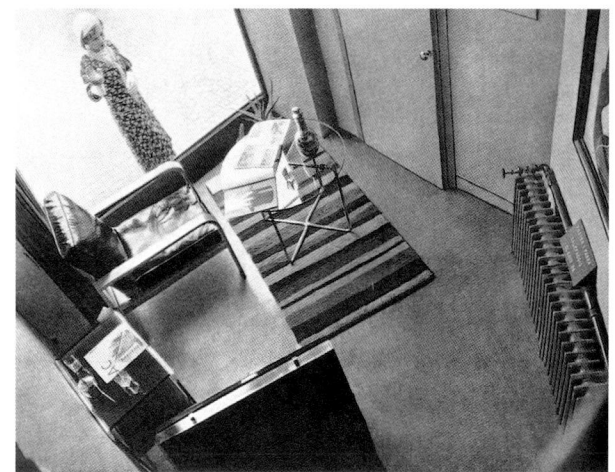

Premises of GATEPAC's Grupo Este, Barcelona, 1931.

and his colleagues included setting up exhibitions as well as releasing statements to the press, interviews with the town mayor, and the publication *A.C.* magazine, whose first issue came out in March 1931. Sert therefore had to become an expert on the techniques and language proper to this discipline. It is for this reason that his attendance at the CIAM meeting in Brussels, held between 27 and 29 November 1930, was so crucial.[62]

From its initial stages, the Congress had already given rise to discussions of a different calibre, which would influence the future thinking of the avant-garde architects of the time. At a preparatory meeting held on 17 May, in the presence of Sigfried Giedion, Walter Gropius, Rudolf Steiger, Marcel Breuer, Karl Moser, etc., Le Corbusier had voiced his

Premises of GATEPAC's Grupo Este, Barcelona, 1931.

opinions on some of the proposals made by the Swiss architect Hans Schmidt, who was in the past publisher of the *ABC* magazine. We do not know what these proposals were about, but what interests us here is what Le Corbusier said at that meeting: 'There is no urbanist doctrine. We are lacking a doctrine of urbanism, and therefore cannot judge specific and individual cases because we do not have a general conception of town planning.' Later he stated: 'I think that we can no longer engage with the architectural issue because the turnover it has suffered is the turnover of urbanism. The only thing that we can address is the issue of how architecture and town planning are linked to social evolution … There is a country that seeks to accomplish this. It is Russia … Moreover, the city of Moscow has commissioned the first plans for a resort town … Since a year ago, Russia with its experts, sociologists, doctors and economists, has been trying to articulate the question of the modern city.'[63]

The USSR was held up as a model where everything could be planned from scratch, where a parallelism existed between the construction of a new reality and the need for it to be organized along intellectual co-ordinates, without the burden that old cities represented for a possibly mechanist city, each of whose parts was to be considered as a com-

ponent of a perfectly functioning organism.

Thus by the middle of 1930, once the novelty of the ideological imperatives had worn off, the same architects who had elaborated and broadcast them began to find them unfulfilling. They needed a framework in which to place themselves, and this was seen as the city, although its antiquated town planning laws presented serious obstacles to the execution of the changes that interested them. The city had to cater for what were considered the urgent needs of the masses. Architects needed a material analysis of the city to understand what these were, and they meant to do that with the help of sociologists, hygienists and economists. Moreover, they understood that they had to unify their criteria of presenting the results so that they could be properly communicated. Thus the city became the focus of interest for the architects whom Sert would soon meet. His training was becoming more complex, since it was not only a question of learning a new vocabulary, but of understanding the new relationships that existed between architecture and the modern city.

For European architects the interest in real cities and their conditions had come to the fore in terms far removed from those of the ideological proposals a few years back, inherited from other traditions. There were no

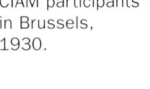

CIAM participants in Brussels, 1930.

longer any preconceptions such as those voiced in *A City for Three Million Inhabitants*, in Le Corbusier's own *Plan Voisin,* or in Hilberseimer's proposals. Now the issue at hand was different and implied other decisions. The first of these was momentarily to forget architecture and its decisive role in the formation of a city. In the words of Le Corbusier at the same meeting in May: 'I think that the architectural revolution that has taken place in the last twenty, forty or a hundred years, has come to a standstill before a crossroads. I think we can no further advance the question of architecture since the issue at hand is that of town planning. It is not a matter of perfecting the investigations recently carried out; this is an absolutely new urbanism.'

Thus at the end of May 1930, faced with the need to deal with a city as if it were a problem that first had to be understood in depth (even though they lacked a clear urbanist discipline), and with the distant hope (fostered by the Soviet situation) that they would be able to participate in change, the best architects in Europe prepared for the CIAM in Brussels. The title of the congress, 'Rational Land Plotting', seems at odds with their main concern at the time. However, a letter from Giedion to Le Corbusier on 25 July 1930, stated that on the third day of the congress 'we

would discuss the programme of the third Congress, which will deal with town planning.'[64] It is probable that the Swiss historian had a momentary lapse and got the number of the congress wrong, since the Brussels meeting was the third one, and therefore everything seems to point to the fact that after having dealt in previous events with 'Minimal Housing' and 'Rational Land Plotting', it would soon be the city's turn.

During the session of 20 May 1930 there were discussions about where the next CIAM should be held. Perhaps as a reaction against the pro-Russian sentiment that reigned at the time, Le Corbusier suggested: 'Why not go to Rome? There are interesting things there to see and to get to know about its organization … I am not proposing Paris because I think it would be a pity at present to do so, and I don't think it is necessary to discuss whether it will be in Moscow the next year. We could also consider Barcelona.' It is not clear why Le Corbusier wished to hold the Congress in cities with such intense political conditions. Even though he might have been well-informed on the Russian and Italian totalitarian regimes, and might have admired the planning capacity they showed thanks to their ruthless totalitarianism, the same could not be said of Barcelona, where the situation was undefined

Cover
of the official
publication
of the Brussels
CIAM, 1930.

CIAM 3
in Brussels,
regrouping
of dwellings.

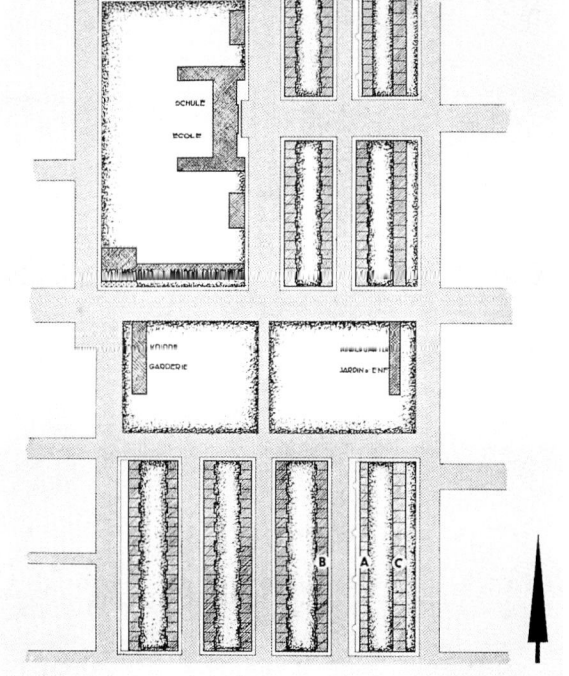

and political tension was running high near the end of 1930. However, what matters is that, thanks to Sert's contact with the Swiss architect, Barcelona cropped up as a possible site for CIAM meetings.

In Brussels there was very little talk about the city itself, since this had been left for a future congress. The title of this meeting, 'Rational Land Plotting', however, inspired an exhibition of examples, as well as a series of speeches on the issue, the most noteworthy of which were given by Gropius and Le Corbusier.[65] The former theorized on the hygienic, social, urban and economic advantages of high-rise constructions in comparison with the garden-city model, suggesting the ideal parameters that would regulate the proportions between the height of the blocks aligned in a row and the distance that should separate them to ensure air, sun and sufficiently extensive green spaces. Le Corbusier defended this thesis, putting forward the model of a stairway tower with a terraced roof, and stressing the urgent need for replotting the ground as the only possible solution to counteract the structure of private property, which would need to be addressed if one were to carry out urban planning on a large scale. He also placed special emphasis on the need for a strong 'authority' that would be able to call on technicians to face the many problems he foresaw.

Thus Sert must have clearly perceived that certain conditions would be indispensable for carrying out his work: the inevitable relationship between architecture and the city and the urgent need for the rational planning of workers' housing were key elements, along with a capacity to master the new language of the modern city. From Brussels on, this type of city began to be identified and defined using a terminology still familiar today. In a typewritten page from the Congress' programme, compiled by Giedion, we read in reference to the activities for Saturday 29 November: 'Afternoon at 3 p.m.: general assembly of the Congress members. Only Congress members will have access on presentation of their membership card. Presentation of the 1931 Congress "The Functional City"; proposals of the Commission and its groups. Distribution of tasks to be carried out for 1931.' Here the new city

was defined as 'functional' and a Congress was planned to focus on this issue. Over-optimistically, the CIAM architects expected it to take place the following year in Moscow, as had been discussed in previous sessions.

Sert seems to have learned the most in the morning session of that day, when the groups from different countries discussed their answers to a questionnaire on minimal housing.[66] The general opinion can be summarized by pointing out the marked deficit of low-cost housing and its poor condition in Europe due to the absence of adequate legislation, the mistrust of new construction techniques, and the authorities' lack of interest in solving the problem. Sert would experience the same situation in Spain when he returned from Brussels.

It is not surprising, therefore, that in the first quarter of 1931, in the debut issue of *A.C.*, GATEPAC's magazine for dissemination and combat, we find a statement on 'Housing Development for Barcelona of the Future': 'From 1854 to 1931, Barcelona has grown following a previously ordained urban layout marked in the Cerdá Plan. The city has surpassed the limits of this plan and as a consequence of this and of the lack of any other overall plan, the Barcelona City Council has adopted the System of Partial Urban Layouts, which reveals certain grave problems: 1) It generally favours private interests. 2) It does not take into account the distribution of the different areas, nor their siting in the future city. 3) It is impossible to link these urban designs in a rational and logical manner … It is

Manifesto for a 'Barcelona Futura' in *A.C.*, no. 1, 1931.

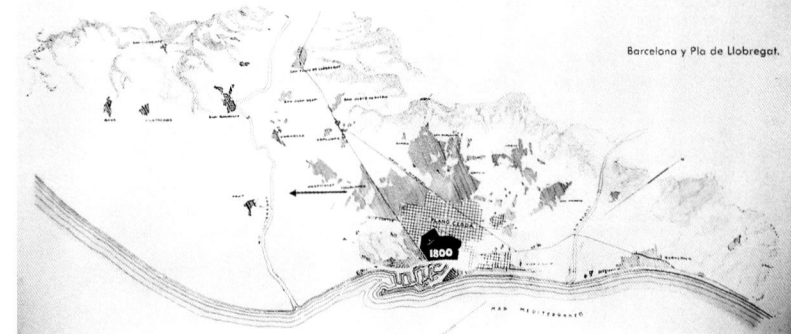

Sixte Illescas,
Casa Vilaró
in *A.C.*, no. 1,
1931.

tions of the masses. So at the end of the text we read: 'Due to the great significance and responsibility of this subject, it is necessary to call a competition.'[67]

In this first issue of *A.C.*, we can observe not only an interest in the city, but also in a particular house, Sixte Illescas' Casa Vilaró. What draws our attention further is the fact that the first photograph of it rings a bell: a vanishing-point perspective in its terrace appears very similar to the photograph on the cover of *Vers une Architecture*. Therefore the content of the first issue, to which Sert certainly contributed, makes clear two tendencies: the fact that it was interested in showing that it had mastered the Corbusian aesthetic style, and a preoccupation with the city.

We can consider Sert's training period as having ended in 1931, when he finished his first three buildings: the casa Duclós in Seville and the apartment buildings of Carrer Rosselló and Carrer Muntaner in Barcelona. The first

Cover
of Le Corbusier's
*Vers une
architecture*.

necessary to create a plan of Barcelona in which the situation is clearly stated, facilitating the growth of each one of the areas that will make up the new city.' Further on we read: 'One cannot pretend to modernize an old city; however, it is necessary to make it hygienic and to link it with the new urban layout by means of circulation routes, with the principal monuments surrounded by present-day constructions.'

With hindsight, it is logical to see this as a first manifesto. The modern architects who were starting to work in Barcelona in the 1930s clearly wanted to intervene in the city and were not willing to accept a way of thinking about it that did not have as its driving force the material data and the living condi-

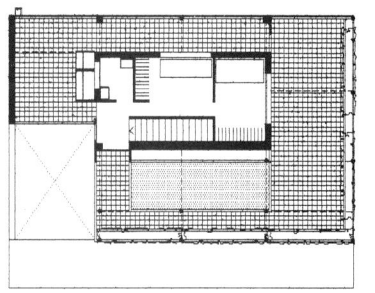

PLANTA TERRADO

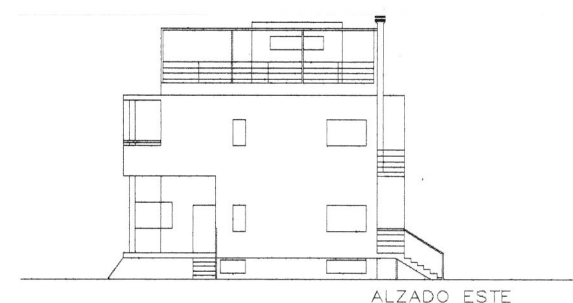

ALZADO ESTE

ALZADO SUR

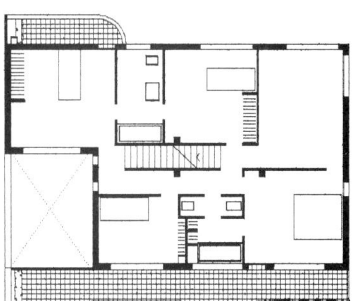

PLANTA PISO

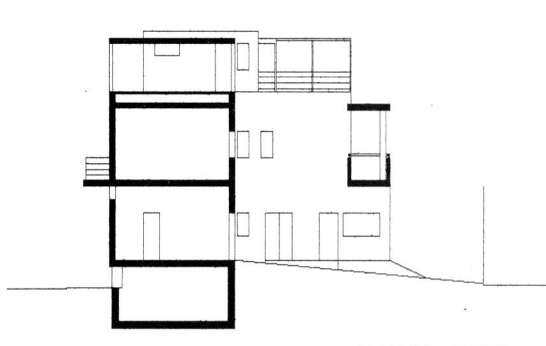

ALZADO OESTE

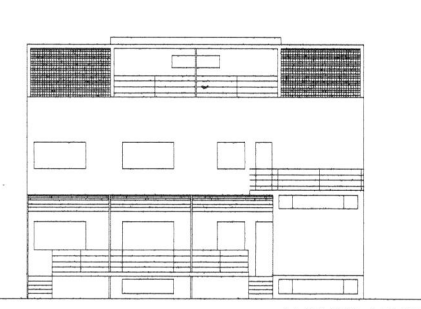

ALZADO NORTE

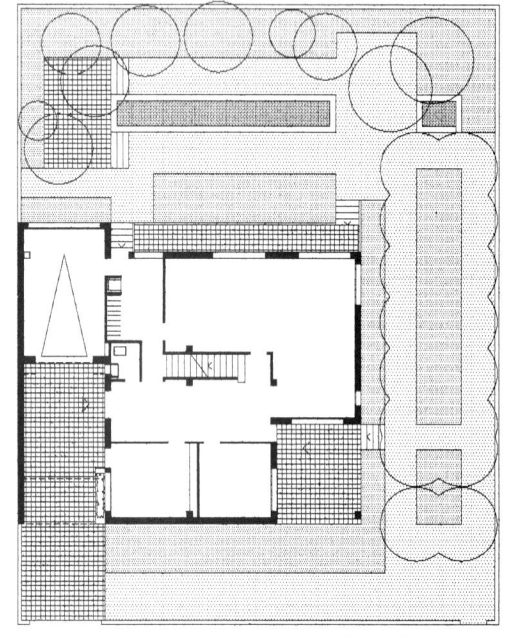

PLANTA BAJA

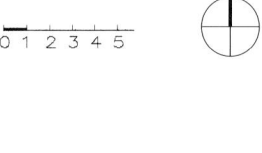

0 1 2 3 4 5

Casa Duclós,
Seville, 1930,
plans, elevations,
sections
and view.

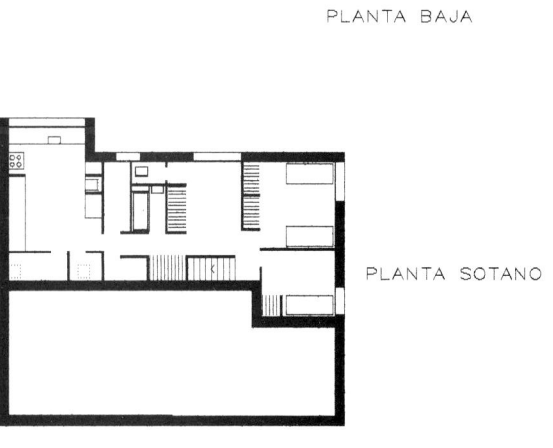

PLANTA SOTANO

of these, carried out for his cousin Benita López, who married the Sevillian physician Francisco Duclós in 1930, is a townhouse of 160 square metres distributed over four floors and built with a metal structure on a strictly modulated grid that determines the volume of the building.[68] From the way in which the building plans are drawn, it seems that Sert was investigating the possibility of freeing the distribution of the ground floor from structural elements: the black marks representing the erasure of pillars would appear to demonstrate this, a worthy effort for someone who wished to learn how to work on Le Corbusier's concept of a *plan libre*.

Thus we can also observe a process of emptying or filling in volumes that anticipates the structure: on the ground floor, in the two corners; on the first floor, in the line of the facade and along the side. When the vertical dimension of the building was finished, Sert reproduced the structure by incorporating certain thin elements that recalled it and gave continuity to the initial idea of solids and voids: the topmost part of the building recedes from the facade line as a continuation of the house. A flat roof and a pure painted volume constitute the finish, which embody the initial restless-

Apartment building on Carrer Rosselló, Barcelona, 1929, interior.

ness of its author, hesitant about the investigation carried out but eager to learn how to express himself, with an echo of Pessac in the background.

A report on the building on Carrer Rosselló that goes beyond mere description was published in the second issue of *A.C.*, along with some plans and several pictures. This seems to have been a text expressly written for the magazine, because the plans are not identical to those appearing in the administrative dossier.[69] The text reads: 'The return to basics, the systematic simplification that reigns today in the manifestations of modern architecture,

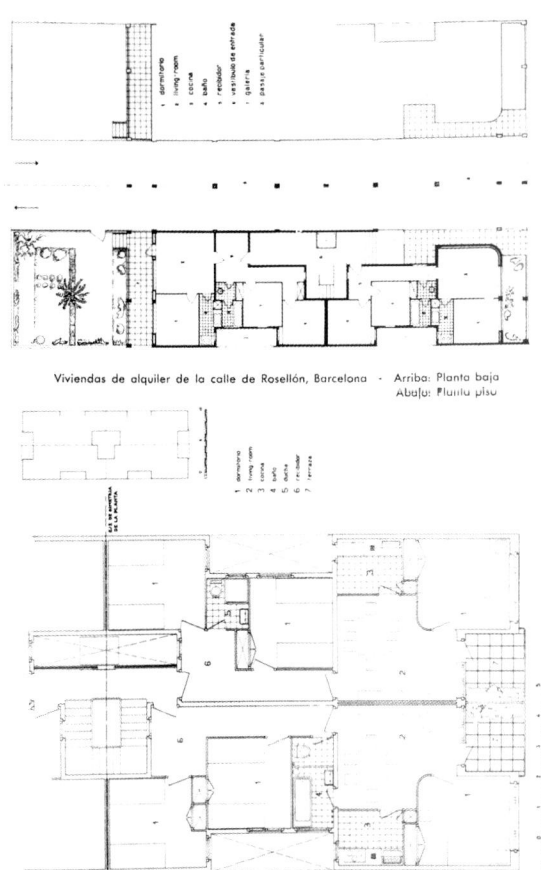

Viviendas de alquiler de la calle de Rosellón, Barcelona · Arriba: Planta baja
Abajo: Planta piso

Apartment building on Carrer Rosselló, Barcelona, 1929, view and plans.

responds to a need.' According to Sert, an avid reader of *Vers une Architecture* and a mindful participant of the CIAM in Brussels, these needs were common to all, and the architect must address them with 'things that are necessarily precise (structure, skeleton, volumes, cubes of empty space, surfaces of light, quantity of ventilation, door and window measurements)', which constitute the first phase of the architecture. Afterwards one would be able 'to start thinking about its aesthetic appearance, a reflection of the complexity of human beings, whose spirit is not wholly satisfied with the austerity of algebraic language … This consideration for the expression of feeling that we proclaim by no means obliterates the knowledge of and admiration for scientific advances. Our times demand this complexity from the architect.' Behind Sert's words was the possibility of joining functionalist objectivity with feeling and aesthetic values that could come from another type of composition.

From this information we can deduce an initial backing up of Le Corbusier's criteria in contrast to the stance of those architects whom the Swiss architect called *Sachklich* and to whom Le Corbusier referred scornfully throughout his career. In one part of the text, Sert uses a term employed in the title of one of his mentor's best-known books: '[The architect] will have to distance himself from all rising academicism (horizontal windows, cylindrical railings, etc.) maintaining the freedom of spirit and form that is the conquest of new architecture.' This recalls the book published in 1933 by Le Corbusier, *Croissade ou le Crépuscule des Acádemies*, in which he encompassed under the epithet of 'academicist' all the architecture habitually carried out by his French antagonists, as well as certain modern German architecture. By 1931, Sert had clearly come to consider that adapting new architectural elements without exercising a critical appraisal of them meant falling into another type of academicism, something against which he fought by means of his public speeches and the pages of *A.C.*, crossing out in red all the architectures that displeased him. However, it was a mistake he could not altogether avoid making himself, since the first step in learning something new implies making it one's own,

and at this stage of doubt and uncertainty, pitfalls are common.

Sert was trying to formulate an objective solution for an apartment building plan. In the descriptive part of the report, he explained in detail why he would not follow the domestic architecture of Cerda's Barcelona Ensanche, in which there was a traditional distinction between the principal facade, usually historicized, and the facade facing the inner courtyard of a city block, which was left as an open balcony. Sert instead proposed two facades that were exactly alike, a logical result of his having placed four flats on each floor. The will to 'express' the interior had gained the upper hand

Cover of *Befreites Wohnen*, Sigfried Giedion, 1928.

38

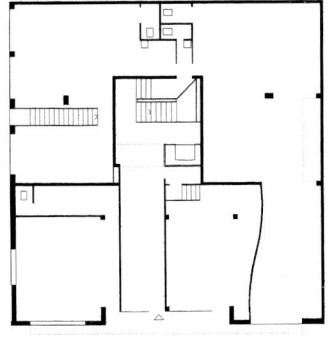

PLANTA BAJA

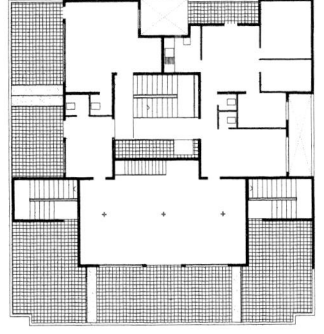

PLANTA ESTUDIOS

PLANTA INFERIOR VIVIENDA

PLANTA SUPERIOR VIVIENDA

0 1 2 3 4 5

Apartment building on Carrer Muntaner, Barcelona, 1929, plans.

in conditioning factors that had to do with image, although this is not the only interesting point. There is also the fact that there are four apartments per floor, of only 62 square metres each, an unusual trait in comparison with the buildings around it, whose living quarters tended to be much larger because they were destined for a relatively wealthy class. It is risky to deduce from this, however, that Sert's intentions were social, and that he wished to offer small flats at a low cost to a public with less purchasing power;[70] it is more reasonable to think that, given the alarming scarcity of dwellings in Barcelona at the time, a greater number of smaller flats would make more lodgings available to renters.

There are other matters that also bothered Sert, but to which he offered no alternatives, perhaps because he was obliged to take into account the profitability of this enterprise and because he was conditioned by the plotting of the Ensanche district of Barcelona, which had an excessive depth in comparison to the small dimensions of its facades. Due to these inflexible factors, Sert created two inner courtyards, of doubtful effectiveness, to ventilate some of the rooms, leading him into a fatal symmetry

that resulted in rooms that had to be ventilated through the stairwell and were therefore excessively drafty.

In the best *Sachklich* tradition, the building reveals a facade without traits, and its metal railings could have been taken from any German magazine of the period; even the way in which it was published seems to have been copied from the huge amount of European publications that Sert must have consulted.[71] Thus, despite his attraction to Le Corbusier, the first building that Sert created partakes of that objective style that his intellectual mentor so disliked.

There are some similar elements, as well as differing ones, in the apartment building for Carrer Muntaner. Published in the fourth issue of *A.C.*, it becomes patent that it was based on the facade of Villa Stein. Here, the same symmetry of floors, this time with two duplex apartments per storey, reveals the Beaux-Arts legacy that Sert had unwittingly inherited during his student days at the School of Architecture, especially if we consider that one of the apartments on each floor had great difficulty in obtaining light and ventilation in many of its rooms.

There were also some functional errors: the installation of the kitchen in the upper part of the duplex, the bad toilet distribution, a window that could never be cleaned, etc.[72] Perhaps it did not matter to him, since what Sert was really seeking to do was to create a facade three times greater in height than that of the villa in Garches and to make a duplex apartment with double-height interior spaces. In other words, he wished to be considered a good apprentice of the Paris studio that had welcomed him, by repeating the facades of his teacher while working on the interior space, coming up with a very similar solution to the one he had employed in the double-height entrance hall of the Hotel on a Beach of 1928; indeed it seems probable that the project for Carrer Muntaner had begun in 35 rue de Sèvres.

One needs only to follow certain points of the report to observe the loose ends left by our architect. In the plans we see three tiny courtyards for ventilation and we read: 'The construction is an adaptation of the modern principles that could be applied given the present-

Apartment
building on Carrer
Muntaner,
Barcelona, 1929,
views.

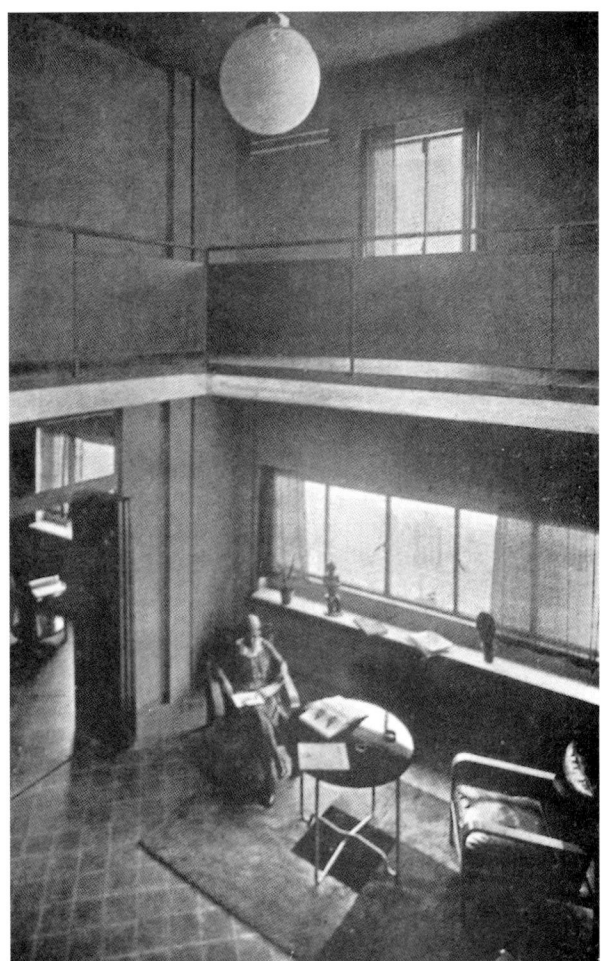

day urbanist system in Barcelona, which did not allow us to do away with the small interior courtyards for light and ventilation, despite their many inconveniences.' These sentences are evidently unjustified given the building's corner location and the family finance it had received. It is also strange that he should boast of 'getting rid of the corridor … badly lit and ventilated', and that later it should turn out that the two corridors that appear per dwelling provide both ventilation and light through the stairwell or through a courtyard of ridiculous dimensions. Even worse, we could speak of the deficient construction of some of the enclosure walls, which are made up only of a double partition wall.

However, contradictions really increase when Sert attempts to present the facade as a logical 'consequence of the interior distribution'; it is impossible for anyone to perceive the alternating play of volumes created by the protruding balcony and enclosed terrace or the displacement of the balcony with respect

to the void of the double height, as anything other than a simple formal play aspiring to please his mentor; nor is it very light-efficient, from the point of view of interior-exterior relations, to put the same window in a place that is spatially fragmented by a double height, such as the living room-dining room area.

We have arrived at the final stage of an apprenticeship in the architectures that were be-

Le Corbusier, Villa
Stein, Garches,
1927.

41

Francesc Macià during the proclamation of the Republic, 14 April 1931.

ing carried out in Europe, and Sert would have time to correct his mistakes so as to make progress in his understanding of and participation in this necessary modernity.

Throughout this survey, we have observed Sert's constant desire to keep up with the times and to work on the persuasion of the public,[73] without losing sight of the possibilities opened up by the political news that dominated it: the proclamation of the Second Republic on 14 April 1931.

[1] Francisco Sert Badía, a native of Barcelona, was born on 16 November 1863 on 25 Carrer Sant Pere més Alt, Barcelona; he was the son of Domingo Sert Rius, a textile manufacturer, and of Maria Badía Capdevila, native of Sabadell, and was baptized in the San Francisco Parish. Genara López was born in Santander and was the daughter of Claudio López López, brother of the Marquis of Comillas, and of Benita Díaz de Quijano Fernández. Information on the industrial activities of the Sert family can be found in a book about the architect's uncle, José María Sert: María del Mar Arnus, *Sert, Conde de Sert*, Edicions Nou Art, Barcelona, 1989.

It cannot be established with any certainty that the birthdate given for José Luís Sert is accurate, since another document contradicting this one was found among the architect's personal papers in the Archives of the Joan Miró Foundation of Barcelona (JMFA). In a trunk containing Sert's personal belongings, which he brought with him from the States, is a varied collection of documents, many of them of a personal nature. Amongst them is a document stating: 'Osvaldo Duyas Romaña, Municipal Judge and Curator of the Registry Office, certifies that in the fourth volume of the section on Births of the Bacuranao Registry Office in Minas, Republic of Cuba, there is a record whose literal tenor is the following: "Number 331. José Luís Sert y López. In the district of Bacuranao at one o'clock in the afternoon on 10 May 1901, Mr Francisco Sert y Badía, native of Barcelona, Spain, of legal age, white, married, merchant and resident in this neighborhood, appeared before Mr Carlos del Castillo y García, Municipal Deputy Judge, and José Martínez Peña, Secretary, to request that the birth of his son be recorded in the Registry Office, and as father of the same, declares that said son was born in the house of the witness on 7 May of this year at 11 o'clock p.m. That

he is the legitimate son of the witness and of his wife Mrs Genara López y Díaz Quijano, native of Santander, Spain, and domiciled in the witness' address. Who on the father's side is grandson of … And that said male child has been named José Luis. The eyewitnesses of the declaration were …" This act having been read to those present in its entirety, and having requested that those who were to sign it read it to themselves if they considered it necessary, it has been stamped … IN CONFORMITY WITH THE ORIGINAL, and at the petition of the interested party, I issue this certificate in Minas, on July 22, 1939.'

What is the reason for these contradictions? Why does neither Sert's date of birth nor his birthplace coincide in the two documents? One hypothesis would be that the second birth certificate was fake, and that in fact it was the architect himself who arranged for it to be written in 1939 so as to possess a document that would facilitate his entry into the United States, presenting himself in that country as a citizen of Cuba, a place 'agreeably disposed' to American policy, and not as a Spanish exile with suspicious political tendencies.

It is certainly true that Sert was in Cuba at that time, as can be gathered from some pieces of correspondence. From Bermuda he wrote to Sigfried Giedion on 21 March 1939 saying: 'Dear Giedion: here I am, heading for Havana! You can write to me at: Angel Segura Solé. Reina 12, 3o., Havana (Cuba) … From down there, my trip to the United States in September will be all the easier.' Archive Sigfried Giedion (SGA). Correspondence with José Luis Sert, 43–K1939–3–21. The gist of the letter is clear: it would be easier to enter the States from Cuba, especially if he could prove that he was born on the island, something that the López family might have been interested in asserting in 1901 and which could therefore explain the presence of the Sert-López couple in Havana, especially considering that the

López family was still involved in banking activities in Cuba in 1921.

A letter from John D. Johnson, the American Consul in Canada, to Gaspare M. Cusumano, Counsellor at Law, written on 12 March 1945, may help dispel any doubts. The letter was sent to clear up questions regarding the residence permits of Sert and his wife Moncha in the USA: 'Please note: no assurance can be given that Mr and Mrs Sert will be found eligible to receive immigration visas when they apply in person. This is due to the fact that Mr Sert admits he obtained a Cuban passport in Havana for his wife by representing her to be the spouse of a Cuban citizen and indicates he obtained a Cuban passport for himself by claiming to be a Cuban citizen' … "I decided to solve my dilemma", he states in connection to an affidavit he has submitted, "by accepting the Cuban passport that my friends suggested I should take … I equally obtained a Cuban passport for my wife, as the spouse of a Cuban citizen. We both got a visitor's visa for six months for the United States. We arrived in Miami on 26 June 1939."' JMFA, Sert's trunk.

[2] Information on some of these personal matters has been forwarded by Josefa Graells, daughter of Sert family's chauffeur, whom I thank for her information, trusting her accurate recollection of events. The pictures of Sert family's cars given to me by Arturo Graells, also a relative of Sert family's chauffeur.

[3] The López Group controlled the Banco Hispano Colonial and the following companies: Transatlántica, Tabacos de Filipinas, Hullera Española and Asfaltos y Portlands. Moreover, they were connected through family ties with the 'best' families of Barcelona. An analysis of the López family's enterprises and those of the upper social class of Barcelona during the second half of the nineteenth century can be found in Gary Wray McDonough, *Good Families in Barcelona*, New Jersey, 1986. Quoted from the Spanish edition: *Las buenas familias de Barcelona*,

Barcelona, 1989, pp. 127–33. The book analyzes the most relevant aspects of this Catalan social class to which the López and Sert families pertained, going from the 'Ley de las tres generaciones' (three-generations law) to the importance given, since 1868, to the possibility of establishing joint-stock companies, as well as reviewing the significance of marriage in Catalonia and the concept of what constituted a *Señor* (upper-class gentleman of social distinction).

Many years before, Jaume Vicens Vives and Montserrat Llorens had already studied in depth some of the Catalan industrialists and their financial and political strategies: *Industrialists and Politicians*, Barcelona, 1958. These authors have referred to the Catalan textile monopoly in Cuba and to the process of nobilization of these Catalan industrialists: 'Thus, in nineteenth-century Barcelona, there emerged a group of some twenty or thirty families who held the reins of economic and political power, and who moreover flaunted a certain aristocratic superiority due to their having received noble titles in recognition of the services rendered to the Restoration and Regency monarchies.' (p. 128).

4 Santiago Barjau, *Enrique Sagnier*, Editorial Labour, Barcelona, 1992, thesis for the History of Art Department of the University of Barcelona.

5 *Centenari de l'Escola d'Arquitectura de Barcelona*, ETSAB, 1977, pp. 95–97.

6 Josep M. Rovira, *La arquitectura catalana de la modernidad*, Ediciones UPC, 1987. Ignasi Sola-Morales, *L'Exposició Internacional de Barcelona 1914–1929: Arquitectura i Ciutat*, Barcelona, 1985. *L'Avenç* magazine, monographic issue published in commemoration of the 50th anniversary of the World's Fair, Barcelona, 1980.

7 Josep Francesc Rafols, *Pere Blay i l'arquitectura del Renaixement a Catalunya*, Barcelona, 1934. On p. 30 we read: 'When some students from the School of Architecture (who by now have become fully-fledged architects) – Josep Bofarull, Sixte Illescas, Lluís Riudor, Josep Lluís Sert and Josep María Clavé – organized a tour of the Tarragonian fields in search of Pere Blay's creations, we were very pleased to accompany them on their trip; the first graphic studies of the church of La Selva date from that time.'

8 Benet's chronicles in *La Veu de Catalunya*, or at least those that interest us, began to appear on 8 July 1925 under the title 'Cròniques d'Art de París'. A critical analysis of the World's Fair in Paris as well as a large quantity of graphic material is offered by Yvonne Brunhamer, *1925, Les Presses de la Connaissance*, Paris, 1976.

9 Rafael Benet, 'Cròniques d'Art de París', *La Veu de Catalunya*, Monday 20 July 1925, p. 4.

10 Benet also quotes Le Corbusier in his Wednesday chronicle of 16 September 1925. On the friendship between Sert and Le Corbusier see Josep M. Rovira, 'Le Corbusier y José Luis Sert: momentos de una amistad', in *Le Corbusier and Spain*, ed. by Juan José Lahuerta, CCCB, Barcelona, 1197, pp. 95–99.

11 See *Cuadernos de Arquitectura y Urbanismo*, no. 140, COAC, Barcelona. On the fifth page of an interview held in Ibiza in September 1968 with Sixte Illescas, Joan Prats, Germán Rodríguez Arias, José Luis Sert and Raimon Torres, Sert stated: 'We used to meet and speak about everything, and then in 1926 we got interested in Le Corbusier. I was in Paris and got hold of Le Corbusier's books, three books.'

12 To illustrate the feelings awakened by this architecture, we can step ahead in time and compare the cover of *Vers une architecture* with the first image published in the *A.C.* magazine's first issue, edited by the Grupo Este of the

GATEPAC. In it we see that the perspective used to photograph the terrace of the Casa Vilaró (designed by Sixte Illescas in 1929) coincides with the perspective of the bridge of the steamer that Le Corbusier chose for the cover of his most influential book.

13 Rafael Benet, 'Art Nou. Cop de Maça', *La Ciutat i La Casa*, no. 6, 1926, pp. 6–7.

14 The author has found these books in his visits to Ramón Puig Gairalt's library, and in the collections of his brother Antoni and Pere Benavent.

15 Rafael Benet, 'Exposició de la 'Werkbund' a Estutgard' [sic], *La Ciutat i la Casa*, no. 7, 1927, pp. 27–28.

16 Le Corbusier, who had been invited by García Mercadal, gave two lectures in the Residencia de Estudiantes of Madrid on 9 and 11 May 1928. Pictures from this trip can be found at the Fondation Le Corbusier. See the FLC dossier 'Le Corbusier on different occasions. Le Corbusier in Spain, 1927–1930.' L 1 (2)10. Among others, is a picture he had taken of himself and Mercadal in the Escorial, L 1 (2)10–8, on a ball of granite, L 1(2) 10–7 with Don Jaime and with Don ?, 'Infant of Spain', L 1(2) 10–12.

17 Quoted in *Gaudí*, Ed. RM, Barcelona, 1958, with a preface by Le Corbusier titled 'Encounter with Gaudí's work'.

18 *Cuadernos de Arquitectura y Urbanismo*, no. 140, op. cit., In a feature on the verdict of the League of Nations Palace competition in Geneva, published in *La Veu de Catalunya* on 30 March 1928, Rafael Benet wrote that two students, whose names he did not give, had invited the Swiss architect to speak. It is not too far-fetched to suspect that Sert was one of them. In a text on Rafael Benet, Alicia Suárez mentions a letter from Ràfols to Benet in which he was requested to find lodgings for Le Corbusier near the Ateneu because Ràfols was in Villanueva due to his father's ill-health. See *Un estudi sobre Rafael Benet*, Fundació Rafael Benet, p. 162.

19 Fernando García Mercadal's activities are reviewed in *Nueva Forma*, no. 69, Madrid, 1971. A commentary on the building called 'el rincón de Goya' can be found in Federico Torralba, *El rincón de Goya en Zaragoza*, Seminario de Arte Aragonés, XXVII–XXVIII, 1978.

20 See *Poesía*, no. 11, Madrid, 1981, pp. 5–66, an issue almost entirely devoted to the architect Fernández Shaw.

21 Martin Steinmann, *CIAM Dokumente 1928–1939*, Birkhäuser Verlag, Basel and Stuttgart, 1979.

22 José Angel Sanz, *Archivo de arquitectura en el país vasco*, Colegio Oficial de Arquitectos Vasco-Navarro, 1990, p. 13.

23 Rafael Benet, 'Hotel en una Platja: Salutació a Le Corbusier', *Gaseta de les Arts*, no. 1, 1928, p. 16.

24 'Le Corbusier a Barcelona. Primera conferència', *La Veu de Catalunya*, Saturday 19 May 1928. 'Le Corbusier a Barcelona', Segona lliço, *La Veu de Catalunya*, Wednesday 23 May 1928.

25 Published for the first time in Alfred Roth, *Zwei Wohnhäuser von Le Corbusier und Pierre Jeanneret*, Akadem, Verlag Dr. Fr Wedekind & Co., Stuttgart, 1927. The Spanish edition has an introductory article by Juan José Lahuerta, 'El año de Stuttgart', *Dos casas de Le Corbusier y Pierre Jeanneret*, Colección de Arquitectura, Colegio Oficial de Aparejadores y Arquitectos Técnicos, Murcia, 1997.

26 On the Geneva competition, see Ilia Delizia and Fabio Mangone, *Architettura e politica. Ginevra e la Società delle nazioni*, Officina Edizioni, Rome, 1992; 'Ginebra 1927', *3ZU*, no. 1, publication of the ETSAB, Barcelona, 1993.

On Le Corbusier's intervention see Ciro Anzivino and Ezio Godoli, *Ginevra 1927: il concorso per il palazzo della Società delle nazioni e il caso Le Corbusier*, Modulo Editrice, Florence, 1979; Josep M. Rovira, 'Le Corbusier en el concurso del palacio de la SDN', *3ZU*, op. cit., pp. 18–35.

27 Le Corbusier-Saugnier, 'Les Paquebots', *L'Esprit Nouveau*, no. 8, p. 848. Also in *Almanach d'Architecture moderne*, Ed. Crès, Paris, 1925, p. 29.

28 Ramón Sastre, 'Arquitectura. Reflexions entorn les teories de Le Corbusier', *Joia*, no. 3–4, 1928.

29 Le Corbusier-Saugnier, 'Pure création de l'esprit', *L'Esprit Nouveau*, no. 16, pp. 1903–18.

30 Juan José Lahuerta, '1928. Le Corbusier en Barcelona', *La tradició moderna*, COAC, Girona, 1995, pp. 109–12. Antonio Pizza, 'Maggio 1928: arrivo di Le Corbusier a Barcelona', *Le Corbusier y España*, op. cit., pp. 83–93.

31 FLC R 3 03177.

32 J.J.P. Oud, 'La evolución de la arquitectura moderna en Holanda, 1922–1923', *Mi trayectoria en 'De Stijl'*, Colección de Arquitectura. Murcia, 1986. On p. 53, we read: 'What is "modern" was to be defined as that which "is changing" in the sense of "what becomes", or in other words, that "which evolves". But at the same time, what is "modern" by no means has to be "new". What is "modern" is what "becomes individual", what is "new" is what "becomes collective"; this is a fundamental distinction in the evolution of art, on whose importance we will again speak throughout this conference.'

33 Hannes Meyer, 'El nuevo mundo', in *El arquitecto en la lucha de clases y otros escritos*, introduction by Francesco Dal Co, Gustavo Gili, Barcelona, 1972, pp. 86–92 (Italian trans: *Hannes Meyer. Architettura o rivoluzione. Scritti 1921–1942*). Meyer starts off with modern world aspects related to the omnipresence of machines and their consequences to explain the profound changes that were taking place in people's lives in the 1920s, and ends up proclaiming the changes that this would imply in an architecture that, in the opinion of some European architects (for whom Le Corbusier felt contempt), could only be objective. 'Cars are circulating on our roads. Around the traffic area of the Champs-Elysées, from 6 o'clock in the morning to 8 o'clock at night, a single metropolitan dynamism has been loosed. The Fords and Rolls-Royces have destroyed the core of the city, have annulled distances and have erased the boundaries between city and countryside. Aeroplanes fly in the sky: the Fokker and Farman increase the scope of our movements and the distance between us and the earth; they ignore national borders and bring nations closer together … We live more quickly and therefore longer. We have a keener sense than ever for speed, and speed records represent a benefit for all … freed from the weight of classical beauty … new era testimonies take over: industrial fairs, silos, music-halls, airports, office chairs, standardized products … They are not works of art. Art is composition, the aim is functionality. The composition of a dock seems an unreasonable idea to us, but what about the composition of a city plan, of a housing building? This functional conception of a building in all of its aspects leads to pure construction. Pure construction is the characteristic trait of the new world of forms. Constructive form is not of any country in particular; it is cosmopolitan and it is the expression of an international conception of architecture.'

34 Hilberseimer's article is reproduced in the magazine *Daidalos*, no. 52, June 1994, p. 127. The text mentioned is on the last page of

Hilberseimer's renowned book *Internationale neue Baukunst*, Julius Hoffmann, Stuttgart, 1928.

[35] Häring's text is in *Daidalos*, op. cit., pp. 130–31.

[36] A handwritten letter without a specific addressee dating from April 1931, housed in the GATCPAC Archives of the Colegio de Arquitectos de Cataluña reads: 'We are awaiting the two printing types from Germany … Each page will have two colours like the *Das Neue Frankfurt*', C–12–75.

[37] Werner Oeschlin, 'Das Neue und die moderne Architektur', *Daidalos*, pp. 114–25.

[38] Joan Sacs (pseudonym of Feliu Elias), 'Arquitectura nova', *Mirador*, no. 13, Barcelona, 25 April 1929. The article is paired with another, entitled 'Els arquitectes joves', by Màrius Gifreda, expressing a similar point of view. The project report by Sert and Torres, along with much photographic material, can be found in 'La nova arquitectura a Catalunya', *Gaseta de les Arts*, May 1929, pp. 111–18. Rafael Benet, under the pseudonym Rafael Baiarola, published a series of seven articles on architecture in the 'Vida Artística' section of *La Veu de Catalunya*. The last three articles review the projects presented in the exhibition at the Galeries Dalmau (24, 25 and 26 April 1929). On the scope of the Spanish avant-garde, see Jaime Brihuega, *Manifiestos, proclamas, panfletos y textos doctrinales. Las vanguardias artísticas en España, 1910–1931*, Cátedra, Madrid, 1979; Serge Salaun and Elisée Trenc, *Les Avant-Gardes en Catalogne*, Presses de la Sorbonne Nouvelle, Paris, 1995; *3ZU*, ETSAB, no. 4, June 1995.

[39] *Arquitectura. Exposició de projectes*, Galeries Dalmau, Barcelona, May 1929.

[40] The catalogue of the exhibition reads: 'In our country's case, where there is an excessive intensity of light but where, just like everywhere else, there is still a need for the widest possible scope of vision, we can soften light intensity by means of cantilevers or balconies that are similar to those that logic has dictated in these climates.'

[41] Antonio Pizza, *Guía de arquitectura moderna en Barcelona*, Ed. Del Serbal, Barcelona, 1996, pp. 45–49.

[42] Le Corbusier travelled to America between October and December 1929. He spent his time giving lectures in Buenos Aires and Rio de Janeiro. These have been gathered in *Précisions sur un état de l'architecture et de l'urbanisme*, Ed. Crès, Paris, 1930.

[43] See *Die Wohnung für das Existenzminimum*, Julius Hoffmann Verlag, Stuttgart, 1930 (reprinted 1933). A selection of the Congress' documentary material can be found in Martin Steinmann, op. cit., pp. 35–71. The small catalogue edited by the Gewerbemuseum, Basil, which housed the Congress panels that had shortly before been exhibited in Frankfurt, put the author's name next to the number of his corresponding panel. Thus, we find that Spanish participation was restricted to the following numbers: 17 (Vallejo), 18 (Zarranz and Madariaga), 51 (Salvador), and 158 (Arralle). Although the numbering is not correlative, it almost coincides with the official publication of the Congress. There is one number, however, that is incorrectly matched: number 158 corresponds to a plan of Karlsruhe, whereas number 150 represents a sketch of Madrid.
The original documentation of CIAM 2 can be found in the Sigfried Giedion Archives (SGA). From it we have gathered that Sert did not attend the CIRPAC held on 2 February 1929 in Basil, in which the first programme proposal was discussed. Aizpurua and Vallejo, however, were present. Concerning the relevance of the Congress with respect to the introduction of new architecture in Spain, see

José Angel Sanz, *Archivo de arquitectura en el País Vasco, Años 30*, Colegio de Arquitectos Vasco-Navarro, Bilbao, 1990. Sanz reports on the National Competition on Minimal Housing, which was announced in Madrid in May 1929: "It was a previous step … to choose the most paradigmatic Spanish projects that would later compete against architects from other European countries in the Critical Exhibition of Minimal Housing Projects and Implementations announced by Ernst May and Mart Stam in Frankfurt for September of 1929. These two architects would publish in 1930 a selection of these projects in the well-known volume *Die Wohnung für das Existenzminimum*' (p. 31). Fifteen works were presented for competition, none of which were Sert's (p. 33). Nevertheless, there is still no clear answer concerning Sert's presence in Stuttgart. A letter written by Walter Gropius to Sert in May 1969 (Sert Collection, SC, E 25), states: 'I salute you as my friend of forty years', but despite these explicit words, we cannot necessarily trust Gropius' recollection.

[44] An analysis of political change in Spain during the 1930s is found in Stanley G. Payne, *Spain's First Democracy. The Second Republic, 1931–1936*, University of Wisconsin Press, 1933, pp. 3–46; Miguel Artola, *Partidos y programs políticos, 1808–1936*, Alianza Editorial, Madrid, 1991. For a survey of the Catalan scenario at the time see Josep Termes, *De la Revolució de Setembre a la fi de la guerra civil*, Edicions 62, Barcelona, 1987, pp. 267–330.

[45] Artola, op. cit., vol. 1, pp. 567–68.

[46] Ibid., p. 568.

[47] The events that took place between Berenguer's rise to power and the proclamation of the Republic are explained in ibid., pp. 570–98. The other texts mentioned also provide good analyses of this.

[48] Municipal Administrative Archives of Barcelona. See dossiers 45347, 3756, in which we find evidence of the vicissitudes suffered by Sert during his first two projects, which experienced serious difficulties in being approved by several municipal commissions. One of these commissions, devoted to ornament, demanded that Sert drew a specific perspective for the building on Carrer Muntaner, which he did in the summer of 1930.

[49] Fulgencio Castañar, *El compromiso en la novela de la segunda República*, Siglo XXI, Madrid, 1992, p. 23.

[50] Javier Tusell and Genoveva Queipo del Llano, *Los intelectuales y la República*, Nerea, Madrid, 1990, p. 96.

[51] Fulgencio Castañar, op. cit., p. 29.

[52] Francisco Grandmontagne, *El panorama político*, quoted in Javier Tusell and Genoveva Queipo del Llano, op. cit., pp. 16–17.

[53] Díaz Fernandez had also contributed to *Post-Guerra* magazine (1927–28), whose aim was: 'To promote the participation of intellectuals in the working-class struggles, to advocate the need for political struggle to transform the bourgeois society into a socialist society, to persevere in the fight for labour unions, to disseminate Marxism, and to involve literature and art in general in these struggles.' See Francisco Claudet, *Las cenizas del Fénix*, Ed. De la Torre, Madrid, 1993, p. 40.

[54] José Díaz Fernández, *El nuevo romanticismo. Polémica de arte, política y literatura*, José Esteban, Madrid, 1985, pp. 55–57. This re-edition of Díaz Fernández's work has an interesting introduction by José Manuel López de Abadia, which offers important information on the author and the context in which the book was written.

[55] See Carlos Diez Fernández, *Proclama de la gen-*

eración del 29, quoted in Claudet, op. cit., p. 79. On the decisive role of intellectuals in this process of change, see J. Venegas, *La revolución española y los intelectuales. La propaganda izquierdista por medio del libro*, Claudet, op. cit., p. 81. Another useful text that helps explain this process is the book by Tusell and Queipo del Llano.

[56] Angel Isac, *Vanguardia al margen. Andalucía años treinta*, *3ZU*, no. 4, Barcelona, 1995, pp. 30–45.

[57] In some undated typewritten pages, under the heading 'Origins, activities and possibilities of the GATEPAC', in the GATCPAC Archives in Barcelona, we find news of the competition, which was held under the title 'Exhibition of Modern Paintings and Architectures'. Apart from paintings by Picasso, Gris, Miró, Dalí, Pruna, Bores, Maruja Mallo, etc., and building plans and models, there were cinema sessions showing films by Buñuel and Giménez Caballero: 'Exhibition of painting and architecture in the old casino of San Sebastian. Architects: Mercadal, López Delgado, Barroso … from Madrid, Aizpurua and Labayen from San Sebastian, Vallejo from Bilbao and the group from Barcelona.'
A letter from Germán Rodríguez Arias to Aizpurua and Labayen from 24 August 1930 reads: 'I am also enclosing a list of the colleagues who will present work in the exhibition and of the works that we are presenting. Since I believe that Churruca is already in Zarauz, you can contact him and he will help you to organize the exhibition.'
There are also witnesses who recall the exhibition. See additionally Rodríguez Arias and Sert in an interview of September 1968, held in Ibiza, which appeared in *Cuadernos de Arquitectura y Urbanismo*, no. 140, p. 5. José Angel Sanz has given a report on this exhibition too. See Sanz, op. cit., pp. 11–14. The catalogue of the architectural works presented at the exhibition is reproduced in *Arte y artistas vascos de los años 30*, Diputación Foral de Guipúzcoa, 1986, p. 138.

[58] GATEPAC stands for Grupo de Arquitectos Españoles Para una Arquitectura Contemporánea (Group of Spanish Architects for a Contemporary Architecture), while GATC-PAC stand for Grup d'Arquitectes Catalans Per una Arquitectura Contemporánia (Group of Catalan Architects for a Contemporary Architecture). It is interesting to note that the words 'new' and 'modern' (which until then had been the distinguishing sign of the architecture that interested them) had disappeared.
A letter from Barcelona to Aizpurua and Labayen in the GATCPAC Archives, dated 18 October 1930, reads: 'The other day we gathered here to talk about the organization of the meeting that will be held in Zaragoza. We wrote a notice of the meeting, which we will send to the architects whom you have recommended in your letter once it has been printed. The summons is for the 25th of this month (Saturday afternoon) in the Gran Hotel of Zaragoza. Don't you think that you should add to your list the names of Bergamín, Domínguez and Arniches? We will do so unless you answer otherwise. We are forwarding you a model of the announcement that we plan to send out. Try to bring something of what your Northern group has been working on. We were delighted with our trip to Germany; we will give you our impressions when we meet up. Hope to see you in our TRASCENDENTAL MEETING.' Taken from *Arte y artistas vascos de los años 30*, op. cit., p. 123.
The same typewritten page mentioned in the letter contains the words: 'October 1930. The Catalan group is established in Barcelona (see Statutes), and the constitution of the G.E.

group (as well as an organ magazine of the group) is launched, also projecting the contribution of industrialists, the creation of standard printing types, press campaigns, and the participation in competitions as a group.' This is followed by: 'On the 25th and 26th, the architects from Madrid, the North and Catalonia who had assembled at the San Sebastian Exhibition held a meeting in Zaragoza for the G.E.; the Statutes are ratified and the group is constituted by G.C., G.N., and G.E.'

The GATCPAC archive houses some press cuttings from local newspapers (the names and dates of the publications, with the exception of one from October 1930 written in pencil, are not included), which seem to suggest a Catalan initiative in promoting this meeting: 'The mayor of Barcelona has also been visited by a group of young architects who initially propose to develop constructions and solve building problems of contemporary architecture following the most modern tendencies … They have told him that they will go to Zaragoza to establish the national group, read the Statutes that they have established, and constitute the Spanish group under a Catalan initiative.'

'On 25 and 26 October, a meeting of architects from Madrid, the North and Catalonia was held in the Gran Hotel of Zaragoza on the initiative of the Catalans so as to establish the GATEPAC affiliated to the CIRPAC. They extensively discussed the statutes presented by the Catalan architects and finally established GATEPAC as a federation of the three subgroups representing the centre, the North and Catalonia.'

The first issue of A.C. provides an explanation as to how the idea took shape at the Exhibition of San Sebastian in September 1930: 'As always, after an exhibition that has required a collective effort, there is an interchange of ideas, a communication among all who have participated in it, and this interchange of ideas among those who are exhibiting is as interesting as the effervescence produced by the exhibition itself … We can therefore say that GATEPAC sprang from the Exhibition of San Sebastian.'

[59] In the file 'Statutes and Regulations C–1/7' of the GATCPAC archives, are two typewritten pages, one with corrections and the other without, signed by Sert and Subiño, in which we can read the GATCPAC statutes. The latter page coincides with the printed declaration of the group's principles and activities, written in Catalan, and is signed in the following order: Sert, Illescas, Alzamora, Torres, Churruca, Rodríguez Arias, Subiño, Perales and Armengou. The Statutes were not printed until 10 February 1936, when they also edited a propagandist pamphlet. C–1/9.

[60] There is a copy in the GATCPAC archives. We will remark on some important conceptual points of its contents without going into its organizational details: 'The aims of the GATCPAC are: a) to assemble architects, engineers and industrialists from the construction branch … to foster and disseminate this architecture and the industries related to it. b) to establish contact with the rest of the Spanish groups for the correct development of this idea both in Spain and in foreign countries. To achieve the aforementioned aims, the group will use the following means: a) to study, by means of the commissions set up, topics related to contemporary architecture. b) to participate, either as a group or as a representative part of it, in the competitions and exhibitions of Spain and abroad. c) to organize lectures, competitions and exhibitions. d) to give publicity, in the

manner most suited to each case and whenever it is considered convenient, to the works created by our associates. e) to write and contribute to a magazine, organ of the Spanish group. f) to select and assemble a group of industrialists (contributors) and to orient them in their activities so as to achieve a 'standard' type that fits in with the guiding idea of our group.' For an analysis of the structure of the group's organization, see Joan C. Theilacker, 'La organización interna del GATCPAC', Cuadernos de Arquitectura y Urbanismo, no. 90, COACB, Barcelona, 1972, pp. 8–17.

[61] It was also mentioned in an interview published in Cuadernos de Arquitectura, no. 140, pp. 5–6. Sixte Illescas states that he and the wife of Fuster i Fabra, a manufacturer of radiators, rented the premises, and that it was inaugurated on 14 April 1931, the day the Republic was proclaimed. In the printed page previously mentioned it states that the inauguration was to be on 13 April. The GATCPAC premises, 99 Passeig de Gràcia of Barcelona, were published in the second issue of A.C., which came out in the second quarter of 1931 (pp. 13–17).

[62] According to the Sigfried Giedion Archives (SGA), in the dossier on CIAM 3, Spanish attendance of the Congress in Brussels was limited to F.G. Mercadal, Sert and Vallejo. Mercadal was still official delegate at the time. In a card from Mercadal dated 10 November 1930 (also kept in these archives), is a list of the thirteen Spanish architects who were CIRPAC members and who had paid their 50-peseta membership fees: A. Salvador, J.M. Rivas, L. Vallejo, F.G. Mercadal, L. Labayen, J.M. Aizpurua, C. Fernández Shaw, S. Illescas, J.L. Sert, R. de Churruca, G. Rodríguez Arias, and Martínez de Aicoitia.

[63] Preparatory meeting in Paris on Saturday 17 May 1930. FLC D2 53–66. There was another meeting in Paris on 5 February and a further one in Palmengar, Frankfurt, on 25 September, to determine the dates of the Congress in Brussels and to decide the programme. SGA. CIAM 3.

[64] Letter from Giedion to Le Corbusier of 25 July 1925. FLC. Correspondence with Giedion. 261. D2 3.

[65] They have been gathered in Rationelle Bebauunsweisen, Julius Hoffmann Verlag, Stuttgart, 1931, pp. 26–47, which compiles all the proposals and speeches of the Congress, with an introduction by Sigfried Giedion. Walter Gropius' typewritten copy is found in SGA, 3–4–42 F.

[66] The Spanish group's answer to workers' housing in Spain is found in the Giedion Archives and is specified as follows: '1. There is no legislation to combat land speculation. 2. There is a lack of knowledge about the problem's magnitude and how it is handled abroad, which could be got through corporations and technicians. 3. There are no standardized elements. 4. The situation of our national urbanism is outdated. There are neither expansion plans nor zoning plans.' SGA, 3–4–61 F.

[67] 'Documents of Contemporary Activity', A.C., no. 1, p. 21.

[68] The Casa Duclós was published in the magazine Hogar y Arquitectura, no. 76, May–June 1968, pp. 57–64; J.L. Sert and the Mediterranean, COAC, Barcelona, 1997, pp. 104–105. We thank Professor Angel Isac for sending us the copies of the plans on this building.

[69] See Antonio Pizza, Guía de la arquitectura moderna. op. cit., pp. 45–48.

[70] In a letter sent by his mother on 22 April 1942, we read the 'consequences' of Sert's gesture: 'The Rosselló flats are doing well, but you know what happens with those flats that have

many renters and the poor ones can't pay.' Archives of Fundació Joan Miró. Sert trunk.

[71] It is not surprising that the railing of the building on Carrer Rosselló appears, for example, on the cover of Sigfried Giedion's book Befreites Wohnen in 1928, nor is it odd that the photographs reproduced in A.C. recall the cover of this same book.

[72] Josep M. Rovira, La arquitectura catalana de la modernidad, op. cit., 1987, p. 194. Antonio Pizza has also remarked on the project's poor structural solution, op. cit., p. 50.

[73] In the Sala Parés of Barcelona, the GATCPAC members held an exhibition of architecture from 27 June to 5 July 1931, organized by the Associació d'Arquitectes de Catalunya. Sert exhibited his buildings for Carrer Rosselló and Carrer Muntaner as well as his Casa Galobart. This last building was published in A.C., no. 8, 1932, pp. 18–20.

Barcelona, the Macià Plan and the CIAMs

In the fourth issue of *A.C.*, another urban project was published, revealing a continuation of the interest in the city already expressed in the first issue. In this case the project focused on solving the housing development of the Avinguda Diagonal in Barcelona. Clearly, *A.C.* believed that there was more at stake than a discussion of the project itself, as can be seen from the way in which it made direct reference to the Brussels CIAM: 'This project has not been developed seeking only the effects of monumentality or aesthetics, but rather it has sprung from a preliminary study of a plan for housing development in Barcelona, which we are preparing for the 1932 Congress in Moscow on 'The Functional City'.[74]

An example of what was discussed there can be found in Walter Gropius' discourse, entitled 'Low, Medium or High-Rise Building?': 'So that the question "What should be the height of rational buildings for the mass construction of popular housing?" may become clearer, it is important to decide on the exact meaning of the word "rational". It is the Congress' duty to fight against the frequent identification of "rational" with "economic". Rational literally means "of good sense" and that is our interpretation of it, because it not only takes into account economic aspects, but also psychological and social ones.'[75] The influence of this text becomes clear in the Diagonal project report written by the GATPAC members: 'The construction must be rational in the sense that Walter Gropius has given it: "of good sense", and not in the frequent sense it is given of being "economic" or low-cost.' Thus, the words 'rational' and 'functional' were already being used regularly in the discourses of Sert and his fellow-believers. In an analogous way, their interest in global town planning and the establishment of grounds for housing, work and rest, as well as their interest in

the social, economic and hygienic aspects of town planning, which are repeatedly mentioned in the project report, were a reflection of the speeches made by Victor Bourgeois and Cornelis van Eesteren during the Brussels Congress.

A glance at the drawings also reveals their need to work on formal hypotheses discussed at the CIAM meeting. The grouping of high-rise apartment blocks separated by a distance that would allow for natural sunlight to reach each apartment and for a depth that would

Macià Plan, diorama (by kind permission of Raimon Torres),

Diagonal Housing development, Barcelona, in *A.C.*, no. 4.

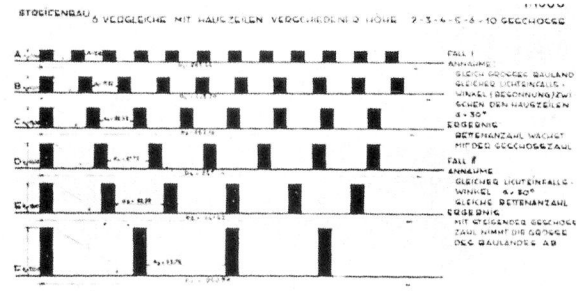

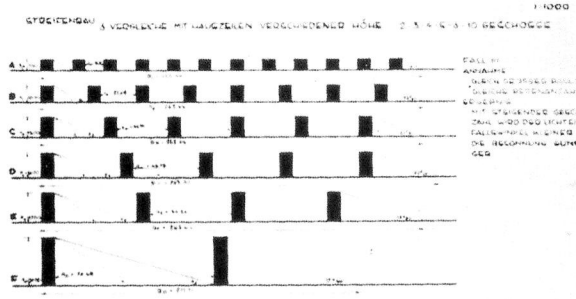

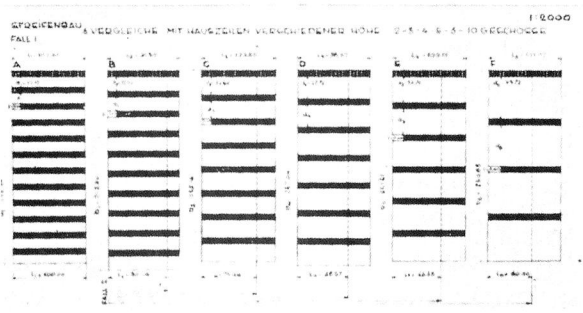

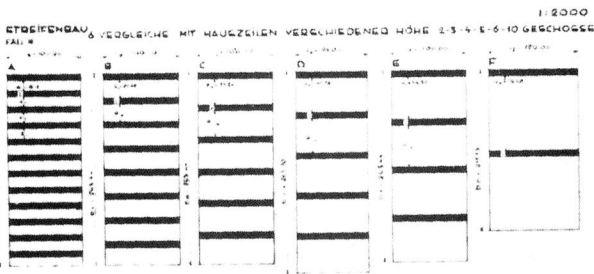

Graphs
by Gropius
concerning
the height
proportions
and free spaces
between buildings
for CIAM 3
in Brussels,
1930.

promote cross ventilation, with the subsequent disappearance of unhealthy light wells, are all options that can be gleaned from an analysis of Gropius' speech and the general atmosphere of the Brussels discussions. Here, Le Corbusier attacked the garden-city idea of individual houses because he thought it contrary to the collective spirit and likely to induce an 'enslaved individualism'. He also defended high-rise buildings, a point that was upheld in the speeches of the architects Boehm and Kaufmann. It is therefore not surprising that the way in which the project was represented by the GATPAC members should be halfway between that chosen by Le Corbusier for his Plan Voisin project and the axonometric perspec-

Drawing
by Gropius
concerning
the height
proportions
and free space
between buildings
for CIAM 3
in Brussels,
1930.

tives presented in the publication of Gropius' text, and that there were none of the expected *pilotis* on the ground floor, nor any terraces being used as gardens: 'The ground floors of the blocks close to the Avenue are to be used for shops and warehouses … Part of the plot space left between buildings may be rented to companies, which may use it for tennis courts, games, swimming pools, etc, its success being guaranteed by the same inhabitants of the area.'

This underlines the interest shown in adapting European models to the city in which they were applied, but one should not overlook the way in which the analysis of the city's specific reality played a part in the development of this proposal. In the project report we also read: 'The preliminary idea of the Diagonal as an avenue for promenades headed towards the former Palacio Real with certain types of low buildings and gardens or detached houses of a certain rank was an absurd and arbitrary idea conceived during the monarchic regime. Since the Palacio Real no longer exists as such, that project no longer has any reason for being, for it is almost impossible to carry out and would be politically disastrous.' In other words, the new political period could precipitate an improvement of the town-planning criteria that would switch from an elitism derived from the monarchic system, which lacked even the most elementary town planning in Barcelona, to a more social vision of the housing problem.

The new authorities, with a different, more open attitude, could back this initiative. The Diagonal project was an experiment with a high dose of naivety, which tried to make the public aware of the advantages of the new ideas and of the possibilities of achieving certain pacts with the authorities concerning the offers that technicians were capable of making, reversing the usual mechanisms of relationships between authority and the proposals of intellectuals. Sert was already familiar with this novel idea from his experience of the transformation of Spanish intellectuals during the preceding period of political upheaval, and he confirmed it by reading the pages of *Plans*, a magazine in which Le Corbusier published in segments his project La Ville Radieuse shortly before the GATPAC members exhibited their Diagonal project to the Barcelona public.

Plans was a magazine that inevitably interested Le Corbusier. With a writing staff whose tendencies were unmistakable, made up of Philippe Lamour, Hubert de Lagardelle, François de Pier-

Cover of *Plans*, no. 1.

refeu and the Swiss architect himself, it was primarily concerned, or so we gather from its first editorial, with reorienting the destiny of France: 'For the understanding and reorientation of the contemporary world, we need an exact measure of the forces and a precise sense of the objectives: a general line of direction is lacking ... The objective of social organization is to afford man a rational material life in which he may develop his personality according to his ends. A society that has collapsed under a series of events is in a state of anarchy that does not allow it to attain this objective. One must order social life; organize man's activities; make of machines a commodity and not a tyranny; have a healthy body in a logical city.'[76]

One can easily read between the lines of a declaration of this type made in a democratic European country during the 1930s, deducing that there were doubts as to whether this type of system could really organize and civilize a country. In fact, one of the constant objectives of *Plans* was to criticize and discredit the democratic system: 'The crisis of democracy makes patent the impotence of individualistic society to adapt itself to the conditions of modern life ... Democracy only acknowledges the individual; it ignores the group ... It is the regime of peasants and the lower middle-class.'[77]

That Le Corbusier shared these opinions and ideology is confirmed by reading his first contribution to *Plans*; in the debut issue he published a text that echoes the above: 'Contemporary society is in crisis ... The world is ill ... A readjustment is called upon, or should I not say readjustment? It is rather a great adventure for humanity, this building of a new world ... because it is urgent ... to build we will look forward.'[78] Moreover, he began to view the metaphor on which he had structured *Vers une Architecture*, that is the machine, as useless when faced with the need to build a new order: 'The mechanist period is already a century old. It has provoked the destruction and desolation of a world; it has brought upon us misery and perils; it has carried out one of its most painful tasks, that of rupture.' After speaking of his mistrust of machines, Le Corbusier went on to describe where architecture stood at the time, referring to it as being at a standstill, something he emphasized again later in the text.

In an unfavourable environment surrounded by a generalized crisis, which the staff of *Plans* referred to as 'disorder' in their writings ('Administrative Disorder', 'Economic Disorder', 'Disorder of the Social Organization'), Le Corbusier considered that in order to deal with town planning there had to be a strong power that would back up, facilitate and process their proposals. He generically spoke of this power, as he had done in the CIAM meeting in Brussels, as 'the authorities', and to these authorities he dedicated the first edition of *La Ville Radieuse*, as well as referring to it in the first issue of *Plans*: 'The city only exists on paper; the act of faith that would make it come alive would be that of the authorities. But the authorities do not concern themselves with urbanism. They have not become aware of what town planning means: to foresee, to prepare … A gesture of the authorities would bring about human well-being in cities … It is a matter of creating La Ville Radieuse.'

A further coincidence enlightens us: just as the staff of *Plans* preferred the political formulas of totalitarian regimes as the only way out of an ineffectual democratic system, Le Cor-

busier would at that point see clearly that it was no longer a matter of trying to persuade powerful industrial businessmen to carry out his dreams: now it was a question of reaching agreement with the political powers, which France did not have and which Sert hoped to find in a Catalonia governed by Francesc Macià after 14 April 1931.

The interest shown by the *Plans* staff in emphasizing the chaos in France led its members to analyze totalitarian regimes of whatever tendency so as to become familiar with those systems that did not reveal the weaknesses of democracies, placing them in a European and world context between the wars, and praising their representatives: 'At least Hitler has a doctrine',[79] as well as their political mechanisms: 'The USSR imposes upon its citizens a heroic life, and thanks to the continuity of its federal regime, it develops through its Plan the only reasonable economy in this world given over to anarchy.'[80]

The possibility of creating a different culture that would allow for the liberation of personal existence through town planning, architecture, work organization and free time was also high-

Buildings of 'The Green City' placed in *redent* and built on *pilotis*.

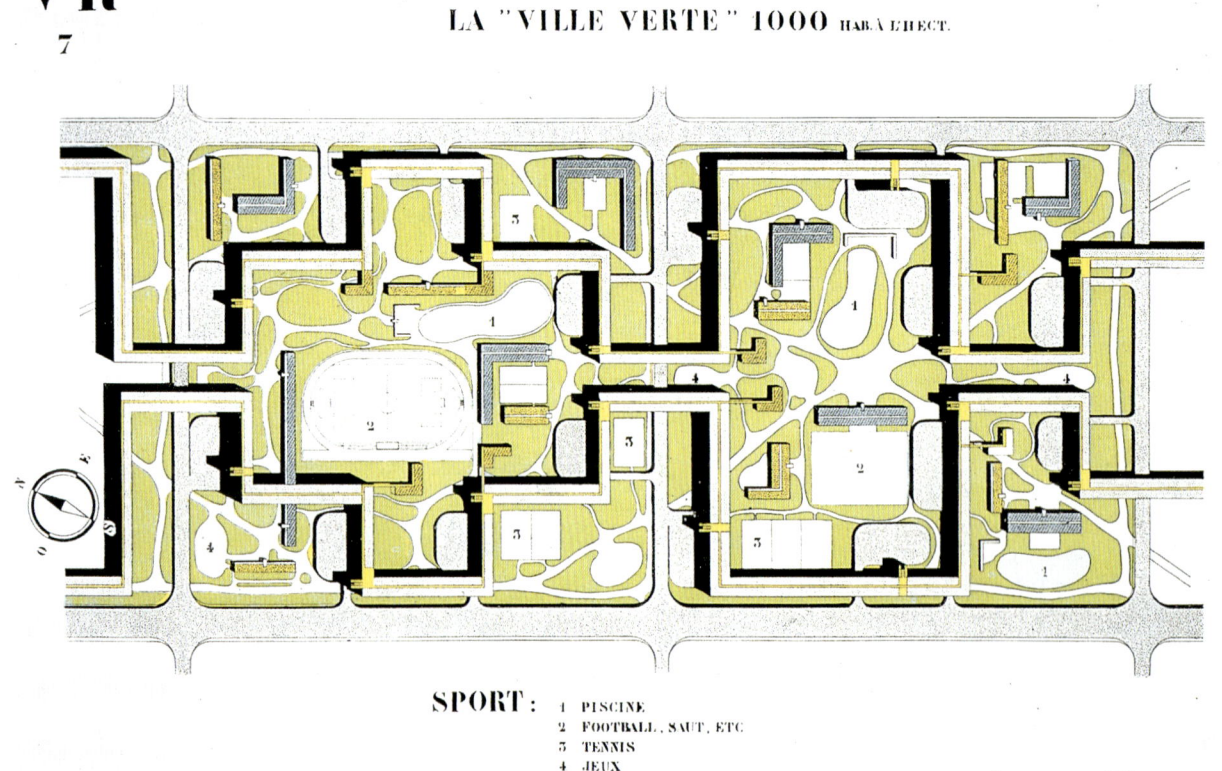

VR
7

LA "VILLE VERTE" 1000 HAB. À L'HECT.

SPORT : 1 PISCINE
2 FOOTBALL, SAUT, ETC
3 TENNIS
4 JEUX

0   100   200'

ly praised. Other constant topics that we find in various issues of *Plans* are the renovation of the educational system and the aesthetic development that the new world should follow.

This is the context in which La Ville Radieuse was being created. Some aspects of it are worthy of attention, such as a fragment of a residential city that Le Corbusier called Ville Verte, which appears in the first and third issues of the magazine, the latter showing more definition and including for the first time a series of residential buildings organized in *redent* and built on top of *pilotis* surrounded by recreational amenities.

The comparison made by Le Corbusier between the closed city blocks in Paris or Buenos Aires and his alternative proposal is one of the issues that will crop up in the Macià Plan and that originates here, when the scheme of La Ville Radieuse had not yet come into being. Le Corbusier wanted to show the French public a new way of grouping residential buildings together, something that we can imagine was linked to a theory that CIAM members always defended, namely that housing is the most important of urban functions, and which had also been the subject of the experiences dealt with in the CIAM meeting in Brussels and in the exhibition that was staged later.

Nevertheless, the way in which housing was focused upon illustrates the insecurities of the Swiss architect concerning urbanism, which he himself thought was still lacking its own discipline. To initiate a disquisition on a city by concerning oneself with the grouping of residential buildings makes one justifiably suspect that there were conceptual difficulties to be solved in his work. And was not this way of initially thinking about a compositional mechanism that could assemble important housing production interventions in a city scandalously lacking in them what led Sert and his friends to imagine the Diagonal project (a project that would later be abandoned) as a point of departure for a new Barcelona? These architects expressed their desire to think about the city as something indivisible, but this idea of indivisibility did not make it easier to solve the problem.

We must wait until May 1931 to observe the first sketch of La Ville Radieuse in the fifth issue of *Plans*. With its functions – businesses, sta-

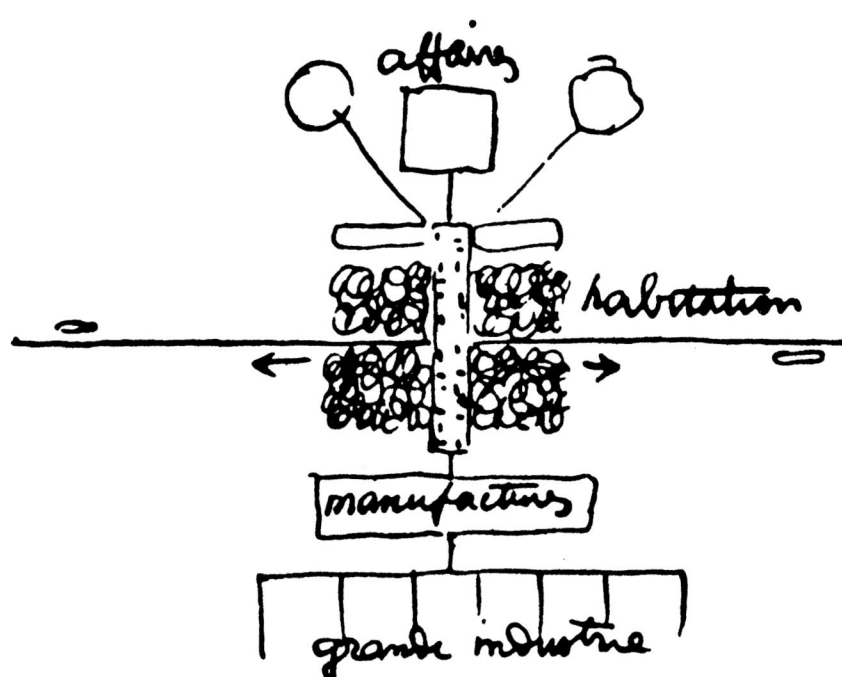

First scheme of La Ville Radieuse (the Radiant City) in *Plans*, no. 5.

tions, hotels and embassies, dwellings, factories, industry – all grouped together in a continuum of parallel strips presided over by the businesses, it recalls an anthropomorphic outline more in keeping with Renaissance plans by Francesco di Giorgio. At the head of the city were businesses on which all the main communication routes converged, the most important one being destined for public buildings construction: entertainment, government buildings, etc. The pact between capital and the political and tertiary sectors was evident in this model of clear Beaux Arts inspiration, which relegated industrial production to the last position and paid much attention to leisure time both in the programme of the radiant city and in many texts that we find in the *Plans* issues.

In addition to pointing out its mechanist outline, which could lead us to believe that we are looking at a layout of Plan Voisin in which the business area of the city has been put at the head of things (in the Plan Voisin it had occupied a central position integrated into the core life of the city, without the elitist and dominating role it now had), it is necessary to remark on the location of the tertiary sector, which is highly significant. Not only production, but also the control of leisure activities and representation, and their location on the best urban axis, is of interest as an urban function that had to be incorporated into the functional city.

All of this was clearly inspired by the urban layouts of French Baroque classicism, especially since we know that during that historical period existed a firm authority that was much to Charles Edouard Jeanneret's liking, and which helps us to understand the name given to the proposal of the city in question: 'Louis XIV … wished to make what was tortuous straight: he rectifies, decrees new layouts, changes the scale … Louis XIV shines, he is the Sun King.'

There is something else that draws our attention to that first drawing of the radiant city. In the outline that we have described, Le Corbusier wrote: 'The highway network laid out here ensures the necessary infrastructure (complete, efficient and sufficient) for a city of a million and a half inhabitants. Each unit of the residential city grid measures 400 metres.' This is the same measurement that would be proposed in the Macià Plan when they tried to organize the city blocks that Ildefonso Cerdá had projected by grouping nine on a square with three of these per side. This was baptized *Nuevo Módulo*, but Le Corbusier chose to call it *Le Carré Espagnol*. The viability of these super-city blocks was explained during the presentation

of the plan: 'The Ensanche must be taken over by this new layout, more in keeping with present-day needs. This new layout will first be carried out in the border areas … it will invade the old city (only with regard to major roads) and link the rest of Barcelona with the new administrative centre.'[81]

We find a more complete development of Le Corbusier's city in the eighth issue of *Plans,* the same in which we are told: 'In Spain, the Socialists, copying with sweet obstinacy the unfortunate example of their Russian predecessors, are allying themselves with the Conservatives in a purely negative sentiment against the royal regime, and they are organizing amongst themselves great chaos, preparing the way for a Spanish Lenin.'[82] The intention of this article is unmistakable: 'A new city replaces an old one.' The scale used for the plan drawing allows us to observe some significant novelties.

The strip that we know was to be used for entertainment and administrative purposes had gained in dimension, and here, without a detailed programme, we observe groupings of buildings that we can conventionally assimilate with the forms that Le Corbusier had essayed

La Ville Radieuse in *Plans*, no. 8.

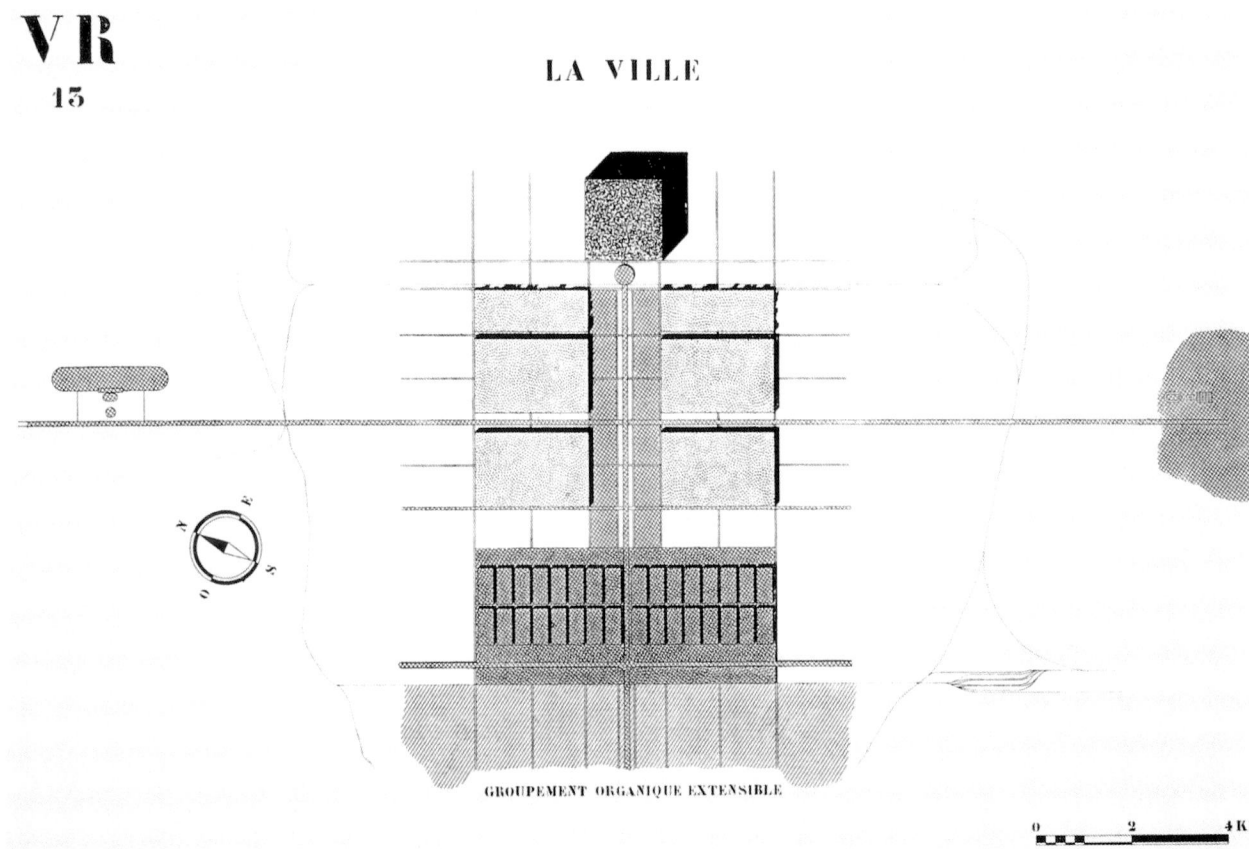

GROUPEMENT ORGANIQUE EXTENSIBLE

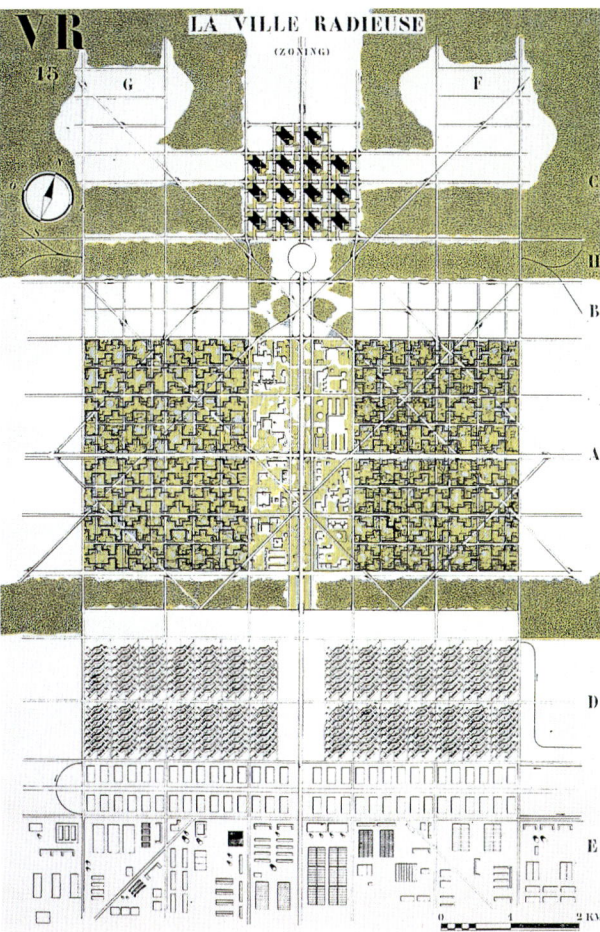

in his monumental proposals for public infrastructures. Elements taken from the Palace of the League of Nations competition project, from the Centrosoyuz and from the Palace of the Soviets competition are distributed along a network of orthogonal streets at 45 degrees, distributed on different levels and occupying exactly the same width as the business centre. One must pay special attention to the layout of some of these islands of administrative infrastructures since they will also show up in what the Macià Plan called the Civic Centre, drawn in detail in January 1935.

Furthermore, in the radiant city, which we know was supposed to replace the old city, the plan for the historic centre was clear. This downtown area, with its deficient hygienic and sanitary conditions and overcrowded population, was to be demolished in a staggered operation. Le Corbusier went so far as to make sociological comments in keeping with his obsession with the new order: 'Crime there is international, that is how things work today! We shall have to send the police in there! 40,000

policemen, Mr Chiappe, with machineguns and hand grenades and gas!' We will understand the source of this desire later, when we see the interest shown by GATPAC members in the improvement of living conditions in the old Barcelona.

The fact that we have made use of diverse information from *Plans* in our survey is due to a comment that Le Corbusier made in his book *La Ville Radieuse*, published in 1935, in which we find five pages dedicated to the Macià Plan within the chapter explaining the Swiss architect's different urban proposals, ranging from Rome to Stockholm, the Plan Voisin, to proposals for cities in South America, as well as the Algiers Plan and the Moscow Plan. The proposals appearing in the pages of this book of texts and plans are a good example of Le Corbusier's interest in the city.

In the short text that accompanies the presentation of the project for Barcelona, which at first he had come up with by himself and had then developed with Sert and other GATPAC members who were also bent on carrying it out, we read: 'I exposed my thesis, my admiration for the city of Barcelona – a conjugation of an unfortunate geographical site for a capital with natural splendour. The intention of this city, and the youthful spirit of its leaders, gave wings to hope: at last, in a thriving spot of the world, modern times could find a refuge.'[83]

Barcelona was thus chosen as the site for the synthesis of modern times with the true belief that the ideas on modern, functional cities, elaborated in congresses and in discussions among the leading European architecture professionals, were to materialize there. In 1935 Le Corbusier believed that those proposals that had always remained on paper, that seemed mere sophisticated dreams with no chance of coming into being, could finally come true in Barcelona.

In the fifth issue of *A.C.*, published in the first quarter of 1932, the wording of the editorial became more radical. Titled 'The Functional City', it manifested a clear will to back up what was being discussed in the preparatory meetings for CIAM 4, which they still thought would be held in Moscow. Here we read: 'The modern city must be, as any being that possesses life, an ensemble of organs ordered according

President Macià with the CIRPAC delegates, Barcelona, 1932.

CIRPAC meeting, Barcelona, 1932.

to their functions. The areas of LIVING, PRODUCTION, REST, with CIRCULATION as the linking element, are determining factors in the forms of urban agglomeration.'[84] Naturally, before writing a text that was so radical in its wording, the GATCPAC members had to ask for help from the place in which this new way of looking at the city was being formulated. This is why Sert addressed a letter to Sigfried Giedion on 25 November 1931, saying: 'I would like to ask if you could give me all possible information on the subject of the Congress in Moscow dealing with 'The Functional City' and if you could send me everything that has been published on this topic or if you could tell me where I might find it.'[85]

The reason for sending this letter could only be Sert's inability to attend the CIRPAC held between 4 and 7 June in Berlin,[86] where the participants discussed topics that had to do with the preparation of the fourth CIAM, as did the meeting held in Amsterdam on 5 December. These two meetings were fundamental for the GATPAC architects, not only because of what they would learn from them but also due to their decision to organize the following CIRPAC in Barcelona, which was to be held from 29 March to 1 April 1932. During those days, the Catalan city would be the centre of attention of the European architectural avant-garde.

The press immediately echoed this, as witnessed by a report found in the GATCPAC archives and dated 2 March 1932: 'The Generalitat has declared guests of honour the archi-

tects attending the preparatory meeting that will be held in Barcelona in mid-March with the object of discussing questions that will be submitted to the Congress in Moscow so as to clearly specify the characteristics of the new organism with respect to the functional housing of workers. The preparatory meeting is financed by the Ateneu and the GATEVAC [sic], a group of architects and technicians interested in the rational resolution of workers'

Sert and Le Corbusier at the Palace of the Generalitat during the CIRPAC, Barcelona, 1932.

housing. This meeting will be attended by, among others, the renowned urban designers Le Courbusier [sic] from Paris, Gideou [sic] from Zurich, Bourgeois from Brussels, Van Eestereu [sic] from Amsterdam, and Baüer from Berlin, who will hold in our city diverse lectures on issues relating to the problems of a 'functional city' with the idea of implementing it in Barcelona.'

Despite the many typographical errors spoiling this report, some of the topics it mentioned are worthy of our attention. The first and probably the most important is the institutional support given to the preparation and monitoring of the meeting. Renowned architects would be coming to discuss the problems of the industrial city, and were to be guided by local colleagues who had been insisting for over a year on the urgent need to solve issues arising from town planning in Barcelona. They had been invited, therefore, by a tacit alliance between the political authorities – those authorities they had so often demanded – and by the representatives of architectural modernity who were starting to construct buildings that their fellow-citizens did not understand, that their academic colleagues scorned, and that, nevertheless, had a broadcasting vehicle which had already published five issues. Considering the short life of most vanguard magazines of the period, this was not an insignificant achievement.

It seems evident that Sert and company had decided to place themselves before the authorities in order to begin proposing solutions, animated by the political and ideological changes represented by the coming of the Republic. We can ascertain this thanks to a letter that Sert wrote to Le Corbusier on 21 January 1932, in which he told him of their firm commitment to start a Plan for Barcelona: 'We have started to work on the town planning for the future Barcelona, although it is very difficult to organize this type of work when we are lacking all sorts of statistics.'

The conjunction of the clear intellectual will of the GATCPAC members and of the favourable circumstances regarding what Le Corbusier called 'the authorities' were thus beginning to be perceived in Barcelona. Something of this is transmitted by Le Corbusier in an extract from *La Ville Radieuse*: 'In the spring of 1932, Luís Sert, who so clearly seems to direct the destinies of the GATEPAC team (a Catalan group for international congresses on modern architecture) in Barcelona, arranged for me to meet with President Macià. The future of the Catalan Republic and urbanism were joined as one in the insightful spirit of the President and the professional people that surrounded him.'[87]

In Barcelona, the CIRPAC delegates did not only discuss the functional city; as well as persistent efforts by the press to publicize the meeting, some of the most famous CIRPAC architects also gave public lectures in an attempt to introduce to the most renowned intellectual circles the new ideas that were being discussed behind closed doors.[88] Thus, during that radiant spring of 1932, it was possible to attend in Barcelona intelligent conferences on issues that until then had been unheard of, or – to put it more mildly – were scarcely known: workers' housing, the scientific and material analysis of cities, the construction of dwellings as if assembling prefabricated parts, etc., became issues that began to penetrate common feeling.

It was not merely a forum for the interests of architects, however. Apart from the specific solutions that the newly arrived CIRPAC delegates seemed to offer, there were other issues yet to be solved in Barcelona, and their presence could be sensed floating in the atmosphere. This can be explained by referring to a work by Francesc Roca, who has investigated some of these subjects: 'Therefore, an analysis of the municipal programmes of the political parties that ran for election in April 1931 allows one to discover an interesting fact: the battle against forced unemployment, the restructuring of municipal administration and urban reform: "cheap housing, hygienic districts, education …" make up a coherent whole.'[89] Thus, technical possibilities and municipal concerns could now go hand in hand, and because of this we can understand why Le Corbusier insisted on defining Barcelona as a favourable city for modern times. Roca has also pointed out another important factor to complete the reasoning: the content of the combat magazines published in the first years of the 1930s – *L'Hora*, *Treball*, *La Batalla*, *Justicia Social*, *La Rambla*. These publications on the

Drawings
by Le Corbusier
for the Macià
Plan, 1932 (FLC,
Carnet C10 and
Carnet C10-636).

fringes of the liberal bourgeois press denounced the precarious living conditions of 'the marginalized', who manifested the urgent needs of the working classes.[90]

Thus, the debates that were taking place in CIAM, Le Corbusier's proposals for his radiant city and the new language and tools with which to face the city coincided with the collective ambition to improve Barcelona manifested by the authorities, technicians and the socially aware. The letter that the Generalitat of Catalonia wrote to Sert on 3 May 1932, and which he took with him to the US, is eloquent proof of this: 'We are pleased to tell you that we are establishing in Barcelona the Commissariat for Workers' Housing annexed to the Generalitat of Catalonia, and since you have been one of the persons designated to integrate it, we ask

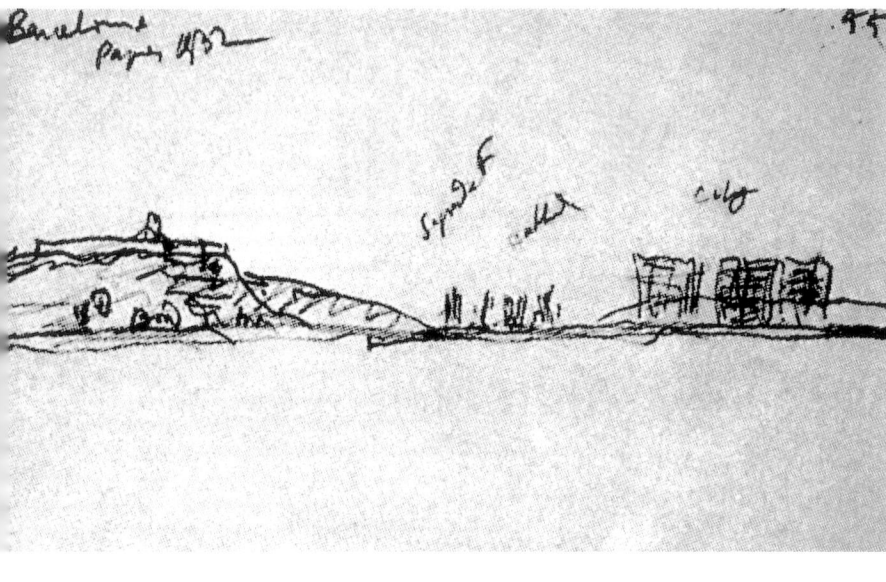

on the President's behalf that you attend the meeting that will be held tomorrow, Wednesday, at 5 o'clock in this Presidence.'[91] This coincidence might have triggered Macià's meeting with Le Corbusier a few days earlier, a meeting that the Swiss architect acknowledged to be the work of Sert.

It is not certain whether the two drawings from 1932 that are considered to be the first ones pertaining to the Macià Plan were done by Le Corbusier in the presence of the old President of the Generalitat at this meeting. One of the freehand drawings is a front elevation view, in which we can see Montjuïc in the background behind what seem to be three skyscrapers of great height, rising from Barcelona's seafront, as seen from the sea, and labelled in Le Corbusier's hand with the word 'City'.[92] Since the 'Business City' was the most important element – the thinking head and economic ruler of the functional city – when it at last seemed possible that this plan could come about, the first gesture was to imagine this governing site in a vibrant landscape, by the sea, competing in lordliness with the mountain and defiantly standing against it. On a variation, or perhaps initial version, of this drawing, Le Corbusier wrote: 'We will need skyscrapers of the same height as Montjuïc.'

It is worth remembering how Le Corbusier had chosen to represent his proposal for Buenos Aires a few years earlier, a representation that became the cover for one of his most influential books: four brilliant, radiant towers against a starry sky, reflected in the Mar de la Plata at night, constituted the new facade for the Argentinian capital synthesized with the world of business.

The second drawing was published in Le Corbusier's book *La Ville Radieuse* and shows the embryo of the definitive Macià Plan, also drawn freehand. Two powerful diagonals, the Parallel and the Meridiana (corresponding to large circulation routes designed by Ildefonso Cerdá), converge at three points located by the sea. These diagonals cross on parallel strips occupied by the housing areas, which are headed, by an extension of the Gran Vía, towards the Llobregat River; the similarities with the scheme of the radiant city are too much in evidence to pass unnoticed.[93] The three points are

Le Corbusier, proposal for Buenos Aires (Conférence - FLC 30304).

the three skyscrapers that make up the core of the 'City' that Le Corbusier had already imagined in front elevation. A classification of the districts from 1 to 13 accompany the drawing, give it the weight of a global proposal, which moreover, is measured by a larger territory than the one marked by the municipal limits. At the base of the three business skyscrapers, which would later be reduced to two, we find a significant addition: a stadium and an auditorium or palace of congress that would undergo various transformations in the process of the project's development. Thus we see in an unsigned

and undated aerial perspective two skyscrapers that Le Corbusier called 'Cartesian'. These are no longer like those he had conceived in the form of a cross for Buenos Aires, which were already included in his project for a city of three million inhabitants and which he repeated in successive proposals that were repeatedly criticized. Now they took on a new form resembling a Y, placed on the coastline, defiantly facing the sea with open wings while turning their back to the city. Thus, Barcelona modified Le Corbusier's conception of skyscrapers, changing the shape of this Cartesian vertical curtain-wall variant, which he would develop in great detail in plans and front elevations and which we again find repeated in other projects that were also published in *La Ville Radieuse*.

Immediately after these two initial drawings, in May 1932, the GATCPAC members published three successive articles in the *Mirador* magazine. One can observe the result of this contact with Le Corbusier in the explicit statement of what the Plan's main guidelines for intervention should be.

Under the general heading 'Outline of the GATCPAC Programme' and with a sole title for the three articles – 'Town Development of the Future Barcelona' – we find a systematic formulation of the city's problems and some schemes that reveal significant variations on Le Corbusier's initial sketch.

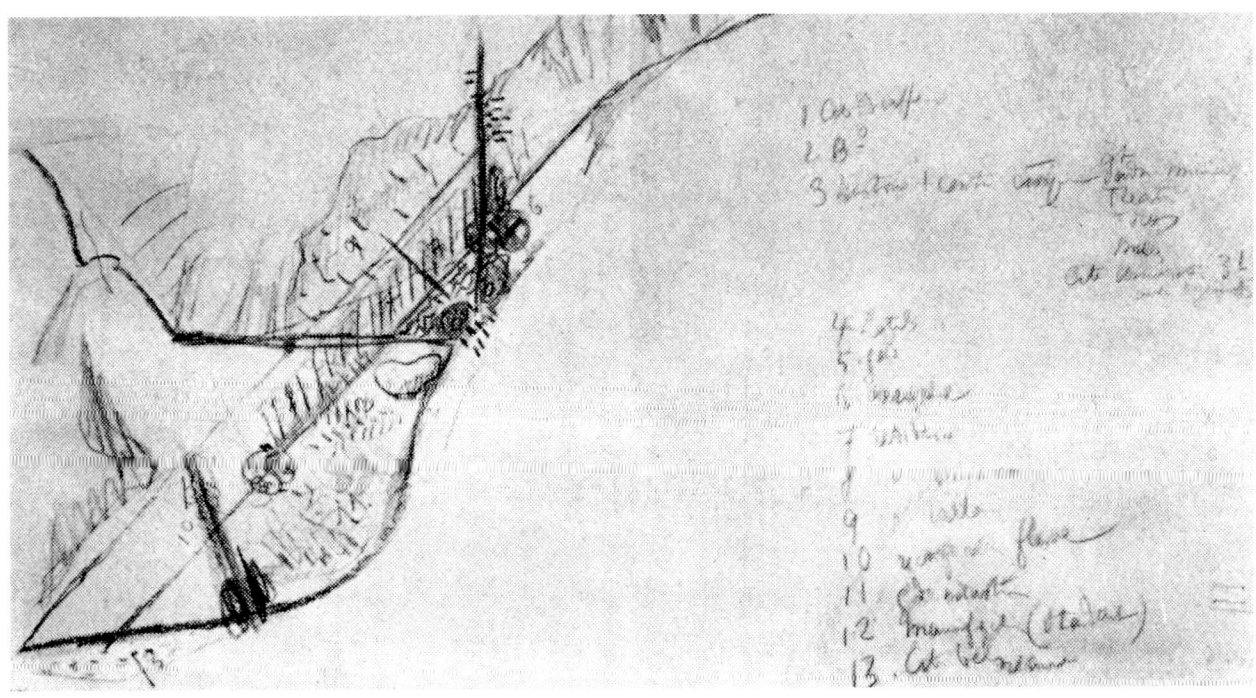

Le Corbusier and Sert, Macià Plan, sketch of the master plan from 1932, published in *L'Architecture d'Aujourd'Hui*, no. 10, p. 32 and in the book *La Ville Radieuse*, 1935, p. 38.

Le Corbusier,
Macià Plan,
sketch of the plan
and aerial
perspective,
1933 (FLC 13213
and 13186).

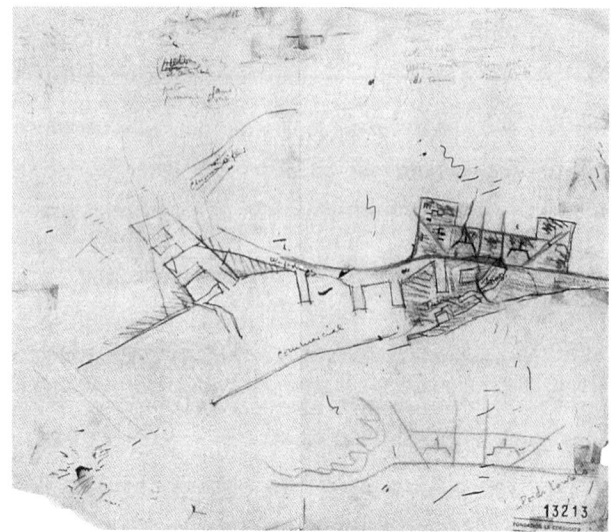

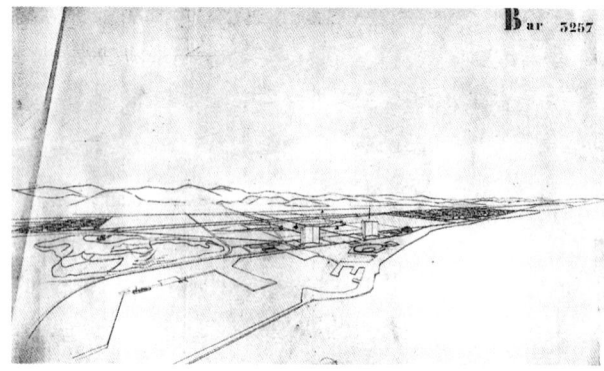

Le Corbusier,
Macià Plan, aerial
perspective,
1933 (FLC
13186).

In the first text, after criticizing the deplorable state in which the city found itself, was a review of Barcelona's expansion in which the principal plans that guided this growth were mentioned. There was specific emphasis on the misapplication of the provisions made by the Cerdá Plan, on the lack of urban efficacy of the Jaussely Plan, and on the serious errors of Rubió i Tudurí's 'Regional Planning'. The text then laid out some considerations concerning the geographic territorial circumference of Barcelona: 'Present-day Barcelona is limited by two natural obstacles that situate it between two parallels: the sea and the mountain. As areas of expansion, it can count only on the plains between its two rivers to the east and to the south.' Although Le Corbusier's parallel strips were based on what was only a theoretical model, they nevertheless obeyed a logic that is worth taking into account.

However, the most decisive point in this first text is made in the last sentence, which introduces the content of the second article. Barcelona is defined and interpreted according to its functions and to the new circumstances through which it was living: 'We are forced to consider Barcelona as an industrial city with a predominance of worker inhabitants, and as Catalonia's port. Our city is also on the point of becoming the capital of an autonomous state.' This autonomy had been developing for some time, since August 1930, when the Catalan representatives gave support to the Republican Committee headed by Alcalá Zamora in the Pact of San Sebastian, with the condition that he committed himself to solving the Catalan problem legally under the formula of an autonomous constitution or set of statutes. After the proclamation of the Republic, the government of the Generalitat called an assembly of representatives of the town councils made up of independents or left-wing delegates, who by 20 June 1931 had already written up the Estatut de Núria, an early version of the Estatut d'Autonomia, which began to be debated in

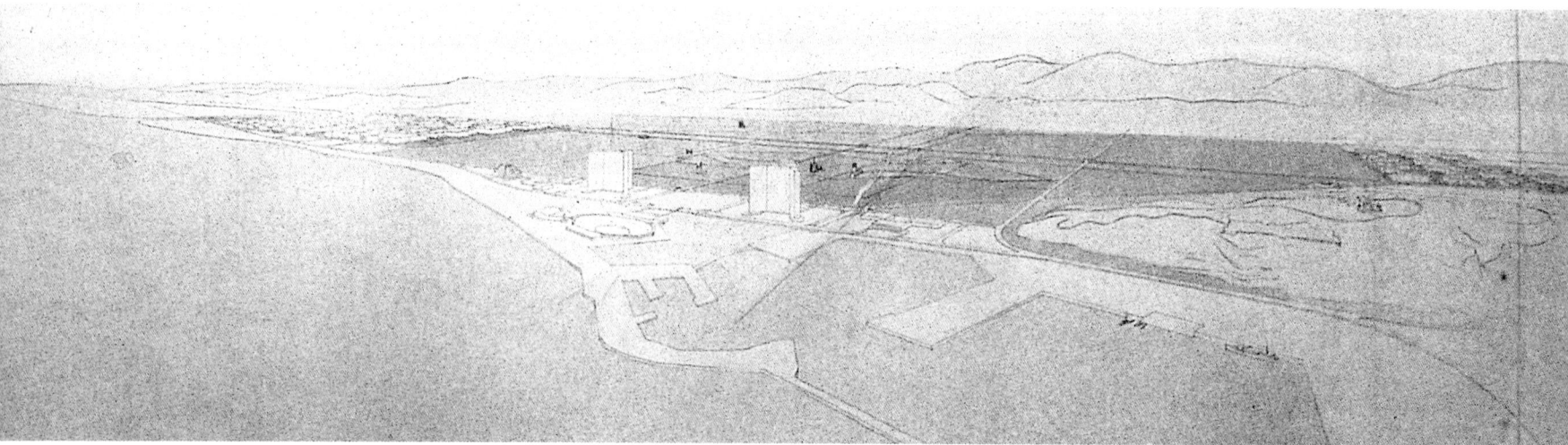

Propagandist
manifesto
of the campaign
to obtain
the Statutes
of Autonomy.

the Courts of Madrid on 6 May 1932. This was taking place at the same time that Sert and his friends were writing their articles for *Mirador*, and it was not a chance coincidence, as can be seen from a letter from Sert to Le Corbusier (which we will mention later) some months afterwards, in which he pointed out the importance of this political event in the defining of the future Barcelona.

The second article focused on resolving the conflict in this industrial working-class city and capital, presenting clearly designated areas accompanied by an imprecise scale drawing: 'In the future city, the following areas must be differentiated: Production, Civic Centre, Housing, Leisure and Traffic.' Each of the parts integrated in this zoning was accordingly described with an explanation regarding its position and conditions. In one of the two graphs that illustrate this text we find some new aspects. A free port was included, with a plotted area called City of Leisure – a term with whose origin we are familiar – whose third section was described as the Beach Area: 'A main area for the

whole city, of great capacity, in which we foresee different services like baths, sports, weekend stations, seasonal dwellings for vacations and sanatoriums for convalescents, which is to go from the pond of Remolà to the Garraf, just two kilometres away from the coast. The highway, an extension of the Avinguda de les Corts, will provide easy access to this area.'

Considering that Barcelona was to be the capital of an autonomous state, it is not surprising that a Civic Centre with a defined programme was proposed, although it was still not shown in the perspective that Le Corbusier had by then corrected. However, in this text it had both a site and a clearly detailed justification: 'The fact that our city will be capital of Catalonia will make necessary the construction of buildings destined for the functioning of the Government, such as Ministries, Administration Offices, Palace of the City, Exhibition Halls, Workers' Associations, etc. They will be located in a green environment near the City, once the "Barrio Chino" at the base of Montjuïc has undergone an adequate process of reclamation, leaving the silhouette of our mountain well-defined.'[94]

The objective of the Plan was to continue the expansion of the capital city, conducting new public life and rationalizing the placement of industrial sites, as well as improving housing conditions – with the 400 × 400-metre city block that was now adapted to the Cerdá city blocks, so that its dimensions were 260 × 400 – while at the same time creating a meeting point in the city, where the businesses and bureaucracy in charge of making the city function efficiently would be concentrated.

Furthermore, this third article proffers an additional provision concerning the interrelationship between Barcelona and its surrounding region, anticipating the contents, debates and resolutions of the CIAM, which was held in the summer of 1933 in Athens. Faced with the rapid and uncontrolled growth of traffic and acknowledging its importance as the functional glue of all modern urban ideas, this was an attempt to order its main strands: railways, car transit and air traffic. It even foresaw two solutions that would be carried out long afterwards: the need for a beltway that would join Molins de Rei, Sabadell and Granollers, and

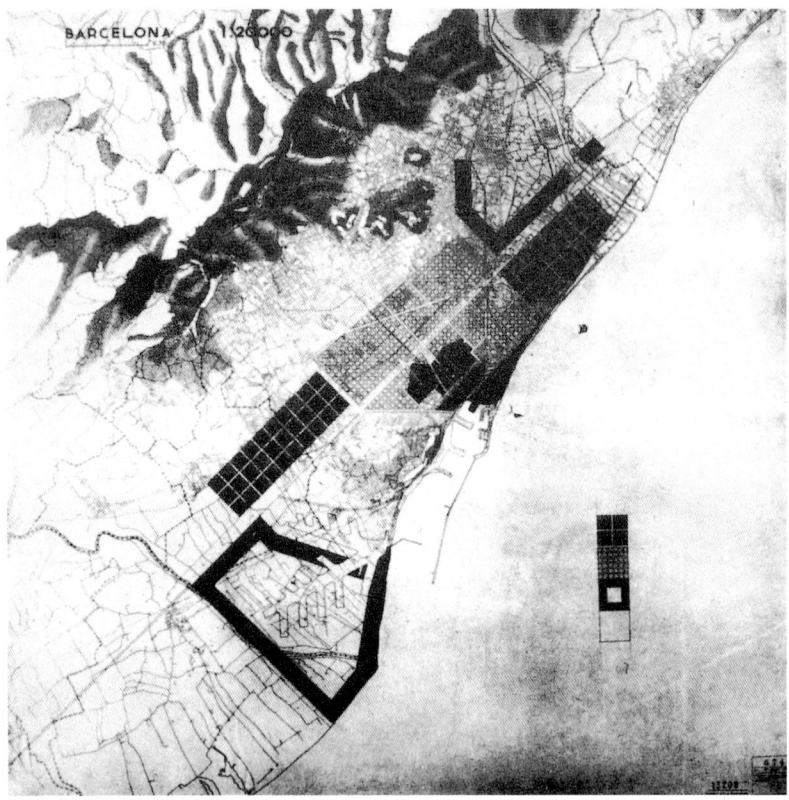

Le Corbusier,
Macià Plan,
overall view, 1933
(FLC 13206).

we furnish our citizens with quick and inexpensive means of transportation to these areas … The governing authorities of the people must take heed of this desire, this need of the masses. And it is their duty, their obligation, to organize, create and structure, by the most modern – functional – means available, the areas dedicated to relaxation and leisure activities in the open before the expansion of the city makes this impossible.' Once more, the architects were making proposals to the authorities based on the analytical methods that they had developed regarding the city's needs. They called on the authorities with the same words that Le Corbusier had used in *Plans*, unaware of the structural weakness of the Republic and trusting its ideological tendencies, or perhaps hopeful that an autonomous state would be able to arbitrate its own urban strategies.

We should not only analyze but also follow the process that was to make this dream come true. The additional tasks to be taken on were many: finding the ideal terrain; creating a preliminary design; taking care of the initial economic provisions and starting to explain the idea to Catalan co-operatives in order to get the attention of the 'marginalized' who would most benefit from the project. To do this, the GATCPAC members designed, constructed and exhibited a small, inexpensive 'weekend' house that could be dismantled and could act as a model for occupation by the masses for leisure and rest by the sea. Foreseeably, the next step taken by *A.C.* was the writing up of a preliminary design called City of Leisure and Va-

the elimination of the railway parallel to the sea heading towards the Besós River.

The seventh issue of *A.C.*, running parallel with these reflections although it came out shortly after these articles were published, in the third quarter of 1932, focused mainly on the organization of the leisure time of the masses.[95] Once again, the format chosen for calling attention to an urban problem that needed an immediate solution was the manifesto: 'It is urgent that we organize areas of rest and leisure that are lacking in cities, and that

Le Corbusier,
overall view of the
Macià Plan, 1933
(FLC 13210).

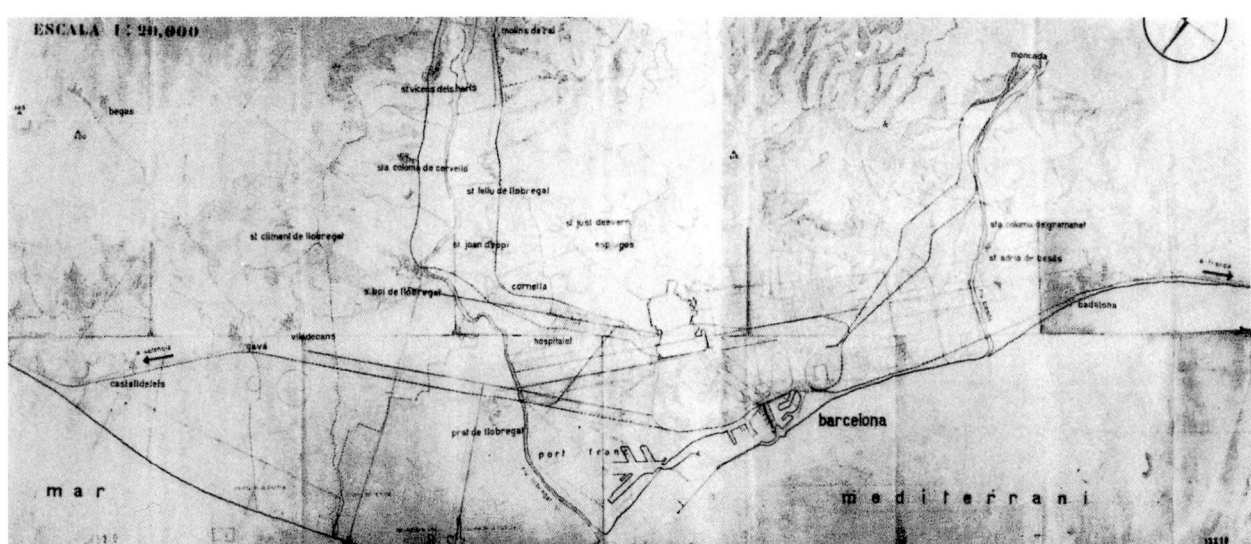

Cover of the seventh issue of *A.C.*, devoted to planning and leisure time.

cations, which included a clear-cut programme and ideology. The former designated a series of areas to meet the diverse needs of the users, leading to the development of a bathing area, a weekend area, a residential area and a health-care area to encompass a wide and versatile functional offer. With regard to the ideology, the intention of the project report is transparent: 'We are not trying to create a new beach

vogue. The general orientation of the project is deeply democratic, steered only towards the social needs of the working classes and middle classes, and there is a total absence of casinos and luxury hotels … Today, the worker aims to satisfy his longing for sunlight and rest … the organization of periodic rest is urgent, and to solve it one must act in a decided manner, appealing if necessary this being a case of public health – to the laws of expropriation'

In the declarations made in La Sarraz,[96] it had already been observed that one of the main obstacles against which the rationalist urbanism was going to come up was land property and its consequences. In France this had been approached in the first meeting of 1928 as follows: 'The chaotic division of land, which has resulted from sales and speculations, from inheritances, must be abolished by means of a methodical and collective territorial economy. This regrouping of land, which is the necessary foundation stone for all town planning, must lead to the equitable distribution of surplus benefits among landowners and the community, which result from the works of common interest.' However, this approach was considered totally insufficient by the modern Catalan architects. Their idea was not the replotting of the land but rather expropriation in the face of the project's collective interest. The need for new rules in the urban game, for a new urban economy, as Sert himself said in 1937, was seen as an urgent issue that revealed the far-reaching scope of the proposals to which a given interpretation of the city could give rise.

A letter from Sert to Le Corbusier on 21 March 1932 gives us an idea of the general tone of their first contacts and of Sert's intentions in preparing the interview with Macià, a few days before the CIRPAC in Barcelona: 'We are working on the plans for Barcelona and would be pleased to have you as a fellow-associate, but I have to warn you that from a practical viewpoint this is not easy because the Government of Catalonia is suffering great economic difficulties and one cannot define anything until the Statutes of Catalonia have been ratified. Nevertheless, I consider your interview with Mr Macià to be very worthwhile; if possible, please bring graphic material to show him.' Le Corbusier's answer to Sert on 24 May, once the meeting in Barcelona had come to an end, is explicit: 'I thought about this on Sunday: don't you think that while your Commissariat on Workers' Housing is being formed I could be named Counsellor on town development and other related issues?'[97]

Sert began travelling to and from Paris in order to design and elaborate the Macià Plan with Le Corbusier. Perhaps an additional factor was that Ramona Longas, or Moncha, Sert's lifetime sweetheart and companion, had signed a rental contract for an apartment on Boulevard de Bon Sejour on 20 December of 1931 (the address to which Sert asked letters to be sent to him when he was staying in Paris).[98] Nevertheless, there were some issues affecting the Macià Plan project that cannot be overlooked.

The background to these was the insistent criticism towards the official town planning of Barcelona City Council, which we have already noted in the first issue of *A.C.* In an article published in the newspaper *L'Opinió* on 4 January 1932, GATCPAC attacked the opening of the Gran Via C, already contained in the Cerdá Plan, which was to cross the old quarter of the city from one end to the other. It instead proposed a more global solution, more in keeping with the style of modern planning, for an area that had been persistently overlooked by the municipal authorities. This proposal was summarized in five points: 'First: the need for roads to link the old quarter of Barcelona with the Ensanche. Second: transversal 'secondary' roads to avoid a 'touristic' layout that would mean crossing the old quarter from one end to the other by means of great roads. Third: distribution of parking lots so as to avoid cars being parked on main streets. Fourth: the demolition and new structuring of the insalubrious quarters of town. Fifth: the setting up of a plan for the new alignment of the whole old Barcelona to avoid new constructions being built on an outdated plan.'

In the sixth issue of *A.C.*, published in the second quarter of 1932, they again drew attention – in terms by now familiar to us – to the tragic situation and terrible living conditions of the inhabitants of the fifth district of the city, the so-called Barrio Chino: 'Today we must expose the cancer of Barcelona, known as the Barrio Chino, as a clinical case that exists in all big cities. What we are saying can be applied to all cities with a large, compact population, since these have expanded without an encompassing plan and are alienated from all functional purposes … having had to solve the enormous crisis in housing and spaces for new industries without any town-planning measures … the housing in these quarters has descended to subhuman levels.' It was not only a matter of denouncing this situation, but also of denouncing the solutions to the shantytown problem provided by the municipal Patronage of Housing in Barcelona: 'This offence against the laws of the most basic humanity very soon provoked criticism and a press campaign against it that led to the destruction of some of these deplorable ensembles, sometimes substituted, as is the case with the Patronage of Housing of Barcelona, with no less deplorable "groups of cheap housing".'

The GATCPAC members' proposal was clear: to lay out and construct a new housing development for the district, building inexpensive dwellings and destroying the most insalubrious streets, providing medical care so as to eradicate diseases, and creating health care centres for the population in the area. With this, the prototype of what would later be the Central Dispensary for tuberculosis came into being, built by Sert, Subirana and Torres.[99] All of this was to be carried out within an encompassing plan that would take into account the guidelines that the leading architects had debated in the CIRPAC of Barcelona, and they stated that this plan would not create a problem for private property, but rather a lucrative business: 'Moreover, consider that these plots of land, once the demolition and the layout of the new town development have been executed, will have considerably increased in value.'

In the conclusions of the first Congress of Architects in the Catalan language, which was held from 4 to 10 July 1932, a series of texts on town planning policies concerning the distribution of the city into zones (so as to embark on their development) were ratified. Thus all the

Ramona Longas, 'Moncha'.

architects working in Catalonia at the time had understood and adopted a different manner of thinking about the city.[100]

All seemed ready for work to begin, and Sert had to collate this with another activity in which he was deeply involved: preparing the fourth CIAM, which was to take place in Athens. The trips between Barcelona and Paris to prepare the Macià Plan took first place on Sert's agenda,[101] and the letters he addressed to the Swiss architect constantly speak of this collaboration. A letter from 29 November 1932 is revealing: 'I have wanted to answer your letter for a long time. Yes, it is a wonderful thing that Catalonia finally has its Statutes, but things here remained uncertain until the elections of the 20th of this month, which have ended in a new victory for President Macià … My intention is to go to Paris for a couple of days after 15 December, and we could then take up again our work on the Plan of Barcelona.' On 20 July 1933, shortly before embarking from Marseilles to the CIAM in Athens, Sert wrote to Le Corbusier: 'I am about to do the schemes of the Barcelona Plan that we prepared in Paris … Since my arrival in February, our group has made a great effort and worked very successfully.' Thus, between the winter and spring of 1933, the first scale drawings of the Macià Plan must have been completed.

The hustle and bustle at this point involved not only the difficulties in finding a definitive place for the Congress to be held,[102] and Sert's efforts in resolving certain professional issues, but also the completion of his work on Barcelona so as to debate it with his European colleagues. Something of this can be gleaned from a letter he wrote to Ernest Weissmann on 21 January 1933: 'It is true, I am hard at work. Our collective organization is starting to take off. They count on us for official competitions and for setting up exhibitions, etc. I hope I will be able to go to Paris next week. You can write to me at 51 Boulevard du Beau Sejour. I will only be staying there for 15 20 days.'[103] On 13 February Sert received a letter in Paris that informed him of an exhibition on the 'City of Leisure' that would be held in the basement of Plaça de Catalunya in Barcelona. A letter from Emery in March of the same year expressed his regret at not having been able to participate in an exhibition of town planning and architecture in Algiers.[104]

On 28 July Sert embarked from Marseilles on board the *Patris II*, headed for Athens to participate in CIAM 4, which was to focus on the Functional City in accordance with the programme that Giedion had sent to the delegates on 16 June.[105] In the session held on 30 July, Sert gave a lecture on the city of Barcelona, which along with thirty-two other cities also analyzed with unified criteria and graphs, comprised the basis of the sessions dedicated to the material analysis of cities that were carried out during the trip to the Greek capital. The plans that were presented for each one of the cities represented in each case the four functions that all cities encompassed, according to the presuppositions of a Functional City.[106] Sert's explanations added nothing new to what we have already seen: he focused on the disorder that had been a by-product of the uncontrolled growth of industry, on the excessive density of population in the old districts of the city, and on the bad conditions of beach areas as well as the lack of green spaces in Barcelona at the time.

On 1 August the delegates reached Athens. By then, while on board the *Patris*, they had talked about issues regarding the organization of the exhibition and their relationship with the press as well as possible work commissions. In the following two days they were warmly

Torres, Moncha and Sert in the Acropolis, 1933 (SC).

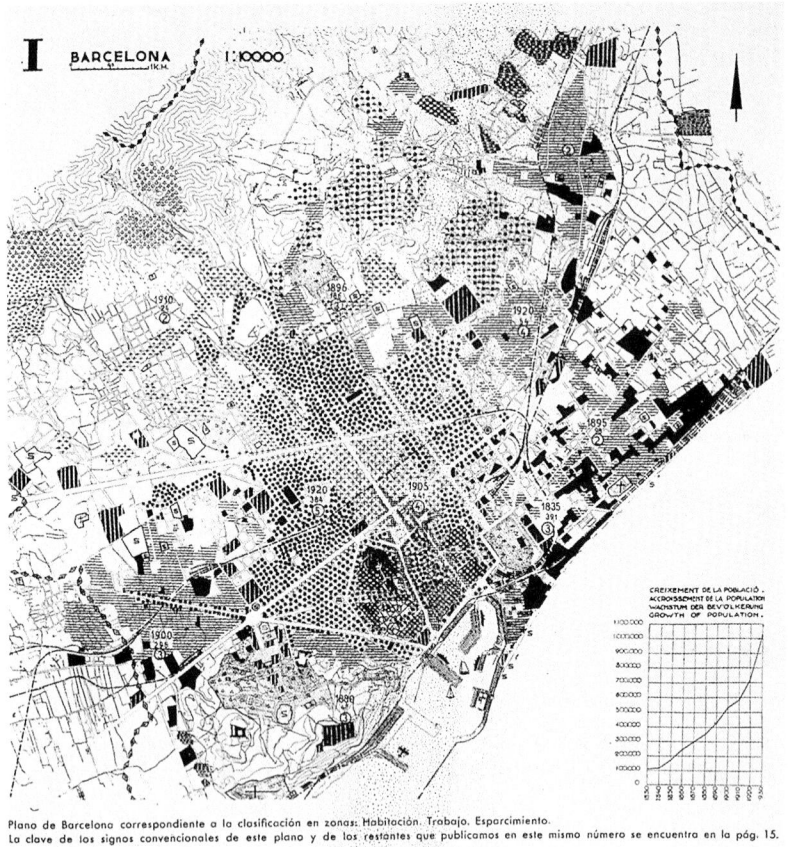

I BARCELONA 1:10000

II BARCELONA 1:10000

Plano de Barcelona correspondiente a la clasificación en zonas: Habitación. Trabajo. Esparcimiento.
La clave de los signos convencionales de este plano y de los restantes que publicamos en este mismo número se encuentra en la pág. 15.

Plano de Barcelona correspondiente a la circulación.

GATCPAC, analysis of Barcelona presented on board *Patris II*; circulation and functions.

received by the Greek authorities, and they also spent time visiting the Acropolis, the dam on Marathon lake, school buildings and the Benaki Museum. On the afternoon of 3 August, the first session of the Congress was held, attended by the Greek political authorities. Van Eesteren's speech on 'The Objectives of the Congress' and Giedion's on 'The Present State of Contemporary Architecture' formed the preamble for the inauguration of the exhibition on the Functional City, which was held in the halls of the new Polytechnic building. After the visit to the exhibition, Le Corbusier gave a lecture whose title was: 'Air, Sound, Light'.[107]

The intentions of the questionnaire[108] that was handed out in Athens on 4 August to 'the authors of the analysis of city plans' and which was to be used to formulate the conclusions on the functional city and to become its 'consideration of principles' are clear: the questions were articulated around the circumstances that surrounded and constituted the four functions of the city – Housing, Leisure, Work and Transport. There was a fifth item under the name Generalities, concerning 'Opinion on Historical Questions' and 'The Future Development

of Cities and the Proportional Growth of their Components'. Between 5 and 8 August, the Congress delegates visited the Aegean Islands. This trip held great interest for Sert, as we shall see later. On 9 August, they embarked on the return trip and on the following day, at 6.45 p.m. there was an Assembly of Delegates that aimed to reach an agreement on the resolutions of the Congress. Present were: van Eesteren, Giedion, Le Corbusier, Sert, Steiger, Moser, Weissmann, Bottoni, Pollini and Wells Coates.[109]

The initial results of the Congress were gathered from this meeting and its debates,[110] which were held from 12 to 13 August.[111] In the first deliberations, after 'a lively and general debate in which all the groups present participated, it was agreed that the Congress had reached a unanimous opinion regarding the evaluation of the conditions in present-day cities. Furthermore, the ideological and indicative character of the Congress was underlined, as well as its fundamental task as a guide in contrast to the demands of a greater scientific precision and a higher degree of specialization … The debate ended with the decision not to publish the results of this Congress in the form of a memoir

José Luis Sert while visiting the Parthenon, 1933 (SC).

including the material information and the work developed, but rather in the form of deliberations.'

The notes of the Congress compiled much of the work carried out during its work sessions and stated many of the elements that would later be considered the Functional City's doctrine. Insofar as the four functions are concerned, the aspects that could be optimized in a possible future plan were enumerated. Thus, for housing, for example, the following was necessary: '1. That residential districts occupy the best areas of the city from the topographical and climatological point of view and in relation to green areas and sunlight. 2. That the distribution of residential districts be motivated by issues of hygiene. 3. That each dwelling have a minimum number of hours of sunlight. 4. That the alignment of construction along traffic ways be prohibited. 5. That modern techniques be used to build at a great distance from each other constructions of a certain height; thus leaving room for large green spaces.' This method of making recommendations to render the city more habitable was also repeated with regard to its other functions.

Concerning the historical areas of cities, the document stated: 'Historical monuments should be protected: a) if they are a clear expression of the preceding culture and if they are of general interest. b) if their conservation does not mean subjecting the people who have to live in them to unhealthy conditions. c) if it is possible that the damage caused by their presence with respect to the impossibility of the city's organic expansion be remedied by changing the direction of traffic or changing the directional centre of the city.'

The Congress had managed to draw up a first draft from which to continue its work in future meetings, but this was not enough, and some points of conflict must have arisen when writing up the fourteen points of the Conclusions. The outcome of this was that two days after the *Patris* had arrived in Marseilles, a commission formed by Sert, Wells Coates, Bottoni, Weissmann and probably Terragni and Torres was set up to work on these points. A letter from Giedion to Le Corbusier of 22 August warned of this turn of events: 'There has been a discussion in Marseilles about the resolutions, that is, the conclusions that were made by Sert, Weissmann, Wells Coates and the Italians. The discussion was serious, and not surprisingly it had political overtones … I am sending you a copy of the resolutions … The press is waiting. We have received many telegrams but cannot communicate the results of the 4th Congress after what happened in Marseilles on Monday afternoon. Nobody was able to finish his intervention. I left for Aix at 11 o'clock at night.'

Shortly afterwards, on 29 August, Le Corbusier sent Giedion a heated handwritten letter, some passages of which were underlined, in which he expressed his surprise at knowing that so many problems had arisen in writing the Resolutions when everybody had acknowledged them on the last day of the Congress: 'These are the ideas that have to be exposed to public opinion. It is thanks to this that our Congress is alive. *If not, it dies.* These objective ideas will be the truth of 1933 for all and in all countries … I think you could have given them a better form, a better order. But I beg you: these are the ideas of our present reality … Besides, the last assembly had accepted these principles. I would have a hard time accepting their suppression due to cowardice or the fear to commit ourselves. *It is time*. Giedion, the world is on fire. Affirmations are necessary. We are *the technicians of modern architecture*. In the name of all that is unique and in the name of this sacred cause, I demand that the resolutions be published.'[112]

Little did the architect of La Chaux de Fonds imagine that so much time would transpire before the Resolutions would be published, but at any rate, we are left in the dark as to the circumstances that made it so difficult. We have only Giedion's vague reference to 'political' issues, although his letter to Le Corbusier on 28 September is slightly more revealing: 'Yesterday I met with van Eesteren, and we again spoke of the Congress' conclusions. The only difficulty was the issue of land organization. In Marseilles there was a conclusory meeting which questioned the existence of our association due to the division of opinions held on this issue by the Italians, on the one hand, and the Spaniards, as well as Weissmann and Wells Coates, on the other … In the conclusions we have an indecisive formula that is full of compromises, which has been proposed by the Spaniards and Wells Coates to satisfy the Italians, who certainly showed themselves to be "fearless".'[113]

What seems certain is that there were problems (at least in tone and form) regarding the issue of private property on urban ground. If we compare the drafts of *Project of Resolutions* with that of the final *Resolutions*, there are noticeable differences in their nuances. In the latter we read: 'It is necessary … to abolish private property in terms of: 1) land 2) built properties 3) means of transport 4) the organization of provisions.' To accomplish this, a provision is necessary 'to satisfy the developmental needs of cities by means of a rational classification of urban elements without consideration for private property.'[114] In the former, however, we read: 'Two antagonistic realities exist. On one side there is a great quantity of work that has to be carried out urgently, and on the other side there are the conditions of the extreme division into fractions of real estate. This contradiction sets forth one of the gravest problems of our time: the need to regulate the access to land so as to satisfy both the vital needs of each individual and the needs of the community. Private interest should be subordinated to public interest.'[115]

Once back in Barcelona (although without a set of resolutions that satisfied all the CIAM members),[116] Sert had much to do: he had to start planning a forthcoming issue of *A.C.* dedicated to the Athens CIAM; he had to continue the work on the Macià Plan, travelling again to and from Paris;[117] he had to direct the final processes of some architectural works and start on others – which, based on the programmes they exhibited, should be viewed within the context of the functional city debate – and he had to design some building projects and begin working on CIAM 5.

On 8 March 1933, the Department of Health and Social Assistance of the Generalitat of Catalonia commissioned the architect Juan Bautista Subirana to carry out a project for a Dispensary to tackle tuberculosis that was to be located in district V of the city, the district that, as we have seen, *A.C.* had denounced for its bad living conditions. However, the true responsibility for this project is not clear. In a letter from Sert to Subirana (who was living in the Hotel Gredos, Madrid) of 18 March, he wrote: 'The day before yesterday I spoke with the President in the morning and handed him directly the minimum budget that we had devised for the Commissariat offices … There is nothing new known about the Anti-Tuberculosis Clinic. Make Dencàs understand too that it is urgent to decide on the site for the building, and then we will work with all our might to finish the project in the least amount of time possible if construction work can start straight away.' It seems clear that Sert was going to actively participate in the project, probably along with Torres, especially given that Subirana was living in Madrid at the time. The licence request is from 29 September 1933, and the person who signed the plans, though we do not know why, was Torres. In another letter from Sert to Subirana written on 18 October of that year, we read: 'This morning I was on the construction site of the Dispensary speaking with Soteras … It would be a good idea for you to send us the structure calculations within the next two or three days at the latest. Dencàs went to the site on Sunday, and if we have to

Sert, Subirana and Torres, Central Dispensary, 1933, section.

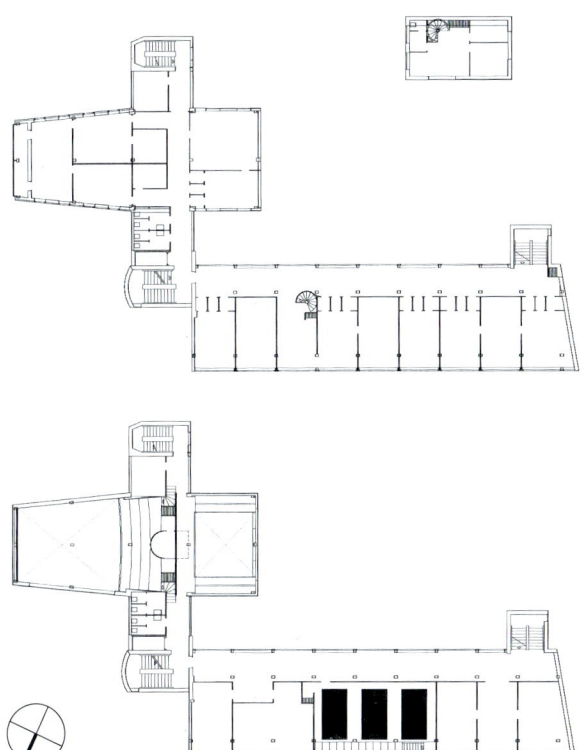
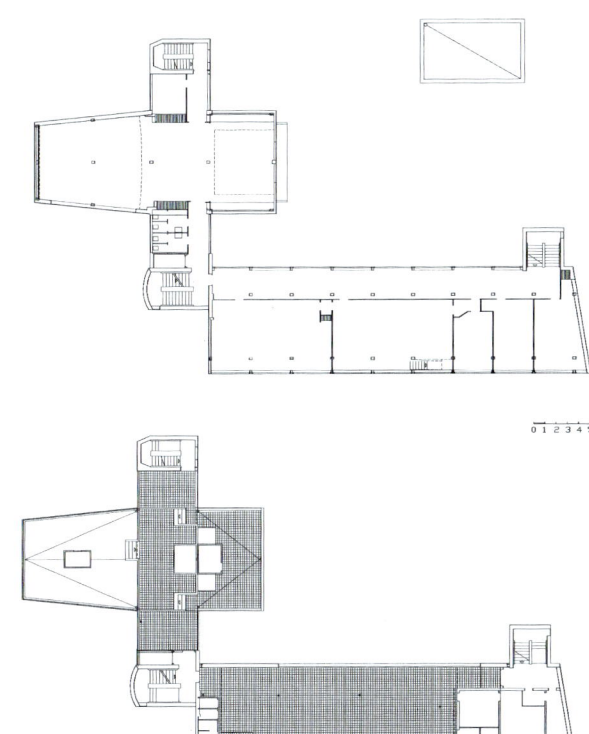

stop construction work again and he goes by again and sees everything at a standstill, he will leave with a very bad impression.'[118] We do not know, since the project had been commissioned to Subirana, why Sert was working on it, why Torres signed the plans, why Subirana calculated the structure, and why Sert always shows this sense of authority in his letters. It is impossible to glean Sert's real responsibility in the authorship of this project, but what is clear, despite the fact that there is no documentary proof of it, is that it existed and was decisive, given the final result of the architectural work. We do know that Sert and Subirana had worked together in the past, as can also be deduced from a letter that Sert had sent to Madrid on 27 January 1933, in which after reminding Subirana that he had to pay the GATCPAC fee, he wrote: 'I sent the school plans to Zurich days ago.' Despite these gaps in our knowledge regarding the real authorship of the dispensary, what can certainly be affirmed is that this tuberculosis clinic is the first architectural project defended by the GATCPAC members, and that it had been based on a specific urban strategy that is present in the preliminary Macià Plan: the possibility of intervening in the drainage and sanitizing of the unhealthy old part of town. Nothing could have been more fitting or representative of this

operation than a clinic, a place in which investigation and education were to be put into practice. The demolition of part of the city (the coach-houses pertaining to the Casa de la Caritat) in order to carry out a new idea, was the surgical task that Le Corbusier had recommended to remedy the ills of Paris, and this is what the *A.C.* members understood and began to implement as soon as it was possible for them to do so.

The project report highlights some key aspects that help us to understand certain questions. The building, for example, was conceived from a territorial perspective and with a desire for widespread planning so as to eradicate the disease: 'As a focus of irradiation for all actions against tuberculosis in Catalonia, it is necessary to install the social headquarters of the so-called "Fight against Tuberculosis in Catalonia", with all its annexes and offices.' And it was

Sert, Subirana and Torres, Central Dispensary, Barcelona, 1933, plans.

Central
Dispensary,
1933, external
views.

for this reason that it was to be a place 'for investigation into tuberculosis in which doctors may become specialists, researchers can be assisted, and nurses be trained.'

The shape that the Central Dispensary was to take narrates this double role of clashing against city opposition and acting as an example of optimizing the fight against disease in a newly inaugurated autonomous state. From the conception of the plan to the use of formal resources that made it up, the building keeps in mind the aspects of its double mission. It would be isolated from the insalubrious part of town by means of a U shape that would facilitate the creation of a protecting courtyard, closed and open at the same time: closed off to the city, open to Catalonia, sending out a message of health from within. At the same time, the final play of volumes offers a protruding body that contains the double-height library and connects with the auditorium. This almost symbolyzes the sense that, just as the good news was preached from its balcony, so research carried out within the building could direct scientific debate, thus offering through medical analysis a message of science to a nation urgently in need of a cure.

Sert, Subirana
and Torres,
Central
Dispensary,
1933, view.

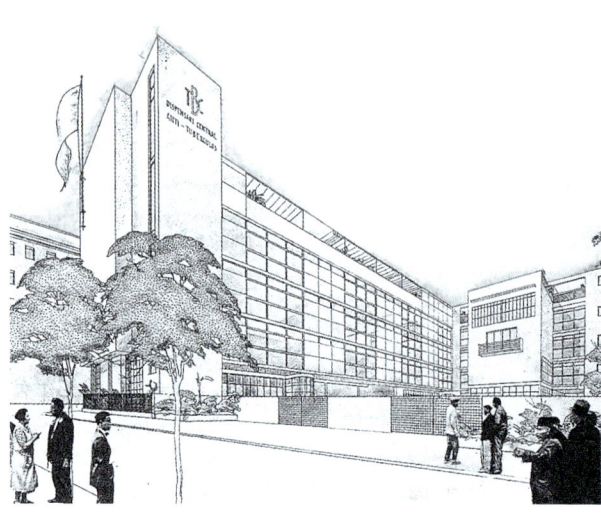

Central
Dispensary,
1933, library
and meeting
room.

Antonio Pizza has provided the genealogy of the model for this hospital, which determines so many aspects of its shape. He has also pointed out the special significance of the location of the common walls and the stairs with respect to the external limits of the building: 'A common wall facing Carrer Torres Amat is cut off in an extremely provisional fashion by a screen of corrugated asbestos-cement boards, and two staircases are placed there, where the construction paradoxically ends (which thus, rather than being a functional oversight in comparison with the third staircase, and clearly conceived as an articulation of the interior of the volumetric configurations, insinuates the directions of possible future municipal developments).' Other aspects, such as leaving the structural steel skeleton visible, indicating the different uses assigned to each part of the building with a different finish on the facades, or the use of 'modern' and 'traditional' materials, are of less interest to us at present. They also show too many contradictions with respect to the building's fundamental mission, due to the fact that the Functional City did not want to express itself through these linguistic topics.

The second building on which Sert, Subirana and Torres were working corresponds to a theme very much in tune with the architectural culture in Europe at the time: workers' housing. We have already seen some of the opinions of the GATCPAC members on this issue, and can now survey the first example in which this ideological positioning becomes a reality. It was put into practice through the construction of ten small houses in the Avinguda Torras i Bages in Barcelona as an experimental prelude to the construction of a project of 207 apartments nearby, called Casa Bloc. This complex was built by the Commissariat for Workers' Housing, which was created by a Decree of 13 March 1932 within a programme to combat unemployment. In the eleventh issue of *A.C.*, during the third quarter of 1933, photographs of the houses that had been built, along with the Casa Bloc plans, were published and signed anonymously with the GATEPAC initials (GE). A letter from Sert to Weissmann of 21 January 1933 almost certainly confirms that the construction work there had been concluded: 'We have built ten small houses for the gov-

Sert, Subirana and Torres, houses on Avinguda Torras i Bages, Barcelona, 1932.

ernment. It has been quite a successful attempt. We have excluded the contractor and have worked with teams provided by the Labour Union.' In another letter (mentioned previously), sent by Sert to Subirana on 27 January, we read that the model for the future Casa Bloc is almost finished: 'The model for the new Commissariat project is advancing. I hope to finish it by the beginning of next week.' It was completely finished by 11 February.[119]

In the eleventh issue of *A.C.*, the houses on the Avinguda Torras i Bages were published under the title: 'Essay on a Minimal Type of Worker's Housing'. Located in a working-class district that formed part of the old municipality of San Andrés de Palomar, these houses were an attempt to accomplish certain objectives, which were expressed in the project report in very clear terms: 'The object of these constructions has been to verify an essay that was to reconduct the problem of workers' housing construction with the support of public organisms, so that it would serve as a base for an economic-type legislation, while at the same time setting the standard for the minimal technical characteristics of these types of dwellings.' Thus, the ten houses, set up as duplexes and with a plan that could have been taken from any book of that period describing these types of programmes, were more than anything a prototype to show the government of the Generalitat the direction that their policies (as yet nonexistent) should take in dealing with one of the most acute problems of industrialized Catalonia during that period. Once again, we are faced with a proposal to the authorities, as always under the auspices of the Macià Plan and made by the GATCPAC architects, who sought a global programme that would give meaning to buildings of near-anonymous appearance.

It seems evident from this that the real designers of these houses, Sert, Subirana and Torres,[120] were interested in questions far removed from their formal value, or at least this is what we can gather from other parts of the project report: 'Given land prices, which are quite high due to this being an already developed area … we had to try to take up as little ground space as possible for each house, which we resolved by building two floors on each of them … Concerning the location, our point of departure was the principle that workers' housing neighbourhoods have to be built in developed areas … The overriding criterion in the preparation of the plan consisted in obtaining the maximum depth possible, as long as this allowed for the direct ventilation of the exterior of all the rooms without counting on interior courtyards or light wells, thus keeping facade surface to a minimum.' After showing their great interest in the co-operative system that had allowed them to do away with the contractor (one more intermediary, who could consequently inflate the product price), the architects published a detailed budget for the construction work, the number of workers employed in it, and the amount of working days invested in building.[121] It seems that the strict 'objectivity' that surrounded the experiment had precise and necessary objectives in mind: to approach the problem in a manner fitting to scientific 'management' that could, when applied to a different discipline, offer a solution to a pending problem in Greater Barcelona.

Things would greatly change when this experiment was transformed into a project of

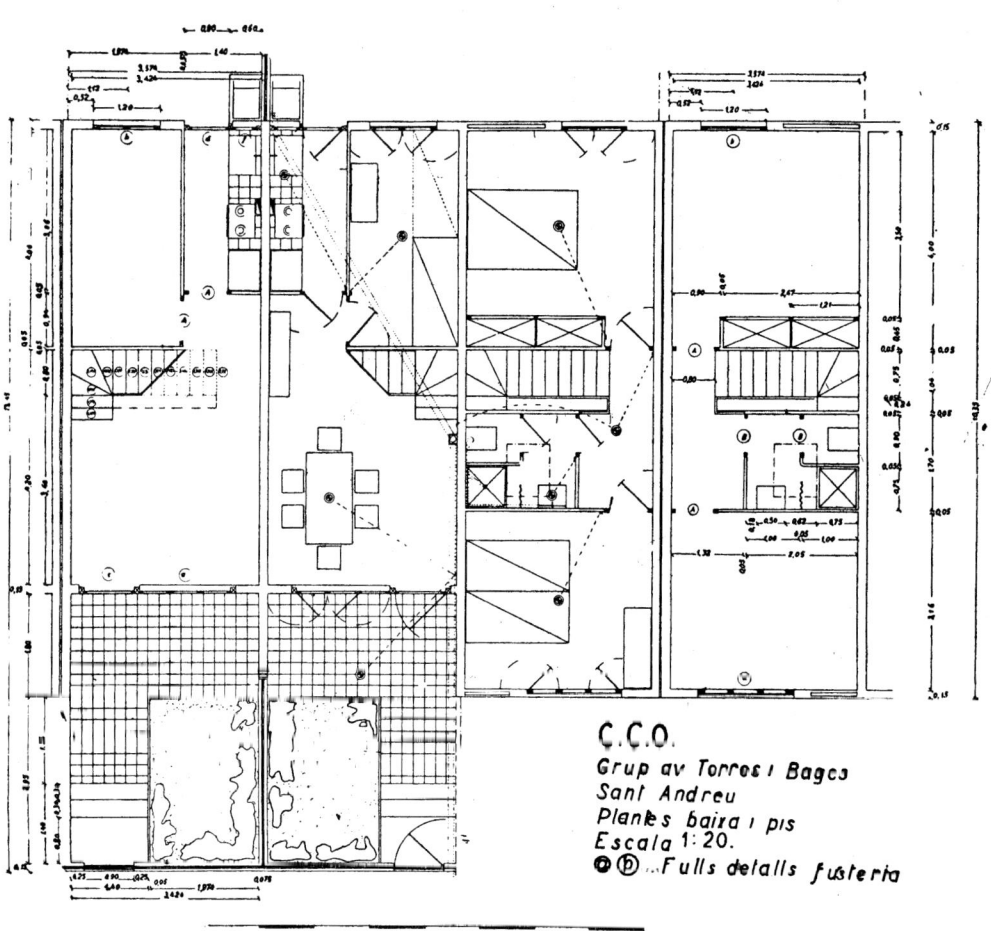

Houses on Avinguda Torres i Bages, Barcelona, 1932, plan.

considerable dimensions, which also had to serve as a cultural reference regarding its authors' intentions. The Casa Bloc was based on Corbusian conventions so as to achieve recognition in the metropolis as a recognizable beacon of modern architectural culture: plan in *redent*, corridor floors, duplex apartments, *pilotis*, etc. The project report for this building, also located on Avinguda Torras i Bages, stressed the uniqueness of its programme for this type of dwelling unit: 'The ensemble of the workers' housing building in the project will be provided with all the annex facilities that a purely social orientation requires, as for example: baths, consumer co-operatives, public libraries, kindergarten, workers' clubs, sports facilities, swimming pools, playgrounds with sandpits and a small children's swimming pool.' Access to the apartments via stairs and elevators was located at the rotation points (corners) in order to form the *redents* of a series of apartments placed parallel to each other, and emphasis was placed on the hygienic parameters of lighting and ventilation in each apartment in order to make explicit the architects' stance on this issue. However, certain conceptual issues in tune with modern times seem to have become important. Thus, for example, though the report stated that the frame would be of iron, we go onto read that: 'The entire structure will be of laminated steel; by doing so we have separated the two functions that the wall accomplishes: to support, a function that the steel frame carries out,

Sert, Subirana and Torres, Casa Bloc, Barcelona, 1933, model.

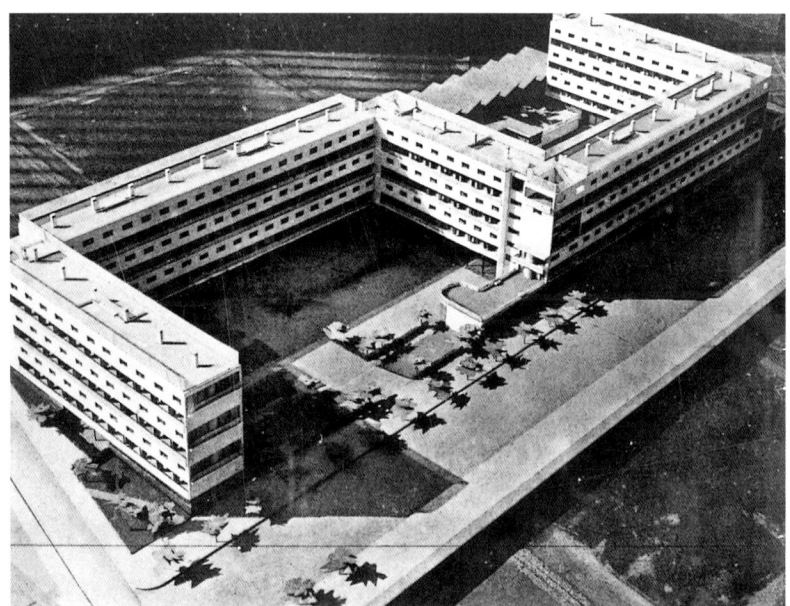

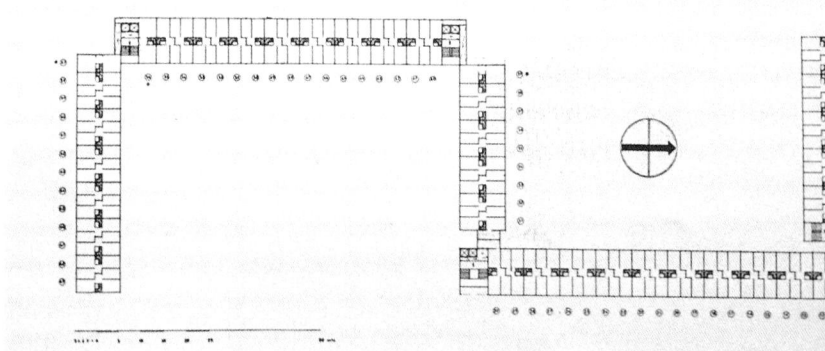

Planta pisos.   Planta inferior de las viviendas con los corredores de acceso.

and to insulate, the only function that allows us to treat the wall in a completely different manner depending on the insulating materials used, so as to achieve the least thickness and weight possible in the wall ... The structure thus conceived will afford us the greatest freedom on the ground floors for the installation of communal services.'

The use of pillars on the ground floor achieves another important objective, apart from allowing the eyes to roam freely over the open space: with this layout the building was 'in accordance with the formula recently approved in the 4th congress of the CIRPAC: free pedestrian circulation in all directions and channelling of vehicle circulation away from pedestrian paths.' The Casa Bloc, like the Dispensary, attempted to provide a model; this reveals the preoccupation shared by Sert and his colleagues with modern architecture's latest forms, and at the same time offers a prototype based on the proposals of a functional city that was concerned with circulation.

Both the interventions in the Cerdá grid system that were proposed in the Macià Plan, and the part of the Macià plan dedicated to workers' housing were to follow models resembling the Casa Bloc solution, and Sert would still find this

Casa Bloc, Barcelona, 1933, plan.

Casa Bloc,
general view.

experience a source of inspiration many years later, when drawing plans for Latin America. The problem of workers' housing in Barcelona was felt to be extremely urgent. In the same issue of *A.C.*, an article devoted to 'An attempt to set up an Ensanche city block in Barcelona based on a type of workers' housing', presented the reader with solutions for intervention in the Cerdá grid that provided alternatives to it by recuperating open courtyards and interior gardens for public use so as to achieve greater hygiene and ventilation in the apartment buildings. These projects were executed 'by petition of the city mayor, Dr Aguadé, to illustrate a pamphlet for his conference on "The Problem of Workers' Housing in Barcelona" published by the Municipal Institute of Hygiene', a fact that indicates that those managing the city were also aware of the problem.[122]

Thus, the Macià Plan continued to advance through parallel experimental architectural attempts and through partial confirmation of the doctrine developed in the CIAMs. Its design progressed thanks to the constant effort of Sert and his friends, along with the interest shown in the project by Le Corbusier. By retracing Sert's steps after Athens, we can follow his evolution.

Between 24 November and 4 December

1933, Sert was in Paris, again working with Le Corbusier on the Plan of Barcelona.[123] On 24 January of the following year, Le Corbusier wrote to Jose María de Sucre to find out whether there was a possibility of a paid commission: 'Would it be possible to continue studying the plan of Barcelona, and especially to obtain a definite contract between the city and the group of Sert and company and myself?'[124] In another letter from Le Corbusier, this time ad-

Casa Bloc, partial view.

dressed to Sert on 20 February, we find for the first time the name 'Macià Plan' applied to their ideas for Barcelona: 'I have also told Sucre that the thing that would make me happiest is that the Government officially recognize the principle of the "Macià Plan" of which the city-spa is one of its elements.'[125] Three days later, Sert answered: 'These days we have been hard at work on our project of the city-spa; the Co-operative that we have recently created … has just organized an exhibition in the Plaça de Catalunya … We will take the President of the Generalitat there as well as all the people who can help us to obtain a decree that declares the project to be of public interest … We have not yet won on this point, unfortunately … The Government of the Generalitat is going through a difficult moment. The economic situation between Catalonia and Madrid has not yet been settled … PLANS OF BARCELONA – Two days ago I gave my first conference and I spoke about how necessary these plans were and what they could provide us with … I spoke of the work that we have carried out together but without revealing all. I think that we have examined the matter well in Paris and should not reveal everything for the time being … We should not speak of a great town-planning project because they may inevitably think of summoning an international competition, and this is not convenient for us. I also think that the conception of our plan of Barcelona is good; nevertheless, there are two things that should be modified, especially the part on the 'Free Port' … It has to do with terrains that belong to the municipality and in which … we would be free to adopt a perfect layout for the work areas; we also have to discuss the location of the industrial area because after having made the plans for the 4th Congress, I realized the importance of the industry that already exists along the shore area. I hope to go to Paris in April with more complete studies … I hope that in May I will be able to organize, with the collaboration of our group, an exhibition of the Barcelona plans, which we will be able to finish together in Paris this April.'[126]

Sert's declarations are extremely enlightening. Through this letter we know that the City of Leisure project was advancing, and that he was trying to get the authorities involved in order to achieve the most important element (and which would not prove possible until much later): the decree of expropriation of the land, without which nothing could be done. Sert and his friends continued with their campaign to raise public awareness of the issue, setting up exhibitions and also giving conferences on the Plan of Barcelona, which Sert did not yet call the Macià Plan. He made use of these strategies without giving away the significance underlying his actions, keeping information on the project to himself while encouraging the public to take an interest in how to solve the city's problems. At the same time he was constantly thinking of the Plan and of the possibilities of improving it, on the basis of the direct observation of the city allowed by living in Barcelona. Moreover, we sense that the political optimism of the last two years had perhaps started to fade. This is confirmed by briefly surveying the troubled events that culminated in October 1934.

On 25 December 1933 Macià died. His funeral was attended by all the GATCPAC members as a body, and Lluis Companys was elected as the new President of the Generalitat on the 31 December. Sert congratulated him in a letter of 19 January 1934, offering him his services. All these events occurred within the framework of November 1933 elections. The results were crucial 'because they mark the change of destiny of the Spanish Republic due to the electoral victory of the centre and right wing over the left, Republican and Socialist.'[127] In this context, Companys was nevertheless able to form a government that concentrated left-wing groups, and with the advent of the municipal elections of 14 January, the myth of Catalonia as a bulwark of the Republic started to take hold. In these elections, the coalition of left-wing parties obtained twenty-six deputies as opposed to the nine on the right wing represented by the Lliga. At that point the differences among the radical nationalists, the CNT and the BOC, all suspicious of Esquerra Republicana's pacts and uncertain stand, took a radical turn, fostered by the high unemployment rate among workers, which had reached more than 50 per cent in the construction sector.

The passage of the 'Law on Harvesting Contracts'[128] and the fact that it was revoked and then passed again revealed a grave ancestral class conflict in the Catalan lands, which the Republic failed to solve, once again demonstrating its structural weakness. On 2 October 1934, the government of Madrid renounced power and a new board with an even more right-wing tendency was constituted. On 4 October 1934, a general strike was proclaimed throughout Spain, and the next day Barcelona came to a standstill. Catalonia rose up against the Republic, and on 6 October, from the balcony of the Palace of the Generalitat, Companys proclaimed the 'Catalan State of the Spanish Federal State'. General Batet answered by imposing martial law and Companys and his government surrendered at 6 o'clock in the morning.

In this atmosphere of tension, Sert and company continued to pursue the new authorities, and to work on the Barcelona Plan, in order to make an impact on public opinion and to involve the new President in the urban problems of the city. On 4 April 1934, Sert wrote to Le Corbusier: 'Our Exhibition on Barcelona's town development will not take place until the month of June … I think that the scheme we made together in Paris should be in this Exhibition at a scale of 1:20,000 and in colour.'[129] He then sent Le Corbusier a list of the plans that would be included in this exhibition, providing us with information on the extent to which the Plan was at that time: '1. Distribution of the city into areas (work, housing, leisure, community life). 2. Limitation of the current city block system of 133 × 133 and adoption of new module. 3. Reclamation of old city quarter (first stage). 4. Linking of Barcelona with the new seaside leisure area by means of the highway of the Carrer Corts (Gran Via), which will be created immediately.'

Between 23 April and 9 May, Sert travelled to Moscow, on the date on which he had planned to return to Paris so as to continue the debates regarding the Barcelona Plan until it was time to go to London for the CIRPAC meeting, to which we will soon return. The thirteenth issue of A.C. – despite the fact that it is registered as having been published in the first quarter of 1934 – must have come out between 21 May and 3 June. In it were the first town maps of the Macià Plan, although they were not published under that name. The mag-

azine's editorial was explicit, stating the need for the teaching of town planning in architectural schools and basing this knowledge on the problems revealed by a material analysis of the city: the arbitrary plot distribution of urban terrains, the irrationality of certain ordinances, the unhealthy barrage of urban functions, traffic problems, etc. It then went on to attack urban layouts and the design of streetlights and benches, marking – as ABC had done – certain proposals with a red cross, and criticizing Sitte.

In an article entitled 'Preliminary notes for a town development study on Barcelona', the A.C. writers offered a great deal of information on the studies that had been developed to make the Plan. The analysis, which gives scientific weight to any urban proposal based on reality, along with the problems it must solve, was presented to readers as an indispensable element. It was through this analysis (and its scrupulously critical content) of the Barcelona of that period that the theoretical conception for the Plan arose, which can be summarized in five different lines of action: 1. Reclamation of the old town quarters. 2. Immediate restriction of the Ensanche project and determining of a new layout in accordance with current needs. 3. Classification of the city in areas that respond to the different urban functions of: housing, work and leisure, which therefore call for the immediate restriction of the so-called mixed areas (annexed towns). 4. Linking of the city to the beach on the Llobregat plain by means of the extension of the Gran Via de les Corts 5. Modification of municipal ordinances.

After this came the schemes for a project, the first among these being the zoning plan, in which we see Barcelona transformed into a functional city in the long term, as can be deduced from the modifications of the Cerdá grid and the importance given to the duty-free zone and the port. The provisions for creating a Civic Centre and an administrative centre, which had only been outlined at that point and will be later examined in detail, encompassed the interventions in the old city (of which we are only told that they planned to conserve 'its buildings and streets of artistic and historical interest'), and shifted the notion of 'centre' that Barcelona had held until that time. For the time being, a programme for the Civic Centre was to be

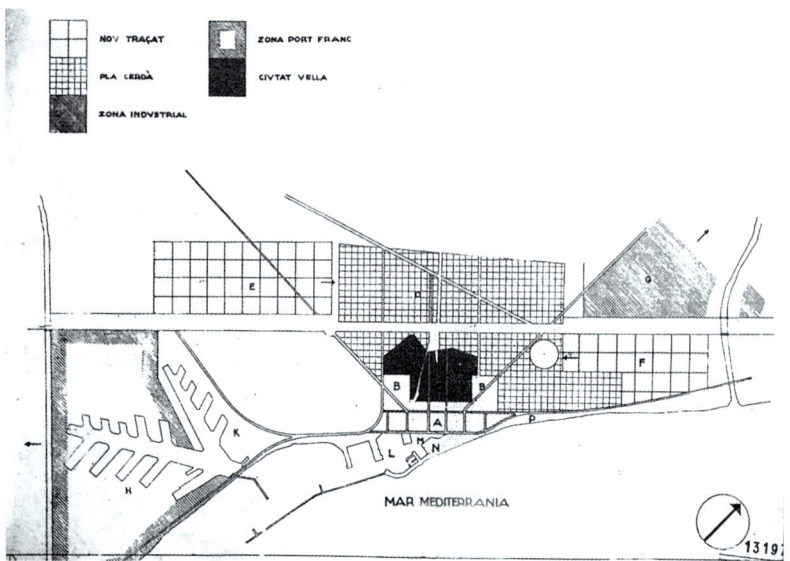

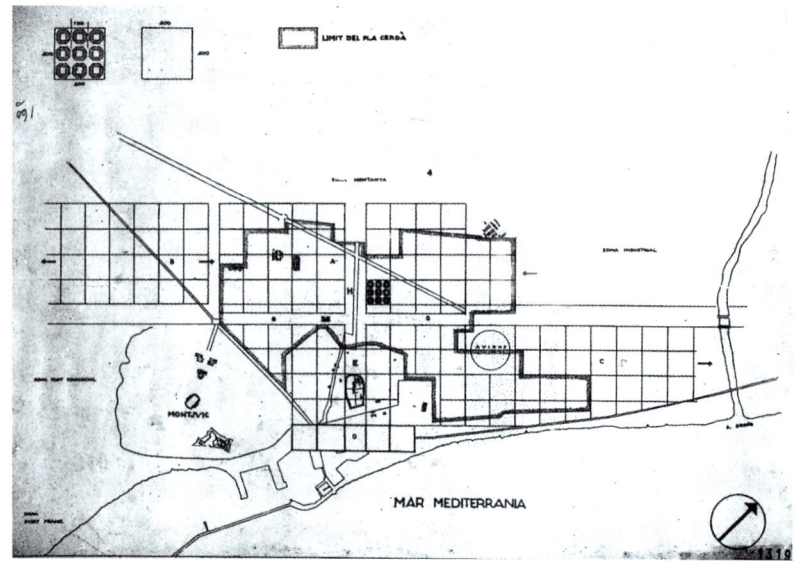

drafted, incorporating: high schools, training schools, museums, libraries, Co-operative Headquarters, Palace of Labour Unions, etc. It was intended to be located in the 'most insalubrious area of the old city, which is to be torn down'. The administrative centre occupied a strip of land of 400 × 1,200 metres from the sealine, and the existing port was to be used for tourism since the commercial harbour and the free port were to be relocated. This centre was to be perfectly connected to the city through the Ramblas and linked to the exterior by the Gran Via Meridiana and the Parallel, which would symbolically converge there. Barcelona was seen as the capital city of an industrial country, in which the businesses arising from its renewal came first; it is therefore not surprising that Sert and Le Corbusier could only imagine

a Beaux-Arts scheme when defining its centre.

Two large areas for workers' housing were established to provide for marked future growth: one of these was located between Gran Via and the sea, up to the mouth of the Besós River, and the other was near the free port. Both were close to the great industrial areas that the Plan had laid out, occupying the edge of the municipal limits: the outskirts of the capitalist metropolis have always been working-class.

Zoning means the segregation of social classes and of urban uses. The trilogy of industry, working-class and capital was resolved in a manner that was as linear as it was implacable. It is also not surprising that the leisure area was not included in the zoning plan; we have to wait for the scheme dedicated to aviation to understand the relationship of the plan to the

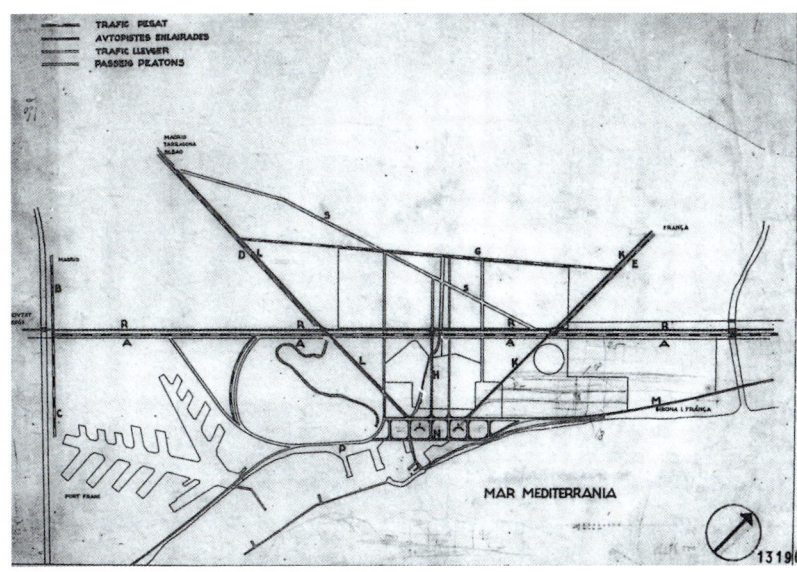

Macià Plan, transportation scheme.

Diputació by demolishing the buildings that separated them; heavy vehicles were to use it to cross the city coming from the Meridiana or the Parallel and heading for France or Madrid, ensuring, from their perspective at that time, that traffic was deviated from the city centre. Evidently, there was also a tendency to remove railways to a greater distance.

Between 15 June and 14 August, the Macià Plan documents and a large diorama of the ensemble (which provoked a great impact) were exhibited in the basement of the Plaza Cataluña in Barcelona. The photograph of Sert showing it to Companys, and the declaration of the President of the Generalitat that if he could, he would destroy the old city quarter with a cannon, eloquently speak of the interest that all of this awoke in the spheres of Catalan political power, and of the fact that technical know-how and the political class were getting closer. It also generated too much optimism among the architects who were behind this urban proposal. Sert's letter to Le Corbusier on 16 July, and the latter's to Ventura Gassol, Counsellor of Culture at the Generalitat, on 7 August, clearly reflect this.[131] What is certain is that despite a last and irrelevant letter of 4 September, epistolary exchanges between Sert and Le Corbusier on the subject of the Macià Plan continued to flow steadily. However, the turn of events in October, including the suppression of the Statutes of Autonomy, created serious difficulties that hindered the possibility of executing the Plan.

location of the City of Leisure and Vacations, a hobbyhorse for the urban proposals of GATC-PAC, which at the time was being exhibited in Barcelona and was criticized by Le Corbusier for its lack of definition.[130] Working-class leisure had never been inserted in areas near the city and this can only be understood from the perspective of a territorial attitude that not only encompassed the city, but also its vast area of influence.

The importance given to traffic in the Plan is notable, specified through three maps devoted to resolving this function: vehicular transit, railways, and sea transport. Vehicular transit was solved by applying different categories to the routes according to their location. All the weight was to be borne by Gran Vía de Las Cortes, which had been widened up to Carrer

On 27 October, Sert, aware that things had taken a turn for the worse, wrote to Le Cor-

Diorama of the Macià Plan (with kind permission of Raimon Torres).

busier: 'I will soon write to you at length to give you details of the political situation here.'[132] However, Le Corbusier did not let his hopes die, and on the following 22 January wrote back: 'I have recently looked at our studies of Barcelona, and I have noticed that in the definitive schemes that you have carried out in Barcelona it seems you have abandoned the idea of leaving the street of les Corts as it is for the light circulation of cars … As a curiosity, I am sending you a small sketch of the old city quarter of Barcelona, which was executed based on your drawings by STREB and of which I will make a negative for my book.'[133] As we see, the Swiss architect continued working, indifferent to political reality, very possibly so that he could include the Macià Plan in *La Ville Radieuse*. Sert's response to this missive on 31 January mentions having received the sketch (from 20 January 1935) of the idea for the old city quarter in which the design for the Civic Centre emerged – a key factor in understanding the Civic Centre projects that he would later execute in South America.

Despite the new political context, the Swiss architect made the most of his friendship with Sucre, and he must have written to him concerning the possibility of going ahead with the Plan. We do not know the content or date of this missive, but we have Sucre's answer to it, dated 22 May, in which he included a rough draft of what Le Corbusier should write to the new authorities, that political force whose ideology – as we know – Le Corbusier considered irrelevant as long as it allowed the architect to develop the projects he wished. 'You asked me a long time ago whether there was any way to reopen the case in benefit of our urban idea. I feel it is my duty to tell you that the moment has arrived and that you would do well to send out letters along the lines of the texts I am including within this same envelope … You had better do it quickly as the occasion might not arise again and one should take advantage of the moment and the people in charge.'[134]

It is not known whether Sucre was referring to the fact that the Lerrouxist Pich i Pon had been made President of the Generalitat in April

Macià Plan, Civic Centre, 1935.

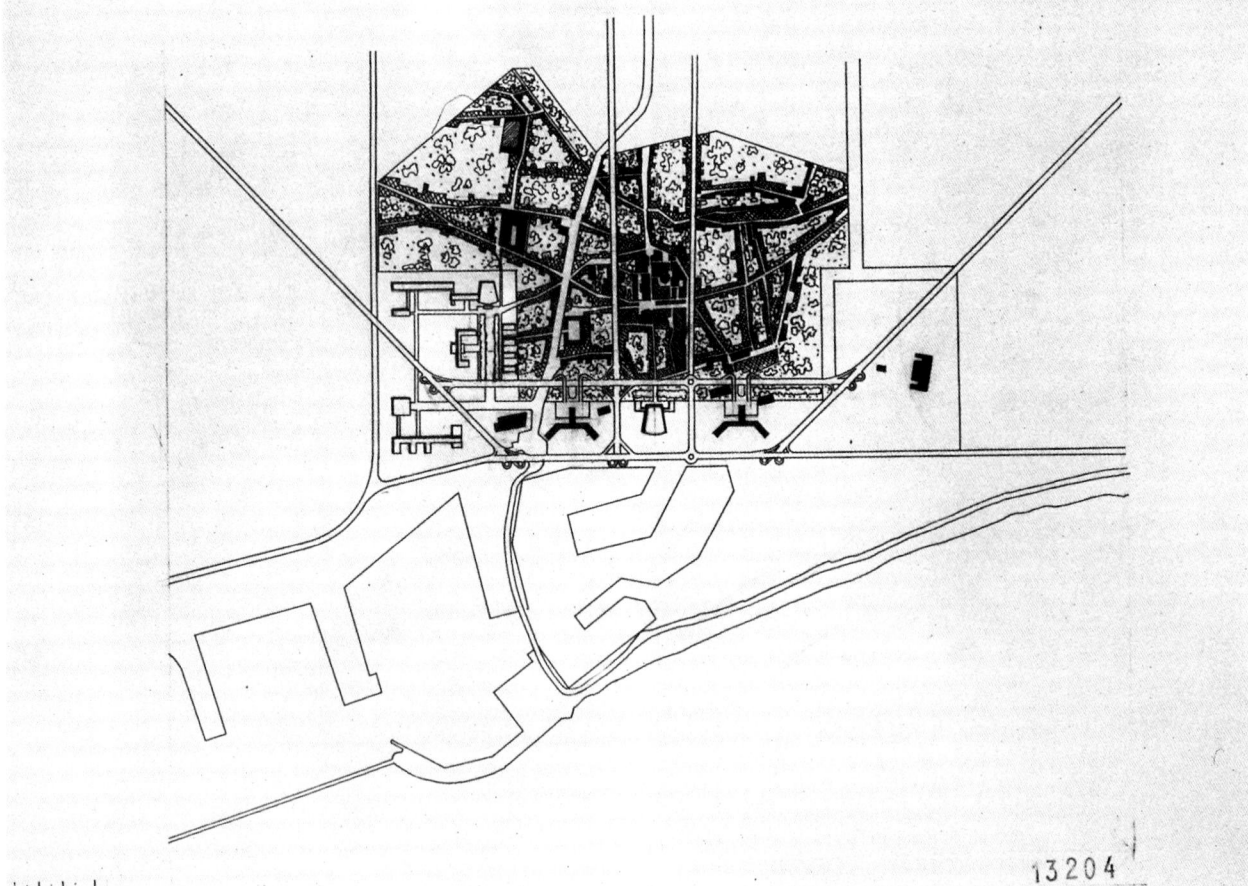

13204

1935, but at any rate his hopes were shortly dashed. Le Corbusier wrote a letter to Pich on 24 May whose contents were hesitant and ambiguous,[135] and to which he received an evasive answer on 5 June, stating: 'I received your attentive letter of 24 May and have passed it on to the Department of Architecture, and as soon as I have analyzed the information that you have exposed to me, I will let you know my answer.'

In a structural interpretation of the Plan, Francesc Roca has expounded on its multiple character: 'It oscillates between the capitalist rationalization of an extensive and problematic area and the manifestation of the impossibility of this rationalization within a framework of economic relations that are predominantly capitalist, but in which the units bound to income from urban soil still carry great weight.'[136]

This explains why the Plan could only be seriously considered during the few months in which Esquerra Republicana was in power (despite the fact that it was never formally commissioned): it had been structured on a popular basis, and it represented a utopia in which it was possible to construct a new reality, something that the Republic and the autonomous Generalitat had seemed to promise. These points no longer carried any weight during the so-called Black Biennial, which is why the Plan, or at least its possibilities for influencing the authorities, came to a standstill. It was again exhibited from 1 to 15 April 1935, but the new authorities ordered that the plans concerning the intervention in the old city districts be removed, since this was where the owners' interests were most at stake.

On the 29 October 1935, Alcalá Zamora provoked the resignation of the Lerroux government; on 7 January 1936 Portela Valladares dissolved the courts, and on 16 February new elections were held. The left won again in Catalonia, this time by a great majority,[137] and this triumph was echoed in the rest of Spain. Azaña became the President of the new Republican government and Companys was freed from jail and re-elected President of the Parliament of Catalonia on 29 February. On 2 March, an excited Sert wrote to Le Corbusier: 'This time things have gone well for us here! This has been a good compensation for our apparent defeat on 6 October 1934. The revolution that began on 14 April 1931 has not come to a halt after all! Companys and all our friends were re-established in the government yesterday … We must act immediately. We will do our best to achieve something practical with our Barcelona Plan.'[138] Le Corbusier quickly answered on 6 March: 'I think it is wonderful that you will make a very serious effort at a time when enthusiasm is still fresh and daily vicissitudes have not yet taken a toll on public life.'[139]

Roca has followed the Plan's fate under the new political power and has shown how some of its aspects were incorporated in municipal budgets, including some of national scope. However, things would change again when war broke out on 18 July 1936, but Sert would not be able to participate in these events;[140] shortly afterwards he left for Paris, continuing his work there.

Nevertheless, he did not abandon his work on the preparations for CIAM 5, a task in which he had been actively engaged since 1933. This Congress was finally held in Paris in 1937, but before that, Sert went to London with Torres to attend the Assembly of Delegates, which was held on 20 and 21 May 1934. On the first day of debates, which was devoted to reviewing the situation in each country,[141] the CIAM delegates made a declaration concerning political issues in which they stated that: 'Since CIAM is a professional organization, its task is not to get involved in political affairs. Its objective is to analyze all architectural and urban data departing from a technical base.' The diversity of political situations in the delegates' countries of origin almost certainly provoked this false declaration (we must not forget that Le Corbusier had just come back from Italy, where he had unsuccessfully attempted to offer his services to Mussolini). By making it, they avoided confrontation among themselves and deviation from their strict and disciplinary intellectual work.

On the following day, they debated the issue of publishing the CIAM 4 documents, agreeing that, in view of what had been presented, a commission (in which Sert was included) would be set up to continue with this task: 'Steiger submits to the assembly a proposition from the Swiss group for the first volume of the publication *La ville fonctionelle* … It is about explaining to the public at large the reflections

CIRPAC in London,
Assembly
of the Delegates,
1934 (SGA).

of the Congress of Athens in the most complete and comprehensive manner possible. A classification of ideas has been made and illustrated with new complementary documentation based on the reciprocal influences of economic factors and conditions of production and technique. Their simultaneous influence on the development of cities is graphically visualized on a big chart. The results of this work are acclaimed by the assembly, which decides that preparatory tasks for the publication will be continued by the commission formed by Le Corbusier, Gropius, Steiger, Sert and Weissmann, designated by the assembly of Paris in 1933, and by Wells Coates.' They then proceeded to discuss where it should be published, and the costs in Spain were considered to be the most accessible, although this was secondary. What is important is that Sert would have access to documents that would later be fundamental for writing one of his principal theoretical works.

As far as the preparatory tasks of CIAM 5 are concerned, Sert again played an important part, submitting to the assembly the Spanish group's proposal on the method of representation, as well as revealing the criteria used in elaborating the plans they were preparing for the Barcelona Exhibition. (Helena Syrkus and

Jan Olaf Chmielewski did the same concerning their Warsaw proposal.) Afterwards they discussed the programme and site for CIAM 5, which at the time they planned on titling 'The Functional City II'. Here they were to show real urban plans from different cities. Whereas in Athens they had more or less achieved a unity of doctrine based on the analyses that had been presented, they now wanted to test it in real cases: 'Having taken as their basis the theses approved in the Congress of Athens, the members of the Congress are charged with applying these theses to urban reality by setting up objective projects for the planning and development of their own cities in the areas that are most urgent or most accessible.' Clearly, Sert had a head start, since he was one of the delegates who could offer the most designed solutions to the problems of his city because he had been working on this for a long time. The delegates also agreed to present a more or less detailed Regional Plan according to the Polish way of working.

There were still many questions and doubts concerning the date and place of the Congress. They spoke of the spring of 1935, and deliberated on whether to hold it in Algiers, Moscow or a Central European city, as van Eesteren proposed. After dealing with other minor issues, they decided that the following CIRPAC meeting would be held in Amsterdam the following fall, a forecast that proved far too optimistic.

As it turned out, the next meeting was indeed in Amsterdam, but they had to wait until the summer of 1935, between 9 and 13 June, and Le Corbusier was not present. As had occurred in London, the delegates informed him of their activities, but now Sert's opinions were heavily influenced by the circumstances[142] we have previously mentioned. They did decide on the four areas of study that were to form the Congress' focus, and on who would head these: A) Regional Plan: S. Syrkus. B) City plan: Sert. C) Reclamation: Steiger. D) Legislation and Regulation: Wells Coates. A closer look reveals the coincidence between these sections and the headings used in the Macià Plan, which from very early on showed a certain regional focus. Sert had devised a questionnaire for this meeting. It concerned the problem of 'Plans for City Expansion', and in twelve points he set forth a

CIRPAC
in Amsterdam,
1953, group
picture (SGA).

series of questions dealing with this aspect of the conception of cities so as to debate it in the meeting and afterwards present it to the Congress if it was considered opportune.[143]

In the midst of the debate, Sert and Syrkus proposed that sections A, B and C be discussed jointly since 'it is impossible to study any urban detail without linking it with the rest of the city, or to study the city without relating it with its region … It is impossible to imagine the region without linking it to all these partial solutions. Sections A and B especially must go together.'[144] After a heated debate, a commission was designated to submit to the Assembly all proposals in graphic form and with sufficiently detailed reports. It was formed by Sert, Syrkus, Weissmann, Moser and Wells Coates. Although the meeting reached few agreements, Sert came out strengthened in his position, since along with the factors that we have already noted, he was able to show his European colleagues the maps that he had drawn up for Barcelona, a city that increasingly seemed, in the eyes of modern European architects at the time, to be an effective laboratory for a functional city in which to experiment with what had been debated in the CIAMs.

The twentieth issue of *A.C.*, published in the fourth quarter of 1935, presented a detailed report of the subjects discussed in Amsterdam, confirming Sert's growing commitment to CIAM. It shows a graph separating the contents debated in Athens from those that were to be discussed in CIAM 5: the City-Region. The important thing about this graph is that it allows us to observe how city functions had grown, a factor that would later be highly important in Sert's work in America. Presumably

Sert at the CIRPAC
in Amsterdam,
1935 (SGA).

as a result of the agreement at the Assembly reported above, six graphics each encompassed a separate function. These functions have grown from four to six: housing, production, provisions, leisure, community life and transport. The graph revealed the transition from the continent in which the city was located to the zoning necessary for any city, passing through the country to which it pertained, the region on which it depended, and its own urban structure.

Thus, at the end of 1935, it seems that the programme of CIAM 5 was to go a step further than the previous one in Athens: it was to analyze the relationship between city and region from the standpoint of urban proposals for the expansion of specific cities, or from the standpoint of problems of detail in which these relationships were necessarily present. In the process, the idea of the district started to take on relevance as a live component of the city. After defining a city's relationship with its country and its region, and of thinking about the urban characteristics of the city itself, they decided to analyze the district focalizing on three points from which to initiate their understanding of this component of the city: its structure, its communications and its population. The pages of *A.C.* went on to offer an 'example' of this way of analyzing cities, using the extensive work carried out in Warsaw by the Polish technical groups Praesens and U.

From a letter written by Giedion to Le Corbusier on 10 September 1935 we know that Giedion and Gropius went to the castle of La Sarraz to speak with Madame de Mandrot about the possibility of holding CIAM 5 there, because they knew by then that it could not be held in Algiers.[145] However, Le Corbusier intervened and proposed instead that Madame Mandrot should allow a CIRPAC meeting in her castle at the end of August, preferring to hold CIAM 5 in Paris in order to take advantage of the International Exhibition.[146] Meanwhile, Giedion's letters to Sert became progressively more pessimistic concerning the possibility of publishing *The Functional City*, perhaps due to lack of capital or energy.

On 30 May 1936, Giedion sent the delegates the CIRPAC programme (the meeting was finally held in La Sarraz from 9 to 12 September) in which the following project presentations appeared: Warsaw as an example of a Regional Plan, Barcelona as an example of a City Plan, and the Langstrasse quarter of Zurich as an example of reclamation.[147] One must bear in mind, however, that September 1936 was for all Spanish citizens a time of civil war, and for Sert a point of no return to Barcelona.

It has been impossible to establish the exact date and circumstances of Sert's departure from Barcelona. In an interview, we read his direct testimony: 'The studio remained open, and officially it never closed. I left and went to France. My situation in Barcelona was rather complicated; there was the whole issue of the family and the Sert house. In the end it was my friends from the Ateneu, Colomer and the rest of them, who insisted: "Come on, don't be dumb and get away, after all, these things happen." I remember that Serra wrote a letter for me. There was a peace congress, and we had a committee of anti-Fascist fight of which Serra was the president, so they sent me to that congress in Brussels. That is when I left Barcelona, and afterwards I stayed in Paris and worked making propaganda.'[148] The contradiction between his professional and political trajectory and his social origins must have worsened Sert's personal position during those times of revolution. Oral witnesses have explained how the Sert family left for Rapallo when war broke out, but not accompanied by the architect.[149] On 18 July 1936, when war broke out, Sert was in the Palace of the Generalitat from where he managed to get the family house protected by the police, handing it over for war activities, thus ensuring that it would not be attacked or burned to the ground.[150] However, all that allows us to grasp the full meaning of the letter Sert received on 1 January 1937 from the Ateneu Enciclopèdic Popular, of which he was Vice-President.[151]

After the official presentations, the CIRPAC sessions opened with a debate on a perpetually outstanding issue: the pending publication of CIAM 4's results, that is, the book on the Functional City, which was hindered by serious financial difficulties. In La Sarraz they came up with the idea of making two editions, one of an inexpensive sort that was commissioned to the French and Catalan groups, and another with a 'scientific orientation', directed by the Dutch

Republican militiamen marching to the front, 1936.

group, which would reproduce all the cartographic material available. The first edition, which was to be called *The City of the Future*, would serve as a basis for the other and was to be ready by the time the Congress was held in Paris. The profits from it were to partially finance the high production costs of the second edition.

The next step was the debate on the programme, which had been accepted, and after Syrkus had explained the Regional Plan of Warsaw, Sert went on to describe his Plan for Barcelona, adding in his report the projects for the Leisure City and the reclamation of the old town quarter. Le Corbusier expounded on his Nemours project; Bottoni spoke on the Regional Plans for the Aosta Valley; Hoste described his town development project for the right bank of the Escaut in Anvers, and Stam explained his analysis of Berlin. Helena Syrkus continued with her idea of publishing a book on a topic that was much to Sert's liking, as we have seen in the project memoirs of Casa Bloc and the Dispensary: the exterior wall in a skeleton-structured building.

The rest of the sessions were devoted to deliberating on administrative aspects and to the preparation of the 'Functional City' exhibition, which was to be held in Paris at the same time as the Congress, and which was to include the cartographic material from the Athens Congress as well as the fifteen plan projects drafted since then, among which the Barcelona project was to have a prominent place. Moreover, they spoke of the topics that would be debated in the Congress, designating the commissions that would be in charge of working on these issues.[152]

There had been many changes in Barcelona, and given the new reality, it seemed feasible to implement some of the Macià Plan proposals, or so we gather from Torres' letter to Sert. This was sent at the end of August 1936[153] and Sert received it after the CIRPAC meeting, once he was back in Paris, from where he scarcely moved until his departure to the US,[154] carrying out a number of different activities until CIAM 5 was held. Torres was looking for finance to publish *The Functional City* in Barcelona, and he asked Sert to take advantage of his privileged situation so as to gather sufficient material for the book and to work on writing the original version.[155] On 7 December Sert wrote back to Torres: 'I am working in this office in the affairs of exhibitions and propaganda. We have inaugurated an exhibition of photographs and documents on Spain and Tourism on its premises on the Boulevard de la Madeleine, and will soon organize another one.' Sert afterwards took charge of an exhibition on Catalan Medieval Art,[156] and started to design and build, along with Lacasa, the Spanish Pavilion for the 1937 World's Fair in Paris (which was inaugurated without having been finished on 12 July 1937). We will come back to this building in another chapter of this book.

For no apparent reason, on 15 December 1936 came out a programme for CIAM 5, which had nothing to do with what had been discussed up until then at the preparatory CIRPACs.[157] It stated that the meeting would be held between 28 June and 2 July and the main theme of debate would have the concise title: 'Logis et Loisirs'. What had happened?[158]

There is only one possible answer. Le Corbusier had decided to take charge of the first Congress to be held in the city where he worked, a city that, moreover, was living through very special circumstances in 1937 as host to the World's Fair. Le Corbusier had been preparing for it since 1932 so as to be an important protagonist.[159] That same year he had drawn up a project for a competition with a made-up title, 'International Exhibition of Housing', which was to be hypothetically carried out in the Bois de Vincennes. The subject was to be the design of a plan for some buildings in *redent* as well as a complex housing, sports and cultural amenities programme, that is to say, a place in which housing and leisure time would be intimately intertwined. In 1934 he had insisted on the same theme, although on that occasion it was for the Kellerman bastion, Paris, and the building was a high-rise residential complex with a Y shape, which was called Unités d'Habitation and which was to be attached to the exhibition. He made another attempt in the same place in 1936, this time with his renowned museum of unlimited expansion dedicated to knowledge, which was to be included in the exhibition 'Art and Technique'. These were all unsuccessful attempts to participate in a fair that had continually closed its doors to him.

This was the case until 15 December of that same year, the very day that the Congress programme was altered. Le Corbusier, recalling this, wrote: 'Robert Delaunay, artist, painter, calls us on 15 December from the office of Monsieur Locqui, general delegate of the Presidency of the Council for the 1937 Exhibition, and tells us: "Come quickly, we are requesting that you participate in the 1937 World's Fair … we have taken on the responsibility of building the Pavilion of Modern Times on schedule"'.

These events were taking place in a Paris that had been struggling for some years with a high unemployment rate, an important strike movement and serious conflicts in some areas out in the country. In April–May of 1936, the Popular Front won the general election after the left-wing parties had gone on a campaign (which had begun back in October 1934) to achieve a minimum of unity. This allowed for a complete turnaround of labour legislation, so that collective conventions, two weeks of paid holidays and a forty-hour working week were all put into force. This radical change in the living conditions of the working classes meant that they could now enjoy their leisure time – a leisure time that would have to be planned. On 4 June 1936 Blum created a Secretariat of State for Recreation and Sports, and Blum himself wrote on 31 December: 'Hope has returned, as has the joy in work, the joy in life.' The historian Georges Duby has explained this new feeling: 'In 1936 there is an exaltation of faith in man, of belief in progress, of a return to nature, of fraternity, which is found in the films of Renoir and in Malraux's novel about his Spanish adventure, which is fittingly called *L'Espoir*.'[160]

There were too many coincidences: on the one hand, there was the commission to Le Corbusier and the possibility of building a Pavilion to broadcast his ideas concerning the city, town planning and the Unités d'Habitation, and on the other was an atmosphere in which housing and leisure could be intertwined to improve the living conditions of the working classes. The time was ripe for insisting on the virtues of the Unités d'Habitation (residential complexes), which according to Le Corbusier was 'the residential building that transforms the conditions of town planning'. He exhibited the Ilot no. 6 in his lightweight, canvas-covered pavilion, resolving and integrating two of the Functional City's aspects (dwelling and recreation). At the same time, the countryside had to be taken into account: 'It is impossible to dream about town development of the cities if one does not develop the countryside', thereby proposing that the Congress should be subtitled 'Cities and Countryside'.

Evidently, Le Corbusier's lecture, 'Solutions of principle', was crucial. Here, the binominal Logis-Loisirs (Dwellings-Leisure) were present-

CIAM 5, Paris, 1937, cover of the official publication.

munity obligation, are a direct extension of public services. 5. So established, the programme for housing opens to the great transformation of the construction industry; housing can now be built in factories, profiting from modern work methods and administration.'

Le Corbusier's programme could not have been more opportune considering the French situation at the time: the need for industrialization in construction was promoted at a moment when spirits were running high among the working class, thanks to a growing confidence in progress and the lessening of physical effort at work. It was also a time when the most suitable sites for housing were obtained by expropriation, doing away with speculation, thus improving living conditions thanks to socialization of land. Confidence in planning also grew, enhancing the force of the Popular Front's leftist ideas.

Sert's speech, called 'Case of Application: Cities', also reflected the singular reality of Catalonia at the time, transmitted to him by Torres' enthusiastic correspondence. It was a suitable time for the unification of technical know-how and social transformation, and for conceiving the whole with the globalist mentality that had characterized the CIRPACs preceding the Congress. 'Only the great technical means of today, based on a new urban economy, will be able to reorganize big modern cities in a harmonious fashion.' In other words, without a

ed as being inseparable: 'TO DWELL – TO RECREATE (Logis et Loisirs). These two functions are indissociable. Leisure-time activities are daily, weekly or annual. Daily leisure-time activities are a direct function of the dwelling.'[161] Departing from this first affirmation, the long text of the Swiss architect flows like a river of words, aspiring to determine the stages undergone by housing production through a five-point outline: '1. The General Directing Plan, based on the real and urgent needs of the population, is the supreme law of urbanism. 2. The creation of grounds for building, favourable to the "logis-loisirs", introduces new principles on the independence of the urban organs of circulation and dwelling. These new principles are: the notion of "artificial terrains"; the separation of pedestrians from cars; the free land recovered from all of the city's surface. 3. For public health reasons, so as to allow the establishment of this plan affording it protection from speculation: freeing of national land. 4. The "logis-loisirs", considered a com-

CIAM 5, Paris, 1937, group photograph (SGA).

new urban economy that facilitates socialization of land property, it is impossible to improve living conditions in modern cities; we should keep this in mind when we analyze the misadventures of the projects for Latin American cities that Sert would draw up in the future.

Sert's speech, now distanced from Le Corbusier's point of view, continued to delve into the issues discussed in Amsterdam and La Sarraz, insisting on enriching the functional analysis of cities, constructing an urban theory that had no immediate possibilities of being carried out in the near future; his condition as an exile did not allow him to hope for many commissions. Thus, his efforts were aimed at enumerating the conditions that a General Plan would have to fulfill, and at defining the aspects that should make up a Plan for Urban Reorganization. A review of this process leads us to the script that defined the last stages of the Macià Plan as we know it. Among the topics mentioned is one of special relevance that would later be developed in a number of proposals for South America: 'The site for a city's community services, administrative centres and civic centres must be studied more in depth, because this nucleus has a great influence on the other areas.'[162] The outline followed in the Plan had become a general working method for a theory that was to be applied to different cases and that had recovered a more complex and encompassing vision surpassing the deterministic classification of the four functions; Le Corbusier's solution in the Ilot no. 6 also had to do with the desire to transform the Ensanche of Barcelona, which is seen in the Macià Plan.

Other interesting points cropped up in CIAM 5. On surveying the rest of the speeches, one becomes aware of how the different political climates or structural realities of the participants conditioned their discourses. The Poles insisted on regional planning and working-class cities, whereas the French emphasized rural urbanism, the need for the construction of 'radiant farms', and harped on old hygienist topics. The Italians also insisted on rural urbanism, while the English focused on what was happening in London, and the Dutch pointed out the irony of everything in general, due to Le Corbusier's abrupt change of agenda and his ambitions to control the meeting, a situation

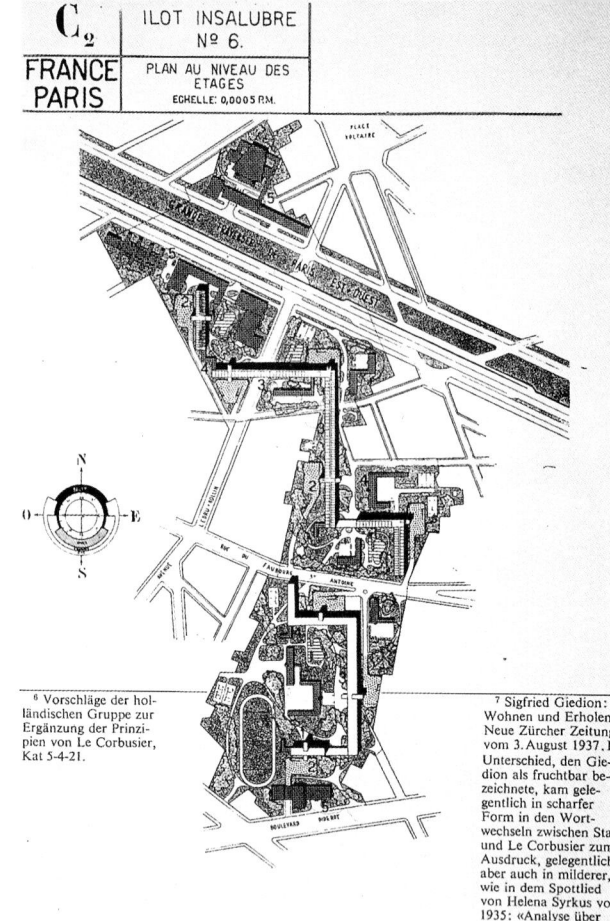

CIAM 5, Paris, 1937, Ilot no. 6

that must have reminded them of the *ABC* days: 'When a Congress confirms the ideas of one of its members, when it publishes them as if they were the conceptions of the whole Congress, these ideas must not have any gaps in them and their publication must give a precise image of them, comprehensible even to those who are not specialists … If Le Corbusier, for example, says that the execution of these colossal buildings is not a technical problem, the Congress must decide whether this idea is true. We consider that the question is not as easy as Le Corbusier depicts it in his enthusiasm for a profound change in our way of building.'[163]

This was a Babel-like Congress with an irregular set of paths to be taken, making one recall with longing the fruitful meetings in Athens and La Sarraz. This can be gleaned from the conclusions, which tried to come to terms with the reality faced by an afflicted Europe in 1937, on the brink of disaster and with the Spanish Civil War 'experiment' baring its teeth. Despite this, and despite its disagreement with Le Corbusier's obsessions, the Congress' conclusions acknowledged the possibility of unifying Logis et Loisirs given the increase of leisure time among the working class, therefore acknowledging the viability of the Unité d'Habitation model. Thus, in 1937, functional integration was already beginning to be perceived as a solution to the schematism of separating functions, and as a solution for old town quarters, as long as a general framework plan could be counted on and there was the possibility of implementing a new urban economy that would free land for the most urgent social needs.

As usual, once CIAM 5 was over, the members started preparing the next one, a task that Sert now had to carry out in precarious conditions while working at the same time on the inexpensive edition of *Functional City*. In an undated circular letter[164] sent by Giedion in 1938 to all the CIAM delegates and members, we read: 'The small publication for the general public is edited by J.L. Sert and Charlotte Perriand; it will be, as we had desired it to be, an ABC book on urbanism, containing clear examples accompanied by photographs, illustrating the DECISIONS OF THE CONGRESS OF ATHENS. The dummy for the work has already been presented in Paris. At present, the publication is proceeding well; in December 1937, Sert and Giedion met with the English group in London, and it was decided that J.L. Sert stay on in London until the publication is ready to be printed.' Thus, Sert travelled to London and stayed there until 15 January 1938, or so it seems from a letter sent on that day to Wells Coates to discuss with the English the final details concerning the publication.

We next find Sert in Paris, where he continued working with the National Patronage of Tourism (as one may gather from a letter to José Gaos on 21 February 1938), at the same time directing the dismantling of the World's Fair Pavilion. On 16 May we know that Giedion wrote to him at 11 bis rue Jules Chaplain. He must have returned to London soon afterwards, since on 13 June he received another letter from the Swiss historian, written to 24 Woburn Square, in which Giedion expressed his concern about his imminent and final trip to the States: 'I am awfully sorry I can't come and work together with you in London, but I am in a great hurry to prepare the lectures for Harvard.'[165] On 5 July Sert wrote to Giedion a letter from London, a missive that we will analyze later.

On 10 July, Sert was again present at the CIRPAC meeting in Brussels (already attending in his post as Vice-President), along with van Eesteren, Bourgeois, Giedion, Schmidt, Le Corbusier, Edwin Maxwell Fry, Mart Stam, Huib Hoste, Louis Herman De Koninck, Renaat Braems and Paul Fitschy.[166] There they deliberated on the organization and programme of CIAM 6, which was to centre on cases applying to the Athens Charter, these being drawn on panels of predetermined size and colour. The document of the Athens Charter as such did not exist yet, unless the low-cost text that Sert and Perriand had been working on had been given this name; at any rate, a 204-page dummy for the book was presented for discussion at the meeting. This allows us to observe the growing complexity of a Plan (such as that which Sert had defended in Paris at the CIAM 5 meeting), which was completed by the presence of the Unités d'Habitation. Here, there is already a breakdown into the Commercial Centre, the Civic Centre and the Administrative Centre, a triad that would later appear in the cities that Sert and his associate Paul Lester Wiener would design for South America.

Sert kept in touch with London to ask for materials, as we have gathered from the letters he sent to William Tatton during the month of August. Meanwhile, Gropius was writing from the United States to declare his interest in holding CIAM 6 in New York.[167] At the end of December 1938, Sert broke his leg, but his economic situation was so precarious that he could not afford to have it X-rayed. On 1 January 1939, he was sent by friends to a physician, Doctor Legard, who was requested to do the X-rays free of charge. Shortly afterwards, on 7 February, he received a letter from Giedion in Paris. It would be the last Sert would receive in the Old World before setting out on his journey to the United States.

74 'Housing development project for the Diagonal of Barcelona', *A.C.*, no. 4, 1931, pp. 22–27. This project was also shown in the Sala Parés exhibition.

75 Extracted from the typewritten copy in French in the CIAM files of the Giedion Archives (3–4–42–F). It is published in German under the title 'Flach-, mittel- oder hochbau?' in *Rationelle Bebauungsweisen,* op. cit., pp. 26–47.

76 'La ligne générale', *Plans*, no. 1, January 1931, p. 9.

77 Hubert Lagardelle, 'Au delà de la démocratie', *Plans*, no. 1, pp. 24, 30.

78 Le Corbusier, 'Invite à l'action', *Plans*, no. 1, p. 51.

79 Aldo Dami, 'Deux après-guerres', *Plans*, no. 1, p. 129.

80 'La ligne générale', *Plans*, no. 2, February 1931, p. 8. To understand how Fascism was evolving in France, see Robert Soucy, *French Fascism: The First Wave, 1924–1933*, Yale University Press, New Haven and London, 1986.

81 'Barcelona. Esquemas para el proyecto de conjunto', *A.C.*, no. 13, 4th quarter of 1934, pp. 21–22.

82 'Vers la deuxième étape', *Plans*, no. 8, October 1931, p. 10.

83 Le Corbusier, *La Ville Radieuse*, Editions de l'Architecture d'Aujourd'hui, Paris, 1935, p. 305. In the copy consulted the publication date is not mentioned, but there are projects from 1934. Concerning the Macià Plan, a plan is published, the origin of which dates back to 1935. It is found in the Fondation Le Corbusier. The first drawings of the Macià Plan came out in October 1934 monographic issue of *L'Architecture d'Aujourd'Hui* on Le Corbusier. In this issue we also find the following eloquent commentary by the Swiss architect, who wrote it from his recollections of his meeting and interview with President Macià in Barcelona in the spring of 1932: 'President, both of us – Sert as a Catalan and as leader of the GATEPAC group, and I as a foreigner who for a long time has felt the grandeur of your city, its force, its intensity, its unmistakable reason for being – we both ask you for the authorization to establish the plan for the future of the city in keeping with the spirit of modern times. It is a gracious request on our part; we do not aspire to any commission. We would simply like to know that the leaders of Catalonia are informed about our initiative, that they know that the Plan will be carried out, a plan that will be like a programme or a guideline, a stable framework from the interior on which the successive decisions of your councils can be inserted. Barcelona is a predestined place, geographically and demographically speaking; Barcelona is one of the active cores of the universe; life palpitates and bursts here. One must channel such latent force to avoid catastrophes, or direct it to channels leading to harmony.'

84 *A.C.*, no. 5, 1932, p. 17.

85 Letter from Sert to Giedion, GATCPAC Archives, C–10/65.

86 Letter from Sert to Giedion, 29 May 1931, GATCPAC Archives, C–10/65.

87 Le Corbusier, *La Ville Radieuse*, op. cit., p. 305. This text is transcribed, although with some small omissions, in Salvador Tarrago, 'El Plá Macià o la nova Barcelona', *Cuadernos de Arquitectura y Urbanismo*, no. 90, Barcelona, July–August 1972, p. 28. The article offers an interesting chronology of the gestation and development of the Macià Plan.

88 The authors and subjects of the conferences were as follows: Le Corbusier spoke in the Saló de Cent of the Barcelona City Council on 'The Urbanistic Possibilities of the Mechanistic Epoch'; Victor Bourgeois spoke in the Escola Industrial on 'Economic Housing'; Sigfried Giedion spoke in the Ateneu Enciclopèdic on 'The Optical Revolution of the Twentieth Century'; Walter Gropius spoke in the Festivities hall of the Colegio Alemán on 'Modern Construction'; van Eesteren spoke in the Escola Industrial on 'Modern Town Development in Amsterdam'. The report of the work carried out in Barcelona is in FLC D 2 5 40, and states: 'The Spanish group GATEPAC is admitted.'

89 Francesc Roca, 'El G.A.T.C.P.A.C. y la crisis urbana de los años treinta', *Cuadernos de Arquitectura y Urbanismo*, op. cit., p. 19. In this article Roca presents both the sanitary analyses and the demographic and economic studies carried out in Barcelona in those days, which help us to understand the tone of the scientific urban studies that encompassed and gave consistency to the proposals of rationalist architects. Another work by Roca should be consulted: *El Pla Macià*, La Magrana, Barcelona, 1977. A work that focuses on the Macià Plan within a twentieth-century Barcelona and shows the changes in its urban structure is Manuel De Torres, 'L'estructura urbana de Barcelona. De les annexions a la fi de la guerra civil', in *Història de Barcelona*, vol. 7, Ajuntament de Barcelona, Barcelona, 1995, pp. 31–70.

90 Some of the publications that dealt with the grave problems of workers' housing should be quoted to get an idea of their tone, ranging from the most conservative to the most radical. Among the first is an outstanding work, *La habitación humilde en Barcelona*, which was published in June 1928 by the Municipal Patronage of Housing of Barcelona, where we read: 'All the Spanish capitals are greatly lacking rooms for rent at a reduced price that also comply with the minimum conditions of hygiene, health and commodity to which any person should have a right … As a consequence of this lack of housing, there has been an agglomeration of people in all the working-class town quarters in which whole flats and single rooms are rented at exorbitant prices … This same problem has given rise to hundreds of squalid shantytowns which circumscribe Barcelona … as a shameful example of a city without culture, and what is worse, without charity.' The work reports on the Patronage's agreement to build 4,000 simple single-family dwellings in the five main areas of the city, where there were approximately 6,748 shacks housing 26,172 people. Of these, only 2,335 or 2,229 were built, according to the article 'Las viviendas para los humildes', published in the magazine *Su Finca*, no. 16, February 1931, p. 38. The alarming number of shacks, and the serious hygienic and social problems this entailed, along with the urgent need to build dwellings for their inhabitants, had already been the subject of a series of four articles under the title, 'Barracópolis' (Shantytown City), signed by E. Mira and published in *Justicia Social, setmanari socialista* in November and December 1923 and January and March 1924. Here it was not of charity that they spoke, but of the right to housing, summoning the working classes to organize themselves so as to combat the problem.
In issue no. 32, published on 12 March 1931, the Communist weekly *La Batalla* published an article by Jordi Arquer titled 'Política municipal de la clase obrera', in which we read: 'If the working classes truly wish to solve once and for all their most urgent problems – inexpensive dwellings, hygienic town quarters, education for their children, etc. – it is necessary that, on the one hand, they take away their votes from left-wing bourgeois parties, and on the other, that they abandon their suicidal inhibition so as to decisively support candidates from the farming and working-class blocks in the coming municipal elections.' We have gone from calling for organization to believing that this can be possible, and that specific political results can be achieved concerning certain issues, foremost of which is housing. In *La Humanidad* of 12 July 1934, we find an unsigned article titled 'The New Barcelona', reviewing the Macià Plan, which was being exhibited at the time.
Parallel publications were to reflect the possibility of change by mirroring the USSR example, which is seen in articles in *La nueva era* or in the article published in *La Rambla* on 6 August 1934. All of these present the symmetry between social revolution and the improvement of working-class living conditions: 'The first task of the Soviet government was to fight against the lack of hygienic conditions in workers' dwellings and to create 'green cities' in the areas surrounding big cities.' We also find references to the connection between architectural language and the political system: 'It is in the USSR that this architecture has found a sufficiently ample ground for experimentation, since it is the only country that has prepared itself to fully accept the principles of modern architecture.'

91 Sert Collection, SC E 0.

92 Oliveras, op. cit., p. 44. In Javier Monteys, *Barcelona, la Ville Radieuse y el mar*, there is also a variant on p. 50.

93 We cannot overlook the fact that the extension of Gran Via and the need for a Free Port had already been taken into account in the Hospitalet Plan proposal made by Ramón Puig Gairalt, the architect who introduced Le Corbusier to Barcelonians. See Josep M. Rovira, 'El plano de Ensanche de L'Hospitalet: resistencia y flirteo frente a la Metrópoli', in *Història Urbana del Plà de Barcelona*, vol. II, Barcelona, 1990, pp. 339–47.

94 For the origins of the name 'Barrio Chino', given to the most squalid part of the old city, and for its history see Paco Villar, *Historia y leyenda del Barrio Chino*, La Campana, Barcelona, 1996.

95 See *Cuadernos de Arquitectura y Urbanismo*, no. 94, Barcelona, January–February 1974. Practically the entire issue is dedicated to the project of The Leisure City. The local press wrote extensively on this plan: *L'Opinió* on 28 July 1932; *La Publicitat* on 22 March 1933, reporting on a conference given by Sert in which he discussed it; *El Mundo Deportivo* on 5 April 1933; and *La hoja del Lunes* on 9 April 1934, in an article written by Comorera.

96 The conclusions of the first CIAM are known to have been written up in two variants, one in French and the other in German. See Martin Steinmann, *CIAM Dokumente 1928–1939*, op. cit., pp. 28–31.

97 Sert answered this letter on 1 June 1932, giving the impression that Le Corbusier's collaboration had already begun during his stay in Barcelona: 'The Commissariat for Workers' Housing has not yet begun to function; we have had meetings and interviews, but things have not got to that point yet. If we manage to make these people see that it is necessary to adopt an overall plan, we will then be able to propose that which you wish … I will soon send you a copy of the plan of Barcelona; I deduce from your letter that you are referring to the plan we made jointly with you.' FLC H3 4.

98 A letter to Sucre on 11 November 1933 reads: 'I am leaving for Paris today … I will come back to Barcelona at the end of the month … I will try to see our friends there and

try to invite Lagardelle to come so that he could give some lectures here if at all possible. My address in Paris is 51 Boulevard Beau-sejour, Paris 16.' On Sucre's relationship with the activities of the Ateneu Enciclopèdic Popular (founded in 1903), see Termes, op. cit., pp. 325–27.

[99] Concerning the chronology and analysis of this building, which will be dealt with later in the text, see Antonio Pizza, *Dispensario Antituberculoso de Barcelona, 1933–1937*, Colegio de Arquitectos de Almería, 1933.

[100] A summary of the issues debated in this Congress is found in *A.C.*, no. 6, 1932, pp. 50–51.

[101] Sert's correspondence is the source for information on all the trips made. A list of these can be compiled from two letters, housed in the GATCPAC Archives, addressed to Aizpurua on 2 and 17 May 1932. The reference to the trips is made just before the end of the CIRPAC meeting in Barcelona.

[102] From 4 to 14 December 1932, van Eesteren and Giedion were in Moscow negotiating with the Commission, which was to promote CIAM 4 and ensure that conditions were suitable for the execution of the Congress. They managed to write up a programme that the CIAM secretary sent to the delegates through a circular on the 26th of that month. Despite this, on the following day Giedion sent Le Corbusier a letter of warning in which it became evident that the USSR was not favourably inclined towards the CIAMs: 'Be that as it may, in the USSR there is a strong reaction against modern architecture. We spoke with architects and the authorities, and our small group found that they had the same attitude … Due to the present reaction, which seems to be increasingly on the rise, Colli has faced remarkable difficulties. He cannot write easily, and has given me a note for you, which I am enclosing.' FLC D 2 4–6. An extensive text on CIAM 4 can be found in the Italian magazine *Parametro*, no. 50.

In the French CIRPAC meeting held on 27 February 1933, it still seemed evident that CIAM 4 would be held in the Soviet capital. On 22 March, Giedion received a letter from Moscow from someone called Weinschenker, in which he was told: 'In the course of our preliminary work we have come to the conclusion, much to our dismay, that the preparations for the Congress would not be ready by the time we had established it would be held. We have therefore all agreed that it is necessary to adjourn the deadline for the Congress … We by no means give up on the idea of holding the Congress in Moscow.' Giedion's immediate reaction to this news was to write to Syrkus and to Emery on 29 March asking whether there was any chance of holding the Congress in Warsaw or in Algiers.

Finally, after receiving a telegram from Moscow on 18 April 1933 with the brief message: 'The Congress is only possible in 1934. Weinschenker', he sent a circular explaining the results of a meeting with van Eesteren, Bourgeois, Le Corbusier, Breuer, Steiger and himself on 23 and 24 April, in which, after informing them of the possible sites for the Congress, he wrote: 'Due to the Congress not being able to be held on time, and due to the fact that the last congresses have not allowed its members the possibility of establishing closer contacts, we have favourably received the proposal made by a navigation company to assemble the Congress on board the ship Patris II.'
An explanation of the difficulties of holding a CIAM in Moscow is found in Anatole Kopp, *Quand le MODERNE n'était pas un style mais*

une cause, École nationale superieure des Beaux-Arts, Paris, 1988, pp. 169–91.

[103] GATCPAC Archives, C 10/67.

[104] GATCPAC Archives, C 11/69. In another letter of 7 March 1933, he again asked Aizpurua to explain how many architects from the North Group would be coming to CIAM 4. Sert was on his own in matters having to do with the Spanish group since Mercadal was not interested in the CIAMs, as can be plainly deduced from this missive: 'I have not heard from Mercadal at all. The CIRPAC members are angry with him and ready to depose him, ridiculing him in front of all the National Assembly of Architects. He truly deserves it.' GATCPAC Archives, C 9/64. A letter from Mercadal to Sert of June 1933 states: 'The GC will not be amongst those going on this "classical" excursion; I have already been to Greece. Have a good time and enjoy yourselves.' GATCPAC Archives, C–11/71. Other letters deposited in the GATCPAC Archives show Sert's organizational zeal concerning the presence of Spanish architects in the CIAM of Athens. C–9/64.

[105] FLC D 2 4 52–56.

[106] Extensive commentaries and plans on the cities analyzed are to be found in Steinmann, op. cit., pp. 132–39, as well as in *A.C.*, no. 12, pp. 15–41. The short text written by Sert and his GATCPAC friends (a first draft, which was probably the one read on board the ship) is found in FLC D 2 4 102. A refined version is found in *A.C.*, no. 12, p. 18.

[107] The activities carried out in Athens, and the texts of the papers given by van Eestern, Giedion and Le Corbusier, are found on twenty-six typewritten sheets in Sert's archives: SC CIAM B3.

[108] FLC D 2 4 202.

[109] FLC D 2 4 221. On the return trip from Athens, Fernand Léger gave a lecture titled 'Architecture's Stand in Life', in which he defended values such as 'feelings' or 'aspirations' for the inhabitants of modern architecture, and proposed the use of colour as a way to humanize it, a point that was taken up in architectural debates after World War II. The December 1940 issue of the *Architectural Record* contains a review of 'The Humanizing Architecture', a text by Alvar Aalto published in *The Technology Review* of the previous November. This is to cite two early examples in which we observe a criticism of the strict functionality of modern architecture.

[110] They are found in *Parametro*, op. cit., pp. 44–45.

[111] FLC D 2 4 251–266.

[112] FLC D 2 4 358–359. A handwritten letter from Giedion to Le Corbusier on 4 September 1933 reads: 'The resolutions of Marseilles were, for the most part, ineffectual.' It goes on to propose alternatives to be debated as to whether the CIAMs were to become simply places for technical discussions or whether they were to be forums for political debate. Near the end of the letter Giedion admitted that it would be better 'to acknowledge the events and details that are repeated in every government. I find that our point of view on the margin of politics is extremely important today to achieve order.' FLC D 2 4 360.
In the CIRPAC session in London on 20 May 1934, it seems that these doubts had been dissipated, as we shall see further on in the text.

[113] Gino Pollini, who attended the Congress, seems to recall the gist of Giedion's words, but he rejects the idea that the Italian delegation did not agree on the point about land availability being absolutely necessary to resolve the great urban problems faced by European cities. See *Parametro*, op. cit., p. 23.

[114] FLC D 2 4 290–292.

[115] The resolutions can also be found in *Parametro*, op. cit., p. 47.

[116] A letter from Giedion to Sert of 4 November 1933 reads: 'The resolutions have finally been completed; writing them has neither been easy nor agreeable.' GATCPAC Archives, C–10/65. In another from Sert to Wells Coates of 5 December 1933, we read: 'The resolutions (last edition in Zurich) are not from our group because they lack clarity and do not express what we did in the Congress. I will make a new project here, based on the last system that we spoke about in Marseilles, plus some summarized notes from Le Corbusier. It must always be clear that these notes are nothing else but principles marking a course of action for the next Congress, from which we will draw the solutions or definitive bases once the analysis has been completed and the new projects have been done.' GATCPAC Archives, C–9/64.

[117] The letter sent to him by Steiger and Hubacher on 18 October 1933, in which they informed him that they were sending the Zurich maps, also reflected this state of affairs. GATCPAC Archives, C–11/72. The letter still shows some doubts as to the validity of the Resolutions of Athens. A missive to Aizpurua on 22 November 1933 confirms this: 'For the 12th *A.C.* we have prepared a special issue on Urbanism, which we believe to be very good … I am leaving for Paris tomorrow.' GATCPAC Archives, C–9/64. In another note to Wells Coates of 27 November, he asked him for maps of London for the twelfth issue of *A.C.* and wrote that he hoped to see him in Paris. GATCPAC Archives, C–9/64. As a matter of fact, no. 12 of *A.C.*, which is registered as having been published in the fourth quarter of 1933 although it must have come out some time later, is monographically dedicated to the CIAM of Athens, and analyzes Barcelona, Amsterdam, Berlin, Madrid, Zurich, Zagreb, Athens and Littoria. The London maps must not have arrived on time or never got there.

[118] See Antonio Pizza, op. cit., p. 77. Relations between Subirana and Sert can be traced through the documents in the COAC Archives. Subirana became Director Member of GATCPAC on 25 December 1932, and resigned on 1 November 1933. He asked to be readmitted as a member in May 1934, but on 7 February 1935 his request was formally rejected. He was *A.C.*'s librarian and Industrial Assistant.

[119] Letter from Sert to José María de Sucre, GATCPAC Archives, C 10/67. Sucre had become 'the strong man' of the Commissariat for Workers' Housing, and due to his conservative worker's union position and the mediation of Sert and Le Corbusier, he came into contact with Hubert Lagardelle and Pierre Winter, whom we found working for *Plans* magazine. Part of the correspondence among them is housed in the GATCPAC Archives. Sucre invited Lagardelle and Le Corbusier to the placing of the foundation stone for The Leisure City, which he naively believed would be executed in May 1934.

[120] In a cutting from *La Noche* of 29 May 1934, we read: 'In the Generalitat of Catalonia there are Departments that are completely unknown to the public … for example … the "Commissariat for Workers' Housing", established by decree on 13 June 1932. This Department, under the management of José María Sucre and the technical direction of the architects Sert, Subirana and Torres, the technician-worker Mr Simó i Piera and the administrator Mr Baró Mas, has, since its creation, developed the following social works: construction of 10 single-family houses, to ensure a minimum of work-

ers' housing in an industrial area, using for its construction the unemployed construction workers from Sant Andreu to reduce forced unemployment.'

[121] Despite the good will of the architects, something must have gone amiss with the budget, as can be gathered from some of the letters found in the COAC Archives. Thus, for example, in the previously mentioned letter from Torres to Sert of 13 February 1933, we read: 'We went to see Dencàs, and instead of answering what we were asking him … he spoke about the results of the Sant Andreu houses, which he said were expensively priced because Piera had not paid attention to his indications.' José Dencàs, leader of the Joventut d'Estat Català, was named Councillor of Health of the Generalitat of Catalonia by the Catalan government that came into power on 24 January 1933.

[122] The Casa Bloc, which was still under construction during the Civil War, was used by Torres as a standard bearer for the new ideas on workers' housing, which were more feasible at that point given that it was a time of revolution. In the second issue of *Nova Ibèria* (February 1937), which was edited by the Commissariat of Propaganda of the Generalitat of Catalonia, an article was published under the title 'La transformació del concepte de l'estatge' (The Transformation of the Concept of Dwelling), which states: 'In today's society, more just and egalitarian, we will again be able to focus quickly on the problems that previous social prejudices did not allow us to solve in a logical manner … Among all the functions that we are obliged to fulfill in a city: dwelling, work, recreation, circulation, etc., etc., the first, that is dwelling, is the most important … To complete the perfect concept of housing, it must be surrounded by all those elements that complete its functioning: schools, parks, nursery schools and children's libraries, free spaces for older children's games: swimming pools, squash courts, sports fields, etc … The present CASA BLOC, located in the St Andreu neighbourhood, which is about to be finished, constitutes a first essay in the execution of this programme, which must undoubtedly serve as a point of departure so as to implant these new housing complexes, which must arise as a result of this new social structuring … In two months' time, CASA BLOC … will be ready to start functioning. It is therefore already a reality.'

[123] In a letter to Giedion of 9 November 1933, we read: 'I will be in Paris on Friday the 24th, and will be very happy to see Gropius there.' GATCPAC Archives, C 10/65. In another missive addressed to Wells Coates on 5 December 1933, we find: 'I have received your telegram from Paris, having arrived in Barcelona yesterday from there.' GATCPAC Archives, C 9/64.

[124] FLC H3–13 9.

[125] FLC H3–13 15.

[126] FLC H3–18 19.

[127] Termes, op. cit., p. 353.

[128] Ibid., pp. 373–77.

[129] FLC H3 13 20.

[130] A letter from Le Corbusier to Sert of 5 July 1934 states: 'On taking a closer look at it, I have the feeling that your conception is still a bit dispersed, and that the whole subject should be redefined to give it the unity and expansion necessary: those are two small things that have to be done, but still, they must be done.' Le Corbusier was already working on the form that the expansion of working-class quarters should take in Barcelona: 'We will send you one of these days the printing of a *redent* executed here with a great deal of care by one of our draftsmen for one of the town quarters of

the Barcelona expansion. This drawing has nothing very absolute about it, but it has a firmer grasp on reality than the simple schemes done until now for the Plan of Barcelona.' FLC H3 13 25.

Le Corbusier published the Plan of Barcelona in the October 1934 issue of *L'Architecture d'Aujourd'Hui*, which was dedicated to his work and to that of Pierre Jeanneret, op. cit., pp. 132–33. The material was finished before the end of April 1934, as we can gather from a text by Le Corbusier within this publication. There we read: 'President Macià is dead. He incarnated the idea, but above all, the ideal. We call this plan of Barcelona (which is just a beginning) the "Macià Plan".'

L'Architecture d'Aujourd'Hui published a text by Sert on Le Corbusier, which in an autobiographical sense, allows us to understand better the important role played by the Swiss architect in Sert's professional training. (pp. 11–12).

[131] FLC H3 13 26. FLC H3 13 27.

[132] FLC H3 13 29. Much later, at the end of the 1970s, in a typewritten text titled 'Living and Working with Joan Miró', Sert wrote: 'In 1935 we visited the eastern coast of Spain and Andalusia, and went to the central prison in Madrid to meet the members of the Catalan government including President Companys.' SC D 27.

[133] FLC H3 13 30. The GATCPAC members also continued working on the Barcelona Plan, increasing the number of panels that they had showed in the 1934 exhibition in Barcelona. They exhibited them in April 1935, amidst the scandal that arose when they were forced to take down some maps, and presented them in Amsterdam one month later. See Salvador Tarrago, 'El Plan Macià, síntesis del trabajo del GATCPAC para Barcelona', *2C*, no. 15–16, 1980. In a letter from Sert to Wells Coates of 16 July 1934, we read: 'We have made 30 big maps and a seven-metre-long diorama.' In another to Mercadal of 26 April 1935, he told him: 'We will present a plan of expansion for Barcelona and a study for the sewage system of the old town quarters.'

[134] FLC H3 13 32.

[135] FLC H3 13 33. The letter states: 'Excellency: On the occasion of the International Meeting of Town Planners that will be held in Amsterdam the following month, may we contact you as representatives of the city of Barcelona, which has been the object of our study and of which we hold very pleasant recollections due to our having held various meetings of our Spring Congress of 1932 there. In our Amsterdam meeting we will once again be dealing with your city, and since a long time has gone by since my last stay in Barcelona without having received any news on the town development projects that we had exhibited in your city, I would like to request, if it is not too much to ask, that you give us your opinion, ensuring you that a renewal of contact with you is for all of us a great pleasure … we would be very happy to collaborate with the works of the distinguished architects and town planners of Barcelona … We will most willingly welcome delegates or official observers from the City Council of Barcelona and from the Generalitat of Catalonia.'

[136] Francesc Roca, op. cit., p. 40.

[137] The seats obtained by the different parties throughout Catalonia were: Esquerra Republicana de Catalunya, 21 deputies; Acció Catalana Republicana, 5; Unió Socialista de Catalunya, 4; Partit Republicá d'Esquerra, 3; Partit Nacionalista Republicá d'Esquerra, 2; Unió de Rabassaires, 2; Partit Comunista de Catalunya, Partit Cátala Proletari, Partit Obrer d'Unifi-

cació Marxista and PSOE, 1 vote each. Termes, op. cit., p. 383.

[138] FLC H3 13 37.

[139] FLC H3 13 38. A letter from Sert to Mercadal of 18 March 1936 is full of these topics: 'I got your letter; we hope that the change in the political situation here will help the GATEPAC; maybe after all these years we will finally get to execute some of the work we had projected.' GATCPAC Archives, C 10/66. Two days later he also wrote to Giedion: 'But political elements here have changed, this time favourably with our plans, which of course means we have much work before us. GATEPAC these days is working to full capacity.' GATCPAC Archives, C 10765.

[140] Francesc Roca, op. cit., pp. 42–45.

[141] In that day's session, Sert said, in reference to the Spanish situation: 'Since Mercadal is alone in Madrid, he cannot form a group there all by himself. Aizpurua promises to reorganize the San Sebastian group with all his might. The Barcelona group (GATCPAC) effectively continues its collective work (commissions and CIAM manifestations with conferences and exhibitions). Among other things, we are expecting to exhibit in the fall the documents of the 4th Congress.' SGA 5–1–23F.

[142] 'After the political change, the Catalan group's work is carried on with great difficulties and we no longer have relations with the government. Some of the members of the Madrid group and from the North Group hold rather important posts in the Ministry, as is the case of Aizpurua. Mercadal is professor at the School of Architecture.' FLC D2 6 133.

[143] FLC D 2 6, 108–9. The Catalan delegates also presented a scheme to determine the necessary plans, and the format and colours for the City Regulating Plan, FLC D 2 6, 112–114.

[144] FLC D 2 6 135.

[145] FLC D 2 6 192.

[146] Letter from Le Corbusier to Mme. de Mandrot of 11 March 1936, FLC D 2 6 195.

[147] FLC D 2 6 201.

[148] From an interview in *Cuadernos de Arquitectura y Urbanismo*, no. 140, Barcelona, 1980. Concerning war circumstances and architects, see Antonio Ferrer y Vega, 'El SAC: Revolución y ejercicio profesional', *2C*, op. cit., pp. 87–95. Josep M. Rovira, op. cit., pp. 59–64. In the first minutes of the 'Libro de Actas del Sindicat d'Arquitectes de Catalunya', which are kept in the COAC Archives and dated 7 August 1936, Sert's name does not appear, perhaps because by that time he was no longer in Barcelona. A letter from Giedion written on 21 August 1936, evidences his doubts as to whether Sert would be able to go to La Sarranz, possibly due to the political situation: 'The absence of Sert and Le Corbusier in La Sarranz will leave a big gap in the collaboration of the rest.' FLC D 2 6 211.

[149] Interview with the Count of Sert, August 1997.

[150] Interview with Josefa Graells, August 1997.

[151] 'The Board of Directors reaffirms its trust in the position you hold with which you honour the institution, and we are sure that in so doing we interpret with justice the feelings of all our members. Having been informed of the circumstances of your expatriation, we would like to let you know the satisfaction it would give the Ateneu to welcome your return to Catalonia and to have you take on anew the revolutionary tasks that you were carrying out from your place of work, study and dissemination. The Revolution, in a moment of passion has perhaps been unfair to you. Once things have gone back to a revolutionary order, the Ateneu, a pioneer in this fight for liberty,

would like to rectify this error that has been perpetrated against its Vice-President. The Ateneu needs your assistance, your work and your advice; at the same time it requests that you come back to our city and will launch a campaign in defence of your name. We would like your return to have all the solemnity that your constant work for the sake of the proletariat and culture deserves. We are preparing an act of disproval that will necessarily be an act of reparation, which will honour us all', SC E2.

[152] FLC D 2 6 230–245. Moser was responsible for the Committee for the Representation of Plans, with the help of Torres, Stam, Mohely, Perriand, Roth, Merkelbach and Burckhardt. Perriand, from the Organization of the Congress, was helped by Charreau, Giedion, Gropius, Sert and Jeanneret. Quétant was to deal with the Committee for the Establishment of the Fundamental Rules of Urbanism, and was helped by Brown, Burckhardt, Forbat, Hoste, Nazarieff and Roth. Roth was responsible for the Committee for Photographic Exhibitions, and was assisted by Pierrand, Jeanneret, Stam and Merkelbach. Samuel was in charge of the Committee of Finances, jointly with Sert, Moser, Kaliwoda, Fischer, Fanti and Fitschy. Giedion was in charge of the Committee of Press and Files, assisted by Bijhower, Fanti, Fischer, Fitschy, Kaliwoda and Morton Shand. Finally, Roth managed the Committee for the Organization of the Circle of Friends of the CIAMs, and was helped by Fry, Perkins and Perriand.

[153] The most significant points of Torres' excited letter state: 'Events have been taking a very sudden turn these days. It seems as if much time has elapsed since the seizure by force of the Col.legi i Associació until now. In the first Assembly we managed to constitute ourselves as an autonomous Labour Union … that will solve the internal labour struggle among architects … We have gone on to the control of all the construction companies in Barcelona. The control in the City Council is verified in an effective manner. I am personally in charge of this. We are involved in everything, we know everything, we control all the technical offices, we ensure that all the projects crossing our minds are written down, among which, as you might have guessed, is the demolition of the Barrio Chino. I have also discovered in the municipal offices the project, which is almost finished, of the extension of Gran Via to the Prat de Llobregat. As you may suppose, I have got it approved immediately, and on Monday the 8th we will start construction work on it … I have achieved a complete victory by being personally designated Delegate of the School of Architecture with all the rights to do and undo … I have got the Architects' Labour Union to approve the dismissal of all, absolutely all the tenure professors of the School of Architecture and on Monday they will carry out the dismissal. At the same time I have achieved a perfect organization of the Architects' Labour Union, through different commissions that execute every Committee's orders with great discipline … We hope to have the new general school plan for the whole Catalonia approved within the next fifteen days … The only architect entitled to receive commission is the Labour Union and it is this body that then distributes these among all the rest.' COAC Archives, C 30/188.
On the collectivizations that were promoted in those revolutionary times see Antoni Castells, *Les col.lectivitzacions a Barcelona, 1936–1939*, Ed. Hacer, Barcelona, 1993. Another interpretation from a different era and point of view is found in Manuel Roldan, *Las colectivizaciones en Cataluña*, Barcelona, 1940.

[154] Josefa Graells insists that Sert returned on a lightning trip to Barcelona during the war, although she does not know the reasons for it nor the exact dates. In some of his letters from Paris he spoke of his wish to travel to Barcelona, but we cannot glean from them that he actually did so. On 12 January 1937, he wrote to Torres from Paris: 'I am planning to come to Barcelona within a month once the exhibition of Catalan art is inaugurated and the project for the 1937 Pavilion is finished.' GATCPAC Archives, C 30/188.
In another letter to Torres of 12 October 1938, he wrote: 'Your last letter, full of enthusiasm, makes me take on the work here with renewed force so I could go to Barcelona as soon as possible to collaborate with you and all our companions.' GATCPAC Archives, C 30/188.
A text written by Sert on 29 October 1938 reads: 'At the end of May [1937], by petition of the General Commissary, the architect Sert went to Valencia to make contact with the people who made up the Organizing Committee for the selection and expedition of material that had to be included in the pavilion.' A transcription of this text is found in Catherine Blanton Freedberg, *The Spanish Pavilion at the Paris World's Fair*, vol. II, Garland, New York/London, 1986, p. 752.
In Sert's trial for war responsibilities after the civil war, one of the causes with which he was charged was the fact that he had come back to instigate the Republican troops. We will return to this later.

[155] Letter from Torres to Sert, 30 September 1936, GATCPAC Archives, C 30/188.

[156] A letter from the President of the Generalitat, Lluis Companys, of 8 February 1937, which is housed in the Sert Collection, says: 'It is my duty to inform you that in the meeting held on the 2nd of this month with the Committee of Medieval Catalan Art Exhibition, you were designated, in accordance with the decree of 26 January of last year, member of the Executive Committee in Paris.' SC E 2. In the Sert trunk of the FJM there is a copy of this exhibition's catalogue, in which we read: 'The General Director of Art Museums of Catalonia, Mr Joaquin Folch i Torres, and the architect J.L. Sert have directed the installation with the aim of emphasizing the value of each piece by setting them in a surrounding of utmost simplicity.'

[157] FLC D 2 6 376–383.

[158] The 'official' explanation for this abrupt change is described in the sixth page of the official publication of CIAM 5, *Logis et Loisirs*, published by Editions L'Architecture d'Aujourd'Hui in 1938. It says: 'The subject matter of the 5th Congress in Paris had been conceived in the summer of 1936 at the CIRPAC meeting in the Castle of La Sarranz. However, when the time came, in December of that year, to make the definitive arrangements for it, the President of the French CIAM Group summoned those in charge of the organization of the 5th Congress: Pierre Jeanneret, Charlotte Pierrand, J. Louis Sert and E. Weissmann. The programme was again examined at length and the La Sarranz proposals were abandoned in favour of a precise subject that could offer interesting points of view and that could decisively intervene on the most urgent problem of this period: housing. To the notion of housing, another term, that of 'recreation', was immediately added as if it were inseparable; the theme of the Congress was thus definitely adopted: "LOGIS ET LOISIRS".'

[159] There are two sources that trace Le Corbusier's activities between 1932 and 1937 in relation to his interest in the Paris World's Fair:

Le Corbusier and Pierre Jeanneret, *Oeuvre Complète 1934–1938*, Artemis, Zurich, 1964, pp. 140–69; Le Corbusier, *Des canons, des munitions? Merci! Des Logis … SVP*, Ed. L'Architecture d'Aujourd'Hui, Paris, 1938. In this last publication we can follow the content of the interior of the Pavilion that Le Corbusier designed. The part dedicated to the history of urbanism was prepared by Sert, Dupre and Masson.

[160] Georges Duby, *Histoire de la France, de 1852 à nos jours*, Larousse, 1987, p. 297.

[161] *Logis et Loisirs*, op. cit., p. 17.

[162] Ibid., p. 35.

[163] Ibid., pp. 77–78.

[164] SGA 6 1 11 F

[165] SC CIAM C2.

[166] A copy of the minutes of the meeting, written by José Luis Sert, is kept in FLC D2 14 32–36. There we find: 'The title of the 6th Congress will be "Specific Cases of Town Development According to the Proposals of the Chart of Athens".'

[167] This can be deduced from a letter that Sert addressed to van Eesteren on 30 September 1938. SC CIAM C2. Between 8 and 11 July 1939, there was meeting in Zurich in which they debated the possibility of holding the next CIAM in the USA. SGA CIAM VI. A letter from Giedion to Le Corbusier of 21 May 1939 makes many references to this subject, stating that there had been a CIAM assembly in New York. In the letter we also find the initial will to create a CIAM group in the States. FLC D 2 14 82. Giedion was referring to the 'Meeting of American Architects and Members of CIAM present in the United States', which was held at the Architectural League in New York on 13 May 1939, in which 'Dr Giedion closed the meeting by asking collaborators to assist Mr Sert in completing CIAM's latest work.'

1942, *Can Our Cities Survive?*

If the information we have is correct, José Luís Sert's book *Can Our Cities Survive?* was published by the Harvard University Press in the last months of 1942.[168] A great number of letters received by the Catalan architect, who was by then residing in New York, seem to corroborate this. The first of these, sent by Richard Neutra on 6 January 1943, reads: 'I hope you have started this new and strange year with fair anticipation, and with satisfaction regarding the fine reception your really splendid work has received. In Los Angeles we have endeavoured to get your book into all high school libraries and I hope the recommendation of the Haynes Foundation in this matter will succeed.'[169] If we take into account the fact that Neutra had written the Sert couple a Christmas card in 1942 without mentioning the book,[170] we can surmise that the Viennese architect must have received it between the end of December and the beginning of January.

Neutra's was not the only letter of congratulation, however. Josef Albers wrote to Sert on 11 January to ask him for a copy of the book for the library of Black Mountain College,[171] and on the 18th of the same month the all-powerful Lewis Mumford (to whom we will return later) sent him a handwritten letter stating: 'I have been ill and overworked, hence my tardiness in answering your letter of November; hence also my delay in reviewing your admirable book for the *New Republic*. I finally succeeded in writing it last week. I hope it has received the attention it deserves.'[172] Moholy-Nagy also congratulated Sert with warm words of praise in a letter of 25 January, in which he invited him to give some lectures in Chicago, for each of which Sert would be paid fifty dollars.[173]

To dispel any doubts as to the book's success, we also have a letter from New York written by Giedion to Gropius on 6 November 1942:

'Sert's book has been impeccably published, and this has made me very happy. His success under the present circumstances is assured.'[174]

Later we will analyze the contents of *Can Our Cities Survive?*, but for the moment we will focus on the intentions and events surrounding its publication. How did an architect who had just arrived in the United States manage to publish a book whose production cost was high (especially if we take into account that it was a time of war), whose contents were so specific, and that partook in a doctrine that was not well regarded by American intellectuals? Why was he interested in doing so? Who, besides himself, in the circles of American architects and urbanists, could be concerned with this work? Answering these questions will allow us to review Sert's book under a different light, as well as making a survey of the preceding years inevitable in order to trace some of the steps that led him to seek the publication of this work.

While he was desperately attempting to get the Republic to pay his honorary fees for his work on the Spanish Pavilion of the 1937 World's Fair,[175] Sert wrote a letter from London on 5 July 1938 to his friend Sigfried Giedion, in which he told him: 'My work on the publication is not as advanced as I would have hoped it to be … Going to Brussels under the present circumstances would mean a special round trip plus my stay, and this is difficult given my current means … Do you plan on coming to London right after the delegates' meeting? In that case we could talk here about a lot of things, as well as about the publication.'[176] Undoubtedly, by referring twice to the 'publication' in this confidential tone, he was referring to something known to his friend (and of which we are also aware, through the evidence gathered in the previous chapter). It is clear

Illustration reproduced in *Can Our Cities Survive?*

93

Sigfried Giedion.

that they understood each other, as is confirmed by a letter from a few years back (dated 16 July 1935 and found in the GATCPAC archives), in which Sert wrote to Giedion: 'I agree with you, we must work assiduously on the publication of *The Functional City*.' The word 'publication' used in reference to this text is also found in another letter from the GATCPAC archives, which Sert addressed to Giedion on 3 December of the same year.

The Sert Collection contains many other interesting data that allow us to trace the publication of which our architect was speaking. There is, in fact, a whole bundle of letters from May to November 1938, either addressed to Paris or to London, that he received on the matter. The objective was always the same: to send Sert material on cities so that he could elaborate the book that was under his responsibility.[177]

Shortly afterwards, on 27 October, when Sert's situation had become more precarious, he wrote a letter to the historian of architecture in decisive terms. After referring to the possibility of holding the following CIAM in the United States, mentioning that the ideal time for him would be September 1939, he again spoke about the publication: 'As to the dummy of *The Functional City*, it is completely finished with respect to its illustrations and composition. It is just a question of finishing the texts. If I return to London next week, I will immediately send you a copy of it to the States … I may have to go back to Barcelona instead of going to London; in that case I cannot tell you exactly when the draft will be finished.'[178] By that time the famous publication had a title, and we can link its contents to the City Planning Chart drawn up at the Athens CIAM of 1933. The letter ended in unmistakable terms: 'The political situation in Europe continues to go badly; I am increasingly interested in going to America. *I'm counting on you!*' Thus, it was also a matter of starting to prepare his departure from Europe due to the turn that events were taking in the Old Continent, and to do so he needed Giedion's support.

Help was immediately offered, almost by return post; on 25 December the Swiss historian answered him: 'We would like to have you in America and I think the optimistic atmosphere, which is so relaxing, will also have a beneficial influence on you. You can count on us, and we will constantly be on the alert for the most propitious moment. Naturally, all posts here are highly requested, but America nevertheless needs to attract creative forces from elsewhere. The great majority of immigrants here have an average level of education, and they cannot be useful to the Americans.'[179]

As time went on, Sert's situation worsened, and Giedion, his trustworthy American contact, was continually updated on the matter. On 13 February of the following year he received another letter from Sert in which there was no more news concerning how the writing of *The Functional City* was going; rather, the Catalan architect centred on his personal situation, given that the Civil War in his country now plainly revealed a reverse of fortune for those loyal to the Republic: on 26 January, the rebel army had entered Barcelona, which must have affected Sert profoundly, and the end of the war – which occurred two months later – seemed imminent. In the letter he states: 'The latest events in Spain force me to take the decision of leaving Europe within a few weeks. I would very much like to stay in the United States for a year … I can only get my visa if I am to do some sort of job, be it conferences, the organization of a congress, etc. Could you speak to Gropius and the members of CIAM in that country?'[180] Sert at the time was greatly afflicted by some terrible news: his friend Josep Tor-

Josep Torres.

res had died 'on 12 January during a bombardment in Catalonia.'

What was Giedion doing in the United States? He was teaching a course on architectural history at the Graduate School of Design, where he had been invited to hold the Charles Eliot Norton Professorship by the New York-born Paul J. Sachs, businessman, Chairman of the Fine Arts Department of the Fogg Museum, Cambridge. Walter Gropius – who had arrived in the New World on 17 March 1937,[181] invited there by Joseph Hudnut, Dean of the GSD – was also a visiting professor in the School. Hudnut had convinced Gropius to accept this job in America while the German architect was in London. Giedion's lectures would be the basis for *Space, Time and Architecture*, published by Harvard University Press in 1941. This was the first of a series of books on the history of contemporary architecture that came to be regarded as a Bible by more than three generations of architects. It was a book that Gropius especially needed, as did Hudnut to a lesser degree.

With his usual ability to pull strings, Gropius managed to arrange for his friend from Zurich to come and visit him. In a letter written on 24 June 1937 from Planting Island, Massachusetts, Gropius told his friend that his university was interested in inviting Giedion to give lectures there, and from that time onwards the correspondence between them flowed without break

to ensure the success of the venture. (Before this they had been writing to each other on a regular basis to discuss issues concerning the organization of the 1937 CIAM meeting in Paris, which Gropius did not attend.) The later letters outline the programme of seminars, the fees, Giedion's fears about speaking English, etc.[182]

Giedion also wrote to Sachs to tie up any outstanding issue in the organization of this venture. On 12 January 1938, he received the first letter from the American, in which he was informed that his classes would start in October, listing the other speakers who had previously participated there and the lectures that had been given in the past. Giedion was also offered the possibility of giving seminars at the Fogg Museum, reminding him at the same time that Charles Eliot Norton had been a Professor of Poetry. Sachs also added a comment that helps us to understand the publication of *Space, Time and Architecture*: 'Within six months after the talks, the manuscript of these lectures shall be delivered to Harvard University, whose property these manuscripts shall then become. These lectures shall be published either by the Harvard University Press or otherwise, as the Corporation of the University shall determine.'[183]

On 4 February 1938, Giedion wrote back to him thanking him for 'my official appointment as Professor to the Eliot Norton chair for the year 1938–39', and offering his interpretation

Joseph Hudnut.

Walter Gropius.

of what was expected of him in these lectures, given that it was not usual to invite someone to speak on architecture: 'I really hope to be able to interpret the term "poetry" like the French expression of *sens lirique de notre époque* and to combine it with our scientific point of view.'[184] He ended the letter by saying he would be at his disposal 'in the first week of October', a fact confirmed in a letter to Maxwell Fry on 2 September 1938: 'I leave Zurich at the end of the present month and sail from Boulogne on 8 October.' In it he gave the English architect Sert's address in Paris: 136, Bis Boulevard Montparnasse. As can be seen in a letter of 17 February, Sachs had travelled to Zurich to outline the contents of the classes and lectures.[185]

The decisive launch of *Space, Time and Architecture* can be gleaned from Sachs' letter to Giedion on 7 June, 1939: 'I am pleased to inform you that the Harvard University Press informs me that your manuscript, as it has been delivered so far, seems to the Press in reasonably good shape, and they add that if the rest of it is as good there will be no difficulty. They tell me that in the event that any trouble should develop, they will let me know … I hope all of this is as satisfactory to you as it is to me and that you will now be in a position to get the rest of the manuscript into the same shape and with the help of the same collaborator.'[186]

That Giedion had gone to America with certain intentions in mind can be deduced from a letter to Madame de Mandrot written on 1 June 1938: 'I am trying to introduce into Harvard a new method of history that will link our modern period with those that have preceded us. It is History seen through our eyes, but with respect for our past. It is our period seen as a part of a long development.'[187] This is probably what he was trying to explain to Le Corbusier when on 18 March 1941 he sent him the first proofs of the book, so that he could revise them: 'I have entirely treated your ideas as if I were a neutral historian, comparing them and relating them with other ideas of our contemporaries. You may sometimes not agree … I have not wanted to do anything other than systematize my point of view and express myself frankly and without hesitation.'[188]

This was an unexpected shift, especially considering that the Swiss historian had shown to be an enthusiast of Le Corbusier's work since 14 December 1925, the date of the first letter of their correspondence. Here, Giedion had written something of great interest, especially given that we are analyzing his work in America: 'I have declared your house Laroche to be the first really modern house. It … aims to unite all rooms on one level, as is the custom in America (I am surprised at not finding any reference to Lloyd Wright in your writings) … Next month I must write a long article on your architectural thoughts for an important art magazine in Germany.'[189] Not long before leaving for the States, Giedion had organized in Zurich one of the largest exhibitions of Le Corbusier's paintings, and had been in charge of editing its catalogue.[190] Their friendship had solidified in the intervening thirteen years through fidelity, through constant correspondence between them, through Giedion's articles in the *Neue Zurcher Zeitung* praising Le Corbusier's work, through debates in which the historian had 'constructed' the architect, through active participation in the CIAMs of which Giedion was secretary, through fighting in favour of modern architecture, especially supporting the architect from La Chaux-de-Fonds. And yet suddenly, those thirteen years had apparently been abruptly interrupted (although, in reality, the two remained friends for the rest of their lives), from the moment Giedion set Le Corbusier up against American architectural production.

Things had certainly changed by 1941, which is why Giedion's words to Le Corbusier sound like a lame excuse. The great admiration that bound him to Le Corbusier had led the historian to attempt a double loop so as not to irritate his friend. On the one hand, before leaving for the United States he had written to Madame Mandrot to announce the pillars of his intellectual project: the idea of history as a continuity, thus distancing himself from the avant-garde's obsession with making a *tabula rasa* of the past. On the other hand, he tried to deny this to the Swiss architect; to pretend that, besides being continuous, history could also be neutral was too much. After all, this 'neutrality' was to be achieved by lumping Le Corbusier in with other architects, comparing his work with other architectures, manuscripts and experi-

Chicago World's Fair, 1893.

ences, seeking thereby to annul qualitative differences by making uniform the responses to the clash between modernity and traditional architecture. The whole question has an underlying meaning that we cannot overlook because of the role it plays in the publication of Sert's book and even the 'convenience' of his arrival in America.

Giedion's own manuscript sheds some light on the matter. America had betrayed itself in the Chicago World's Fair of 1893, in which the 'regression' to a Beaux-Arts aesthetics had caught by surprise many architects who had staked their bets on a different way of doing things; the 'great white cloud', as Louis Henry Sullivan called it, had engulfed a naive America. It had not yet been possible to recover from that blow, or at least that was what Giedion wished university students and American architects to believe when they heard his views in 1938 and later read them (and have continued to read them since 1941). Europe had taken the lead, a lead always vied for by the Americans, and Giedion plainly supported them in this, basing his ideas on a text by Gropius from 1913: 'But in America, the cradle of industry, there are great industrial constructions which, in their unconscious majesty, surpass even the best German buildings of this type.' Is it possible that Giedion just happened to recall this detail of the text, or was it perhaps that 'someone' reminded him of it or fed him the information?[191]

Gropius was thus presented to the American reader as the person who had first intuitively seen that the European vanguards were in debt to American architecture; it was only many years later that Ozenfant and Jeanneret would publish slightly touched-up images of these same American industrial elements in one of the first issues of *L'Esprit Nouveau*. It was also the German architect who had insisted that Dean Hudnut invited Giedion to Harvard, because Gropius considered him a key person not only in his project of converting America to the cause of modernity, but also in his need to attain an influential position in modern architecture as the only means by which he could achieve recognition from this new society so as to be able to work professionally for its people. Though not stated in plain words, these reasons can be gleaned by consulting the correspondence between them.

The exchange of letters began on 16 January 1937 when Gropius told Giedion that he had been appointed Professor of Harvard, the place in which 'I am allowed to have a decisive influence'[192] and where he planned to start a crusade in favour of the modern, as if this were a sacred mission that called for the support of high priests: 'Everything seems to be going our way, and I think it is wonderful that at least one of us will have an important teaching post from

American silos reproduced in the *Werkbund Year Book*, 1913.

97

which we can disseminate our thoughts to the new generations.' Clearly, Giedion was amongst those who were to help Gropius avoid isolation. This is why the German architect's next step was to promote Giedion's transfer to the States. In a letter written on 23 December 1937, we read that Gropius' efforts had been successful: 'In the University of Harvard there is a so-called "Norton Lecturer Fund", which has considerable renown. A specially designated commission chooses important people from all over the world. Hudnut informed Breuer and me that this time he would be on the commission, and that he would try to bring over an architect. After several conversations we decided to put you in first place and I have assembled everything I know about your life and works and everything I could find about you in books. Just imagine, it has worked! You are the first on the list and Thomas Mann is the second.'[193]

As if by magic, the possibility of inviting an architect had become an invitation for Giedion to travel to the States. This is even more remarkable considering that Giedion was completely unknown to the Committee, which meant that Gropius had to come up with a curriculum vitae for him so that Hudnut could defend his candidacy. When Gropius said '*we have decided* to put you in first place', we are left with no doubts as to the pressure he must have exerted on Hudnut to achieve his objective. After all, inviting another architect might have endangered his interests, whereas bringing Giedion over could be doubly beneficial, not only because he was to be an effective force in

fighting for the cause of the architectural project that had been developing in Europe since the 1920s, but also because the historian could explain this movement with the apparent objectivity of someone who had nothing at stake, neither the desire for commissions, nor the need to defend one's work: 'I think no one is more qualified than you to make a lasting impression on minds and to offer truly fundamental clarifications of our movement.'

Eduard F. Sekler tells us the names of the members who made up the committee that decided to invite Giedion, and expresses his doubts concerning their knowledge of Giedion's work apart from the information that Gropius had compiled for them.[194] It was only thanks to Hudnut's insistence, with Gropius in the background, that Giedion was finally and miraculously considered to be more important than Thomas Mann. This miracle could not fail, for much was at stake, as can be gathered from Gropius' almost rude insistence: 'Obviously, I hope you will accept because it is <u>something important</u> [underlined in the original] that will not only give you great publicity, but will also in one fell swoop propagate your ideas in far-reaching circles.'

An intense correspondence by letter began after Giedion had naively expressed his gratitude: 'That you have dared to assume responsibility for me is the greatest proof of friendship I have ever been given.'[195] In these missives Giedion revealed his intentions and asked for advice on what subjects he should focus in his lectures at Harvard, to which Gropius respond-

Walter Gropius, Fagus Factory, Alfeld a.d. Leine, 1911–25.

Walter Gropius,
Bauhaus building
in Dessau,
1925–26, private
collection.

ed by urging him 'to adapt himself' to his suggestions.[196] Given Gropius' biased interest in concentrating on history,[197] it could not be otherwise.

Gropius, who occupied an eminent teaching post from which he exerted considerable influence, and who was moreover keen to be perceived as the standard-bearer of modernity in the United States, had seen his dream of being modern come true thanks to America. He himself was convinced of this, as is deduced from the letter he wrote on 9 March 1937 when leaving England. Apart from thanking Morton Shand for the exhibition of his works at the RIBA and for the English translation of his book, a circumstance that had opened America's doors to him, he also wrote: 'I have been to America only once in 1928 ... I went there to study the extraordinary American building organization, which is at present unsurpassed in the world. It has provided an instrument of wonderful perfection, so that any architect would feel inspired and ready to take part in the great task of forming the American architecture of the future ... I feel very much attracted by the enthusiasm and engerness [sic] of young Americans ... I like their optimistic and undaunted spirit and feel certain that we shall get on with each other ... I hope my ap-

pointment will be a further proof of the American ability to reconcile and amalgamate the most diverse types of people to create a new form of life of typical American stamp.'[198]

The enthusiasm for the American way of life that Gropius so fervently expressed is probably due to a combination of several hypotheses: either Hudnut and Conant, Dean of Harvard, had been very persuasive in their invitation, or they had promised him a substantial salary, or Gropius foresaw a hopeless future for himself in England. At any rate, he wished to achieve certain objectives in America and had stated so plainly, and the best way to accomplish this was for someone to reaffirm him in America as one of the best (if not *the* best) European architects. This was what he intended Giedion to do through the pages of *Space, Time and Architecture*.

Thus, in this book we read how 'in the Fagus Factory, Gropius succeeded in bringing together the results he had obtained in the last fifteen years ... He bridged the gap that separated feelings from intelligence, which had been the marrow disease of European architecture.' Gropius was presented before the American public as the connecting link between modern technique and architectural form that had been separated during the nineteenth century (a claim that Giedion made without offering any substantial proof). Gropius, or one of his architectural works, even served as the inspirational source for the final title of the book, since it is in the Bauhaus building that the architectural avant-garde and painting converge,

Walter Gropius,
Bauhaus building
in Dessau, view.

Pablo Picasso, *L'Arlésienne*, 1911–12.

and it is there that the revolutionary concept of 'space-time' demonstrates the far-reaching scope of the German architect's proposal: 'The transparency is so fully carried out that we are in the position of seeing the interior and exterior simultaneously, *en face et en profile*, like Picasso's *Arlésienne* from 1901–12; there is a multiplicity of levels of reference … and, in one word, simultaneity, the concept of space-time.' This is the Bauhaus that Gropius had managed to introduce to the American public at large through the renowned exhibition that he had organized jointly with Josef Albers at MoMA, New York, in 1938.

It is clear that Gropius had initiated a manoeuvre of far-reaching scope to decisively open the way for modern architecture in the United States, and to achieve the consolidation of his own situation within American academic circles. The foreseeable arrival of Sert was very possibly of help to him in concluding the operation successfully. Now it would not only be a question of architecture, but rather of importing the CIAM debates on the city, and Sert had been working on this subject during the last years and therefore had substantial documentary material on the issue.

While Giedion was busy writing his book in the States, Sert continued to correspond with him there, as is evidenced by a letter of 21 June 1939. Shortly before this, on 6 June, the Catalan architect married Ramona Longas in

Havana, in order to have more 'convincing' papers when presenting themselves in the United States as a matrimony in need of asylum.[199] On the 21st, Giedion sent a letter to Sachs in which he took leave of him before his trip to Chicago, and in which he informed him that the translator (someone by the name of Callaghan who was the third to be assigned to the project) 'has sufficient material to work until my return', furthermore specifying that his CIAM colleague Morton Shand would be supervising all of the translation work. He also thanked the Norton Committee 'for the confidence shown in me for the publication of my book', and announced that he would be back in Cambridge by mid-August, thanking Sachs for his kindness with these words: 'I cannot express as I wish my appreciation of both objective and personal connections at Harvard in my field. It has opened new ways for my own specific interests.'[200]

While Giedion was gathering pamphlets on industrial propaganda – which would later be essential in the writing of *Mechanization Takes Command* – and admiring the buildings of Sul-

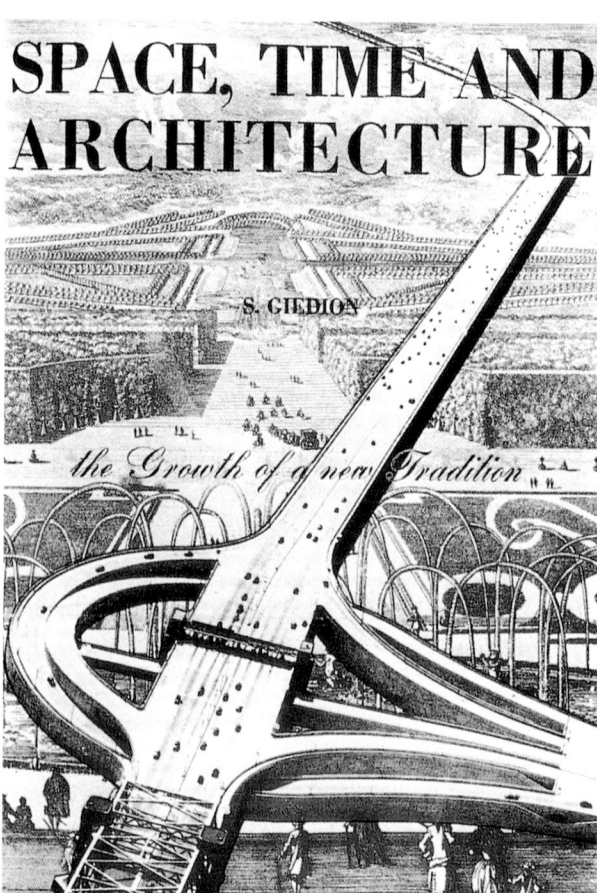

Cover by Herber Bayer for Sigfried Giedion's *Space, Time and Architecture*.

livan, Richardson and Lloyd Wright, Sert and his wife arrived in New York.

To continue with our analysis, we must look for other sources of information. Sert first asked for help in his letter of 27 October 1938, and Giedion quickly came to his aid, apparently finding a job for his Catalan friend, who was residing in Paris at the time. This is what we can deduce from Giedion's letter to Le Corbusier on 23 November 1938: 'Do you think that it would be possible to hold a Congress given the political situation in Europe? According to Sert, it should be planned for the month of September. Later than this is impossible because once the academic year starts at the end of September, no more dormitories will be available at Columbia University.'[201]

Despite the terrible situation in Europe, Giedion did not lose time. He again attempted to establish an American CIAM group despite Gropius' discouragement, and this must certainly have interested Sert. In a letter from Cambridge on 7 February 1939, Giedion wrote to the Catalan architect: 'I almost hesitate to write to you these days. In America we are also extremely depressed about the events that have occurred these last days. All of Europe will pay dearly for these atrocities. One cannot think of the future but with horror. Despite all of this, we are trying to set up a place here for the CIAM. Gropius and I were in New York fifteen days ago and tomorrow I must go back by myself to see whether it is possible to assemble American architects with an objective in mind that is not economic.'[202] The idea was not only to establish this group, but also to publish the manuscript on the Athens agreements, that is, 'The Functional City' resolutions, which Sert had not sent to his friend although Giedion had requested this material on 15 December. Sert had been keeping this documentation under his custody, but Giedion was very interested in it being published, writing in a letter to him: 'I have now managed to get an important publisher (one of the most international ones) interested in our small publication'

Before arriving in Havana, Sert had made a stopover in Bermuda, and from there he had written a letter to Giedion on 21 March 1939: 'Here I am, heading for Havana! There is nothing for me to do in Europe after the last events

in Spain … and Paris is no longer the Paris that we all love! My trip will be much easier from here to the States in September. I have the dummy of the book with me; you will soon have news on this subject.'[203] At the end of the letter he wrote down his future address in Cuba in the hope of receiving information about what he would need to enter the United States, and shortly after he had received it, revealing how successfully Giedion and Gropius had worked to help him.

While Sert was waiting for this news to arrive, he was also awaiting something else: apparently it was a parcel, or so we gather from a letter that Koen Limperg sent to Le Corbusier on 5 May 1939: 'I received a wonderful letter today from Sert in which he gives me his new address … He has requested that I send him a package with all the documentary material gathered for his publication of the CIAM Congress. You no doubt recall that I had sent this package with another package (another book) addressed to Sert to your studio in Paris. I would beg you to change the address on both packages and to send the material to Sert in Cuba.'[204] The content of the parcel is evident: it is the material compiled for the publication of *The Functional City*. We do not know exactly why Limperg refers to it as 'his publication', as if it had been agreed that Sert could take possession of a work that had been in great part collective and which had been developed throughout various congresses. At any rate, in the credits that appear in the first edition of *Can Our Cities Survive?*, the names 'Sert and CIAM' appear both on the cover and spine of the book. On the first page, the author's name is written in bold letters, and the book is also credited to 'the proposals formulated by the CIAM.'

Further enlightenment concerning this point is provided by a letter from Giedion to Sert (by then in Havana as the date of the letter – 26 March 1939 – indicates). After informing Sert of a possible CIRPAC meeting to be held during the New York World's Fair of 1939, Gidieon wrote: 'Our President, C. van Eesteren, in Amsterdam, is not able to come and we need your personal assistance, Mr Sert, not only as Vice-President, but also because you have prepared the publication concerning our town-planning problems, which is to be published in this country this year.'[205] This letter to Sert was thus almost an invitation of entry into the United States, where supposedly he would be welcomed with open arms and where the publication of *The Functional City* seemed imminent. Just in case Giedion's letter was not sufficient to convince the officials in the US Immigration Office, other invitations were quickly forwarded to him.

On 28 April James Johnson Sweeney wrote to him in Havana: 'The Institute of Fine Arts of New York University is planning a symposium on architecture to take place on 12 May … We would be very grateful if you could possibly arrange to participate. Besides those who are at present residing in the US, such as Walter Gropius and Walter Behrendt, we hope to have the collaboration of Aalto, Markelius, van de Velde and others.'[206] This was both an appropriate and useful letter of recommendation if by chance Sert needed to present one to the authorities.

Shortly afterwards, on the 29th of that month, Joseph Hudnut, Dean of the GSD, sent Sert a letter to the Havana address that Giedion had given him. The message was concise: 'In planning our lectures for the present academic year, which ends in June, it occurs to me that it might be possible for you to come to this country and participate in our lecture courses. On behalf of the faculty, I extend a very cordial invitation for you to do so.'[207] Sert and his wife could now truly count on obtaining a green card to enter the United States; the architect could show before the American consulate in Havana the invitations of both Sweeney and Hudnut as proof of having a salaried job in that country.

The date of his arrival was to be the end of June 1939, or so we are led to believe by a letter from Stamos Papadaki on the 18th of that month: 'It will be a pleasure to see you in New York. Since there is no specific arrival time for the buses, to make sure that we meet the best thing would be for you to call … we will come to pick you up. Have you tried to get a plane from Cuba to Miami?'[208] A document from the US Department of Justice confirms this: on 3 October 1940, Sert paid sixteen dollars head tax to the US Department, and an 'alien pas-

senger arrived on the *SS Florida* on 26 June 1939', adding that he was prolonging his stay in the country until 26 December 1940.[209]

With the road paved for him by his good friends, Sert immediately went to work. Thus, by 29 September 1939, while living in the Hotel van Rensselaer on 17 E, 11th Street, New York, the architect had already written a letter to Giedion informing him that Gropius had invited him to give a lecture in Cambridge, an invitation that he evidently accepted. After telling his friend that on 17 October he planned to visit Alexander Calder and his wife, he proposed that they meet on his return from Chicago.[210] The fact that we find so few letters in Sert's papers throughout the following year suggests that he spent most of 1940 in libraries and institutions, researching material for his book, whose content is to a large extent American images, information and bibliographies.[211]

Sert also spent his time exploring the possibility of creating an American CIAM, as well as pragmatically looking for jobs on other horizons far from Europe and the US, as we can gather from his letter of 9 December to Le Corbusier, in which he expressed his doubts as to the feasibility of a CIAM of American architects: 'Sacrifices scare them, since they tend to look only for positions that are sure, allowing them a comfortable life … The studies of our Congresses seem to them too abstract, and they do not commit themselves to collaborating except in the tasks that guarantee an immediate result … To stake everything for an agreeable and easy life entails certain risks, as the world has unfortunately come to realize in the last months; I do not think that they will learn from this lesson … I am making plans to go to South America; friends down there inform me that there is much activity in the construction sector and that we have chances of succeeding by forming a group of young architects … I believe you would have enormous possibilities if you were to decide someday to go to South America.'[212]

Thus, by the time *Can Our Cities Survive?* was ready for the printing press, Sert had already tried to establish his future work possibilities (which also depended on the success of his book) in Latin and South American countries, as we can see from the letter Juan Larrea

First cover and final cover by Herbert Bayer for *Can Our Cities Survive?*, 1942.

Can Our Cities Survive? An ABC of Urban Problems, Their Analysis, Their Solutions was the complete title of Sert's book, whose cover was designed by Herbert Bayer. Since the manuscript was to be finally published in the United States, the references to urban issues analyzed in the book evidently had to be specifically American. It is necessary to know American cities and their failings in order to be able to contrast these with the experience of urban phenomena that Sert had acquired professionally in Spain and in his dealings with the CIAM meetings. He had in his suitcases valuable documentary material with images and graphs to be included in his publication, but it had been devised with Europe in mind. Now that he had to make an impression on the American public it was absolutely essential that he make a great effort in establishing links between the European urban crisis and the American one, one of the underlying issues of his manuscript.

It makes sense, therefore, that the first picture in the book is an aerial view of New York,[214] followed by three images that reproduce the plan of Amsterdam and its region as a demonstration of the level achieved by the Europeans in the material analysis of cities. These graphic advertisements summarize the content of the manuscript, which after the author's preface presents the Athens agreements, organized according to the four city functions established, starting with that of housing.[215] Throughout the book, the comments, images, statistics and bibliography evoke the problems of the city, with special emphasis on studies centring on American cities, which are often compared to their European counterparts.

Sert visited the New York libraries in search of material that could aid him in explaining the points that had been approved in Athens, and succeeded in intertwining the works that he found with the materials he had brought with him from Europe (data, graphs and images of Barcelona, Paris and London). The problems he had experienced in Barcelona turned out to be the same in any other city of the world, and squalid districts could be found everywhere. What had been debated in Athens therefore took on the status of an international diagnosis that could be applied to the disas-

sent him from Mexico on 21 January 1941: 'I spoke with Neruda about the subject you're interested in. He told me that the best thing would be for you to speak *in his name* to Mr Aníbal Jara, the Consul of Chile in New York and a good friend of his, who will give you all the information necessary. Ensure him, or so Neruda counsels you, that you have the necessary means to live and establish yourself, because the fear of all consuls is to allow people to enter Chile who might afterwards become a public burden because of their lack of employment ... Obviously, though, with a friend like Rodríguez Arias there, everything will become much easier.'[213]

Illustrations reproduced in *Can Our Cities Survive?*

trous living conditions in certain city quarters, from Chelsea to Harlem.

His text necessarily became critical when analyzing, for example, Queensbridge Houses, a neighbourhood that had been completed in 1939, or when tracing American legislation on housing until the creation of the Housing Act, or when presenting data on the brutal expansion of the suburbs in Paris when the population had increased in its centre. It also tried to point out the superiority of high-rise buildings where there was a great density of inhabitants, which had more amenities and green spaces in comparison with American residential areas made up of endless garden-cities. It is at this point that Sert included a picture of Casa Bloc in his book, proving himself capable of offering answers emerging out of his own experience.

Our architect used the same strategy for each of the city functions, and thus, when it was the turn of 'Recreation', he first briefly introduced the subject using arguments similar to those that had appeared in the feature in *A.C.*, but on a different scale. The photographs of the masses in Barcelona that had appeared in the magazine looked like nothing in comparison to the number of people on the New York beaches (which Sert showed in a sufficiently graphic manner), or in comparison to the number of people who went to Paris on vacation. 'Work' and 'Transport', the other two functions, were treated in a similar fashion; the

images of traffic jams in London, for example, spoke eloquently for themselves, as did the problems caused by railways crossing the city, another problem that was common to cities all over the world, which desperately needed new road-network layouts.

Once the analysis had been concluded and the possible solutions had been proposed, Sert added: 'Having analyzed the four primary functions of cities, examining their present conditions and presenting proposals for their amelioration, we feel the need for a wider view encompassing the city as a whole – that is, the city and its surroundings – in order to comprehend both the interrelationships of urban functions and those of city and region.'[216]

Illustrations reproduced in *Can Our Cities Survive?*

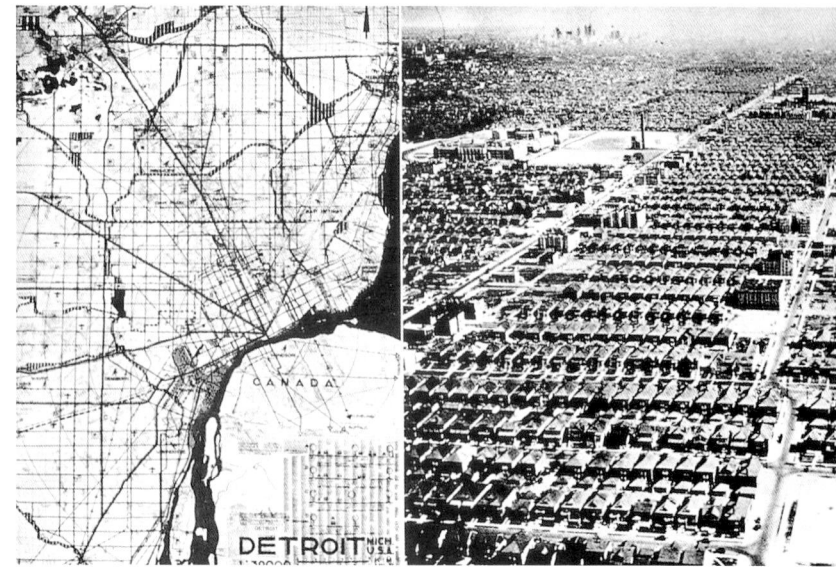

Illustration
reproduced
in *Can Our Cities
Survive?*

The gist of this was to offer a vision of the metropolis and its area of influence so as to confront the ineluctable need to control the growth of cities, something that American urban culture must have found difficult to understand, as we will see in the third chapter of this book. It also emphasized the need for planning as the only real possibility of survival for our cities, which Sert exemplified by means of a new city in the Soviet Union, designed by Mart Stam. The heading of the last chapter of the book, 'Towards the Functional City', leaves no room for doubt, transforming his work into a manifesto by illustrating it with images that showed changes in the historical centres of Coventry and Cambridge, as well as including the plan of Amster-

dam and a couple of sketches of his beloved Macià Plan. The European lesson and the lesson that the author himself put forward were to serve as an example to wavering Americans, who were now handed an organized and rational doctrine with which to define their cities as well as being offered the contributions of an architect who, in two key moments of the book, had demonstrated his professional experience and capability in dealing with urban problems.

Can Our Cities Survive? must have been finished by November 1940, although Sert continued working on the manuscript, as is deduced from some bibliographical references he used, sometimes dated July 1941. A letter from Lewis Mumford to Sert gives more weight to this hypothesis. Dated 28 December 1940, it alludes in places to the issues we are analyzing. Thus, after initially praising Sert's successful establishment of 'the guiding principles about modern planning', Mumford pointed out several problems: 'The four functions of the city do not seem to me to adequately cover the ground of city planning: dwelling, work, recreation and transportation are all important. But what of the political, educational, and cultural functions of the city: what of the part played by the disposition and plan of the buildings concerned with these functions in the whole evolution of the city design?'[217] Although he did not offer many alternatives, or at least did not specify the real scope of his words, Mumford substituted the functionalist abstraction of cities that had been forged in the CIAMs, at its

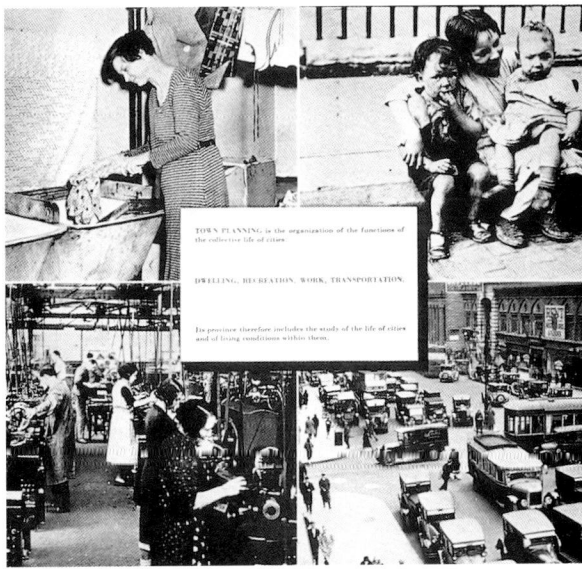

Illustrations
reproduced
in *Can Our Cities
Survive?*

LE GROUPE CIAM-FRANCE

URBANISME DES C.I.A.M.

LA CHARTE D'ATHÈNES

avec

UN DISCOURS LIMINAIRE

de

JEAN GIRAUDOUX

PLON

Cover of *La Charte d'Athènes*, 1943.

peak in Athens and perfected in later CIRPAC meetings, with a functional amplification of the city's use.

As if implying that the CIAM members had overlooked the complexity of uses that a city comprised, Mumford corrected their mistake by listing more functions that were not mentioned in the functionalist reductionism that Sert presented. Without these, he argued, the city was merely 'an urban mass'. Culture, politics and education were activities that polarized functions, since in the city 'all the economic organs … exist, ultimately, to support this civic nucleus.' He added: 'Unless some attention was paid to this as a field, at least, for future investigation, I should find it very difficult to write the introduction that you suggested', thus revealing the reason why Sert sent his manuscript to one of the most influential writers on American cities and their clash with modernity.

Sert thought it absolutely essential that Mumford should write this introduction if his manuscript was to be well-received in the US and be published quickly and effectively by a prestigious American publishing house, espe-

cially considering the circumstances at the time. Despite his criticism, Mumford acted kindly towards Sert, acknowledging the efforts he had made as well as recommending strategies for its possible publication, among which he suggested: 'The first thing to decide is whether the plan volume and the explanatory volume are to be uniform. If they are to be published at the same time, I think that this should be highly advisable. Unfortunately, from the publisher's standpoint, the cost of the graphic volume is almost prohibitory.'

Following these suggestions and a warning not to publish with any private publisher due to the elevated cost of the book in combination with its being a work on architecture (that is, the type of book not aimed at a wide public), he suggested the name of an institution that might be interested, and offered to act as mediator so that the enterprise could succeed: 'The Carnegie Corporation would, I think, be interested in this book, and I would be glad to put the matter before Dr Keppel and his assistant … I would be very happy to recommend the book to Harcourt, or to give a recommendation to any other publisher you may select, but I feel it would be a waste of time until we have worked out more carefully the whole matter of costs.' Sert must have understood from this that, despite his refusal to write the introduction, Mumford was willing to promote the publication; in other words, the favourable reception of his work by the American architectural and town-development intelligentsia was guaranteed – something that, as we shall see, Mumford himself was keen to achieve. The American critic's letter also helps us to understand how Sert had initially structured his work: there was to be a volume devoted to graphic material – probably the city plans that CIAM members had drawn up – and another with commentaries on the parts that made up and defined the 'functional city'.

Soon afterwards, in a letter written on 8 January 1941, Gropius corroborated Mumford's interest in the manuscript: 'I had a very friendly letter from Mumford, praising your book by saying that it is "the best statement of the method and objective of modern city planning that anyone has made", so I think that he is really interested. I wrote him back that we both agree.'[218] If we thought before that Gropius had a good deal to gain through the publishing of Sert's book, it now seems completely certain: by agreeing with Mumford, Gropius knew that the manuscript would not experience any problems in the American market, and that it would be warmly welcomed in the corresponding spheres, thus consolidating his position even further.

That Gropius went on weaving his web, can be gleaned from his words: 'Meanwhile I had a long talk with Hudnut. We decided to write to Keppel of the Carnegie Foundation and ask for an appointment *very soon*.' Though the meeting that he and Hudnut were organizing had not yet materialized (a meeting Gropius thought feasible thanks to a letter of presentation on his behalf from Mumford to Keppel), Sert was to write a summary of his intentions in the book and send it to Gropius along with a curriculum 'of your life'. He emphasized for Sert not to worry, since 'we will do the rest', and that one of the principal difficulties would be estimating the cost of the book: 'Do you think one thousand dollars would be suitable?' Between 14 January and mid-February 1941, the letters and telegrams sent among Sert, Hudnut and Gropius give us an idea of the intensity with which the three got down to work. It is plain that relations between Sert and Gropius were excellent, as is suggested by a letter from the Catalan architect to his German counterpart on 13 February, in which he not only explained all the work he was carrying out to ensure the publication of his book, but also added: 'We had a very nice time with you in Lincoln. Thank you once more for all your kindness and help.'[219]

The efforts of Gropius and Hudnut, however, were to no avail. Despite their perseverance and despite the fact that they were two highly significant figures in the American architectural and cultural world, they did not succeed. This can be deduced from a letter sent on 28 March by the Carnegie Corporation to the Dean of the GSD of Harvard: 'I am sorry to have to report that our Grants-in-Aid Committee did not find it possible to take favourable action on your suggestion as to the publication of Mr Sert's manuscript. Frankly, the reports of our advisers were not enthusias-

tic … We are returning the manuscript to you by express, and should appreciate it if you would let Mr Sert know that we are not in a position to help.'[220] We do not know who the advisers of the Carnegie Corporation were, nor have we found their reports, but it is evident that they were not impressed either by the book's renowned advocates, or by the contents of the book itself.

Despite the fact that this first attempt had failed, neither Hudnut nor Gropius lost hope, continuing to look in other directions, especially one to which they had greater access. This was the Harvard University Press (HUP), which was directed by Dumas Malone from 1935 until 1943 and, thanks to his management, of whose Board of Directors Sachs was a member. Malone's beliefs regarding HUP's remit were clear from the beginning: its mission was to publish books that compiled the most important research work emerging from Harvard University's departments, and these had to be capable of interesting a wide readership, even if sales figures were not very high, so that the most important thing would be that ideas and discoveries 'should be shared with whatever portion of the public is capable of appreciating them'.[221]

Malone saw the University publishing house as an intellectual, educational institution with similar aims to those of the University itself. He undoubtedly published many books with very little commercial gain, but it is also certain that he obtained a remarkable number of editorial successes. While he was director, two of the books he published eventually sold more than 100,000 copies. One of these was *Space, Time and Architecture*, which by 1984 had sold in the hardcover English-language edition alone more than 129,000 copies. It must have impressed Malone that following the first edition of March 1941, a second edition had to be produced in August, a third in February 1942, and a fourth in April 1943, shortly before Malone agreed to resign from his post on 17 July 1943. This is perhaps why, when he received the first letter from Hudnut and Gropius on 11 June 1941, he saw it as a chance to repeat the same success story, especially if we take into account the content of the letter and the fact that those signing it had been Giedion's main supporters. In the letters, the two men wrote warm words of praise concerning their Catalan friend's work: 'We examined this book with care and were convinced that its publication could be of very great value not only to students in the American schools of architecture, but especially to that large body of laymen who are becoming interested in city planning. There are many books on city planning but none which, in our opinion, presents the subject so clearly and so intelligibly. We think that Mr Sert's book deserves a wide circulation.'[222] They could not have been more explicit: the book they were offering him had an enormous market potential which spanned from students of architecture (those who were snapping up the first edition of *Space, Time and Architecture*) to town planners and the lawyers who intervened in the complex administration of any town-planning project, etc. Moreover, the book was intellectually impeccable.

The letter could not have been better written. By making a reference to cultural values, it was possible to make a convincing case to Malone, who was always interested in the quality of his editorial production. By alluding to its commercial possibilities, Gropius and Hudnut presented a golden panorama to Malone, who at the time was having serious difficulties with William H. Claflin, HUP's treasurer since 1938. Strictly speaking, Claflin was a businessman; he had been president of a sugar-producing company, was an associate of a brokerage firm that operated in Boston, and his interests were plain: it was a matter of protecting the University's finances from the continuous losses generated by its Press. Max Hall describes it thus: 'He had no close knowledge of publishing problems and probably had little opportunity to appreciate the importance of the books Malone was publishing.'[223] Indeed it was in June 1941 that things came to a head between Malone and Claflin, evidently for economic reasons, and it was also in that month that Malone tried to convince the treasurer of his ideas on what the HUP's aims should be. One of the eight questions that he put to Claflin could not be more enlightening: 'If the publishing department of the Press renders an academic service, is it just that it should receive no direct financial aid from the University?'

The tug of war between the two men continued throughout that year until 14 February 1942, when Sert's book was being printed. Claflin finally had the upper hand and succeeded in putting an end to one of the aspects of HUP that Malone had been most proud of: the HUP was to be separated into two separate entities, the Press and the Department of Publications, so that books could be printed anywhere depending on the prices dictated by the market. Even so, the publishing house had a deficit of 26,000 dollars on 30 June 1942, which made Malone's stance even more questionable; Claflin was not prepared to tolerate a deficit above 20,000 dollars.

The HUP situation must have been known to Gropius and Hudnut, making even more comprehensible the text of the letter recommending *Can Our Cities Survive?*, since Malone could put Claflin's mind at rest that it ensured a wide reading public, and the precedent of Giedion's book guaranteed the economic benefits of publishing meticulously printed architectural books. The letter furthermore stated in plain terms: 'It is our belief that this book would be a practical success. We think it is possible to reduce the cost by making some changes in the arrangement of the manuscript. In this matter you could count upon the assistance of the Faculty of Architecture.'

Gropius would again approach Malone after this first contact, and he did so on his own as we can see from a letter he sent to Sert on 16 July 1941: 'After Mr. Malone had come back from vacation, I had a meeting with him this morning and I must say that my impression was very favourable. He seems to be keen to get the book printed and all will depend only on the costs involved, I think.'[224] He suggested that Sert define the number of illustrations the book was to contain, since the cost of the edition depended on this, and he set up a meeting between Malone and Sert for 28 or 29 July: 'I think it would be of the greatest advantage for the book if you could manage to come to Cambridge and then we could both go to the press and see it.' Gropius also confessed that he had played the card of emphasizing the profitability of the book to Malone, and added: 'As the Giedion book is going very well and has a second edition, he thought that the estimate of

2,000 [the number of copies to be printed] may be right but I am sure they will investigate further. As a whole, they took everything very seriously and Mr Malone finished by saying "this book looks awfully interesting to me".'

However, as we know, the financial problems were grave. This explains Malone's answer on 26 September 1941 in a letter addressed on that occasion to Dean Hudnut (thus confirming their interchangeability concerning their interest in publishing Sert's work): 'As I told you, this will be an expensive book to produce, owing to the large number of illustrations.'[225] After specifying the costs for the 2,000 copies to be printed – approximately 5,000 to 6,000 dollars, which meant that the price per book would have to be 7.50 to 8 dollars per copy – he insisted on the fact that it would be impossible to sell it for more than 5 dollars, which meant that either the number of illustrations would have to be reduced or that they would have to ask the university for 2,000 dollars of aid so that the operation could succeed; therefore HUP would be in charge of promotion and sales costs. Evidently Sert would not receive any money for its publication, but he was assigned 10 per cent of the profits if sales surpassed 2,500 copies, and 15 per cent if they surpassed 3,500 copies.[226]

Shortly afterwards, on 2 October, Hudnut wrote to Sert explaining the conditions established by Malone, and also informing him that the University had agreed to invest the 2,000 dollars requested by the HUP. Hudnut's protection and Gropius' insistence had clearly been responsible for getting the publication underway, and Hudnut said so frankly: 'It is my expectation that the book will appear early in the spring – perhaps as early as March first. Mr Malone will confer with you from time to time in respect to the book and you may be sure that Gropius and I will both take an active interest in it.'[227]

It was time – it is certain that Sert was in no position to choose and that therefore the conditions agreed between Hudnut and Malone were acceptable to start thinking about the book's structure and to put the finishing touches to its contents. Hudnut would again write to Malone insisting that Sert wanted Herbert Bayer to be in charge of the typography, a point

that interested the HUP editor because he was convinced that *Space, Time and Architecture* had been such a success precisely due to the innovative graphic design achieved by this former Bauhaus professor. Likewise, possibly in deference to a person who had done so much for the book's publication, Sert asked Hudnut to write the preface, which initially Mumford was to have done. The introduction was to be Giedion's responsibility, which would allow readers to see a continuity between the architectural books and the town-planning books edited by HUP.

On 7 January 1942, after some last-minute modifications requested by its promoters had been carried out, the definitive version of the book was basically finished. Sert explained it thus to Hudnut in a letter written on that day: 'I sent the corrected and complete copy of the manuscript to Mr Malone on 29 December. I have mailed today more than one third of the illustration material (37 pages) ready for the engraver. I will send the rest the day after tomorrow, with the exception of fifteen pages for which I must design some graphs and collect some documents … I have tried to simplify matters for the printer.' After this he put himself entirely at the publishing house's disposal: 'I will be available any time they need me, to solve no matter what difficulty. I also have the greatest interest for the book to be out next spring.'[228] The following correspondence over the months of March, April and May of 1942, shows the activities in which Sert was involved, obtaining illustrations and the relevant permissions for their publication, as well as revealing that he spent the months of June and July correcting proofs.

Dated 29 October, a letter from the Catalan architect to Hudnut reveals that the book was about to come out: 'I received the promotion folder of my book last week and hope to see the book out soon', adding: 'I should very much like Lewis Mumford to review it.'[229]

That *Can Our Cities Survive?* was going to be published soon is confirmed by a letter from Hudnut to Sert on 21 November 1942, which already contained the congratulations of the GSD Dean on its publication.[230] Mumford reviewed it for *The New Republic*, speaking revealingly of its intentions and objectives: 'An ideal book for the reader who wishes to understand the problems of the modern city … The whole argument for urban reconstruction is carried out with sanity and human insight … I have nothing but admiration for the way in which Mr Sert has presented the essential technical problems and their solution.'[231] Gropius and Hudnut must have breathed a sigh of relief after reading Mumford's text, and for Sert it meant that his process of integration into American architectural culture would be somewhat easier, and that his future in the country in which he had chosen to continue his professional career could now be viewed under a more optimistic light.[232]

[168] Sert's book was originally to be called *Should Our Cities Survive?*. Both this title and the final one seem to have been taken from Sigfried Giedion's article 'Can Expositions Survive?', published in New York *Plus* magazine in 1938.

[169] SC E 2.

[170] SC E 2.

[171] SC E 2.

[172] SC E 2.

[173] SC E 2. According to Moholy-Nagy, Sert was supposed to speak on 'Urbanism versus Suburbanism' in Chicago while he was staying in Detroit.

[174] SGA 43–K–1942–11–26.

[175] Catherine Freedberg Blanton, *The Spanish Pavilion at the Paris World's Fair*, op. cit., vol. II, pp. 744–75. In these pages we find a transcription of a letter from 20 May 1938, which says: 'I have wanted to write to you for a long time on the details of the dismantling of the Spanish Pavilion … I have intentionally left for the end of my letter the matter about the payment of my fees. Once having completed the dismantling, I am forced to insist, despite my unwillingness to do so, on this matter which has now become so embarrassing. I need you to forward the francs owed to me, because as I have told you on previous occasions, I have been living in Paris paying francs and not pesetas the whole time, and I have been lent in francs amounts that I meant to pay back the day I received my fees, never believing that I would have to wait so long to have been paid. I have thrice written to Lacasa without his ever having bothered to answer a single time my queries on this matter.'
The matter must not have been resolved, for on 29 October of that same year, Sert wrote a petition to complain formally about the debt he was owed and to request that his fees be paid once and for all: 'The architect Sert has worked for ten months on the writing of the project, direction of construction work, dismantling of the same, and the organization and re-shipment of the material. On 7 April 1937, the architect Sert received the amount of 5,000 francs in advance of his fees. From the month of September 1937 onwards, the architect Sert has constantly been requesting the Commissary General to settle the fees or monthly salaries owed to him, and he has done so on every new visit made by the Commissary General to Paris … Once the dismantling of the Pavilion had been carried out without his having achieved the settlement of his fees and without having been informed as to the motives for such delay in receiving his payment, Sert wrote to the Commissary General on 20 May insisting that the 25,000 francs still owed to him be settled once and for all. Not having received an answer to this letter, Sert once again addressed himself to Mr Gaos on 20 September without having received a response up to the present date.' Ibid., pp. 752–53.

[176] SGA 43–K–1938–7–5.

[177] SC C 2. We find the following letters, all of them from 1938: William Tatton Brown wrote to him in London on 7, 28 and 31 August. Helena Syrkus wrote to him in Paris on 2 August and on 27 November, and van Eesteren wrote to him in Paris on 30 September.

[178] SGA 43–K–1938–10–27.

[179] SGA 43–K–1938–12–25.

[180] SGA 43–K–1939–2–13. Charlotte Pierrand has recently published a text in which she makes reference to certain moments in Sert's trip to Paris after 1937, gathered from the Austrian historian's recollections of this period. See Charlotte Pierrand, *Une Vie de Création*, Editions Odile Jacob, Paris, 1998.

[181] Winfried Nerdinger, *Walter Gropius*, Electa, Milan, 1993, p. 204.

[182] SGA 43–K–1937–6–24.

[183] SGA 43–K–1938–1–12.

[184] SGA 43–K–1938–2–4(6)–1/2.

[185] SGA 43–K–1938–2–17–1/3.

[186] SGA 43–K–1939–6–7.

[187] SGA 43–K–1938–6–1(6)–1/2.

[188] SGA 43–K–1941–3–18(6).

[189] SGA 43–K–1925–12–14(6).

[190] The exhibition was held at the Zurich Kunsthaus between 15 January and 6 February 1938, under the title: 'Le Corbusier (Oeuvre plastique). 1919–1937. Tableaux et Architecture'. The catalogue contains a long essay by Sigfried Giedion on Le Corbusier's work.

[191] Marcel Duchamp was one of the first Europeans to declare his fascination with architecture in the USA, although there are others whom we should not forget, such as Adolf Loos, who was deeply impressed by the lifestyle in that country. In the *Boston Evening Transcript* of 18 September 1915, Alfred Kreymborg published an article portraying Duchamp, in which he described the Frenchman's liking for Americans: 'They are like big children, like the French. They turn everything into a game: from baseball to business, from inventions to art and literature … American architecture is the only true architecture at present.' See Jennifer Gough-Cooper and Jacques Caumont, *Effemeridi su e intorno a Marcel Duchamp e Rrose Sélavy, 1887–1968*, catalogue of the Duchamp exhibition at the Palazzo Grassi of Venice, Bompiani, Milan, 1993.
The fascination that American grain elevators and silos held for Gropius, and their influence on European architecture is discussed in: Reyner Banham, *A Concrete Atlantis*, MIT, Cambridge, Massachusetts, 1986.

[192] SGA 43–K–1937–1–16.

[193] SGA 43–K–1937–12–23.

[194] Eduard F. Sekler, 'Sigfried Giedion at Harvard University', in *The Architectural Historian in America*, National Gallery of Art, Washington, 1990, p. 266.

[195] SGA 43–K–1938–1–18. In this letter Giedion explained to Gropius the order in which he would give the contents of his lectures at Harvard University, and he also talked of his interest in American architecture, hoping to improve his knowledge of it: 'The fact that I will be able to fill in this gap is already a special recompense.'

[196] SGA. See correspondence between Giedion and Gropius from 21 January to 21 March 1938.

[197] Winfried Nerdinger, 'Walter Gropius: De l'américanisme au nouveau monde', in Jean-Louis Cohen and Hubert Damisch, *Américanisme et Modernité*, Flammarion, Paris, 1993, pp. 147–70.

[198] SGA 43–K–1937–3–9.1/2.

[199] The original copy of the marriage certificate of José Luis Sert and Ramona Longas (issued in Cuba, where they married before departing to the States) is kept in the Sert trunk of the JMF Archives. It may in fact have been the second time they got married (so that they could present these documents on their entry to the United States), since it is likely that they married years before in Paris. A letter from Sert to Le Corbusier dated 8 March 1941 seems to confirm this: 'I wrote to Pierre on 27 January asking him to send me with his legalized signature a document certifying that he was one of the witnesses of my marriage because I cannot obtain the certificate from the town hall of the 6th district of the Paris commune.' FLC R 3 O 3 185.

[200] SGA 43–K–1939–6–21(6)–1/3. Hudnut recommended Robert C. Weinberg as the English translator of Giedion's manuscript because he had already translated Hegeman's book on town planning. SGA 43–K–1939–5–6(6)–1/3. We know about the trip to Chicago from a letter Giedion sent to someone by the name of Carter on 21 June: 'I expect to return to Europe in October. In the meantime we shall see a bit of the country, stopping at Chicago en route to the coast. Chicago is the keynote of the whole American development.' Through this letter we also discover that Giedion meant to call his book *Interrelations between Art, Architecture and Technique*. SGA 43–K–1939–6–21–(6)–1/3.

[201] SGA 43–K–1938–11–23(6)–1/2.

[202] SC C 2.

[203] SGA 43–K–1939–3–21.

[204] FLC D 2 14.

[205] SC C 2.

[206] SC E 1.

[207] SC E 1.

[208] SC E 1.

[209] JMFA. Sert trunk.

[210] SGA 43–K–1939–9–29.

[211] In a letter from Gropius to Giedion of 10 July 1940, when the latter had already returned from his trip to the States, we can catch a glimmer of the lifestyle Sert was leading that year (which will again crop up in the third chapter of this book): 'We had a wonderful weekend on Long Island with the Herberts, Serts and Xantis, Harrison from New York and some friends of Marion's. It was a feast like one of the old days, in one of those open courtyards and everybody was in high spirits.' SGA 43–K–1940–10–17.

[212] FLC R 3 O 3 183.

[213] SC E 2.

214 José Luis Sert, *Can Our Cities Survive?*, Harvard University Press, Cambridge, 1942, p. 3.

215 It seems unavoidable to draw a comparison with the *Charte d'Athènes*, published in April 1943 by the Librairie Plon with an introduction by Jean Giradoux. This is, after all, the orthodox text on the functional city, perhaps because its author is Le Corbusier, although he did not sign it. Despite the date of publication, on pages 237–39 of the original edition, we read: 'The Athens Charter is commented on for the first time in the present work, which was published in France in 1941 … In France, therefore, the country in which the spirit of grandeur and the sense of beauty have always manifested themselves through the buildings and monuments that have graced the world with their brilliance, the Athens Charter comes out right on schedule with its National Revolution.' Although Le Corbusier did not assume authorship of the book, in its last page we find: 'The elucidating explanations of the Athens Charter articles have been written by the first French delegate of the CIAMs and by Jeanne de Villeneuve, Baroness of Aubigny.' Thus it seems clear that Sert's book follows the points of the City Planning Chart programme, but it changes the commentaries and their order, enlarging on them and adapting them to the American reality.
In 1973, Sert wrote the introduction for the English version of the Athens Charter in which he spoke of the trip aboard the Patris and in which he reaffirmed the validity of many points that were agreed upon in the Greek capital: 'The problems in outlines are still very real today, and the trends prevailing then have only been aggravated in the four decades elapsed. In this sense, the document, in spite of its oversimplified statements and its considerable gaps, may serve as a starting point for the formulation of a "Charter of Urban Rights", which is badly needed.'

216 Sert, op. cit., p. 195.

217 SC E 1. On 23 November 1940, Lewis Mumford wrote Sert a letter excusing himself for not being able to meet him until 5 December and offering to see him in his editor's office on that day at 3 o'clock. It was probably during this meeting that Sert showed him the manuscript and asked him to write an introduction. SC E 1. Sert would write an obituary greatly praising Mumford in October 1979. SC D 29.
In a letter from Giedion to Le Corbusier of 20 February 1940, we find: 'Sert has almost finished his manuscript on the Congress of Athens and has named it *Should Our City* [here there is a correction in Le Corbusier's hand, who wrote 'Cities'] *Survive*. The work is excellent, and we have used all of our influence to find a publisher, and have finally found one.' SGA 43–K–1941–2–20(6).

218 SC E 2.

219 SC E 2.

220 SC C 1.

221 Max Hall, *Harvard University Press: A History*, Harvard University Press, Cambridge, 1986, p. 68.

222 SC C 1.

223 Hall, op. cit., p. 90.

224 SC C 1.

225 SC C 1.

226 In a letter to Gropius from W. W. Smith, business manager of Harvard University Press, dated 17 February 1949, he specified that 5,314 copies of Sert's book had been sold. SC CIAM C 5. On a folded piece of paper found in the Sert Collection, we are told that by 10 March 1954, 7,000 copies had been printed and 6,333 sold. SC C 1.

227 SC C 1.

228 SC C 1.

229 SC C 1.

230 SC C 1.

231 Quoted on a book-jacket of the fourth edition of *Space, Time and Architecture*, published in April 1943.

232 In the October 1942 issue of the *Journal of the Society of Architectural Historians* Carl Feiss, Director of the Denver Planning Commission, reviews Sert's book, complaining about the paucity of information offered about the CIAMs and their history and pointing out that 'there was no reverberation of the activity of the CIAM in this country … the CIAM did not receive any important place in any American architectural journal of the period.' This article was answered by another from Giedion, published by the same magazine under the title 'On CIAM's Unwritten Catalogue', in which he explained the reasons for the scarce interest raised by the CIAMs in the USA. *JSHA*, no. 1–2, January/April 1943. In SC E 2, we find a number of letters addressed to Sert from diverse sectors who were interested in the book.

Latin America

Prior to the publication of Sert's book, Paul Lester Wiener, an architect of German origin who was to be Sert's associate until 1959, was introduced by his father-in-law Henry Morgenthau, Secretary of the Treasury for the Roosevelt administration, to the Secretary of State, Cordell Hull. The purpose of this introduction is specified in a letter written by Morgenthau to Hull on 17 December 1940, in which we read: 'The reason I am writing to you is that [Lester] could be made useful in the cultural field in the capacity of adviser in Architectural Planning for Latin America, or in the field of Art and Design.'[233] This is how Sert's associate came to have the opportunity to work in a vast new field of development and in a unknown territory, although some time would elapse before this actually occurred.

The correspondence between Lester and the Department of State between 1941 and 1943 allows us to trace how the two architects approached and drew nearer to Latin American countries during this time, initially doing so through lectures. In a letter addressed to Edward G. Trueblood of 28 April 1941, Lester revealed the ideological intentions behind this operation and also described the possible subjects that would guarantee the success of this educational activity. Having begun his letter by stating that it was important that the United States should get closer to its South American neighbours given the recent victories of the Nazis, he continued: 'Small but powerful intellectual groups, however, may have real influence in sustaining our points of view.' Despite admitting that 'cultural efforts are not the most effective answers to these problems', he nevertheless affirmed their usefulness to a certain degree: 'The lectures which we discussed could in a small measure help to meet the considerations just mentioned. It would be important to

include men of importance in the audiences. Our enormous capacity to produce would convince many "doubters".' After these introductory notes, Lester went on to include, under the generic title of 'Architecture and Planning', a long list of possible subjects to be developed in the lectures: '1. Does Architecture Express Our Daily Life? 2. Designing-Planning for Industry. 3. Designing-Planning for the Future. 4. Public Works for Peaceful Expansion. 5. Public Works for Defence. 6. Modern Theories on Large-Scale Territorial Planning. 7. New Techniques for South American Construction. 8. New Materials. 9. Welfare of the People: Hospitals, Recreation, etc. 10. Architectural Design Culture of the Americas.'[234] In this way, Lester wrote, it would be possible to show these countries factories, hospitals, schools, highways and to demonstrate how this infrastructure, along with the scientific and technological advances of a developed country, could help to improve the quality of life there. By

Paul Lester Wiener.

TPA (Town Planning Associates), Pilot plan of Tumaco, Colombia, 1948–49, perspective drawing of the church.

achieving this end, the effectiveness of these lectures was demonstrated.

Brazil[235] was to be the first country of destination in South America, and Sert and Lester were to be its visitors, charged with spreading the 'good news'. That Sert accompanied his associate in this venture we can gather from another letter sent by Lester to Trueblood: 'I thought you might be interested to see the enclosed announcement of a series of lectures which Mr Sert and I will give in about twenty universities this winter. Do you think any of them would be of interest to the people in Brazil?'[236]

Thus, the two architects' first contacts with Brazil were established in the course of this trip, which lasted all winter and which they devoted to speaking about the issues described above. The trip must have made quite an impression in certain Brazilian university circles, as can be deduced from the letters that Lester regularly received from that country.[237] The practice continued to be encouraged by the North American Department of State throughout 1943, the year in which Lester wrote an opuscule with the unequivocal title: *Una Nova Era Cultural para as Americas* (*A New Cultural Era for the Americas*). The following year continued along the same basic lines, as can be gleaned from documents, including a letter from Gropius to Lester that attests to the interest aroused by these trips in certain professional circles.[238]

All these visits to Brazil finally bore fruit in the form of a commission, of which we have some specific details, thanks to precise chronological references. In the Lester Wiener Archives we find evidence of the visit of a Brazilian engineer to the office of Sert and Lester (which would become known as Town Planning Associates, or TPA), who was to travel to the United States to study the problem of 'our projected industrial city';[239] this is confirmed by a letter from Sert to J. Vilanova Artigas of 10 July 1944, in which we read: 'We also have a visit from a Brazilian engineer from the Motors Factory in Rio in order to give him whatever advice we can towards building a new industrial town.' The visit must have taken place, since in another letter of 21 June 1944, he wrote that the Brigadier Antonio Guedes Muñiz had communicated to his government 'the friendly and noble gesture of the distinguished architect Paul Lester Wiener, who has offered his precious collaboration and that of two of his colleagues in favour of the Cidade dos Motores.' This collaboration was considered even more valuable since it was made 'without any desire for remuneration', a fact that was not altogether true.[240] Another certain source of information is the 'Study Analysis and Anteproject', which is dated 10 September 1944, a date that is consistent with what has been surmised so far, and proves that Sert and Lester worked on writing it between June and September of that year, as can be deduced from a letter sent to Le Corbusier on 12 April 1945.[241]

This is how it came about that the Brazilian government decided to build an industrial city attached to a motor factory near Rio de Janeiro, a decision that was inserted into a vast programme of modernization in the country. It was developed under the authoritative mandate of Getulio Vargas, the man responsible for the creation of a strong state, the so-called Estado Novo, from the revolution of 1930 on, but especially between 1937 and 1945. This was a centralized, populist and repressive state that followed in general lines the Mussolinian model. It was a state that, by nationalizing politics and protecting national industry, intervened in the planning of public health and education, and in the supply of electrical energy,

The Town Planning Associates' Office on West 42nd Street, New York (PLWC).

as well as promoting the iron and steel industry, the rationalization of transport and the production of trucks.

This was a business state with which the armed forces, who had finally subordinated the military police to the general staff and who had united themselves into one army, identified. It was a state that kept judicial power under its control and that firmly intended to promote the capitalist development of Brazil and steer away from excessive dependence on its cotton and coffee crops; in other words, it meant to weld agriculture and industry. The Charter of 1937 clearly marked the boundaries and set the norms between the public and private sectors: 'State intervention in the economic plan is only legitimate in order to fill in deficiencies of individual initiative and to co-ordinate the factors of production and to avoid or resolve its conflicts and to introduce in the development of individual competency the idea of the Nation's interests represented by the State.'[242]

Vargas had a special predilection for the manufacture of iron and steel, as he manifested in Belo Horizonte on 23 February 1931: 'We will have accomplished much in a brief time if we manage to free ourselves from the import of iron artefacts, producing what is necessary to meet the country's needs. By nationalizing the iron and steel industry we will be taking a big step towards the great destiny that awaits us. Our growth has to come from the soil, from the intense development of agriculture, but the effort to accomplish this would be sterile if the machines, from the plough to the vehicle that transports the crop production, have to come from abroad.'[243]

This industry was to manufacture iron artefacts, the main reason being to provide weapons for the army. It clearly devoted itself to this task, as is revealed by Vargas himself in November 1939: 'Within a short time we will start simultaneously to export iron mineral and to fabricate steel in sufficient quantity and quality for our present needs, including those needed by the defensive military apparatus, and we will install specialized metallurgical factories and set up the supply of necessary material for transport.'[244]

The beginning of the war in 1939 saw Brazil controlling its enterprises with an iron hand. From that time on, to this control were added large sums of North American capital, since as we have seen, the United States was also very interested in controlling the Brazilian territory. The result of this interest was the creation in 1940 of the Commission for the National Iron and Steel Plan and in 1941 the foundation of the National Iron and Steel Company, actions that when added to the 'Special Plan of Public Works and Rigging of National Defense (DASP)' of 1939 helped to frame the 'need' for the Cidade dos Motores. The DASP had clear objectives: to order the priorities of public expenditure, to differentiate ordinary budget from special budget (expenses from public investments) and to link the devising of budgets to economic planning: 'A budget is a plan turned into money'.[245]

The specific actions of the DASP took a shape that is of interest to us. The plan, in its will to industrialize the state so as to defend its sovereignty, made clear its interest in reinforcing the army under the slogan 'Progress and National Security', and thus 45 per cent of general expenses were dedicated to the Ministry of the Army and Navy, and the same quantity was allotted to investments in transport, energy, oil, the National Factory of Motors and the management of Electrical Energy.

The construction of the Factory began in 1943 in the Baixada Fluminense as part of the regeneration of a region located forty kilometres south of Rio de Janeiro. The past five years had been spent draining the marshland areas most affected by malaria and freeing them from this disease. The Cidade dos Motores, attached to the National Factory of Motors, was to be the regional centre and was to attempt through its influential presence to modernize and mechanize agriculture in the adjoining territory. It is not by chance, therefore, that a second factory for tractors was to be added to that of aviation motors, nor is it surprising that the manager of the whole operation was a military man, the Brigadier-General Antonio Guedes Muñiz, head of the aeroplane factory in Brazil, who not only asked the United States for technical help, but also for financial and engineering aid. According to Sigrid de Lima, the Motor Factory used American production-line methods and received supplies from the States through a credit of 1,220,000 dollars granted by the Export–Import Bank, although the construction was financed with Brazilian funds. Likewise, technical assistance was provided by diverse US enterprises, especially by Pratt and Whitney.[246] This US military man liked to simplify matters with statements like: 'By building tractors for agricultural necessities and for road construction, the country will in a few years increase the productive capacity of the 45 million Brazilians entirely lost today in more than 9 million kilometres of this immense country.'

Although we are mainly concerned with the industrial facet of the city, there are other aspects linked to it that deserve attention and that frame it in its overall context. In Getulio Vargas' policy, the issue of workers' housing was highly important within the general programme proclaimed in 1939 and aimed at the working classes: 'In this programme [of projects having to do with work and provision], the New State has not limited itself to developing a policy of social protection, which was begun in 1930. By expanding on its guidelines, it deliberately promotes an appraisal of the national workers' situation, taking on not only legal issues inherent to work contracts but also and especially social and political aspects of this question. Aside from acknowledging the basic rights of workers guaranteed by these contracts, the present legislation wishes to give them living conditions that are compatible with human dignity, raising their cultural level, ensuring that they have dignified dwellings, and improving the quality of their nutrition.'[247] The interest in workers' housing therefore seems clear, not only in political declarations but also in the construction work carried out by Penha, Castillo, Pedregulho, Cascadura, Ipiranga, Realengo and others.

These works, whose meaning and ideology helped to corroborate the contents and political scope of Vargas' project, were intensified during the World War II period by placing technicians of a reformist mentality in the Ministry of Work. Thus, while reinforcing the idea that the State was responsible for the housing issue, a social perspective on the matter also arose. This can be perceived from the words pronounced in the Pacambeu stadium on the 1 May 1944: 'Once concluded, the phase of experimentation and consolidation of the Institutes and the Savings Banks, whose reserves are being applied based on the criteria of immediate security and certain benefits, it is time to initiate a more long-term policy with respect to the use of the accumulated funds … With the collaboration of municipal administrations, which will introduce the respective projects within their town planning, we will build model cities near the big industrial centres with public health installations and professional, educational and sports facilities.'[248]

Thus, by this time there were already references to model cities, which were to be developed near big industrial centres; it is evident that the Cidade dos Motores of Sert and Lester Wiener pertained to this new political orientation in the Brazilian government. It was in these cities that the *novo homen* whom the regime sought to create was to flourish, and where rationality and modernity were emphasized. The State took on the building of social amenities, a basic part of the process of controlling and standardizing the behaviour and social issues that mattered to the working population. Brigadier Guedes Muñiz also made this clear: 'Social hierarchy depends on the individual value of each person, which is the most effective way to negate Communist promiscuity.'[249]

These model cities were to be strictly modern; in other words, they were to be different from garden cities and individual housing, and nearer to the postulates of functional urbanism, which had in the past, in diverse ways, disagreed with the former model and which offered, in some publications, models for intervention. Guedes Muñiz, with the help of the architect Atílio Correia Lima, who was in charge of the preliminary sketches for the Cidade dos Motores, understood the matter in this light: 'We therefore consulted Atílio Correia Lima, the brilliant urbanist … Correia Lima and the book *La Ville Radieuse* of Le Corbusier totally convinced me. In the same area of land where we could shelter five thousand people in modest individual houses, it was possible to shelter twenty to twenty-five thousand people in comfortable and modern apartments. Instead of a tiny and individual plot of land, workers could have at their disposal big parks

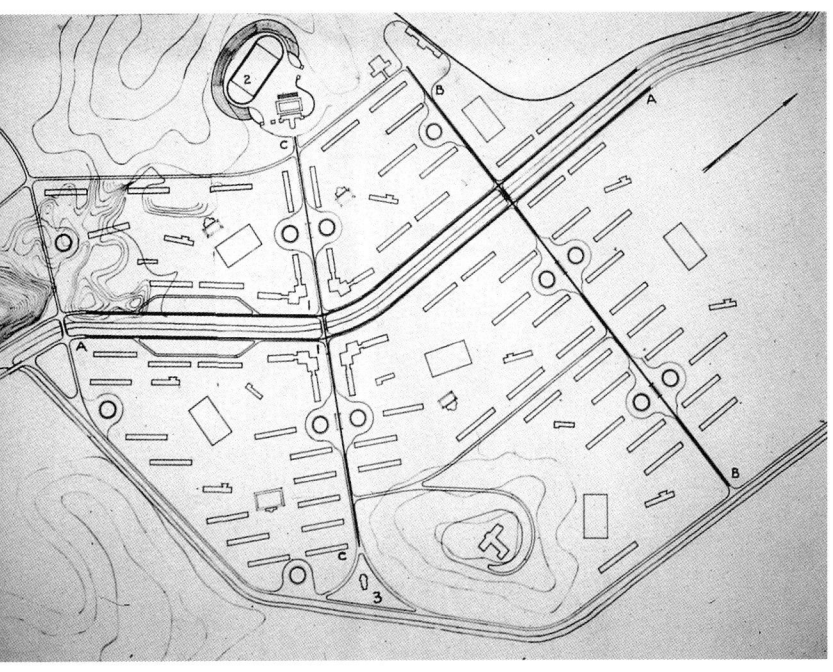

Atílio Correia Lima, first project for the Cidade dos Motores, Brazil, 1943 (PLWC).

with swimming pools, gardens, sports fields and recreational areas.'

In August 1943, three days before his death, Correia Lima wrote the first report for the Cidade dos Motores, a manifesto in defence of modern planning. Both the plans and the project report were an attempt to convince Guedes Muñiz, seeking to identify the proposal with the modernity necessary to implement Vargas' ideology. From this report we can extract: 'The mass-production constructions that form building compounds present the same advantages as industrial mass production, lowering the unit cost and adding more to the dwelling unit, allowing for the creation of communal parks of great dimensions … with a different social life and a sports field right next door … The industrial era that is now beginning in Brazil, of which the FNM (the National Motor Factory) is one of the most audacious pioneers, must not carry along with it all that is secondary. New Spirit! Creating new industry! In a new setting! These must be the criteria so that the formidable cycle of Brigadier Antonio Guedes Muñiz's interventions may be completed.'[250]

The link between the new spirit and the new architecture was something with which modern architects were familiar, having read Le Corbusier, who had been markedly influential among architects in Brazil. This new architecture was to introduce a new way of dealing with the housing issue from the formal, productive, social and cultural points of view. Along with the errors and naivety to be expected at that time in Brazil, a dualistic vision between what was backward and what was modern predominated, and it was considered of utmost importance to foment different habits in the working classes from those observed in rural life. Modernization was equal to industrialization and therefore to deruralization. Contributing to this task meant constructing a 'rationalized space and offering a new way of dwelling, symbols of a new period in which the working class would live and in which it could spend its so-called leisure time in a more socialized manner.'[251] Thus, in the same way that they had needed advice in the aspects previously mentioned, the Brazilian military men and engineers must have come to the conclusion after Correia Lima's death that they needed the type of assistance offered by the two visitors, who some time before had spoken to them about urbanist town planning based on functional criteria, one of whom, moreover, had written a book on the subject that was known in Brazil.[252]

Furthermore, in Brazil there was a tradition of inviting well-known foreign architects to act as consultants,[253] and it had a considerable architectural production of its own, which at the time was being exhibited in New York's best cultural showcase, the Museum of Modern Art.[254] Not too long after the period about which we are speaking, Lester tried to hold a CIAM in Brazil,[255] a country that had been open to the renovation of architecture and town planning for some time. Besides the groups of workers' housing, which were the offspring of so many urbanist proposals of the 1920s in Europe, this renovation had to go through certain unavoidable stages, ranging from Lúcio Costa's text of 1934, *Razones de una nueva arquitectura*, to the first verifications of this renovation, such as the proletariat apartments in Gamboa, also by Costa in collaboration with Gregori Warchavchik in 1932; Costa's 1934 project for a working-class quarter in Monlevade; the building for the Ministry of Education and Culture by Le Corbusier, Costa and

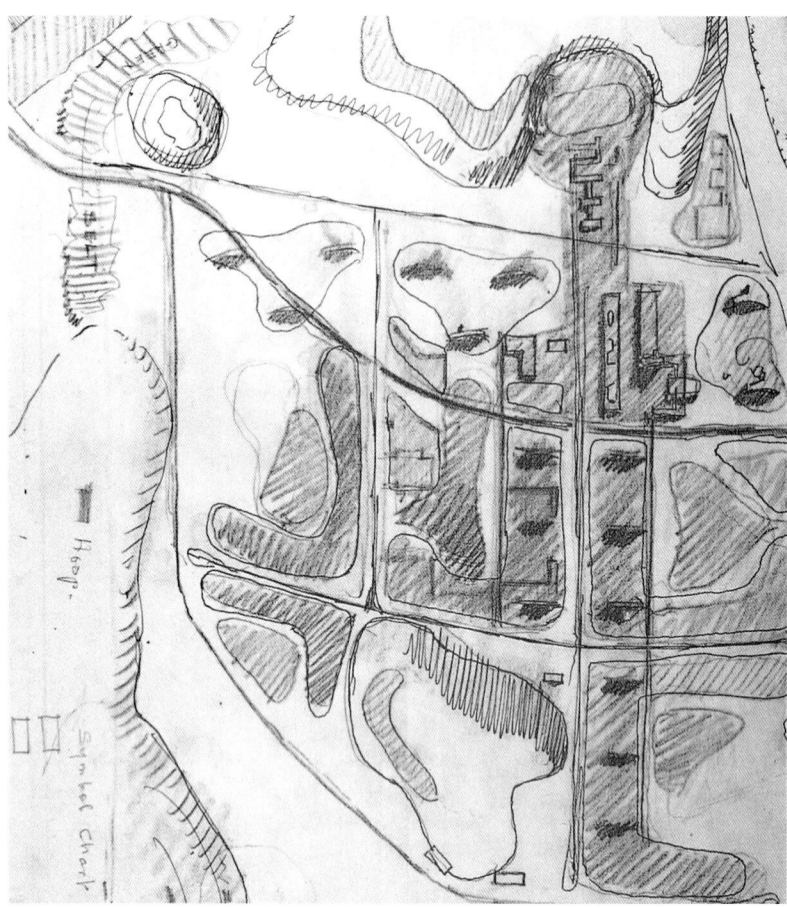

Cidade dos Motores, sketch from the first project by Lester and Sert, 1943 (SC).

furthermore remark that these recover 95 per cent of the constructed area … Their employment ensures that all apartments have a view of the horizon and contact with nature. Workers who now have nothing to keep themselves busy with, and lack a better social surrounding, are drawn by gambling in bars, where vices and bad habits reign. The *pilotis* therefore resolve even this problem, which is of great social importance, since in that pleasant and agreeable area, in constant contact with nature, people can gather at night during their hours of leisure and organize various activities, games, debates, etc.'[256]

Porto also mentioned the functional and economic advantage of duplexes, and pointed out both the possibilities offered by new techniques of mass construction and the complexities of the programme of new interventions, already alluding to the idea of neighbourhood units, a concept that Sert and Lester would so often put into practice in their South American experiences: 'The problem to be solved consists of a project for a town with 2,000 inexpensive dwellings to be built serially through rationalized processes. It seems that the most adequate solution in this case is that of "neighbourhood unit cells", that is, urban complexes that are self-sufficient … In each one of them its inhabitants must find everything they need except for work – each neighbourhood-unit cell will therefore have its own school, church, playgrounds and shops.'

Niemeyer in 1936, and the ensemble of projects for the University Campus in the same year.

By 1938, the time was ripe for what concerns us here, as is evidenced by the book *O Problema das Casas Operáias e os Institutos e Caixas de Pensoes*, written by the architect Rubens Porto, technical advisor of the National Council of Work, responsible for the standardization, inspection and approval of various IAPS (reports from the area of social planning) in the field of engineering. In this book he laid out guidelines for the intervention of the Institutes in the area of housing. Closely tied to the Catholic Church and a defender of greater state intervention in housing issues, Porto was strongly in favour of modern solutions to these questions, something that is patent throughout the pages of the text, in which there was already a rejection of individual housing and a defence of free-standing, low-rise buildings – no more than four storeys high – to avoid the cost of putting in elevators. The moral significance he attached to *pilotis* is symptomatic of his beliefs: 'Concerning the use of *pilotis*, I must

Cidade dos Motores, adaptation of the first scheme to the topography of the area.

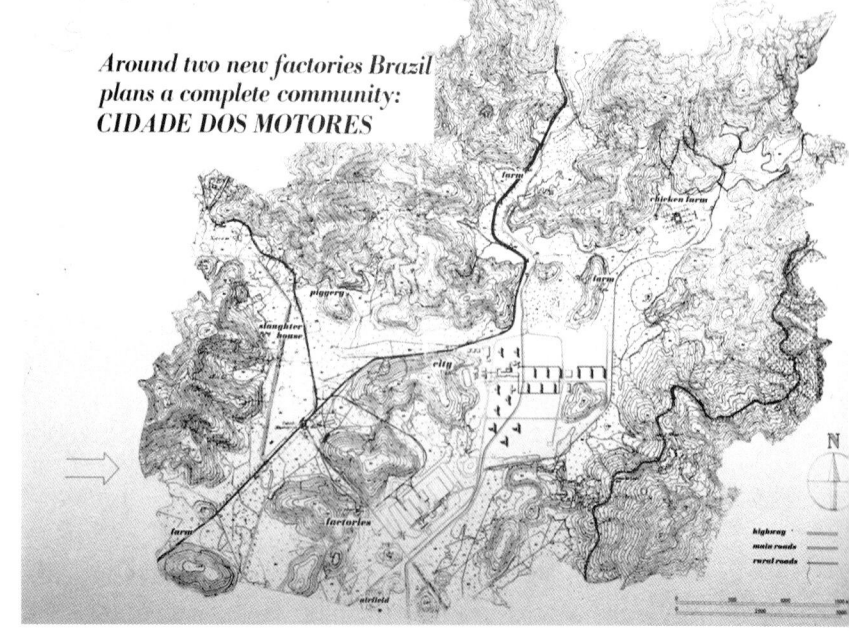

Around two new factories Brazil plans a complete community: CIDADE DOS MOTORES

He also acknowledged that the construction of housing compounds meant drawing up urban plans in which the importance and differentiation of the road network had to be taken into account, furthermore insisting on the need for modern furniture that would fit into dwellings of small dimensions. This programme was to be fundamental to the development of the projects promoted by the governments of Vargas and Dutra, and it paved the way for the Cidade dos Motores proposal. One could say that what they presented to Guedes Muñiz fitted in well with the high degree of urbanist and architectural culture that had characterized Brazil since the 1930s.

The proposal was formulated based on a critical analysis of the preliminary design drawn up by Correia Lima, of which there is a photographic copy in the Lester Wiener Archives. In this preliminary design we can observe the excessive functionalist reductionism present in the new large-scale Brazilian housing schemes. The Cidade dos Motores outlined by the Brazilian architect limited itself to placing a series of free-standing blocks that were set up without any preordained order on the enormous plots of land located among the main traffic routes. A hypothetical city 'centre' was located in the worst site possible, with the simple gesture of placing four blocks in an L shape that magnified the junction of the highway linking Rio and Petrópolis with one of the two main streets, the one going from the stadium, which was oriented to the east. The stadium, nevertheless, was placed in such a way as to take advantage of the special topographical conditions of the area, and Sert and Lester kept it in the same location in the three proposals they drew up.

The first proposal was basically a simple sketch drawn with coloured pencils, which was then done to scale to demonstrate the strict dependency on the topographical conditions of the area, an issue on which Sert and Lester always insisted. In both sketches there is an initial laying out of isolated blocks, although this time they are linked by the presence of order, hierarchy and composition, which is easy to perceive due to the use of colour in the first sketch. The 'communal' areas of the project appear in blue, such as the stadium and what is presented as the Civic Centre of the future city.

To the right of the stadium a red blotch indicates another functional area whose purpose is not indicated, but which is identified in the second scale plan as the Industrial Area. Some brown splotches cover the free-standing buildings that are laid out in two different ways and with two different shapes. One of the layouts is understood to be the continuation of the Civic Centre through the circulation axis that connected them, formed by high-rise buildings with rectangular floors and a presumably separate nucleus of access. The other was contained by encircling lines, formed by the two nuclei of three buildings, which one might suppose were to be high-rise; one of these had a Y form, like the Macià Plan skyscrapers. This was the initial contact established with the programme and the terrain, showing greater contention in the number of buildings to be placed there; what surfaces is the idea of a plan in which circulation routes take on a different meaning, due to linking up (without overlapping) the key sites that were being introduced: the Civic Centre, the stadium, and the industrial area. The project had more behind it than this, however, since we can already see that there was a decided will to create a true centre, in other words, to build on the idea of communal life, with its moral and ideological consequences for the working population that we have seen in previous declarations made by the political authorities and technicians responsible for planning.

Le Corbusier, Nemours Plan, 1934.

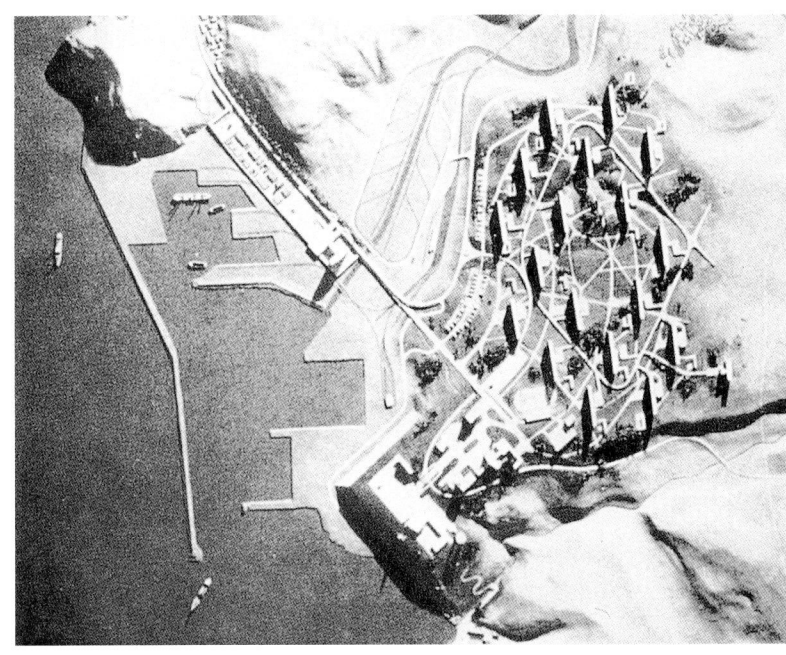

Eric Mumford has pointed out the influence exerted by Le Corbusier's Nemours Plan on this project,[257] which seems to be true if one compares this first proposal with that of the Swiss architect, both being alarmingly schematic. Nemours also had a Civic Centre, a stadium, schools and a hospital in a city of 50,000 inhabitants, twice the estimated population of the Cidade dos Motores. Nevertheless, we must also take into account the Hellocourt proposal of 1935, in which we find high-rise apartment buildings with a Y form, an element also present in the Macià Plan. We should not forget that in 1934 there was frequent contact between Sert and Le Corbusier due to their joint work on the Macià Plan, which was of much greater complexity and which had a far more elaborate programme, as we have seen, and as will become evident in the future development of the Brazilian city. We should also remember that Le Corbusier presented the Nemours Plan at the La Sarraz CIRPAC, which Sert had attended. It is not surprising that Nemours, Barcelona and Hellocourt were present in Sert's mind.

Departing from these initial guidelines, and having rethought the shape and enriched the programme of their project, Sert and Lester presented their second proposal, a graphic development of a text that Sert published in 1944, probably as a result of the lectures given between 1943 and 1944 as Professor Consultant for Planning in the Fine Arts College of Yale. We should briefly analyze this text before moving on.[258]

Two issues clearly surfaced in the text. On the one hand, there was a programmatic will to move away from mechanist schemes: 'It is useless to try to represent these future cities as abstractions detached from those conditions, as new cities in which the machine would be the sole transforming agent. We cannot pretend that machines alone can offer the solutions to all the ills of cities as we know them today. It is the forces behind the machines that count, and the purpose to which these forces put the new mechanical devices, and whom they want to favour with them.' On the other hand, there was an interest in specifying the possible conditions of urbanism in a democracy, at a time when the war was developing favourably for the Allies: 'We must ask ourselves right now, for whom do we intend to plan? In a democracy there can only be one answer: we should plan for the people, or the community as a whole. The moment that we agree on this premise, the human factor becomes the main guiding element in our plans.'

Sert later became interested in searching for historical models for this new city, and he believed he had found them in medieval cities, since they occupied a 'limited and well-determined area' and did not have suburbs. In them 'one or more civic centres (political, religious, cultural and recreational) were clearly distinguishable', and distances could easily be covered on foot. These three characteristics would be incorporated in the second and third projects of the Cidade dos Motores, thus enriching the panorama of references in this first Latin American experience.

Furthermore, Sert employed the concept of an organic, living city, which was to be achieved through a balanced social structure, '... transforming the actual inorganic shape of our cities into an organic and living body. This can only be accomplished by breaking up the cities and their suburbs into well-defined and well-planned units.' These units are then developed into 'the neighbourhood unit, the sub-city or township, the city proper, the metropolitan area, and the economic region.' It is interesting to note that these programmes of neighbourhood unit and Civic Centre coincided exactly with those contained in the future Cidade dos Motores projects.[259]

The second proposal, which according to the memorandum and plans was already drawn up as an ante-project, attempted to elaborate a plan that would provide solutions for the different parts of the city by creating four neighbourhood units, whose construction was to be staggered over time and which were to be articulated by the Civic Centre, which Sert had also defined in the article: 'This civic and cultural centre constitutes the most important element of a big city, it is its brain and governing machine. It is at the same time the highest exponent of civic life. Its influence surpasses the city limits and should extend across whole regions.'

Each one of the neighbourhood units was to house between 6,000 and 7,000 inhabitants,

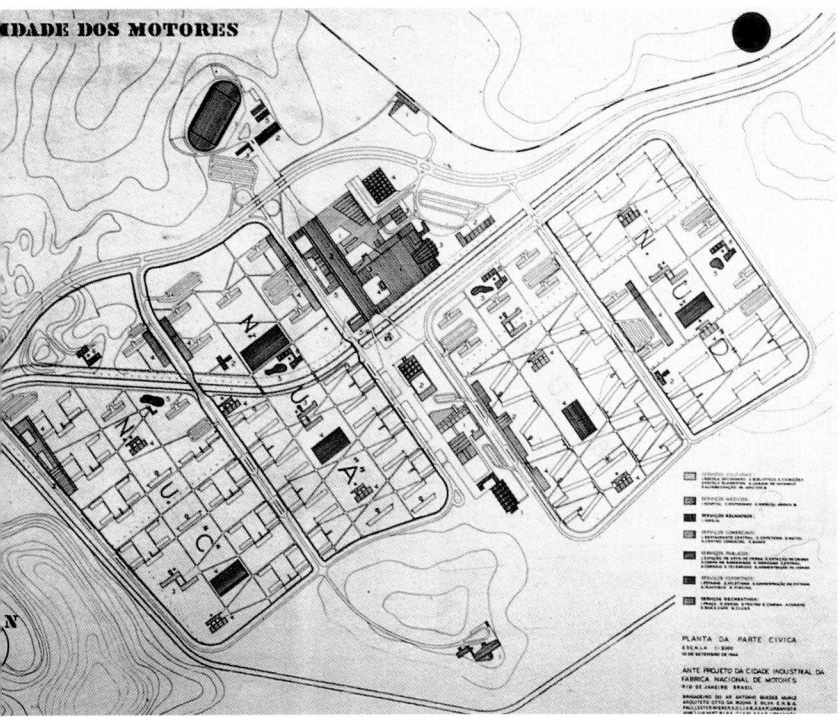

Cidade dos Motores, second project (PLWC).

who were to live in apartment buildings joined by ramps and corridors. These were to be either one-floor or duplex apartments, depending on each case, and there were to be special buildings for bachelor residents. We are not told the buildings' height, but we can deduce that they were to be from two to four storeys high, depending on the apartment typology. The space below the corridors and ramps was to be used for storing bicycles or any necessary administrative facilities.

Along with the apartments, Sert and Lester included in each neighbourhood unit a programme made up of shopping centre, sports club with baths and swimming pool, a classroom for adults and playgrounds for children, two nursery schools, an elementary school with twenty classrooms that could be used in two shifts, a sports field, a restaurant and a cafeteria, a dispensary, a soccer field and a radio station as well as parking lots near the small shopping centre. This programme was extracted from those that were standard in the United States, as Sert cited in the bibliographies included in all of the plans that he elaborated for Latin America, a bibliography with which he had become familiar while writing *Can Our Cities Survive?*[260] Each neighbourhood unit was crossed by two interior streets, with more running along its perimeter. In their design, the ar-

chitects followed the indications of the Interregional Highway Committee, which determines 'the width of the pavement, the width of separation strips, the turning radii at curves and intersections, and the channelization of intersections.'[261] All the streets were connected by other diagonal roads that crossed among themselves to facilitate the diversity of routes, creating a grid that attempted to connect the different apartment buildings and the amenities of the neighbourhood unit, many of them placed near crossings.

This pedestrian network and the special design of the apartment buildings grouped into four, each two having different dimensions, made it possible for an urban configuration to appear in which all of its components were linked, creating a continuity through which the different functions flowed. This is far removed from the initial schematism of the first proposal; here there was a desire to create a city, to find a way in which to connect the functional complexity that went on in each neighbourhood unit. The housing area, therefore, was no longer reduced in urban presence to simple buildings placed in parallel, something that had seemed fine when it was first proposed at the CIAM in Belgium before the wide eyes of the young Sert; now the housing area must show itself as a living part of an organized city.

The Civic Centre was to be the hub that gave meaning to the urban ensemble, manifesting itself as the communal focus par excellence, not only because of the programme it contained but also due to its position in the plan. In the report accompanying the preliminary design we read: 'The Civic Centre is based on the traditions of the Brazilian and European *PRAÇA* [square] and *CORSO* [promenade] … The Civic Centre aims for the first time to combine the pleasant features of the traditional *PRAÇA* with scientific planning.' Divided into three parts, namely sports area, shopping centre and cultural centre, it occupied an elongated central space between two groups of neighbourhood units. The sports area had a soccer stadium whose tiers were adapted to the slope of the mountain, a swimming pool and a parking lot. In the shopping centre was a train station, business buildings, a restaurant and a bar, a hotel, a theatre and a cinema, a central

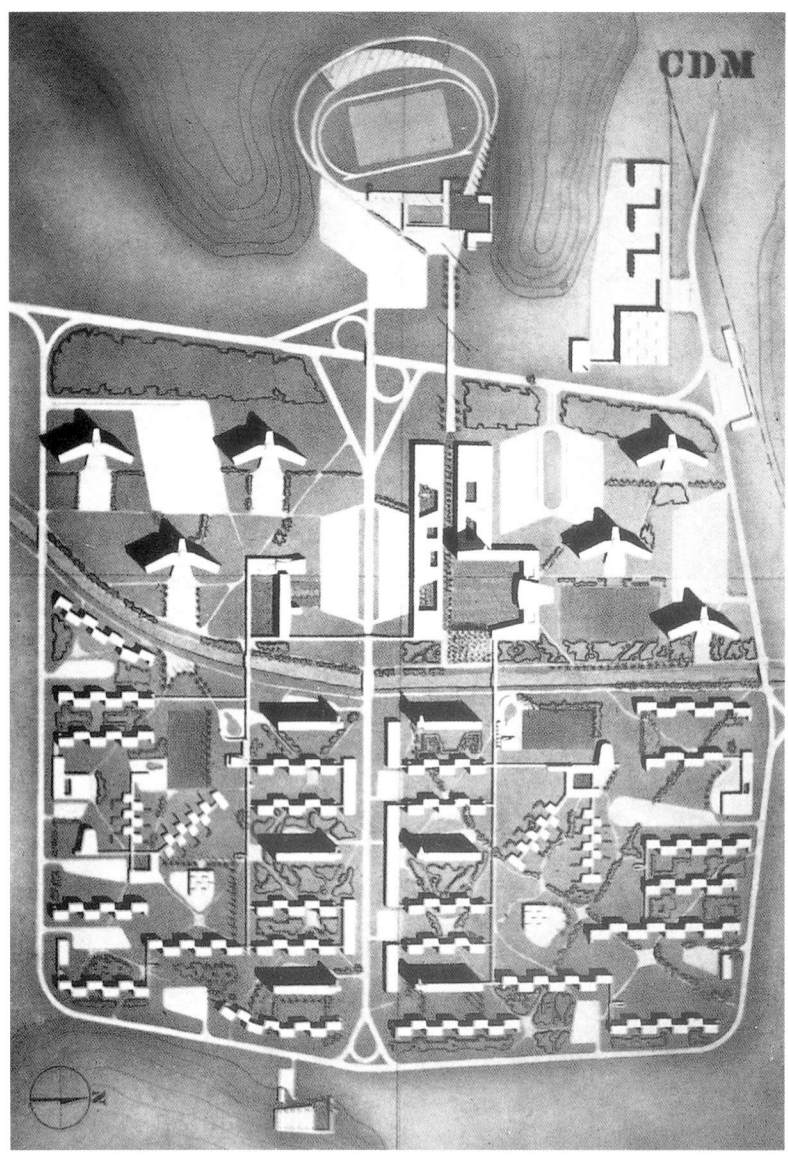

CDM

he asked the American architects for something that occupied less ground surface, increasing the height of the buildings and sensibly lowering the cost of infrastructures. This would be the third project devised by Sert and Lester for the Cidade dos Motores,[263] which the architects came to define very precisely. The differences between the last two proposals are significant although the programme was almost identical. At this point it was a matter of concentrating uses and of creating spatial hierarchies. In this way, the Civic Centre's programme was split into two, no longer being a continuous urban space. The canal that crossed the city separated functions, giving greater social and formal coherence to the project. In the area adjacent to the stadium and the pool was an enormous square that was closed to the east by a technical school. The *corso* departed from this square, passing through the shopping area of the Civic Centre and ending in an enclosed square.

To the right and left of this part of the Civic Centre were nine free-standing buildings with a Y form. Each of these was nine floors high and destined for bachelors, housing 801 men, who supposedly had more leisure time to be outdoors, therefore making greater use of the infrastructures offered by the city. The first two floors had rooms for five people at a time, reached through a corridor on the western facade of the building. In the floors above these a double corridor allowed access to single cells for two or three people. The central nucleus of the building was linked to its overhanging

market, a bus station, a post and telegraph office, a warehouse and a parking lot. A *corso*, partially covered, which joined this area with the sports area, ended in a great square surrounded on two of its sides by the hotel, the bar and the theatre, with a bandstand in the centre. The *corso* continued towards the east and arrived at the third area of the Civic Centre in which the library, exhibition hall, a monument (probably to Getulio Vargas), the high school, the church and the parking lots were located. We do not have a model or an aerial perspective of this second project to analyze its volumetric results, and in all likelihood the architects did not get the chance to reach this stage of definition in their project.

The scale of the proposal and its cost must have shocked Guedes Muñiz,[262] and it seems that

Cidade dos Motores, aerial perspective of urbanist configuration.

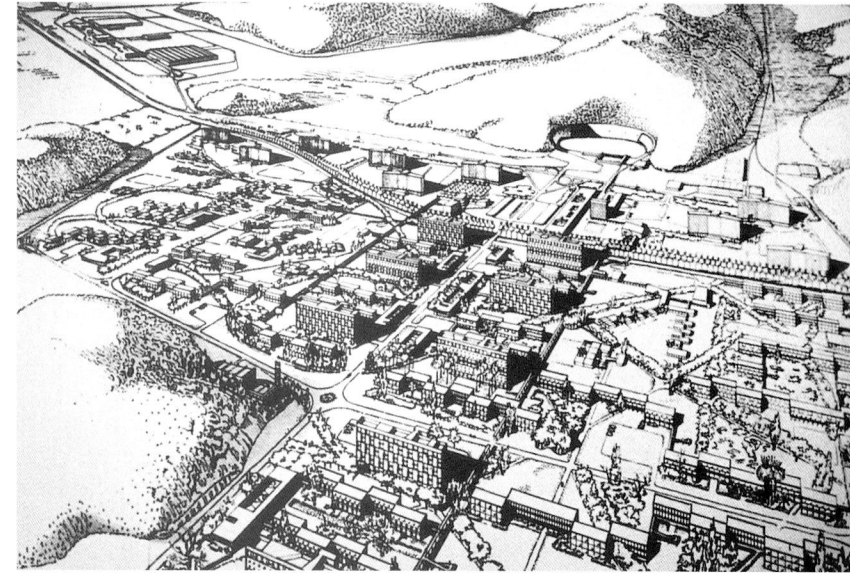

Cidade dos
Motores, third
project,
specifically the
Civic Centre (SC).

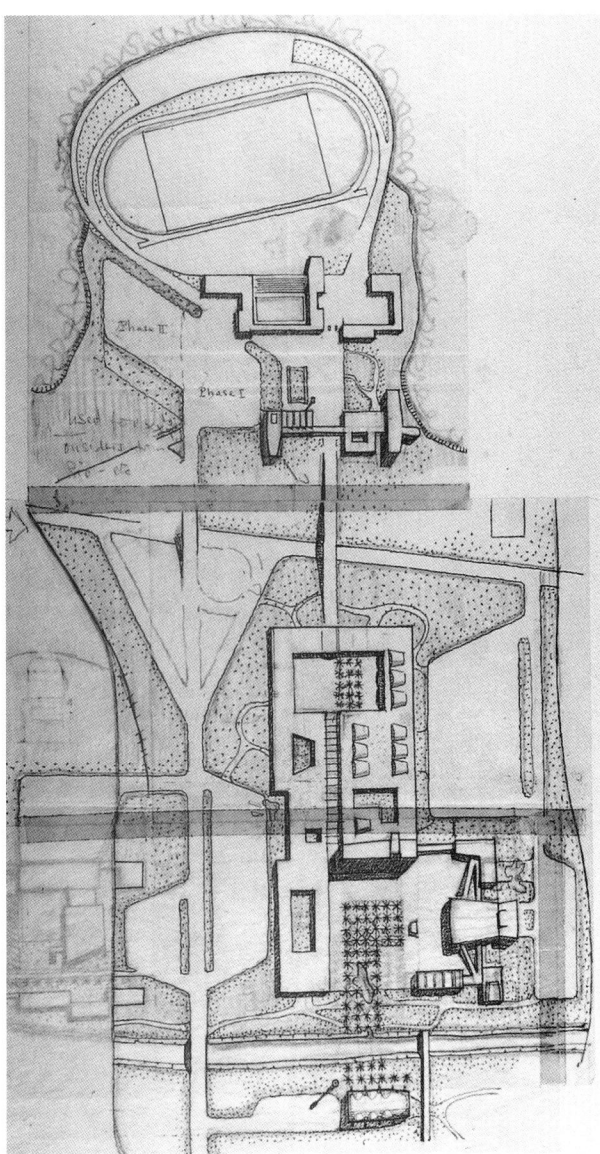

would distance them from a mechanical repetition; it was a matter of initiating plastic experiences that would do away with any image that might recall the times in which architecture was conceived as a machine for living.

To do this, besides the mechanism mentioned, Sert and Lester designed three different types of enclosure wallings,[264] which apart from being adapted to the tropical climate, introduced with their different forms and textures a visual sensation of uniqueness at different points of the city. This formal strategy was complemented by three-floor buildings that

Cidade dos
Motores, bachelor
apartments,
elevation, plans
(SC).

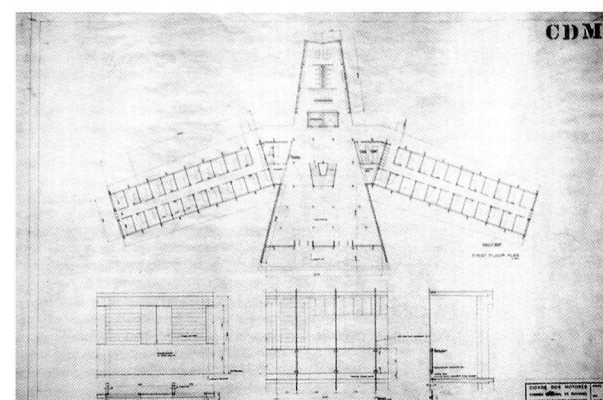

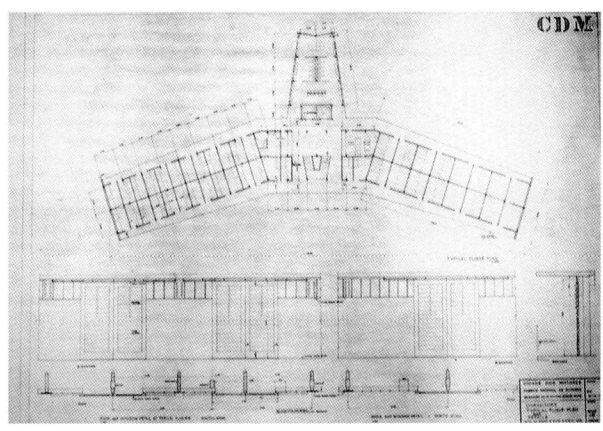

wing, where the vertical accesses and communal amenities were placed.

The cultural part of the Civic Centre organized another axis, along which eight buildings, made of eight floor each were placed, four on each side, embodying the strong tempo of the city. These were also free-standing buildings that contained three-room family apartments set up as duplexes, combined with small one-room apartments with all the amenities, and alternating with two-room simplex apartments. Access was through an outside corridor; the stairs and elevator occupied a separate volume of the base of the parallelepiped located on its western facade. In these buildings the architects essayed some atypical solutions in order to achieve formal effects in which the variation, created by alternating a series of modules,

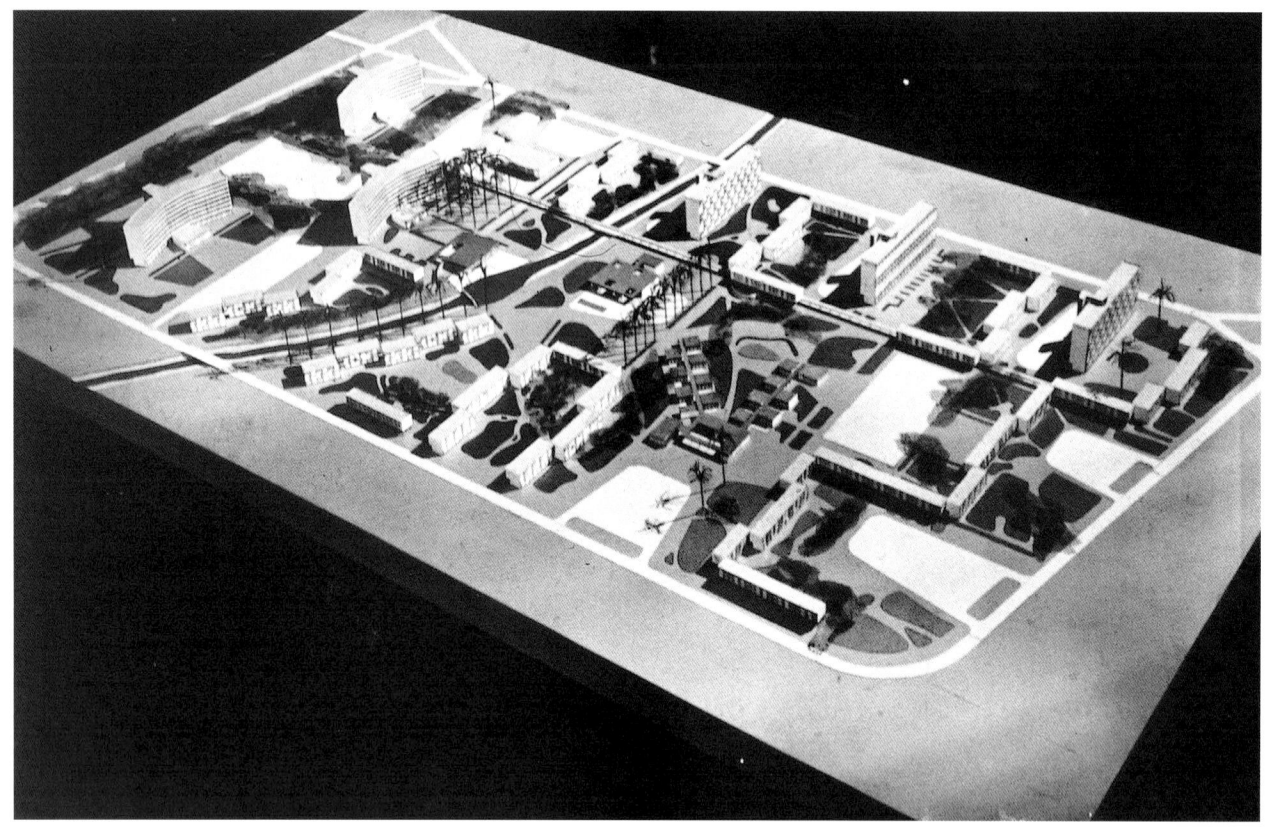

Cidade dos Motores, neighbourhood unit, model.

were interjected among the other buildings, thus willfully breaking up the rigid shape of the parallelepiped by spreading themselves out as timid *redents*. An outside corridor provided access to these apartments, set up as duplexes or simplexes, a combination that in the architects' opinion helped to lend a variable appearance to the city facades. Once this spatial structure had been consolidated, the city went on to ex-

tend itself through pedestrian routes lined with tropical vegetation. These pedestrian paths, set up diagonally, went from the long covered promenades with porches to the amenities of each one of the neighbourhood units and to the rest of the three-floor buildings that closed off the confines of the city, reaching the streets along the city's perimeter. The elementary school, which offered the possibility of holding

Cidade dos Motores, apartment buildings, plans and elevations (SC).

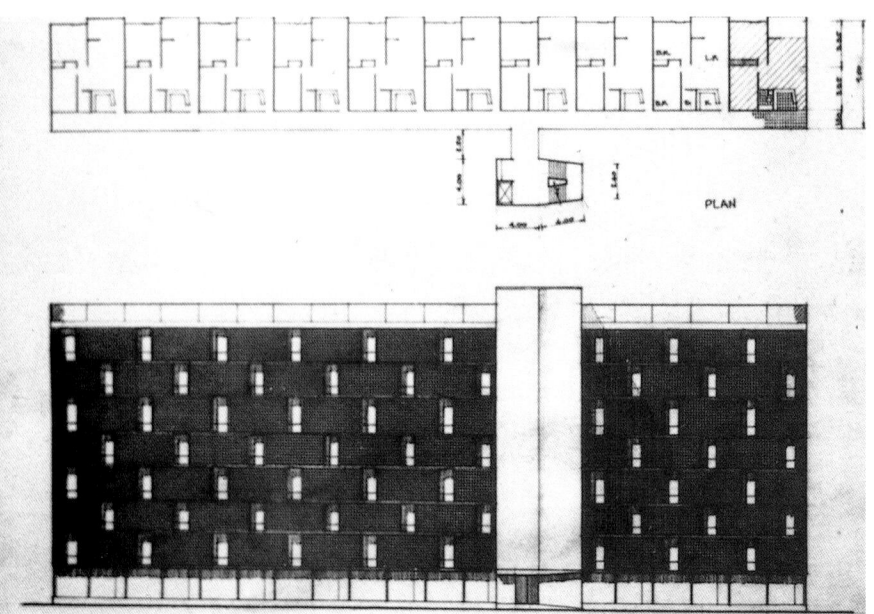

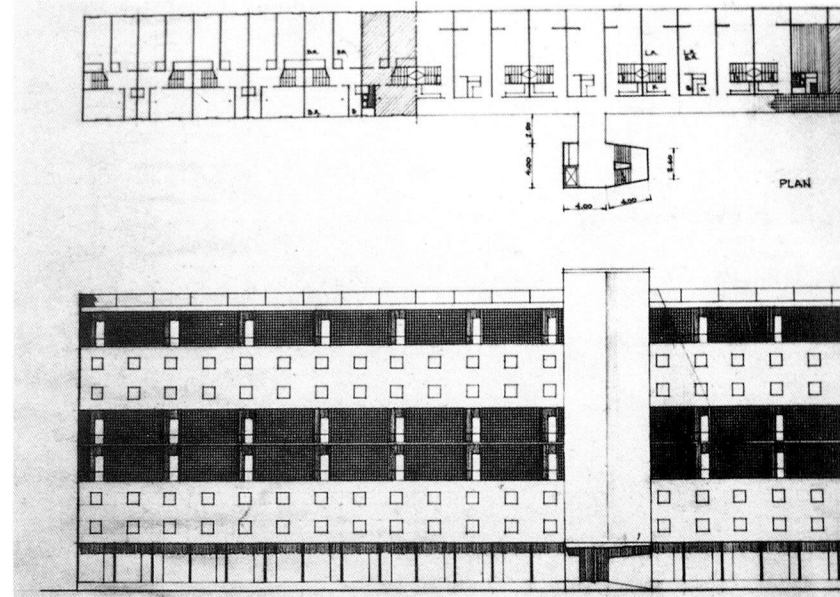

Cidade dos Motores, apartment buildings, elevations (SC).

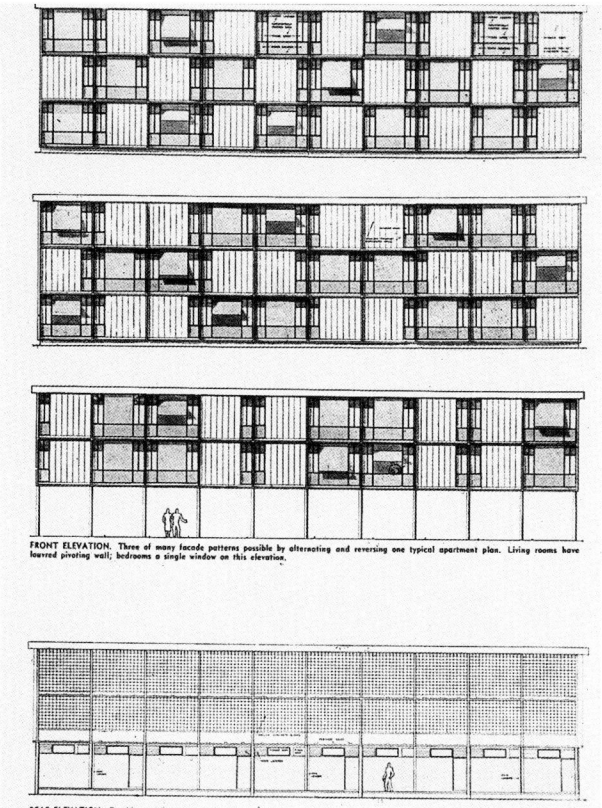

FRONT ELEVATION. Three of many facade patterns possible by alternating and reversing one typical apartment plan. Living rooms have louvred pivoting wall; bedrooms a single window on this elevation.

REAR ELEVATION. Outside corridors are protected by pierced masonry units.

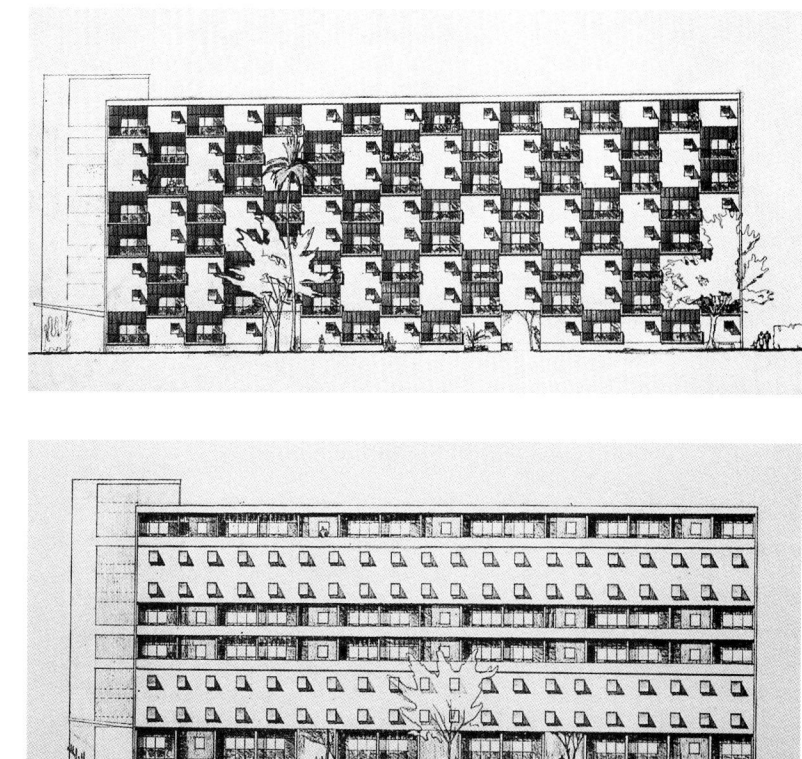

8 Story apartment - (S.C.)

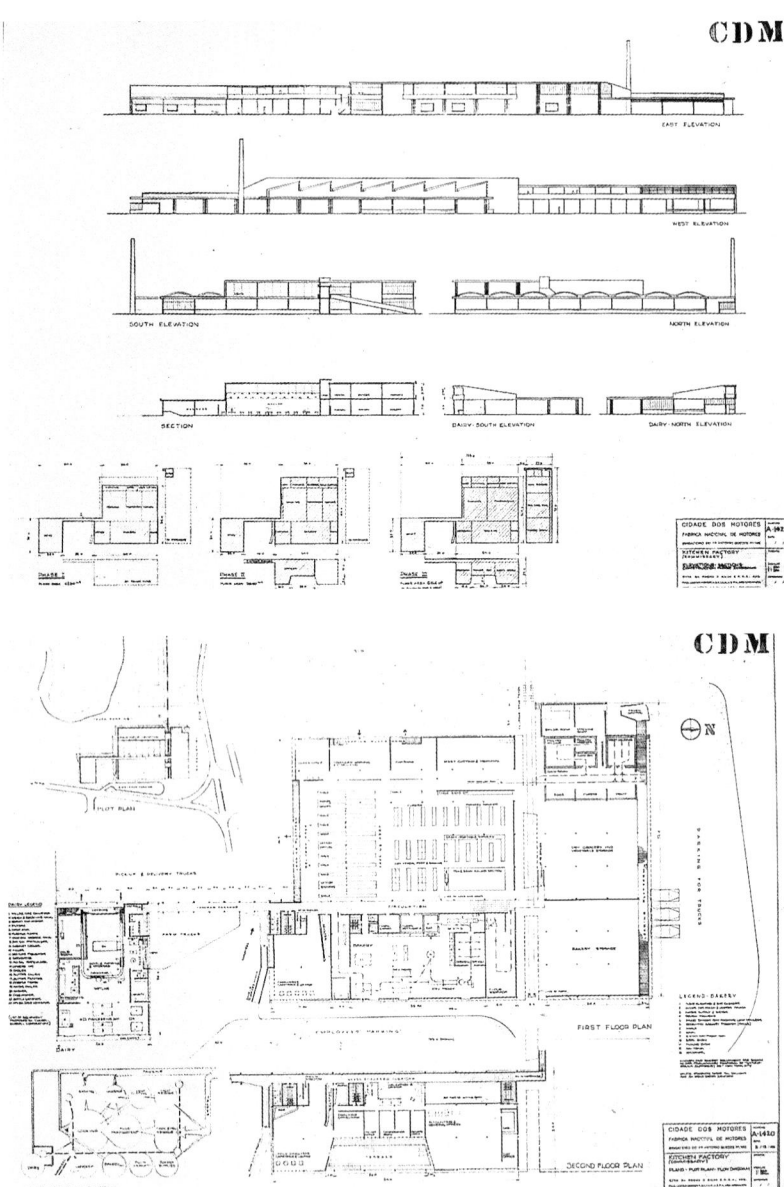

Cidade dos
Motores,
kitchen factory,
elevations, plans,
sections (SC).

classes out in the open, followed the direction of one of these diagonal roads, thus helping to maintain direct contact between the road system, its use and the architecture.

Although this description of the urban configuration is based on the formal and compositional schemes that are observed in the aerial perspective of the complex, the city had been conceived on the basis of criteria similar to those observed in the second proposal, that is, it concentrated its attention on the possibility of building it from neighbourhood units housing 6,200 inhabitants. In these units we observe the same generous standards that had been included in the previous project, in a city that was to have a population density of 100 inhabitants per acre.

To the right of the Civic Centre, an element reappeared that had been included in the first project but had disappeared in the second. This is the 'Kitchen Factory', a place in which to prepare the agricultural products coming in from the previous planning of the Baixada Fluminense area. To understand this process, it is enlightening to read the information offered by Sigrid de Lima: 'The government has already set up an organization to feed and care for the population, including the poultry farm, piggeries and cattle ranches. The poultry farm has an average of 8,000 chickens producing 3,000 eggs a day and more than 1,760 pounds of meat a month. Pigsties with 600 pigs provide the aeroplane factory cafeteria with some 2,640 pounds of meat a month, while 300 head of cattle supply all present needs for milk.'[265] The minimum nutritional needs of the city were thus covered, and the cafeteria set up by the architects in the centre of the industrial area was to offer healthy food and a balanced diet.

It was a model city 'conceived for its inhabitants … to fully satisfy the physical and moral needs of the population', as its architects wrote and as was affirmed in the pamphlet-style proclamations of Vargas and Guedes Muñiz. All was based on a human scale and was to contribute to the happiness of humankind, everything functioning correctly according to the provisions offered by the plan. The life of a typical family of Cidade dos Motores was described as follows: 'Since man is the measure of all things, let us take a family of four, consisting of father, mother and two children, and see how their lives can evolve within the twenty-four hour life cycle.'[266] The text went on to narrate the activities of each family member in this idealized city, in which the man could get to the factory in a few minutes thanks to a bus he would have taken after a pleasant walk under the porches, which offered protection from the glaring tropical sun. In the factory he would be able to eat in the cafeteria while his wife would have dropped off her younger offspring at the nursery while the older child would go to elementary school or kindergarden. Naturally all of the children would enjoy healthy balanced meals, and if the woman was pregnant, she would receive medical attention in the dispensary near her home, whose access was through an exclusively pedestrian street.

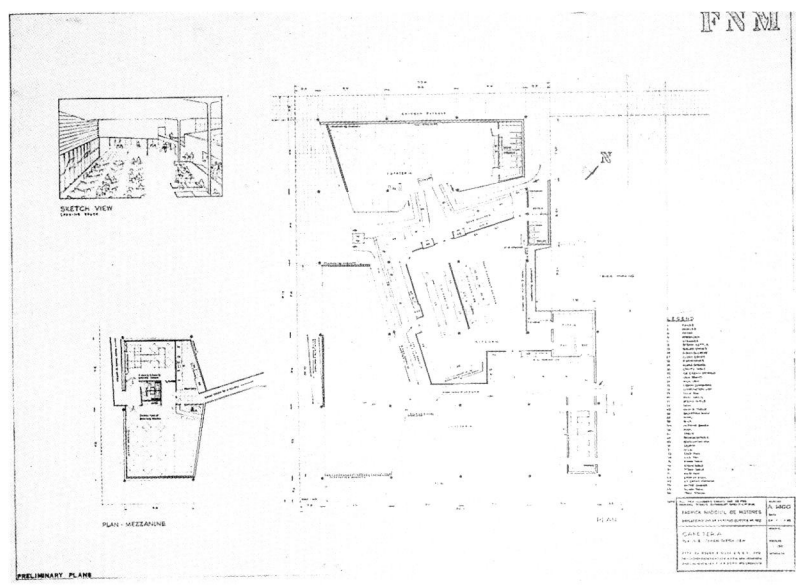

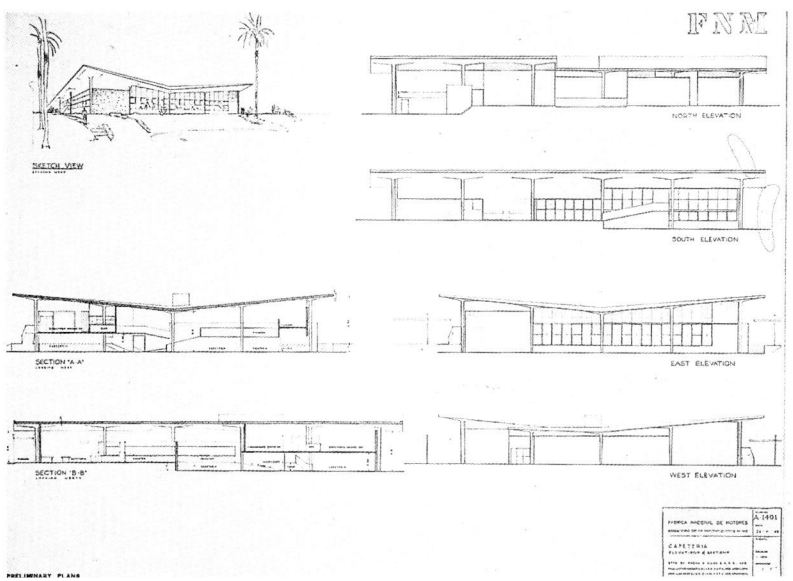

Cidade dos
Motores,
cafeteria, plan,
elevations,
sections (SC).

At night, once the family had gathered, they could go for dinner to a restaurant in their neighbourhood unit or spend time at the club. They could walk around the square of the Civic Centre, attend concerts, go to the movies or watch a soccer game, activities reserved for the weekends. The Civic Centre revived the Spanish tradition of public spaces in a city that 'will be the first modernly planned city that maintains this good traditional feature, bringing it into relationship with present-day life', and whose planning aspired to create 'a physical and spiritual background against which the modern Brazilian way of life may be carried on, with ever greater health, happiness and efficiency.'

These words reveal an astonishing naivety coupled with an unconditional faith in the advantages of a functional city that can no longer be perceived as schematic: the combination of uses and the diversity of its offer made the construction of the city seem possible within the interventionist policy carried out by the Brazilian government, although it turned out to be more difficult for it to take shape once it was faced by more complex structural parameters. The high degree of amenities proposed elevated the quality of life to standards that were far removed from the workers' true destiny: after all, from the viewpoint of capitalist logic, the only strict obligation of a working-class city was to ensure the reproduction of its labour force. Conditions in Brazil made one think more of survival than a state of well-being.

A letter that Lester wrote to the Colombian architect Jorge Gaitán on 25 June 1948 reveals that the city would never become a reality: 'The Fabrica Nacional de Motores of Rio de Janeiro was converted into a private enterprise. The officials with whom we had to deal with on behalf of the Brazilian Government are no longer there. The activities of the factory at present have ceased and a new private company is about to take over.'

After the factory became a private enterprise and the officials in charge had been made redundant due to political changes, nobody was interested in the proposal of Sert and Lester. Since 1946, moreover, both architects had been busy with other commissions and private concerns. Shortly afterwards the factory closed its doors, so that any remaining hope of seeing the *novo homen* materialize was definitively lost.

On a personal level, Sert was going through a difficult period due to the sudden illness of his mother, which obliged him to go back to Barcelona much sooner than he could have imagined,[267] and at the same time he had to initiate the process of his professional registration as an architect in the United States,[268] while refusing continuous invitations from Le Corbusier to work with him in his Paris studio.[269] He was also in charge of preparing his participation in CIAM 6, which was to be held in Bridgwater between 7 and 14 September 1947 (and in which he would be designated Presi-

Chimbote, Peru,
aerial view.

dent, a post that he occupied until the Congress' disappearance). A month before Sert travelled to England, moreover, he and his associate had received at their West 42nd Street office in New York the contract commissioning them with the Master Plan for the Peruvian city of Chimbote.[270]

Located on the Pacific coast, Chimbote had reaped the benefits of a vast programme of industrialization, which had taken off some years before in its area of influence. This programme involved the exploitation of the area's coal mines and of its fishing industry,[271] the reorganization of its railway infrastructure, the construction of a hydro-electric factory with 125,000 kilowatts of power, by making use of the waterfall in the Cañón del Pato, the installation of an irrigation system and the construction of a port equipped with modern utilities to export coal. Next to it an industrial complex was to be installed for the treatment of ferrous metals.[272] The hydro-electric project ensemble involved the irrigation of 10,000 hectares of the Río Santa region.

Chimbote had 4,000 inhabitants and was ordered on a sixty-block grid as a result of the layout plan set up by the American architect Henry Meiggs in 1860. Here the problems faced were different from those we have seen in Cidade dos Motores. The question was how

to intervene in an existing city, remodelling the urban layout so as to adapt it to the abrupt expansion that would foreseeably occur, something that was taken into account in the specifications of the Master Plan. In it, Sert and Lester made a list of the population according to their occupations in the future city:

Fishing industry, ceramics, electrical products and small industries
Employees   300–400

Larger industries that may use the electrical energy available since February 1944
Employees in 1950   4,000
Employees in 1952   3,500

With the irrigation of the area between Chimbote and Versique, 4,000 hectares of agricultural land will be available
Inhabitants   6,000–9,000

The railway that links Trujillo with Chimbote will make it a port for the export of products from the State of Liberty with an annual movement of 300,000 tons
Inhabitants   5,000

In the next fifty years, the city will reach a population density of 50,000 inhabitants.

With these provisions as guidelines, Sert and Lester wrote the Plan report, stressing the importance of a zoning that still bore in mind the four principal functions, and stressing the advantages of ensuring privacy, good ventilation, absence of noise and open spaces for children to play in. They also included, as usual, a copious North American bibliography on urban issues. The zoning they spoke of 'follows well-proven precedents of modern town planning, and in particular the town planning chart of CIAM Athens, 1933, and the findings of the last Congress held in Bridgwater, England in 1947.' This complicates matters, since it entails an analysis of what took place in that English city in order to ascertain in what measure the declarations made there influenced the form of the Plan. However, we will proceed with the report, which indicated that Chimbote was a 'slum area' without good sanitary conditions in which there abounded diseases, vices, immorality, delinquency and crime. This 'squatter population' was to be integrated into the new destiny of the city: 'It would seem important to

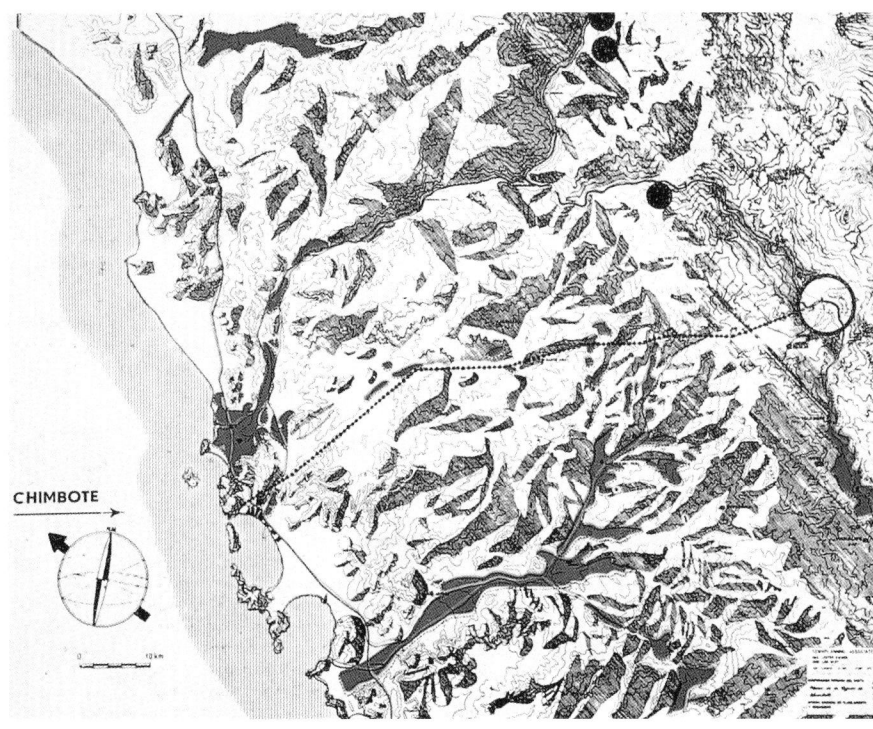

CHIMBOTE

Chimbote, orography.

convert this population into productive people (producers and consumers) as it will become necessary to use this resource of manpower to serve the industries of Chimbote.' Sert and Lester designed a special area for these people, with three groups of forty-eight very simple brick courtyard houses, each group separated by six-metre strips of green areas that could be cultivated, plus communal amenities, a school and an outdoor chapel. The New York architects also pointed out that the cost of the investment was minimal in comparison with the availability of labour force that would result from it.

The first sketches of the project (dated October 1948,[273] although this does not seem likely) proposed the optimization of scarce natural resources such as water, which was to become the key factor of a central park that, along with the road system – once again a main protagonist – defined the four neighbourhood units. In these were articulated the residential areas and the Civic Centre, which would be located facing the sea, as in the Macià Plan. In the Pilot Plan report, the road system was broken up into roads, avenues, streets, cul-de-sac parking areas and pedestrian paths, justified by economic reasonings that place them in contrast to the existing 'costly and unnecessary' grid, which did not correspond to 'the needs and hazards of motorized traffic'.

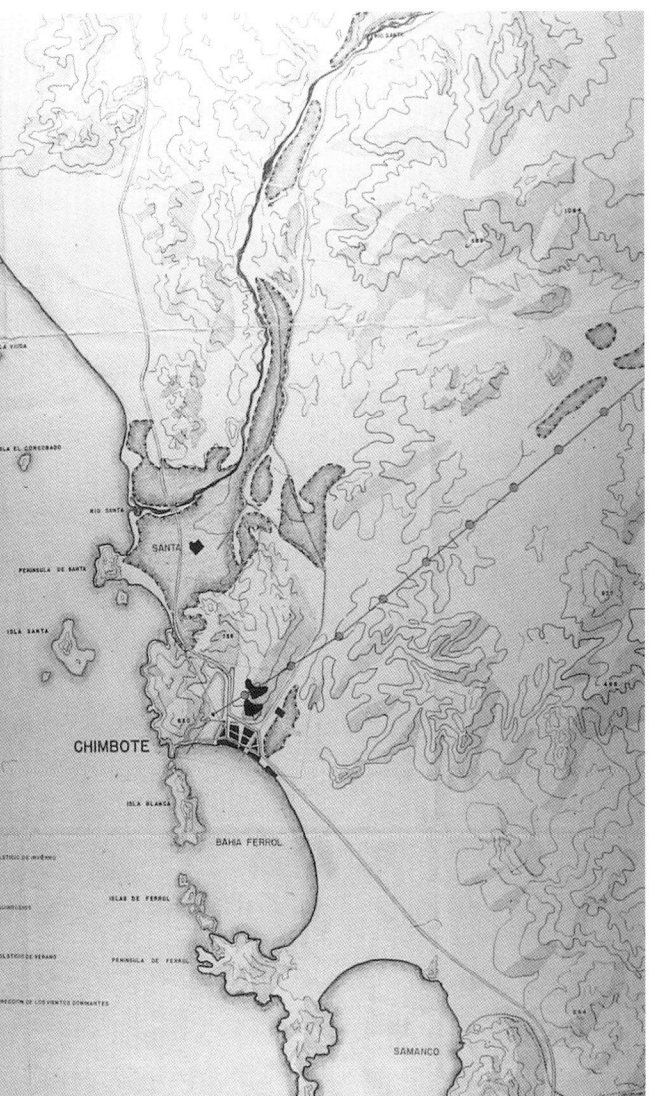

Chimbote, geographical location.

CHIMBOTE

129

TPA (town
Planning
Associates), Pilot
Plan of Chimbote,
1946–48, plan
prior to TPA
intervention
(PLWC).

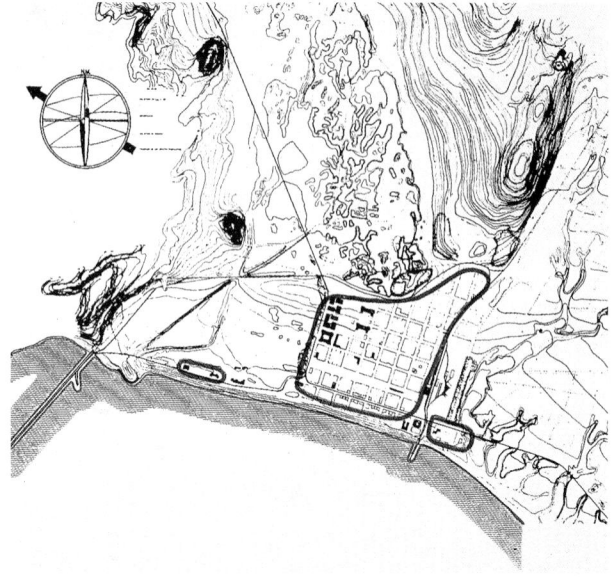

Towards the north, and separated by a fifty-metre green belt, was the industrial area – the site having been chosen by the Peruvian Corporation of Santa – organized around the port and provided with a sophisticated programme: warehouses, train station, mineral-processing factories, chemical industries and thermal power plants, steel factories, refineries, a hospital and a workers' residence. That Sert and Lester dreamed that this industrial area would be exemplary can be deduced from the Pilot Plan report: 'The port of Chimbote and its industries, of great importance for Peru, will

surely be visited by people who will come to admire the place and its magnificent bay. One must therefore take into account the embellishment of the factories and its routes of access so that its exterior appearance corresponds to the technical perfection of the work coming out of them.'

In the residential area, the importance of the neighbourhood units as protagonists[274] is evidenced by the ranking they were assigned in the Plan report. The programme for each one was written in full detail, specifying the different types of dwellings they would contain and the number of inhabitants who were to live there; it also specified the process of intervention that was to slowly transform the existing grid into open blocks, which would include among the dwellings the ample presence of green spaces and a high level of amenities – something that in the Macià Plan had merely reached an embryonic stage. There was also a study of the square metres destined for construction, a matter that had already cropped up in the project for Brazil. There are two issues of interest for a cross-analysis with Bridgwater:[275] the insistence on the idea of neighbourhood units and the presence of a wide range of dwellings and systems for grouping them.

The circumstances of living in a post-war period and its consequences were key matters

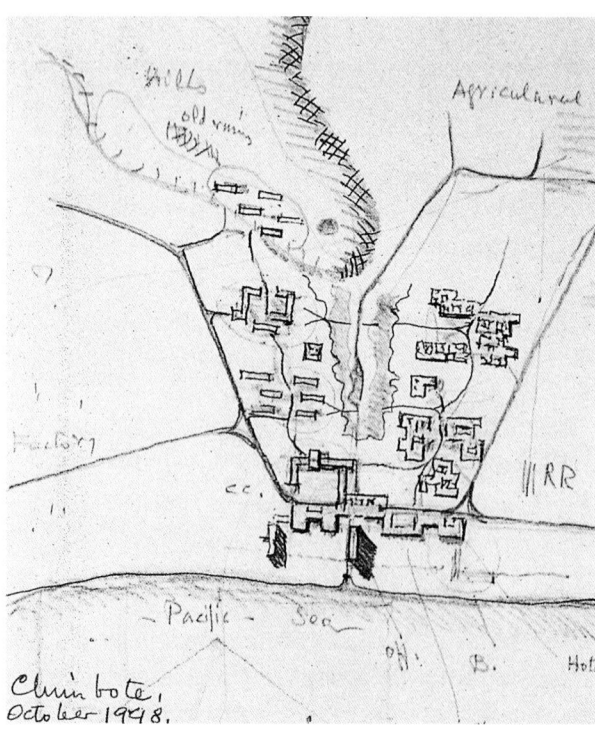

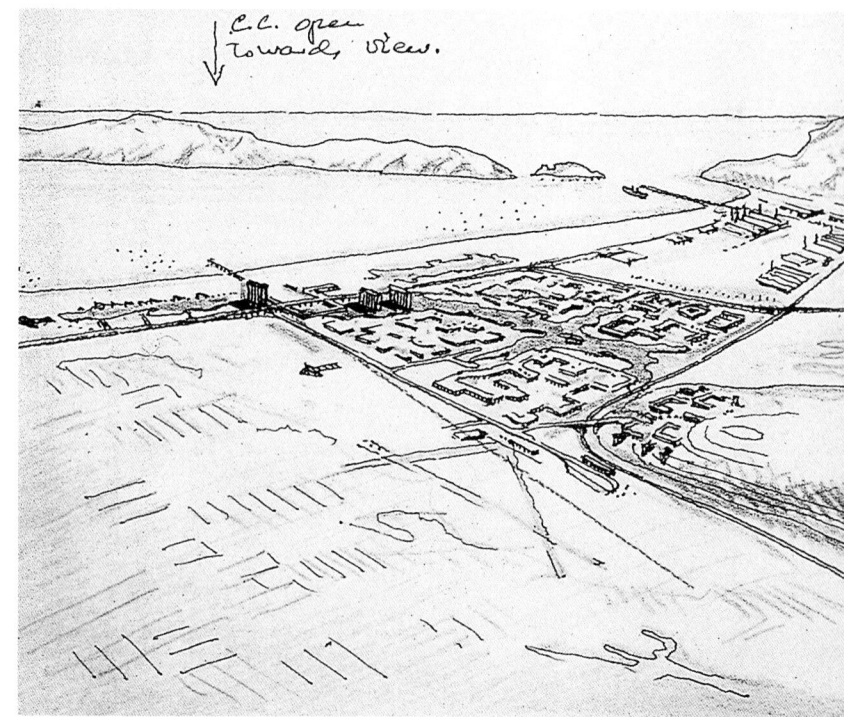

Sert, Giedion and van Eesteren at the Bridgwater CIAM, 1947.

Chimbote Pilot Plan, general plan and urban centre plan.

ties that had predominated in Sert's work over the last years?

Our architect worked with Gropius on Commission III, which dealt with urbanism, from whose text we can extract the following: 'The Athens Charter gave a clear line of principles to be followed for the planning of towns, but since then two important fields of physical planning have been opened up: the broader field of national and regional planning and the more localized field of neighbourhood planning.'[277]

Once again, it is clear that the Congress' interests coincided with Sert's latest urbanist concerns; for some time he had been praising the neighbourhood unit as one of the strong points of his urban work, as was the case in Cidade dos Motores. Thus, although Sert mentioned the Congress' important influence on the Chimbote project, we can suggest another reading of this: it was in CIAM 6 that Sert tested his ideas, discussing them in debates with his colleagues, laying out the projects for Latin America that he was developing with Lester, especially since in Chimbote the neighbourhood unit was to be used in conceiving the city's living and leisure space. A survey of the questionnaire on neighbourhood units devised at the Congress shows that the type of questions put there run parallel to those manifested by Sert and Lester in the reports connected to their plans.[278]

to be dealt with at CIAM 6: 'We are faced with an enormous task of rebuilding the territories devastated by the war, as well as in raising the standard of living in undeveloped countries where great changes are now taking place.'[276] The CIAM participants also felt the need to make a proclamation worthy of its best days, declaring that the meeting would attempt 'to work for the creation of a physical environment that will satisfy man's emotional and material needs and stimulate his spiritual growth.' Human needs and attention to underdeveloped countries – were these not the ideas and reali-

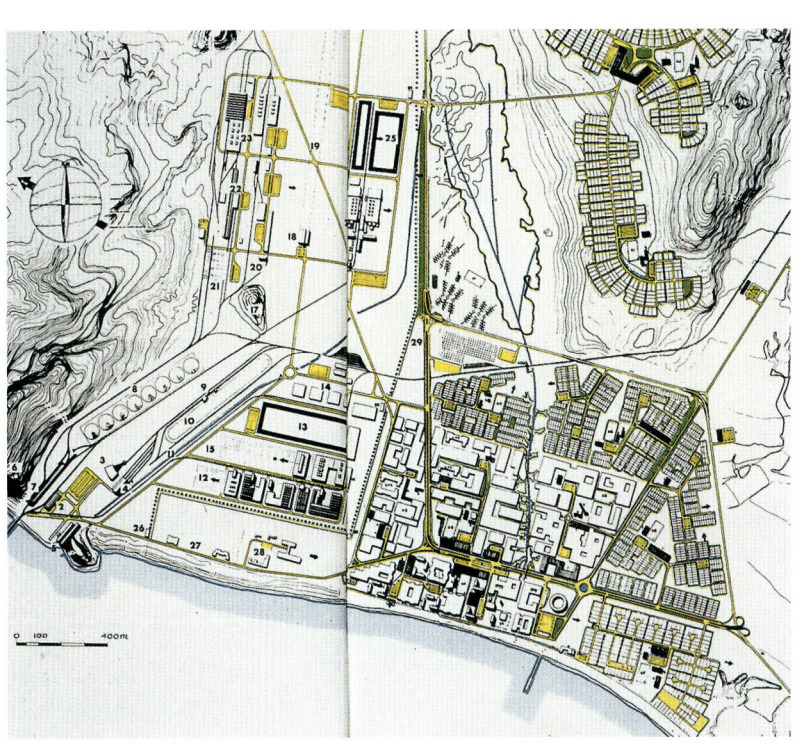

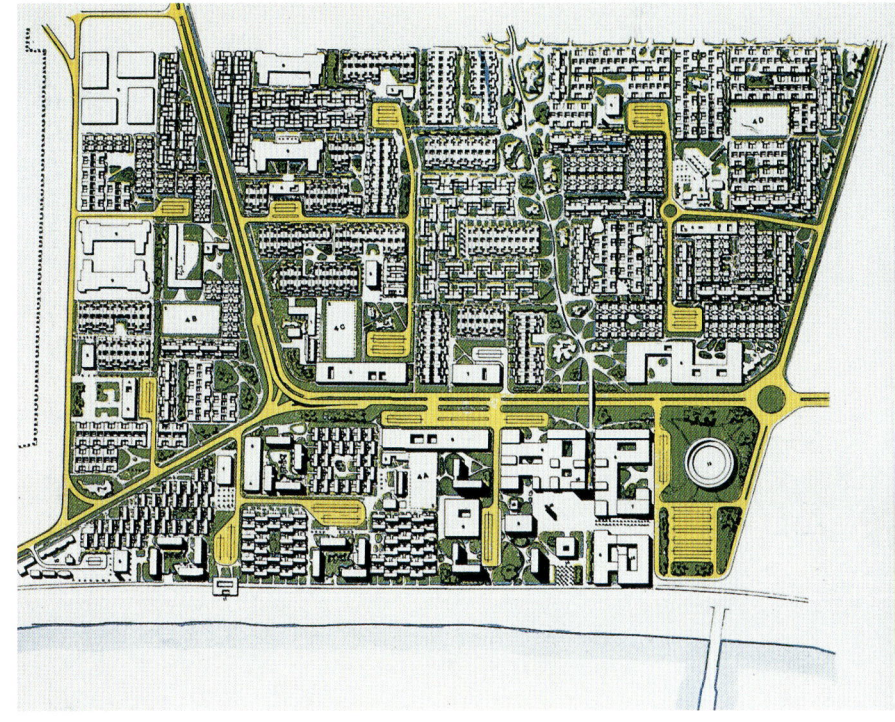

There are other aspects of interest in the Bridgwater meeting that have to do with the excessive zeal in showing the variety of dwellings present in Chimbote, far greater than in the Brazilian experiment. CIAM 6 also dealt with architects' education and organizational problems resulting from the affluence of professionals,[279] and it gave priority to issues concerning formal aspects of architecture, a discussion that CIAM had avoided throughout its existence. Commission III was specifically charged with 'Architectural Expression' and all the different aspects deriving from it, and these matters as well as the lectures given are of great interest to us. There were three main topics: 1. The impact of technical advances. 2. The impact of social advances. 3. The impact of related arts. As usual, they served to elaborate a questionnaire that was to be answered at CIAM 7.

The third topic, the longest, was very important because it spoke about the possible integration of painting, sculpture, architecture, and the use of colour, materials and structure in architecture. This was far removed from the need for abstraction of the 1920s, and from the distaste for ornamentation that all leading architects had shared at that time. The participants began to show a collective interest in 'the relationship of natural and artificial light sources to sculpture', or to wonder whether it was possible for the 'architect, painter, and sculptor to co-operate from the very beginning, so as to strengthen the emotional and symbolic content of architecture.' They put questions that would have been unthinkable at any previous moment: 'How can light be used as an emotional expression not merely to satisfy functional requirements? … Do you consider that we could profit from the experience of the Theatre in the use of artificial light for the creation of special atmospheric or emotional results, internally and externally?'

This climate led Le Corbusier, in a speech given at the General Assembly of this Commission, to utter the brave words: 'To make the poetical phenomenon break loose! This is a collective enterprise. Poetry! The word must be pronounced.' This was a poetry dedicated to and produced by humankind, the creation of an individual addressing others like himself in order to impart emotion and art: 'This man goes to-wards the unknown, but to unknown things that exist, that are there, that await and for which EMOTION and ART are as necessary as bread and water.'[280] Things had taken a new turn in Bridgwater: architects were interested in offering other values that surpassed the functional postulates that had allowed them to dissect the needs of cities. This path was covered in a similar fashion to that in which Sert clearly perceived the linear relationship between the functional complexity of the neighbourhood unit and human happiness. Le Corbusier wished to convince himself that with all the experience accumulated he could now think about poetry and beauty without falling into the trap of the old academicist formulations.

Other key speeches were those of the young Aldo van Eyck and the English architect James M. Richards. The former insisted on the need to get over functionalist reductionism: 'The old struggle between imagination and common sense ended tragically in favour of the latter … Imagination remains the only common denominator of man and nature, the only faculty capable of registering spiritual transformation simultaneously, and thus of significant prophecy … The more tangible functions – those implied by the word "functionalism" – are only relevant insofar as they help to adjust man's environment more accurately to his elementary requirements. But this, after all, is no more than a necessary preliminary.'[281]

Two aspects of Richards' intervention directly concern us. The first is that he was interested in revealing the contrast between monotony and the serial style that standardization would produce: 'Does prefabrication require more flexible types of component, designed without respect to the size of the separate dwelling, as a way of ensuring variety of architectural form, or can monotony be avoided and an added sense of enclosure be achieved by varying the height and density of the buildings in a given area?'[282] The second aspect was his interest in regionalism, a term that will reappear further on in this book: 'It is in keeping with the spirit of modern architecture and its necessarily mechanistic quality to make use nevertheless of the effect of time and weather on building materials, or to encourage a return to some kind of regionalism in architecture, to use the local materials and the incorporation of forms traditional to particular localities, especially those that can still be regarded as valid because they are derived from conditions of climate, social custom and the like, which still exist.'[283] After these interventions it seems understandable that Sert referred to the Bridgwater CIAM in his Chimbote report: after all, much that had been discussed there had been included in his project in Brazil and in the one underway in Peru. It was necessary to exploit a path that had been gaining acceptance and consistency among architects who after the war were still bent on continuing the task that had begun in La Sarraz twenty years before. Sert showed himself to be a pioneer of this new direction, something that is corroborated by a statement in the Chimbote Plan report: 'We have wanted to rationalize and avoid a monotonous appearance.'

The point was to be taken up over and again, benefiting from the overlapping knowledge and accumulated experience that so many years of debates and meetings had generated, as has become evident in this analysis. Perhaps now the reasons for the excess of the different housing typologies and meticulous design of the dwellings in Chimbote become clearer: it was a matter of seeking out the effect of variation and difference, a formal mechanism that led Sert to flee from anything that could be interpreted as repetition or might evoke the mechanistic past that was currently being questioned. It is therefore not surprising to discover eight different proposals, the use of 'modern' and local materials, diverse housing combinations, and the inclusion of the patio as an element that gives

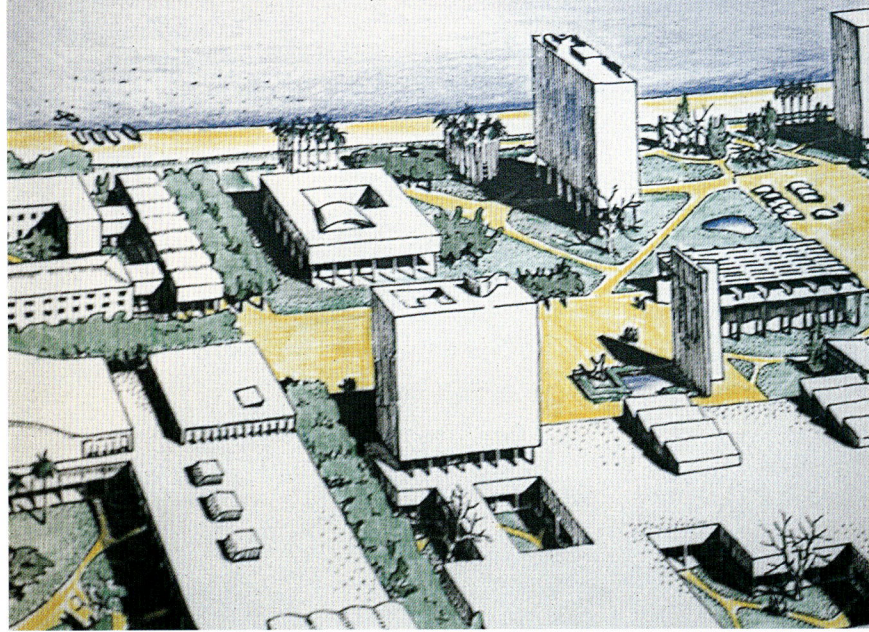

Chimbote, Civic Centre, perspective (SC).

flexibility to the mixed construction types, all of these elements being employed to resolve the residential function of the city. Examples are one-floor buildings of 72 and 85 square meters with a 28-square-meters patio, combined with others of 110 square meters with a 26.5-square-meters patio, or others of 97 square meters and 84 square meters with 63-square-meters and 136-square-meters patios respectively. There were also family houses built with a flat roof, a gable roof or with a brick barrel vault, an element consistently favoured by Sert.

By incorporating the patio in the facade, and varying the design and material of its walling as well as modifying its alignments, it was possible to achieve a diversity of aesthetic effects that made one forget the strict modulation set up by the architects. Duplex dwellings whose surface was similar to that of their patios were to be placed next to four to six-storey buildings that would contain smaller apart-

Chimbote, model of the Civic Centre.

Chimbote, Civic Centre plan.

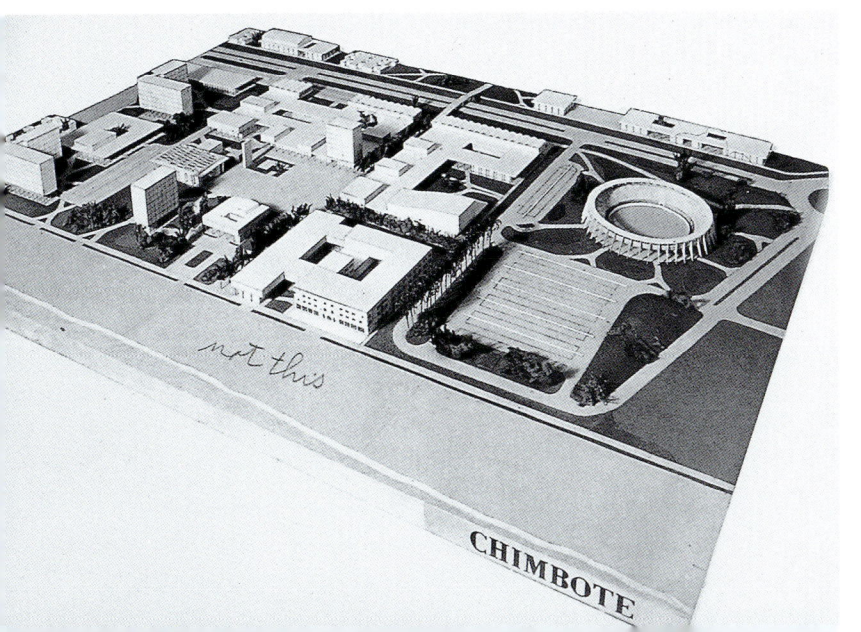

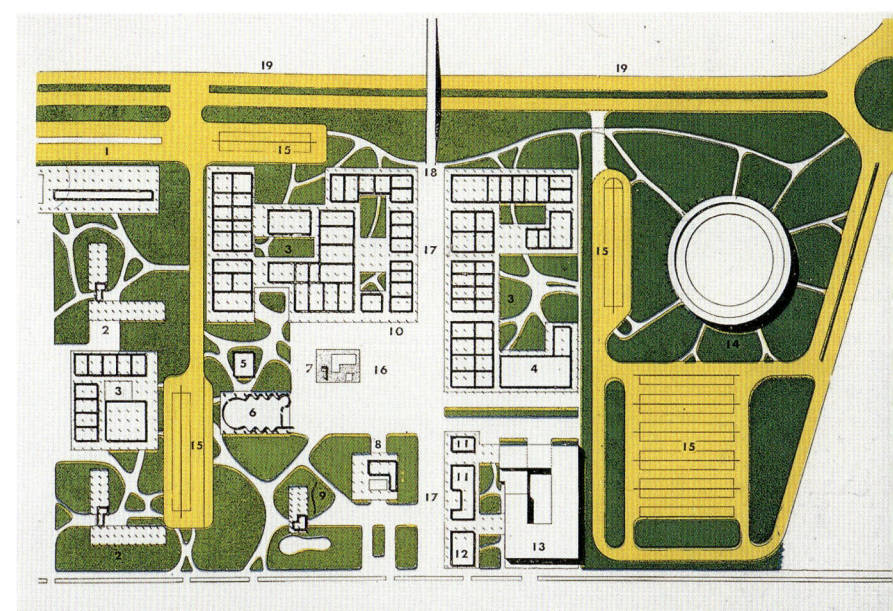

ments. In the empty spaces freed by this combination there were to be green areas and diverse common facilities that would enclose the programme of each neighbourhood unit.

The Civic Centre was located by the sea, and the design of the road system as well as the central park made it seem as if the city were trying to converge on it. The programme for Chimbote was completed by this Centre, whose monumental aspect,[284] resulting not only from the volumetric contrast of its buildings but also from the special shape of some of them, was to become the image of the city. In the Plan report a word cropped up that had been applied before in this context, but which would later become controversial in urbanist vocabulary: 'The Civic Centre is located and designed as the "Heart" of the future Chimbote.' The project, in some ways similar to the one for the Cidade dos Motores, took into account and integrated the Chimu Hotel. It also proposed a main square that aimed to recuperate the traditional *plaza de armas* of colonial cities, and included a bullring and a church, a Town Hall and administrative buildings of different heights set up as glass towers or as one-storey complexes covered by brick vaults that were placed around courtyards, creating what Sert called a 'vegetation tapestry'.[285]

The programme in Chimbote was enriched by elements that draw our attention to the path taken by Sert and Lester to improve the strict zoning of the functional city: there was a cemetery, a market, a hospital and an airport. But once again there was an excess of optimism and confidence in the future of this timid industrialist takeoff, which made the architects dream of offering the city's inhabitants, who were to be essentially working class, amenities more suited to other ambitions. And there was another problem. In the Pilot Plan report, Sert and Lester warned of the need to dispose of the urban land, necessary to carry out the Plan: 'It would facilitate matters if a definitive agreement could be reached with respect to the property titles, which are at present in litigation, persuading many families to exchange their terrains and present dwellings for other sites in the new housing developments that will offer them greater security and more comforts than the ones they have today. This would facilitate the construction of the first sections drawn up in the Pilot Plan.'

Difficulties arose earlier than foreseen when the managers of the Corporación Peruana de Santa were removed from their posts. In a letter from C. Morales, President of the Society of Architects dated 11 July 1949, we read: 'I must inform you, according to the information of a trustworthy source, that in the Ministry of

Public Works the Chimbote project that you have elaborated has been reviewed and considered to be impracticable.'[286] In another letter from Luis Dórich and Carlos Belaunde on 12 September, the news was just as pessimistic: 'The new management has not received from you a direct presentation of the project and knows it less well, and naturally does not feel linked to it by any filial ties.'[287] This was further aggravated by reluctance in paying the architects' bills due to a weakening of the *sole* in relation to the dollar.

Sert and Lester hired the lawyer Celso Pastor to defend their interests in Peru, who informed them on 24 February 1950 that the Plan was undergoing ever greater difficulties: 'The engineer Torres Belón has told me that the reason for not paying your professional fees is not only due to a lack of dollars … but also to the fact that the project you executed does not meet the needs of the Corporation … The Corporation also faces a grave problem, which is the Government's rejection of the Corporation's petition to dispose of the Chimbote lands.'[288] Soon afterwards it became evident that the Plan would never be carried out when a grave obstacle arose for the Corporation 'by virtue of the Decree-Law number 11324, which adjudicates the Municipal Council of Chimbote the property of the urban lands of Chimbote.'[289] This Decree of 14 April 1950, 'obstructs the plans of the Corporation and dismantles the urban projects that you have developed.'[290]

While the process of defending their Chimbote proposal was failing to prosper, Sert and Lester were busy with other concerns and activities that were going on in their office. Since the beginning of 1948 they had been working on a project for the Colombian city of Tumaco, which had been razed to the ground by a fire on 17 October 1947. The first evidence we have of this project is a letter that Lester wrote in Lima to the Colombian architect Jorge Gaitán Cortés on 10 January 1948, followed by a second missive on the 19th, in which he stated that they would be working on the Tumaco project between February and April after having visited Colombia, a visit that Lester feared would be extended, according to a letter sent to a woman by the name of Marian, whom he informed that he had another project in Bo-

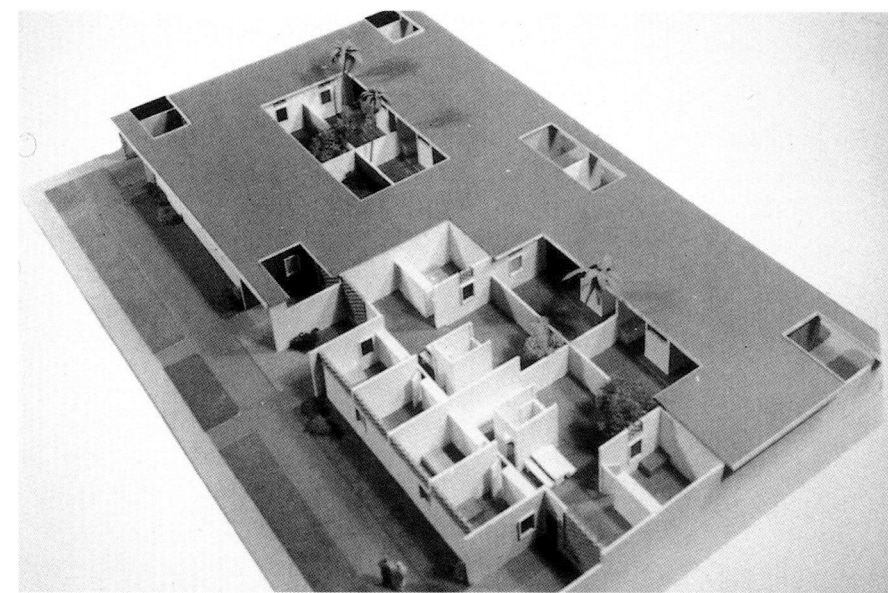

135

gotá, perhaps referring to the Tumaco project or possibly to one in Medellin: 'Another city for the government of Colombia. This will keep me a little longer in South America, but I hope to be in New York no later than 2 June.'[291] The interest in planning had switched to a different country, and it is interesting to analyze the reasons for this change.

Since 1930 and until 1946, the liberal party had been in power in Colombia and had established its particular ideology as a governmental system after a long period of conservative rule. Javier Ocampo summarizes it thus: 'Their interest in social problems is presented as the standard-bearer for all social reforms: workers' legislation, public aid, agrarian reform, protection of workers and farmers, etc.'[292] This liberal party was to rule from the 1929 crash in the US and its unfavourable consequences until the end of World War II in times of agrarian crisis due to the sudden fall in coffee prices. Its protectionist policy was referred to variously as 'national concentration' (1930–34), 'revolution in progress' (1934–38), and 'The Great Pause' (1938–42). The objectives of this policy were to promote the development of local industries so as to do away with any colonial vestiges as well as to protect the internal market, thus creating a nationalist bourgeoisie 'willing to contribute to socio-economic reforms in a country that already shown that it was heading towards modernization', thereby promoting greater distance between the popular masses and the upper and middle classes.

This reform period propitiated this chasm, which was partly hidden by the populism of the liberal leaders, and involved changes in the tributary, constitutional, educational, international and judicial areas, in keeping with the atmosphere that enveloped many Latin American countries during those years. It was also a time of conflict with the native population, especially between labourers and landowners in the great *haciendas* of the Cuca and Santander valley. In this climate, 'a marginalized population with multiple urban problems had sprung up around the four cities of Bogotá, Medellin, Cali and Barranquilla, each with more than 100,000 inhabitants, and had expanded to the outskirts of other cities that were initiating the industrialization process. It was a dissatisfied group due to President López's patchwork reform, suffering from unemployment and misery and increasingly carrying out activities to bring about radical change.'[293]

This situation worsened between 1942 and 1946 as a result of the grave economic world crisis,[294] and as a result of the consequences of the war, which ensured a new 'stability' for the world by putting into gear the Cold War.[295] This process culminated with the return to power of the conservative party in 1945 under Alberto Lleras, and with the elections in 1946, which were won by Mariano Ospina, directly linked with the highest economic circles of industry, coffee production and the large land estates. The conservatives initiated a period of confrontation by breaking previous pacts between the government and labour unions. It was a question of searching for other alternatives in order to exert power with the blessing of the international scene and backed up by the high industrial spheres and the Church. The strikes of the Textiles Montserrate and of the Río Magdalena workers marked the beginning of an escalation of violence that had two climactic moments, coinciding precisely with the increasingly frequent trips to Colombia undergone by Sert and Lester.

The first of these was the assassination of the liberal leader Jorge Eliécer Gaitán on 9 April 1948, and the popular revolt it provoked, leading to the burning of the capital's centre, a circumstance that caused Sert and Lester to postpone the visit to Bogotá stipulated in their Tumaco work contract. Shortly before his death, Gaitán addressed 100,000 people in Bogotá on 7 February, in a heartrending speech that helps us to understand the situation more clearly: 'All that we ask for is that our country stop behaving in such a way as to shame us before our eyes and those of foreigners. We ask this for the sake of charity and civilization … We plead for this persecution on the part of the authorities to cease … Put an end, Mr President, to all this violence. All we are asking is that human life be guaranteed, which is the least a nation can ask for.' The second incident originated in a parliamentary debate on whether Parliament could function during the state of siege following Gaitán's death. The debate became extremely heated and the session of 8 September 1949 ended in the shooting of two of the liberal party representatives. Ospina closed Parliament on 9 November.

Sert and Lester thus found a conflict-ridden climate in their trips to Colombia, a situation that the Catalan architect, in a letter of 30 June 1948, transmitted (with great foresight) to Le Corbusier, from whom he had sought advice on the alarming urban problems suffered by Bogotá: 'We have insisted … that the present situation in Bogotá needs your emergency plan and that the great problems of this city cannot be remedied by a partial and provisional solution. The piecemeal reconstruction of Bogotá will be a catastrophe! … But I have the impression that this reconstruction of the city has become a political affair and the struggle between "liberals" and "conservatives" dominates everything, and the mayor himself hardly has any freedom of action within all this … In all honesty, I do not think they will take any decision aside from that of following their immediate course of action, which mainly consists of street realignment. Within this programme of 45,000,000 pesos, they use up 20,000,000 for expropriating the land necessary for enlarging the streets! … Our work is going slowly.'[296]

On the economic scene, however, things were improving, at least statistically, and only for those benefiting from the process: exports increased, coffee prices went up, and the reserve of funds was notably augmented; between 1945 and 1950 there was a growth in production of 11.5 per cent, which must have pleased the industrial sphere. However, inflation and unemployment rose, further punishing the working classes. This situation provoked a great rural exodus to the cities, which increased at the beginning of the 1950s due to the incipient civil war that the country was facing and the lack of safety in the countryside due to guerrilla activities.

In this climate, ordering the city seemed a difficult but necessary mission, although any notion of rational planning now seemed almost like a joke. At any rate, the fact that the country hailed it as an absolute necessity is witnessed by the editorial of the first issue of *Proa*, a Colombian magazine on urbanism and architecture headed by Carlos Martínez and Jorge Arango, which first appeared in August 1946 when the conservatives came into power: 'This new publication is the contribution of its editors to the study of issues concerning Urbanism and Architecture in Colombia, since our country is also participating, more or less intensely, in the world ills caused by the chaotic and rapid growth of cities … These problems and tasks deserve to be widely studied and known, and for this purpose we have created this magazine. We hope to influence through it the urban and architectural orientation of the country, if we are able to count on the support of our colleagues.' From this declaration onwards, *Proa* was to document the urban problems in Colombia and their possible solutions, publishing the projects that were most relevant to the need for urgent urban planning.[297]

The call for a solution to the situation began with a cry for Le Corbusier's help in the pages of *Proa* in 1946, with an eye to the Brazilian example that we have previously analyzed: 'To hope, to hope that some day, here amongst us, something might happen that seems like a miracle today, but which is not out of this world since it has been accomplished in Brazil, where there exist, both in official organisms as well as among individuals, people who have decided to face forwards and look real architecture in the eye.'[298] The magazine also insisted on the pressing need to explore in depth the idea of planning and its connections to urbanism: 'Thus, planning is, in other terms, the just relationship between official works of public service and the satisfaction of collective needs.' It looked for politically diverse examples from which to learn: 'Planning, as a present-day science, has in its grasp a great number of important accomplishments. Let us look, among others, at the Five-Year Plan of the Russians … We could delve into the plans of Fascist Italy, such as "the Battle of Grain" or the "Swamps of the Agro Pontino" or of the "Electrification of Italy" … We could reproduce the English plans that were carried out in devastated areas … We could summarize the extraordinarily interesting American project and integral planning carried out in the Tennessee Valley.' It also attempted to define the main concerns for a city in any planning process: 'In the last century, the machine as an element of work provoked upheaval in the industries, whose last manifestation was the great concentration of the working masses in certain sectors … Back then they spoke of "garden cities", "linear cities", "worker cities", "hexagonal cities", and then the intervention of architects who presented studies, projects and conceptions that tended to resolve the problems were accepted. That is how another of architecture's legitimate branches, URBANISM, was born.'[299]

In its third issue, of October 1946, the magazine featured an apartment building in Barcelona: none other than the Casa Bloc. We will not ask whether or not Sert was behind this, since his name did not appear in the publication and at this time there is no evidence that he had any contact with Colombia. What is more relevant is that the article accompanying the building was as opportune for the Colombian panorama as it was inaccurate: 'Barcelona managed to become a modern city. There was a will and a desire to carry out the necessary works. Catalans are a people of action. Their city was uncomfortable, congested and dirty. In a short time the authorities had enlarged the circulation routes (*ramblas*) and had provided gardens and promenades: rundown quarters of town were demolished or moved and in their place appeared buildings with sunlit and comfortable apartments. Gardens and flowers blossomed where before there was only vice … We have chosen to taken Barcelona as an example for the study that we will now introduce [an article called 'Bogotá Can Become a Modern City']. Had we been inspired by the meritorious interventions in cities of North, South and Central Europe, we would have been overwhelmed by protests: Horror, Communism! Horror, Nazism! … Horror, Fascism! For those backwards people, there is yet another good excuse. They will answer: when a FOREIGN TECHNICIAN arrives, this or that problem will be analyzed correctly, but in the meantime, why make plans if nothing is going on in Bogotá?'

It is clear that the example of Barcelona was to some extent invented by the dynamic writers of *Proa*, although we are not told whether they found this example in the Macià Plan, free from any shadow of totalitarian policies due to the character of the Second Spanish Republic, an aspect that was viewed favourably in 1946. It is also clear that the Colombian scene had no intention of budging until the technician-redeemer appeared, that figure inscribed in capital letters, that demigod whose genius would be able to solve the problems of the Colombian cities. We cannot, of course, deduce from this text alone why Sert, Lester and Le Corbusier received invitations to work on the planning of Colombian cities, but what is certainly true is the description of the Swiss architect's arrival in Bogotá.[300] It seems that the presence of European town planners was considered absolutely necessary to give impulse to an issue that was having difficulty getting on its feet, and in this sense *Proa* made a decisive contribution with its campaign to put this into action.

The success of this campaign was largely due to a favourable climate for new architecture that had begun in Colombia with the foundation of the School of Architecture in 1936 and the orientation given to it by the architect Carlos Martínez, 'at the time an enthusiastic youth in favour of rationalist ideas, especially Le Corbusier's work, despite his academic training, of an eclectic and historicist nature, which he had acquired in the Beaux Arts School in Paris.'[301] New architecture in Colombia was being taught by young professors who had studied in the United States under the European emigrés who had fled from the war for various reasons. In the words of Germán Téllez: 'But rationalism in its primitive state, in its original European medium, is not the same as this version of it, filtered by the professional and academic North American world. What was taught in Colombia during the 1940s was already an eclectic mixture with interpretations of its own of the European rationalism that arrived via the United States.'

The National University campus, which was called the White City when it was initially projected by the German architects Leopoldo Rother and Erich Lange, and later developed by the former along with the Colombians Alberto Wills, Eusebio Santamaría, José María Cifuentes, Carlos Cristancho and Julio Bonilla (who were in charge of constructing the campus buildings from the end of the 1930s until the beginning of the 1940s), was to be the first coherent operation of what was called modernist architecture in Colombia. The campus was built at around the same time as the building of Nel Rodríguez in Medellin, and the works of Bruno Violi. This was taking place when the country's architectural patrimony was being destroyed, leaving Colombian architecture without a tradition with which to face the new architecture.

One last point is worthy of our attention: since 1942, the Institute of Territorial Credit, originally created to deal with problems of housing and rural amenities, switched strategies to concentrate its actions in the field of urban housing. This new orientation gave rise in Colombia to the first projects for neighbourhood units, which were carried out by a team of architects led by Jorge Gaitán, and which suffered a number of different fates over the course of time. However, this proves that the mechanisms of functional urbanism were already present in Bogotá at the time that Sert and Lester began to visit it.[302]

The city of Tumaco began to be 'officially' planned in the Colombian capital in February of 1948,[303] and we find initial analyses of the urban problems in the reports that Sert and Lester wrote after each of their trips. In the Lester Wiener Archives there are three preliminary sketches in coloured pencils made in Cali in January of that year. In two of these we observe a preliminary approach to the circulation plan,

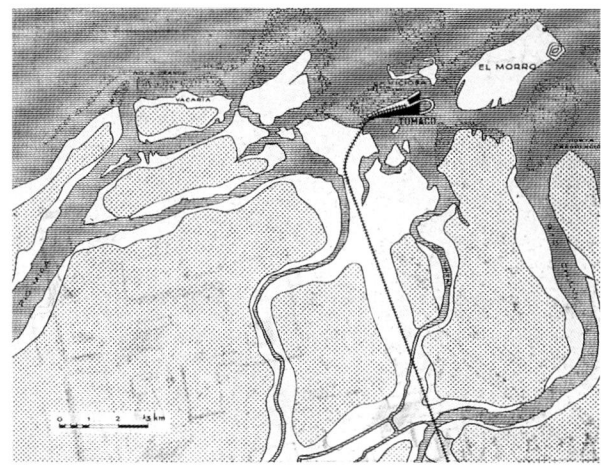

The Tumaco region of Colombia.

with similar schemes to those seen in previous cities, and a first sketch of the Civic Centre, this time intimately linked with the first neighbourhood unit, the only one that was eventually designed. In these drawings we do not see the totality of the Isla del Morro, probably because there was still no global vision of it.

The architects' first trip lasted from 14 February to 1 March, and during this time, after the official presentations had been made, they assembled all the architects designated to the project[304] and flew to Tumaco in a military plane on 21 February,[305] managing to hand in their Pilot Plan model 'a few days after our return to Lima'. The site for the island constituting Morro's new port, the extension of the railway from

Tumaco and the Island of Morro, aerial view.

They worked in what they considered a scientific fashion, looking at the urban phenomenon from the viewpoint of a material analysis of the city, a method that Sert had been employing ever since he had faced the problem of Barcelona. This allowed them to continue saying with pride what they had already pointed out in previous reports: 'This pilot plan is based on the application of the principles laid out in the International Congresses of Modern Architecture – CIAM – in the Athens Charter formulated in 1933, as well as on the guidelines of the last CIAM Congress held in Bridgwater, England, in 1947.'[307] Although the problems were different, the architects continued to respond to them, at least along general lines, in a similar fashion.

TPA (Town Planning Associates), Tumaco Pilot Plan, 1948–49, configuration prior to the fire, and preliminary study (PLWC).

Tumaco, fishermen's houses and the old port.

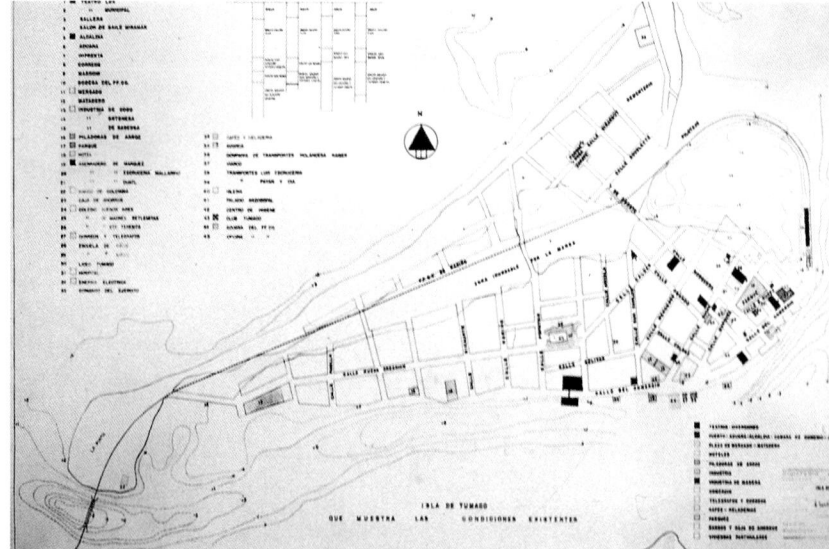

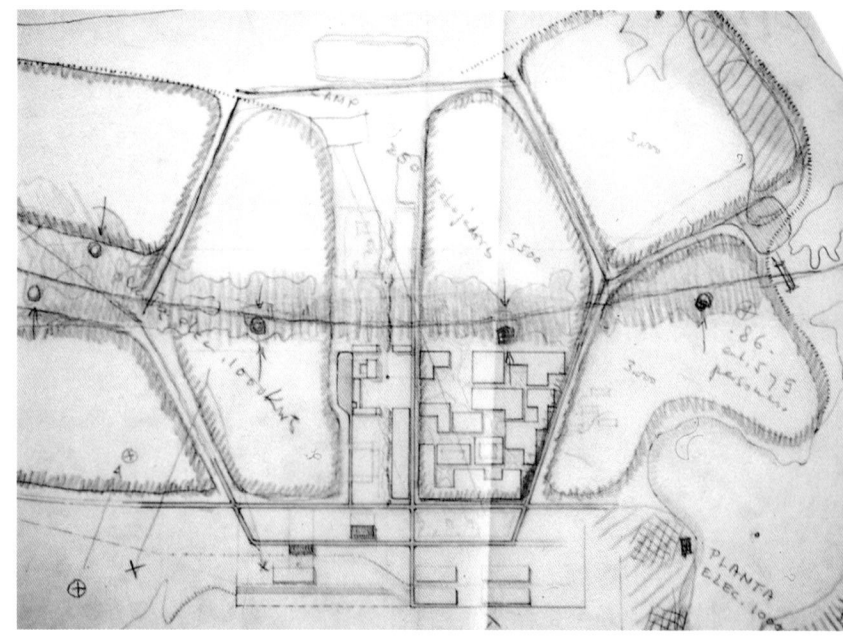

the island of Tumaco, and the site for the airport had all been decided by the time the architects arrived.[306] During their visit, they analyzed geographical, geological and climatological data provided by the National Geological Services of the Ministry of Mines and Oil, the proposal for the reconstruction of the Tumaco port and the construction of the new one in Isla del Morro, as well as studying the functioning of the existing port, the population graphs of the Tumaco municipality and the analytical map of the old city's activities prior to the fire, so as to determine the programme of services for the future city.

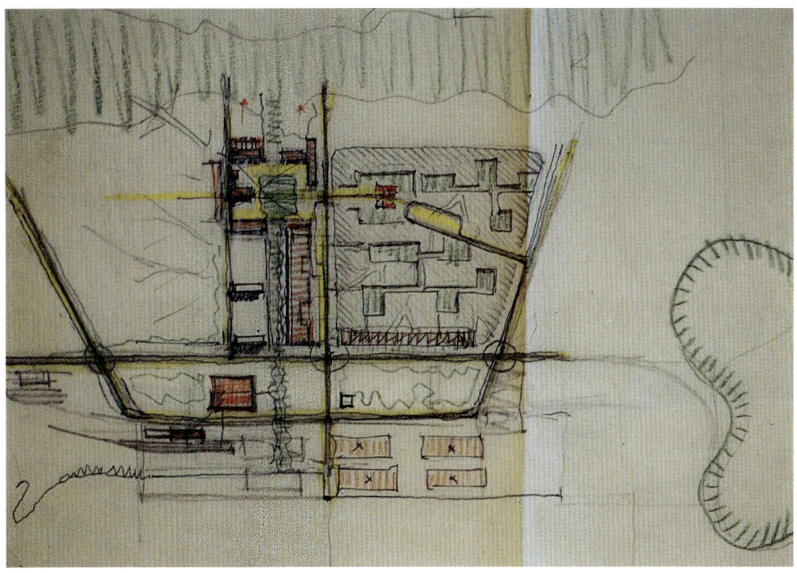

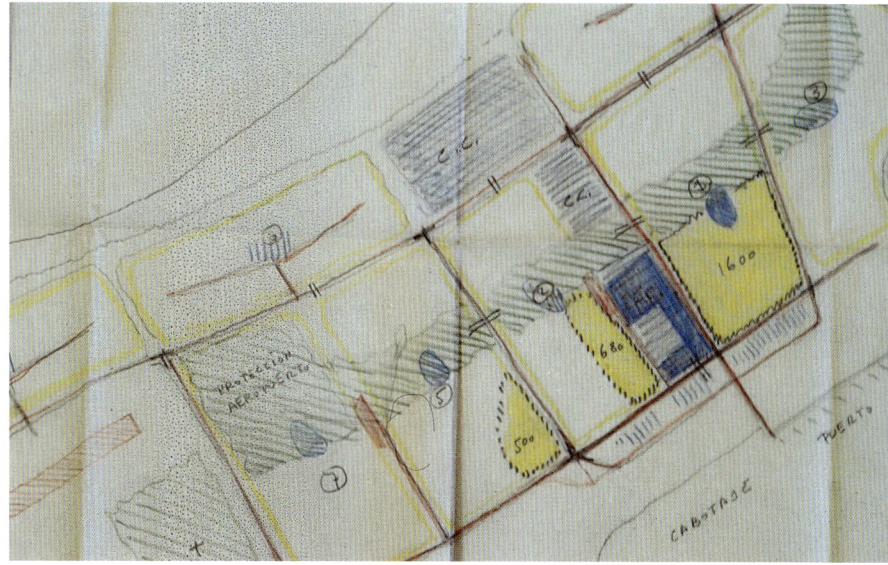

Tumaco Pilot
Plan, initial
scheme
and plans (PLWC).

The result allows us to observe even in the first scale drawings that there was a plan for a road system along with a proposal for a Civic Centre and for the first neighbourhood unit, organized on different systems of grouping dwellings and their amenities. The rest of the neighbourhood units were yet to be determined, although they were taken into account. We can also see how the remainder of the Isla de Morro was occupied by an industrial area and its extension, a military zone, a coastal trade port, a naval base, a layout for the railway and its outbuildings, a landing strip, etc., aspects that the architects would hardly have had the opportunity to carry out.

Despite this, *Proa* enthusiastically acclaimed the proposal, excessively approving the structural and future possibilities 'of the new port as

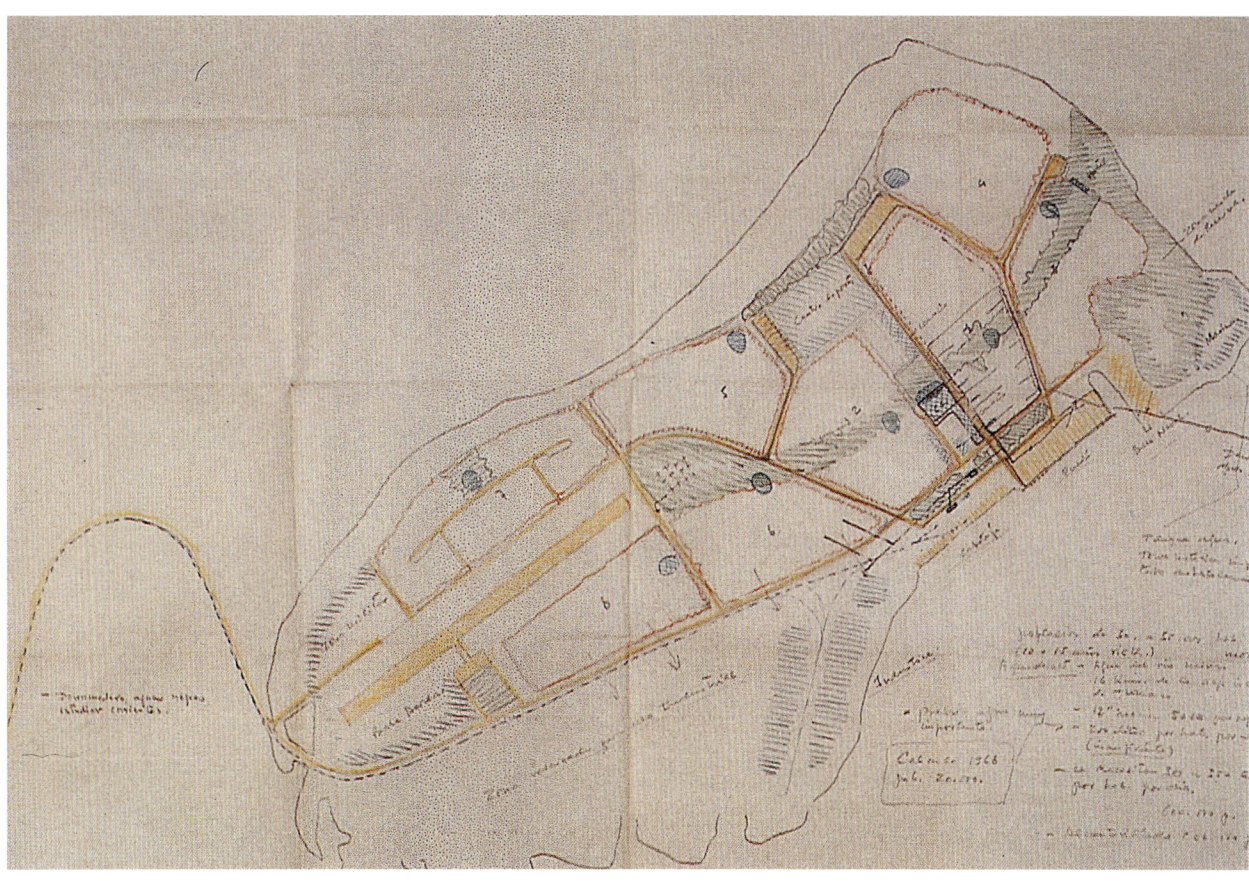

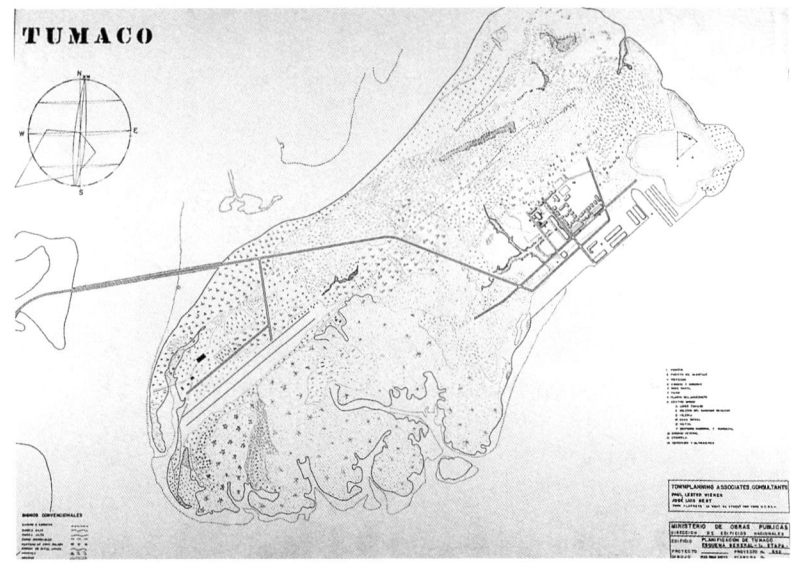

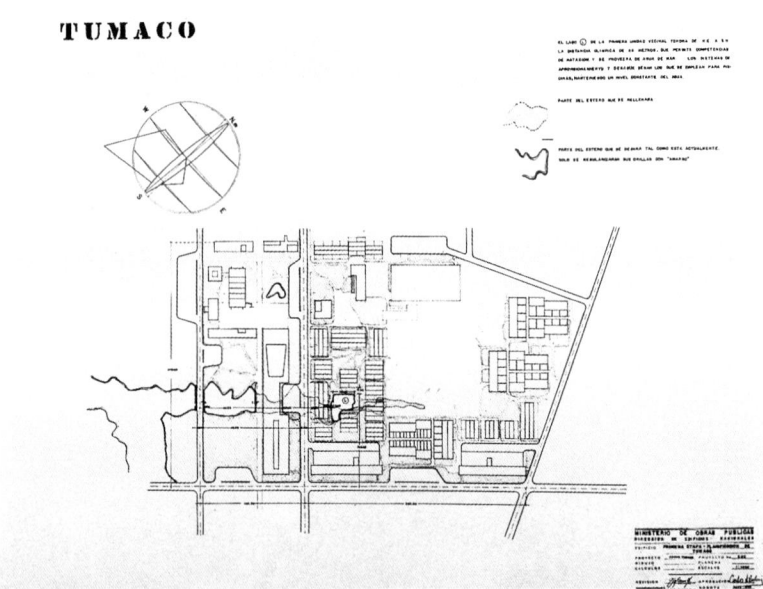

Tumaco Pilot
Plan, overall plan,
urban centre
and Civic Centre
model (SC).

a site of commercial exchange among the region of Nariño and Alto Cauca, the region of Alto Amazonas, the other ports in the country and the rest of the continent … In the very near future the basin of the Alto Amazonas will be an enormous source of wealth … a study of the conditions and possibilities of the matter easily allows one to establish two basic points from which to export products, one to the north of Peru (already under study by the Peruvian authorities) and one to the south of Colombia in the surroundings of the Mira River, which could very well be Tumaco.' *Proa* also pointed out local considerations incorporated in the project: 'In the elaboration of the project, the technical, social and economic aspects were meticulously considered … that is why the result is a plan that is adjusted to dwelling and spiritual needs. The inhabitants of Tumaco will thus be able to exchange their degraded huts without hygienic and aesthetic attributes for agreeable, rational and clean dwellings designed to suit the demands of the climate, the economy and the local customs.'

As might be anticipated, the plan for Tumaco was described in the same words that we saw used in their previous experiences. They again refer to 'the four main functions of urbanism', starting with a description of the residential areas. This time, however, in contrast to what we saw in Brazil or Peru, three types of intervention were considered: neighbourhood units, apportioned residential areas for the sale

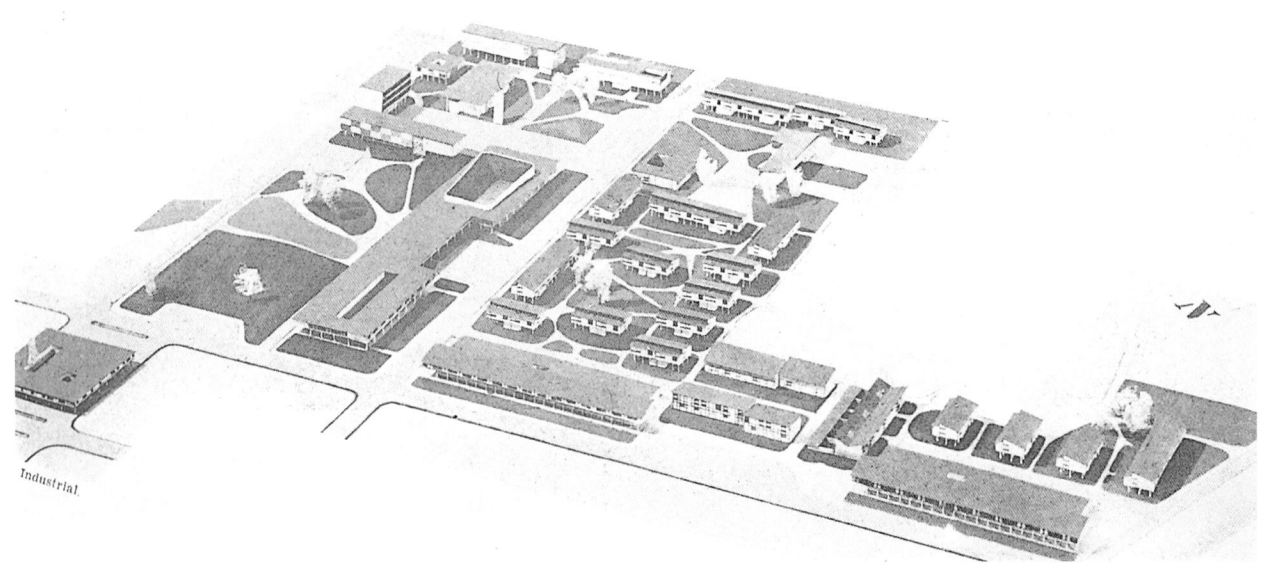

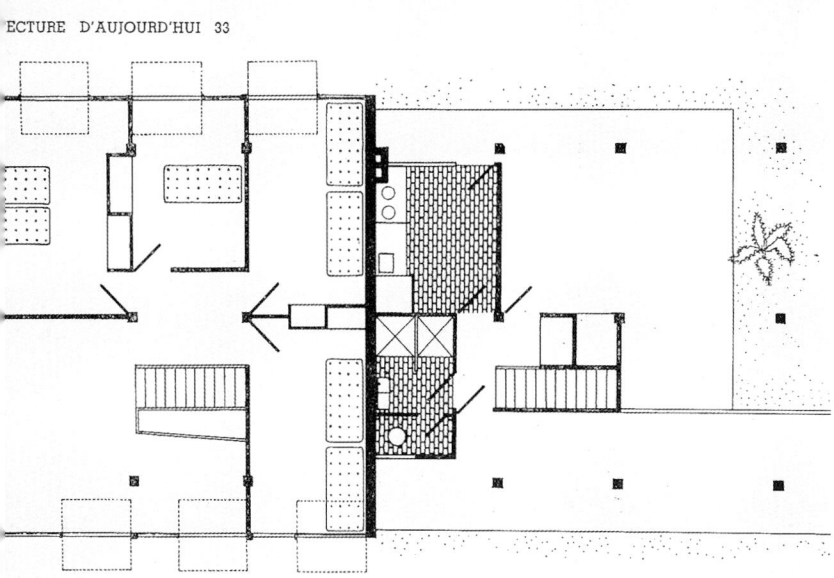

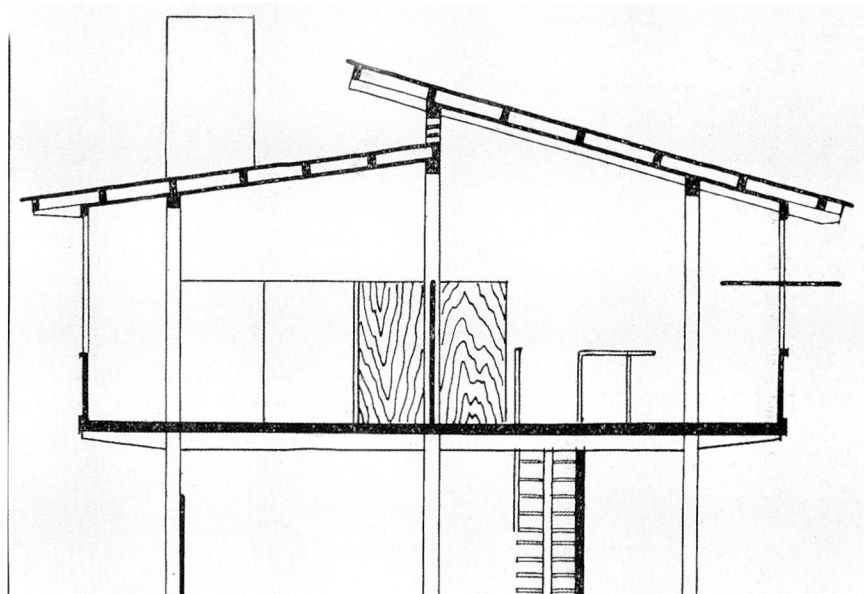

Tumaco,
individual family
house, plan
and section.

of plots, and residential areas for the naval, military and aviation bases.

The areas of work were divided into industrial, commercial, port, market and agricultural districts, and their distribution in the plan located them in the areas closest to where they were most useful, mixing them with other functions where necessary. Thus, for example, in coming up with a site for certain commercial needs, they wrote: 'The commercial activities directly linked to dwellings (a very characteristic and frequent element in the old Tumaco) can be located in the different neighbourhood units, whose access will be through small commercial streets in *cul de sac* … We have planned small lo-

cal markets (of the type found throughout the United States) in the neighbourhood units and residential districts that are farthest from the port.' In the section on recreation, which was defined as a place to cultivate both mind and body, there were health and hygiene services, as well as cultural activities, educational services, nursery and elementary schools, sports fields, a theatre-cinema and meeting places of all types, from cafés and restaurants to billiards and centres of worship, spread out among the neighbourhood units, the Civic Centre and the port area; once again, the supposed rigidity of urban functionalism showed its flexibility. However, there were 'excessive' amenities, an idea con-

Town of Tumaco,
commercial
buildings.

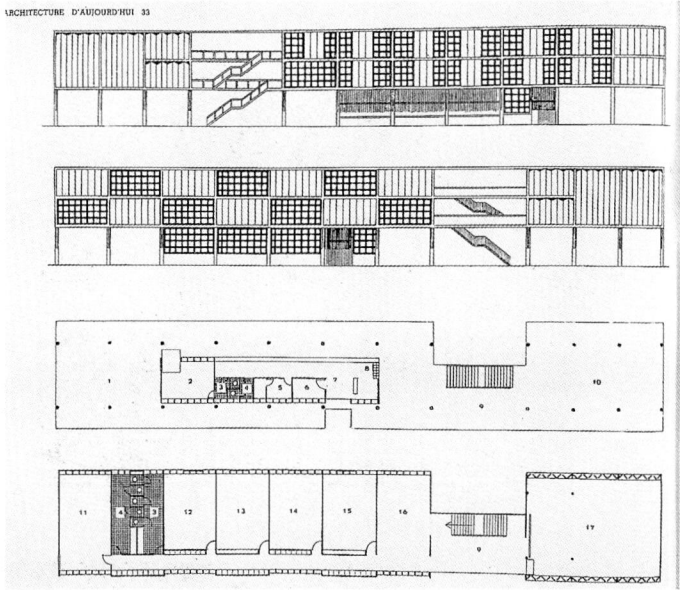

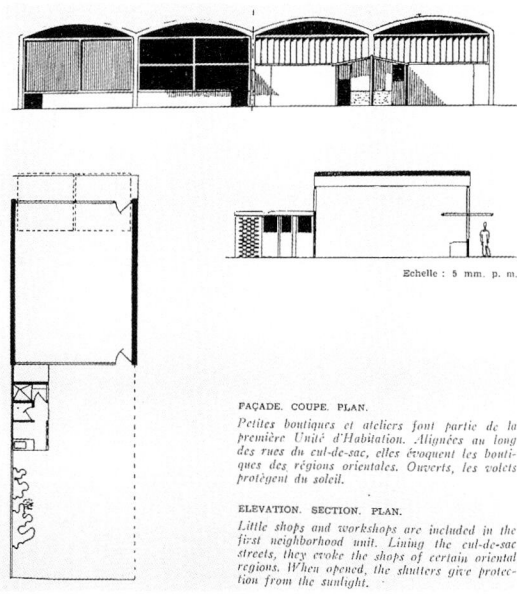

FAÇADE. COUPE. PLAN.
Petites boutiques et ateliers font partie de la première Unité d'Habitation. Alignées au long des rues du cul-de-sac, elles évoquent les boutiques des régions orientales. Ouverts, les volets protègent du soleil.

ELEVATION. SECTION. PLAN.
Little shops and workshops are included in the first neighborhood unit. Lining the cul-de-sac streets, they evoke the shops of certain oriental regions. When opened, the shutters give protection from the sunlight.

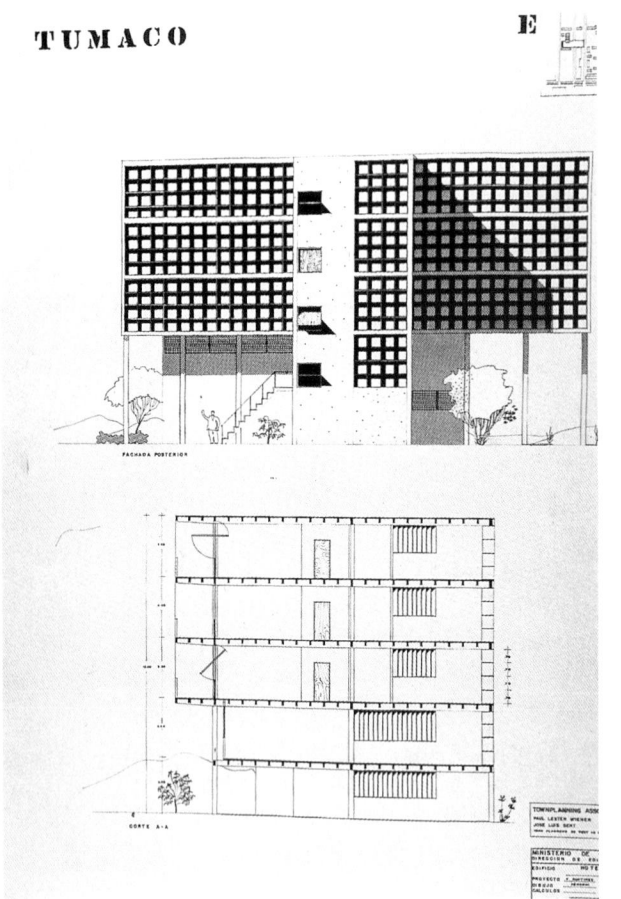

Tumaco, apartment building, elevation and section.

civic and commercial centre: 'In it there will be many important activities of a cultural, recreational, commercial, administrative and religious nature. This centre will constitute the heart of the new city.' In the project, two areas were established: the central square surrounded by public buildings, following the old style of the *plaza de armas*, and another square devoted to commerce, according to the principles applied by American town planners to commercial centres.

Once the report had been written and the first scale maps for building a model had been made, Sert and Lester began to face obstacles in returning to Bogotá between 2 May and 1 June (a trip that complied with their contractual obligations) due to the political circumstances in Colombia mentioned previously. By the time they returned, the people who had formerly been in charge had resigned. Santacruz and Gaitán had been substituted by Jorge Arango and Gonzalo Samper. The second part of their report was written in disquieting terms: 'The Tumaco plan and the work programme were reconsidered due to the changes

stantly defended by Sert and Lester to ensure the correct use of the city, but which made the proposal unfeasible.

Despite this, their faith in the success of the enterprise was unbroken: 'When the population of Tumaco has grown until it occupies the greater part of the Isla del Morro, the Civic Centre and the sports centre will have to be joined, constituting a linear layout of communal services that will go from the beach on the Costa Norte to the port area.'[308]

Circulation was defined in familiar terms, starting with the separation of its objectives into a main highway, avenues, streets, roads, secondary roads and parking areas. It also included bicycle and pedestrian paths, a railway network, a pier, bus services and an airfield.[309] This was all laid out in the plan in such a way as to avoid uncomfortable or dangerous intersections and specifying that it was a 'layout that could be called organic or branch-like to differentiate it from a rigid and inorganic layout based on a grid system.'

The Tumaco Pilot Plan report ended with a description of the area corresponding to the

TUMACO

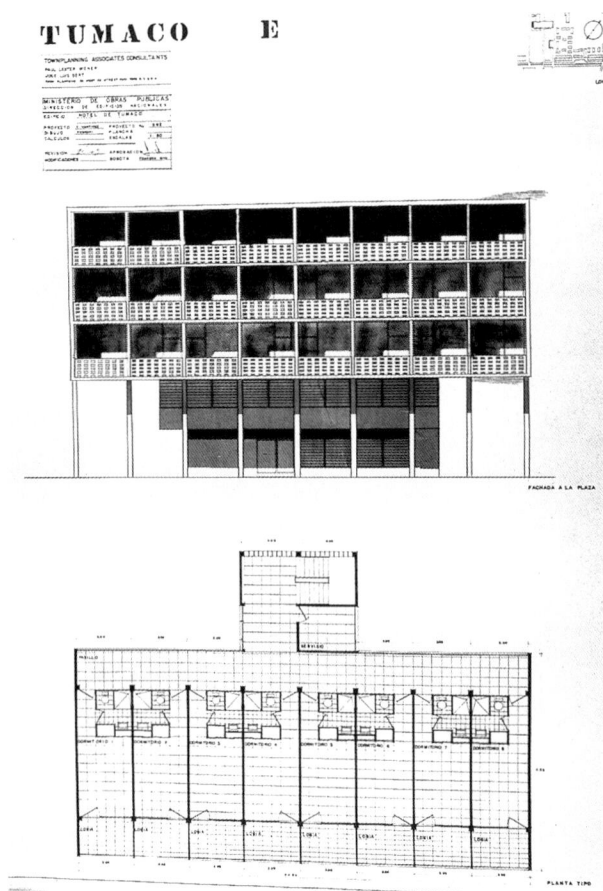

Tumaco, apartment building, elevation and plan (SC).

Tumaco,
perspective
and model
of the church.

put in pivoting wooden windows that facilitated transversal ventilation and protection from the sun, eliminating glass panes and hinges. The common walls were to be of brick or cement to avoid the propagation of fire, in case of future disasters, and the houses were to be covered by asbestos-cement boards, whereas the shops and workshops would have vaulted ceilings, probably of reinforced concrete.[311] Despite certain differences, this proposal was not unlike Chimbote; in Tumaco, due to temporal and financial pressures, it was not possible to study the other neighbourhood units so as to consider the combination of dwelling types and thus continue to offer diverse images, though we do see a reiterated interest in varying the enclosure wall systems.

Some construction phases were then determined with respect to the Civic Centre buildings (of which we have a fairly detailed plan), and the New York architects even drew some sketches of the church, a building of undulating roof and walls derived from the 1942 Oscar Niemeyer's project for the chapel of Saint Francis of Assisi in Pampulha.[312] Before leaving Bogotá, Sert and Lester left a plan for the road and sewer systems, and met with the new construction manager of Tumaco, Carlos Santacruz, who not only showed his agreement with the proposals he received but moreover asked them for a study of other dwellings within the same neighbourhood unit for families with greater purchasing power.

that occurred during our absence. They unanimously decided that, due to time and financial limitations regarding the works, the most convenient thing would be to dedicate the second stage of our trip to the study of an immediate programme for construction.'[310] During this visit, Sert and Lester devoted themselves to examining the proposal for the first neighbourhood unit, the only one they had drawn, along with the Civic Centre. In the definitive version of the new Tumaco, the Civic Centre would cross the island from north-northeast to south-southeast, acting as a central backbone surrounded by dwelling units and having on one extreme the stadium, open to the best beaches on the island and where the greater part of the its residential area would be located; on the other extreme would be the coastal trade port and the railway station.

The housing typologies and their programmes were based on the data obtained by the architects from the Ministry, which indicated the number of individuals in each family, their occupation and their annual salaries. Due to climate conditions, it seemed advisable to

A clause in their contract obliged Sert and Lester to return to Bogotá to work on the Tu-

Tumaco, sketch
of the church
(PLWC).

maco Plan between January and February 1949, and that they did so can be deduced from a letter they sent on 19 January of that year from the Colombian capital: 'We are again in Bogotá having finished the town plan for Chimbote and the Pilot Plan for Lima. Our work here consists of planning the town of Tumaco and the Master Plan for Medellin.'[313] We have no report of this third trip, in which they continued to discuss the Tumaco plan, but nothing seems to have changed much, if we compare *Proa* with what was published in *L'Architecture d'Aujourd'hui* two years later.

It is possible that the interest in the Medellin Plan, on which they had been working since at least May 1948,[314] had by then become the focus of their attention. It is also possible that the full-time involvement of Colombian architects in the Tumaco works, coupled with the status of Sert and Lester as consultants, allowed them to conclude that their contribution was over once the decisions at the last work meeting had been agreed by the local architects. At any rate, in a letter of 5 April 1949 addressed to the engineer Humberto Suito we read: 'We are actually organizing a planning workshop to carry out the plans of Medellin, Cali and Bogotá.' As we see, Tumaco was no longer on the worktable of Town Planning Associates, which due to an excessive demand to take on commissions had been forced to move offices, something we can gather from a letter from Sert to Giedion dated 4 May 1949: 'We have organized a new workshop where we have more space to develop our plans for the Colombian cities. We keep our old office for reception purposes.'

What is certain is that when construction of Tumaco began, it was not under the direct supervision of Sert and Lester. We can deduce this from a series of handwritten pages with photographs in the Sert Collection at Harvard,[315] along with another factor, with which he ended this text: 'The problem of land property is still afoot. The "landowners" of Morro do not wish to reach any agreement, according to their lawyers. Some of them, however, have made similar proposals to that of Márques, trying to make exchanges for a plot on the Snare beach. In my opinion, this would be the best, and I have said so to the lawyers, as long as they submit themselves to the pilot plan and the regulations on construction of the Ministry of Public Works, section Tumaco Plan … This must be resolved quickly because many people not directly affected also want plots of land in Morro. The railway co-operative of Nariño also has ready cash for 100 houses and wishes to build them in Morro, and industrial companies want to buy land in this area to build factories. Among these is a specific proposal from a big factory of products derived from the mangrove tree for tanneries: half a million pesos of initial capital is not a bad deal for Tumaco.'

Thus on the one hand there was the usual confrontation between rational planning and private land property (like in Chimbote), and on the other it seems that there was an initial interest in carrying out the project, with some funds being destined for the reconstruction of Tumaco. This issue was treated with great caution by Carlos Arbeláez in a letter with a Ministry of Public Works seal addressed to TPA and written on 15 September 1949 during a period of extreme violence in Colombia. After reminding them that the construction work was to be financed with the budget of the Railway Funds from the years 1947, 1948 and 1949, he complained that the National Buildings section 'had not received anything corresponding to 1947 and was therefore fearing that by 1950 it would be unable to get the money, so that we would be forced to suspend construction … Moreover, the present minister, who does not know the works because he has been unable to make the trip, does not feel any connection with them, and it seems that he hardly believes in the future of the city. He told me not to ask for anything until the coming year.' However, not everything was as catastrophic as it seemed, since he ended the letter by stating that 'the representatives of Nariño needed to invest the money of their Department, a matter that would solve things, apart from there being some additional financial allotments that could be invested in the works of Tumaco.'[316] The letter concluded with an eloquent: 'From today on I commit myself to informing you regularly about everything that happens, so that our team does not lose contact with either of you.' Nevertheless, it is evident that they did lose contact: there is no more mention of Tumaco in the correspondence received by Sert and

Lester, who continued to visit Colombia but were unable to keep working on the city of the Isla del Morro, another project whose possibilities had fizzled out.

Some pages earlier we mentioned other concerns in which Sert was becoming interested while travelling back and forth to Latin America and promulgating the advantages of the Functional City. Since 1947 he was CIAM President, and as such was one of the top figures in charge of organizing the following Congress, which was held in Bergamo between 23 and 31 July 1949. While the Tumaco project was still on the TPA worktable, Sert was busy managing the development of CIAM 7, a task he had begun as soon as he got back from Bridgwater. He also had some parallel concerns, which emerge in his correspondence during this period.

In a letter to Giedion from 22 October 1947, apart from discovering that Sert even had time for trips of a cultural nature, we read: 'We arrived on Sunday evening from Rome after a wonderful stay in Italy … I have seen Papadaki, Holm and Herman Field and we have talked about CIAM matters … I had a long talk with the Milan group … I talked to them about holding the Congress in Italy … Bergamo seems the right spot and they believe accommodations can be found there and facilities for meetings, etc.'[317] In another letter, of 19 November, he expressed how pleased he was that the French magazine *L'Architecture d'Aujourd'hui* wished to dedicate a monographic issue to the Bridgwater Congress. He was also interested in its publication in Spanish: 'The fact that Bloc also prints a Spanish edition is extremely important. The Latin American groups will be more numerous in the coming congresses and every architect and many government offices in South America are subscribers. I think we cannot continue to consider central Europe as the main field of interest for CIAM … I have written to Gropius on the work of the commission for Architectural Education … We are willing to centralize the secretariat for the American continent here and can have all documents distributed in multiple copies, which will facilitate distribution and reduce expenses. I am in touch with Gropius, Chermayeff and Neutra for the organization of

local groups.'[318] These were the matters with which Sert was concerned while he was preparing the CIAM in Bergamo and which cropped up in his correspondence during this period: to get the Bridgwater CIAM published,[319] to attempt the creation of a genuine group in the United States, and in Latin America. This would help to consolidate the Functional City's possibilities: in the United States, it would combat the opposition they had found, and in South America it would widen their field of work by introducing the architects there to CIAM ideology and inviting them to attend the congresses.

Sert eventually had to accept and agree with Gropius' mistrust and fatigue concerning the possibility of setting up a possible and effective CIAM group in the US;[320] but he seemed hopeful about the possibility of organizing a Latin American group.[321] Moreover, another obstacle had arisen to make matters more difficult: the division of the world into two blocks made it difficult to count on the participation of Poles, Czechs and Hungarians, who had representation in the CIAM Council, and it was likewise very difficult for North American citizens to get a visa that allowed them to visit these countries.[322]

In Bergamo certain issues arose that seemed significant cause for concern. On 22 July 1949, a day before the inaugural session of the Congress, a meeting of Council members was held in the library of the Palazzo della Ragione, a session entirely devoted to bureaucratic problems concerning who could vote and who could not, to the admittance of new groups and the conditions imposed on them, as well as to the drawing up of a list of the delegates pre-

CIAM 7 Manifesto, Bergamo, 1949.

José Luis Sert, Le Corbusier and other architects in Bergamo, 1949.

searches for the means to correct the confusion reigning in the domains of architecture and urbanism, which for the Congress are one and the same thing.'[324] Nevertheless, it was clear that there was an effort to understand these changes. Sert recalled that CIAM meetings prior to the war had dealt with only one subject, whereas now different issues were being laid out and worked on individually by a series of commissions.

The question he asked during this opening session was significant: 'To what extent have we been able to apply the principles of the Athens Charter?' This indicates his determination to put the functional city proposal on trial in different situations through a universal and objective method of analysis: the *grille*, that battle-horse of the Congress.

When speaking about the synthesis of visual arts, Sert expressed an incipient self-criticism: 'The problems of town reconstructions and those of the creation of new civic centres focus the attention and are the object of study of many architects. Modern architects who in their beginnings had studied low-cost houses and hospitals have acknowledged with the passing of years that the principles in which we believe cannot be enframed within the rigid framework of the so-called functional architecture such as it has been interpreted by most people. Spiritual satisfaction is an eternal need that no period, and even less ours, can ignore.'[325] With regard to the education of future architects, he focused on the current situation: 'The education within the framework of official schools of architecture has nothing to do, or in the best of cases, little to do with post-war realities.' After this speech, Le Corbusier's excessive zeal in explaining the *grille*, and his emphasis on the amount of time spent on developing the charts and data for its application seemed to dilute this interest in delving into the new conditions of cities.[326]

The work sessions of the commissions followed this first meeting. In Sub-Commission A of Commission I, presided over by Le Corbusier, who was in charge of applying the *grille* to specific cases, the architects analyzed, among other things, the proposal for the town of Tumaco (despite the fact that in the Congress minutes it was specified that this project had

sent. The principal activity of the Congress was to be the application of the Athens Charter through an analysis of cities based on the *grilles* (grids), which had been developed in France by Le Corbusier and the ASCORAL members,[323] leaving issues of architectural education and the synthesis with the visual arts as secondary matters. This session foreshadowed a Congress that would not contribute many advances to what had been debated in Bridgwater, being mainly concerned with the arrival of more than two hundred architects from all over the world; it would be almost impossible in the future for the architects to meet as a group of friends who could speak about common problems from nearby geographical locations.

In the inaugural session, Sert emphasized the chaos of modern cities resulting from their disorderly and unplanned expansion, comparing this with Bergamo, a city that he considered to be made on a human scale. Despite his failures in Latin America, he was still confident enough to maintain his beliefs. The first part of his speech was more like a sermon than a structured vision of the new challenges that had to be faced in the post-war period, or of the new experience of working in areas of the world that were geographically distant and whose conditions and demands were extremely diverse: 'We as town planners and architects revolt against this state of affairs. The work of the CIAM congresses is the result of this spirit of revolt coupled with a constructive spirit that

Cover,
explanatory grid
and scheme
of application
of *grille*
for CIAM 7.

been presented without the *grille*) and the Chimbote proposal. Both were explained by Sert. The conclusions of this sub-commission reveal a complex development of the programme from the purely outlined grammar of the Athens Charter. The discussions on the cities exhibited served to demonstrate and enumerate, by classification, the extreme irregularity of the functions at work in cities. The

architects pointed this out in their discussions in light of the findings and solutions that others had come up with in the most diverse circumstances and faced with very different problems. This document could now be used as a point of departure when thinking about the city, but it had to develop so as to encompass the complexity and diverse geographical and structural situations that a city might present.[327]

Sub-Commission C, presided over by Sert, was in charge of disseminating the application of the Athens Charter, and its members discussed the mechanisms for presenting urban plans, as well as the order, format and number of maps, the colours to be used and the graphic scale with which to represent them. Once again, it was considered of utmost necessity to establish a prior and common order for all, something that had come up in the CIAMs of Frankfurt and Brussels. Meanwhile, Rogers was in charge of directing the third Commission, which debated the education of architects, a question that did not greatly interest Sert at the time, although, as we will see, he would later make use of various questions debated there, when he became interested in the presence of history within academ-

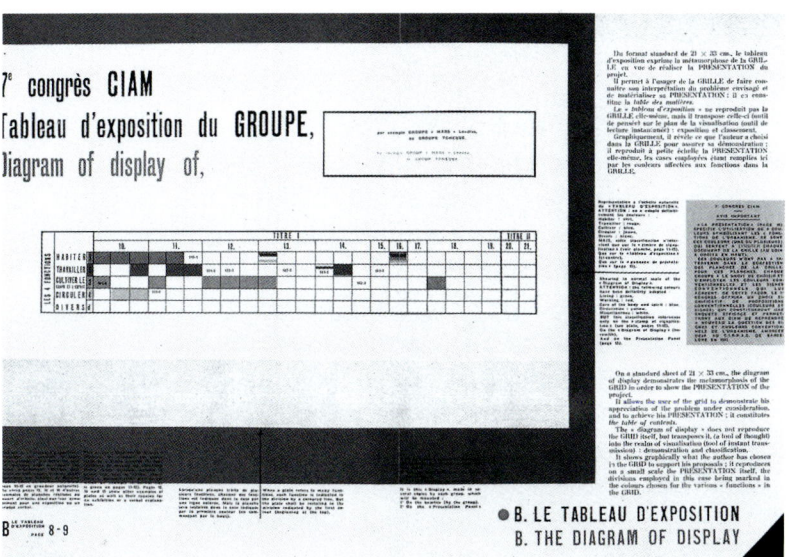

ic courses.[328] History must have been very much on his mind at this time, recalling old ghosts that now, disguised by political opportunism, threatened to make a comeback, and which had to be conjured away.[329] The Congress thus came to an end without having had time to debate any other issues.

On his return to the States, Sert seemed fairly optimistic. In a letter to Gropius dated 8 September 1949, he wrote: 'The Congress went well as a whole, and we had about 200 people. Discussions were very lively, and I think that CIAM has now recovered from the disorganization caused by the war.'[330] Perhaps this moderate happiness in having recovered control of the congresses had to do with the way in which his Latin American planning projects were going, since at that time they were facing a decisive turning point. He was currently in charge of planning the cities that constituted what was called in Colombia the 'Golden Triangle', formed by Medellin, Cali and Bogotá, a sample of cities that had doubled or tripled in population between 1838 and 1951 as a result of the consolidation of industry; this process would become even more accelerated between 1951 and 1964. In the words of Carlos Niño: 'Bogotá and Medellin have been the main economic and industrial centres, and have therefore expanded the most, receiving the greatest quantity of immigrants. Barranquilla has also been another important industrial centre, as well as Cali, especially for the sugar-producing industry … With the consolidation of Cali as an industrial centre, the "Golden Triangle" was formed, with the resulting rise in the importance of its three poles.'[331] In 1938, Bogotá had 332,000 inhabitants, whereas by 1951 it had reached a population of 665,000. In the same period, Medellin grew from 155,000 to 398,000 inhabitants, while Cali underwent spectacular growth from 91,000 to 245,000.

As we have mentioned, Sert and Lester had been working since May 1948 on the Pilot Plan of Medellin, and through a letter from Lester to the Town Council of that city on 5 April 1950, we know that they had been commissioned with the technical consultantship for the development of the Master Plan, 'the term of a year starting from today's date'. In a letter from Jorge Gaitán to Paul Lester dated 12 May, the Colombian architect mentioned the programme to be developed for working on the Cali Plan. In the same letter, Gaitán informed the American architect that he would take care of ensuring that the fees for the first part of the Bogotá contract were paid.[332]

On 20 September 1950, the Pilot Plan for Cali was handed in, and after that we know nothing about its influence on the planning of that city. On 21 April 1951 the architects wrote an eleven-page resumé to summarize the meeting that was held concerning the regulating plan of Bogotá. On 20 June 1951, they wrote a similar report for the city of Medellin.

They worked on the Bogotá proposal at least until 17 February 1953, since we know from a letter addressed to Le Corbusier that they were debating the width of the streets 'to give the finishing touches to the Plan', a work that presumably ended in May of the same year.[333] We lose track of their work for Medellin after 13 June 1952, the date on which Lester wrote a memorandum for this city. In the same folder dedicated to Medellin is an undated handwritten letter from Lester to Sert in which we read: 'I see no chance of moving the Mayor from his position towards us.' There is also an account of the mayor's refusal to give them a new contract. In a letter of 31 March 1953, which Lester sent to Ariel Escobar, we read that the Medellin Plan was no longer in their hands.

Thus, between 1948 and 1953, Sert and Lester had worked intensely on the plans for the three Colombian cities, at a time when a right-wing shift in politics was turning the country into a para-Fascist dictatorship, wholly under the power of the United States.[334] Considering the situation, it seems unnecessary to examine these proposals at any length, except to point out that the projected mechanisms announced for the cities are similar to those seen in previous projects, aside from natural differences derived from the geographical and urban context of each case. The cities in question already existed and had consolidated urban structures despite the precarious conditions they faced, and therefore the objective was to avoid the uncontrolled expansion they had been undergoing, and to assign different uses to some existing urban centres.[335]

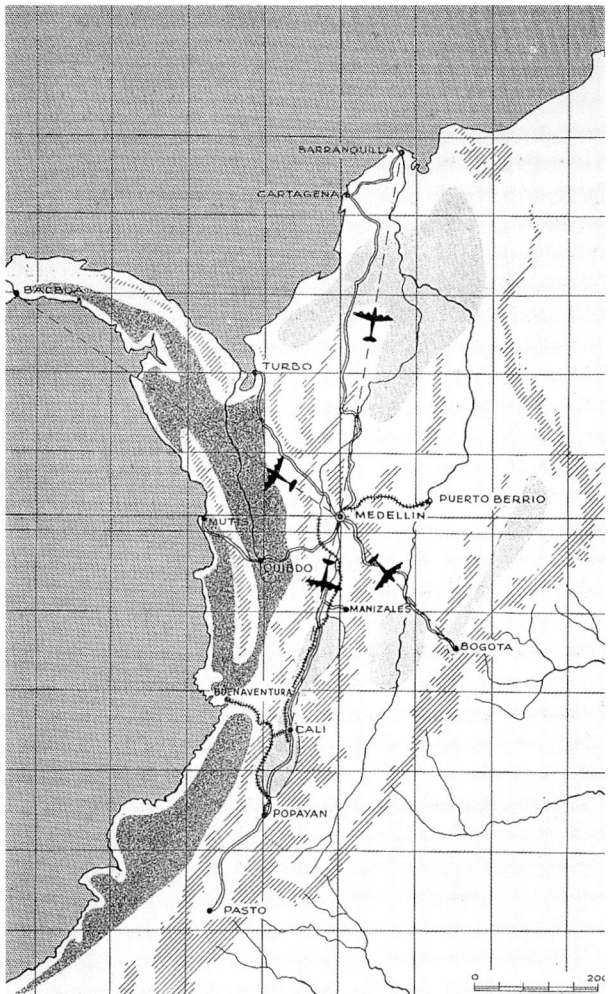

Geographical map of Medellin, Colombia.

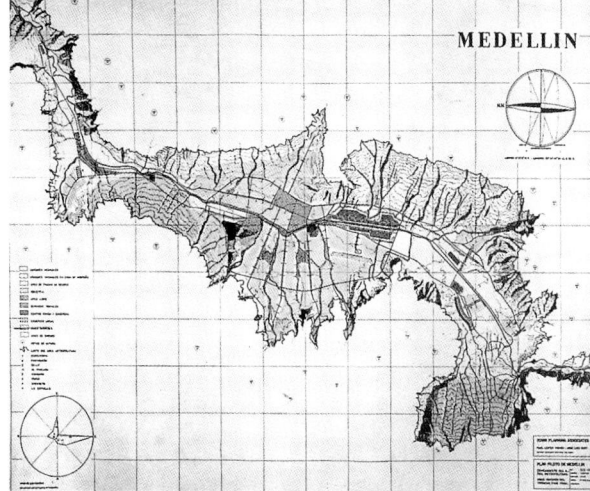

TPA (Town Planning Associates), Le Corbusier, Pilot Plan of Medellin, 1948–52, sketch of the plan.

Medellin Pilot Plan, overall plan (SC).

In Medellin, a city with a limiting topography due to its location in a valley surrounded by mountains, the idea was to control the flow of the river and its tributaries, and thus gain vast extensions of land necessary for urban expansion. This would facilitate the functional delimitation of areas, and would enable a correct treatment of the disorganized location of industries, as well as the design of a transport network with a great access road that would follow the river course and would become the main axis of the whole network. The neighbourhood-unit strategy was again employed, some of these units being placed on hills and others in the flatlands, their limits being defined by a main road. They had all the green public spaces and services of the other projects, being designed in order to offer variety, a well-known characteristic element. There was a Civic Centre with a programme similar to the previous ones, and its design took into account the relocation of the railway station and the

market. It was situated on a strategic intersection, thus enlarging the centre of the city, to which it would be linked by commercial streets that would converge in a public square where Sert and Lester meant to place a great church that would be a replica of the cathedral erected at the other end of the Avenida Junin.

The thirty pages that make up the Cali Pilot Plan report also contain information about the serious problems the city was experiencing

Medellin, Civic Centre (SC).

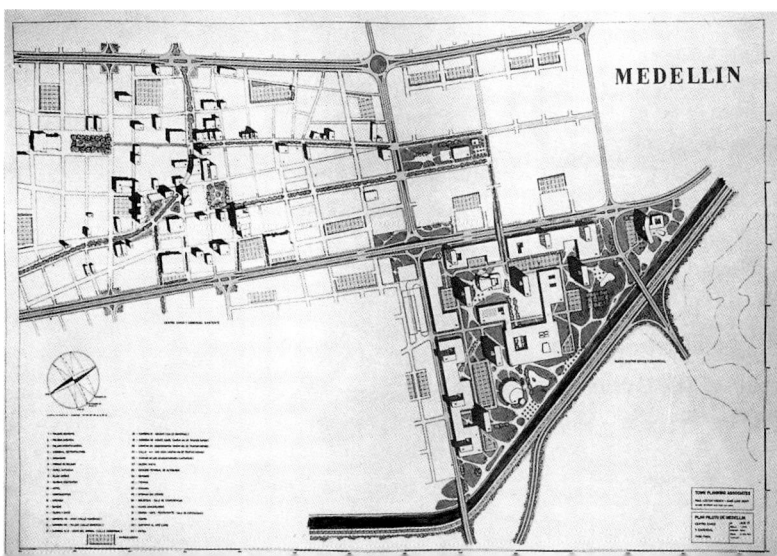

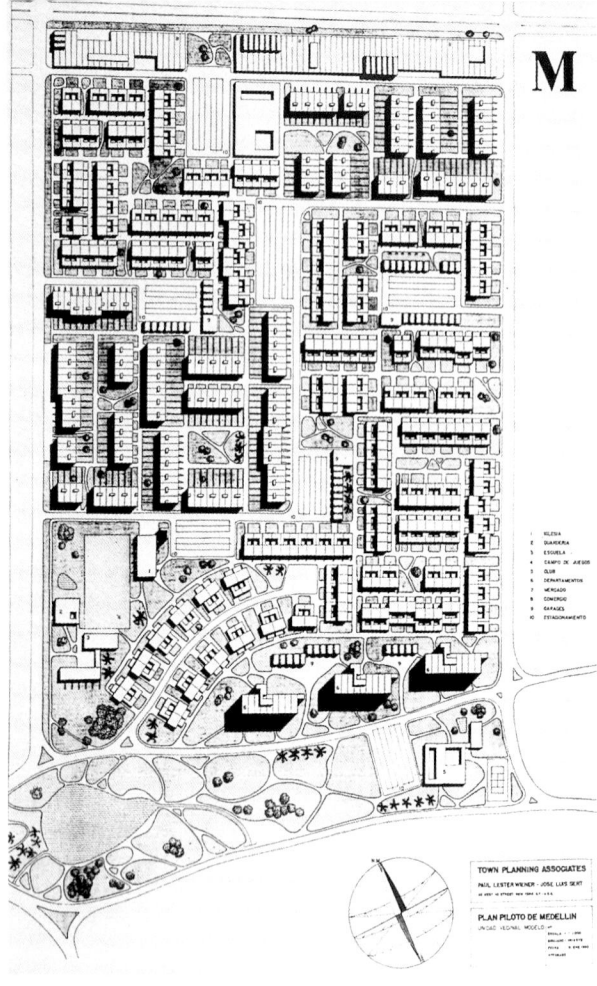

Medellin,
residential area.

isting location of the railway station and its outbuildings, and it was to grow along what they called the Valley Highway, which would go from north to south and would be separated from the neighbourhood units by a wide green belt.

Before entering the city, the highway was to head towards the Cauca River; in this meeting point between the highway and the existing urban grid, the Civic Centre of Cali would be situated. There was also to be a beltway avenue that would start out from the north end of the highway and would converge in the Civic Centre, crossing it. The neighbourhood units, which were not designed but whose extension was marked so as to be able to lay out the road system, were to be distributed between these two roads. Once again, faced by an expansion in which 'industry and housing are mixed in perfect disorder on both sides of the railroad tracks … the commercial area is badly defined … schools and other social centres are not adequately set up to meet the needs of the areas they are to serve … the city has grown without harmony and order', they insisted that 'the only way to correct this state of things is by establishing a zoning plan, giving each sector of urban territory the use that corresponds to it within the ensemble.'[336]

The intervention in the Bogotá Plan allowed the TPA associates to meet with Le Corbusier, who visited the Colombian capital a second time between 2 and 30 March 1949.[337] They worked together with the Colombian ar-

due to constant floods from the Cauca River, therefore prompting the proposal of an urban expansion towards high areas to avoid this problem, as well as proposing a sewage system for waste water. To do so, 'it was advisable to give Cali a Linear City shape instead of the radial one that the city would adopt if it expanded towards the Cauca River.' This linear expansion was proposed in opposition to the ex-

Medellin, aerial
view, buildings.

chitect Herbert Ritter on this project in France from the beginning of August 1949 until the 23rd of that month, once the Bergamo CIAM had come to an end. The stages and responsibilities for the Regulating Plan of Bogotá were established by that time. Sert and Lester were to work as consultants at the information stage, which would be carried out by the Office of the Regulating Plan of Bogotá (OPRB). The basic scheme would be executed in Cap Martin with Ritter, the director of the OPRB. Le Corbusier would develop the Master Plan in Paris until August 1950 with Lester, Ritter and Sert as consultants. This explains Le Corbusier's two visits to Bogotá, the first from 16 February to 8 March 1950, and the second from the beginning of September until 30 October of the same year. In his first visit he met up with Sert, and in the second with both TPA architects. The Regulating Plan was the responsibility of Sert and Lester, who were to develop and discuss it with the OPRB in two meetings in Bogotá, one in February 1951 and the other in February 1952.

This was stipulated in the contracts consulted, but there is in any case no doubt that Lester and Sert made constant trips to Bogotá, as can be gathered from correspondence in the Lester Wiener Archives and in Le Corbusier Foundation's, a fact that alters the 'official' chronology of these visits. On 9 April 1951, Sert wrote to Jacqueline Tyrwith: 'We are working very hard these days on the Bogotá plans. The pilot plan has been officially approved and the necessary legislation passed.' From 10 May 1951, Le Corbusier, Lester and Sert were in Bogotá to write the 'Resumé of Meetings held in Bogotá from 11 May 1951', which consisted of eleven typewritten pages indicating the general guidelines from which to develop the regulating plan.[338] On 2 March 1952, Sert wrote an optimistic letter to Lester in which he foresaw the possibility that the Plan would prosper: 'Work in Bogotá is good; the boys and the Mayor seem satisfied. Had an interesting conference with Dr Trujillo last week and will see him again tomorrow. Established first-phase plan for roads, markets, free areas, industry, Quiroga houses.' Shortly afterwards, however, things took a turn for the worse, especially because in Sert's opinion the Bogotá offices did not know how to develop a master plan. These conflicts increased between May and June of that year. In a letter of 10 March, Sert wrote to his associate that interest in developing the Plan was waning, and in another undated letter from Lester to Sert we read: 'I will try to conclude the matter as best as I can.' The remaining data that allow us to establish the chronology of the Plan have already been mentioned.

The Bogotá Plan developed on a different

TPA (Town Planning Associates), Le Corbusier, H. Ritter, Bogotá Pilot Plan, 1949–53, overall plan and in-depth study of a residential area.

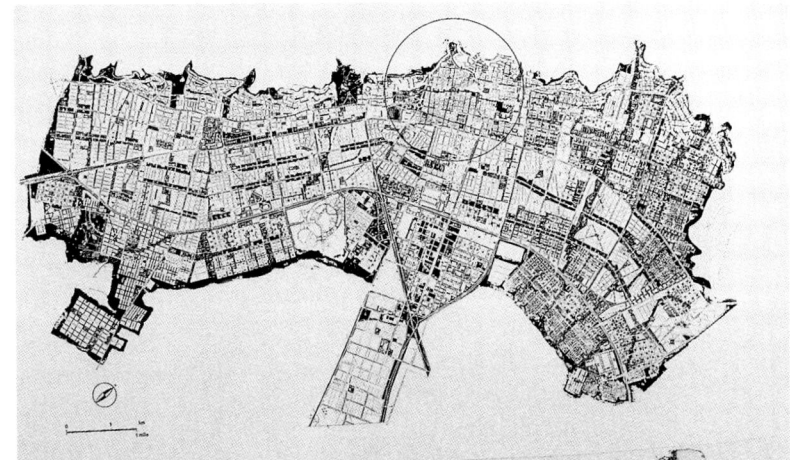

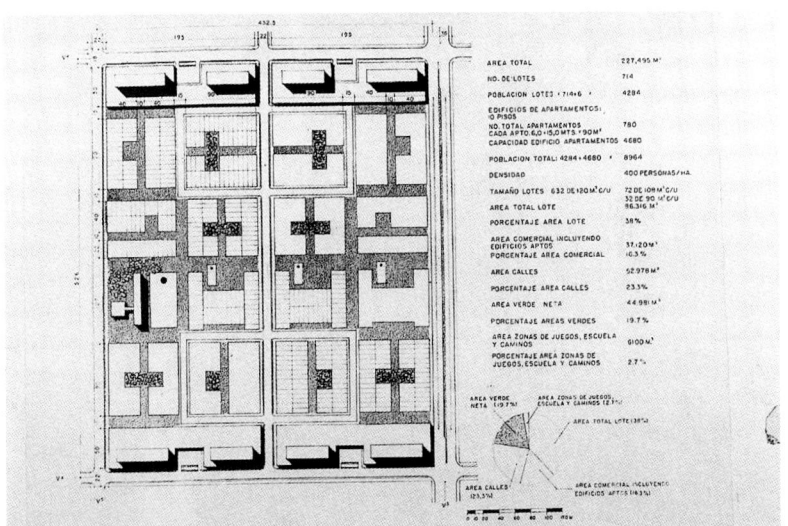

scale the functional city ideas that Lester and Sert had put into practice in other cities that already had a consolidated urban structure. They limited the expansion of the city towards the west, and divided its plan into thirty-five urban sectors of greater capacity than the previous neighbourhood units, since each was to house from 25,000 to 75,000 inhabitants. These sectors were determined by the localization of the main road networks of the structural traffic

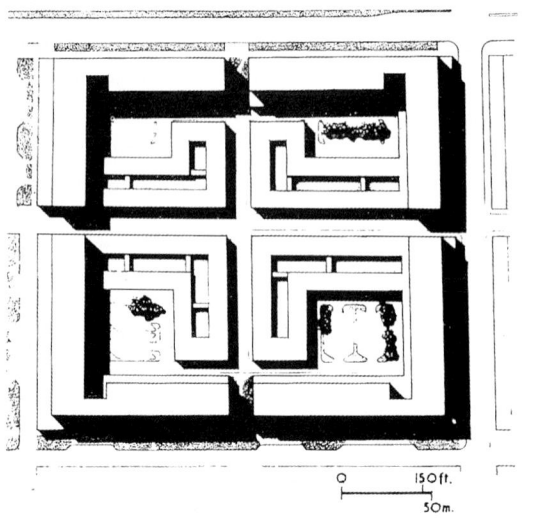

routes, which were modified according to the Corbusian system of seven-road classification ('Règles des 7V'), adapted to the functional needs of each sector. It was necessary to intervene in each of these sectors to ensure their drainage, and in order to equip them with services, nonexistent until then; by invading and redeveloping the blocks of the colonial period they offered variations of dwelling systems, both in high-rise buildings and in compounds of low-rise residential buildings surrounded by ample green areas, which were the equivalent of large interior courtyards or acted as green belts.

The urban centre was divided into three areas: that which contained the political and religious centres, located on Plaza Bolívar, which conserved the Cathedral and the Parliament and where they proposed a Palace of Justice, a new Town Hall and the Presidential Palace jointly with a Ministries building; the area that was to hold the business centre, with medium-sized arcaded squares flanked by new buildings; and the district that would offer the cultural and touristic centre, with free-standing buildings dispersed across a vast park. Linked together, these areas attempted to revive the idea of a promenade that we have seen in other projects, but on a scale of a city of 750,000 inhabitants, which was growing too quickly.

Sert and Lester soon received criticisms of their Colombian projects. In a letter from Jorge Gaitán to Lester dated 4 January 1949, we learn of a press campaign against the plans of TPA and Le Corbusier.[339] Not everyone was congratulatory regarding the possibilities of the functionalist town planning developed in Latin America, an urbanism that was also criticized at CIAM 8 when it was held a few months later. The criticisms they received are still voiced today: 'When Sert and Wiener handed in the regulating plans of Bogotá and Medellin in 1952, a heated debate sprang up: the lack of knowledge they showed concerning the physical, social and even topographical realities of these Colombian cities made it evident that "long-distance" plans by international experts, no matter how well-known they are, are not the most adequate for solving the urgent urban problems of Colombia.'[340]

In reference to the Tumaco project, Carlos Niño has written: 'Today, following criticism voiced against CIAM's town plans, we can see that the Plan did not have well-defined or well-shaped spaces, that it did not create streets or squares with any adornment, and that monuments were concentrated in the centre while the rest became a dormitory-suburb. That was its planning. Today we know from experience that many CIAM principles were too abstract and incorrect: zoning became desolate and anti-urban … The reduction of urban complexity to its mere four functions seems simplistic.'[341]

The lack of in-depth knowledge of the problems and the excessive abstraction of the proposals are criticisms that can be applied to the idealism of functional urbanism. For the economies that aspired to gain rapid profits from almost nonexistent investments, and from governments shamelessly bound to capital, Colombian cities, with their uncontrolled growth, were

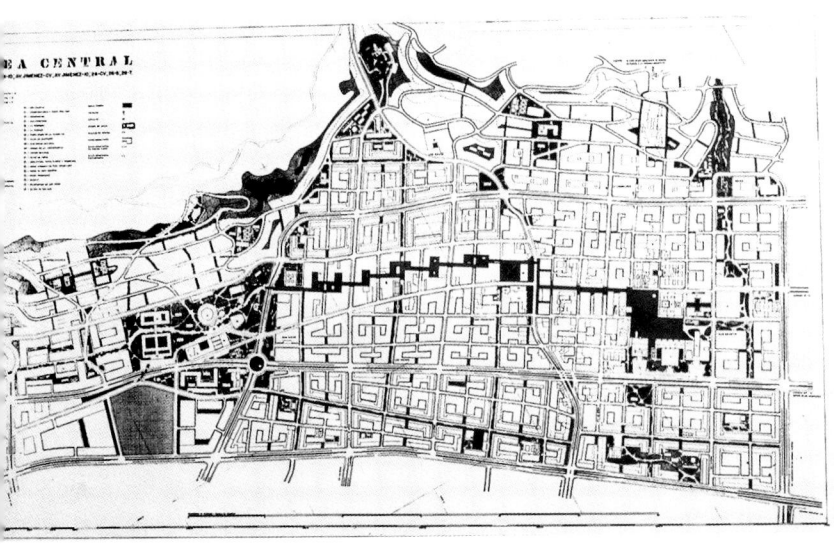

Pilot Plan
of Bogotá,
modification
of the central
sector (SC).

Thus, controlling urban expansion, offering housing at walking distance from work, thereby lowering transport costs, monitoring conditions at work, thinking of services and amenities that would make life more liveable, imagining good hygienic conditions, offering possibilities to enjoy leisure time, etc., pertained to an ideology that was impossible at a time of crazed capitalist industrial expansion and exploitation of the labour force.

The TPA architects were still convinced that they could contribute with their new urban ideology to improve life in the cities, just as Sert had attempted to do in Barcelona. Their hopes and naivety (or arrogance) made them forget the difficulties encompassing these projects and the ruthless enemies they would have to face. Although some crucial aspects of their theses reveal certain flaws or gaps, however, to criticize their town planning on the sole basis of the terms used above seems unacceptably limiting.

the ideal place for the failure of any provision that did not respect the following conditions: the over-exploitation, the underground economy, and the illegal occupation of terrains. These were the rules of the game of urban survival that denied planning any possibility of succeeding.

[233] Paul Lester Wiener Collection (PLWC), Incoming Correspondence, box 14, Correspondence with US Department of State. Shortly before this date, on 9 December 1940, Sert wrote a letter to Le Corbusier in which he commented on the possibility of working in Latin America: 'I am making plans to go to South America; friends down there tell me there is great activity in construction and we have the opportunity to succeed in forming a group of young architects.' FLC R3 O3 183.
[234] PLWC, Outgoing Correspondence. We mention only two details that give us an idea of the USA's interest in being present in Latin America during the 1940s. During the 1939–40 school term, the Boston University School of Law offered a new course with a title that speaks for itself: 'Commercial Law of Latin America', directed by professor Charles P. Sherman. In Henry Wallace's speech on 12 September 1946, we find: 'We should welcome the opportunity to help along the most rapid possible industrialization in Latin America, China, India and the Near East. For as the productivity of these people increases, our exports will increase.' See R. James Andrews and David Zarefsky, Contemporary American Voices, Longman, New York, 1992, p. 3.
Even on 21 March 1945, Lawrence H. Levy, General Council Co-ordinator of Inter-American Affairs, wrote to Lester: 'This will confirm our understanding that you will make a lecture tour of approximately three months' duration of certain of the other American Republics including Peru and Brazil ... This Office will pay you $500 upon the submission of your report, payment to be made upon a public voucher prepared for you.' PLWC, US Department of State. This invitation was repeated on 30 June 1955, in which he was offered $700 monthly to give lectures on Architecture and Urban Planning in South America. On 6 June 1956, the Department of State congratulated him on the favourable comments that his lectures had received.

[235] Le Corbusier had visited Brazil on previous occasions, so that the Brazilian architectural intelligentsia must have been updated about his recent production of modern architecture. To better understand the circumstances of this trip, see Roberto Cavalcanti, Le Corbusier, la France et le Brésil: influences réciproques, in Le Corbusier: Europe et la Modernité, Editions Corvina, Budapest, 1991, pp. 106–9.
[236] PLWC Outgoing Correspondence, letter to Trueblood, 29 July 1941. Previously, on 7 May of the same year, Lester had sent a letter to Sert in which he told him that the contract was only in his name, although despite this: 'We share the benefits and obligations under this contract equally.'
[237] Paul Lester received various letters of invitation from diverse Brazilian Schools of Fine Arts and Universities, which are found in his archives among the correspondence from the 1940s and 1950s. He even gave a course on Urban Planning at Columbia University in 1965–66.
[238] Letter from Walter Gropius to Paul Lester of 25 April 1944, PLWC. The ex-director of the Bauhaus spoke of his interest in hearing them talk about their experiences in Latin America in a CIAM meeting that they were preparing for May. In this letter Gropius mentioned not only Brazil but also Peru.
[239] PLWC Box 4, Cidade dos Motores folder, Contracts.
[240] In the PLWC are the receipts for the payments to TPA for their work on the Cidade dos Motores project. Oswaldo Bittencout Sampaio, Director of the Brazilian Government Aeroplane Factory Commission, paid $6,000 on 26 September 1945, and the same sum on 2 November of that year, as well as paying $6,000 on 23 April 1946, all of which corresponded to an 'agreement in official letter no. 828', dated 29 May 1945, presumably the date of the official contract.
[241] FLC R3 O3 186: 'Last summer we were

commissioned to design a plan for a new town in Brazil. It is a city for 24,000 inhabitants near the new aviation factories. The preliminary design was well received down there, and we are speaking about developing the first phase. Wiener has gone to Brazil to settle these questions.'
[242] Raimundo Faoro, Os donos do poder, Ed. Globo, 1973, p. 722.
[243] Ibid., p. 721.
[244] Ibid., p. 722. To put the economic plans of Getulio Vargas within their historical context, see Nelson Werneck Sodre, Formaçao histórica do Brasil, Ed. Bertrand, Brazil, 1987, pp. 315–93.
[245] Amélia María De Oliveira Reynaldo, A especificidade da industrializaçao e da formaçao do Estado nacional no Brasil, typewritten text, 1990, p. 24.
[246] Sigrid De Lima, 'Brazil Builds a New City', in The American Journal of Economics and Sociology, pp. 337–38.
[247] From a speech by Getulio Vargas extracted from Nabil Georges Bonduki, Origens de Habitaçao Social no Brasil, 1930–1954, typewritten Ph.D. thesis, School of Architecture and Urbanism of Sao Paulo University, 1994, p. 194.
[248] Ibid., p. 195.
[249] Ibid., p. 231.
[250] Atilío Correia Lima, Parecer sobre o plano de cidade operaia de FNM (24 August 1943), in Arquitetura, no. 4, August 1963.
[251] Bonduki, op. cit., p. 233.
[252] Letter from Paul Lester to Oscar Niemeyer on 18 November 1942, telling him he will send him Sert's Can Our Cities Survive?, which had just been published. He also mentioned the work he was carrying out with his associate, which at the time was known as the Ratio Structure project.
[253] The most significant work for a basic understanding of how new architecture was introduced in Brazil is Yves Bruard, Arquitetura contemporânea no Brasil, 2nd edition, Ed. Perspectiva, 1991. For a closer examination of this phenomenon during the years of which we are

speaking see José Artur d'Alo Frota, *El vuelo del Fénix. La aventura de una idea: el movimiento moderno en tierras brasileñas*, unpublished Ph.D. thesis, ETSAB, 1997.

[254] The exhibition of Brazilian architecture at MoMA, New York, in 1943.

[255] The letter from Lester to Neutra of 21 September 1945 is plain: 'I suggested that CIAM may be interested in holding its next Congress in Brazil.'

[256] Quoted in Bonduki, op. cit., p. 239.

[257] Eric Mumford, 'CIAM and Latin America', in *Sert, arquitecte a Nova York*, MACBA, Barcelona, 1997, pp. 48–75. A more generalized survey of rationalist urbanism in relation to the CIAM congresses and to some specific interventions can be found in Eric Mumford, 'CIAM Urbanism after the Athens Charter', in *Planning Perspectives*, no. 7, 1992, pp. 391–417. In a monograph on Le Corbusier, edited by Stamos Papadaki, we find an article by Sert under the title 'From Architecture to City Planning', pp. 81–113. In this article, accompanied by a large number of illustrations, Sert showed that he was familiar with all the town-planning projects of the Swiss architect. See *Le Corbusier: Architect, Painter, Writer*, Macmillan Company, New York, 1948.

[258] José Luis Sert, 'The Human Scale in City Planning', in Paul Zucker, *New Architecture and City Planning*, Philosophical Library, New York, 1944, pp. 392–414. Sert would later insist on this relationship in two more essays: 'The Human Scale: Key to the Measure of Cities', 23 April 1957, typewritten text in the Sert Collection, D17; 'The Neighbourhood Unit: A Human Measure in City Planning', undated typewritten text. This is a report for the 'Housing and Town and Country Planning Section, Department of Social Affairs, United Nations', which Sert signed as Dean of the GSD of Harvard (thus it must have been written in 1953). Sert Collection, D100. In some texts that were to be read at conferences we also find references to this subject: 'The Human Factor in Architecture and Urbanism' for the Boston Society of Architects, 12 May 1953, and 'The Human Factor in Urban Design' for the Detroit Institute of Arts, 5 March 1956. These texts are translated into Spanish in *Cuadernos de Arquitectura y Urbanismo*, no. 93, Barcelona, November–December 1972, pp. 18–21. We have abundant material on Sert's classes at Yale from the correspondence consulted in the Sert Collection of Cambridge. On 22 March 1943, Sert received a first telegram from Yale inviting him to give classes at the university. On 29 March they sent him another letter in which they specified that they could pay him $300 for six lectures, which the University qualified as a 'modest honorarium'. On 17 February 1944, they again invited him, and renewed the request on 21 March. In March 1943, Sert gave some lectures in Chicago thanks to an invitation from Moholy-Nagy, to which the *Chicago Sun* dedicated a laudatory article. He was also invited to Black Mountain College, as we can gather from Theodore Dreier's letter of 26 May 1943 and Josef Albers' letter of 31 January 1944. Sert must have been very busy at the time, unfortunately for Gropius, because he was ill and wanted Sert to substitute him at Harvard while he recovered. In a letter he sent Sert on 17 April 1944, he said: 'Sorry that you weren't able to take over my class here, but I rather expected this because I know how busy you are just now. We have made another arrangement with Professor Wagner and Christopher Tunnard.'

[259] To explain the parameters of these neighbourhood units, Sert wrote in footnote eight of the first text mentioned in the note above: 'The different characteristics attributed to these neighbourhood units and townships by different authors show the need for adaptation of general standards, which the living conditions of each country can determine … The English planners fix the population of neighbourhood units in figures ranging from 6,000 to 10,000 inhabitants and agree on townships of 50,000 minimum population. (See figures given by the National Council of Social Services, 1943, MARS group, "Study for Master Plan of London", 1942; Patrick Abercrombie's "County of London Plan", 1943). In the US the suggested population figures for neighbourhood units vary from 3,000 inhabitants to about 10,000 … (See figures given by Clarence Perry in *Housing for the Machine Age*, Russell Sage Foundation, New York, 1939, "The School-Neighbourhood Nucleus" by N.L. Engelhardt from *Architectural Forum*, October 1943, and "Studies for the Replanning of Corpus Christi, Salt Lake City and Tacoma" in *New Pencil Points*, August 1943).' In 1945, Le Corbusier published 'Manière de penser l'urbanisme', in *L'Architecture d'Aujourd'hui*. A close examination of the contents of pages 67 to 71 allows us to observe how Sert's programme for neighbourhood units coincides with that which Le Corbusier called the *prolongement du logis* (the extension of dwelling). In the US we also find references concerning the interest awoken by the neighbourhood units. In 1944, Louis I. Kahn and Oscar Stonorov published *You and Your Neighbourhood*, Revere Copper and Brass Incorporated, New York. This work shows the degree to which rationalist urbanism had come to interest some North American architects. We even find some samples of this method of urban design in the 1940s. See 'Toledo, A Model of Proposed Changes in the Transportation Pattern Arouses Citizen Interest in Planning the City's Future', *Architectural Forum*, August 1945; 'Riverfront Redevelopment for Cincinnati', *Architectural Record*, February 1947; 'Redevelopment Plan for Grand Haven', *Architectural Record*, February 1948; 'Cultural Centre', *Architectural Forum*, June 1945. In the *Architectural Record* editorial of August 1945, titled 'Planning, too, is for People', Kenneth K. Stowell defended rationalist urbanism, mentioning the Saint Dié project and alluding to the meetings held by professionals of that sector, among which he spoke of Sert. The Princeton Congress was also mentioned in the *Architectural Record* of April 1945.

[260] As a summary and example of this bibliography we can cite that of 'Neighbourhood Unit', August 21, 1951, which is found in SC CIAM C 12.

[261] PLWC, Cidade dos Motores folder, 'Study Analysis and Anteproject'.

[262] On 25 May 1945, a strange letter from Lester to Antonio Guedes Muñiz foreshadowed some future disagreements between the associates and their client, though it is not clear what consequences this had on the third project that Sert and Lester Wiener drew. However, if we consider how near in date this letter is to the official contract, it may just have been an explanatory missive concerning what works were to be carried out in the third project: 'Only the experience of the United States of North America, where billions of dollars have been expended in the past ten years, and with its specialized departments, its compiled statistical figures, its experience in actual performance – rejecting solutions that at first sight would appear ideal and adopting those that in practice proved adequate to the necessities of the times in which we live, an era in which the welfare and improved standard of living of the worker who produces must be promoted – affords the essential conditions for the success of so unusual an undertaking as that of the Fábrica Nacional de Motores, the National Motor Works. It is the function of a perfect plan to adjust, co-ordinate and provide in modern terms for the various requirements of a city … It is not the right thing to open up streets, squares, services that are not for the immediate use of the population. As our inquiry has had in view a city that from the beginning shall be low-cost, with only that which is absolutely essential and which shall grow naturally like any living thing, it is easy to see what this represents in sheer economy. Avoiding everything non-essential, giving to everything its functional size and dimensions, seeking to standardize in order to facilitate execution of the plans to the maximum, introducing overall savings in time and money, these are the necessary features of a scientifically planned project'. What is undoubtedly certain is that in a letter to his associate on 2 April 1945, Sert explained to Lester that he was working on the Cidade dos Motores project reform. It is also a fact that in another letter of 19 June 1945, which Lester sent to a man by the name of Fernando, he told him concerning the Cidade dos Motores that 'Construction of the new town is beginning'. On 20 December 1945 Lester told Antonio Guedes Muñiz that he was sending him plans for 'A) Water Distribution B) Sewage System C) FNM Industrial Tract D) FNM Factory and Cafeteria E) Commissary and Milk Plant F) Kindergarten G) Services Buildings for Neighbourhoods A & B.' He mentioned that he would send him more plans with 'inexpensive methods of sun protection for dwellings' and that 'at present we are working on a version of the complete city including the factory industrial tract', for which he added that they would need his approval.

[263] This is the project that is the most well known. It is best described in *Progressive Architecture*, September 1946, which features the article 'Brazil Builds a New City', pp. 52–75, and in *L'Architecture d'Aujourd'hui*, no. 9, 1947, pp. 100–119, useful for the reader who wishes to consult further detailed descriptions and graphic documents not found in this work. The Belgian magazine *Chantiers. Editions arts et techniques* of February 1946 also published 'Le Brésil construit une ville nouvelle, La Cidade dos Motores'. This publication contains a presentation of the project made by Le Corbusier, in which after referring extensively to himself and to the influence exerted by the CIAMs, he states: 'The work of Paul Lester Wiener and José Luis Sert, an architectural and urbanist work admirable from all points of view, attests to this. I have regarded their plans with great joy; I have looked on them with extreme pleasure. It is a well-done work: landscape, climate, geography, topography, science of the engineer and of the architect combined, make for a harmonious and scrupulous whole that inspires trust … It is good to see the principles of a healthy doctrine put into practice. One perceives that the rule is not a brake but rather a tool that liberates from disorder. Unity reigns, that unity that man obtains when he is master.' In 1947 an exhibition was held at MoMA in which two urban plans were compared: that of the Cidade dos Motores and that of Chicago. There is an article on this exhibition: 'Planning in North and South America' in the MoMA Bulletin of June of 1947. Here we again find a description of Sert's and Lester's project. In the April 1947 issue of *Architectural Forum*

156

cited in footnote 259, we find an article on the meeting prepared to celebrate the bicentennial of Princeton University, which assembled 'the foremost US architects and planners to spend two days talking about Planning Man's Physical Environment'. Among those invited were Sert and Gropius, Wright, Hudnut, Chermayeff, Howe, Neutra, Johnson, etc. The publications on the project for Brazil had borne fruit. Nevertheless, in a letter from Giedion to Le Corbusier from 18 April 1946, we read: 'Has Sert's city found an artistic solution? I have only seen the first project and I have found it too schematic, and I have criticized it to Sert for this reason.' FLC D 2 15 101.

[264] See *Progressive Architecture*, September 1946, op. cit., pp. 62–63.

[265] De Lima, op. cit., p. 341.

[266] Paul Lester Wiener and José Luis Sert, *A City Measured by its People*, in *Progressive Architecture*, September 1946, p. 74.

[267] On 26 June 1946, Sert received a telegram from his brother Francisco, which said: 'Mom's health requires your presence immediately.' Another telegram from 15 August indicates that Genara López was suffering from a prolapsed womb, aggravated by a nervous crisis, and that there was a visa for our architect to enter Spain. Sert set up an ingenious strategy to ensure that the police would not detain him in that country by having Gropius and Hudnut send him letters to the US consulate in Barcelona 'requiring' his presence at Harvard University. Sert was truly worried by the unforeseeable consequences of his trip, and in a letter to Gropius on 9 July 1946, he even asked him to have CIAM, ASA or RIBA intercede for him if things went awry. On 7 October he received authorization to return to the US, and through a letter to Gropius of 25 October 1946, we learn that he had returned. Sert therefore spent two months in Barcelona, from mid–August to mid–October of 1946. Existing documents in SC, E3. According to the oral account of Josefina Ribera, the nurse who took care of Genara, it was Sert who requested that his mother be taken to the Fuster Clinic in Barcelona so that she could be operated on and cured. She recovered well, and lived eight more years until her death 10 October 1954.

[268] The correspondence on this matter is in SC, E3 and E4 in the following order. On 15 November 1946, just after returning from Barcelona with certificate stating his Spanish architectural degree, Sert made a petition to register as architect on the National Council of Architectural Registration Boards of the US. This institution asked him, through a letter of 14 June 1947, to prepare 'a photographic exhibit of executed work'. In a letter of 9th December of the same year, he excused himself for not being able to take the examination because he was in Lima. He was finally summoned on 21 July 1948 at 11.15 a.m. to take the 'Senior Examination'. On 19 August 1949, he was informed that he had passed the exam and was asked to send the documents that proved he was a US citizen so as to grant him the corresponding certificate. Proof of Sert's architectural degree from Spain was released by the Chief of the Spanish State, Francisco Franco, on 5 August 1947.

[269] Le Corbusier insisted on various occasions that Sert come and work in his studio in Paris. The first invitation we have found is in a letter sent from the Hotel de la Paix in Vichy on 18 January 1941: 'My dear Sert, I have always dreamed of working with you because you are loyal and wise. We would understand each other very well. I hope that the occasion will arise.' Four years later, on 23 June 1945, he

again insisted in a letter he addressed to Moncha: 'I would love that Sert come and take a part in this and that we be a team.' The following day, he sent a letter to Sert that said: 'I have just come from seeing a friend of yours, Duarte … To my question: "Will Sert come and work with me?", he told me that you would certainly do so. I have already written once to you about this subject.' SC E28.
Sert's answer was clear, as is evident from the letter of 20 August 1945: 'It is impossible for me to join you right now in your new workshop for constructors. I have just signed a contract to draw up the plans for a new city in Brazil and I have a lot of work.' FLC R3 O3 187. Six years later, Le Corbusier again insisted. In a letter of 13 June 1951, in which he commented on the possibility of being commissioned with the Plan for Lisbon, we read: 'I am ready to undertake this work with you.' FLC R3 O3 215. Sert's refusal simply shows that he had found professional stability in the United States and was not willing to travel to Paris to work as Le Corbusier's assistant, although he certainly did not wish to distance himself from the Swiss architect, to whom he was bound by a deep friendship. We also know that at the time they were collaborating on the Bogotá Plan.
Five years later, we find another letter from Le Corbusier to Sert dated 29 February 1956, in which after announcing that he had the chance of being commissioned with the housing development of the new federal capital of Pakistan, he offered: 'Before getting in touch again with the Embassy of Pakistan I would like to know if this affair would interest you and Wiener.' The letter went on to specify the tasks that Sert and Lester would be in charge of developing, based on their vast South American experience. SC Sert E4.

[270] The TPA's involvement with Peru started with the lectures given by Lester in that country, as we can gather from a letter sent by the architect Fernando Belaunde to Lester on 4 January 1945, in which he suggested the subjects that would be of greatest interest in that country. The first clue that sets us on the track of the Chimbote project commission is a letter that the Peruvian Corporation of Santa sent to the US Embassy of Brazil addressed to Lester, thanking him for 'your kind offer to co-operate with this corporation and your suggestion to compile all the data on hand to prepare a long-range Master Plan of Chimbote and surroundings.' PLWC, Peru Folder.
A letter from the architect Luis Dórich dated 8 July 1945, corroborates the notion that the Chimbote commission was a certainty. In another missive from 18 September 1945, addressed to David Dasso, Director of the Peruvian Corporation of Santa, there is already a petition for working data, such as the building costs, ordinances, etc. PLWC, Outgoing Correspondence Folder, 1945.
The 1946 correspondence reveals the contacts established with Luis Dórich and David Dasso to obtain information on the city and its area of influence and to specify technical aspects for the drawing up of the Plan. A telegram to Dasso of 2 August 1946 testifies that the TPA office would begin the study of Chimbote in the following months. A letter to Dasso from 2 May of the same year thanked him for having sent nineteen photographs of the city plus the Chimbote census. On 29 May Lester sent Dasso another letter with the future programme to develop the project. PLWC, Outgoing Correspondence Folder, 1946.
The date of the contract, written in Spanish and English and signed by the Director of the

Peruvian Corporation of Santa, who at the time was Manuel Vázquez Díaz, is 7 August 1947. It specified an honorary fee of $28,700, with all expenses covered except for three round trips to be made by Sert and Lester, and it also specified the form of payment and the conditions in which the work was to be carried out.
The engineer Luis Dórich sent them a report on the climate and geographical conditions of Chimbote on 25 March 1947, according to the explanations of Sert and Lester in the Plan memorandum. They also explained that the engineers Torres y Ortiz and Zevallos had made reports, but did not specify what these were about. There was an account of the conversations held with the engineers Dasso, Quiñones and Ballón, and with the technicians from the Peruvian Corporation of Santa. The Pilot Plan was handed in on 14 February 1948, and was approved by the Corporation of Santa on 31 March, and by the Ministry of Public Works on 15 June of that year. The deadline for the Master Plan was 2 January 1949, and its report bears the date of 31 December 1948.
The archives offer some clues as to the huge amount of time that Sert and Lester spent travelling back and forth from Latin America in 1948, a fact that allows us to observe the increase in commissions as well as to clear up their chronology. On 15 December 1947 they travelled to Lima, as we can gather from a letter that Sert wrote to Le Corbusier on 28 November of the same year (FLC R3 O3 191). On 7 March 1948, Sert wrote to Le Corbusier from the Hotel Chez Victor in Lima, beginning his letter by informing him that he had just returned from Bogotá and that he had to be back in the Colombian capital by 18 April, where he would be staying until 30 May so as to continue work in Tumaco (FLC R3 O3 193), a trip that was postponed for political reasons, as we shall see. On 30 June 1948, Sert told Le Corbusier that he had spent six months in Latin America (FLC R3 O3 195). In another letter to Le Corbusier of 5 October 1948, he again spoke of a trip, this time to Medellin and Lima (FLC R3 O3 199).
An article about CIAM 7 from the Italian newspaper *L'Eco di Bergamo* on 19 July 1949, was accompanied by a picture of Sert and Lester whose caption read: 'American architects; the first is the current CIAM President and is the author of the great project of the Cidade dos Motores; both architects are building new neighbourhood units in Peru.' FLC D2 17 335.

[271] 'The most serious urban example, in terms of expansion, is that of the city of Chimbote, north of Lima, which registered an explosive growth intimately bound with the accelerated development of fishing (especially the fishing industry), because this promoted a marked migration during the time it was flourishing. This also explains the lowering of the population growth rate between 1972 and the following years. Chimbote grew from 4,000 inhabitants in 1940 to a population of 253,000 in 1985.' Franklin Pease, *Breve historia contemporánea del Perú*, Fondo de Cultura Económica, Mexico, 1995.

[272] See 'Urbanisme en Amérique Latine', in *L'Architecture d'Aujourd'hui*, December 1950–January 1951, pp. 33–45. The situation in Peru prior to the industrial growth is found in José Carlos Mariategui, *7 ensayos de interpretación de la realidad peruana*, Amauta, Lima, 1975 (first edition 1928).

[273] In the second half of 1948, the political situation became especially tense in Peru: on 27

157

October, President José Luis Bustamante was removed from office, and a military council headed by General Manuel A. Odría took over, ruling the country for the next eight years. Pease, op. cit., pp. 210–11.

[274] Interventions based on neighbourhood units were known in Peru, since neighbourhood unit 3 of Lima had been projected in 1945 and completed in 1948. In a letter of 8 May 1946 from Luis Dórich addressed to Lester, he says: 'Very soon after the new government had taken office last year, President Bustamante called together a group from the Instituto de Urbanismo and asked us to make the projects for six neighbourhood units for 1,000 families each. The first neighbourhood unit is already under construction and the projects for two more are completed. The remaining three are not yet projected as location has not been decided. The programme we have adopted for each unit is based of course on the elementary school and the installation of all the services including civic, social and shopping facilities.'
Sert wrote an undated article on the neighbourhood units, 'The Neighbourhood Unit – Its Creation, Improvement and Conservation'. SC CIAM C12.
This was not the only sample of modern architecture in Peru. There was also the isolated works of architects such as Alfredo Dammert, who had studied at the Bauhaus, or Augusto Guzman, both showing by the end of the 1930s architectural works derived from European modernity. In March 1947, the Agrupación Espacio wrote its Manifesto. This group was led by the architect Luis Miró Quesada, who in 1946 had organized a university course titled 'Analysis of the Architectural Function' to teach these new ideas. A letter from Luis Dórich to Sert of 29 January 1949 expressed the Agrupación Espacio's interest in being CIAM members. PLWC, Peru Folder.
In 1946, in a climate of openness fostered by the Frente Democrático under José Bustamante that would continue until October 1948, the National Office of Planning and Urbanism, as well as the Housing Corporation, were established. In 1947, the architect Fernando Belaunde Terry, with whom Sert and Lester were in contact through letters, gave a university course entitled 'The National Housing Problem'. See Javier Sota Nadal, 'El movimiento moderno en Perú'; José Beingolea, and Marco de la Torre, 'La arquitectura de la modernidad', in *Revista Hurca*, Universidad Nacional de Ingeniería, Facultad de Arquitectura y Urbanismo, Lima, 1980.
[275] As early as June 1945 we find letters concerning the relaunching of the CIAMs; some are addressed to and others are written by Le Corbusier. See: FLC D2 15 37, FLC D2 15 40, FLC D2 15 98, FLC D2 15 126, FLC D2 15 127, and FLC D2 15 130. Meanwhile, Sert, Giedion and Papadaki were attempting to set up an American CIAM. FLC D2 15 41, FLC D2 15 42, FLC D2 16 52, and FLC D2 15 154. The programme to be developed in Bridgwater was already outlined in a letter from Giedion to Sert of 18 January 1947, in which we read:' We totally agree with the English that the CIAMs have to play a leading role in aesthetic questions … After many long meetings, the English are now writing the questionnaire on "Architecture and the Common Man", and I have finally finished the questionnaire on "Relationship among Architecture, Painting and Sculpture" … I spoke in London in the great RIBA hall on our old subject, "The Need for New Monumentality" … *The Architectural Review* wants to publish a special issue on "The Need for New Monumentality", in which it

will publish my article along with that of Léger, and, I hope, an article by you.' SC CIAM C4.
In the meeting held in Zurich between 26 and 29 May 1947, the content was further specified, although it was generally acknowledged that the main function of the Congress 'would be simply to get CIAM going again after the war, and whose programme of work would only be preliminary to a full-dress congress in 1948.' *Documents of the Sixth Congress*, SC CIAM B4, p. 3. Also in FLC D2 16 1.
[276] *Documents of the Sixth Congress*, Report of Commission I, SC CIAM B4.
[277] Report of Commission III A. Urbanism, *Documents of the Sixth Congress*, SC CIAM B4, p. 18.
[278] Ibid., pp. 20–22.
[279] Eighty-five architects from many different countries were present at CIAM 6. This made its leaders aware of the future difficulties of organization that would come about from such massive attendance. A letter from Le Corbusier to Giedion on 2 May 1947 warned about this circumstance. FLC D2 20. One of the Commissions of the Congress was devoted to this issue, and foreshadowed a process that tended towards the bureaucratization of the CIAMs. See: *Documents of the Sixth Congress*, SC CIAM B4, pp. 13–17. The new CIAM statutes are found in FLC D2 18. An example of the bureaucratic problems is the fact that Le Corbusier had to submit himself to the Congress' rigid discipline concerning his request to invite his closest friends to the meeting. See letter from Le Corbusier to Giedion and Sert on 21 November 1947, FLC D2 56, or the minutes of the meeting in Paris between 28 and 31 March to prepare CIAM 7, FLC D2 16 210.
[280] Le Corbusier, *Séance de l'Assemblée Genérale sur l'expression architecturale*, Bridgwater, 13 September 1947, FLC D2 16. The report in which we are told that Sert is 'President in power', which was prepared by the press delegate J.M. Richards is also highly informative. FLC D2 16, pp. 45–46.
[281] Van Eyck's intervention is included in Sigfried Giedion, *A Decade of New Architecture*, Editions Girsberger, Zurich, 1951, p. 37. The book as a whole compiles a great part of the CIAM 6 speeches. On pages 217–25 it is possible to see different types of neighbourhood units, among which is a picture of one of the neighbourhood unit models from the Cidade dos Motores project.
The book must have come out at the end of 1951, as we can gather from a letter that Sert wrote to Giedion on 28 December of that year, in which we read: 'Thank you for the *Decade*, which finally arrived through our friend Janice … The book looks very good and I am glad that there is so much information about the Congress in the first part.' SC CIAM C10.
[282] J.M. Richards, 'Architectural Expression', in *Documents of the Sixth Congress*, op. cit., p. 28.
[283] Ibid. Although it was written eight years later, it is useful to consult Sigfried Giedion's, 'The New Regionalism', in *Architecture, You and Me*, Harvard University Press, 1958, pp. 138–53, original edition in German, *Architektur und Gemeinschaft*, Rowohlt, Hamburg, 1956.
[284] Between 1943 and 1944, Sert, Giedion and Léger worked on the writing of some texts dealing with monumentality. These texts, the manifesto *Nine Points on Monumentality* (1943) by Giedion, Sert and Léger, and *The Need for a New Monumentality* (1944) by Giedion, are compiled in the book by Giedion that appears in the previous note. In both essays there is a defence of the cultural value of monuments

and an appeal to reverse their vilified collective value. A fragment of the 1943 text summarizes this change of mentality, allowing us to approach the relationship between architecture and city from this viewpoint: 'Monumental buildings will then be able to stand in space, because, like trees or plants, monumental buildings cannot be crowded upon any old lot in any district. Only when this space is achieved can the new urban centres come to life.'
On the basis of the idea of a new monumentality, Sert supported Le Corbusier in the United Nations building affair. See letter from Sert to Giedion of 4 December 1947, SC C4.
In the November 1950 issue of *Architectural Forum*, the subject was again taken up in relation to the construction of the United Nations building.
[285] The perspectives for the Saint-Dié Civic Centre that Le Corbusier executed in 1945 demonstrate his interest in playing with the volumes of representative buildings in the city centre. The Swiss architect, whose programme was functionally less sophisticated and not clearly linked to the rest of the city, inserted elements of his repertoire by demolishing what had remained standing after the war. The *Oeuvre Complète* (vol. 1938–46, pp. 132–9) states that the Plan was exhibited in the US in 1945 at Radio-City Hall and at the Rockefeller Centre, New York, suggesting that Sert and Lester must have seen it.
[286] PLWC, Peru Folder, Incoming Correspondence (1945–52). The Report on the Master Plan of Chimbote, from 31 December 1948, is found in PLWC. In it we see the great care shown in defining the neighbourhood units and in explaining local construction systems and the mechanisms for sheltering the 'squatter population'.
[287] Ibid.
[288] Ibid.
[289] PLWC, letter from Celso Pastor to Lester and Sert, 25 IV 1950, Peru Folder, Publicity.
[290] In Pease's work we read how the law was formulated 'in 1950, a Mining Law openly in favour of promoting investment, in which the tax burdens were lessened and profits were granted to foreign investment', op. cit., p. 214. Despite all of these facilities, the Chimbote project was filed and forgotten.
[291] PLWC, Outgoing Correspondence, 1948. In fact, it is possible to consider that these matters had already arisen some time before. A letter from Gaitán Cortés to Lester of 4 January 1948 stated: 'I have had the opportunity to speak with the architects of the Department about the Tumaco Plan proposal you handed me in Cali.' PLWC, Incoming Correspondence, Box 14.
The commission for the Tumaco project, which appears in PLWC, is dated 16 February 1948, and specifies some issues that are of interest. Sert and Lester had a contract 'as consultants in the Department of National Buildings of the Ministry of Public Works, to offer assessment to this Entity in the elaboration of the projects for the Pilot Plan of Tumaco that the Ministry of Public Works is developing in accordance with Law 48 of 1947.' The law the contract mentions is from 26 December 1947 and called for the elaboration of a Regulating Plan of Urbanism in each municipality that had a budget superior to $200,000. This regulating plan was to indicate 'how future housing development was to be continued and how new quarters of town were to be built.' This law may explain the growing interest shown in Colombia concerning planning during this time: Bogotá, Medellin and Cali were cities

'planned' by local architects in conjunction with the TPA and Le Corbusier.

The contract specified that Sert and Lester, who were called 'contractors', were responsible for: '1. Undertaking the revision and resolving any consultations that in this first stage of the contract the Department of National Buildings may make regarding the programme, the general documentation and the preliminary schemes for the Tumaco Plan, for which reason the contractors will remain in Bogotá for two weeks corresponding to the month of February of the current year. 2. Undertaking the revision and resolving any consultations that in this second stage of this contract the said Department may make regarding the plans for the initial phase of construction of the new city on the Isla del Morro, for which reason the contractors will remain in Bogotá for six weeks during the months of April and May 1948. 3. Undertaking the revision and resolving the consultations that, in the last stage of this contract, the said Department may make regarding the development of the Plan, for which reason they will remain in Bogotá for six weeks during the months of January and February 1949 … As a fee for their services, the Nation will pay the contractors the sum of $12,000 in the following manner … The Government, moreover, commits itself to covering the contractors' transport expenses in the three trips they will make to Bogotá.'

A letter from Sert to Le Corbusier of 7 March 1949, corroborates some of these points: 'On returning from Bogotá … we started talking about the Tumaco Plan and quickly executed a preliminary design on which we worked jointly with the group from the Ministry of Public Works … We have to go back to Bogotá on 18 April and will stay there until 30 May to continue our work on Tumaco.' FLC R3 O3 193.

[292] Javier Ocampo, *Historia básica de Colombia*, Plaza & Janés editores, 1995, p. 286. The Presidents from the Liberal period were: Enrique Olaya (1930–34), Alfonso López (1934–39), Eduardo Santos (1938–42), Alfonso López (1942–45) and Alberto Lleras (1945–46).

[293] Ibid., p. 294.

[294] It was a crisis whose consequences for Colombia are described thus: 'The war provoked difficult economic conditions. The United States took advantage of the occasion to impose the lowering of prices of the products sold by Latin America, and just as had been the case with copper and tin – which because they were catalogued as strategic materials had to be exported at ludicrous prices, consequently damaging the economies of countries such as Bolivia, Chile and Peru – so it was with coffee, the main export product of Colombia, which suffered from the lowered prices imposed in the market controlled by North America. In September 1940 a pound of coffee was being exported at nine cents. The demand created by the American army pushed the price of coffee up to 16 cents a pound; at that point the price-regulating office of the United States fixed a maximum price, which was maintained throughout the war until 1945. This notion of supporting the war effort by means of contributing to the well-being of North American consumers implied for Colombia a loss of a billion dollars.' See Jorge Orlando Melo (co-ordinator), *Colombia hoy. Perspectivas hacia el siglo XXI*, TM Editores, Bogotá, 1995, p. 160.

[295] Even during the 1942 elections, or in other words, at a time of uncertainty as to the result of the war, there were alliances between the Communist Party of Colombia and the Liberal Party, a fact that may surprise us but that is consistent with specific historical circumstances: 'The Colombian Communist Party gave its unconditional support to the government of López, which was on the Allies' side, a collaboration that had its ideological implications … Our party widely disseminated first the articles and then the books of Browder, at the time General Secretary of the Communist Party of the United States, who used the glorious anti-Fascist flag to cover up the contraband of a revisionism well-disguised as tactical considerations. Browder affirmed that a new historical era was dawning, one of close collaboration between the Soviet Union and the United States in the war and after it, and that this ensured a world without economic crises and without armed conflicts, the gradual change from capitalism to socialism, and the pacific development of underdeveloped countries with the financial support of North America.' Ibid., p. 154.

[296] FLC Correspondence, R3 O3 195.

[297] The articles in the first issues of *Proa* before the Tumaco project was published were explicit and generally dealt with proposing alternative solutions to those of the government, or with denouncing terrible realities: 'Problemas de Urbanismo en Bogotá. La Carrera 10', 'Para que Bogotá sea una ciudad moderna', 'Las futuras grandes avenidas de Bogotá', 'Bogotá puede ser una ciudad moderna', 'El plan urbanístico y regulador de Villavicencio', 'Las calles de Bogotá fueron ANCHAS pero se estrecharon', 'Las calles de Bogotá fueron RECTAS pero se torcieron' and 'Reconstrucción de Bogotá'. The references are diverse, ranging from Soviet planning to more or less noteworthy Beaux-Arts ideas: 'La reconstrucción de Stalingrado', 'La ciudad universitaria de Caracas', 'Caracas y su progreso urbano', 'Nuevas ciudades para Gran Bretaña', etc.

In the ninth issue, of November 1947, a translation of the Athens Charter was published, possibly as a result of Le Corbusier's first trip to Bogotá from 16 to 24 June 1947. These echoes resound clearly in the article 'Planos criminales', which appeared in the same issue. In the following issue, emphasis was placed on the terms used by Le Corbusier when he compared the actions of a city planner to those of a physician or surgeon: 'Physicians, before they make a diagnosis and medicate a patient, write up a "clinical history" of the patient. An urbanist is a physician of cities.' See 'Segunda lección de urbanismo', *Proa*, no. 10, March 1948.

In other magazine issues we find statements like: 'There is no problem as current, as fundamental and as urgent as urbanism', *Proa*, no. 9, November 1949, or: 'Urbanism is economy, is happiness, is living with hope, is light and is hygiene', *Proa*, no. 3, November 1946.

Thanks to the architect Fernando Torres for sending the *Proa* documentary material.

[298] José de Recasens, 'El otro Le Corbusier', *Proa*, no. 2, September 1946, p. 13. Recasens is probably one of the three Spanish architects who emigrated to Colombia after the Spanish Civil War.

[299] Eupalinos, 'La planificación. ¿Quién planifica a los planificadores?', *Proa*, no. 3, October 1946, pp. 9–11.

[300] 'When the plane landed in Techo airport, almost all the architects and students of architecture of Bogotá, about two hundred people, were waiting for Le Corbusier with welcoming placards and with shouts of "A bas l'Académie!", "Vive Le Corbusier!" For the *Proa* generation – Carlos Martínez, Gabriel Serrano, Vicente Nasi or Rafael Obregón – Le Corbusier was the great Master whom they had finally been able to bring over to Colombia. For the younger ones – Jorge Arango, Carlos Arbelaez, Hernando Vargas or Jorge Gaitán – Le Corbusier was a legendary figure whom they had learned to respect in Leopoldo Rother's classes at the University … With Le Corbusier's visit, the confidence and faith of Bogotán architects was renewed … No gesture of the great architect allowed them to guess at the doubts that were gnawing away at him inside.' Silvia Arango and Jaime Gonzalez, 'Le Corbusier: realidades y representaciones', in *Le Corbusier en Colombia*, Cementos Bocaya, Bogotá, 1987, p. 152.

[301] Germán Téllez, 'La arquitectura y el urbanismo en la época actual', in *Manual de historia de Colombia*, Instituto Colombiano de Cultura, 1984, pp. 352–53.

An attempt to link the times and architecture so as to evaluate the scope of modern architecture in Colombia during the period that interests us is found in Carlos Niño, *Arquitectura y Estado*, Ed. Universidad Nacional de Colombia, Bogotá, 1991, pp. 225–312. Also noteworthy is Silvia Arango, *Historia de la arquitectura en Colombia*, Centro Editorial y Facultad de Artes Universidad Nacional de Colombia, Bogotá, 1989, pp. 209–28. Another interesting book with contributions from various critics is *Contexto histórico de la arquitectura en Colombia*, Asociación colombiana de facultades de arquitectura, 1985.

[302] Téllez is referring to the neighbourhood unit projects of Muzu, Quiroga, Los Alcazares and the so-called Antonio Nariño Urban Centre. He explains how the first two 'were quickly and profoundly transformed by their inhabitants (so that they are barely recognizable), generally tending to re-establish the previous urban situation (orthodox road network and plots, similar to those in adjacent and pre-existing quarters of town); regression to a ferociously possessive attitude concerning purchased plots of land, abandonment and destruction of the free communal areas; failure of the "Civic Centres" proposed for each sector, etc.' Los Alcázares had better luck, perhaps because it was occupied by the middle class, while the Antonio Nariño Urban Centre was to be 'the country's first attempt at a highly dense housing compound in the style of those that were built in all European countries after World War II … It was the first Colombian version of the celebrated notion of juxtaposing enormous high-rise buildings in vast green areas.' Téllez, op. cit., pp. 377–78.

[303] The Tumaco project is published in 'Reconstrucción de Tumaco', *Proa*, no. 14, July 1948, and 'El proyecto del nuevo Tumaco', *Proa*, no. 15, September 1948. It also came out in *L'Architecture d'Aujourd'hui*, December 1950–January 1951, pp. 20–32.

[304] The architects who worked in conjunction with Sert and Lester on the Tumaco project were: Gonzalo Samper, Eduardo Mejía, Hernán Vieco, Alvaro Pradilla, Luz Amorocho, Fernando Martínez and Edgar Burbano. PLWC, Tumaco Folder 'Informe sobre las consultas referentes al Planeamiento de la nueva ciudad de Tumaco', p. 1.

[305] From the Tumaco trip we have the following description: 'We were able to fly low over the islands of Tumaco and del Morro, which could be clearly examined from the plane thanks to the excellent weather we had. This allowed us to confirm through the terrain itself the data that had been used as the basis for the Pilot Plan. We landed on the Isla del Morro, visited sectors of it, and crossed to the island of Tumaco to inspect the sector of the city destroyed by the fire as well as the main streets that had not suffered damage. This allowed us

to get a general idea of the population and their means of life and habits.' Ibid., p. 3.

[306] As had been the case in the Cidade dos Motores, there was an outline of a plan for the new city, which was made by the Frederick Snare company. Due to this circumstance, on 16 February the architects were requested to meet technicians from the Ministry and the Frederick Snare representatives. Sert's words are eloquent: 'These presented a map for the future city of Tumaco. As we had just arrived in Bogotá and had not had time to study the problem, we did not want to make any comments about this map until we had become more familiar with the problem. This map, which was simply a schematic visualization, was nevertheless carefully studied and analyzed by us and by the group from the Ministry. Our reaction to the Snare proposition is contained in the counter-proposition of our preliminary pilot plan, which was afterwards approved by the Ministry. This plan is based on modern town-planning principles, which are totally different from those that served as the basis for the plan presented by the Snare company. We wish to add the following comment: the project presented by the Frederick Snare Company is, in our opinion, absolutely at odds with the economic reality and the special living conditions of the Tumaco population. If the problem is studied in a scientific manner, the said map can only be viewed as a preliminary drawing without any real basis … the Snare map is conceived as a simple visualization and not as a consequence of a serious investigation of the problem. Certain town-planning points such as the paths on a level with the railroad that cross the main avenues, the dispersion of services, and the lack of scale in their planning as well as their overblown importance, could be the object of a new report if the Ministry desires it.' Ibid., pp. 6–7.

[307] Ibid., p.10.

[308] Ibid., p. 17.

[309] The differentiation of circulation uses in the city was an issue that had recently started to be analyzed. It was formulated in a 'definitive' manner in Le Corbusier's book Le trois établissements humains, Editions de Minuit. In it we find the following comment on the regulation for the 7 routes: 'The regulation of the 7 Routes established in 1948 by request of UNESCO constitutes a respiratory and blood circulation system. The "7 Routes" become the models of hierarchy that are capable of regulating modern circulation.' Le Corbusier then went on to describe the importance of each one of these roads. Quoted from the French 1959 edition, p. 48.

[310] Informe sobre las consultas referentes al Planeamiento de la nueva ciudad de Tumaco, p. 26. Through a letter from Gaitán to Lester of 26 May 1948, we are informed of the Colombian's decision to participate actively in politics within the Liberal party.

[311] The architect Fernando Martínez headed the special study on housing and its groupings. He proposed three types of housing, A, B, and C, which were conceived for similar programmes with some variations, and these dwellings were to be developed mainly as duplexes with a patio that would connect the buildings to the services, and the workshop on the ground floor. The rooms located on the floor above were to be connected by a terrace that would unite them, forming a porch. Special attention was paid to the presence of houses-cum-workshops: 'The study of the Tumaco population's activities convinced us of the necessity to connect housing and the workshop or store sites directly in some cases. The type of houses-cum-workshops organized on the basis of the work carried out by a family therefore does not force the different family members to abandon their dwellings and the care of their children. This system can be compared to the handicraft organization of life that still exists in many European cities. This has made us project groups of housing with the workshops or stores located at the end of the patio. The workshops in these cases are connected to accessways ending in parking areas.' Ibid., p. 30.

[312] See d'Alo Frota, op. cit., pp. 316–18.

[313] PLWC Outgoing Correspondence, 1949. The letter is addressed to two people who are only referred to by their first names: Sergio and Emilio.

[314] The first news we have of the Medellin project comes from the letter to Marian from 3 March that we have previously mentioned. However, it is in the letter of 14 May 1948 addressed to Colonel Abadía, Mayor of Medellin, that we find a proposal for the elaboration of a Regulating Plan. From then on, there would be constant correspondence with Jorge Restrepo, Chief of Assessment, concerning the Medellin Plan. In a letter from Sert to Sigfried Giedion of 26 July 1948, he states: 'We received a wonderful contract for the master plan for the city of Medellin in Colombia; 275,000 inhabitants, slightly smaller than Zurich and the fastest growing city in the southern continent after Sao Paulo.' SC CIAM C5. In October of the same year, Sert and Lester visited Medellin with their wives. After January 1949 we are able to track down the chronology and fate of the proposal for this Colombian city through their correspondence with Nel Rodríguez. We also read in a letter to Giedion of 5 October 1948: 'We are starting our work in Medellin and will stay there for two weeks; will go from there to Lima were we will be staying from the beginning of January '49 … After that, we have to go back to Bogotá to finish our work there. We won't be back in New York before the middle of March.'

[315] This without date or signature, although it was probably from before September of 1949 given that it mentioned Carlos Santacruz, who resigned around this time. It seems to be a report sent from Colombia to the TPA office concerning the progress of the Tumaco works, and included original pictures glued onto the pages. This can be deduced from comments such as the following: 'The wall foundations and pad foundations of the columns are made by the commercial groups H.J. … The shell roofs will be made out of reinforced concrete, as well as the walls. The bulldozer finally arrived in Tumaco, as did the grader and the other dumpers, and we then saw that we had the possibility of filling in part of the cove … In the houses that are being finished we are installing water from four wells … The engineer Charria is going to Tumaco during Easter Week. We still don't know what we will do about the waste water … Type A houses: I did all I could to accelerate their completion by employing mass production (which was not being done because of lack of machinery) for all the elements possible … Thanks to the mechanists' workshop, the fabrication of hardware for the balanced levers has been greatly simplified.' There are annotations in Sert's handwriting alongside some of the report's points. SC Tumaco B 68C.

[316] PLWC, Incoming Correspondence, Box 14. The aforementioned letter specifies these financial allotments: 'We were also able to obtain an allotment of $500,000, which by mistake had been sent to the Snare Company. With this money and a carryover of $270,000, plus the monthly allotments that are available, we have organized a work programme to effect works which, once they are completed, will give the ensemble the appearance of reality that it should have.' It went on to specify the works that had to be advanced after cancelling the pending debt that 'considerably hinders the progress of construction'. It also spoke of Carlos Santacruz's resignation and the appointment of someone by the name of Ariel Escobar.

[317] SC CIAM C4.

[318] SC CIAM C4.

[319] Alma Morgenthau, Paul Lester's wife, generously helped him by contributing $5,000, as Sert told Giedion in a letter of 4 December 1947. SC CIAM C4. In the book A Decade of New Architecture (op. cit., note 281), which ended up being the publication for CIAM 6, there is a note thanking her for her contribution: 'The publication of this book was only made possible by a generous gift of money from Alma Morgenthau.'

[320] In a letter of 24 November 1947, Gropius wrote to Sert: 'I am going to sound out my group here about the formation of a local CIAM group in Boston. I can do it only if I am not expected to be the driving force as I simply feel unable to take more on my shoulders than I have already. I will be glad to give advice but the work in that group must be done by younger men. You know how difficult the building of such a group is in this country but at least I am going to make an attempt.' SC CIAM C4.

[321] A letter to Giedion on 16 December 1947 confirms this: 'From Lima I hope to be able to work for CIAM by organizing a local group there and establishing closer contact with all Latin American delegates. I also believe it would be possible for us to do some work for the next congress with a young group in Lima … I am pessimistic about the situation of our groups here. It is more and more difficult to get people together, and as usual, nothing can be started unless a grant from a foundation is obtained.' SC CIAM C4. These reasons are repeated in another letter, which Sert sent to Giedion on 18 March 1949, SC CIAM C6. In a letter of 4 May 1949, the full names of the Latin American participants in CIAM 7 are specified. SC CIAM C6. Sert wrote a letter to Gropius on 21 June 1949, when the Bergamo CIAM was about to be inaugurated, in which he explained his intentions of holding CIAM 8 in a Latin American city: 'Cuba, Bogotá or Lima would be possible meeting places, and I am sure we would get a lively Congress, although many people from Europe would be unable to attend.' SC CIAM C6.

[322] See Giedion's letter to Sert of 27 June 1948, and Sert's answer on 15 July of that year, in which the impossibility of holding CIAM 7 in Prague or Warsaw was already becoming evident. SC CIAM C5. For this reason, and despite it had been announced some time before, we can say that it is in this second letter that Sert finally decided to hold the CIAM Congress in Bergamo: 'We will have to decide on Bergamo, supposing members of Eastern countries can go there.' In the circular letter that Giedion sent to CIAM Council members on 14 August 1948, it was officially decided that the Congress should be held in the Italian city. FLC D2 20 88. The CIAM Council was formed by: van Eesteren, Giedion, Steiger, Sert, Gropius, Le Corbusier, Syrkus, Fischer, Havlicek, Rogers, Samuel and Emery. The agenda of the CIAM session in Bergamo is found in FLC D2 17.

[323] For aspects of the *grille* that were proposed by ASCORAL, see *Grille CIAM d'Urbanisme*. It is an explanatory pamphlet published by *L'Architecture d'Aujourd'hui* with a text of June 1948 titled 'Les Instructions aux Groupes'.

[324] 'VIIème Congrés CIAM. Séance d'ouverture', FLC D2 17 88.

[325] Ibid., D2 17 90.

[326] Le Corbusier's intervention in the inaugural session was far too long, going into detail regarding the functioning of the *grille*, which according to him had taken fourteen months of work in conjunction with the ASCORAL group. Ibid.

[327] It is easy to observe in the enumeration of this programme's complexity the functional itemization that Sert and Lester carried out in the South American cities analyzed so far. See 'Essentials of Town Planning', by Commission 1A, CIAM 7 BERGAMO, SC CIAM B5.

[328] In the minutes of Commission III in Bergamo we find: 'The teaching of the History of Architecture must be freed from its isolation and be shown to be the functional expression of the general history of mankind. The student will then understand that architecture is the most faithful witness to contemporary social, cultural, economic and political conceptions, past and present. He will acquire pride in his own period and will disdain to imitate others.' SC CIAM B5, Report and Discussion of Commission III, 1071–73. In his speech for Commission III, contained in this report, Sert 'stressed the importance of a study of history and the effects of history as a means of understanding contemporary life.'

[329] This can be deduced from the possible effect produced on him by a letter that Sanchez Arcas sent him in Bergamo through Helena Syrkus. In it, the previous champion of rationalist architecture said: 'I have been in Warsaw for the last two years representing the Government of the Spanish Republic, which is akin to the Popular Republic of Poland. During this time I have seen the city, the new capital of the Popular Republic, stand on its feet again amidst the ruins to which Fascist barbarians had reduced it … I daily observe the enthusiasm of the new builders of the capital, who are creating for the Polish people a new future of happiness … I am sure that you will defend the principles that were agreed in the last Congress of Peace Partisans held in Paris. I therefore beg you to aid and support the proposals that our good friend Helena may make, as well as any other similar suggestions that may arise … In this progressive sense I would be very glad if you were to adhere to the most advanced principles of socialist realism, which are the most humane and the most in agreement with the present development of culture towards a superior stage.' SC E4. For Sánchez Arcas, rationalist experience did not make sense at the time, and the historicist proposal that prioritized the reconstruction of Warsaw seemed to him the best way to erase the horrors of war undergone by the Polish people. We are faced a city whose problems were very different from those confronted by Sert in the South American cities on which he was working, and we are also faced with a use of history that Sert abhorred, and which came from one of his most extremist travelling companions from his Spanish period. This radical change must have affected him. Sert also received through Helena Syrkus a letter from Pablo Neruda in which he suggested that the Bergamo Congress should reach an agreement to back up world peace by giving its support to the Peace Congress of Paris.

[330] SC CIAM C6.

[331] Niño, op. cit., p. 243.

[332] PLWC, Letters from Gaitán Cortés, Box 14.

[333] Lester and Sert wrote this in a letter to Augusto Tobito of 16 January 1953, so that he would go to their New York office to finish the Bogotá Plan, which was to be completed by May. PLWC, Outgoing Correspondence, 1953.

[334] President Laureano Gómez, who was elected in 1949, sympathized with Fascist ideals and was a great admirer of the Spanish dictator Francisco Franco; he invented the Colombia battalion that fought side by side with the 7th US Army in Korea from May 1951 until October 1954. His economic policy promoted the entrance of foreign capital and gave support to national capitalism. On 13 June 1953, in a climate of civil war, he was deposed by General Gustavo Rojas Pinilla's coup d'état. See Orlando Melee, op. cit., pp. 165–75.

[335] Two works by María Rubert attempt to point out the common characteristics in the South American urban projects of Sert and Lester: 'Cinco esquemas de la ciudad funcionalista', in *Arquitecturas Bis*, Barcelona, March 1985, pp. 2–7, and 'Ciutats a América Llatina. L'obra de Town Planning Associates 1943–56', in *Sert. Arquitecte a Nova York*, MACBA, Barcelona, 1997, pp. 77–101. A comparison of the five civic centres of these cities is found in 'Five Civic Centres in South America', in *Architectural Record*, August 1953.

[336] The contract to execute the Regulating Plan of Cali bears the date 23 March 1949, and for their city planning Sert and Lester were to receive a fee of $45,000. To fulfill the contract they were to carry out the commission in four phases. The analysis of the city and its area of influence would be executed in conjunction with the members of the Office of the Regulating Plan of Cali. The preliminary design of the Pilot Plan was to be done by Sert and Lester with the assistance of the Office members. The Master Plan or Overall Plan reversed this, with the Office carrying it out and with Sert and Lester acting as supervisors. The Development of the Plan was the responsibility of the Cali Office. PLWC, Box 4.

[337] Le Corbusier's diverse activities in Bogotá as well as his Pilot Plan proposal for the Colombian capital are described in *Le Corbusier en Colombia*, Cementos Bocaya, Bogotá, 1987.

[338] PLWC, Outgoing Correspondence, 1951. In the Sert Collection there are many letters from Le Corbusier concerning their mutual collaboration on the Bogotá Plan starting on 19 January 1950 and continuing until 29 December 1951. SC E 30. In one of 23 January 1951 we perceive that Le Corbusier was tired of the treatment he was receiving and was considering devoting himself to the Chandigarh project, having signed a contract for this commission on 20 December 1950: 'I received an explanatory letter from Arbelaez. I am very disappointed about having to go to Bogotá in the spring; I would love to limit the trip to New York, or if I am forced by all means to go to Bogotá, I will demand that they formally commission me the architectural works of the Civic Centre.' SC E 31. Sert replied on 30 January 1951, asking his colleague in Paris to be patient so that matters would not be further aggravated. SC E 31. The letters from the Fondation Le Corbusier help to fill in chronological gaps concerning their collaboration in the Bogotá Plan. On 30 October 1951, Sert and Lester wrote to him: 'After five weeks, we arrived at determinations that appear on the composite plan that you may have received. These definitions have now been issued by decree of law, which was signed by the Mayor and Governor of Cundinamarca. Naturally the principles of the Pilot Plan have been maintained.' FLC R3 O3 228. On 6 December 1951, Le Corbusier wrote to Sert: 'I have no news from Arbelaez concerning your recent sojourn to Bogotá. I have received no plan from the Office nor any copy of the decree signed by the Mayor and the Governor.' FLC R3 O3 230. On 25 February 1952, Sert wrote to Le Corbusier: 'I had to leave Bogotá to go to Caracas in January … The Plan matters are proceeding slowly, but the office is consolidated and the Mayor always helps us. Some decrees have come up concerning the new avenues, building heights, etc. Nothing is yet known about the Civic Centre but the extension of the 10th road will soon be carried out … Concerning the Presidential Palace, they have not yet done anything but the government does not want to change its present location.' FLC R3 O3 238. On 24 September of the same year, Sert wrote to Le Corbusier: 'I received from your office a copy of the tracé du capitol Chandigarh. Perhaps this was sent by mistake and you wanted to send the centre of Bogotá … We would like to have your latest plans to incorporate them into designs of the central area that are now underway in this office … The situation in Colombia is very critical. It may be better that things explode soon and matters clear up because with this political mess it is difficult to get anything through.' FLC R3 O3 245. Le Corbusier wrote to Sert from Chandigarh on 26 November 1952 in reference to the design of the Civic Centre of Bogotá: 'It does not seem admissible to me to start the new studies of the Civic Centre again without a precise programme. My plan (Heart of the City) is flexible and sound. The one you sent some time ago, covering only two city blocks, does not seem sufficient to me. It looks poor on account of the absence of the third block.' FLC R3 O3 248. In a letter of November 1953 sent by Sert and Lester to Le Corbusier, they informed him that the Plan of Bogotá had been accepted, although that did not mean that it would be executed, nor was it clear whether they would be commissioned to undertake the Civic Centre. FLC R3 O3 271.

[339] In the Hoddesdon CIAM, the architects Vieco and Samper criticized in the presence of Le Corbusier, Gropius, Sert, Roth, Chermayeff and Giedion the bases for the Bogotá Pilot Plan, which were not adapted to the social and cultural framework of the Colombian capital. See *Le Corbusier en Colombia*, op. cit., p. 15. News of this appeared in *El Tiempo*, Bogotá, 8 August 1951, from an article by Arturo Laguado called 'Lo que dijeron del Plan Piloto'.

[340] Arango, op. cit., p. 215.

[341] Niño, op. cit., p. 312.

LA HABANA - NUCLEOS CIVICOS

PLAN DE ENLACES

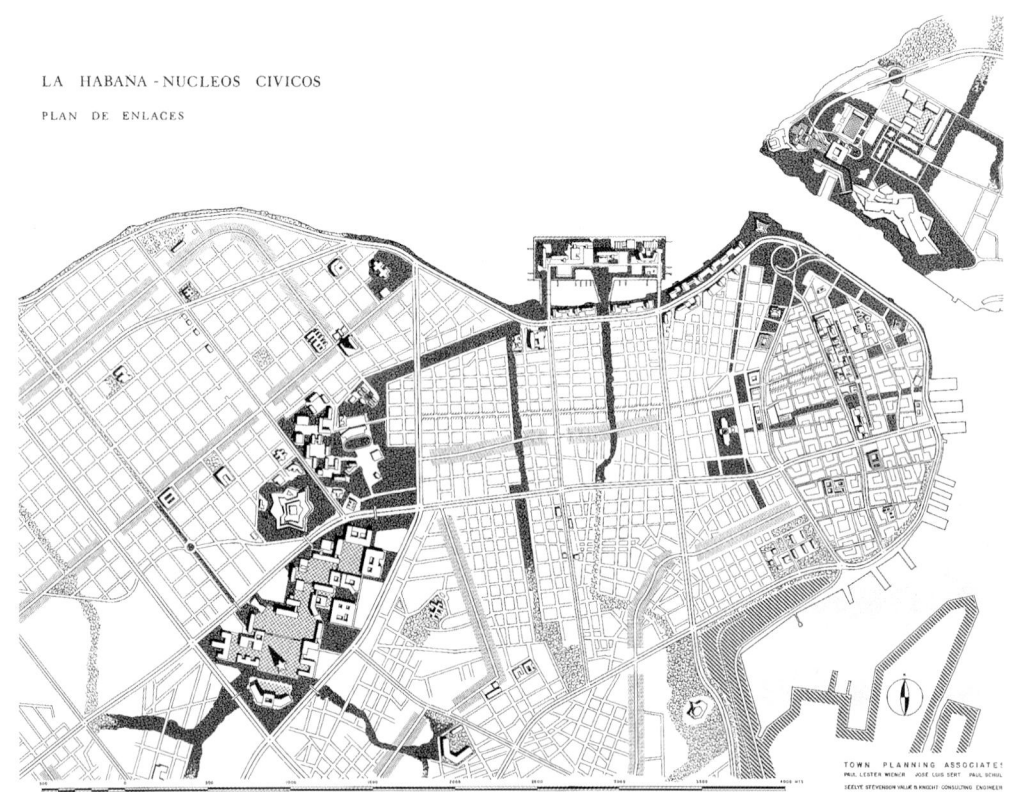

TOWN PLANNING ASSOCIATES
PAUL LESTER WIENER   JOSÉ LUIS SERT   PAUL SCHULZ
SEELYE STEVENSON VALUE & KNIGHT CONSULTING ENGINEERS

Last Commissions and End of the CIAMs

TPA (Town Planning Associates), Seelye, Stevenson, Value, Knecht, Pilot Plan for Havana, Cuba, 1955–58, urban centres (AJFM).

José Luis Sert and his associate continued to find their town planning ideas beset by obstacles. This also occurred in the projects for Venezuela that they undertook in 1950 for the Orinoco Mining Company (OMC), a society funded with American capital that was established to exploit the great iron ore deposits in Cerro Bolivar near the Orinoco River. The idea was to build two cities for the exploitation of the mines, one of which was to be Ciudad Piar, situated at the foot of the mines, and the other, Puerto Ordaz (named after Diego de Ordaz, the discoverer of the Orinoco Valley), which was to be built in the small harbour that had been constructed to transport iron to the US Steel Company, an American factory located at the convergence of the Orinoco and Caroní rivers. Both cities were connected by a railroad that transported the mineral from the first city to the second. On 7 December 1950, Sert and Lester received a letter from Francisco Carrillo Batalla, who promised to prepare and

TPA (Town Planning Associates), Carlos Guinand Baldo, Moisés Benacerraf, plan for Ciudad Piar, Venezuela, 1951–53.

compile all the documentary material so as to start negotiating their collaboration on the projects commissioned by the OMC. On 27 January 1951, he sent them an advance fee of $2,000, but by April problems had begun to arise, and these were to increase as time went on. Concerning the Puerto Ordaz project, the clients protested against their attempt to control the 'parasitic population', complaining that the Venezuelan administration would not tolerate

Puerto Caroni, Venezuela, aerial view.

Ciudad Piar, aerial view.

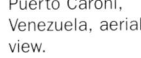

discrimination between Americans and Venezuelans, and that the existence of two civic centres was contrary to the idea of an integrated city.[342] This conflict would recur throughout the spring and summer of that year, when TPA handed in its partial plans for Puerto Ordaz.[343] The contract came into force on 3 September 1951,[344] shortly before Carrillo's criticisms reached an intolerable level. The letter that he sent to TPA on 9 September leaves no room for doubt as to the gravity of the situation. Carrillo complained about the height of the apartments (2.4 meters), about the exterior corridors for access to the apartments, about the lack of exterior stairwells, about the fact that the apartments were duplexes, about the fact that wash rooms were communal and kitchen-dining rooms were arranged together, about the use of the barrel vault, etc. Faced by this avalanche of protests, Sert and Lester modified some drawings and offered another plan for Puerto Ordaz, but this did not placate Carrillo, who by October was complaining about the Puerto Ordaz school plans and about some issues concerning Pomona, another small Venezuelan city designed by TPA for the Banco Obrero de Venezuela, which was financing low-cost housing throughout the country.[345]

Pomona, apartment buildings.

In February 1952 the situation became more critical as Sert and Lester had to modify many aspects of the projects they were drawing. Sert hastened to Pomona at the last minute to hand in the construction work plans. The technical documentary material for the school and commercial centre were to be completed by February 1953, according to a letter of 2 February in which Carrillo told them that their drawings had been modified

TPA (Town Planning Associates), Carlos Guinand Baldo, Moisés Benacerraf, building complexes in Pomona, Maracaibo, Venezuela, 1952–53.

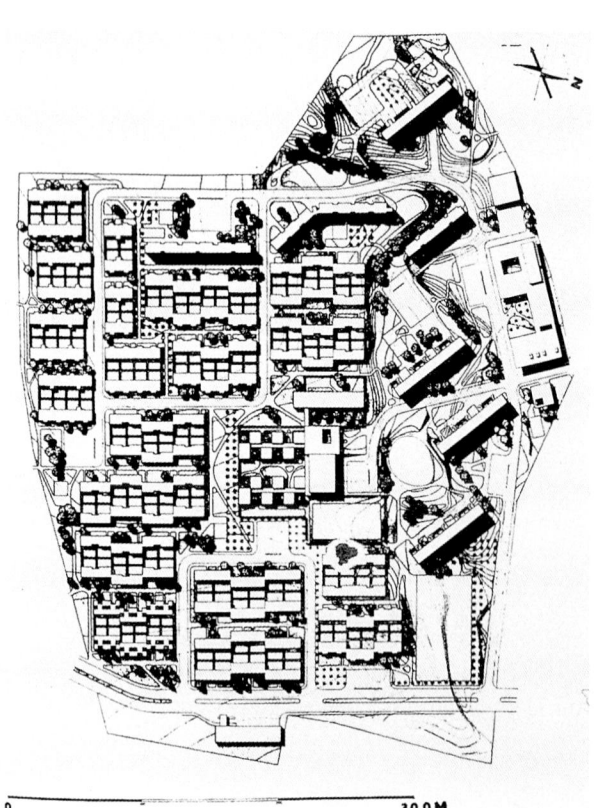

Pomona, apartment buildings.

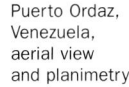

Puerto Ordaz, Venezuela, aerial view and planimetry.

TPA (Town Planning Associates), Civic Centre of Puerto Ordaz, 1951–53, model.

due to 'the use of local materials for maximum economy'. The final rupture came about in a letter of 25 August 1953, after it became known in Venezuela that Sert and Lester had published the OMC projects in the *Architectural Record*. Not only did the local architects feel deeply affronted by the American architects' breach of contract clause 15, which expressly forbade publishing any material without the consent of the OMC, they also felt they had

been made to look ridiculous because they were referred to merely as assistants. On 27 October, Sert's and Lester's presence in Venezuela came to an end when the OMC requested the original plans from TPA, since according to the signed contracts, these belonged to them.

A quick survey of these plans is sufficient to avoid repetition of comments on already well-known aspects. It is nevertheless useful to ob-

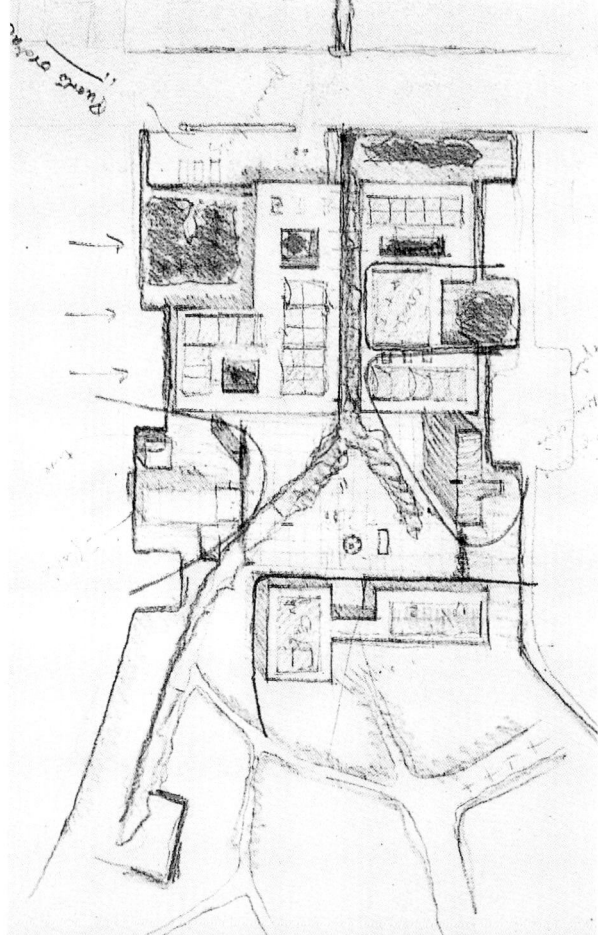

Puerto Ordaz, preliminary study of the Civic Centre (SC).

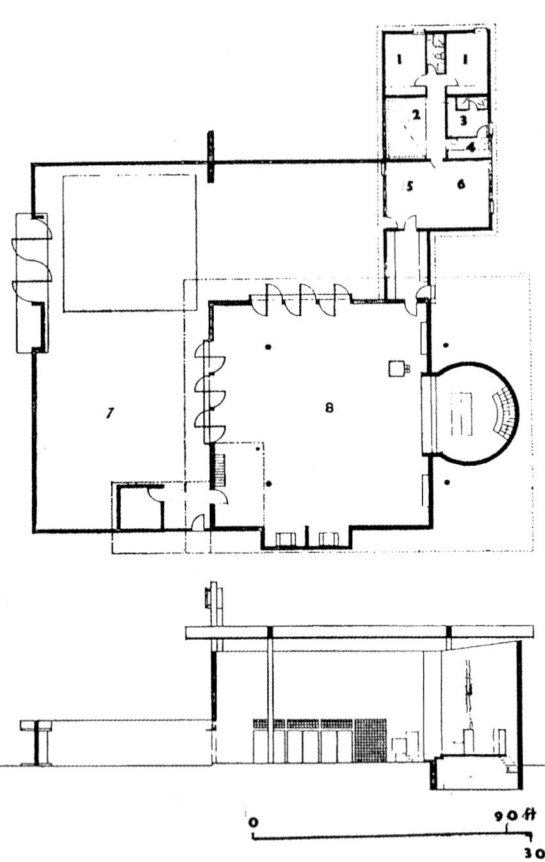

TPA (Town Planning Associates), plan for the church in Puerto Ordaz, 1951–53.

great number of people to attend religious services sheltered from the street while at the same time having the potential to serve as a recreational area for the parish school or as an outdoor classroom. The movement from closed space to courtyard allows for a different axial play from the one seen in religious spaces in Western Europe. Inspired by a Peruvian tradition of lining the roads with symbols from Christ's passion, Sert placed these emblems (ceramic and painted concrete ornamental reliefs) on a 12-metre high bell-tower following the usual Modulor proportions.

The church is a white cube topped by a roof that has no contact with the walls, vaguely based on the racetrack of La Zarzuela in Madrid, and formed by four concrete vaults that Sert conceived as an umbrella to give shel-

Puerto Ordaz church, views of the model.

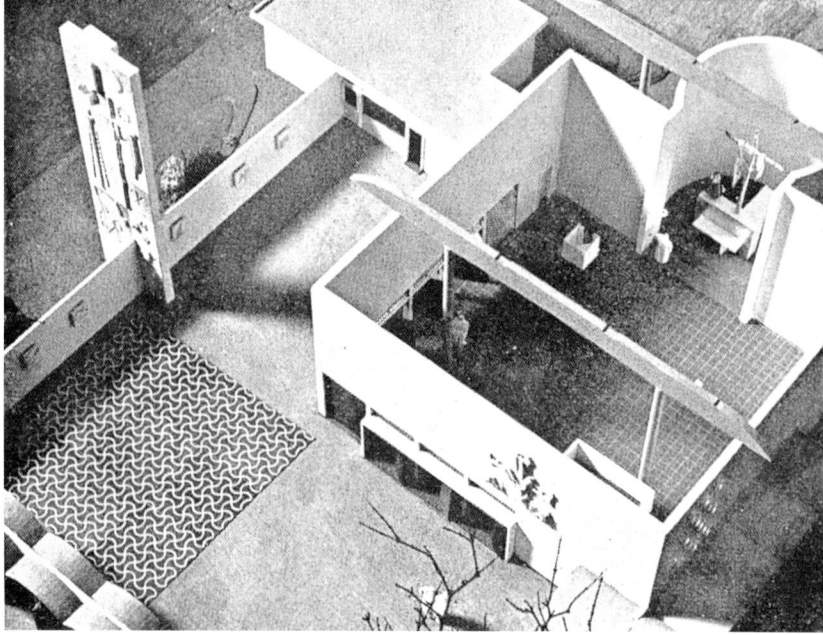

serve how Sert and Lester resolved the floor plans and facades of different housing groups, making use of compositional mechanisms in which the taste for variation is a determining factor and where at last they could test the aesthetic results of such a choice, since in this case the greater part of their proposals was built.

The project for the church of Puerto Ordaz, of which there are plans and a model, is one of the best elements of the architecture from this Venezuelan period. Sert made a minutely detailed explanation of its characteristics in the report he wrote: 'In trying to solve the problem presented by the church in the civic core of Puerto Ordaz, we have attempted to design a structure that avails itself of the knowledge of modern engineering and the advantages of modern materials … The proportions of old structures, colonial and others, were carefully considered. Scaling became the main concern … The Plan is simple. The basic shape used is the square; the different parts are related to the golden mean, in this particular case, Le Corbusier's Modulor.' A white wall circumscribes a patio from which one can enter directly into the church building, and which allows for a

ter from excessive sunlight, while stating that the apsidial form that covered the ensemble was inspired by Romanesque or Mudejar churches in Spain.[346] In this building, the ideals of new monumentality and the urgent need to recover history so as to formulate new architectural proposals become so evident that it is impossible not to notice this conceptual change in the way of thinking about architecture in relation to what we have seen so far.

Meanwhile, Sert was busy with the preparation of CIAM 8 and with the publication of a book on urban planning, which was a result of the debates in Bergamo. Concerning the former, it seems that Sert, President of CIAM, decided what theme would dominate the debates in Hoddesdon, the English city in which the Congress was to be held. This can be gleaned from the

Habitat Charter change the theme by calling it civic centre.'[347] A disagreement within the fold of the CIAM leaders had arisen, and there was no longer a unanimous opinion as to the subject that should be chosen for the upcoming Congress. On the 27th, Sert wrote to Giedion: 'Honegger tells me in his last letter that the Council meeting has been postponed to 11 April. I hope to see Corbusier before that date in Bogotá and talk with him about the subject and the place for the next Congress. In the meantime, I would like to state the following: as you know I am very interested in the subject of Civic Centres, and when the Dutch group suggested it as the theme for the next Congress I put this motion to a vote, and all other groups … voted for the other proposal, that is, for "Charte de l'habitat"; this included the British

Puerto Ordaz, club.

letters prior to the meeting, in which details of organization and subject matter were discussed.

In a letter of 12 January 1950, which Le Corbusier sent to Godfrey Samuel, an architect who formed part of the English MARS group and who was in charge of preparing the Congress, we read: 'I have to tell you that Emery and I are totally against the MARS proposal: the civic centre. The General Assembly, following the Directing Council in Bergamo, voted on the theme of the 8th Congress: the Charte de l'Habitat … So far as I'm concerned, I will not permit that a group in charge of organizing the

group.'[348] However, the most important aspect had become clear: Sert was eager that CIAM 8 should focus on the Civic Centre, an issue on which he was an expert thanks to his work in Latin America, and which consolidated his position as the ultimate arbiter of the next Congress' theme.

We are not sure what happened after this, but what is certain is that the next CIAM document that Sert kept was the minutes of an American CIAM group meeting held at the TPA New York office on 5 June 1950. In it we read: 'The meeting discussed the proposed programme for CIAM 8 in London, 7 to 14 July 1951. It was agreed that "Core" was not the happiest term for the theme. "Centres of community life" gave a clearer expression to the idea.'[349] Moreover, Sert had managed to convince Le Corbusier that the upcoming CIAM should not focus on the Charte de l'habitat. The pressure Sert must have exerted to get the civic centre theme approved for the CIAM is confirmed in a letter that he sent to Giedion on 9 November 1950: 'A book on Town Planning in general, including regional planning, etc., presents many difficulties and a unified system of presentation is very expensive to achieve without the co-operation of CIAM members … I therefore think it would be better to abandon this idea and replace this book with the Core publication, which would be more stimulating for the Congress and have good public acceptance … I will send you a brief outline of the book as I see it.'[350] Thus, instead of trying to synthesize what had been debated in Bergamo, as should have been the case, Sert was more interested in reversing this decision so as to advance a publication on the heart of the city as soon as possible: the CIAM President was determined to debate his professional and intellectual concerns with all the architects interested in the matter, and it seems that he had prepared the ground well in advance.

Our suspicions as to the possible connections between his interest in the heart of cities and his failures in South America, along with other interests derived from post-war Europe, seem to be well founded: the theme of the heart of a city made possible the convergence of architecture and city, as well as bringing together collective values and artistic expression, and it was also one of the important issues to keep in mind in the reconstruction of devastated European cities. All of this distanced the debate from global plans, which would have difficulty in progressing for the reasons stated above. It was impossible to think that there would be an economic system that would seriously consider providing a city with the infrastructures it needed for the correct development of human life within it, but it did not seem far-fetched to imagine that in the centre, or centres of it, the coincidence between pro-

fessional, representative and political interests, would revitalize the studies and work on cities that modern architects had been carrying out since 1930.

Giedion quickly showed his agreement with Sert's proposal,[351] and the writing of the text went ahead with the valuable collaboration of Gropius, who expressed through his correspondence with them his doubts as to the effectiveness of Le Corbusier's and Ascoral's *grille*.[352] In February 1951, Sert was still trying to convince Le Corbusier of the great relevance of the 'Civic Centres' subject, asking him to hand in his contribution as soon as possible: 'The good response seems to show that the problems of the Core is considered important by CIAM architects in many parts of the world. I personally feel this subject is one of the things we have till now left unexplored, and one that requires urgent study … You will see that I have provisionally included your name on the attached synopsis of the book. I hope very much that you will be willing to contribute an article, and the title I have suggested may be a guide for you.'[353]

This book took shape under the patient guidance of Jacqueline Tyrwhitt, since, apart from the task of planning the Congress, Sert was finishing the manuscript for a book on Gaudí and had no time to prepare the CIAM panels.[354] These were very different times from the Barcelona period; by then the excess of commissions and the huge amount of time he had to spend travelling to the South American continent did not allow Sert to control in a thorough manner all the issues in which he was involved. Times had changed, and the CIAM founders were looking for new ways in which to continue their work. This desire for continuity will be one of the key factors that will help us to understand some aspects of the CIAMs' demise, and we will come back to this point later.

Sert soon saw that the book on the heart of the city would not be ready in time for the Congress, and would have to be postponed until it was over. On 27 June, when he already had his tickets to fly to Europe, he was still asking Gropius for his article,[355] having finished his own introduction shortly before.[356]

CIAM 8 was held in Hoddesdon, Hertfordshire, on the dates set by the programme.[357] The central theme of the Congress, whose designation varied from 'Core' in English to *Noyau* in French, was to be debated by four commissions, who would approach the matter from different angles: the social and historical medium, urbanism, ethics and aesthetics, and legislation and financing. The commission dealing with urbanism placed great emphasis on selecting a precise term for the main theme of the Congress: 'The English word "core" has been translated into French as *noyau*; your commission prefers the word "heart", which is much closer to the aims sought. There is another term, that of "centre".' As secondary subjects, they were to deal with the Habitat Charter, architectural techniques, education and structures.

The session on 9 July is worthy of mention. Here, Le Corbusier insisted on the need to motivate the participation of post-war society in the collective problems presented by all cities: 'We have confirmed the worst: that modern society has become passive in all matters, suffers the arts and sports of others, but does not itself participate. We think CIAM could play a useful role by inviting modern society to procure itself the means with which to stimulate its members, a means that should be on a human scale.'[358] This became a leitmotiv of the lectures written for the Congress, which would later form the core of the book on the heart of the city and whose importance was manifested in the Congress' conclusions.

Sert's lecture, which bore an elucidating title ('Centres for Community Life'), would become the first article in *The Heart of the City*.[359] The text began with a long quotation from *Revolt of the Masses* by Ortega y Gasset, an author whom Sert deeply admired and of whom we shall speak later. Sert stressed the need to think about the civic centre after reviewing the concerns that had marked the course taken by CIAMs since 1929. According to him, the city needed a strong process of recentralization so as to avoid the dismembering that it had suffered in the course of daily wear and tear and the destruction caused by the war, which had effaced the personality of many places that had represented the collective values of the cities. 'The social function of the new community centres or cores is primarily that of uniting people and

facilitating direct contacts and exchange of ideas that will stimulate free discussion.' He then went on to enumerate the meeting places that he considered exemplary for the development of these functions, such as Trafalgar Square, Piccadilly Circus, the Galleria Vittorio Emanuele in Milan, the Ramblas in Barcelona, etc., going on to propose the need for a constellation of minor community centres that would be dominated by the main centre: 'The resulting pattern should then be organic and different from the shapeless growth we have today. Each of these sectors or parts of the city needs to have its own centre or nucleus, and the system as a whole results in a *network or constellation* of community centres, classified from small to large, one main centre being the expression of the city or metropolis as a whole, *the heart of the city*.'

The heart of the city was to be the place in which that mythical fusion of all the arts was to be accomplished, as had been the case in

Cover for the original edition of *The Heart of the City*.

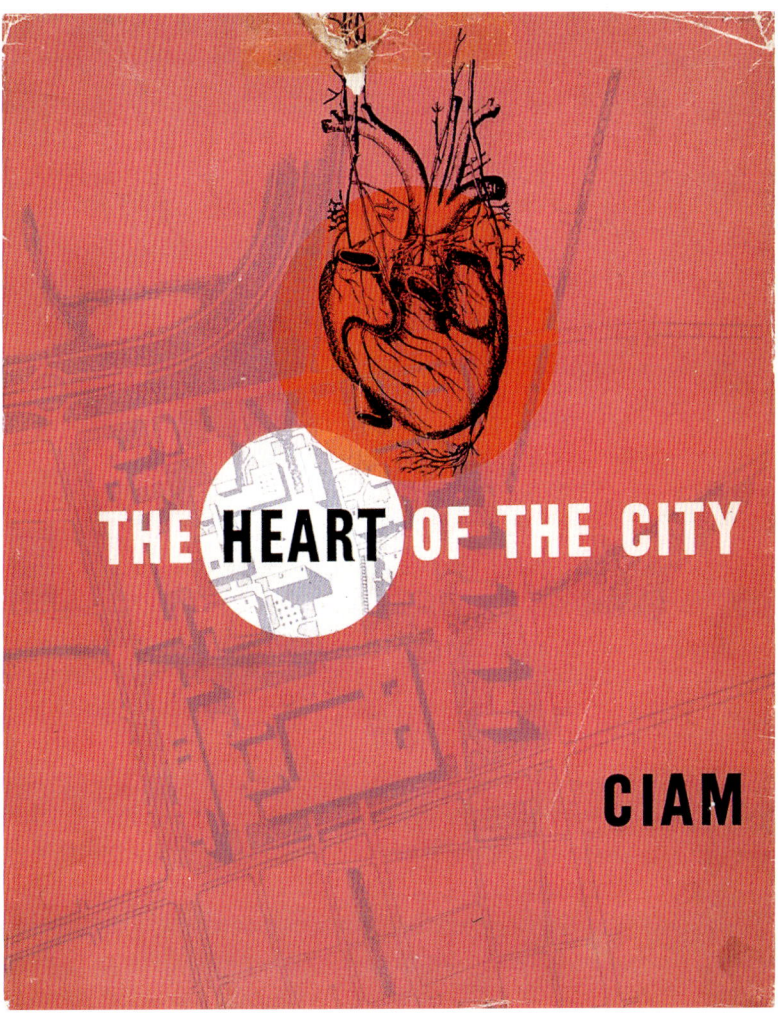

THE HEART OF THE CITY

CIAM

Athens according to Léger, and now this theoretical conception was taking form: 'In these centres of community life, the city planner-architect deals with civic design, uniting planning and architecture … Throughout history it is in such places of public gathering – the *agora*, the forum, the cathedral square – that the integration of the arts has been most successfully accomplished.'

Sert again emphasized the fact that functionalist ideas could take second place, and that the heart of the city was the site that could serve as a catalyst to facilitate new ways of expression for the unexplored formal possibilities of modern architecture, which in this way would free itself once and for all from its dependency on the 'machine' metaphor: 'The functional aspects of contemporary architecture are now fully appreciated by a great many people, and it has become generally accepted for utility buildings of all sorts, such as low-rent housing, hospitals, schools, factories, etc. But these same people cannot imagine its possibilities if applied to groups of public buildings because there are no examples of this type. On the other hand, most contemporary architects are now well aware that the period of house-cleaning of the 1920s is over. We have outlived that period when architecture aimed solely at expressing function. New trends are now apparent towards a greater freedom of plasticity, a more complete architectural vocabulary. No matter how beautiful structure alone may be, should we forget that flesh and skin can be added to the bones? The need for the superfluous is as old as mankind.'

Once again, therefore, we observe in Sert a will to synthesize the architectural moment, professional practice and cultural concerns. In this matter he had a headstart, as his experience in designing urban centres for South American cities invested his discourse with an authority that is evidenced both in the articles that made up *The Heart of the City* as well as in the examples he presented at the CIAM Congress, which were compiled and published in this book along with the Chimbote, Medellin and Bogotá projects.

Once Sert had returned to the US, completing the book became the main focus of interest, and Jacqueline Tyrwhitt in London and Rogers in Milan worked jointly with Sert to finish it. The intense correspondence between Tyrwhitt and Rogers allows us to trace the progress of its publication. Sert, who was somewhat disappointed with the Congress results, was very interested in controlling all aspects of the book's production: 'The civic character and social importance of the main core or heart of the city has not been stressed enough, and all our resolutions refer more to the smaller local cores … The task of the city planner to create an appropriate container for all activities in the core has not been stressed clearly enough … Please send me, at your earliest convenience, a copy of the dummy you have made with Rogers.'[360] After receiving the parcel, he wrote to Tyrwhitt on 8 August to stress his desire to supervise the whole process: 'I received your long communiqué … I agree to the table of contents as you sent it, but I enclose a new copy of it with a few minor changes.' On 7 September he wrote to her again regarding the final title for the book: 'Haven't we finally agreed that the title of the book should be *The heart of the city*? I really believe that CORE is an unpopular and meaningless word and I definitely believe that it is a mistake to use it in the title.'

By 22 September the first part of the book had been completed,[361] and a month later Giedion complained about the speed and egotism that had characterized the production of the book, making him feel excluded from the enterprise.[362] Thus it is clear that small frictions continued to surface among the old CIAM leaders. By mid-December, Tyrwhitt was requesting the last illustrations for the book and proposing a title for the second part while finishing the translations; she was hoping to have everything ready for printing by January 1952.[363]

By then it was time to start preparing CIAM 9, which was held in Aix-en-Provence from 19 to 26 July 1953. From the very beginning of its preparation, however, tension was in the air, and this situation did not improve until the Congress itself was held. A letter from Giedion to Sert of 19 March 1952 expresses foreboding regarding this: 'I am increasingly worried about the existence of the CIAMs. We must avoid at all costs handing these over to people of compromise, and the CIAMs are full of them now. The young members who should take the reins have not shown a truly active spirit … I would rather be in favour of dissolving the CIAMs than leaving them in weak hands or in the hands of the newly arrived.'[364] Perhaps the effort undertaken in the last meeting had been conceived as the legacy that its founders were capable of leaving to the younger generations: debating on the heart of the city was a way of formulating a vanguard idea that distanced it from the old functionalist concepts, thus ensuring a continued commitment to architectural ideology and reality.

Sert's answer on the 31st of that month is full of similar doubts, although he tried to offer logical explanations regarding the changing ideals upheld at different times: 'If CIAM has to be dissolved because no one can continue our work, only the Congress as a whole can decide … There is no doubt that world matters have changed and that young people are not living under the same conditions that we did twenty years ago. It is not only lack of interest, but we should not forget that working conditions have changed and that the fight for Modern Architecture cannot be engaged on the same basis as before … The problems they have to face are those of better building techniques, materials and different social approaches to the whole matter … They do not see what the Congress has to offer them.'[365]

By May, doubts concerning the efficacy of the CIAMs and the roles of the different generations had become more generalized. On the 8th of that month, Sert wrote Giedion a letter in which he defined the programme to be followed until the Congress was held. He was clearly not convinced that the younger generation was willing to take over: 'The reaction has always been that they do not seem prepared to take over and they want the older members to continue.'

In the preparatory meeting to decide where CIAM 9 should take place, which was held in Le Corbusier's studio on 10 and 11 May 1952, they specifically debated 'The Departure of the "Ancient" CIAM Members and the Passing of the Torch to Young Members', employing terms that seem to indicate the veterans' need to unburden themselves of their workload, feeling that events and new areas of study had surpassed their capacities. In Le Corbusier's

words: 'I consider that those present are too old and can no longer "conquer" … right now … the problem of city planning implies such a harmonizing of different disciplines that we no longer have the necessary flexibility for it. We are no longer the "Conquering Generation".' Tyrwhitt read Sert's letter to Giedion and added: 'We must therefore continue by giving our assistance and our experience to the young members … We could hand over the organization to the young members and remain as spectators-counsellors.' In Gropius' opinion, 'the evolution must be carried out very slowly and with a great deal of patience … The old members will attend the Congress basically as spectators. It will be a Congress of transition.' Giedion nevertheless insisted on old theories: 'One must consider the CIAM problem as a problem of continuity. No one must dream of leaving the CIAMs in a theatrical way.'

Something was clearly wrong, for if in the past preparatory meetings were held in order to debate the theme that would be developed in the Congress, now a preparatory meeting was being held to debate the need for such a gathering and for the Congress to take place at all.

A possible explanation for this change was the feeling of failure that had accompanied many of the experiences of functionalist urbanism, and this can be gleaned from a letter that Sert wrote to Le Corbusier shortly before the Paris meeting, which he was unable to attend: 'We realize it is difficult to convince Governments and foreign companies of the need for starting new towns in agreement with CIAM principles and to provide, from the very beginning, the necessary social services and amenities, etc.'[366]

That matters had become more complicated under these circumstances is confirmed by a letter from Sert to Giedion of 12 June,[367] and by the results of the Sigtuna meeting held on the 25th.[368] On 11 November, faced with this outlook, Sert wrote Le Corbusier a long missive (of which there is an English version in the Sert Collection and a French one in the Fondation Le Corbusier), in which he attempted to recompose the conflicts and offer a way out of them: 'After having examined the minutes of the Sigtuna conference … I would suggest the following: CIAM members and groups make no distinct classification between young or old members, continuity being one of the important factors in the work of CIAM … The new groups of CIAM, formed by the younger elements, should start their work with the greatest possible independence, but under the guidance of an "advisory committee" formed by the senior members … An architectural revolution, like any revolution, goes through preliminary phases, the formulation of doctrines, definitions, programming, manifestos, etc., but that period is now over, it came to an end with the last war … Our first meetings … dedicated many hours to matters of semantics and definitions. A time that could have been put to better use dealing with realities. We have also consumed much time on philosophical arguments … The younger generation is, I believe, also rather disturbed by the use of vague terms such as "core", "habitat", etc. … We should not forget that Modern Architecture is very far from reaching its goal.'

Thus, for Sert it was a matter of understanding that new objectives for modern architecture were to be sought, and that these were to be chosen based on reality, leaving aside other issues and integrating the younger members under the protective mantle of the senior group. To carry this out, Sert designed a plan of action to revitalize what looked like a lost cause, specifying six main points: 1. Revision of the Bridgwater Statutes 2. Re-establishment of the CIRPACs 3. Replacement of the Council by an Executive Committee of fewer people 4. Creation of an Advisory Committee for the CIAMs 5. Promotion of CIAM workshops in diverse universities and architects' offices 6. Re-examination of the work done by the CIAM commissions since the Bergamo Congress.

It seems clear that it was not the founding members of CIAM who would be in charge of renovating architecture, not only because they were weary and overburdened, but also because of the younger members' innate instinct for independence, their certainty that they would be able to face the new times by themselves. Tyrwhitt's letter to Sert on 2 December announced that the third issue of *TEAM*, edited by Norberg-Schulz and Neuenschwander, was proposing to hold the first Congress of young CIAM members after CIAM 9 had been held

in the coming summer, and added: 'PLEASE take no action that will discourage this. Even if *TEAM* itself and some of the active youngsters seem a bit green, please let them have freedom to try to work things out for themselves.'[369] It therefore seems that there were two alternatives: the supervision of the renovating work of young members on the part of senior members, or the granting of total freedom to the younger elements so as to give continuity to the existence of a group that would collectively re-orient the possibilities of post-war architecture.

We have previously spoken of the excess of work taken on by the CIAM veterans and of their fatigue due both to the passing of time and to their many occupations. In Sert's case, a new intellectual concern was added to his numerous other responsibilities at this point. In fact, from a letter that Giedion sent to him on 30 January 1953 we gather that he had just been designated Dean of the Graduate School of Design of Harvard: 'First of all, my congratulations on your victory, which is also a victory for the CIAMs. It is formidable to know that you are the head of the school of architecture, and all I can hope is that you will take advantage of the struggles that Gropius had to undertake against the backward forces that made his life so difficult in Harvard.'[370] Sert thus had one more reason to abandon the CIAMs, although he would insist on working to organize the following Congress, possibly due to the obligations he had undertaken as President of the organization.

Things went back to normal[371] in February after the Paris meeting had been held. At the Locust Valley meeting of 3 May, attended by Sert, Giedion and Tyrwhitt, the Congress programme was drafted, and those present agreed to ask Giedion, Le Corbusier, Sert, Gropius, van Eesteren, Rogers, Georges Candilis and the MARS group to prepare lectures for the Congress. Of these, the majority formed part of the veteran group, a fact that was not much in keeping with the spirit of renewal that had been manifested shortly before and that hardly seemed to offer any possibilities to the young members; apparently, the senior members were not willing after all to let go of the reins and trust the capacities of newly arrived members.[372] Moreover, in a letter of 3 July 1953 that Le Corbusier addressed to the Ministry of Reconstruction and Urbanism in France, we find: 'The President Mr José Luis Sert, at present in Spain, has asked me, as Vice-President for Europe, to request permission to organize on Saturday 25 July an activity for this Congress in the Unité d'Habitation of Marseilles so as to celebrate there in the evening the 25th anniversary of the CIAMs.'[373] As Jos Bosman has described it, those present, on Gropius' petition, gave Le Corbusier a standing ovation,[374] an act that Bosman has interpreted as the last physical demonstration of the Modern Movement. In our opinion, however, this homage seems more like the final gesture of a veneration that few were willing to perpetuate.

Bosman cites, without identifying his source, a moment during the meeting of the CIAM Council in Aix in which Sert proposed that a Committee of Transference be created, 'which co-ordinates and evaluates the decisions to be taken so as to transfer the CIAM responsibilities to the younger members while maintaining the CIAM spirit.' Bosman gives an account of the surprising reaction of the younger members to this proposal: 'Candilis, Aujaume, Ecochard, and Bakema affirmed that the CIAM spirit depended on the constant presence of the senior members … The CIAM Council was the spirit of the CIAMs … The young members were enthusiasts, but one could hardly say they had a common spirit … It was not necessary to separate the two components … A revolutionary change was not necessary … just a greater incorporation into the Council. After a second count, Wogensky and Bakema were elected.' Bosman goes on to relate that the other candidates were van Eyck, Neuenschwander, Norberg-Schulz, Ernst May and Ecochard, and that the rest of the Council members remained in their posts. Without its founding members, there was no chance of this, as young members were thinking along other lines far removed from the 'continuity' of something that did not pertain to them. This is confirmed by the total lack of agreement reached when they were charged with organizing CIAM 10 in Dubrovnik, or at the meeting at Otterlo, but this matter, as well as the meetings of TEAM X (a group formed by the Ali-son and Peter Smithson and Jill and Bill Howell), are issues that do not concern us here.[375]

The lectures at Aix were developed around the theme of 'Habitat', which was worked on by the six permanent Commissions in accordance with a text written by Sert for the Congress Programme.[376] In it, we again observe a concern for defining the scope of the term 'to inhabit', since the function of living was constantly changing and that of planning was not the sum of its parts but rather an integrated whole that needed to be organized. He proposed debating specific projects presented on a common basis, recalling the development of the CIAM in Athens, and hoped that as a result of the collective discussions they would be able to draft the long-awaited Habitat Charter. There was a surfeit of nostalgia in this text, especially when one considers it in relation to the absurd content of Le Corbusier's lecture, in which he demonstrated no intention of creating an organized body of knowledge around the idea of habitat, and showed no desire to contribute to the writing of the CIAM 9 publication, which in fact was never published.[377]

Some of the other lectures hold a certain interest, especially due to the novelty of approach to certain issues that had seemed unmovable. One example is the lecture of Subcommission 1 of the Commission on Urbanism, in which we find: 'The house will be an instrument that can open like a flower in the interior so as to reflect the life of the cell that is the family … The house will be an ensemble that will open to the exterior so as to express the grandeur of nature and the life of a city through its shapes and colours.'[378] Another example is found in Subcommission 1b: 'We observe a need for greater differentiation between the functions of the dwelling and the *unité d'habitation* … The expression of such visual elements will help man to conserve his identity despite the greater numerical extension of the problem.'[379] In Subcommission 1c's report we read: 'Outside of the dwelling – where the intimate role of the family takes places – there is a need for a framework in which to play an active role in communal life. The apparition of the machine breaks up the existing harmony between individual life and communal life.'[380]

There are also striking elements in the findings of Commission II, dedicated to the Synthesis of Visual Arts, which dealt with the role of aesthetics in the habitat. It no longer focused on intermediate disciplines such as painting or sculpture, but concentrated instead on elements proper to architecture and to the design of the city, thus distancing itself from the objective-rationalist determinism of the 1930s and recovering some Corbusian formulations for which it was necessary to have 'a new visual sensibility, a new development of its sense of rhythm and of its capacity to appreciate the play of volumes in space … The exercise of this faculty based on the superiority of these visual relationships should form part of university education.' This new sensibility called for a return to the primitive as a liberating mechanism from so many modern proposals: 'A hut in Cameroon has more aesthetic dignity than do most pre-fabricated houses.'

Gropius presented a disjointed lecture with rehashed content in which he jumbled issues such as the need for human scale with others such as the users' participation in urbanistic plans, at the same time praising the advantages of team work and asserting the rights of pedestrians.[381]

Finally, the Commission on Social Issues spoke about the rights of all humankind to have decent housing, and again the old ghost that had arisen in CIAM 2 and which had since then stalked the Congresses, came to the fore: 'The present form of real-estate property, of building property as well as land occupation and dwelling rights, are the main obstacles for the necessary evolution and transformation of the habitat.' This is further complicated when we read: 'Contemporary habitat no longer measures up to the possibilities of modern technique.'[382]

It seems evident that the veterans no longer had anything new to say. CIAM 9 therefore demonstrated, both through the emptiness of its content and through the failure of its basic initial intentions, the impossibility of continuing the Congresses.

There was more to it than that, however, since the contributions made by some of the young participants at Aix, such as Jacob Berend Bakema, van Eyck, the Smithsons and the Howells showed how alienated they were from the

ethical obsessions of their elders and how much more concerned they were with new definitions and paths that could propose different forms and resolve new problems. Thus, for example, the Nagele project on which van Eyck was working when he participated at Aix was based on the idea of achieving a space within a space instead of thinking about functional ends, or on investigating the aesthetics of numbers as Richard Paul Lohse was also doing at the time. According to van Eyck, this was due to the fact that he did not consider that the concepts of the individual and the collective were opposed, as was proposed in a mechanical interpretation of the functional city, and that he wished 'habitat' to be understood as a dynamic entity, a theory that has led Francis Strauven to apply Bergsonian concepts of relativity to the understanding of this Dutch architect's contribution.[383]

The idea that habitat should be studied from the point of view of the coherency of its internal relationships, the rapport among its components, brought about a change in the orientation of projects. If before it had been a matter of ensuring the standards that Sert and Lester had proposed for their Latin American cities, now it was a matter of thinking about how to intervene in the intermediate spaces between those pure constructed volumes so as to address the physical, human and spatial relationships that could be derived from their confrontation. The proposal of the Smithsons and Howells took off from a clear statement: 'The basis of our work should not be to study the functions, but to study the groupings and phenomena of human relationships',[384] and their text for the Congress attempted to analyze relationships that departed from human terms, which were established based on dwelling, street, neighbourhood and city, so that 'street' was defined as 'a community in physical contact', 'neighbourhood' as 'a community of acquaintances', and 'city' as 'a community of intellectual contacts and common interests'. Thus, in a street one could 'probably make a friend', in the neighbourhood one could 'probably make some friends', and in the city 'various friends'.

It is not pertinent at this point to evaluate the scope of the Dutch and English proposals, but it is certain that in the context in which they were formulated they created a profound awareness of the need for a new language that would substitute the old ideology.

This became so clear that it was common for people to speak of 'before' and 'after' Aix. In an anonymous text found in the Fondation Le Corbusier, we read: 'We the young have received a shock at Aix in seeing to what degree the marvel of La Ville Radieuse has vanished from CIAM … Today each one of us recognizes the existence of a new spirit.'[385] In another, which is in the Sert Collection, and whose heading reads 'CIAM 10', thus leading us to assume that it was written at the start of the preparatory work for the Congress held in Dubrovnik in August 1956, we read: 'We think, especially "after Aix", that the time has come to let the CIAM movement drink from the "fountain of youth", so as to arouse it and re-orient it towards its tradition and its destiny – a path traced by its founders Corbu, Gropius, Giedion, van Eesteren, Sert, etc … We are afraid that old age, weariness, and mediocrity are taking over CIAM. On examining the Aix Congress, from the point of view of a Congress of work and from its results, one must have the courage to speak the truth … The results are from all points of view worse than mediocre … We must renovate and we want to have a chance at it … The majority of us belong to the post-war generation, and we are involved in today's reality.'[386]

The young members offered to orient and organize, but always under the veterans' guidelines. The most they hoped to achieve was the elimination of the commissions, instead encouraging all Congress attendants to come prepared. Concerning organizational questions, they proposed: 'Introduction by the President and by Team X in a lively spirit; exhibition, projections, debates.' This may not have been much, but it did seem clear that they were now willing to work for the Congress, dissipating Sert's fear that they would not collaborate. Thus began the preparation of CIAM 10.

This Congress again began with the work of the veterans. Sert wrote a letter to Giedion on 8 February 1954 in which he spoke of meeting in Europe the following summer 'to talk about the next Congress. Dates, etc. should then be determined as I already have quite a few people requesting that information.' Giedion's answer from Iraq on 19 March dealt with many organizational aspects, such as whether the first preparatory meeting should be in La Sarraz or in Paris. Finally, on 4 July 1954, a meeting was held attended by Sert, Giedion, Le Corbusier, Honegger, Tyrwhitt, Bakema, Howell, Steiger, Candilis, Rogers, P.A. Emery and André Wogensky. Once again there was significant veteran representation, the young members being exclusively represented by those they had elected as Council members. They all agreed that the theme of CIAM 10 should be: 'Habitat problems: first CIAM proposal, findings, and resolutions', and that there should be a calendar of meetings for its organization. On 29 July the Smithsons and the Howells met with Tyrwhitt 'to discuss the progress that had already been made towards formulating the programme for CIAM 10.'[387] In the minutes of the meeting we are told that the 'CIAM 10 Committee consisted of Bakema, Smithson, Candilis and Gutman', and that a meeting would be held on 28 and 29 August to draw up a CIAM 10 programme that would be discussed with Giedion and Sert on 14 September in Paris.

It seems that the younger members had decided to go on; the meeting did in fact take place, and Team X attended along with Candilis, Bakema, van Eyck and van Minkl, while Le Corbusier and Giedion went as representatives of the Advisory Group. This time there was a majority of young members facing the veterans who gave them advice; the transition was taking place, and it was being carried out without theatrical gesture or excessive trauma. In this meeting they debated the proposal for CIAM 10, which the younger members had prepared by setting up four work groups: House, Town, City and Metropolis. In each one of these groups there would be a Council member, lecturers from that group, and a Team X representative.[388]

The differences of orientation between the English and Dutch members became more marked, as is seen in a letter that Bakema sent to Sert, Gropius and Giedion on 28 December, in which he insisted on his and van Eyck's way of working,[389] and this motivated an answer from the three senior members demanding that they reach an understanding.[390] Considering this situation, it is not surprising that Le Corbusier wrote a text in English on 9 May 1955, organizing the Congress on his own,[391] nor that Giedion sent Sert a handwritten letter on 24 April – which along Le Corbusier's lines proposed that 'the veteran CIAM' write the Habitat Charter and that Sert act firmly to avoid repeating the Aix failure – nor that Bakema carried out a war between both factions, organizing at the same time the UIA Congress, which in Giedion's words was a copy of the CIAM programme.[392]

Between 8 and 10 September, a great number of delegates – who thanked Team X for its contribution, encouraging it to continue its work on preparing the Congress under CIRPAC guidelines – assembled in La Sarraz to prepare a declaration on habitat and to write the CIAM 10 programme. The text that was approved was symptomatic of the odd times through which the CIAMs were passing: 'The meeting has decided to give this declaration the following title: Habitat. Declaration of Principles. This declaration will contain in exergue an extract from the Athens Charter, a manifestation of the continuity, vitality and modernity of the CIAM works.'[393] Once again, the old CIAM spirit resisted breathing its last, still longing for manifestos and continuities with a past that it continued to believe could provide guidance in the 1950s; it therefore seems that we are faced by parallel developments of interest that would sometimes meet and converge, but which do not foreshadow collective agreements. A proof of this is Giedion's lecture, in which the Swiss historian wrote: 'The notion of "relations" is one susceptible to furnishing a structure, a valuable support to CIAM 10, which will deal with this aspect of habitat. And by relations one naturally understands those between the functions of town planning … for example the rapport between habitat and their extensions, those between the different elements of the city and its structure.' Giedion's speech served as a springboard for the investigation of this idea, and by November 1955 they were working on showing these relationships through a system of four panels on which van Eyck and others presented their projects in Dubrovnik.[394]

For the CIAM President, it was clear that matters were drawing to a close. In fact, in a letter of 16 July 1956, addressed to Le Corbusier, we read: 'I have a lot of work at this moment and it is no longer easy to take part in the Congresses, but since this will be the last under my presidency, I believe it is my duty to go to Yugoslavia.'[395] He then summarized the reality that we have been unveiling: 'As you know, CIAM is undergoing a very serious crisis, and we must be there to help it surmount present difficulties for the sake of its prestige.' Le Corbusier attempted to help out by sending Sert a handwritten letter[396] and a manifesto to Dubrovnik in which he tried to present the crisis as a generational problem, a problem of people born in different times and with different concerns, and in which he called upon the younger members to take over. Believing that this would be easier for them to achieve without his presence, he decided not to go to Dubrovnik.[397]

On 3 September Sert wrote to him: 'Your message, I believe, has put things in their place, and I hope that everything will go well. At present the Council and the Committee of Reorganization must work together … Team X is willing to propose that the new Secretariat be in Paris … I agree with you, we must not let the CIAMs get lost in a Nordic haze.'[398]

While Sert was contemplating CIAMs loss of meaning, he was also at work drawing up the Havana Plan, the last of TPA's town planning proposals for Latin America. His professional contacts with the Caribbean island went far back in time: from 1949 on, we find his uninterrupted correspondence with Eugenio Batista, a founding member of the ATEC, who was also very interested in CIAM. However, Sert would have to wait until 1953 to go back to Cuba, and from then until 1958 he would travel back and forth from the island on professional matters during the political construction of Fulgencio Batista's dictatorship, which had taken over with almost no resistance on 10 March 1952.[399] Batista was interested in creating a new architectural image representative of power in the capital and in setting up the conditions that would allow the island to become the target of national and North American partnership investments, drafting to this end the Law of General Planning.[400]

This was the ideal terrain for TPA's entry into Cuba. In an interview that appeared in the March–June 1953 issue of the Cuban architectural magazine *Espacio*, Sert, who did not hesitate in making use of his familiar strategies to get a commission, declared: 'In Latin America, architecture has liberated itself and has achieved in certain countries a personality of its own, and one can already say that a Latin American formula for planning is being developed. In Colombia, Peru, Venezuela, Argentina, Uruguay, Brazil, Chile and other countries there are independent technical organizations for national planning that, with the help of national and foreign technicians, are working on the integral study of regions and cities that include regulating plans, economic and legislative studies, etc. … Due to its geographical conditions, Cuba is a country that facilitates planning because it is all one region with quite uniform characteristics.' Concerning the debate organized on the architecture of Havana's Plaza Cívica, he said: 'A pilot plan for the city could be prepared in a short period of time, and even before it is finished it will be possible to know for certain where such a centre should be located … The study necessary for choosing the best location should not take more than two months.'[401]

Shortly after these declarations, on 26 July 1953, the Moncada barracks were attacked – a sign that many people on the island were dissatisfied and did not believe that Batista's planning was seeking solutions for the most destitute. It was necessary to speed up the process so as to demonstrate to impatient potential investors that things were working out according to a carefully designed plan that would ensure profitable capital growth and the well-programmed touristic development of the island. Thus, by 22 September 1953 Sert and Lester were already writing the first Memorandum on the island. This they addressed to Nicolás Arroyo, who would later become Director of the National Planning Board of Cuba, which was created by Decree Law 2018 on 27 January 1955.

In the architects' text we read: 'City planning has become increasingly essential during the last twenty years because of the rapid growth of complex problems such as the use of land, traffic conditions and many others. Cities became increasingly unmanageable due to a lack of planning resulting in financial chaos.

Growth of cities was accompanied by increase in slums, crime, physical and mental illness, traffic congestion and many other chaotic conditions … Legislative procedures to effect the Master Plans have been established in most countries, thereby greatly assisting Governments and their administrative functions, tax structures, etc … for the benefit of all citizens, rich and poor.'[402] Reading this text, one can have few doubts as to what intentions lay behind the planning of Cuba: it was to be an indispensable instrument that would solve social ills, and that, albeit mysteriously, would benefit all thanks to the intervention of the government, that authority for whose protective legislature the rationalist architects in the 1930s had called. However, because of its special character and location, Cuba presented an altogether new aspect for the TPA architects, since it is here that they saw the possibility of conceiving a regional plan for the whole territory: 'As national regions and cities become more closely linked through increased motor traffic and modern technology in general, it becomes necessary to integrate National and Regional resources and services, the use of the land, and a proper network of highways and road systems.'

The memorandum sought to organize the incipient needs that Batista considered appropriate for Cuba. Thus, Sert and Lester devoted themselves to formulating the planning, or in other words, to thinking about how many and what type of people were to make up the Metropolitan Offices of Planning, what departments these would consist of, and which would be their consulting institutions. They then defined what was meant by a Pilot Plan and a subsequent Master Plan, also making reference to the problem-solving programmes that constituted them and the minimum plans necessary for their resolution. The TPA architects offered to train Cuban architects in their New York office while the physical and material situation of Cuba was being analyzed, so that when these architects returned to their own country they could hold important posts in the planning office and in turn train their colleagues.

Sert and Lester concluded their report with an indication of the work they were to be assigned, which they divided into two phases. The first had to do with the elaboration of the Pilot

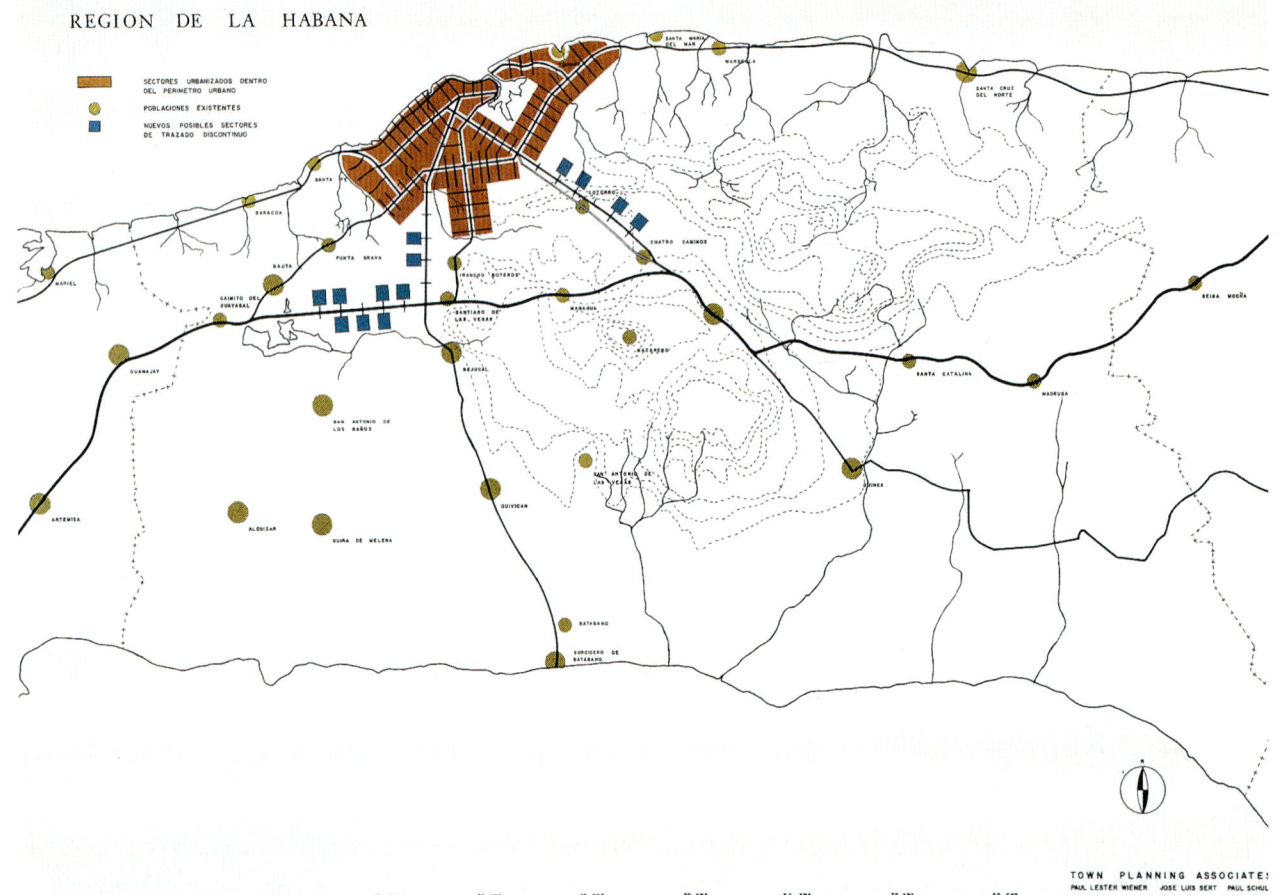

TPA (Town Planning Associates), Seelye, Stevenson, Value, Knecht, Havana Pilot Plan, 1955–58, the Havana region and the old town plan (AJFM).

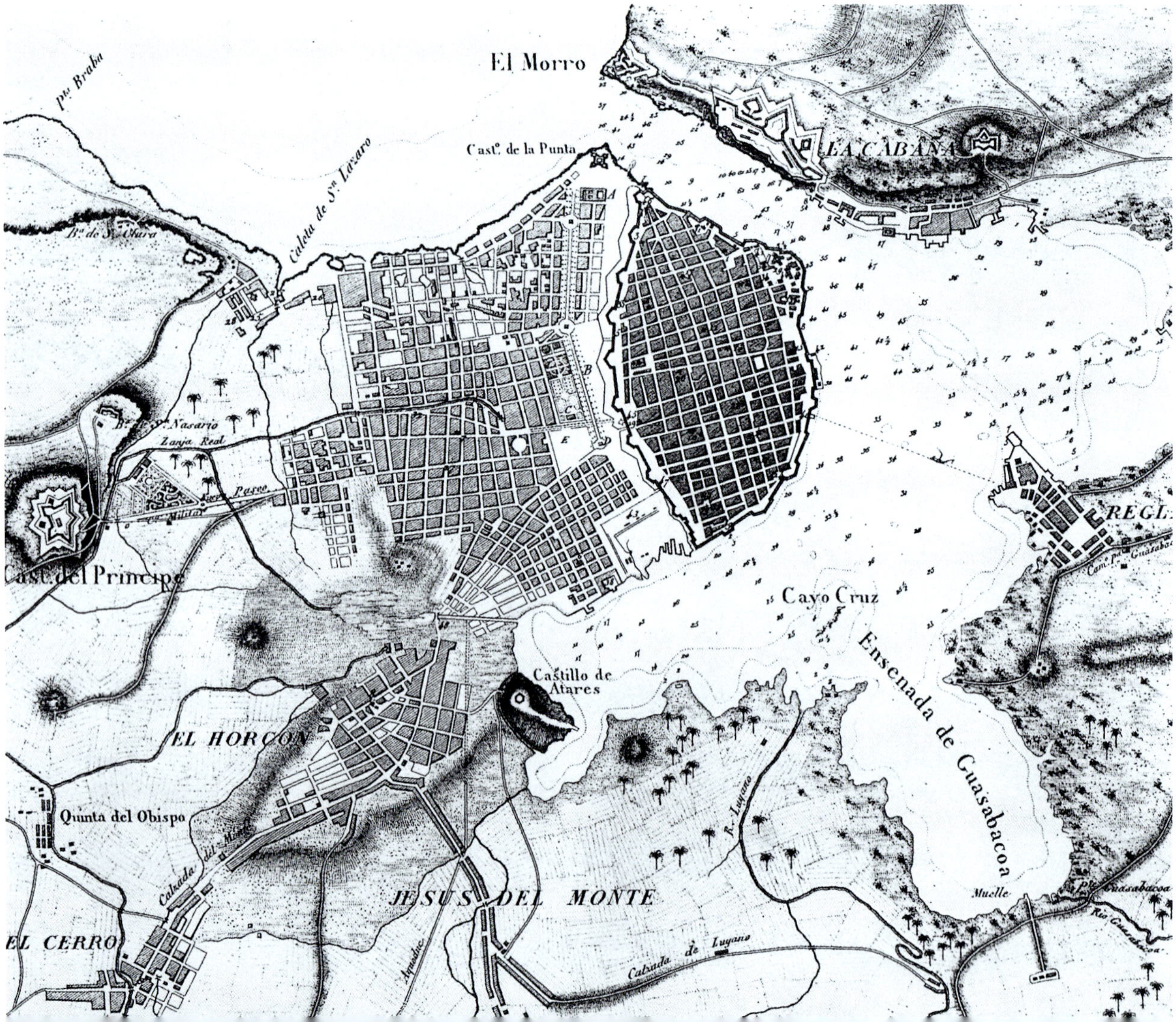

REGION DE LA HABANA

SECTORES URBANIZADOS DENTRO DEL PERIMETRO URBANO

POBLACIONES EXISTENTES

NUEVOS POSIBLES SECTORES DE TRAZADO DISCONTINUO

TOWN PLANNING ASSOCIATES
PAUL LESTER WIENER   JOSE LUIS SERT   PAUL SCHUL
SEELYE STEVENSON VALUE & KNECHT·CONSULTING ENGINEER

El Morro

LA CABANA

Cast°. de la Punta

p™ Braba

Caleta de S™ Lazaro

B™ de S™ Clara

Nasario
Zanja Real

Paseo

Cast. del Principe

EL HORÇON

Quinta del Obispo

Castillo de Atares

Cayo Cruz

REGL

Ensenada de Guasabacoa

Muelle

JESUS DEL MONTE

EL CERRO

Calzada de Luyano

Plan, the organization of the consultant offices and analysis work, etc., and for this they stipulated a fee of $95,000, excluding travelling expenses. The second phase was to work on supervising the Master Plan proposals, which would be drawn up in the Cuban offices during a two-year period, and their fee for this was to be $30,000. The self-assurance that Sert and Lester exhibited in connection with their planning experiences elsewhere, which is patent in the last lines of the report, was an attempt to hide the failures of these previous plans, and, more to the point, the failure of the city model they had been defending: 'These plans have received approval by their respective municipalities and most of them are now in operation. Our work has gained international recognition and constitutes an important contribution to International City Planning.' The truth is that their report was merely attempting to sell an intellectual labour force in order to provide a sure and profitable business for the investments that Batista desired: 'It will be readily understood that the cost of organizing the analysis and designing of the Pilot and Master Plans for Havana are very small in comparison to the benefits that the city and its people will derive from these plans.' That this sales pitch was bought is evidenced by the different commissions they received, ranging from the housing development of Quinta Palatino[403] and of Isla de Pinos[404] to the attempted planning of the Varadero area,[405] although the one that calls for special attention is their Havana Plan. Sert and Lester travelled to the island's capital on 27 June 1955, and remained there until 1 September. They returned on 15 November, staying on until 19 January 1956 to collaborate on the organization of the National Planning Board of Cuba shortly after Batista had decreed a general amnesty and the leader of the Moncada assault, Fidel Castro, had been freed from jail. A coloured-pencil sketch of 16 May 1955 bears the significant caption: 'Historical zone. Integration of financial, residential, office.' By 13 July 1955, Lester had drawn in coloured pencils the perimeter that was to circumscribe their work on the Pilot Plan.[406]

Until 8 October no more detailed plans were drawn, although there was a sketch captioned: 'Preliminary study of present-day Havana so as to determine the boundaries of the

Aerial view of Havana, period photograph.

sectors and the structure of the future road network.' We can therefore assume that the Havana Plan initially took off around these dates, since by 20 December 1955 Lester had written to his associate Paul Schulz: 'We have made some progress with the initial Scheme of Havana but I have not yet shown it to the Minister and to the Junta, waiting for José Luis to go over the minor changes and supporting data.'[407]

The TPA prepared a spectacular folder of twenty-two full-colour, large-format pages that contained the Havana Pilot Plan, and this is the best document available for an analysis of their proposal.[408]

The opening sentence of the report could not be more indicative of its contents: 'Town Planning Associates follows in these guidelines as it has in all its previous works, the principles and rules established by the International Congresses of Modern Architecture (CIAM), by the Athens Charter (1933) and its post-war congresses.' In other words, in this time of marked crises for architecture and for modern urbanism, which were directly manifested at the CIAMs, we still find a will to resist the inevitable. What in previous projects would have

Havana Plan,
central area
(AJFM).

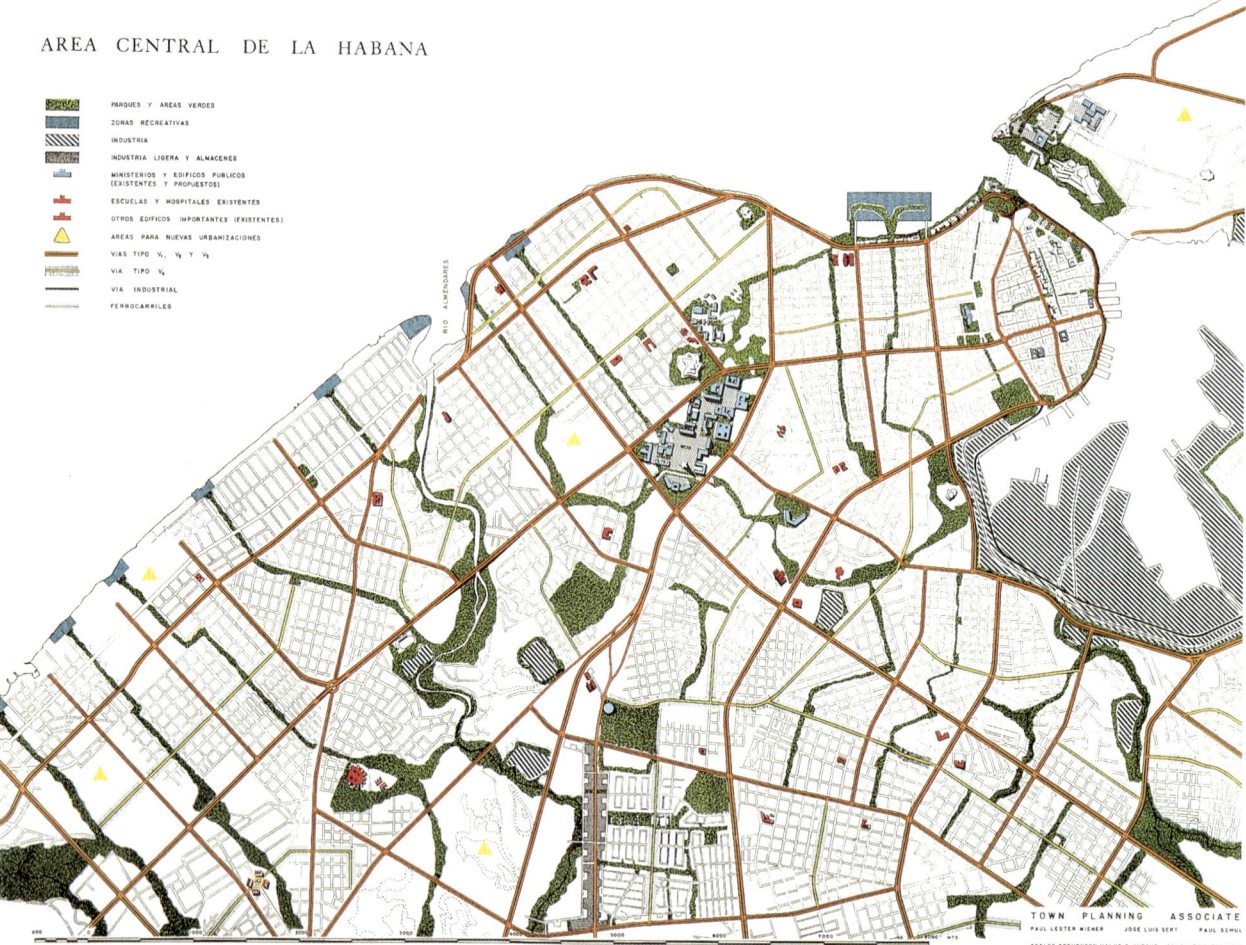

been understood as a research proposal, now seemed, with the passing of time and the evolution of discourses, to be a project alienated from its time and oblivious to the criticisms that architectural students were making against the proposals of the National Planning Board of Cuba. The Board was totally uninterested in promoting low-cost housing, in preserving the scarce spaces left for public use, or even in controlling the vast speculation that was going on, a fact that Sert was to experience for himself in the Quinta Palatino project.

The basic points of this plan for a city conceived according to North American depredatory uses of tourism and the organization of gambling and prostitution were as follows: the modern-oriented redesign of the Plaza Cívica; the promotion of expansion towards the east and its virgin beaches thanks to the construction of the bay tunnel; the construction of an artificial island for recreational use in front of the Malecón (something that had recurrently interested Sert since the Macià Plan); the design of a Presidential Palace in a location that made patent the political connotations of power; the in-depth remodelling of the old city and the

industrial area near the port, placing the humblest dwellings in this industrial area on its periphery; and the promotion of new high-rise residential sectors to provide for the population growth during the next thirty years.[409]

The last two architectural lessons developed in the previous CIAMs, that is to say, the discourse on new monumentality and the debate concerning the heart of the city, took on great, albeit belated, relevance in the Havana Plan. Sert and Lester traced an itinerary through five main centres that ensured the representative historical commemoration of certain city institutions, and which were not only intended to parade the imperturbable passage of time before the eyes of Havana's inhabitants, but were also meant to act as legitimating agents for the Plan's productive and economic basis. The idea was to establish connections between the Plaza de la República, the University Campus, the boulevard that would be built on the land gained from the seashore, the Recreational Centre, the Economic Centre (which was to be established in the old part of the city) and the Presidential Palace. The old city quarter was to be remodelled in depth, with a re-

LA HABANA - NUCLEOS CIVICOS

PLAN DE ENLACES

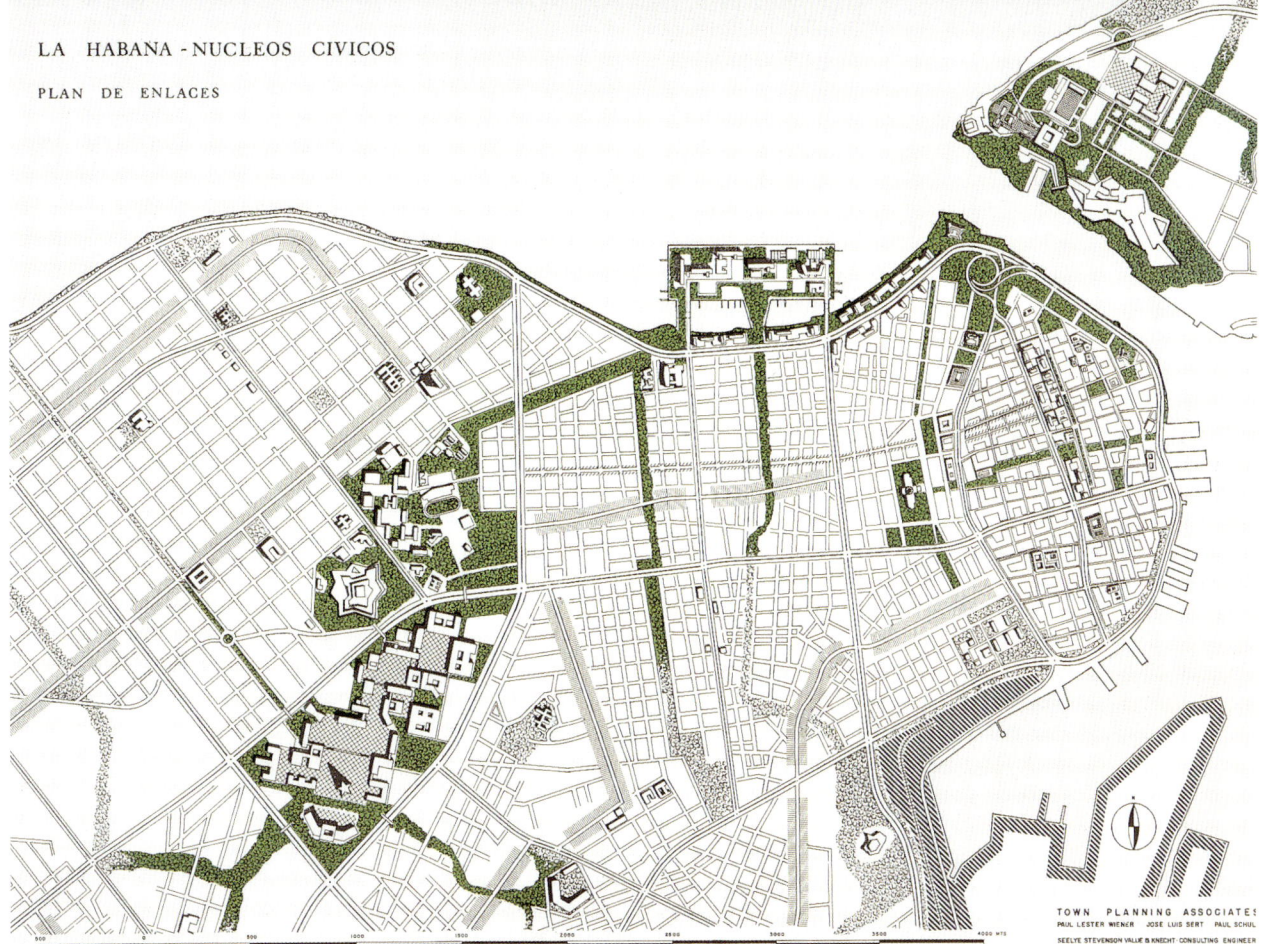

designed road network and provision for the separation of pedestrians from motorized traffic, the inclusion of a great banking and commercial centre, and the redesign of housing, with the voiding of the central area of the housing blocks to create TPA's familiar patios.

This intervention aimed to preserve the most significant buildings, as had been done twenty years before in the Macià Plan for Barcelona, but it was not well received, an attitude voiced by Roberto Segre: 'There is no doubt that the aspect of the plan open to the greatest criticism is that which has to do with the intervention in the Malecón and the transformation of the historical centre. Here, the precepts that Sert declared in *The Heart of the City*, those of respecting "the customs of a people and their lifestyle" and the pre-existing dwelling typologies that conform to the historical memory of society, have been forgotten … The dialectic homogeneity of Havana's historical centre, emphasized by its narrow streets and the alternation between modest colonial houses and pretentious eclectic buildings as well as by the welcoming air of its squares, would have been lost had Sert's solution been applied.'[410]

The delirious palace of Batista,[411] designed by the architects based on the late-Baroque architecture of Enlightenment despotism, was the element that gave the city a new focus in its dialogue with the business centre installed in the historic city and with the island reclaimed from the sea, with its casinos and nightclubs. Its mistake was not only that it served to promote the deplorable figure of the dictator, but that it used the outdated arts from which modern architecture had fled, and broke with the modern concept of monumentality previously discussed.

Thus in the Havana Plan, Sert and Lester reverted to an old vocabulary, employing a depleted discourse without daring to take risks, thus exhausting the cultural and propositional value of the Functional City. And this was just what had occurred with the CIAMs, which had received their mortal blow at Aix. That TPA was no longer capable of keeping up with the times is confirmed by a naive letter that Lester sent to someone by the name of Charlie on 13 January 1959, a few days after the Castro Revolution: 'I naturally have many friends in Cuba belonging to the Castro Party, and am hopeful that I will

181

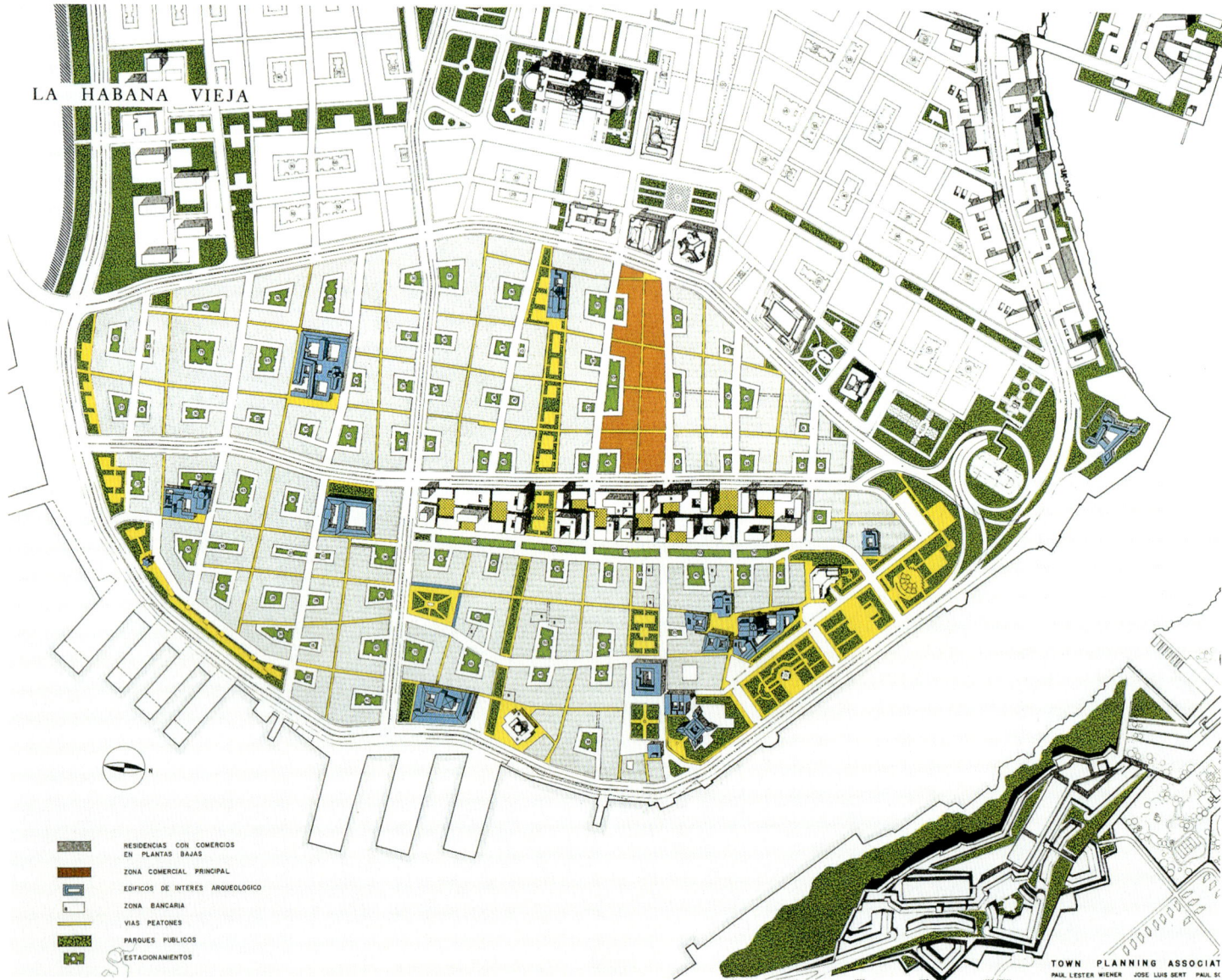

LA HABANA VIEJA

RESIDENCIAS CON COMERCIOS EN PLANTAS BAJAS
ZONA COMERCIAL PRINCIPAL
EDIFICOS DE INTERES ARQUEOLOGICO
ZONA BANCARIA
VIAS PEATONES
PARQUES PUBLICOS
ESTACIONAMIENTOS

TOWN PLANNING ASSOCIAT
PAUL LESTER WIENER   JOSE LUIS SERT   PAUL SC

Havana Plan, proposal for the old city quarters (AJFM).

meet with the new president within the next few months to acquaint him with the work we have done in Cuba … I understand that the Planning Office is intact. Only the top man will be changed. It would be a great pity if our plan could not be put into action.'

It was time to move on, and that is what Sert did, devoting himself to his university work in his small office at Harvard, a job that absorbed most of his time. On 31 March 1959 Lester addressed a letter to Mr Ludwig Prosnitz announcing the dissolution of TPA: 'Due to the course of Mr Schulz's incurable illness and Mr Sert's preoccupation with Harvard, we have decided to liquidate Town Planning Associates as of 31 March 1959 … To effect this liquidation, the attorney requires an accountant's statement

as of 31 March so that the partners of TPA may sign general releases from each other.' Shortly afterwards, through a letter from Sert to Bakema of 4 September, we discover that the Catalan architect would not be attending the CIAM at Otterlo: 'Just a line to wish you and all the CIAM friends a very successful meeting. I am sorry that I cannot be with you, but I believe that it is in many ways better that there are more new people than old ones at the meeting.'

The end of TPA almost coincides with the formal dismantling of the CIAMs, a fact that can be seen from the letters that Giedion sent to Sent at the beginning of 1960, after the events at Otterlo. On 8 March he had received a letter from Sert suggesting the idea of making a declaration of principles and sending it to

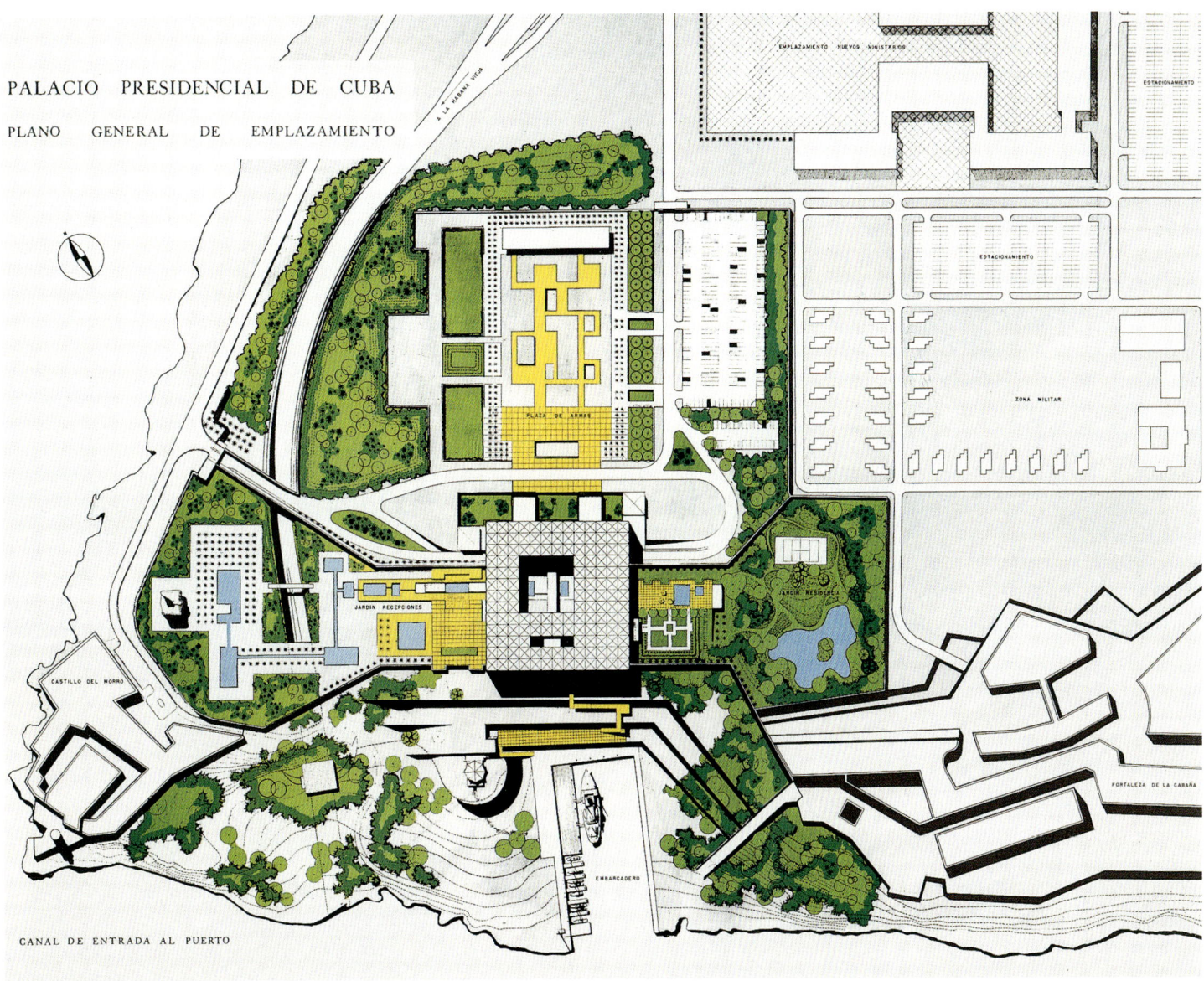

PALACIO PRESIDENCIAL DE CUBA

PLANO GENERAL DE EMPLAZAMIENTO

CANAL DE ENTRADA AL PUERTO

Havana Plan, Presidential Palace (AJFM).

architectural magazines.[412] In a handwritten letter to Sert of 14 March, possibly a response to this, Giedion expressed the need for the senior members advisory committee to make a formal declaration to put an end to the constant quibbling between the English, Italians and Dutch, 'a letter in view of the existing confusion and contradictory statements signed also by you, Gropius and Corbusier. But before doing so I should have some points as to WHAT FORM this clarification should take to avoid the difficulty of making a controversy of CIAM against CIAM.'[413] On 23 April he proposed a meeting with Le Corbusier in Paris to draft the definitive text that they would send to the architectural magazines: 'We will then send our letter about the attacks on CIAM together

with the new Charter to all important journals with the demand that they publish it simultaneously with the charte [sic].'

The text written by Sert, Gropius, Le Corbusier and Giedion, from which we will extract just a few sentences, can be seen as the last will and testament of CIAM.[414] After declaring what the Congresses' aims had been, given the circumstances in 1928, it stated: 'We came together because in our opinion the pressing contemporary problems of architecture and planning had received too little attention by universities, institutes of technology and administrative bodies ... Our intentions could only be realized by enthusiastic, voluntary work on the part of the individual members of CIAM, since the organization was never in its

183

whole history supported by any substantial endowments.' It then went on to list all of the meetings held and the publications that had sprung from them.

However – it went on – the passing of time now called for another type of organization: 'The founders of CIAM felt that the time had come to hand over the organization to a younger generation. One of the reasons was that their own ever increasing activities and responsibilities did not allow them to carry on their CIAM obligations with their customary intensity and they therefore clearly expressed their wish to retire at the congress at Aix en Provence in 1953 … The meeting at Otterlo, Holland, in September 1959 was the first one to be entirely conducted under the responsibility of a "Committee of Reorganization", consisting mainly of members of Team X.' Rather than serving to find harmonious continuities, this Congress had underlined confrontations, concluding with a declaration that had not been to the liking of its founders: 'A statement issued at Otterlo to the press by a minority group … contained the passage that "it was concluded that the name of CIAM will be no longer used in relation to the future activities of the participants" … The "Statement of Otterlo" cannot, therefore, be considered the conclusive opinion of the present members of the organization … Repeated attacks on the leadership and policies of the previous CIAM meetings and congresses made in various publications by members of Team X led us to give this short account of the past activities of CIAM.' The expunging of their name had marked the end of a discourse that had been exhausted for some time: it was the end of the intellectual validity of the functional city criteria that will nevertheless always shine brightly in the history of modern urbanism.

[342] Letter from Francisco Carrillo Batalla to Paul Lester of 13 April 1951. PLWC, Incoming Correspondence, Box 14. Information that helps trace the chronology of their work in Venezuela is found in Sert's letter to Giedion of 2 January 1950, which states in closing: 'There are many other things I want to talk to you about. I hope to do so when I return from Venezuela in April.' SGA 43 K 1950 1 27. Another letter that Sert addressed to Giedion on 21 April 1950, while the Swiss historian was teaching at MIT, seems to corroborate this: 'I arrived from Caracas last Sunday. I hope you received the letter I sent you from Bogotá. The trip to South America was very interesting and I have many things to tell about it. Venezuela would interest you especially. I do not think there is any other country in the world where the clash of past and present is so evident, and where mechanization is disrupting the life of seven million people.' SGA 43 K 1950 4 21.

[343] In a letter from the OMC manager, M. Lake, to Lester dated 4 July 1951, we read: 'We hope that the plans for site B of Puerto Caroni and the variant of Cerro Bolivar will be finished within the next two weeks, as José Luis offered to do by phone.' Shortly before, in a letter of 27 June, Sert had written to Jacqueline Tyrwhitt: 'Some more work has developed for Venezuela.' SC CIAM C8.

[344] Letter from Carrillo to Sert and Lester. PLWC, Incoming Correspondence, Box 14. In it we read: 'The architects Paul Lester Wiener and José Luis Sert commit themselves to the execution of the following works, which are under their direct responsibility and for which they will provide the necessary personnel and office space in New York: A. Preparation of the town planning maps for each of the two cities in accordance with the requirements established in the aforementioned contract clause, with the exception of the public services and levels map. B. Preparation of the preliminary projects for the following buildings: Workers' Housing, Employees' Housing, Executives' Housing, Bachelors' Housing, Guest House, Manager's House, Schools, Churches, Cinemas, Clubs, Mess Halls, Civic Centres, Police Station, National Guard Barracks, Gasoline Station, Laundry Services, and Maintenance Buildings, in accordance with the requirements of clauses 1, 5, and 7 of the aforementioned contract. C. Supervision and assistance in the preparation of all architectural specifications and details of the buildings whose contract plans will be prepared by Carrillo Batalla, Guinand & Benacerraf. D. Supervision and assistance in the preparation of landscape and gardening plans after a study of the soil and the plants most suited to it has been carried out in Venezuela. E. Assistance in the incorporation of equipments in the buildings and verification of the equipments and accessories manufactured in the USA, which can be used in this project.' In return for their work, the TPA architects were to be paid 50,000 US dollars plus 10,000 more for office expenses during the first year.

[345] PLWC, letters of 15 and 16 October 1951.

[346] This is explained in nine typewritten pages found in the PLWC, which deal with the iconographic details that accompany the rest of the project areas, such as the walls, the main entrance, the decoration of the back part of the apse, etc. A reference to the La Zarzuela racetrack is found in Antonio Pizza, *Guía de la arquitectura española del siglo XX*, Electa, Milan, 1997, pp. 302–03.

[347] FLC D2 20 169. In a letter from Samuel to Le Corbusier, which could be the answer to the one mentioned formerly, since it is dated 26 January 1950, we read: 'I understand from the MARS delegates who attended the final Council Meeting in Bergamo that this question was dealt with at the very last moment and that there was no full discussion of your suggested theme or the two alternatives … We will certainly adopt your present suggestion that our point of view should be put to Sert.' FLC D2 18 47.

[348] SGA 43K 1950 1 27. Sert ends his letter by belittling the importance of the specific proposal made by the MARS group for CIAM 8: 'I think there are many subjects that might follow logically on the Athens Charter: it is really a matter of particularization after that general statement on Town Planning. The "London Charter" or the "Centres Charter" is merely one such alternative. I would stress that what we understand by Centres is something much wider and more fundamental than the conventional Civic Centre.' Nevertheless, in a letter of 6 March 1950 from Sert to Giedion, we read: 'I have been talking with Le Corbusier here about CIAM 8, and have convinced him that the subject for the next Congress should be the "Civic Centre" and not the "Habitat Charter". He also agrees that the Congress should take place in London and that the MARS group should organize it.' SGA 43K 1950–3–6–1/2. This proves Sert's interest in the subject and also his persuasive skills with the Swiss architect.

[349] SC CIAM C7.

[350] SC CIAM C7. That same day he wrote another letter to Jacqueline Tyrwhitt, with whom he would afterwards prepare the definitive book. Seeing how far advanced the project was, it is evident that Sert had been mulling over these ideas for quite some time: 'We have no substantial co-operation from CIAM members for the book on city planning … we should reconsider the matter and replace this book with the civic centre publication that I mentioned in my letter of 18 July … The title could be *The Core of the Community* or *Centres of Community Life*.' He then proceeded to explain the index of the book and the title of various articles that would be included in it, and ended by saying: 'I think we should make a

rapid decision on the subject. We could prepare this book with you and Albert here in New York … The dummy of the book could then be presented to the Congress in July, practically in final shape, leaving some space for additions that the Congress would advise.'

351 In a letter from Sert to Giedion of 28 November 1950, we read: 'Thank you for your letter of November 21. With your approval we are going to proceed on the work for the new publication on *The Core of the City*, SC CIAM C7.

352 This can be gleaned from Gropius' letter to Sert of 17 January 1951: 'I have not been able to get a group to do the necessary work on adjusting to the CIAM grid. I wonder whether you have already seen the January issue of the AIA paper, which is completely devoted to our Harvard Planning efforts. There is a lot of material in it that would be desirable for the CIAM meeting; but neither my own Architects Collaborative nor the various classes in Harvard are in a position to do the necessary drafting as there are so many other commitments to be fulfilled. I remember that in one of your letters you wrote that there might be the possibility to have some work done in New York if the essential information is given. I wonder if that is so. I very much wish that a good American example, dealing with specific American problems so different from those of the Europeans, would be in London next July.' SC CIAM C8.

353 FLC D2 20 218.

354 A letter to Tyrwhitt of 9 April 1951 states: 'I am finishing work on the Gaudí book and I am afraid that I won't be able to give you my contribution to the book before leaving for South America, but I promise to send it to you from there very soon … As I told you, I expect to be back by the end of May and hope to be able to work with you then. In the meantime, I will give instructions to Alberto about the book and *grilles* for Chimbote and Medellin to be presented to the Congress. Please give him a little help in this too.' SC CIAM C8.

In 1958 Tyrwhitt and Sert published a book called *The Shape of Our Cities*, which had been prepared for the Fund for Adult Education and was presented at the United Nations Seminar on Regional Planning held in Tokyo in June 1958. The book was edited as a series of 10 fascicles, whose initial title was *The Shape of American Cities*. SC C 3a, 3b.

The correspondence between Tyrwhitt and Sert over many years allows us to trace Tyrwhitt's professional course. *Ekistics* magazine devoted two issues to Tyrwhitt: vol. 52, nos 234 and 315, September–October and November–December 1985.

355 'It would be very interesting if you could have it finished before the Congress. I hope you will do your best, because this will facilitate the publication of the book immediately after the Congress is over.' In the same letter, Sert told Gropius that the best definition of 'Core' was found in a passage of Ortega y Gasset's book *La rebelión de las masas* (Revolt of the Masses). SC CIAM C8.

356 A letter of 27 June 1951 to Tyrwhitt confirms this: 'My introduction is finished. It is about sixteen typewritten pages and will have six illustrations. I will naturally bring it with me to England, together with the dummy and whatever material I can gather here.' In the same letter we also find the first indications of the Congress' programme. SC CIAM C8. The later correspondence with Tyrwhitt allows us to observe the evolution of the book on the heart of the city. By 8 August 1951, the outline of the book was finished, and in May 1952 they met in New York to work on it together.

We know that it was finished by the end of that year from a letter that Sert wrote to Giedion on 28 December. SC CIAM C9–10–11.

357 There is a typewritten copy of it in FLC D2 18 3–10. This demonstrates that everything had been well calculated and that the organization was impeccable.

358 FLC D2 18 47.

359 The work was published in English in 1952 under the familiar title of *The Heart of the City* by the Lund Humphries publishing company. The Italian version was published by Hoepli under the supervision of the architect E.N. Rogers. It was published in Spanish in 1955, a second edition coming out in 1961. Both editions were published by the Editorial Científico Médica of Barcelona.

360 Letter to Tyrwhitt of 1 August 1951. SC CIAM C10.

361 See letter from Tyrwhitt to Sert and Rogers of 22 September 1951: 'The text for the first part is now absolutely in order.' SC CIAM C10.

362 See Giedion's letter to Sert of 19 October 1951: 'The Sunday after the Congress I spoke with Rogers at length and also with my publisher Hoepli about the publication of *Core*, which was done so quickly and with such ardour – very much in contrast with the *Decade* book … it will be very important for the future of CIAM … the books from the Congress must be written by CIAM, and that means that in the future nothing can be printed without having been debated and screened by the assembly … I will propose in the next Council that no article be published that has not passed through the forum of the Congress. Without this step everything resembles an anthology of celebrities.' SC CIAM C 10.

363 Letter from Jacqueline Tyrwhitt to Sert, Rogers and Giedion of 13 December 1951. SC CIAM C10. In March 1952, despite all of their efforts, the book had still not appeared in bookshops, as is evidenced by Sert's impatient letter to Tyrwhitt on the 14th: 'I would very much like to know something about the book and how far work has advanced on it … It is tremendously important that this book appear soon; we should, by all means, avoid delays in publication similar to those of the *Decade* book.' SC CIAM C11.

It seems that the publication was completed in November of the same year. In a letter from Giedion to Le Corbusier of 11 November, we read: 'I guess you also like *The Heart of the City* and I believe it will do more to orientate the officials than any CIAM publication before.' FLC D2 20 314.

364 SC CIAM C11.

365 Letter from Sert to Giedion of 31 March 1953. SC CIAM C11.

366 Letter from Sert to Le Corbusier of 9 May 1952. FLC D2 20 236. In Paris, they drew up the minutes of the meeting (SC CIAM C11) in which some important facts were stated, such as the senior members' desire to leave the preparation of the congresses in the hands of the younger members: 'The theme and organization of CIAM 10 (1955) is to be placed in the hands of the new generation of architects. This would give them both time and opportunity to show how far they are able to develop the aims of CIAM.' It also stressed the role of the young generation in a section whose heading was 'The New Generation of Architects', in which the role of architects' education was remarked on and in which it proposed the idea of a second 'CIAM Summer School', which could be held in Venice under the direction of Albini, Gardella, Rogers and Samonà, with Candilis and Howell, who would be in charge of getting youths to join their work groups.

The act ended with a section devoted to 'The Ideology of CIAM', symptomatic of the crisis through which it was passing, in which we read: 'It was reported that there were divergent views on the direction in which CIAM should go, and the stand it should take in today's world. This was especially confusing for the young generation, and the hope was expressed that the Stockholm meeting would allow time in the programme of CIAM 9 for a discussion on the ideology of CIAM. It appears that certain groups – especially those that have existed for more than 20 years – contain germs of "conformity" and even of "academicism". This has led to confusion and the Council welcomed the steps that are already being taken by a few groups to eliminate such germs in order to maintain the principles that continue to provide the underlying force of CIAM.'

367 Sert complained that many commissions were taking unilateral decisions, pointing out how angry the MARS group had been about the work programme that was to be developed in the Swedish city. He put forward all these motives, pressing Giedion to make an effort to attend the meeting, but Giedion did not go. FLC D3 O1 21–23.

368 There is a written record of the aforementioned meeting, but it does not deal with the issues that concern us. We also do not see a programme for CIAM 9. FLC D3 O1 31–35.

369 SC CIAM C12. The letter stressed the idea of giving the younger members freedom of action: 'But please reconsider your recommendation that the new groups of CIAM should work under the guidance of an Advisory Committee of senior members … they do not want these older members with them all the time; they have reached a stage when they need to be on their own. Also, of course, the actual "older members" who comprise (who would be willing to serve on) an Advisory Committee would seldom be those who had won the open or secret reverence of the youngsters.' The letter proceeded to comment at length on Sert's proposal for the reorganization of CIAM (which we have examined previously). Concerning the meaning of the terms they were employing and the difficulty of reaching an agreement as to the universal validity of their usage, Tyrwhitt was openly critical: 'Here again I do not agree with you that the use of a new word for a new concept "disturbs" anyone except those who are bothered that a new concept should be raised at all. The danger that I see is that words (like Core and Habitat) may in time become as rubbed and misused as Neighbourhood or Green Belt so that we can no longer use them with any certainty that they mean the same thing to the person whom we are addressing. Of course, at the moment we are not entirely clear of the meaning ourselves of Habitat. That must wait till after CIAM 9. But we are now fairly clear of the meaning of Core.'

Giedion expressed himself in similar terms in a letter to Sert on 9 December 1952. He also expressed his agreement with the six points that Sert had devised for the reorganization of CIAM. SGA 43K 1952–12–9 (6)–1/2.

370 SC CIAM C13. In the same letter, Giedion disagreed with the proposal that the Congress focus on habitat, and suggested instead the term 'human environment' as a way to improve the reductive aspects of the main function of the functional city: 'that which interests us more than anything is: to point out and define the relation between the individual and collective spheres, between the home, housing and the formation of social life. Habitat is not enough.'

[371] At least this is what we gather from Giedion's letter to Sert of 27 February 1953: 'The Council Meeting has worked as it always works when those who know how to direct it have clear-cut ideas and assemble together. It was very interesting psychologically that after one hour and ten minutes of quite heated debate, Corbu remarked: "It is always so in CIAM meetings; at the end everyone agrees" ... We again determined that the title would be the old one: HABITAT CHARTER ... Let me speak openly with you. I am not afraid about CIAM 9, but we were all at a loss because the grid proposition that Wogensky was to take care of was not prepared. We had to improvise a grid at that same meeting.' SGA 43K 1953 2 27 (6) 1/2.

[372] FLC D3 O 138–139. In the CIAM 9 programme proposal, which is dedicated to Habitat, we find the different angles from which the theme was to be approached: 'A. Habitat envisaged as a universal problem: it exists in all countries. B. Means to express the rapport and interaction between the human cell and its surroundings. C. The degrees of isolation necessary. D. The evaluation of a vertical integration of homogeneous groups: up to what point are their needs complementary or opposed? E. The advantages of compact planning in contrast to a continuous dispersion. F. The kinship between habitat and core. G. The means to express its bond with the past while giving opportunity to future variations. H. The need to give vivacity to the habitat.' In this same meeting they planned to write a book, formulating the sections of which it should be composed, decided what the Congress' debate commissions should be, as well as suggesting the possibility of holding an exhibition of architecture in Paris in 1955.

[373] FLC D3 O1 552.

[374] Jos Bosman, 'I CIAM del dopoguerra: un bilancio del Movimento Moderno', in Rassegna, no. 52, December 1992, p. 17. In general all the articles in this issue deal with the demise of CIAM. A handwritten letter from Sert to Le Corbusier bearing the date 29 July 1953, seemed to emphasize the relevance of the act: 'I spoke with Giedion suggesting he send you a word of thanks for the events on Saturday the 25th; this acknowledgment was also to express the deep impact that the Unité d' Habitation had made on the CIAM ... The unanimous opinion of the members and delegates present at that evening party is that this building represents the greatest achievement of contemporary architecture and the materialization of the principles that we defend. The visit to the Unité d'Habitation has given the "young" and less young CIAM a greater confidence in the future and greater courage to continue fighting for what we are involved in.' FLC D3 O1 557–60.

[375] Other publications that may be useful in the examination of the last moments of CIAM and the Team X meetings are Oscar Newman, CIAM '59 in Otterlo, Karl Kramer Verlag, Stuttgart, 1961, and Alison Smithson (ed.), Team X Meetings, Publikatieburo, Faculteit der Bouwkunde, Delft, 1991.

[376] See: FLC D3 O1 62–68. The final programme is in SC CIAM B8.

[377] FLC D3 O1 395–400. Le Corbusier's text, written in Chandigarh, began thus: 'To pose the question of modern habitat is to pose the problem of the art of living nowadays. Does this art exist? To live with the body and with the spirit. To feel the joy of living and not despair. Then, to take a stand regarding work: friend or enemy.' The rest of what follows is a series of short disjointed sentences that the

Swiss architect jumbled together, and which sought strange ways of connecting diverse human actions in daily life, ranging from the way in which we dress to the crease in a pair of trousers, or from the way we eat to the sun's path across the sky. Possibly his contact with Oriental culture had provoked a reaction whose consequences were not foreseen in this text.

[378] FLC D3 O1 433.

[379] FLC D3 O1 435.

[380] FLC D3 O1 436.

[381] Gropius' lecture was titled 'Scope of Total Architecture'. There is a typewritten copy in SC CIAM C13.

[382] FLC D3 O1 503.

[383] Francis Strauven, 'Il contributo olandese: Bakema e van Eyck', Rassegna, no. 52, op. cit., p. 54. A document from June 1954 signed by 'De 8 en OPBOW' deals with the organization of CIAM 10 and insists on the idea of rapport, although removed from the notion of relationships that the Smithsons had proposed in Aix: 'Planning of habitat is not only a question of expressing relationships within and between spatial grouping of society, like villages, neighbourhoods or towns; it is also – or should be – the expression of other "forms" of the relationships in society: forms of production, forms of social behaviour, forms of science, forms of art ... Our task is not only to express relationships between man and thing and between man, society and the universal; our work has to be an expression of the most advanced principles of society: of industrial production, of social organization, of management, and also of demolition and replacement of our structures today.' SC CIAM B9.

[384] FLC D3 O1 507.

[385] FLC D3 7 1.

[386] SC CIAM B9.

[387] SC CIAM B9.

[388] FLC D3 7 11.

[389] The text read: 'More precise directives were proposed by the Dutch part of the CIAM X Committee, but refused by the English part. Van Eyck and myself therefore took the responsibility for a Dutch supplement by which groups are invited to give their own more precise ideas about the work of the proposed working parties. The Dutch group thinks that it is useful to study the problem of habitats in fields of human associations indicated by the words: homestead, village, town, city. CIAM X has to define the existence of new fields of human associations, expressed by the new patterns in architectural planning. This by recognizing the key problems, indicated by the words: interrelationship (of inner and outer space), aesthetics of numbers (repetition, rhythm), growth and change (flexibility).' SC CIAM C14.

[390] SGA 43K 1954 12 16.

[391] SC CIAM C14.

[392] Letter from Giedion to Sert of 16 May 1955. FLC D3 7 156–157. Shortly before, on March 25, he had sent him a letter written during the train ride from Paris to Basilea in which he had manifested his concern about the way the Paris meeting had turned out, a meeting that had made patent the overall lack of organization. SGA 43K 1955 3 25.

[393] SC CIAM B9.

[394] CIAM and Team X meeting, November 1955, SC CIAM B9.

[395] FLC D3 O7 171. Le Corbusier answered this letter on 18 July 1956: 'I am very tired and will not go to the CIAM Congress declaring once again that the young must take over, and if this makes everything founder, let it founder!' FLC R3 O3 289.

[396] FLC D3 O7 108–111.

[397] SC CIAM B9.

[398] FLC R3 O3 292. Apart from their interest in ensuring that the 'Mediterranean party' should continue to control CIAM, yet another letter from Le Corbusier two days later seems to insist on keeping a firm grip on CIAM: ' I take it upon myself to point out that I do not think it is a good idea that the Secretariat be in Candilis' hands ... I have found jointly with Wogensky a combination ... a third party apt for the post, a young man totally devoted to CIAM, perfectly loyal.' FLC R3 O3 294.

[399] See Jean-Pierre Clerc, 'Una democracia dos veces asesinada', in La Habana 1952–1961, Alianza Editorial, 1995, pp. 84–98.

[400] On Batista's relationship with the architects and architecture, and on the climate of acceptance or rejection of modern architecture in Cuba, see: Roberto Segre, Lectura crítica del entorno cubano, Havana, 1990, pp. 117–53 and pp. 313–38.

[401] Cited in Segre, op. cit., pp. 132–33.

[402] PLWC, 'Pilot and Master Plan for Metropolitan Area of Havana', Box 5, Cuba Folder.

[403] The Lester Wiener Collection holds abundant information on the planning project of this enormous estate located in the municipality of Santa Teresa, Havana, which was the property of someone by the name of Pedro Abreu. In March of 1954, they had already made contact to undertake the preliminary design. The preliminary design for the sewer network drainage system and the preliminary design for the housing development of the Quinta Palatino area circumscribed by the streets Primelles, Avenida de Santa Catalina, Calle Albear, and Calle Fomento, are from 10 May 1955. The programme for this housing development was comprised of the design of 188 group houses, 1,318 single houses, and 296 apartments. On 30 April 1954, through a letter to Rita Gutierrez (the architect who co-ordinated the works between the office of Sert and Lester and Havana), we discover that Pedro Abreu did not even want to hear any talk of building a school in the area despite the fact that it was obligatory by law, and that he ordered that the games field be eliminated, also drastically reducing the green public spaces, doing so in order 'to gain greater economic benefits'. Abreu travelled to New York on 18 May 1954, and a letter from Sert on 15 June demonstrates that TPA acquiesced to the speculative interests of the project's sponsor. On 9 October they were paid the rest of their fee for the drafting of the project. Graphic documentary material on the Quinta Palatino project is found in Architectural Design, June 1957, op. cit., p. 210–11.

[404] There is documentary material on the Isla de Pinos project dating back to 29 April 1953, when we know that they were paid for the preliminary design, and there is graphic documentation on the project in the June 1957 issue of Architectural Design, p. 213, and in the Harvard archives: SC 82 a 82 g. On 23 April 1955 Lester was still working on the preliminary design.

[405] The Varadero proposal occupied Sert and Lester from October 1954 until June 1956, although the obstacles put in their way by the proprietor of the terrains made it impossible for them to carry out the project. There is more information on the subject in PLWC, Box 5, Varadero Pilot Plan Folder and in Varadero Folder, Miscellaneous, Notes and Clippings.

[406] In the PLWC are the contracts for the drawing up of the Pilot Plan and Master Plan for Havana, of which we have different drafts (one in

English and the other in Spanish). The former is from 14 January 1955, and the latter is from 1 July. The English version specified the works that were to be undertaken by the TPA associates, the scales that were to be used in the graphic documents, and their annual fee of $50,000 over the three years for which the work was to continue. A sub-contract at the end specified the fees they would receive for the Varadero Plan. The text, written in Spanish, specified in a much more detailed manner the tasks that the American architects were to perform, and also stressed the need to elaborate a bibliographical list, an element that TPA had systematically incorporated in all of its South American town planning projects, moreover assigning a fee of 120,000 pesos to TPA, each one of the three members receiving 40,000 pesos. Apart from executing a Regulating Plan for Greater Havana, they were to present a proposal for Va-

radero and La Trinidad, as well as assisting the National Planning Board of Cuba with any other urban plans that it undertook while their three-year contract lasted. In the PLWC Folder devoted to 'Analysis of Consulting and Programme for the Future' dated 15 December 1956, there is a first summary of the overall planning for the island, followed by another text called 'Cuba. Work and Future Programme'.

The bibliography that TPA prepared takes up three spiral-bound books. The titles of these are: vol. I. *Reference material for national, regional and city planning with bibliography*; vol. II. *Traffic and parking*; vol. III. *Urban land policies and implementation of the Master Plan*.

[407] PLWC, Outgoing Correspondence, Folder 1955.

[408] A copy of this proposal is found in the Sert trunk of the AJFM Archives. The Havana Pilot Plan is published in *L'Architecture d'Aujourd'hui*, no. 88, February–March 1960, pp. 62–71.

[409] An analysis of the Havana Plan is found in Roberto Segre, *La Habana de Sert: CIAM, ron y cha cha cha*. This is a typewritten text that Segre sent us himself. As to how the invasion of American tastes was perceived in Havana, independently from the National Planning Board's provisions, see Gilberto Segui, 'Los olores de la calle', in *La Habana 1952–1961*, op. cit., pp. 33–45.

[410] Segre, ibid.

[411] In the PLWC is a Presidential Palace memorandum from 9 July 1956. A letter of 25 January 1958 addressed to Sert indicated that in two or three weeks' time they would be paid for this project. PLWC, Incoming Correspondence, Folder 1958.

[412] SGA 43K 1960 3 81/2.

[413] SGA 43K 1960 3 14.

[414] A typewritten copy of the same is found in SC CIAM C17.

2. The Mediterranean

Noucentisme and the Classical Option

In 1949, Fernand Braudel described the Mediterranean in terms far removed from the ideological positions and cultural and political projects that were in vogue at the time. The French historian's purpose was to contribute to the reconstruction of a damaged post-war Europe, questioning and attempting to understand in a new way, through more enlightening techniques, a geographical scenario that had witnessed successive human cataclysms since ancient times and could now begin to hope for a different reality.[1]

In his long text he suggests that the Mediterranean sea can only be understood in conjunction with the mountains and lands surrounding it: 'The Mediterranean is, by definition, a sea surrounded by lands, confined by them.' This statement lends a more 'scientific' quality to the opening words of his book: 'I love the Mediterranean, perhaps because I have come to it from Northern lands, like so many others and after so many others ... [T]he reader who wishes to approach this book in the way that I would like it to be approached would do well to bring to it his own recollections and precise images of this inland sea, tingeing my writing with his own nuances, actively helping me to recreate this vast presence ... I believe that this sea, as each person regards it and loves it, is still the most valuable document to illustrate its past life.'

Braudel was probably weary of the manipulations that had been carried out since the end of the nineteenth century in French cultural spheres (and in the cultures that modelled themselves on the French one, such as the Catalan culture to which Sert belonged), all in the name of this sea that he so loved. This would explain why he wished to carry out the painstaking task of 'discovering exactly what type of historical character this Mediterranean Sea is', a sea that does not lend itself to easy interpretations when looked at from a historical point of view: 'A hundred warnings from trustworthy sources inform us and put us on guard: the Mediterranean Sea is not this, or the other, or even that: it is not a world sufficient unto itself, nor is it a field with well-defined borders.'

Braudel's warning alerts us as to what would follow in this work. Prior to Braudel, many of those who lived on the shores of the Mediterranean had attempted to interpret it ahistorically, brazenly appropriating it to suit their own ends without understanding it, and employing its name as the ensign that would represent the culture they wished to foster. They had erected an ideology that had spread widely in Catalonia and that had permeated Sert's education, leaving a deep imprint on him.

According to Jaume Vallcorba[2] and Jaume Aulet,[3] those most in need of this ideological construction were certain French intellectuals, who at the end of the nineteenth century wished to change certain aspects of their immediate surroundings, figures who would be decisive for many of our own thinkers, who looked to them for guidance in their initial approach to certain questions.

For example, Vallcorba has detected in Jean Moréas' *Le Pélerin Passionné*, published in December 1890, 'the blossoming of a new point of view ... of new aesthetics based on a rediscovery of autochthonous sources that had previously been rejected', an observation that had already been voiced in the French literary criticism of the period, which analyzed Moréas' text in the following terms: 'Moréas brings to mind two predecessors, Ronsard and Chénier. Like them, he has sought the Greek-Roman Renaissance and attempted to bring back sunny blue skies to our literature, threatened as it is by too many fogs. In Moréas, there are no Saxon mists or hazes, no British snows, but rather a depth of Greek clarity.'[4] We are left in the dark as to exactly what he

The Muntadas House of Josep Puig i Cadafalch in Barcelona, 1901.

meant by the 'Graeco-Roman Renaissance', but this is probably fitting, since it was not so much a matter of recalling the obscure origins of specific forms, but rather of evoking the echoes of its climate, its chromatic reflections, and most of all, of turning to Greek civilization for inspiration.

Perhaps the time had come for literary men to put an end to the neglect, professional sectarianism and backwardness of the French architects who had been looking at Greek forms from a perennially romantic standpoint for many years. They also examined them from a historicist point of view, for like Viollet, they were interested in rebuilding classical Greek *temenoi*,[5] preserving them exactly as they were instead of using them as a springboard for new proposals. Thus, saving the Greek heritage from intellectual heirs who were not profiting from it must have seemed a worthwhile task to Moréas and company. And company there was, very soon and in ever-growing numbers, to the extent that these literary figures were labelled the 'Ecole Romane', an appellation immediately echoed by the national press and accepted in manuals on French literature.[6]

Greece or Rome; the difference between the two did not seem very important to Moréas and his followers, despite the fact that Ernest Renan's enigmatic text *Prière sur l'Acropole* had been extremely enlightening for an architect who played a crucial role in the previous chapter. Renan's work traced a path that Le Corbusier would later follow, travelling eastwards and spending more time than he had foreseen under the shadow of that rock full of mysteries, discovering that presence that would haunt him for the rest of his life. What was important is that these 'Latinists' felt that they formed part of a new and modern movement that could revive the French language and that could be joined by those fleeing from literary forms that no longer aroused interest, such as the Parnasian, naturalist, symbolist, romantic, or simply barbarian forms (by the latter we mean that they came from other geographical latitudes, or in other words, were not French).[7] This movement was soon echoed in the visual arts, as Vallbona has pointed out in reference to a small terracotta figure by Aristide Maillol from 1900, which was baptized with the unmistakable title, *Mediterráneo*, and which was exhibited at the Salon d'Automne in 1905 along with another figure bearing the more noncommittal title, *Mujer*.

Aristides Maillol, *Mediterráneo*, 1900, terracotta.

Two years before, Louis Bertrand had written: 'We affirm a faith before the universe, since it is absolutely certain that we Latins, direct heirs of Rome and Athens, are the Civilization!'.[8]

It is not hard to discern the impact made by this way of thinking on Catalan intellectuals at the beginning of the twentieth century. At the time they were involved both in launching the concept of a cultural identity and in structuring the shape of a political project (which would become more defined during the first decade of the century). This must be willing to encompass and combine tendencies that were at the same time distant and neighbouring, different but capable of being integrated, such as those represented by two key figures of modern Catalan culture: Eusebi Güell and Eugeni D'Ors.

One merely has to read Juan José Lahuerta's book on Gaudí, which tears the blindfold from the eyes of those who believe in establishing artistic and academic categories, to understand this capacity for integration.[9] In the shape of the hypostyle hall of Gaudí's Parque Güell, formed by archaic Doric columns, and in the planimetry that Sellés drew of it, labelled with the words 'Teatre Grec', Lahuerta spots one of the first built results of this aesthetic shift that had begun in France. To further corroborate it he goes on to offer other cultural manifestations linked with different artistic disciplines or with literary publications.

One of the most outstanding manifestations was the first and only rendition in Spain of the *Hymn of Apollo*, which had been found in 1893 in

Antoni Gaudí, hypostyle hall in Parque Güell, Barcelona, 1900–14.

Delphi, home of the Greek god. By organizing this musical event, 'Eusebi Güell demonstrated the same passion for Greek things that had overtaken the salons of all of Europe, although by choosing to interpret the sacred hymn, this archaic music, he eliminated from the act any vestige of wordliness', a fact that allows Lahuerta to establish metaphors with other spaces conceived by Güell: 'But that temple in which Apollo's praises are sung with the authentic sound of antiquity, is not only present in the salon under the cupola of the Güell Palace; it has another headquarters … The Teatre Grec of Parque Güell is the theatre of Apollo, but it is also, in its way, the temple of this god.'

We have gone from literary themes to the architecture that builds the spaces in which these images can be visualized: 'The Teatre Grec of Parque Güell was destined to be the stable headquarters of a new Catalan lyrical theatre, of an essentially Mediterranean nature.'[10] Lahuerta ties its Doric colonnade into the role that Güell may have played in the process of Catalonia's reawakening, thus rejecting the notion that it 'could become an emblem of social virtue'. This archaic Doric colonnade mirrored the image of the oracular shrine at Delphi, the centre of the world, near to which Güell chose to live out the last moments of his life. It was a world in which Mediterranean memory was summoned to legitimize the delusions and strategies of Güell and the social class he represented.

Eugeni D'Ors' attitude, also examined by Vallcorba and Lahuerta, was different. He was well versed in the Ecole Romane and the work of the majority of its members, as well as being acquainted with the political faction Action Française, to which Maurras belonged. Both Vallcorba and Lahuerta have pointed out another instance of theatrical representation in Barcelona at the turn of the century, that of the opera *Emporium*, which was composed by Marquina and Morera and which opened at the Liceu of Barcelona on 19 March 1906. *La Veu de Catalunya* promptly announced the news of its opening through its commentator 'Xènius', the pseudonym of Eugeni d'Ors: 'Emporium … Empúries … A blue horizon that extends its serenity to the Mediterranean Father. Mediterranean Father, Our Sea! … Although frivolous people speak lightly and sardonically about *discovering the Mediterranean Sea*, I on the contrary tell you it is an arduous and lofty task … Medieval Europe had to undergo centuries of grief to arrive here. Sometimes I even think that the ideal meaning behind a heroic deed that redeems Catalonia could be that of *discovering the Mediterranean*, of discovering what is Mediterranean about us, and declaring it to the world, disseminating it to all men through imperialistic works.'[11] After briefly focusing on certain moments in the opera, Xènius laconically concluded: 'And that is why I believe that, despite the *Emporium*, the Mediterranean has still not been discovered.'

Cover of *Glosari* by Eugeni D'Ors, 1906.

EUGENI D'ORS

GLOSARI

MCMVI

VOLV NTAS

AB LES GLOSES A LA CONFERENCIA D'ALGECIRAS Y LES GLOSES AL VIURE DE PARIS

PROLECH DE RAYMON CASELLAS : CARICATURA DEL GLOSADOR PER ''APA''

BARCELONA

This long quotation is indicative of a key moment in Catalonia's resurgence. To use Empuries, the Greek city within Catalonia, as a point of departure was not a casual choice. The ruins of this city were being excavated under the supervision of Puig i Cadafalch (an architect, writer and politician whose activities are fundamental to understanding the relationship between the political programmes and architectural forms of that period, in which the Lliga was the leading party). As D'Ors explained in the inaugural conference of the CADCI (Centre Autonomista de Dependents del Comerç i la Industria) in 1911, he had come up with some extraordinary archaeological finds: 'An Aesculapius [Roman god of medicine identified with the Greek god Asklepios], a Venus that is perhaps Diana: how they sound within our hearts, how they make our blood race, these sounds that are the sounds of humanity and that signify all over the world, be it Athens or Paris, Rome or Oxford, Boston or Heidelberg, the essence of culture! … The findings ennoble us, make us become new men because they turn us into men of antiquity … it is often said that the town festivals, brethren festivals to those held by our Greek ancestors, were of two types: to celebrate the gods and to celebrate the cities. We have already celebrated the gods … We will also celebrate the cities.'

The city, that entity that Sert and the GATC-PAC members would later attempt to reform, was the scenario and metaphor for modern times, centre of all the tensions that a correct and relentless political programme was to rechannel, a place whose progress depended on the contribution of the knowledge and expertise of all, and a collective work to be contemplated as the fruit of all: 'Now, soul, you will stop to contemplate this marvellous creature of energy that is the City.'[12]

In a Catalonia civilized from its very beginnings by the Greeks, therefore, the cultural blessing bestowed on it by this fact would appear to legitimize its affairs; moreover, its origins were now above suspicion. Catalonia had a father, the Mediterranean Sea, that protected it and linked it to the beginnings of civilization, a father who still had to be discovered, or put another way, a father that could possibly be turned into an ideology that would integrate the projects of the so-called Industrial Party. Discovering this could help to redeem Catalonia, distance it from the catastrophic Spain of 1898, and move it away from its previous ideals. It was a matter of self-discovery for Catalonia, removed from the Spanish nationalism carried out overseas that touched on disaster and made Spain lose the little credibility it had left after relinquishing its last colonies. Therefore, despite the beneficial effects that Emporium might have, there was still much work to be done, and D'Ors' text was a sermon – which would be followed by many others in the pages of *La Veu de Catalunya*, the official newspaper of the new ideology – to get the project into gear. From 1906 on, 'a cultural policy would be integrated, therefore setting the basis for the existence of an organic intellectuality.'[13]

The 'Tragic Week' of Barcelona, 1909.

Enric Prat de la Riba.

194

At this point 'the concept of classicism was raised again. It was no longer just the aesthetic selection of the main French poetic currents, which had led to the classicist synthesis; now an ideological content was added that was linked to the political interests of bourgeois conservatism. It is only when these conditions are given that one can speak of *Noucentist* classicism, and not before.'[14]

On 16 November 1904, the poet Josep Carner gave a lecture whose title was 'The Necessity for Young Catalan Writers to Study the Classics'. It portrayed classical authors as the supreme masters of all previous literature, constituting a good source from which to evolve, thus ensuring that Catalan souls following in their wake would adopt the virtues of stability, serenity and grandeur inherent to their character. On 6 January 1908 Carner published a text in the form of a letter to the Three Wise Kings (who bring Catalan children their gifts at Epiphany) with the title: *The Kings in Barcelona: A Tale for Grown-up Children*. In it, he made twenty-five petitions, which constituted a complete political programme. The following are the most outstanding among them: 'A National Philosophy. An Imperialism … A Polytechnic University. An Interior Reform Movement. Connections. A National Catalan Library. A Classicism. An Autonomy.' Thus, it becomes clear that he was not only requesting a political system and the spaces that would generate learning and culture, but also demanding an aesthetic system – classicism – that would en-

velop everything, shaping it according to its canons, and whose key words would be 'order' and 'harmony'.

In 1909, when the terms *Noucentisme* and 'Mediterranism' had become commonplace, this vindication of classicism lost force after the well-known events of the Tragic Week events and the cruel repression of popular uprisings. The advocates of a different ideology would not tolerate this situation or denounced it, a fact that Joaquim Folch i Torres later recalled when identifying those who most clearly manifested difficulty in accepting classicism: 'Casellas was utterly convinced that he belonged with the others and not with the new people, and he listened distrustfully to voices and read between the lines the new words cropping up in the young people's language … Painting likewise underwent a change of direction … They started speaking about a "Mediterranean school", although we are not sure what this meant.'[15]

The many manifestos mentioned previously had not achieved obvious results, and this was very probably due to *La Nacionalitat Catalana*, a fundamental text by Prat de la Riba from 1906, which had made patent his mistrust of certain aspects relating to classical forms. The repeated associations between classicist architecture and Spanish centralism that were found in Prat's text, as well as his praise of architecture that came from the land, such as the *masies* (country houses), facilitated the upsurge of certain forms that Puig i Cadafalch employed in various projects and con-

Catalan *masia*.

Baroque Catalan church.

195

struction works executed for residential buildings in Barcelona at the beginning of the century.[16]

The following is a quotation from Prat's text: 'The integration of country folks within Catalan public life gave rise to the *renaixença* (renaissance). The force that had been accumulated during so many generations could not remain lifeless. The enterprising second-born sons from the *masies* renewed and strengthened with new blood the city and town populations.'[17] Not everything revolved around the *masies*, however; genuine Catalan art, and Romanesque architecture, also received attention, so that by 1907 Puig i Cadafalch had completed a four-volume study of this style.[18] Prat said of this art: 'The unity of the artistic ideal of our nationality was also embodied by the very severe, simple and well-proportioned naturalism of Romanesque art, which is the art of our people, the one that has flourished most in all Catalan-speaking countries.'[19]

Thus, *masies* and the Romanesque style were upheld as autochthonous products that genuinely sprang from the Catalan land. It seems that the model of D'Ors and Carner on the one hand, and that of Prat and Puig on the other, were at odds, at least in 1906, a fact that is especially patent in the scorn expressed by the President of the Mancomunitat Catalana (Catalan Union) towards at least some classicist architecture. In another part of Prat's text we read: 'The ideas and feelings that ruled the world at the time directed

Ramón Casas, drawing of Josep Puig i Cadafalch.

men towards great mechanical units of violent formation: classicism, royalism and centralization were the new ideals of those generations.' Although we are not sure of the exact meaning that Prat gave to 'classicism', it seems clear that it pertained to the realm of the artificial, and this he believed was also true of monarchies (which Prat had previously analyzed in the same work); according to him they were not founded on anything other than dynastic interests. One can easily read between the lines of Prat's text that the Spanish monarchy (identified as a purely cunning

Josep Puig i Cadafalch, the Muntadas House, Barcelona, 1901, and the Trinxet House, Barcelona, 1905.

and artful creation) had adopted classicist forms to express itself; while this was happening and the Spanish state was organizing itself, 'Catalonia was taken over by the Renaissance'.

However, it was almost immediately evident that the language that could be drawn from the *masies* of the Catalan countryside would not be of much use to urban architecture, despite Puig i Cadafalch's attempts to adapt it in the Muntadas house (1901) and in the Trinxet house (1905). It is also clear how difficult it was for the language with which the Romanesque style expressed itself (with the notable exception of the works by the American architect Henry Hobson Richardson) to uphold this architecture as the main source of inspiration for a political party that wished to be labelled industrialist and that furthermore wanted to appear modern in the eyes of its voters.

Faced with this paradox, it seems necessary to go back to D'Ors and to some other points of his programme, expressed through many passages of his novel *La Ben Plantada*, which was published in 1911. In one of these passages we read: 'And now that I have spoken of Count Arnau's Adelaide, I have started to meditate on the ways in which La Ben Plantada [the good-looking one] may or may not resemble her. Both come from a strong breed, but I think that whereas Adelaide represents the sense of touch and colour, la Ben Plantada is Measure. Both mean instinct … Adelaide would have continued to be as she was, only needing the ground and sky of her homeland. La Ben Plantada, however, might not have been what she is today had Ausias March not existed. From a different point of view, we could say that Adelaide is from the mountains and Teresa is from the sea. Or looking at them from still another angle: Adelaide corresponds to Romanesque architecture, whereas Teresa corresponds to Neoclassicism.'[20] D'Ors' text expresses a rejection of everything that had to do with a romantic interpretation of the medieval world: once Catalonia had 'refounded' itself as a nation anchored to the values of Ripoll and Guifre el Pilós (a Catalan king considered to be the first to be motivated by nationalistic ideals) and represented by the Romanesque architecture that so pleased Prat, it seemed time to move on.

It was no longer an issue just for literary men or politicians. This was the moment at which artists and architects entered the scene, and it was up to them to propose the identification of what was modern within the Mediterranean through forms that were based exclusively on one repertoire, the only one that according to D'Ors could possibly fit into this equation: classicism.

In June 1908 the painter Joaquín Torres García published an article in the twelfth issue of *Empori* magazine. That it took as its theme 'El literat i l'artista' ('The Writer and the Artist') is not surprising considering the course of events reviewed so far. In the article, he raised issues that take on special significance within this Mediterranean-classicist tendency. In the first place, this new artist, who was still being awaited, was to be highly educated: 'It is most convenient that the artist knows a great deal about many matters, studied methodically and even with a certain scientific spirit (which is like saying that they have been studied scientifically) … All of this is essential, as well as being a good base for a well-rounded artistic education … All the benefits of this positive knowledge and positive moral education, however, may not be sufficient to counter the damage done to him by a literary education.'[21]

Thus, the artist whom Catalonia needed was to act with a rational certainty that resulted from his many studies and the knowledge acquired through them. He was to train himself to reflect on all matters, and this reflection was to be the source of his creativity. The *Noucentista* civil work, instead of originating in excessively individualistic intuitions that could lead to the creation of a work of genius, was to be standardized, a calculated exercise in manipulating forms selected from the abundant material provided by so-called classicism. It was to do away with the excessive literature that had so far encompassed the *Noucentista* project, since literary images and metaphors did not afford a steady and sure method for reflection on form. The course embarked upon to develop such a method had to take the art form as its exclusive starting point.

To do so, the first and most urgent task was to discard the romantic course and its obsession with the synthesis of the arts. Organization and new order implied the need to think about division, about the autonomy of disciplines, about the sectorial participation of each one of these fields of study in the common task: 'Literature can only give the artist the theme for his work, but its conception has to be absolutely plastic … this is the starting point

Cover of *Notes sobre Art* by Joaquim Torres García, 1913.

for the sculptor or the painter. Therefore, artist, study natural forms and the works of the great masters, and limit your art to the sphere to which it belongs.'[22] The systematization of this new way of making art was not formally set forth until five years later, when in 1913 Torres García published his well-known work *Notes Sobre Art* in which we already find a clearly outlined aesthetic programme that Vallcorba has summarized well (readers are referred to this source for an evaluation of the programme's scope).[23]

Torres considered that imbibing knowledge from the great masters was absolutely essential; however, few architects in Europe at the time bothered to do so. Charles Edouard Jeanneret, the most influential person in Sert's development, an avid reader of Renan, was well aware of this, and he was one of the few architects who did so. His trip east in 1911 had an initial objective that one must not forget: to flee from the architecture that was being carried out in Europe in the studios of the best architects in Paris, Vienna and Berlin (the most dynamic cities on the continent) where he had been trained. He wished to find himself face to face with the architecture of many centuries before, that which it was impossible to emulate formally, and to distance himself from what was being done at the time, no matter how prestigious.

Le Corbusier's itinerary began with a missive of 1 March 1910, which he addressed to the critic, writer and diplomat William Ritter: 'You have lately evoked in a masterful way our great fascination with Latin and classical light … During these last months my spirit has been so open to understanding classical genius, that now my dreams obstinately take me down there … Is it not true that, more than ever before, our current epoch looks towards these joyous lands where clean-cut marbles, vertical columns and entablatures running parallel to the line of the sea shine in all their white splendour? Now, I finally have the occasion to make my dream come true. To conclude a life of study, I am preparing a very important trip.'[24] To travel to the origins of architecture meant discovering the order of orthogonal lines that harmonized with the Mediterranean Sea and with a white marble that was abstract and pure and that did not easily accept chromatic claddings or unnecessary textures.

Many years later, this trip of initiation that had so deeply touched Le Corbusier's soul would leave its imprint on the speech he delivered at CIAM 4. At a time when new architecture was seriously endangered, and the Functional City theory (to which Le Corbusier had decisively contributed) was being formulated, the Swiss architect declared: 'I have tried to act and to create a harmonious and human work. I have done so with the Acropolis, which I carry within me, in my entrails. It is the Acropolis that has turned me into a rebel. This certainty has remained with me: remember the Parthenon, bare, clean, intense, violent, and recall the outcry let loose in a wise

Le Corbusier, *La Cheminée*, 1918 (FLC tableau no. 124).

country made of grace and terror. Force and purity.' That this certainty never left him we can gather from what he wrote in July 1965, shortly before he died, after swimming in the waters that he so loved: 'I am strongly Mediterranean. The Mediterranean ... Light and space. The key event for me is my encounter with Athens in 1910. Decisive light. Decisive volume: the Acropolis. *La Cheminée*, my first painting, executed in 1918, is the Acropolis. My Unité d'habitation in Marseilles is its extension.'

Let us go back to the reality of Catalonia at the beginning of the century. 1913 was a useful date on which to linger and to analyze Torres' text, but it does not coincide with the search for an architecture that would represent the Catalan industrialist party; in this context, 1913 is too late. The publication of a book and the summoning of an open competition two years before this were to alter the flow and development of this architectural quest. This was the same year that D'Ors was writing the *Gloses* de *La Ben Plantada*, that literary image that from the very first descriptions provided by its creator had come to be identified with a familiar name and with architectural forms that would later be taken up by GATCPAC architects ('And that is why I would like to talk to you about la Ben Plantada, who in these golden days of heat has blossomed and grown taller than the rest in a humble summer resort town, very small and white, that is right next to the vast blue of the Mediterranean').[25] The book was *El Palau de la Diputació General de Catalunya* by Puig i Cadafalch and Miret i Sans, which was published by the Institut d'Estudis Catalans, and the competition summoned was the 'Open Competition to Build the Post Office of Barcelona', in which Puig himself participated, though unsuccessfully.

This book is essential for understanding how one of the greatest advocates of the *masia* and of Romanesque architecture came to change his opinion and to regard classicist proposals in a better light. The Palace of the General Council, in which so many programmes to modernize Catalonia were being formulated, a building that Catalans identified with the nationalist conquests of their leaders, presented an unmistakable classical facade. It is therefore not surprising that it was chosen as a local example to redirect attention towards other architectural forms whose cultural affiliations were more or less known. The undertaking, however, was carried out with a certain degree of mistrust.[26]

The text began with Puig and Miret following in the wake of Prat de la Riba's discourse, but then shifted perspective as they began to voice their doubts regarding the effectiveness of medieval art in portraying a power that was increasingly organized around the idea of trust in progress and industry. Medieval architectural aspects were highlighted for their capacity to transmit feelings, whereas the classical parts that Pere Blay and Pere Ferrer had added to the building were exalted not only for their connotations of power and perfection but also for the praise they had received from citizens, students, scholars and professors of architecture. Puig understood that his preferences for what he called 'feeling' would have to take a different rank in his scale of values, and that he had to confront the reality of building a new State, urban and civic architecture that could encompass with its forms not feeling but objective realities that were to be, in Puig's words, 'erudite, patient and submissive'. 'Erudite' was understood to signify what Torres García had expressed in 1908; patience was necessary because they did not yet know which interpretation of classicism was possible; and submission was called for because, instead of seeking individual genius, what was sought was a collective civil work that could be integrated within an allegedly coded and geographically extensive language, which for the time being we may agree to call classicism.

Puig put his words into action by participating in the open competition. His former student and assistant, Josep Goday, presented a building of unmistakable classicist inspiration.[27] The watercolour perspective that Puig submitted to the competition shows a central element that had been awkwardly added on and was characterized by the pell-mell presence of classical elements, topped with a winged Mercury, probably chosen as a symbol of the communications represented by the Post and Telegraph Office. All of this was contained in a symmetrical composition completed by balustrades. Puig's proposal was too similar to the compositional system employed by Blay on the facade of the building facing Plaça Sant Jaume (now the Palace of the Generalitat), an opinion corroborated by the fact that Puig spent time investigating and looking into the documents of the construction of the Palace, and must therefore have

Josep Goday, Central Post Office, Barcelona.

known about the two turrets (nonexistent today) that topped the towers of the building corners. The allusions to certain aspects of Otto Wagner's architecture only added confusion to an architectural conception that Puig had still not mastered. This last point is hardly relevant, however; what does matter is how the project was presented.

In the perspectives he drew, Puig devoted much attention and a great deal of space to the facades of the Borsa (Stock Exchange), one of the few neoclassical buildings in Barcelona that was sufficiently prestigious, and this premeditated gesture reveals much about his intentions. Puig wanted to em-

phasize the natural continuities of classicism in Catalonia, and this was accomplished by linking the Palace of the Generalitat, the Stock Exchange and even the future Post Office: thus, classicism was not, as it had been portrayed until now, an alien entity in the Catalan cultural patrimony.

Moreover, it was in the Palace of the Generalitat that the Renaissance-style addition had eclipsed the pre-existing Gothic presence, minimizing it from an urban point of view. It is also in the Bolsa building erected by Sellés in the eighteenth century on the site of the old Exchange building that we find that a magnificent medieval

Josep Puig i Cadafalch, watercolour perspective presented at the open competition for the Post Office building.

Pere Blay, Palace of the Generalitat, 1596, facade.

arcade has been surrounded and engulfed by a classical envelope, which has functioned as the image of a place that had been and would continue to be representative of noteworthy events in the urban history of Barcelona dating back to the sixteenth century, when city walls were built right up to the sea and the Puerta del Mar (the gate opening to the sea) was erected.

At any rate, there is sufficient evidence to prove that it was not historical treason to believe that the most suitable architecture for Catalonia from 1911 onwards was that based on classical parameters, without this being considered an affront to nationalist feelings.

It is not worth reviewing here what happened from this moment until 1929; various other authors have studied the different meanings taken on by classicism and the different sources on which it fed as it developed in *Noucentist* Catalonia.[28] We have had the opportunity to observe the first formal manifestation of a new ideology that would remain in force for a long time, with the Mediterranean waters both as its witness and its convincing alibi. As we have seen, this was the cultural atmosphere of admiration for the classics in which Sert studied architecture – it was dur-

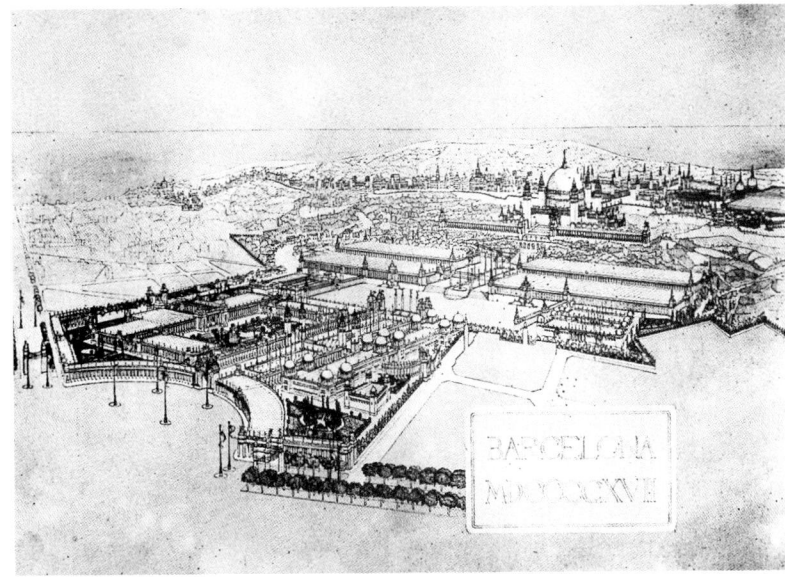

Josep Puig i Cadafalch, perspective from 1917 of Barcelona's World Fair project.

ing this period that the Fundació Bernat Metge published in Catalan all the texts of the classical authors. But despite its positive aspects within Catalan culture, it had become stifling for this young student of architecture, who was subjugated to a universe of classical forms that his professors not only wanted him to study, but obstinately insisted on having him copy, as they themselves had done in their studios.

[1] Fernand Braudel, *El Mediterráneo y el mundo mediterráneo en la época de Felipe II*, Fondo de Cultura Económica, Madrid, 1980. The quotations are from the Spanish edition.
For the influence of the Mediterranean Sea on Sert's architecture see Josep M. Rovira, *Urbanización en Punta Martinet, Ibiza, 1966–1971*, Colección Archivos de Arquitectura, Colegio de Arquitectos de Almería, 1996; various authors. J.LL. *Sert y el mediterráneo*, 'El Mediterráneo es su cuna', COAC, Barcelona, 1997, pp. 46–75.
[2] Jaume Vallcorba, *Noucentisme, mediterranisme i classicisme. Apunts per a l'història d'una estètica*, Quaderns Crema, Assaig Minor, Barcelona, 1994.
[3] Jaume Aulet, *Josep Carner i els orígens del noucentisme*, Curial, Barcelona, 1992.
[4] Vallcorba, op. cit., p. 12.
[5] For information on this subject see: *Paris-Rome-Athènes. Le voyage en Grèce des Architects français aux XVIII et XIX siècles*, Paris, 1982. In this book one can see the works of Loviot, Nénot, Lambert, Lebouteux, etc., who were bent on imagining the original colours of Greek temples and their reconstruction.
[6] Vallcorba, op. cit., p. 15. Moréas even declared that his school had surpassed symbolism, and therefore called it 'Roman': 'We are no longer symbolists; I have found another name for our school, and our school will be the school of Roman poetry.' Other members of this school besides Moréas were Maurice de Plessys, Raimond de la Tailhède, Charles Maurras, Ernest Raynaud and Hugues Rebell.
[7] Vallcorba, op. cit., p. 14. Charles Maurras expressed himself thus in a text of July 1891, whose title was *Barbares et Romans*.

[8] Ibid., p. 26. Vallcorba quotes extensively from part of the text in which one immediately notices the use of epithets such as 'race', 'order', 'harmony', 'composition'; there are also disparaging comments on the supposedly pernicious Germans and Slavs, which transform Le Corbusier into a reactionary who continued to manifest these ideas even twenty years later when he felt that his leadership in the architectural field was being threatened by German proposals.
[9] Juan José Lahuerta, *Antoni Gaudí, 1852–1926*, Electa, Milan, 1992, pp. 143–71. The references are taken from the Italian edition.
[10] V.M. Gibert, *Gaudí, músico potencial*, quoted in Lahuerta, ibid., p. 155.
[11] Eugeni D'Ors, *Obra completa catalana. Glossari, 1906–1910*, pp. 53–54. An interesting interpretation of D'Ors can be found in Norbert Bilbeny, *Eugeni D'Ors i la ideologia del Noucentisme*, La Magrana, Barcelona, 1988. D'Ors made his admiration for Moréas clear on a number of occasions. See *Glossari*, op. cit., pp. 1312–19.
[12] Ibid., pp. 362–63.
[13] Aulet, op. cit., p. 290. In this section of Aulet's work there is an analysis of the events that led to the splitting up of the Lliga in 1904 and the development of a programme based on social classes in 1906. It is worth remembering that in 1906 Prat de la Riba published *La nacionalitat catalana*.
[14] Ibid., p. 309.
[15] Jordi Castellanos, *Raimon Casellas i el modernisme*, Curial, Barcelona, 1983, vol. II, p. 51.
[16] Josep M. Rovira, *La arquitectura catalana de la modernidad*, Ediciones UPC, Barcelona, 1987, pp. 117–25.
[17] Enric Prat de la Riba, *La nacionalitat catalana*,

Col. Biblioteca Popular, Barcelona, 1906, p. 20.
[18] A. de Falguera, J. Goday and Josep Puig i Cadafalch, *L'arquitectura romànica a Catalunya*, Institut d'Estudis Catalans, Barcelona, 1909.
[19] Prat de la Riba, op. cit, p. 97.
[20] Eugeni D'Ors, *La Ben Plantada*, re-edition by Edicions 62, Barcelona, 1980, p. 38.
[21] Joaquím Torres García, *El literat i l'artista*. Taken from *Notes sobre art*, Francesc Fontbona (ed.), Edicions 62, Barcelona, 1980, p. 31.
[22] Ibid., p. 32.
[23] Vallcorba, op. cit., pp. 42–47.
[24] Quoted in Gresleri et al, *Le Corbusier. Il linguaggio delle pietre*, Venice, 1988, p. 23. On Le Corbusier's relationship with the Acropolis, see Josep M. Rovira, 'Le Corbusier i l'Acròpoli', in *Les cases de l'anima*, exhibition catalogue, CC-CB, Barcelona, 1997, pp. 139–44.
[25] D'Ors, op. cit., p. 19.
[26] For a better understanding of this text, see Josep M. Rovira, *Renacimiento y arquitectura. El Palacio de la Generalitat de Catalunya*, Ediciones UPC, Barcelona, 1998.
[27] Concerning the competition, see Josep M. Rovira, *La arquitectura catalana de la modernidad*, op. cit., pp. 154–57.
[28] Among the most outstanding: Oriol Bohigas, 'L'arquitectura a Catalunya', in Enric Jardí (ed.), *L'Art Català Contemporani*, Proa, Barcelona, 1972; Ignasi De Sola, *L'Exposició Internacional de Barcelona, 1914–1929: Arquitectura i Ciutat*, Fira de Barcelona, Barcelona, 1985; Josep M. Rovira, *La arquitectura catalana de la modernidad*, op. cit. We do not include the catalogue from the recent exhibition on *Noucentisme* at CCCB because it offers no new interpretations. It is useful, however, for its illustrations.

Another Mediterranean Reason

The Mediterranean Sea would serve as the starting point for the manifestos of another generation – that which, as previously described, had been trained with its cultural and natural landscapes as a backdrop. As we have seen, this generation wished to go against its upbringing and to start with an architectural *tabula rasa*, an approach reinforced by trustworthy precedents such as Le Corbusier, one of the architects who would be their mentor, and by his friend Sigfried Giedion, the historian of modern architecture. Certain articles can be enlisted to clarify the meaning of their new interpretation of the Mediterranean.

The first of these has to do with Le Corbusier's initial reaction to Barcelona and his first contact with members of this generation there in May 1928 (previously reviewed in this book).[29] After Le Corbusier had given his lectures in Barcelona, he went for a long walk around the city and its environs, accompanied by Marius Gifreda, a commentator on art and architecture for *La Publicitat*, who jotted down some of the Swiss architect's thoughts for his newspaper. Thus, we are able to read what he thought about medieval Catalan: 'Your Gothic has won me over, and I dare say that I prefer it to ours.' For anyone who has even a superficial knowledge of Medieval architecture and calls to mind French cathedrals, a declaration of this type might sound absurd. But it seems less so if we consider that up to 1928 Le Corbusier had repeatedly voiced his reservations about culture in the Middle Ages and his lack of interest in medieval cities,[30] as well as declaring that in Gothic cathedrals '*le barbare est trop proche*'.[31] He was, moreover, less receptive to Northern cultures than to Mediterranean ones. However, these reasons do not seem quite sufficient, and we will come back to them later.

Le Corbusier believed that Northern cultures were alienated from the ideal of order that the Mediterranean civilization seemed to offer, and which, since his trip to the East in 1911, he had idealized, crystallizing it in the image of the Parthenon, the genuine protagonist of *Vers une architecture*. Gifreda's article makes explicit reference to this with the quotation: 'The architecture that I admire is essentially Latin because it is a mathematical equation and has clarity of conception.'

For the young students who heard him, Le Corbusier's words must have been inspiring. Here was one of the most genuine representatives of modern avant-garde architecture, and he was referring to a tradition in which they could share and that could encourage them to move away from the official architectural historicism that was tightening its grip on the city due to the 1929 International Exhibition. After listening to Le Corbusier, they understood that it was possible to undertake this venture without losing sight of their roots.

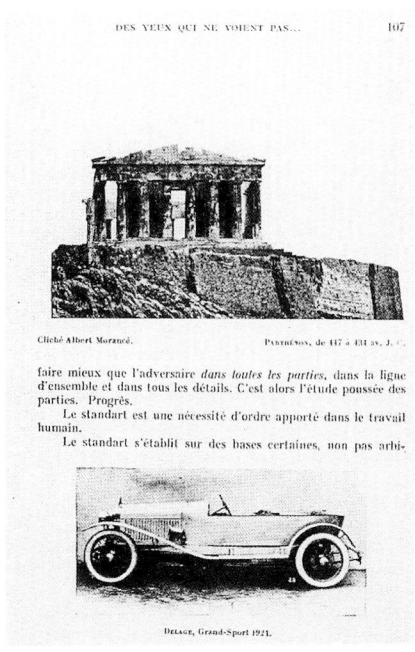

Le Corbusier, *Vers une architecture*, the Parthenon.

J.L. Sert (with the GATCPAC) The City of Leisure and Vacations, Viladecans-Gavà-Castelldefels, Barcelona, 1931–35, aerial perspective.

This was a step in the right direction, and in the first projects publicly presented by these students in 1929 there were clear references to an unmistakably Mediterranean theme. As we know, Sert exhibited the 'Project for a Summer Resort Town in Levante' alongside other proposals by his companions, at the Galeries Dalmau, extensively reported on by Gifreda in *Mirador*.[32] Thus, while the dodecaphonic babel of linguistic eclecticism apparent in Barcelona's street architecture was making an impression on the gullible visitors to the Exhibition, a small art gallery in the city was displaying the embryo of radical architectural change, which attempted to take the lead while rooting itself in common cultural ground. However, considering the warm welcome that Le Corbusier received from the official *Noucentista* intelligentsia,[33] it does not seem that this change provoked any great upheaval, something on which the future GATCPAC members, the authors of this architectural proposal, had counted.

Le Corbusier's admiration for Mediterranean culture and prejudice against Northern ones becomes more evident when examining his correspondence with close friends. In a letter to Giedion on 24 January 1930, he wrote: 'Look, at the bottom of the bottom, at the end of the end, there is art … [T]he [Savoye] house in Poissy lives up to my expectations. What a way of thumbing his nose[34] at the Sachlichkeit!'[35] Scoffing at the Germans and differentiating himself from them was a priority for Le Corbusier, He wished to distance himself from these representatives of New Objectivity because by doing so he was also distancing himself from those who had eliminated the word 'art' from the configuration of architecture (something that he would never renounce) so as to concentrate on the objective elements of a project: its function, its costs, the construction, etc.

This confrontation with the architectural conception of 'those Northerners' would become an obsession with the Swiss architect, an attitude he would again express to Giedion in another letter of 2 July of the same year: 'Your article in *Cahiers d'Art* is very good, but the shadow of the Sachlichs bears down on you. I protest in the name of architecture: what is Sachlich is what is evident and indispensable. *But there is no architecture there*. I am sad in the Sachlich atmosphere, and on the other hand I feel I have created more things than these youths who shout, and I've invented technical things that have freed my poetical side.'[36] Le Corbusier not only affirmed that there was no architecture in the buildings by Northern architects, but that he had been a pioneer in bringing together technique and art, a matter that held no interest in Sachlich circles. It is as if he were vindicating his role as leader, which, as we know, other theorists and designers including Teige and Stam were not willing to grant him. Thus Le Corbusier would have to head South in search of disciples willing to follow him and to make his work more meaningful.

Le Corbusier, Villa Savoye in Poissy, 1929–31.

VILLA SAVOYE 1929

La villa est entourée d'une ceinture de futaies

Group of fishermen's houses in the village of Sant Pol de Mar, in the first issue of *A.C.*, 1931.

Le Corbusier feared that he had lost the contest with the Northern architects through his absence from the Frankfurt Congress of 1929, in which form was not debated at all, instead focusing on the exhibition of different minimal housing models that were drawn in a uniform and anonymous manner. Despite this rivalry, however, Giedion considered that the dialectics of the confrontation could be fruitful, and he made this clear in a letter he sent to Le Corbusier on 5 November 1930, when they were preparing CIAM 3 in Brussels: 'We are glad that you are coming to the Congress. This is also beneficial for an equilibrium between the Latin and the Germanic spirit.'[37]

Clearly Le Corbusier's Mediterranean-based ideology had become an intellectually powerful project in opposition to Germanic or Sachlich conceptions. Giedion apparently understood matters in this light when he wrote in 1932: 'But very soon they saw preliminary signs of a new vitality in the Mediterranean basin, not only in Italy but also in Algeria and in Spain, especially in Barcelona.'[38]

Some time later, on 7 September 1934, Le Corbusier sent a letter to Ventura Gassol, Councillor of Culture of the Generalitat of Catalonia, in which we read: 'On the other hand, in the last years we have been observing a Mediterranean reawakening that is extraordinarily interesting; I am working right now on the plans of Nemours, which is on the Algerian-Moroccan border; I am fighting for my plan in Algiers, which you might already know about.'[39]

Thus, between 1930 and 1934, in the midst of confrontations between ideology and reality, to which were added the complex vicissitudes faced by modern architecture during this period, Le Corbusier had convinced himself, and must also have convinced his unconditionally admiring Catalan followers, of the importance of making the Mediterranean the common ground from which to launch an architecture based on the solid tradition that united them. This coincidence is both odd and suspicious, but it is comprehensible from the standpoint of a strategy to control the destiny of architecture in Europe, the origins of whose international roots were suddenly and mysteriously displaced southwards.

The Catalan rationalist architects, officially called the Grupo Este (East Group) of the GATEPAC, had the advantage of a level of energy and capacity for work that was overwhelming in comparison to that of their colleagues from Northern and Central Spain. The

first task that the Grupo Este tackled was that of seeking a solid formal tradition in keeping with the geography of their Eastern territory, and this was reflected in the first issue of *A.C.*, which was published in Barcelona in March 1931. In this issue we find a couple of pages featuring fishermen's houses in the coastal town of Sant Pol de Mar. The terms used in the analysis were clear: concepts that were of unmistakable *Noucentist* filiation were announced in capital letters: 'CLARITY', 'ORDER', 'ARCHITECTURE'. These words correspond so patently to the ideological repertoire discussed in the first part of this chapter as to render further comment unnecessary, except to point out that the supposed vanguard had not carried out its intentions of making a *tabula rasa* from the ideology that had preceded it despite its clamorous declarations.

In this *A.C.* article, moreover, which had reduced ideology to its minimum expression, a new and surprising opinion was forwarded: the architecture of the Catalan fishermen's dwellings was standardized – that is to say, it was perfectly integrated within the model of mechanist production. This can be deduced from the following paragraph: 'The problem has been solved with the greatest simplicity, taking into account the climate and the inhabitants to give an appropriate scale to the different elements: doors, windows, etc. *The Standard appears*. There is a total lack of aesthetic preoccupation: fantasy, originality, historical styles, "scholastic culture", individualism.' The typographical distinction of the word "standard" cannot be overlooked. From this text, one would gather that popular architecture was being developed with a series of prefabricated elements that were repeatedly used, and that this was in keeping with the assumptions of architecture at the time, which tried to avoid fantasy as well as focusing on collective interests rather than on individual proposals.

Earlier we saw classicism's prevailing need to formalize the Mediterranean ideal. Now it was the turn of popular architecture (that which, represented by the *masia*, had been rejected as a source of formal inspiration by *Noucentista* ideology) to continue the mythicizing process. Both traditions had been invented to undertake projects that were as intellectually and politically different as were the times in which they were conceived.

Inventing a tradition is a phenomenon that has formed part of the Catalan cultural way of working since the second half of the last century. This has been studied from diverse angles that provide a historical framework for the different motives behind it.[40] Hobsbawn and Ranger have defined it thus: 'Invented tradition is understood to be a series of practices normally ruled by norms that are explicitly or tacitly accepted, and by rituals of a symbolic nature that try to inculcate certain principles and norms of behaviour by repetition, which automatically implies continuity with the past … To invent traditions … is essentially a process of formalization and ritualization characterized by its reference to the past, even if it is only accomplished by means of repetition.'[41] For these authors an even more interesting tendency associated with the former phenomenon is that of employing ancient material to invent new traditions with new objectives.

This was the attitude demonstrated by the manifesto of the Catalan rationalists in the first issue of *A.C.* To be able to integrate themselves within the European architectural panorama, despite the delay with which they did so, meant that they had to fulfil certain conditions. The first was to show that they were capable of accepting the principles that had dominated architectural debates since 1920. By speaking of clarity and order, they proved that they had understood the message that Le Corbusier and Ozenfant had broadcast from the pages of *L'Esprit Nouveau*, and by making reference to the need for a standard form they were showing their willingness to conceive the construction of architecture as a process of assembly, the result of mechanical production, or in other words, of modern production. The second condition was to prove themselves, and consequently to prove the professional avant garde they wished to join, that they had in their land a cultural background that made them equal or superior to the rest.

Thus, the whole issue was reduced to a simple detail of chronology: they were the newcomers because of their age, but they were bursting onto the architectural panorama because it was their right to do so, and they proved it by showing that the culture to which they belonged had, from its origins, expressed the very concerns that had been voiced in the last years. And to demonstrate that they were not lagging behind their vanguard colleagues despite their youth, the *A.C.* staff did not hesitate to identify the fishermen's houses in Sant Pol with the facades of J.J.P. Oud's 1927 project on the Weissenhof hill in Stuttgart.

Oud's buildings apparently presented 'the same needs, the same characteristics, making use of the advantages afforded by modern construction techniques'. The claim that a German inhabitant of Oud's houses had the same needs as a fisherman from Sant Pol borders on the absurd. It seems even more so if we read the detailed report written by the Dutch architect about his project, in which he emphasized with great detail and many specific observations the functional nature of his proposal.[42] Likewise, it seems nonsensical to identify those popular architectural forms with Oud's refined design and the meticulous conception of his plan. This is beside the point however; what matters is that Sert, Torres and company were convinced that in their country there was something emanating from the land that gave them the wings to dream up these manipulated identifications, and this allows us to consider other possible interpretations of the rationalist phenomenon in view of what we have so far observed.

The ability of Catalan culture to identify with certain aspects of European tradition stretches far back in time. Indeed, Joan Lluís Marfany has traced this attitude all the way back to Valentí Almirall and Pompeu Gener, and has pointed out how much more productive it was at that point than the classicist reductionism previously examined. A quotation from Gener exemplifies this attitude: 'The elements of the Catalan race, not counting the primitive indigenous element, are: the Celts, the Greeks, the Romans, the Goths and last of all, the Franks. Strong, intelligent and energetic races.'[43] Gener places classical and Northern elements side by side and gives them equal importance, and the Catalans are depicted as a people capable of incarnating this magical synthesis. It is therefore not surprising that the rationalist architects saw Gener's declaration embodied in the fisherman living in Sant Pol, fascinated as they were in

J.J.P. Oud, Houses in Weissenhoff, Stuttgart, 1927.

1931 both with Le Corbusier's teachings and with the architectural production of the Germans, Swiss and Dutch, whose works and projects would often be featured in the pages of their brand-new magazine.

These architects formed part of a Catalonia that had years ago manifested its will to be European. We find the 'justifications' of this desire in a text written in 1904 by Joan Bardina: 'The practical and singular spirit ... was acquired from the Romans, since Catalonia was the area that was most directly influenced by the Romans ... From the Greek and Phoenician colonies first established on our coasts, we inherited our commercial temperament ... And our commercial temperament coupled with our practical spirit has inculcated in our people a tendency to work that has become widely known, and which also characterizes Anglo-Saxon people who, due to this quality, are leaders in matters of progress.'[44] This was an easy and attractive way to identify with an internationalist approach that was not yet in decline. Since Catalonia was able to integrate various nations into the makeup of its character, it could consequently be considered the most international part of Spain, and could therefore confidently attribute this approach to itself.

Marfany stressed the natural consequence of these affirmations: 'In the end, the land is what makes a nation.' In 1931, this nation began to aspire to its own statutes of autonomy, and to an architecture that belonged to its roots and its land. The fishermen's houses that had so pleased the *A.C* staff, were intended to reflect Catalonia's desire and right to establish a free and open dialogue with Europe, both because it was a product of past migrations, and because it had been capable of retaining and integrating the positive aspects of these.

Macià's new government must have approved of the manifestos of these youths, for they coincided with its own interests in ensuring land and shelter for those worst off within the system, especially due to the shortage of workers' housing at the time. From the point of view of land and shelter, Sert and his friends had made a skilful and inspiring choice: to achieve these objectives for a great number of workers was a way of proving Catalonia's ability to continue providing what history showed that it had always produced: popular architecture. It was also a way of approaching the problem of workers' housing, an issue that had been cropping up in European political regimes for some time, and which in 1931 had begun to form part of the programme of some of the political parties running for municipal elections in Barcelona.

When Le Corbusier received the first issue of *A.C.* in his studio on rue de la Sèvres, shortly after Sert's visit, he must have understood that he was faced with a group of devoted followers, although he would not have fully grasped the identification made between the fishermen's houses in Sant Pol and those of the Stuttgart exhibition. This was secondary, however; what did matter was that these youths were his allies, they lived in Barcelona, and were Mediterranean. Moreover, they exhibited their popular architecture with great pride, as we have seen. They could back him up, as would indeed be the case on future occasions, and could also work in constructing the myth of the Mediterranean as the indispensable cornerstone of new architecture, removed from the fogs of the North and its obsessions with objectivity. If the matter were well orchestrated, they could, in fact, control modern architecture. Possessing the Mediterranean was the same thing as owning the new architecture.

We briefly spoke of this 'possession' in the previous chapter, and now we can begin to un-

derstand the scope of its meaning. The City of Leisure and Vacations project, completed in 1935, which had been conceived for the Mediterranean vacations of Barcelona's working classes, was a way of making tangible the importance that leisure time was gaining, while showing the functional efficacy of an ideology that we now know was integral to the Catalan mentality.

As stated earlier in this book in relation to *The Heart of the City*, Sert was a keen reader of José Ortega y Gasset. This author had influenced Sert in his student days because he could easily identify with his portrayal of the 'social aristo-

The City of Leisure and Vacations, front and back cover of publicity pamphlet.

LA CIUDAD DEL REPOSO

Entre las grandes obras que en Barcelona se proyectan figura, en primera línea, el planeamiento de «La Ciudad del Reposo» sobre la magnífica playa de Castelldefels (12 kilómetros de longitud bordeados de una faja de pinares de 300 metros de anchura), marco insuperable al proyecto estudiado por el grupo de arquitectos GATCPAC. No se trata de crear una nueva playa de moda, ya que con la orientación general del proyecto profundamente democrática, se trata de satisfacer una necesidad social de las clases media y trabajadora, prescindiendo por ello de casinos y hoteles de lujo. En contraste con la pasada generación proletaria que pasaba los días festivos en locales de espectáculos o de juego, el trabajador de hoy busca la manera de satisfacer sus ansias de luz y descanso al aire libre en el cultivo del deporte. Hoy, los regidores de la ciudad moderna, han de dar realidad a este tan justo deseo, mejorando el ambiente de vida de las masas en todos sus aspectos, figurando la organización del reposo periódico entre los más apremiantes. Se trata de un caso de urgencia para el proletariado barcelonés el salvar esta zona, evitando pueda ser objeto de una explotación de tipo capitalista. El programa del proyecto queda desarrollado, en sus aspectos urbanísticos y constructivos, en los trabajos que son objeto de esta exposición.

1. Necesidad de las zonas de reposo en las grandes ciudades.
2. Las playas actuales barcelonesas y sus defectos.
3. El único emplazamiento para la futura playa de Barcelona.
4. Dos criterios urbanísticos:
   a) Urbanizaciones de carácter individualista.
   b) Urbanización de carácter colectivo (sistema adoptado).
5. Zona de influencia de la futura playa.
6. Distribución de zonas y su función.
7. Índice del conjunto.
8. Los sports.
9. Circulación.
10. Axonométrico de conjunto.
11. Etapas de realización.
12. Vista aérea de la zona de baños y «fin de semana».
13. Hoteles sanatorios para cura de reposo.
14. Cabinas para baño.
15. Hoteles «fin de semana». Bloques de viviendas familiares.
16. Casa desmontable «fin de semana».
17. Casa mínima.

SALÓN DEL MUSEO DE ARTE MODERNO · PASEO DE RECOLETOS · EDIFICIO DE BIBLIOTECAS Y MUSEO

crat' and intellectual in 1930, a time when the need for the new intellectual was being proclaimed. Ortega's comments on the Mediterranean in *Revolt of the Masses* may help us to understand his discourse and his influence on Sert: 'If we observe public life in the countries in which the masses have most visibly triumphed – and these are the Mediterranean countries – it is surprising to observe that they have no long-range political plans.'[45] Near the end of the text, we find: 'The city is the super-house, the surpassing of the house … It is the republic, the *politeia*, which is not made up of men and women, but of citizens … In this way the city is born, at least as a city-state. In certain ways, all the Mediterranean coast has shown a spontaneous tendency towards this type of state … Our Levant falls into the rut of regionalism whenever it can, which is a bad habit left over from that very ancient inspiration. It would be interesting to demonstrate how in Catalonia two opposing inspirations vie with each other: European nationalism and Barcelona's "sense of city", in which the old Mediterranean tendency towards this type of state continues to survive.'[46]

A strange contradiction envelops Ortega's words. On the one hand Mediterranean countries are depicted as incapable of sustaining a political project for any reasonable duration. On the other, it seems that in these countries there is a natural tendency for people to organize themselves, to invent the *oikos*, and taking off from there, to build states. In the modern Catalonia in which Sert lived, this tendency became tinged with complementary nuances when nationalistic ideas merged with the strong personality of the city. This *Gross* Barcelona, a term coined by Maluquer i Nicolau, became a political and intellectual project that from 1914 onwards came ineluctably to identify city with nation. J. Bofill voiced this idea in *La Veu de Catalunya* between 8 and 20 February of that year: 'If we cherish dreams of imperialism, if we aspire to the reconstruction, or better said, the construction of a "Greater" Catalonia, we had better start preparing lovingly and carefully the compendium of being the capital, the metropolis, the Greater Barcelona, of which Barcelona on its own is merely the nucleus.'

It is now, when the masses are in power, that things have to be redirected, and to do so the Mediterranean spirit offers a solid history from which to learn and obtain resources, a model from which to instruct the masses who must be reoriented. Thus the Mediterranean serves as an example of a social organization that goes back to ancient times.

Ortega's text consistently attempted to orient the masses towards an orderly, directed and controlled solution at a time (the modern period) in which these masses had risen to power: 'There is a fact which, for good or ill, is of utmost importance in European public life at the moment. This fact is the accession of the masses to complete social power. Since the masses by definition should not and cannot direct their own existence, and even less govern society, this means that Europe right now is suffering from the greatest crisis that can afflict peoples, nations and civilization.' Moreover, an increasing agglomeration of people was manifesting itself in the daily spheres of life: 'The cities are full of people. The houses are full of renters. The hotels are full of guests. The trains, full of passengers. The cafés, full of consumers. The boulevards, full of passers-by. The offices of renowned doctors, full of patients. The shows, unless they are exceedingly untimely, full of spectators. The beaches, full of bathers. Lack of space, which before did not tend to be a problem, is now increasingly becoming so.'

To direct and plan so as to bring order to this chaos, Ortega called on the aristocracy, an aristocracy whom he labelled 'social' as a measure of the fact that its task set it apart from the ancient aristocracy, that dead and rotten class that was epitomized by Versailles. This social aristocracy was to redirect the man from the mass 'whose life lacks a project and rambles aimlessly'. It was to achieve its objectives by means of 'liberal and technical democracy'.

Technology, which for Ortega was the result of putting together scientific experimentation and industrialism, was to be in the hands of a ruling class made up of select men: 'The select man or excellent man is he who feels the intimate need to seek from within himself a norm that is beyond him, superior to him, and which he freely chooses to serve.' This was the 'new nobleman', in Ortega's words, an individual who aspired to achieve 'order and law', the new intellectual who was to save Spain from the chaos that monarchy and dictatorship had wreaked on

The City
of Leisure
and Vacations,
graphic images
of leisure time
in issue no. 7
of *A.C.*, 1932.

coastal city par excellence, will not waste the opportunity to have a park on the seashore that is better than any other city's in the world.' At the same time, this park would be a sports area, the scenario of possible competitions in the future that would concentrate massive public attendance in a common precinct. Leisure and entertainment were to go together so as to channel the energies left over from the working day, or to provide a break from a too strenuous schedule, and this was made possible because the city was close enough to allow access to the complex every weekend: 'Competitions of a multiple and complex nature may be organized there to attract the multitudes, and these, thanks to the facilities they are offered, will be able to practice various sports instead of having to stick to one.'

the country. Ortega believed that, faced with this new nobleman, the masses 'would at a given moment have the grace to accept his leadership, especially regarding very difficult issues.'

If we review the images that accompanied the presentation of the project of La Ciutat de Repòs i Vacances (abbreviated to CRV, and meaning the City of Leisure and Vacations), we begin to understand how Orteguian concepts tie in with the GATCPAC architects' ideas: queues of people waiting for buses, on the train ladders, on crowded beaches, etc. Similarly, if we read the report of CRV, we find terms that establish its Orteguian affiliation. The opening sentences show the will of Sert and his colleagues to guide the masses and direct their leisure time. They had not received this commission from any organization, thus it had sprung from their own 'aristocratic-social' tendencies. If their initiative succeeded, the CRV would become a collective project: 'There is a need to organize the leisure and rest of the working-class generations based on a work created and sustained by the people, free from all speculative and interested tendencies. We hope that they and society at large will contribute to this work that will bring prestige to the name of Catalonia. The CRV is the conception of a series of problems that deeply concern all authorities.'[47]

The construction of a coastal park in an area without any apparent owners, which therefore allowed these lands to be occupied without speculative ends, fits in with the need of designers to connect with the Mediterranean and with the desire to open the city to the sea: 'Barcelona,

This was to take place within a context that was socially favourable to these types of proposals, and in this idea it was easy to detect the presence of the Orteguian discourse: 'The right of all workers to a vacation period is already an accepted principle in our nation … [I]t is time to emphasize the need to organize these vacations for the great proletarian masses, for whom there is nothing prepared on a large scale. It is necessary to present the different possibilities offered for these vacations so that the working masses may plan how to make the most of their resources … The problem that we are faced with is the following: how should workers employ these vacations? One very quickly becomes aware of the disorientation of the proletarian masses. That is why popular organisms have to take the lead in this matter and find a solution that is most in

The City
of Leisure
and Vacations,
images portraying
the difficulty
of reaching
the beaches near
Barcelona,
in issue no. 7
of *A.C.*

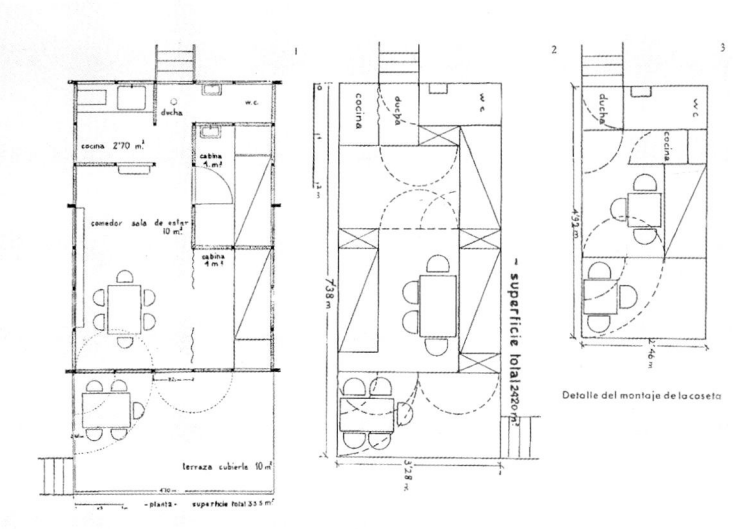

The City of Leisure and Vacations, plan of demountable house.

keeping with workers' needs, and these in their turn, if the strategy is skilfully and carefully executed, will slowly follow the path traced for them without being aware of doing so.'

The next step for Sert and the GATCPAC architects was to explain the CRV programme. It was to include weekend school areas for low-budget families, and semi-permanent school camps that aimed to strengthen children with health problems, as well as providing vegetable gardens for growing one's own produce, a tradition that people from Barcelona had been practising since the nineteenth century in the surrounding towns that were later annexed to the city. There were also bathing areas with huts and swimming pools nearby, following a suggestion that Le Corbusier had made in a letter to them on 5 July 1934, as well as outdoor cinemas and

free spaces for fairs and attraction parks. The weekend areas were made up of demountable houses and dwellings of very small dimensions with adjoining sports fields, 'camping' spaces and school pavilions. The residential areas were to include modest hotels and small houses that could be rented seasonally. The programme also introduced installations for rest therapy, with sanatorium hotels designed to include great terraces to facilitate sun and open-air cures.

The planning for all of this was extremely precise, with a clear distribution of the different uses within a strip 10 km long by 2 km wide, designed facing the sea: bathing areas, weekend areas, residential areas, and rest therapy areas. The great stadium held a central position within this hierarchy, organizing the ensemble, and the masses were to converge there for important public acts. The architecture of the buildings, for which there is documentary material, cannot be taken for anything more than a generic preliminary design, and it is therefore difficult to assess it. We can, however, look at some of the buildings that aspired to be more than just part of the manifesto.

The four typologies of minimal housing proposed solutions that had already been offered on other occasions, or that were being elaborated at the time; these will be analysed later. The most atypical dwelling was the biggest one, a house set on top of *pilotis* with a pressed glass parapet on the upper floor, like that of the tuberculosis clinic, and with a general composition to which Sert would revert in the 1950s. Under the porch, the maid would take the meals to the table where the couple with their child and dog would be waiting,

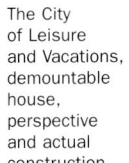

The City of Leisure and Vacations, demountable house, perspective and actual construction.

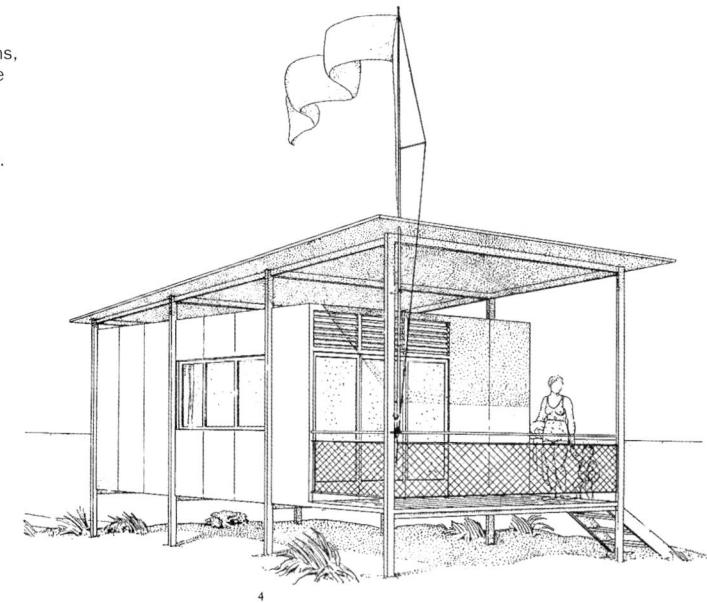

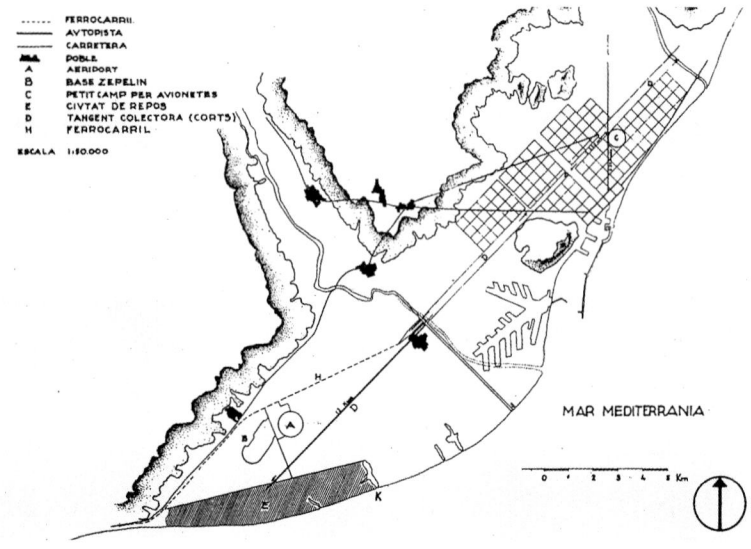

The City
of Leisure
and Vacations,
location on map
of Barcelona,
and plan.

very possibly sitting on chrome-plated iron-tubing chairs. A car would also be present in this scheme. This model does not seem to correspond to the typical Catalan working-class family, but there is no indication that middle-class people could not also make use of the CRV. The weekend hotels and the sanatorium hotels simply limited their structure to repeating as often as was necessary the cell typology, and to placing the vertical accesses within the changes in direction of the floors, a feature that we have already seen in the Casa Bloc. At any rate, they were seen as 'machines for resting', buildings without attributes, as would also be the case with the bathing huts.

As we mentioned earlier, these were building-manifestos, which were supposed to showcase a modernity that was bent on organizing the leisure time of the masses and that attempted, through exhibitions, publications, conferences and propaganda, to draw the attention of the authorities. The latter, however, were incapable of

coming up with effective ways to help and were frightened of veering even slightly away from the capitalist liberalism that defended land property to the hilt; moreover, their coffers were empty and they therefore had no resources for carrying out such a plan.

The CRV was almost a dream come true; to carry it out, the GATCPAC architects set up a co-operative that assembled more than 600 associations throughout Catalonia with a total number of members that exceeded 800,000. However, the decree for the expropriation of the terrains, which was a simple procedure, was never issued: the liberalism expounded by Ortega showed its true nature. The naivety of Sert and his friends was made patent in the futility of their gesture, which had only managed to outline this illusory complex on the Mediterranean Sea that would never become a reality.

In a letter dated 7 August 1943 to Ventura Gassol, Le Corbusier, travelling companion in

The City
of Leisure
and Vacations, aerial
perspective and
photomontage.

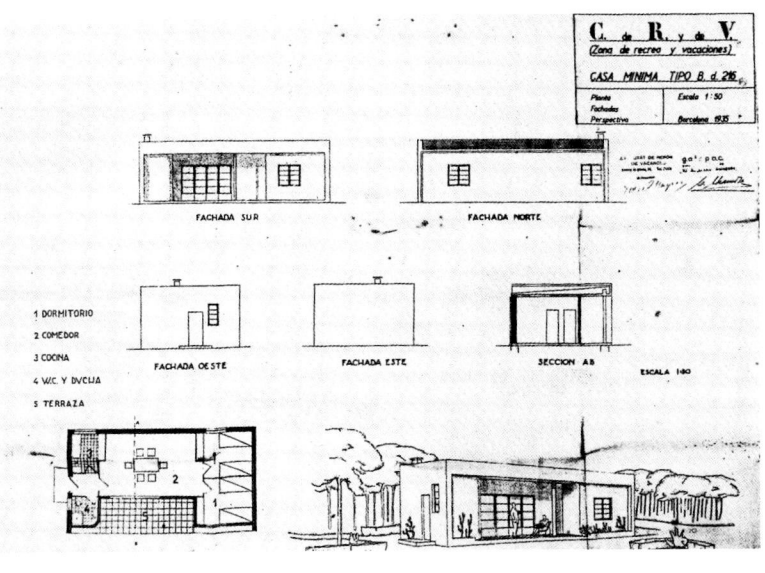

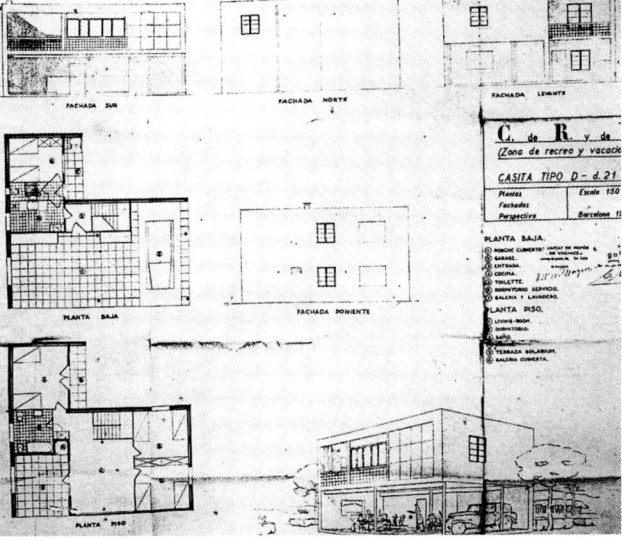

The City
of Leisure
and Vacations,
minimal housing,
weekend hotel
and sanatorium
hotel.

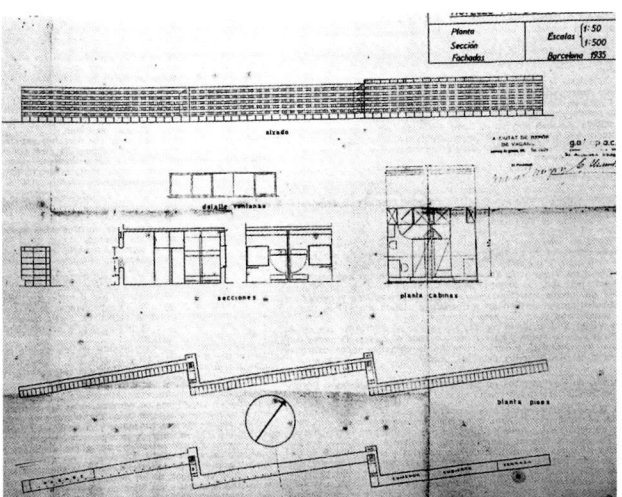

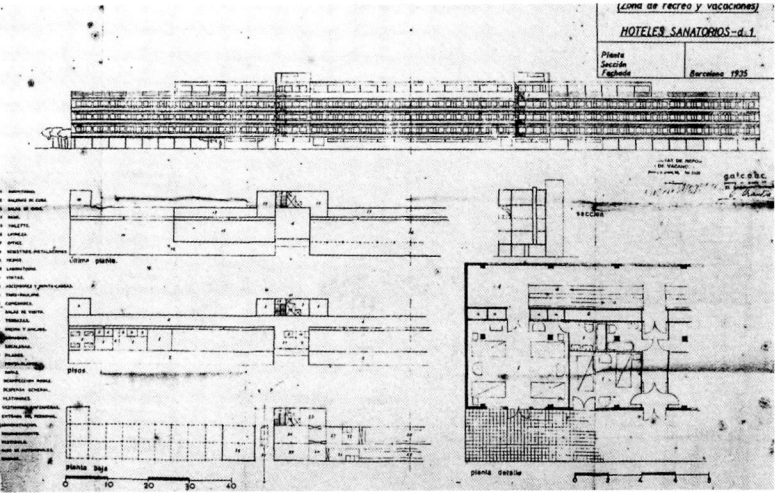

this Mediterranean overview that we are preparing to investigate, expressed himself in optimistic terms for what we know of his projects in progress: 'Besides in these last years we are assisting an extremely interesting Mediterranean awakening: currently I am involved with the town planning of Némours, on the frontier between Algeria and Marocco. I am fighting at Algiers for my project that you perhaps know about.'[48] It will nevertheless be necessary to look elsewhere for the fruits of this ideology, in environments where the same circumstances cannot repeat themselves.

[29] Le Corbusier, *Encuentro con la obra de Gaudí*, in *Gaudí*, Edition RM, Barcelona, 1958.
[30] Le Corbusier, *Urbanisme*, Editions Crès, Paris, 1924, pp. 5–11.
[31] Ibid., p. 33.
[32] See Màrius Gifreda, 'Els arquitectes joves', published in three successive issues of *Mirador*, no. 13, 25 April 1929, no. 14, 2 May 1929, and no. 15, 9 May 1929. The aforementioned project appears on page 42 of the seventh issue of *A.C.*, published during the third trimester of 1932.
[33] Juan Jose Lahuerta, 1928. 'Le Corbusier en Barcelona', in *La Tradición Moderna*, COAC, Girona, 1995, pp. 109–12.
[34] In the French original, Le Corbusier used the word *pied-de-nez*, which is the equivalent of the Catalan *pam i pipa*: the mocking gesture of pressing thumb against nose and waving around the fingers of the open hand.

[35] SGA, Correspondence with Le Corbusier, 43–K–1930, 1–24.
[36] Ibid., 7–2.
[37] SGA, Correspondence with Le Corbusier, 260–D2–3.
[38] Sigfried Giedion, "Uno straniero parla de la trienale" in Lavoro Fascista, 23 September 1932.
[39] GATCPAC Archives, COAC, Barcelona. Reproduced in *Cuadernos de Arquitectura y Urbanismo*, no. 90, Barcelona, 1972, p. 35.
[40] See Eric Hobsbawn and Terence Ranger, *L'invent de la tradició*, Eumo, Barcelona, 1988. Although it does not directly deal with issues linked to Catalonia, it provides a useful general theoretical framework. See also Llorenç Prats, *El mite de la tradició popular*, Edicions 62, Barcelona, 1988; Joan-Lluís Marfany, *La cultura del catalanisme*, Empúries, Barcelona, 1995.
[41] Hobsbawn and Ranger, op. cit., pp. 13–15.
[42] These are found in one of the publications

that came out at the time of the 1927 German Werkbund exhibition in Stuttgart. See *Bau und Wohnung*, Wedekind, Stuttgart, 1927, pp. 87–96. The picture published in *A.C.* also appears in this publication. There is an Italian translation: *Construire Abitare*, Kappa, Rome, 1992.
[43] Pompeu Gener, *Herejías*, 1887, quoted from Marfany, op. cit., p. 196.
[44] Joan Bardina, *Política de Kábila II*, quoted in ibid., p. 200.
[45] José Ortega y Gasset, *La rebelión de las masas*, 1930, quoted from the 1979 edition, Alianza Editorial, Madrid, p. 77.
[46] Ibid., p. 168.
[47] The most exhaustive report of the CRV project, which corresponds to the final project of 1935, was published in *Cuadernos de Arquitectura y Urbanismo*, no. 94, Barcelona, January–February 1973.
[48] FLC H3 13 27.

DOCUMENTOS DE ACTIVIDAD CONTEMPORANEA

A.C. 21

PUBLICACIÓN DEL G. A. T. E. P. A. C. · AÑO VI · PTAS. 3,25

Ibiza and the Avant-garde

Although by now certain issues that we have examined previously may seem somewhat remote, it is worth going back to them to assess some different approaches. Not all *Noucentistes* considered classicism to be the only possible formal strategy for the construction of something new. We have already seen this in a passage from *La Ben Plantada*. In another text of unmistakable affiliation to these ideas, the *Almanach dels Noucentistes* of 1911, we find a contribution by the intellectually renowned Josep Pijoan, which constitutes a clear precedent for this alternative approach. In the poem *De les Terres Velles*, we read: 'Menorca, your white houses, the labyrinthine walls of the island painted all in white, render lighter the grey slabs of stone emerging from the sea. The people who live there look for the shade offered by the low houses and the squalid fig tree rooted in the midst of rocks.'[49] Thus, we see that there were not only two alternatives – that of the *masia* or that of classicism – to enrich urban architectures. There was also the charm of the white Menorcan houses that tinge the countryside with their paleness, making uniform the geography of the island and offering refuge. The chromatic presence and a well-resolved habitat that provides shelter were both image and function, offered on archaic terms: pure, primitive, without form or style. This time the Mediterranean symbolized another type of proposal, one that would long remain latent but which we cannot overlook in search for all the possible antecedents.

The paths we will follow from now on will not be those of the island depicted by Pijoan, but those of its neighbouring Ibiza, which attracted various representatives of the European avant garde and which had notorious repercussions in the pages of *A.C.*

In the 1930s it became customary for artists, philosophers, architects and writers to travel to Ibiza, and this habit continued during the following decades, recalling past eras in which the island had been frequented by other famous travellers with very different interests. Antonio Colinas summarizes it thus: 'It was always a place crossed and visited by many civilizations – Greeks, Carthaginians, Romans, Arabs, Catalans – but it always maintained its aloof serenity. There are many who believe that Ibiza was a sacred land back in antiquity; some say this is due to the total absence of harmful animals on its fields; or to its intensely red earth, which travellers would carry away with them to show when back in their own lands … Since the

Cover of *A.C.*, no. 21.

Cover of *Almanach dels Noucentistes*, 1911.

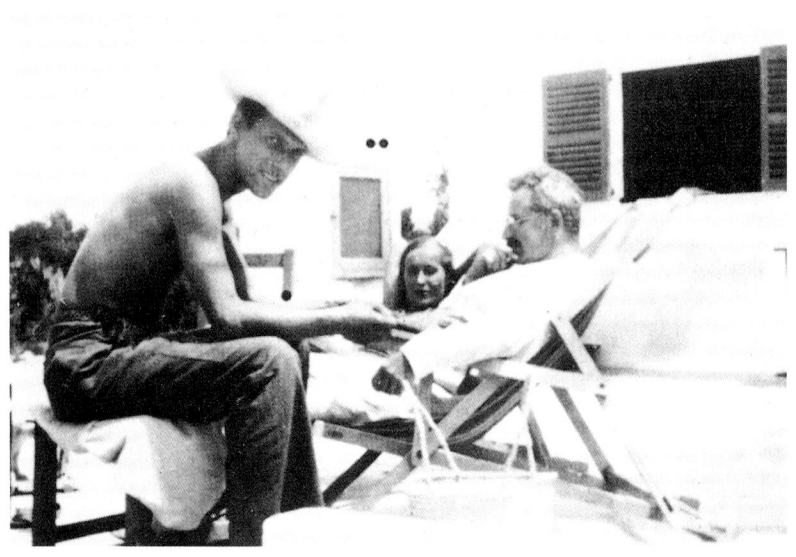

Walter Benjamin and Jean Selz in Ibiza.

sixth century b.c., Ibiza has been a densely populated island, and its sanctuaries, its very fertile orchards, the beauty of its fields, its pleasant climate, had already made of her what she would be blown up to be in the last decades of the twentieth century: an international centre of travel and cultural exchange, inhabited, as Diodorus of Sicily put it, "by barbars of all sorts, especially Phoenicians". It was also an island of many gods, but which has been ruled essentially by two of them: Tanit, the primeval goddess of fertility and of bounty, and Bes, an unclassifiable minor god, considered by some to be evil.'[50]

Walter Benjamin, Albert Camus, Will Faber, Adolf Schulten, Raoul Hausmann, Man Ray, Tristan Tzara, Jean Seltz, José Luis Sert, German Rodríguez Arias (who, according to local lore, first came to the island in 1928 to get away from the overcrowded beaches of the Costa Brava, and later introduced it to his friends), Sixte Illescas, Erwin Broner, Rafael Alberti, Teresa León, von Puttkamer and others were drawn to the island for different reasons, and all visited it at some point during this period.

At the beginning of the 1930s the island was depicted as being somewhat backwards, an image that the *Diario de Ibiza* did not help to dispel: 'Our island needs good roads and walkways to be built.'[51] It was an island that had no sewage system and no running water, with many stray dogs sharing the streets with hens; it was also an island that greeted the arrival of the telephone enthusiastically: 'Today is a day of great joy … All of Ibiza backs up this new en-

terprise, which marks a new stage in our path towards a splendid future, and which arrives like the dawn of a new era of prosperity for our beloved island.'[52] Even in those days the island was seen as a resource that could be exploited, as we know it was to be, and ruthlessly so, much later: 'Ibiza deserves to be visited more, to be better known, for in my opinion it has great potential, but the people of Ibiza must first of all decide to build a hotel, or various hotels',[53] so that 'when we can finally count on the basics to ensure the comfort of our visitors, tourism will certainly become a very important source of income for the island'.

The fact that Ibiza was still so primitive must have increased its charms in the eyes of its illustrious visitors, who in some way or another sought to flee from the large industrial cities that either from technical or political reasons were becoming increasingly uninhabitable.

Walter Benjamin expressed himself along these lines in the first letter he wrote after his arrival in the island: 'I have withdrawn to the most recondite corner, whereas you veer your eyes towards European cities.'[54] In the same letter he described how inexpensive it was to live there, and how unspoiled the landscape was – despite the fact that in further missives he would voice his indignation about the buildings that were being constructed in San Antonio, as well as expressing his hope that the whole operation to attract tourism would fail. He also pointed out how archaic the interiors of the country people's houses were: 'Three chairs along the wall of the room that faces the entrance are placed there in offering to the visitor with the same self-assuredness and solemnity that could be accorded to three Cranachs or three Gauguins hanging on the wall.'

His fascination with the forms of these dwellings is reflected in a number of passages in his correspondence: 'The nicest thing about it is the view from the window: it overlooks the sea and the rocky island whose beacon illuminates my room at night and whose inhabitants are separated from one another by a skilful layout of space and walls about a metre thick that block all noise.'[55] In comparison with the German architecture to which he was accustomed, the houses of Ibiza had an added value, which he recorded in *Suite ibicenca*: 'In our well-equipped houses, there is no room for what is valuable because we lack the margin of freedom for it to render service.' The island also offered other lessons: 'I sometimes learn more here about the origin and nature of people than I had after several years in Berlin.'[56] Moreover, the landscape was 'incomparably more secret and mysterious'.

While Benjamin was writing about his impressions of the island's popular architecture during his two sojourns to Ibiza between 1932 and 1933, *A.C.* also featured an extensive report on the island in its sixth issue, published in the second quarter of 1932. Not surprisingly the terms of analysis were very different. For GATCPAC members, the Ibizan houses were perfect and did not need renovation. They faced the east, the best possible direction for light, they were Latin, built on a human scale, and made logical and rational sense; moreover, some of them were 'minimalist', and their volumes simple. They were also unmarred by inopportune styles, were well suited to the climate, and were clear, orderly and clean, so that

they constituted 'a sedative in our times of stress and speed'. All of this made Ibiza a modern architect's haven for meditation and rest.

A.C. did not publish any pictures of Ibizan interiors, nor did they bother to list the lack of sanitary facilities in these houses or their constructional problems. These issues were unimportant to them. In fact, they were almost attractive, in the sense that they created a distance from the agitated urban lifestyle of the metropolis. It was on the analysis of the volumes that they focused. The popular architecture of Ibiza, in a similar way to the fishermen's houses of Sant Pol, interested them because its form coincided, if this is not a contradiction in terms, with some European avant-garde architectures: it was without ornamentation, displayed pure volumes, and was conceived logically for a certain lifestyle, beginning with its rational choice of geographical orientation. There is also another reason latent in all of this: popular Ibizan architecture could be added in a modern way to the rich compendium of Mediterranist ideology, some of whose aspects we are now fa-

miliar with. This architecture was therefore called upon to implement the Mediterranean traits to which modern architecture 'owed' its proposals. Expected to take on this surprising task, it was to facilitate continuities and overlappings between modernity and tradition, essential for the ideas of Sert and his friends. It is evident, however, that these constructions were also expected to fulfil excessively high levels of efficiency, which would have been better suited to other approaches not so bent on immediate return profit, a factor that the GATCPAC

Popular architectural typologies of Ibiza in *A.C.*, no. 6.

The photographer Raoul Hausmann.

members necessarily had to include in their pragmatic analysis.

One such approach was that of the dadaist Raoul Hausmann, who from 1933 to 1936, the years he lived on the island, looked at these architectures from another point of view, which he afterwards captured in a series of photographs, pencil sketches in his diary and some writings that have been fortuitously discovered.[57] Hausmann was also attracted by certain issues that coincide with those mentioned earlier. One such example was the surprising ease with which the binomial form-function appeared before his eyes when contemplating the chairs that were made by the Ibizans: 'The wooden skeleton of an empty body now represents the idea of a chair which takes shape … So that they become authentic chairs, the carpenter has the seat of the chair plaited with rope; when this has been done, he takes the chairs over to his neighbour the rope maker who plaits the cordage artistically in square shapes that diminish as they reach the centre … Three chairs were finished, solid in their structure, irreproachable, standing on the workshop floor … The carpenter has placed three chairs in the empty space of the big hall. Made of wood and of rope, a function has taken shape.'[58]

Naturally, Hausmann could not avoid all the cultural and linguistic features of his period, and when he observed the Ibizan chairs – which would later be redesigned by Sert and Arias and made by the carpenter Vicarías to furnish the dwellings of the Can Pep Simó

housing development – he fell back on the anachronism of looking at them through a prism that had long since been adopted by architects as an ensign of the modern. However, there were other aspects that were not so obvious, such as the interest in handicraft, the collaboration between the different crafts or trades in a 'collective' work, the old classical distinction between bones (skeleton) and meat (body) that is part of all works, the anthropologist's and ethnologist's regard filtered through dadaist modernity.

Other passages in his initial writings constitute obvious parallels with *A.C.* For example, in 1934 he wrote jointly with Walter Ségal: '[This architecture,] through its external forms recalls in a striking manner our architecture of today.' It seems that the past is being constructed through the filter of present-day concerns. However, he seems to have had no motive for doing so; Hausmann, as we know, did not intend to use the past to suit his interests. The following year he significantly altered his earlier opinions in an article for *L'Architecture d'Aujourd'hui*. 'These primitive conditions and the patriarchal structure of the family are reflected in an architecture that exerts on us a much greater attraction in the sense that the purity of its lines and cubes discovers our love of truth and simplicity … We will not speak here of the analogy between the Ibizan house and the modern architecture of our days. This analogy would be purely superficial.' The fact that Hausmann refused to take the same approach

Raoul Hausmann: hand-crafted Ibizan chairs.

Raoul Hausmann:
Ibizan houses.

as the architects facilitated his discovery of a fertile path for achieving an in-depth knowledge of an architecture whose usefulness was not measured solely by its application to the worktables of modern architects.

The dadaist was much more interested, for example, in identifying the origin of the architectures that fascinated him: 'The predominance of elementary forms in the rustic constructions of the island of Ibiza clearly indicates that its present-day architecture has its origin in the caves that were the dwellings of its primitive settlers.' The house showed highly original systems of construction 'from the tribes that inhabited Asia Minor during the primitive era and which were imported by the Phoenicians when they settled in Ibiza'.

Hausmann pointed out that it was not the concept of the project but rather time that was the factor that made or consolidated rural architecture, and that it was important to trace the process and techniques that had patiently built up this rural architecture: 'The rustic dwelling is a building constructed during different periods of time; we are not dealing with one single dwelling whose plan has previously been traced, but rather the ensemble is truly a group of rooms that has grown according to the needs of its inhabitants … First the dormitories are built, and at a right angle the kitchen is added … In primitive times, the kitchen was built out in the open, right next to the rooms in a place that was duly protected from the wind. The hearth had a U form, was sunken in-

to the ground, and this is where the fire was lit, with the smoke blown away by the wind … The living room is set up in the angle formed by the dormitories and the kitchen … [W]hen there are no longer any free dormitories on the ground floor, the same process of expansion begins to take place on the upper floor … With this process, the primitive rectangular plan has lost its purity with the addition of balconies, floors and columns.'[59]

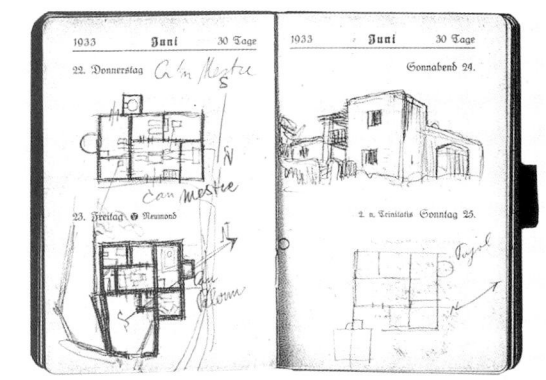

Sketches
of houses in Ibiza.

Cuaderno de notas Kleiner Notizkalender, 1933   Quadern de notes Kleiner Notizkalender, 19

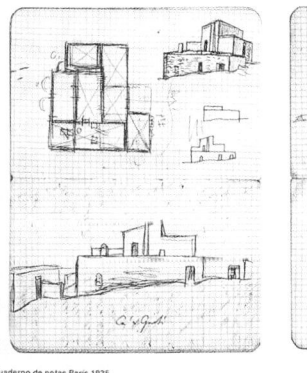

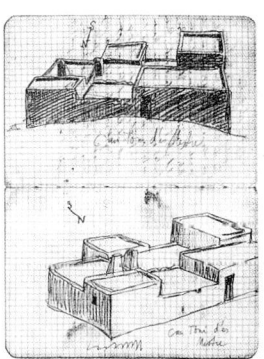

Cuaderno de notas Paris 1935   Quadern de notes Paris 1935

Yves Michaud has explained the possible meanings behind this interest, linking it to cosmic aspects of the monistic philosophy that partook of a trans-individual vision of the subject, in which the arrival of the new man also meant the advent of a new community that would surpass individuals. For Hausmann, as for many other artists, architects, anthropologists and historians of the first two decades of the twentieth century, art was to have an essential role in the creation of the new individual in the mechanist civilization.

To represent that civilization, art would necessarily have to respect certain conditions, which Hausmann has conceptualized thus: 'In the first period of humanity, the representation of the human environment was not naturalist, it was not a simple reproduction, but rather the comprehension of all of man's relations with the world, and of his perceptions of the world and the powers emanating from it, which were grasped, condensed and transported in a symbolic and magical fashion.'[60] The indissoluble union between history and geography that Hausmann observed in the houses of Ibiza, the capacity to synthesize art and life that they demonstrated in their slow construction process, led him to conceive a model that materialized aspects of his thinking regarding the construction of his time or epoch. It was an epoch that was defined by many, but which was best explained by the historian and GATPAC sympathizer Sigfried Giedion; in his opinion, it was a time that forced those who wanted to conceive it to position themselves 'against the I'.[61]

To inhabit a world of machines and to grasp all the possible relationships with this world necessarily forced a radical modification of the subject in the face of time-imposed conditions. Hausmann saw in those primitive cultures a model of equilibrium that modern times would not be willing to tolerate, although it was a model that the dadaist-philosopher always clung to; even in 1957 he still recalled his days in Ibiza as the happiest of his life. His was a call for utopia. This is why he felt such contempt for the operative simplification of the young Catalan architects, who, anxious to find roots *a posteriori* to justify the validity of modern aesthetics, and moreover conscious that architecture was undergoing difficulties that were hampering its development in an increasingly torn Europe, had turned to the Mediterranean as a source of cultural value.

Hausmann made clear his stand against simplification and opportunism in a text published some time later, in 1944: 'It is evident that biological theory will prevail over other theories that wish to establish circular houses as being the ancient form of Western dwellings for the Mediterranean race, and that wish to present the house of a square shape, with a sloping roof and with a porch as being the superior product of the Nordic race.' The point was to know the buildings in depth, not simply to linger on their surface or their cubic forms.

Jean Paul Midant has detected in this attitude certain implications that tie in with the vicissitudes of the difficult 1930s: 'Faced with the rise of totalitarian powers, new man can no longer produce the house-manifesto, nor is it the technocrat who plans the future. It is the present-day man, the architect without an office, the one who, without being tied to his worktable, takes his time to totally rethink the meaning of his project. It is the man who, with irony and ingenuity and without having to prove anything, makes the community aware of the complexity and fragility of his culture.'[62] Following what we have seen so far, Midant's words may now help us enlighten the differences we are interested in, on which bases we should analyze the architectures that were developing at the same time from the architects working in Ibiza.

The cover of the eighteenth issue of *A.C.*, published in the second quarter of 1935, featured an eloquent photograph of a ceramic vase and a wickerwork basket, subjects typically linked to Mediterranean culture. The heading of the editor's note, 'Popular Mediterranean Architecture', corroborated this, and the terms of discussion presented little that was new. However, certain events had taken place that should not be overlooked.

During their trip to Athens for the CIAM meeting held there in the summer of 1933, the Catalan architects were able to see the great resemblance between the architectures of the Greek islands and those of Ibiza, which they knew well. They were also able to observe the impact of these buildings on Le Corbusier and many other architects of their generation who attended the Congress – very few of whom were 'architects from the North' – who considered that this architecture complied with the requirements that characterized what was modern. But in 1933, what was modern was the International Style, or so it had been announced on the other side of the Atlantic, at MoMA in New York by some future friends of Sert. The modern was an architecture that had already achieved worldwide recognition for its formal qualities. And all styles need to find roots that certify their belonging to a culture. All styles need to show that they are anchored within a formal trajectory that is often given the worthless but handy name 'evolution'.

Style, therefore, was the purest end product of a formal evolution that had developed over a long period. When Le Corbusier made reference to the Parthenon in various issues of *L'Esprit Nouveau*, he always did so as if it were the end of a centuries-long voyage, portraying the Acropolis of Athens as its apex. The trip to Athens also had ulterior meanings for Sert. In the GATCPAC archives is a letter from 20 July 1933 that Sert addressed to Le Corbusier before leaving for Marseilles, which includes an enigmatic sentence whose full meaning we will understand later: 'I think it would be very interesting to establish the basis for bringing the French, Italian, Spanish and Algerian groups closer together. Don't you think so?' The idea was to unite the peoples of the Mediterranean to create a common front at a time when modern architecture, after having passed through its programmatic stage, was being accorded little credibility. It was to be a common cause that would grant this architecture a new foundation, with Sert as one of its main ideologists and Le Corbusier as its steady beacon, while doing away with the sterile discussions with 'Slavs and Saxons'.

By 1935, modern architecture was no longer avant garde; style was. Therefore, modern architecture needed to find ancestral roots that would install it in the history books; it needed to become a 'historical vanguard'.

As a result of the voyage on the *Patris* to Athens, the 'Mediterranean party' gained force and cohesion. This was despite the fact that they experienced serious difficulties in reach-

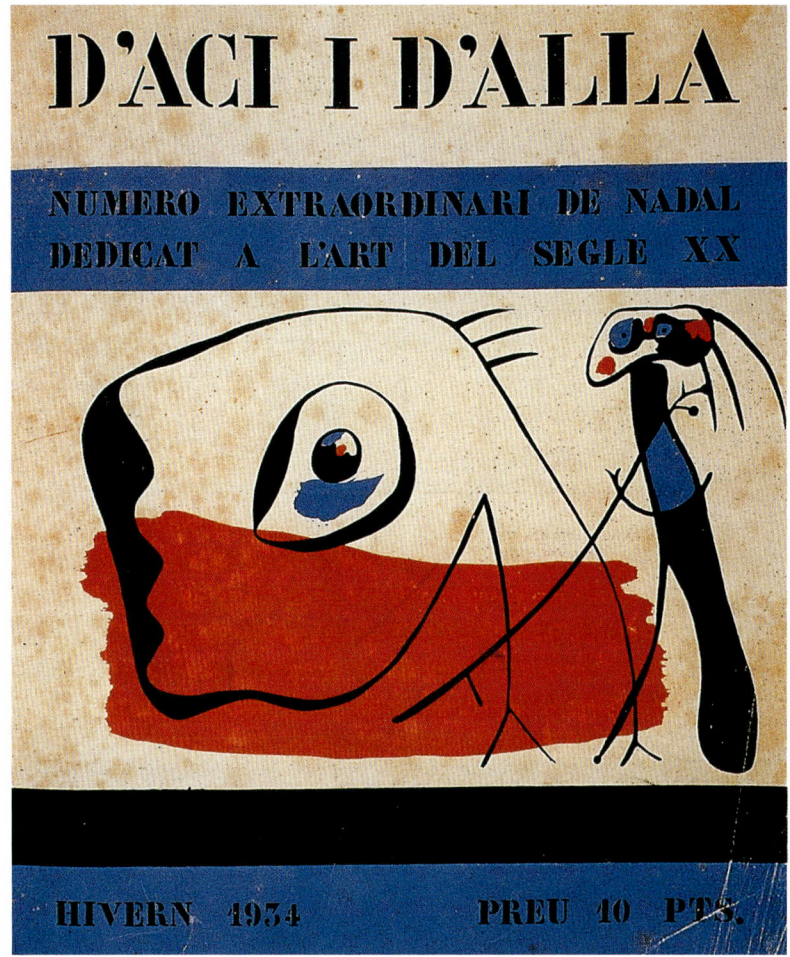

Cover designed by Joan Miró for *D'Ací i D'Allà*, no. 179, 1934.

ing agreement concerning the conclusions of the Congress and their publication. Now, however, due to this reinforcement, the Mediterranean form, which was at the base of some architectures, could aspire to become the foundation stone of all modern architectural forms, the common place from which to head towards new horizons. Some time later, on 20 February 1934, Le Corbusier wrote to Sert: 'The situation takes on very definite contours at an international level: the Latins again take up the ensign of modernity and the Nordics assimilate this without complaining.'

Another important event that should not be overlooked also took place in 1934: Sert worked with Joan Prats on the preparation of issue no. 179 of *D'Ací i D'Allà* magazine, which was dedicated to twentieth-century art. Among its contributors were Christian Zervos, Josep Vicenç Foix, Sebastià Gasch, Carles Soldevila, Luis Fernández, Sindreu, Cassanyes and Jakowsky.

The first existing document relating to this

publication is a letter from Sert to Luis Fernández at 4, Rue Commandant Leandri dated 13 September 1934. For Sert it was a time of intensive work on the preparation of this issue, and of a determined will to establish Mediterranean ideology as a mechanism that would overcome the schematic functionalist approaches of modern architecture. Here we read: 'Everything you propose seems to be a good idea, although I have to make the following observations: a) If you don't have time to prepare the pages summarizing DADA and Marinetti or others of this type, let us prepare them here; we have information at hand to do so b) The "summary on the evolution of art throughout history" has to be a diagram, as we had agreed, that can fit into a page of the format of *D'ací i D'Allà* … c) Ask Jakowsky to let me rewrite the three articles into one … They will have to be abbreviated when written as one because there is not enough space to publish each one of them in its entirety d) Tell Arp that we will not be able to publish Tristan Tzara's text with his pictures because the page has already been set up … Please send all the material as soon as possible because by now we are running short of time and I think it would be very interesting for this issue to come out by Christmas.'[63] These requirements regarding the supervision of the publication show that Sert had taken this job very seriously.

On the 21st of that same month, Sert asked Giedion to send him graphic material, and some of these pictures were included in the magazine.[64] It seems evident that Sert meant to make use of the occasion to broadcast the ideology behind the new architecture to a more varied public than that of *A.C.* On 10 October he asked Fernández to send in any material still missing[65] and on the 23rd he wrote to Theo van Doesburg's wife asking her to send one of 'your husband's paintings'. He received no letter from Alexander Calder until 31 December, when he wrote to tell him that he was sending him material, although it was not published because the information arrived too late, as was also the case with illustrations of Alvar Aalto's work.

The motives for the publication of this issue were set forth by Carles Soldevila, the editor of the magazine: 'We have become aware that no effort has so far been made in Catalonia and in Catalan to offer a brief yet incisive synthesis of the new tendencies that invade, fragmented and disordered, our publications, our affairs and our institutions.' After insisting on the need to offer an orderly vision of modern artistic movements, Soldevila gave Sert credit for having taken on the responsibility of editing the issue, and did not once mention Prats, whose name nevertheless appeared in the credits as co-editor next to the architect's name: 'We have asked Josep Lluis Sert, one of the GATCPAC founders, the man who has most ardently championed this idea within Catalonia, to take charge of editing this special issue with no restrictions or conditions on his work.'

In this issue, painting, new architecture and town planning were all shown in depth. Three works by Le Corbusier were included, as well as two by André Lurçat, one by Gropius, two by Steiger, one by Leender van der Vlugt and Joannes Brinkman, two by Moser and one by Ginsburg and Syrkus. We see a large representation of Sert's friends from the CIAMs, but no Mies, Loos, or Wright. To represent Spain, Sert showed the school complex of Manresa by Pedro Armengou, the single-family dwelling by García Mercadal in Madrid, the Yacht Club by Aizpurua and Labayen in San Sebastian, and the facade and interior of the Roca jewellery shop in Barcelona that he himself had designed in 1933. Naturally, a reference to the New Barcelona (which was yet to become known as the Macià Plan) was also included, and this was done by offering both the image of the diorama made by Torres Torres and an image of the gradual transformation that the Ensanche blocks were to undergo, as outlined in Chapter One.

Sert offered translated excerpts from *Vers une architecture* as well as information on the previous CIAMs before getting to his own article, which bore the title 'Arquitectura sense "estil" i sense "arquitecte"' ('Architecture Without "Style" and Without "Architect"'). This text dealt with Mediterranean architecture, which had steadily been gaining followers since CIAM 4 in Athens. In Sert's text we find the same mechanisms to evaluate popular architecture that had appeared in the first issue of *A.C.*: 'This popular architecture has eliminated

Popular architecture of Cordoba.

all ornamental elements and owes all of its interest to the combination of simple and clean shapes, to a magnificent and very free composition, which is tremendously varied, and to a correct human scale that is absolutely free from harmful ostentation and false concepts propitiated by the architects' schools and academies.'

Sert insisted on the presence of standard elements, as he had done with the Sant Pol houses, to showcase strictly Mediterranean values that appeared in the pictures accompanying the text, all of which were from Ibiza with the exception of one depicting white architecture from a Greek island: 'In Mediterranean countries, this architecture shows some traits that have reached our times, with all of their purity; geometric shapes, pure prisms, creations of human spirit starkly contrasted against a natural and irregular background.'

This architecture, therefore, was the legacy of a sea located in the south of Europe that shared, throughout the coasts bathed by its wa-

ters, the same type of thousand-year old constructions that unified these areas and established bonds between them, and which moreover Sert did not hesitate to define as modern: 'These architectures executed without recipes or academicist formulas, are perfectly modern; they are found scattered from one end of the Mediterranean region to the other, from the islands of the Ionic Sea to the Balearic islands, from Mikonos and Skios to Menorca and Ibiza.'

At this point Sert ventured a hypothesis that must have sounded new and unfamiliar: 'The architecture of today, freeing itself from old scholastic prejudices, and seeking the way to rediscover the types of constructions that can first of all satisfy human needs … again finds the right path and the consistent elements that are maintained throughout time in that architecture without style and without architecture.' In other words, new architecture was derived from popular architecture, a fact that had not yet appeared in any historiographic record. Instead of appealing to the machine or to objectivity, or to the social and functional criteria of the *existenzminimum*, or even to the purist aestheticism of volumes under light, we are now told that it is necessary to rediscover popular Mediterranean architecture in order to establish correct genealogies.

Apparently the dart was aimed at German architecture: 'Architects and theorists, especially Germans, took functionalist attempts to absurd extremes.' This was almost the last sentence and was not integrated within the rest of the text. If we have any doubts, we will have to wait for a new formulation of this idea before we can clear them up.

The issues that Sert had pointed out were quickly echoed by the writers of the eighteenth issue of *A.C.*, who in the opening lines of the editorial wrote: 'For these reasons, popular Mediterranean architecture possesses consistent traits that are repeated throughout all Mediterranean countries. Egypt, the Greek archipelago, Italy, the coast of North Africa, the southern and eastern coasts of Spain, Mallorca, Ibiza, etc., all countries springing from the same civilization, show in their popular constructions similar types, founded on strictly rational bases.' Thus, the experience of Ibiza had widened their horizons. Not only the architecture found on a small island, but indeed all architecture built on the shores of this sea in many lands could now be understood to spring from a clear-cut rationality, an attribute that would henceforth be interpreted as one of its trademarks.

After this internationalist introduction, the comments that followed were predictable and sometimes repetitious: 'without ornamentation', 'functional', 'natural', 'on a human scale', 'without composition', etc. This architecture was beginning to run the risk of having its forms reduced to a sterile picturesque quality due to their amoral use by certain followers of the academic-popular tradition. Their zeal in proving that they were the only valid interpreters of the popular is clearly evidenced by this attitude and by their obsession with proclaiming these architectures as the only predecessors of the modern. Thus, through well-chosen images in which everything flowed without apparent discontinuity between the different places represented, *A.C.* readers could observe how the repertoire had grown, that there were houses in Cordoba that had a corridor that acted as an accessway, others in Cadiz with a flat facade, and still more in Tarifa organized around the patio.

The title of the anonymously authored feature article immediately revealed the core of its contents: 'Raíces mediterráneas de la arquitectura moderna' ('The Mediterranean Roots of Modern Architecture') here again insisting on the internationalism of these architectures and in the oft-repeated purity of their forms and volumes. Now, however, the emphasis on the differences between Mediterranean and Northern cultures – which when enunciated in *D'Ací i D'Allà* had seemed to bear no relation to the rest of the text – was a new factor that added interest to the initial approach. The article began without hesitation: 'It is interesting to confirm that the farther away one is from the Latin sea, the more this architecture loses those "consistent" traits that we have mentioned before. The primary shapes, if they exist, are masked by a profuse decoration. Sculpture-like ornamentation sometimes covers the whole building, as can be seen in the cathedrals of Northern Europe, in Oriental and Indian temples in general, in Portuguese Baroque constructions in the westernmost part of Europe, and in primitive temples in Central America.'

Following these declarations it becomes easier to understand the origin of Le Corbusier's words in 1928 when he announced his preference for Catalan Gothic architecture over the French version. In case any doubts remained, *A.C.* seems to have taken up the baton of the Swiss architect's discourse by echoing, seven years later: 'Santa María del Mar and the Monastery of Pedralbes in Barcelona, are, among many others, good examples of this perfectly Mediterranean Gothic, adapted to the Latin sea.' Thus, it was not only that the further away from the Mediterranean the architecture the more overly decorated it became, but also that the architecture most directly under the beneficial influence of the sea, even forms that had traditionally exhibited excessive ornamentation, became subdued, and as if by magic, lost their redundant ornamentation, thereby achieving an improved formal result.

The praise continued to flow: 'The people who built their dwellings with this magnificent architecture were not familiar with the theories of Vitruvius or Vingnola [sic] … The elements that comprise these constructions … Are mass produced.' We are not sure what Vignola's theories might have been, but what is clear is that this text attempted to leave aside the classical connotations of these buildings, whereas if we were to follow Hausmann, it would be easy to speak of a Phoenician-Greek tradition. Moreover, it seems somewhat excessive to confuse the handcrafted means of production used in these buildings with the ideology of standardization and Taylorism employed in the construction of modern habitats that had so seduced modern architects.

According to the GATCPAC members, this modern habitat avoided unnecessary representative rituals and was instead based on objective principles, such as the best orientation, the best site, etc. Thus it was possible to achieve a native architecture 'based on existing elements, an architecture for a specific climate, light and landscape'.

The point with the greatest ideological weight was left for the end of the text: 'If after having examined various examples of popular

Mediterranean constructions, we compare them with the best creations of modern architecture, we will not be able to overlook common traits, not in details, but in those constant characteristics or "vital signs" that imbue architectural work with their spirit. Then why is it that modern architecture has been called Germanic? This spirit, these common characteristics that we have dealt with, do not pertain to Germanic constructions ... These peoples used different materials from those employed by Latin peoples, materials imposed by a different climate and a different landscape ... Modern architecture, technically speaking, is in great measure a discovery of the Nordic countries, but spiritually it is Mediterranean architecture without style that has influenced this new architecture. Modern architecture is a turning back to pure, traditional forms of the Mediterranean. It is another victory of the Latin sea!'

This passage is worth quoting at such length because its contents are extremely relevant and no explanatory comments are necessary. It also sheds light on the meaning of Sert's enigmatic sentence cited above. Now we understand that he was advocating that modern architecture should be reappropriated by the group of people who had produced it, namely those who had always moved in Le Corbusier's orbit.

All of this was in keeping with the historical context within which these architects were living: the situation in Germany and Russia did not encourage great expectations for modern rationalists, whereas in Italy and Spain things were going better, and it also seemed they would also be able to count on Greece and possibly on Algeria. Even more pertinently, the article was accompanied by a great number of pictures of popular Ibizan architecture, which thus gained status as a formal reference for what was Mediterranean. On the previous page the staff of *A.C.* had written a long manifesto defending the island's architecture from the impending destruction that menaced it, asking the National Tourist Board to take a stand on the issue.

By 1935 the identification between Mediterranean and Ibizan architecture was an undeniable fact for the GATCPAC members. They had suddenly become the owners of a

Cover of *A.C.*, no. 21.

Erwin Broner.

OCUMENTOS DE ACTIVIDAD CONTEMPORANEA

A.C. 21

BLICACIÓN DEL G. A. T. E. P. A. C. · AÑO VI · PTAS. 3,25

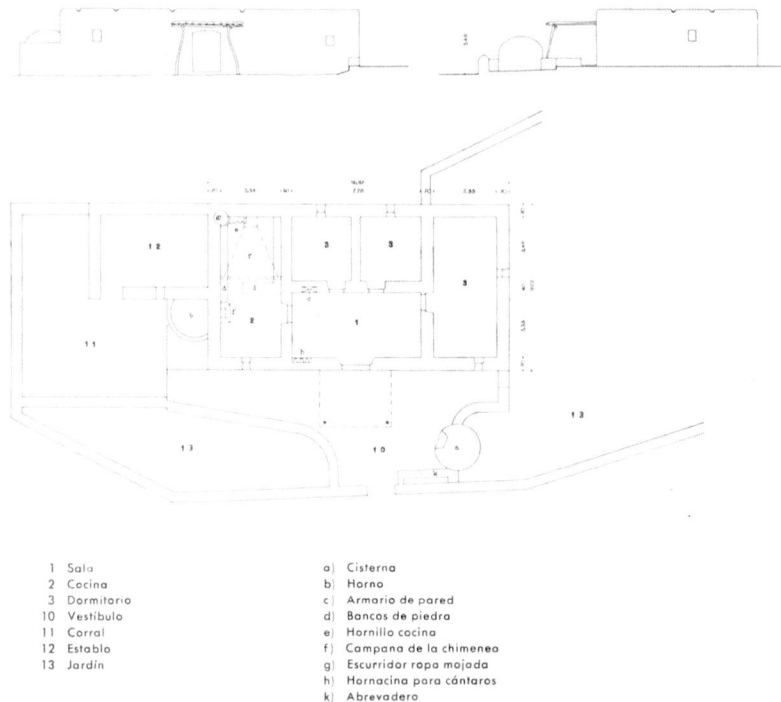

1 Sala
2 Cocina
3 Dormitorio
10 Vestíbulo
11 Corral
12 Establo
13 Jardín

a) Cisterna
b) Horno
c) Armario de pared
d) Bancos de piedra
e) Hornillo cocina
f) Campana de la chimenea
g) Escurridor ropa mojada
h) Hornacina para cántaros
k) Abrevadero

Erwin Broner, plan of an Ibiza's 'country house'.

tradition that had interested the best minds in Europe, and on which, by a strange manoeuvre, modern architecture had come to be built. This was an important feat, and the twenty-first issue of *A.C.*, published in the first quarter of 1936, was again almost wholly dedicated to these buildings, moreover including articles by Hausmann and Erwin Broner[66] who was still signing himself Heilbronner, a surname he would later reject for obvious reasons.

Broner, architect and painter, was the oldest of three siblings in a family of Jewish bankers from Munich, and had graduated as an architect in Stuttgart. He left Germany in March 1933 shortly after the fire in the Reichstag led to mass detentions of left-wing supporters and Broner found out that the police had visited his house. In October 1933, when he was thirty-five years old, Broner arrived in Barcelona. After a trip to Mallorca he got to know Ibiza and settled there in the summer of 1934. He would become one of the many people who found a safe, inexpensive and hospitable refuge on the island at a time when things were not going well in Europe. He preferred to settle in the city instead of going to the countryside like most of his companions, and many years later, in 1960, he built his own house at the foot of Dalt Vila.

It is to Broner that we owe the first scale drawings, plans and sections of Ibizan houses, and through these we can observe the way in which they were organized, which Benjamin and Hausmann had already described.

In contrast to Hausmann's opinions, which we have already examined, Broner attempted to reconcile the views of the dadaist with those held by the *A.C.* staff. This led the German artist and architect to write: 'The typical Ibizan house, which sometimes seems to show certain complications, is in fact a logical consequence of the country-folk's needs and possibilities from all points of view: climate, work, means of building, economic means, etc. In conclusion, it is a perfect and essentially functional dwelling in harmony with the economic situation of our days, which have not greatly varied on this island.'[67]

Thus, after exhibiting a thorough knowledge of the subject by presenting the elevation of seven 'country houses', Broner could affirm that the Ibizan house was solidly rooted in the island's traditions, had been built based on the

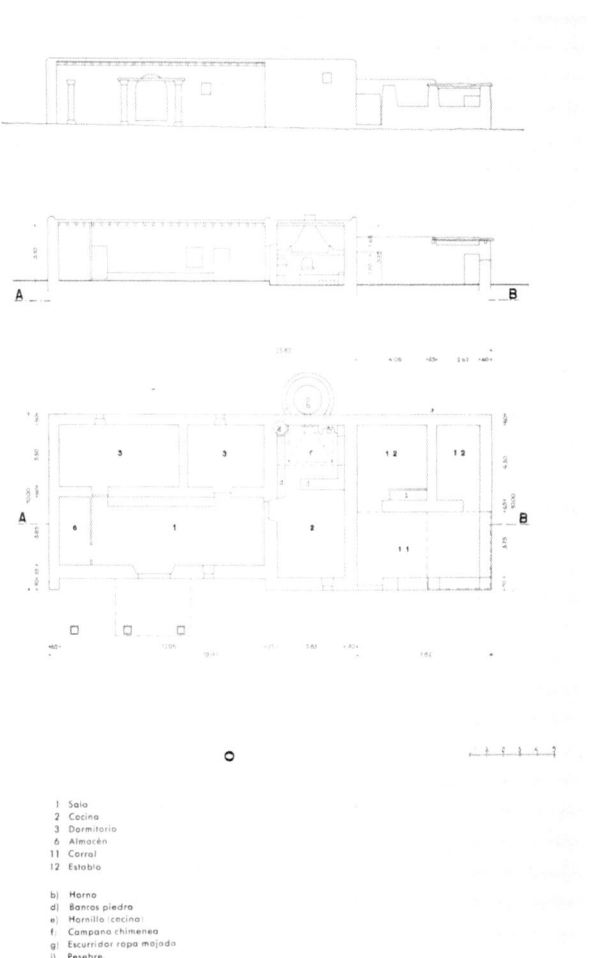

Erwin Broner, plan of an Ibiza's 'country house'.

1 Sala
2 Cocina
3 Dormitorio
6 Almacén
11 Corral
12 Establo

b) Horno
d) Bancos piedra
e) Hornillo cocina
f) Campana chimenea
g) Escurridor ropa mojada
i) Pesebre.

people's living conditions, and could be interpreted as a timeless product due to the special conditions of its development and those of the surroundings in which it was built. Anthropological considerations and pragmatic manifestos are intertwined in Broner's discourse: 'These dwellings of the Ibizan country people come as a surprise to the modern architect, who is forced to solve complicated problems of a technical, social and functional nature, and is therefore very enthusiastic about the simplicity and austerity of these constructions out in the country.'

For Broner (and we should keep in mind that he was German), the idea was not to confront cultures so as to give clout to certain intellectual projects. Nor was it a matter of searching for models that were immediately efficient: instead, the Ibizan house was seen through the eyes of someone fascinated by the strong anthropological component of this tradition, which was represented through architectures that 'are simply adapted to their object', and who sought to get to know these architectures in depth by drawing their plans, elevations and sections.

All of these reflections, regardless of their tendency, were to leave a deep imprint on those who would later conceive and build architectures for the island.

[49] Josep Pijoan, *De les Terres Velles*, in *Almanach dels Noucentistes*, 1911, reprinted in Barcelona, 1980, by Franscesc Fontbona, . We should not overlook a text by the architect Fernando García Mercadal: 'Arquitectura mediterránea', in *Arquitectura*, Madrid, 1927.

[50] Antonio Colinas, *Rafael Alberti en Ibiza*, Tusquets, Barcelona, 1995, p. 35.

[51] *Diario de Ibiza*, 2 January 1930.

[52] Ibid., 19 March 1930.

[53] Ibid., 1 April 1930.

[54] Walter Benjamin, *Correspondance, 1929–1940*, Aubier Montaigne, Paris, 1979, vol. II, p. 64.

[55] Ibid., p. 67.

[56] Ibid., p. 82.

[57] See: *Raoul Hausmann, arquitecto*, Ibiza, 1991. The texts on popular Ibizan architecture by this author are include: 'L'architecture de l'ile d'Ibiza', *Oeuvres*, no. 9, Lausanne, September 1934; 'Ibiza et la maison méditerranée', *L'Architecture d'Aujourd'hui*, no. 1, Paris, 1935, p. 33; 'Elementos de la arquitectura rural de la isla de Ibiza', *A.C.*, no. 21, Barcelona, 1936, pp. 11–14; 'Arquitectura sense arquitecte', *D'Ací i D'Allà*, 1936; 'Nouvelles recherches ethno-anthropologiques sur les Pityuses', *Revue Anthropologique*, Paris, 1938; and 'Recherche sur l'origine de la maison rurale à Eivissa', *Revista de tradiciones populares*, Madrid, 1944.

[58] Ibid., p. 15. The text reproduced is a fragment from *Hyle. Ein Traumsein in Spanien*, a novel by Hausmann set in Ibiza. There is a Spanish translation: *Hyle: Ser-sueño en España*, Trea, Gijón, 1997.

[59] Hausmann, *Elementos de la arquitectura rural de la isla de Ibiza*, op. cit.

[60] Hausmann, *Die Neue Kunst*, 1921, quoted in Yves Michaud's text in *Raoul Hausmann arquitecto*, op. cit., p. 22.

[61] This is the title that Giedion gave to one of his first texts: 'Gegen das Ich', published in *Das Junge Deutschland*, Berlin, 1918. There is a Spanish version in Josep M. Rovira (ed.), 'Sigfried Giedion. Textos escogidos', in *Colección Arquitecturas*, no. 33, Murcia, 1997, pp. 47–50.

[62] Jean-Paul Midant, 'Raoul Hausmann, ¿arquitecto?', in *Raoul Hausmann arquitecto*, op. cit., p. 36.

[63] COAC Archives, C–10/65. In reality, this letter was written in order to request specific items and it proves that Sert was already working on that issue. It is therefore not the first letter in which we find references to the matter at hand, there being a former one from 4 September, which he had written to Le Corbusier: 'At present there is another enterprise: the Catalan magazine *D'Ací i D'Allà* has asked us to supervise the publication of its next issue, which will be entirely dedicated to modern art.' C–10/65. In the same file of the GATCPAC Archives we can follow the stages of this issue's publication. Sert was a member of the board of directors of ADLAN (Amics de l'Art Nou, or Friends of New Art). C–10/68.
In 1934, in a lecture that Sert gave to the Alumni's Association of the School of Architecture of Barcelona, we find another remark that demonstrates this dedication to Mediterranean themes: 'We have to defend an architecture of climate and a Mediterranean setting made for intense sunlight, for a pristine clear atmosphere, and for a benevolent landscape. Architecturally speaking, we cannot respect other boundaries than the natural, geographic, eternal ones. If we analyze the works created in Mediterranean lands, creations of the spirit that has characterized different time periods, we will observe that they are linked by characteristics that are repeated thousands of years later and which are found throughout all the coastlines of this sea. These characteristics form the backbone of good Mediterranean architecture. This must not be a concern for us, since a work well conceived and executed in our country will undoubtedly have these qualities … The path to be taken at present should not be that of being or imitating the architectures of other epochs or historical styles, nor the decoration of ships, nor badly understood functionalism.'

[64] In this letter from Sert to Giedion we read: 'I would need for you to send me as soon as possible some pictures (three or four) chosen by you from amongst the most characteristic works of the mechanist movement (for example the Crystal Palace, the Eiffel Tower, etc.) … They are to appear in a special issue of the Catalan magazine *D'Ací i D'Allà* entirely dedicated to Modern Art, of lavish format, of which I have been asked to take charge.'

[65] Letter to Luis Fernández of 10 October 1934, COAC Archives, C–10/65. 'What I need to get from you before anything else are the Picassos, Braques, what is left of Gris, Giacometti, etc., in other words, the ones having the greatest representation. We can only dedicate one page to Constructivism, Futurism and Dadaism, so their manifestos have to be very briefly summarized … I need to have the article on Zervos as soon as possible.'

[66] On Broner, see: *Erwin Broner. Ciudadano, arquitecto, pintor*, Colegio de Arquitectos de Baleares, November 1980.

[67] Erwin Heilbronner, 'Ibiza: las viviendas rurales', *A.C.*, no. 21, 1936, p. 15.

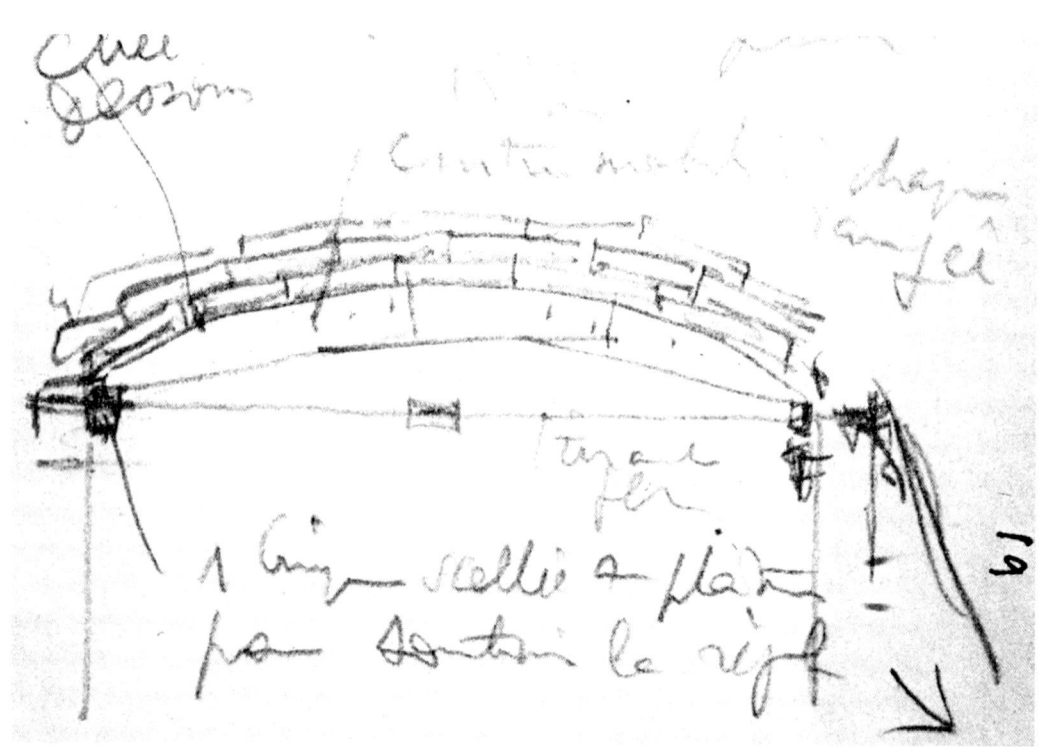

Interpretations

The first evidence of the interest shown by the rationalist Catalan architects in Ibiza can be dated back to 1932. At this time, in the eighth issue of *A.C.*, appeared a proposal signed by Sert entitled Two Minimal Housing Typologies for the Beach, which was also one of the four projects of this type for the CRV (Leisure City). The need for rational solutions to solve the problem of workers' housing in European cities was an issue that required sophisticated urban and constructional strategies. All of this, when applied to Ibiza, was transformed into a house for the weekends in which the casual outdoor and holiday lifestyle required a simple programme that encompassed easy cleaning, a marked contact with the exterior and a multipurpose plan.

As we know, 1932 was still too early to start proclaiming manifestos of a Mediterranean-oriented ideology, and for this reason the plans that Sert came up with are closer to those we saw in the publication that came out of CIAM 2 (held in Frankfurt) than to other proposals, characterized by a generalized tendency to assign to the living-dining room a distributive function that would help reduce the surface to be built and would lower housing costs.[68] To these housing typologies a porch was added that brought all the rooms together, improved the climatic conditions inside the dwelling, and ensured the possibility of being outdoors, a necessary function to be taken into account for vacation periods.

However, it is possible to see a timid approach to the building systems used in Ibiza and a direct reference to popular architecture, leading us to conclude that the first observations that sprang from Rodríguez Arias' trip (if oral accounts are correct, and these are corroborated by the fact that Sert always stated that it was his friend who had 'discovered' the island) must have begun to bear fruit: 'The walls facing east, north and west can be built using materials from the region,

Constructional details of the Catalan brick vault; sketch by Sert (FLC, Carnet E 21).

bricks or stone; these dwellings, inspired by popular houses that are seen throughout Ibiza, were conceived for the Balearic islands, where they use regional limestone, which is easy to cut, for building walls.'

One hardly knows what conclusions to draw from this paragraph. It is strange that they tried to identify a constructional system as being common to the Balearic islands when the only reference was to Ibiza, nor do they specify the characteristics of Ibizan architecture upon which Sert remarked. Moreover, his proposal encompassed the whole dwelling in one volume, whereas we know that popular dwellings were made over time, so that in the final result it was always possible to trace the overlappings of the different bodies of the project as it had evolved.

An excess of glass surfaces foreshadowed air-conditioning problems in the summer, but it also indicated a different objective for the house, turning the contemplation of the landscape into one of its programmatic points. Reinforced concrete was to be used, and a thin almost invisible pillar of metal was to guarantee the continuity of the porch and its formal unity. On the other

Two minimal housing typologies for the beach, in *A.C.*, no. 8, 1932.

hand, Sert did not make use of the traditional system of enclosure walling and air chamber that must have functioned well in the Mediterranean climate, instead opting for walls of excessive thickness yet dubious insulating capacity. Sert seems to have preferred mixing different techniques of construction to achieve a result that would allow him to create a great void in which a subtle column would share space with an unnecessarily curved wall, two formal elements that could be identified with similar ones found in many of Le Corbusier's proposals during this period. The perspective of the project leaves no room for doubt as to its avant-garde ambitions: a woman in a bathing suit with a towel in her hand is going up some stairs, which are not included either in the plans, the section or the axonometric projection illustrating the building. She has obviously been out for a swim, immediately making patent the role of the house as a holiday home. On the porch an athletic man dressed in summer wear awaits her, hand in his pocket, as he looks out at the landscape; a second woman dozes in the chaise-longue designed by Le Corbusier and Charlotte Perriand. The inhabitants of the house are thus identified with the sophisticated world of avant-garde furniture and habits. Hausmann himself travelled to the island in the company of two women, Edwig and Dora. The house is for the denizens of that world, and therefore what is shown to the outside world must belong to that sphere: iron, glass and designer furniture. There was nothing or barely anything of Ibiza in the first period of contact between the Catalan avant garde and the island's architecture.

In the nineteenth issue of *A.C.* (the issue published immediately after the one dedicated to popular Mediterranean architecture examined earlier), we find two items of interest. One is the article on Rodríguez Arias' house in the Ibizan town of San Antonio, and the other is the publication of the houses that Sert and Torres had built in the Garraf area.

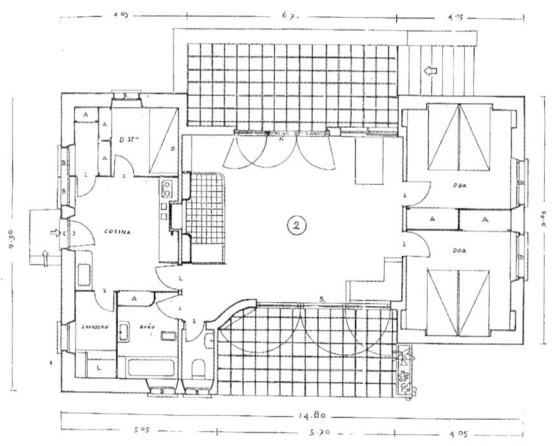

Rodríguez Arias, house in San Antonio, Ibiza, views of the exterior, plan, view of the interior, in *A.C.*, no. 19.

The problem with the specific site chosen in Rodríguez Arias' single-family dwelling is revealed in the contradiction between the best view and its optimum orientation for light. The architect solved this by placing the living room-dining room in the centre of the house, spanning a double view, facing two terraces that ensured sunlight and view respectively, something that had never been taken into account by those who had built the island's farm houses because they had been concerned with other matters: once again, we are dealing with a holiday home.

Rodriguez Arias was apparently pleased with his solution, and the biggest picture published was that showing the interior of this living-dining room, which was furnished with typical chairs whose wooden structures were made of cypress and whose backs and seats were made of esparto cordage, the same chairs that Hausmann had described so poetically and that had also captivated Benjamin. However, the rest of Rodriguez Arias' house lacked definition, perhaps a side effect of his way of working as an architect, not considering plans to be the central issue of his approach.[69] It is clear that this was not minimal housing, since there is a servants' dormitory, and the total surface area of the house is generous; despite this, the origin of the dwelling's distribution can probably be traced once again to the CIAM 2 publication on minimal housing. There are other obvious incoherences: the disastrous location of the lavatories, the fact that the living room is essentially a hall in which it is impossible to carry out any activity because all of its space is given over to circulation; the lack of comfort around the fireplace, the excessive space allotted to the washing room, etc.

If we read the report offered by the architect we are in for even greater surprises, for he dedicated almost all of his text to issues of little relevance, such as a description of how a water tank gathers rainwater or the explanation of the solution adopted for the roof. The facades, however, show a preponderance of solids over voids, with most of the windows having small dimensions to offer protection against the heat, and one also sees the usual rounded edges typical of popular architecture.

Whereas Sert tended towards modernity in his front façade and in the clothing and the furniture of those who were to inhabit the dwelling, Rodríguez preferred to emphasize the repetition of popular shapes. Now, both Hausmann's demand for an anthropologist's respect for tradition and his recommendations to carry out a thorough analysis are revealed in their full dimension: the superiority of a genuine ancestral culture leaves the modern without an alternative answer when it tries to imitate it, and authentic traditional culture makes patent how clearly these attempts fail to come even close to the elements that it had meant to use.

In this same issue of *A.C.* we find another interpretation of Mediterranean values, this time by Sert and Torres, and on this occasion away from Ibiza although reminiscent of its traditions. It is interesting to analyze this proposal because it would be reflected in some later architectures. The project in question was some weekend houses in El Garraf, built on a terrain that was owned by Sert's mother's family.[70] It is important to start the analysis by first looking at the report written by the authors, to which they attached photographs of the final results.

Sert and Torres, plans of weekend houses in El Garraf, Garraf coast, Barcelona, 1935.

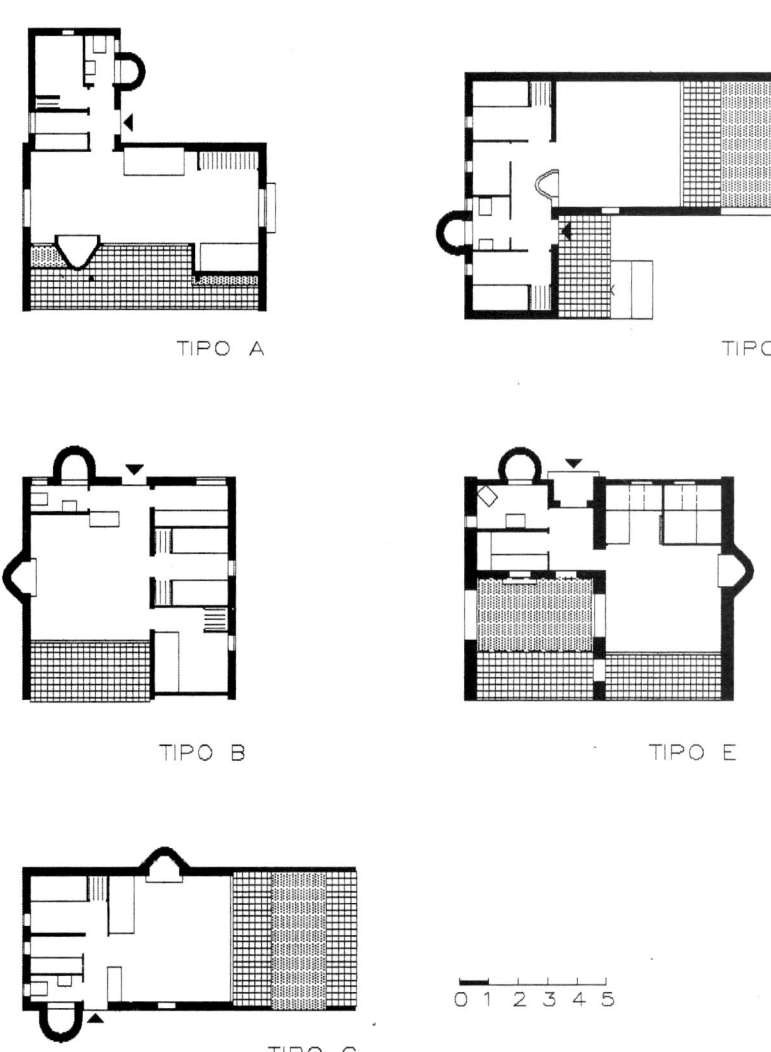

TIPO A

TIPO

TIPO B

TIPO E

TIPO C

0 1 2 3 4 5

Here we find some statements that allow us to understand certain issues that lie behind the project. 'The modern organization of life and the wish to get away from the city … justify the great vulgarity of these dwellings, which would have been incomprehensible and useless fifty years ago.' These were small and therefore relatively inexpensive houses that allowed contact with nature and distance from the city and its noise and stress. The proposal is from 1935, when GATCPAC already had a well-developed CRV project, which they had located at the foot of the Garraf mountain on the beaches of Castelldefels, Viladecans and Gavà, and which was to cater for the massive exodus from the city of the Barcelonian working class. At around this time the architects' material analysis of the industrial and capitalist city of Barcelona had led them to formulate a fairly catastrophic general picture, and the result of their reflections, in association with Le Corbusier, had been to come up with the Macià Plan. Thus we see that in all the cases in which they had to come up with an architectural solution, the reality that they were facing was considered a key element in contextualizing

Houses in El Garraf, in *A.C.*, no. 19.

their work. Some characteristics of modern times also appeared as determining factors in their assessment of the problems they had to face.

It is therefore not surprising that we read further on in the pages of *A.C.*: 'Few people today have the means to build a house in which they can spend their summer holidays for the rest of their lives … Those who can afford it prefer, following the dynamic impulses of our generation, not to be tied down to the same place each summer, instead trying out a new place every year, something that has been greatly facilitated by cars and other quick means of transportation …

A "weekend" house must not be more expensive than a normal car, which means they can be sold and rented easily … Just as the concept of the car has changed greatly in the last years, so that small, low-consumption models are now in vogue … So the concept of a summer residence can evolve too.'

Thus a weekend house was for modern citizens, who would use it sporadically and would not return to the same place every year. It was to be as cheap as a car, and was intimately linked to automobile evolution, which offered parameters for its conceptualization but not for its construction, as is evidenced by the fact that Sert and Torres opted for a traditional system of walls and roofs, insisting on the use of the traditional Cata-

Houses in El Garraf, in *A.C.*, no. 19.

lan barrel vault in certain residential typologies.

The buildings basically responded to three different typologies, not so much regarding their programmes, which were similar, but with respect to their relationship with the exterior, since essentially the objective was a weekend house located in a Mediterranean setting.

The Type-A dwelling had an L-shaped plan in which there was a separation between an area of rigid functions – where we find the kitchen, bathroom and a single bedroom – and a more flexible and informal area, where we find the living room, which could be used for different pur-

poses, given that weekend activities are unpredictable. It therefore had two areas of contact with the exterior: that found between the two arms of the L and that of the front terrace, similar to the one we saw in Sert's house for Ibiza.

Type B followed a similar programme, this time inscribed within a 7×7 metre square, and offering a less flexible solution that was somewhat lacking in terms of circulation, with a kitchen and bathroom whose location was probably not the most fitting. In this case, the geometry was chosen before the project was developed as part of a process of experimenting with different ways of solving plans.

Type C seems to have been the one most concerned with investigating the relationship

between living room and exterior; it proposed a specially designed terrace open to the landscape, in which the changes in the materials used for the pavement and the treatment given to light coming in from above or from the sides provided varying gradations of luminosity on its surface.

We cannot be certain, but it seems likely that the decision to make the volumes of the shower and chimney jut out of the facade originated in popular Ibizan architecture, in which the bread oven and the water tank were cylindrical volumes added on to the main body of the building.

Auguste Perret, warehouses in Casablanca, 1909 (?).

It is worth pointing out some other interesting aspects of these buildings: for example, the architects opted to cover type C with a Catalan brick vault, something that Sert himself had essayed shortly before in the project of a kindergarten for Viladecans. Le Corbusier had already proposed this type of low vault in a project for the Atelier Perret in 1919 and in the Monol houses, and he would come back to it at different points of his professional career.[71] Nevertheless, the vaults of the French architects were made of concrete, so that although their silhouette was rooted in the Mediterranean culture, the technique used to build them was different. Since it was such a typical product of Mediterranean culture, an element that is to be found in many countries in this area, Sert and Torres proposed to revive it, and thus we read in the report: 'Roof in the form of a braced vault, which is made up of three layers, two of thin bricks and one of hollow bricks.'

In a drawing by Sert from 1951 (Carnet E21), which is found in the Fondation Le Corbusier, the Catalan architect indicated to his Swiss colleague the construction details of the Catalan brick vault, providing him with the name of an exiled compatriot, Domènech Escorsa, who could clear up any further doubts that he might have. Le Corbusier would use in various projects this element of Mediterranean tradition, rediscovered by rationalist Catalans and applied to these small weekend houses.

This takes us too far into the future, but it does indicate the longevity of Mediterranean themes in the elaboration of many buildings carried out by Sert after World War II. For the moment we are more interested in examining the first manifestations of this Mediterranean tradition, recovered at a time when the conquests of the modern movement were endangered and many issues were being questioned again, and at a point when the experiences of the Catalan rationalist architects were providing a decisive impulse to this cultural debate about modern architecture.

The stone socle of the Garraf houses helped influence many of the schemes that characterized the vanguard: an archaic material, handcrafted by artisans, created a base for the buildings so that they could 'naturally' spring upwards from the ground. They left aside that which years before had interested Gropius and Le Corbusier: namely the idea that architecture, like industry, should be assembled. The times of Taylorist optimism and of confidence in machines were not in tune with the reality of 1935.

The furniture shown in the pictures of these houses would lead us to a similar discourse: wood and wickerwork are mixed with ceramic

Constructional details of the Catalan brick vault, sketch by Sert (FLC, Carnet E 21).

amphoras and straw baskets, emphasizing the ubiquitous Mediterranean presence. The furniture was no longer of chrome-plated iron tubing and leather, as if for display in a publication, but instead sought a natural appearance in keeping with its use and tradition. However, in these interiors other things were exhibited, such as a Léger painting or a small black sculpture, which, as Juanjo Lahuerta has pointed out, displace themselves without moving,[72] thus abolishing time and bringing together worlds that are very far apart.

In Sert's houses, probably inhabited by himself, Torres and another common friend, elements from the avant-garde world and elements from the Mediterranean tradition shared the same space, and did so in interiors designed for and by its authors. A dangerous autism was beginning to make itself felt, verifying the hypothesis that the Mediterraneanist discourse was only an ideology, something without contact with reality and only practised and felt by those who had invented it. They looked for a place from which to contemplate the possible Leisure City without ever having to rub shoulders with the exploited masses for whom it was conceived; the social aristocracy of Ortega, despite the immense generosity shown by Sert and Torres, could not do otherwise.

Although the pure volumes of these buildings do in fact bring to mind those connections between modernity and tradition that we have previously analyzed, the way in which the authors chose to present their houses leaves little doubt as to the meaning of their gesture. This makes us wary of those who claimed to have invented categories such as 'critical regionalism' (we will address this issue in the next chapter) to dazzle architecture professionals and naive critics at the end of the twentieth century.

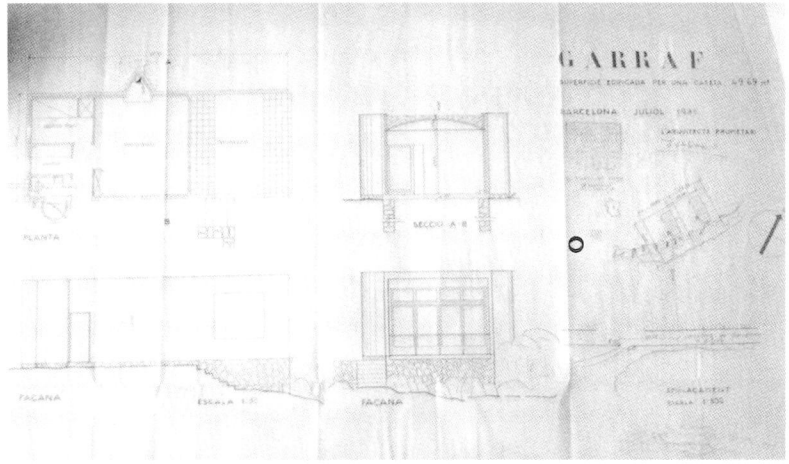

Houses in El Garraf, project specifications.

In a dossier of construction work from 1935 are the plans for two more type-C projects. The Architects' Association application form, dated 9 July of the same year, specifies that the project was for Sert himself, probably to avoid administrative complications. He requested a licence on 11 July and it was granted on the 22nd. We do not know whether the imminent war impeded their being built, or whether they were destroyed in the bombardment mentioned by Genara López in a letter to her son.[73]

Through Sert's correspondence and some drawn references, we gather that Sert had another project for the island of Ibiza. In a letter of 28 April 1933, addressed to Isaac Saporta, residing in Athens, we read: 'I am glad to have news from you and am very interested in the material you've sent me. It will be published in *A.C.* as soon as there is room for it and don't worry, we will return the pictures you have sent us to their respective owners, including yourself. Your project is interesting and it has pleased me to see that you have come up with exactly the same distribution of bedrooms and galleries in a body set apart from common services that I had also conceived for a project for a hotel in Ibiza.'[74]

Sert and Torres, Hotel in Ibiza, 1933.

We can see a parallelepiped that corresponds to the forty rooms announced to Saporta, whose solution is based on a grid that probably comes from a porticoed structure. This volume is joined to a body of other characteristics: it is formed by two planes of different height that define what appear to be different uses. There is a terrace with windows that frame the landscape, a double-height space, terraces of generous dimensions, and finally a great horizontal plane that affords a privileged view over the sea.

Thus, in Sert's work one can observe both the functions grouped in series as well as the different ways of conceiving the treatment of parts, revealing a way of thinking about architecture that is far removed from the experience of the Garraf houses and closer to his first Ibizan project. What is clear is that by 1933 this current of thought was the inheritance of all those who were carrying on a dialogue that depended to a lesser degree on traditional legacy and that did not mean to give up what corresponded to them from modern culture. We have been constrained to move between these two extremes, extremes that Sert himself was caught between, to avoid offering reductionist interpretations of the relationships between modernity and tradition that would continue to pursue our architect during the first years of his residence in the United States.

In the sixth volume of his *Gesammelte Schriften*, Benjamin, friend of the Mediterranean and guest of Ibiza, wrote: 'To historically articulate the past does not mean to know it "as it has truly been". It means to recall a remembrance just the way it shone out in a moment of peril.' In 1937 this peril was clear enough: it was possible that the Republicans would lose the war.[75] And there was another threatening circumstance looming over Sert: it would be difficult for him to return to his native city, no matter how the war turned out. These were two factors that would influence the form of the Pavilion of the Spanish Republic for the Paris World's Fair of 1937.[76]

The war explains why the message that the Pavilion was intended to transmit was understood as a manifesto: 'The Pavilion tries to show the life of Spanish peoples, who in these dramatic hours when their new existence is being decided, reveal more clearly than ever their unique personality. We aspire to make known the evolution of the Spanish nation from the moment that the Republic was proclaimed.'[77] To project and build a pavilion in times of war principally meant erecting an architecture that accepted the role of support for this kind of message, or to erect a speaking architecture that would communicate the message through its strict disciplinary mechanisms.

To accomplish this feat it was important that the right architect should be chosen to carry out this task. The respective roles of Luis Lacasa[78] and Sert in the authorship of the project has been discussed and clarified in other writings from which we will choose some excerpts, and we will also make use of some forgotten details to complete the picture of their contributions. Problems first arise because certain facts are stated in some sources in such a jumbled way as to lead to misinterpretation. One such case is a text by Luis Araquistain, a writer and Socialist activist who had been designated Spanish Ambassador in Paris by Largo Caballero in September 1936. Araquistain was pressing the Republic to specify Spain's exact participation in the Fair: 'It would be most convenient to begin preparing Spanish participation at the Exhibition as soon as possible, and if it does not seem feasible to do so, to communicate this decision immediately to the French Commissary … It would seem a good idea to participate in the Fair and to take the necessary steps to do so, thus providing a feeling of stability … It would be advisable to create an inexpensive though dignified pavilion and to exhibit works of art, propaganda, etc.' To do so, they had to rely on an architect, and Araquistain therefore proposed 'one of the young architects of prestige who moreover are totally on the government's side (for example, Manuel Sánchez Arcas or Luis Lacasa, etc.).' It seems that the government was considering these two architects, not only because of their youth and renown, but especially because they were staunch Republicans.

In Lacasa's autobiography we read: 'During the Civil War, the Government of the Republic sent me to Paris to project and build the Spanish Pavilion for the Paris World's Fair of 1937. I was advised to get in touch with the Catalan architect J.L. Sert. who was living there and who knew how the job could get done because he was familiar with the building industries there … Without being aware of it at the time, I came out in defence of organic architecture of brick and stone, Spanish style, but I had to give up the idea because of the speed needed for the construction … Although I had fought … Le Corbusier's principles and … did not share the formalism of Sert's architectural composition, I did not consider the occasion to be appropriate for picking a fight … I also thought that in an exhibition in which buildings must necessarily be of a provisional nature, Le Corbusier's simplistic approach was more acceptable.'

In an interview with Catherine Blanton on 15 July 1971, Lacasa's son said that when his father arrived in Paris, Sert had already made the first sketches of the Pavilion. In a previous interview with the same writer on 26 January 1971, Sert insisted that he had been working on the project of the Pavilion since the fall of 1936 and that it was the Office of Cultural Affairs of the Embassy in Paris that had given him the commission, a commission for which we have found no documentary proof.[79] Furthermore, the first written reference we have on the Pavilion is a handwritten letter to Torres of 27 December 1936: 'The project of the '37 Exhibition is going well. We have an office in the Chamber of Spanish Commerce in the Avenue of the Opera …

the programme is quite advanced. Organizing the programme one clearly sees the importance of the content. The architecture has to be subordinated to the content at all times. Lacasa agrees in making this Pavilion the glorification of all the peoples of Spain, in keeping with the notes we had prepared.'[80]

There are more documents to be taken into account, however. Through a letter to Torres of 12 January 1937 we know that: 'The preliminary design is almost finished. In Valencia they are not specifying matters nor are they confirming Lacasa's designation or that of the Commissary … Despite this, Roces, Under-Secretary of State Education, has told Lacasa to go on with the project.' In a postcard of 21 January 1937, Sert wrote to Torres: 'I suppose you have seen the plans of the Pavilion kept by Miravitlles; I'm interested in hearing your opinion.' Sert continued to mention the Pavilion in his correspondence with Torres. Thus, in an undated letter we read: 'Tomorrow we will finish the skeleton of the Pavilion; the work on the ground floor is finished and the rest can be completed in twenty days.' In a previously mentioned text written by Sert in May 1938, we read: 'I started working on the project of the Pavilion jointly with Lacasa at the beginning of December 1936.'

Sert and Lacasa, Pavilion of the Spanish Republic at the Paris World's Fair of 1937, plans.

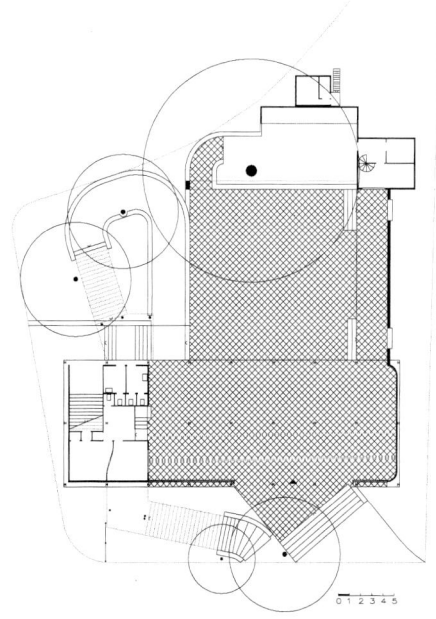
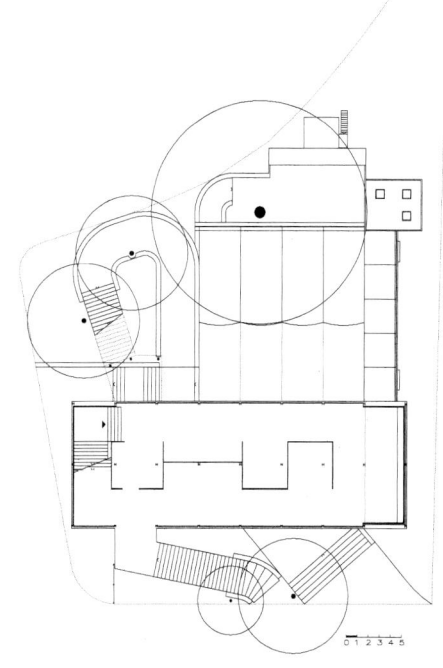
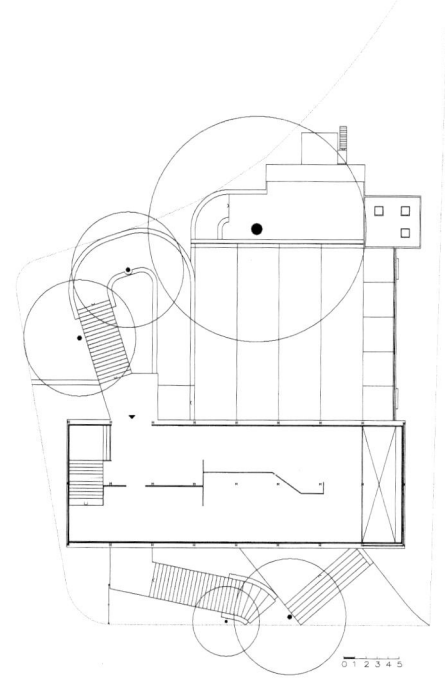

Sert and Lacasa, Spanish Pavilion at the Paris World's Fair of 1937, main facade.

It seems that that there was a problem of co-ordination among some official organisms established in Valencia and other Spanish delegations, such as the National Institution of Tourism and the Office of Cultural Affairs, which were actively working in Paris and with which Sert was in contact, sometimes obtaining work from them. However, the chronology seems to coincide (except for Lacasa's son's testimony, which gives greater protagonism to Sert): the project of the Pavilion took off in December 1936, and was finished by the end of 1937. Another postcard from Sert to Torres of 3 February 1937 corroborates this: 'Yesterday Dalty has gone to deliver the plans of the Pavilion of the World's Fair; they are addressed to you; ask Miravitlles for them.' In the Salamanca Archives there is a photographic reproduction of the first project signed by both architects, which shows some differences with respect to the final result, such as the design of the theatre and its attached rooms, the relationship with the existing tree, the presence of a covered portico to the right of the entrance, which was not carried out, the solution of the display case for propaganda and the skylights on the second floor.

Basing his arguments on Lacasa's activities after 1936 in the Agit-Prop section of the so-called 5th Regiment, Fernando Martín maintains (minimizing the role that Renau must have played, which we cannot analyze here), that 'Sert was basically the author of the design of the formal aspect of the building, whereas Lacasa was the author of the ideological side,

the way of focusing it and of distributing its contents, and on the part of both architects there was a mutual acceptance of each other's respective design and ideology.'[81] The construction of Pavilion, a place in which vanguard artistry and vanguard politics were to coincide, commenced on 27 February 1937, three months before the official inauguration of the Paris World's Fair.

In case this documentary material has not eliminated all doubts as to authorship, there is the architecture itself, which is the most definitive of documents: the final form of the Pavilion fits in with the reflection and approach that most interested Sert during those years. The interest in showing the skeletal frame – something that, as we saw in the report of the Dispensary for Tuberculosis, served to emphasize the 'sincerity' of a building and the role played by each one of the parts that made it up – is intertwined with the presence of the patio and its regional-Mediterranean component, although here the parts were assembled in a different manner.

View from an angle.

The first vision that a spectator glimpsed when approaching and entering the Pavilion after having passed Alberto Sánchez's sculpture *El pueblo español tiene un camino que le conduce a una estrella* (*The Spanish Peoples Have a Path Leading Them to a Star*) was that of a parallelepiped formed by a metal structure. In this structure, the enclosure walling elements changed according to the function they were meant to carry out: on the ground floor there was latticework, on the first floor, glass, and on the second, fibreboard, since the lighting of the interior was achieved through a skylight of highly sophisticated design. On the corner and headwall, the modulation of the grid was interrupted to allow for the installation of written messages and photomontages of propaganda that were changed throughout the course of the war in this exhibition space with mobile partitions. The pavilion, which was placed between those of Norway and Germany, offered a clear initial image: the authenticity of assembling with prefabricated elements offered concepts of economy, speed, pragmatism and efficiency, characteristic of war times, and was further enhanced by a sculpture that called for hope.

Sert's attempts at prefabrication, along with those of the GATCPAC, had started with the small demountable house for the CRV project and the demountable library and kindergarten on which they had worked, all of which clearly attests to their interest in some aspects of 'objective' architecture. During this special political period, their experiments had an evident significance. To enter the Pavilion, one had to pass under this mute manifesto. Far from the sensation of welcoming arms provided by the floor plan of the Dispensary, the experience was as much symbolic as it was historic; symbolic for the reasons given above, and historic because Sert obliged the visitor to follow the path of architectural modernity by presenting some of the most radical and striking manifestos of its beginnings: those against the academies, against composition, in favour of on-site assembly, etc. Once under the porch, the visitor reached a fountain by Calder, in front of which the structural grid was broken.

The sculpture by Alberto Sánchez, Picasso's *Guernica*, and Calder's *Mercury Fountain* in the Spanish Pavilion at the Paris World's Fair.

Spanish Pavilion
at the Paris
World's Fair,
1937.

The courtyard,
Sert and Picasso
during the
construction
of the Pavilion,
interior view.

Next came the patio – an empty element with a square, autonomous plan that did not form part of the porch at the entrance, though at first it might have seemed to do so. In this space, with its terracotta pavement, diverse outdoor activities and shows were held when the weather was good. As the central element of the pavilion, the patio articulated the building's activities and offered itself as a place of obligatory contemplation when reaching the ramp on its left. With its closed and precise delimitations, the patio evoked Mediterranean latitudes, those that, as we have seen, had taken up the torch of modernity. And it achieved this without form, without copying anything and without construction. By arresting time, Sert seemed to be foreshadowing the catastrophe that was drawing near and which for him

Julio González,
La Montserrat
in the Pavilion
of the Spanish
Republic at the
Paris World's Fair.

Sert explained that the last-minute elimination of a pillar was carried out in order to offer a better view of Picasso's *Guernica*. This leads us to see this as an architecture that accepts its role as a means to an end, no longer having to advertize its message – which had been sufficiently expressed on the exterior – and showing the advantages of its conception: between the homage to miners' work represented by Calder's *Mercury Fountain* and the horrors of the war depicted in the *Guernica*, it can disappear without trace.[82]

Joan Miró,
El Segador and
the propagandist
manifesto
for the Pavilion
of the Spanish
Republic at the
Paris World's Fair.

downstairs to the remaining halls of the exhibition. In these, visual arts and handicrafts were placed together with Renau's propagandist photomontages, which evoked the tragedy of the Republic, the endangered artistic patrimony, and the value of work. At the end of the trajectory was a double space in which one could see a huge map of Spain flanked by references to Catalonia and Euskadi, the nations that had the highest level of industry in the country and were responsible for the degree of modernity achieved by Spain. When the visitor once again came out in the open via some stairs, another Catalan presence gave a last farewell: the sculpture by Julio González known as *La Montserrat*. Thus in the empty spaces where there were no exhibits – no propaganda or display of art and craft – the patio, *El Segador* and *La Montserrat* formed a triad with their own discourse. This was transformed into the essence of the Mediterranean land, which must be nurtured so it can bear fruit, in which one must live in harmony with the universe, in which to grow and become better people, and which one must not abandon nor allow to be taken away; a land that stands for a nation.

would mean a long exile and the difficulty of going on with the work of investigating form that so interested him.

Visitors to the pavilion would inevitably sense the 'Mediterranean atmosphere'. Joan Miró's *El Segador*,[83] depicted with a Catalan (and therefore Mediterranean) *barretina* on his head, accompanied the visitor on his way

[68] See *Die Wohnung für das existenzminimum*, Hoffmann, Stuttgart, 1933, third edition.

[69] See *A.C.*, no. 15, 1934, p. 30.

[70] In a letter written by Genara López on 22 April 1942, we read: 'I have to tell you that the little houses in Garraf have been left half destroyed after the war.' Sert trunk, AFJM.

[71] See Fernando Marza and Esteve Roca, 'La volta catalana a l'obra de Le Corbusier', in *Le Corbusier i Barcelona*, Barcelona, 1988, pp. 110–29. In an interview which John Peter held in 1959 we read: 'My first modern design at the School in Barcelona was a building with a vaulted roof because in Catalonia these very thin vaults were not new, they were very old.' *The Oral History of Modern Architecture*, Harry N. Abrams, New York, 1994, p. 249.

[72] Juan José Lahuerta, 'Instantáneas de viaje', in *J.L. Sert y el mediterráneo*, op. cit., pp. 192–207.

[73] I wish to thank two students of architecture, Jaume Bermejo and Carles Prieto, for providing me with this material on the two Type-C house projects in the Garraf.

[74] COAC Archives, C–10/67.

[75] A good work for understanding the Spanish Civil War (1936–39) is Hugh Thomas, *La guerra civil española*, Grijalbo and Mondadori, Barcelona, 1995.

[76] Apart from Catherine Blanton Freedberg's text, which we have already mentioned, the main bibliography on the Pavilion of the Spanish Republic in Paris is Víctor Pérez Escolano, Vicente Lleó, Antonio Martín and Fernando Martín, 'El Pabellón de la República Española en la Exposición Internacional de París, 1937', in *España: Vanguardia artística y Realidad social: 1936–1937*, Barcelona, 1974, pp. 26–44; Fernando Martín, *El pabellón español en la Exposición Universal de París en 1937*, Universidad de Sevilla, 1983. There is an undated handwritten text by Sert in the collection in Cambridge: *The Spanish Pavilion*, SC D 112. The architecture of the pavilion has been reconstructed in Barcelona. Concerning this reconstruction, see 'Reconstruir un mito: el pabellón de 1937, de París a Barcelona', *Arquitectura Viva*, no. 21, Madrid 1991; 'Reconstrucción del Pabellón Español en la Exposición Universal de París de 1937', *ON*, no. 140, Barcelona, 1993; Josep M. Rovira, 'D'un roig encés ... ', *Diversa. Revista Universitaria de arte y arquitectura*, no. 2, San Sebastian, 1994.

[77] Blanton Freedberg, op. cit., p. 421.

[78] A biography of Lacasa can be found in ibid., pp. 223–27. Lacasa's autobiographical notes should also be consulted in *Luis Lacasa: Escritos 1922–1931*, COAM, Madrid, 1976. Carlos Sambricio's introduction is absolutely essential to an understanding of the development of rationalism in Madrid.

[79] Blanton Freedberg, op. cit., p. 135.

[80] COAC Archives, Correspondence with Torres. After an interview with Sert, Blanton Freedberg explained that the premises on the Avenue de l'Opera did not last long, and that the project was then continued in the Passage Alésia, near the Porte d' Orléans. Sert's influence in the development of the construction work and in the elaboration of some of the points of the iconographic programme must have been very important. This is attested by a letter housed in the Sert Collection from Dalí to the architect, written in faulty Catalan, in which the artist complained that his work had not been included in the pavilion: 'I am surprised that you have said nothing nor proposed anything for the Spanish pavilion and I would like to talk to you about this matter. Zervos tells me that you have to leave for Barcelona.' SC E 0.

[81] Fernando Martín, op. cit., p. 49. For questions regarding the relationship between art and politics at the time of the Civil War see Miguel Gamonal, *Arte y Política en la Guerra Civil Española. El caso Republicano*, Granada, 1987.

[82] In a text by Sert of 4 October 1981, we read: 'We decided to eliminate a metal column to give it the visual space which its monumental scale demanded. At six o'clock in the morning on the eve of the inauguration, after hanging a supporting structure from a girder of the roof, the pillar was taken away and the deflection turned out to be minimal. We breathed a sigh of relief after the critical moment had passed!' SC D 15.

The friendship between Calder and Sert endured for the rest of their lives. The details of how the *Mercury Fountain* for the Spanish Pavilion came to be commissioned are narrated by Sert in an undated typewritten text. See SC D 7.

[83] A correct interpretation of the figure of *El Segador* is found in Blanton Freedberg, op. cit., pp. 525–77.

Immersed in Melancholy

In the May 1938 issue of *XX Siècle* magazine, which appeared shortly after the Spanish Pavilion had been dismantled, the painter Joan Miró was quoted as saying: 'My dream, once I have been able to establish myself somewhere, is to have a very big studio, not for reasons of lighting or because of the Northern light, to which I am indifferent, but because I would like to have room, lots of canvases, because the more I work, the more I want to work. I also want to try sculpture, pottery, engraving, and to have a press. I would very much like, in the range of my possibilities, to go beyond the painter's easel, which in my opinion has a petty objective, and to draw closer through big works of art to the masses, whom I have never stopped thinking about.' We do not know whether his friend Sert read this article, but we can certainly witness the artist's budding desire for what would be his studio in Mallorca, although almost twenty years would pass before his dream came true.

We have already examined many of the activities that Sert carried out during his first years in the United States; it is now time to analyze the book he wrote on the architect Antoni Gaudí, which he published jointly with James Johnson Sweeney in 1960.[84] Near the end of the text we find: 'Work on this book was started in the fall of 1946. The discovery by the authors of the remarkable photographic files of Gaudí's work assembled by Joan Prats and Joaquim Gomis suggested the idea of a presentation of this material, new and unknown to the public, that would show Gaudí's work in a new light.'[85]

Since we know that Sert returned to Barcelona between September and October 1946 due to the illness of his mother we can take this statement to be true. In a letter written in French that Gomis sent from Liverpool on 18 February 1950, we read: 'Even though he had especially come back to see his mother, the Countess of Sert, who at the time was gravely ill, he had a second motive and need: to see Gaudí's work again, of which he had kept an indelible recollection during his absence.'[86]

It therefore seems evident that the idea of writing a book on Gaudí dates backs to this period, and that the publication rather than the writing of the book was held back. Gomis also states that the publisher Skira was interested in the book and had seen the dummy, which confirms the notion that the book must have been finished by 1949.[87] In 1953, negotiations with Skira came to an end without an agreement having been reached, and finally, in 1957, Sweeney managed to interest a German publishing company, Gerd Hatje, in publishing the book. A letter of 6 March 1959 confirms that it was finally going to be published jointly with an American publishing house.

Sert became interested in analyzing Gaudí's work, along with the other activities that were keeping him busy, between 1947 and 1949. It is not difficult to imagine why. His motives ranged from a sentimentality typical of the exile who returns to his land and admires that which makes him feel most international, to the melancholy that is characteristic of one who pensively reflects on an identity and memory that may be useful in his or her creative work but which seems far distant and in danger of being lost. It is the kind of melancholy professed by Jacques in Shakespeare's *As You Like It*: 'I have neither the scholar's melancholy, which is emulation; nor the musician's, which is fantastical; nor the courtier's, which is proud; nor the soldier's, which is ambitious; nor the lawyer's, which is politic; nor the lady's, which is nice; nor the lover's, which is all these: but it is a melancholy of mine own, compounded of many elements, extracted from

Maeght Foundation, Saint-Paul-de-Vence, 1959–64/ 1974–79.

243

many objects: and indeed, the sundry contemplation of my travels, in which my often rumination wraps me, is a most humorous sadness.'[88]

It was a melancholy brought on by his many travels, by his nomadic lifestyle, by the learning that had to be rechannelled to fit new situations; it was the sad product of knowing too much, of someone who arrived in a halfway civilized United States where the products of his own background must be tempered by the North American reality. Additionally there was the difficult situation faced by architecture during those years, a time when it was willing to modify its pre-war attitude but found itself at a difficult crossroads, as evidenced by the CIAMs of that period.

Gaudí interested Sert at that time because his architecture went beyond a simple demonstration of the power of technique, of objectivity or of strict rationality: 'Gaudí offered an unashamed stress on the extra-technical, imaginative elements. And as a consequence, his work indicates the way to the architecture of today – not to imitate his solution, but to emulate his approach towards a living flesh in which the spiritual material elements are fused to a building's bare bones of glass and "bars of iron"; he anticipated several problems that have grown in scale.'

After reviewing in the first chapter the structural rationalism of Viollet le Duc and his great influence on Gaudí, Sert dedicated the second chapter to the culture of his land, in which he offered a condensed history of Catalonia. In it he sought both to emphasize the aspects that differentiated it from the rest of Spain, and to draw closer to American readers. He did so by opening this chapter with a quotation from the words of Richard Ford in 1845: 'The Catalans are neither French nor Spaniards, but a distinct people both in language, costume and habits.' These differences were further remarked upon by going back to the history of the principality and pointing out: 'Catalonia has always been a problem to those desirous of a unification of the Iberian peninsula … As a single nation Spain held together for over four hundred years. Yet there has always been an essential division between the Catalans and the rest.'

Gaudí, like Sert, belonged to a country that was different, and this difference was a positive

one, which granted it industrial predominance over the rest of Spanish peoples, a detail that was not lost on Ford. Moreover, it was a country in a geographically determining place, an eminently Mediterranean location, which gave it the right to exhibit the special constructional tradition of which Sert had made use in the houses of Garraf: 'We see evidence even today that they early became familiar with the building methods from the Mediterranean extremes as well as from the lands beyond the Pyrenees. Up the coast of the Peninsula and into her harbours came builders from eastern Mediterranean countries who were familiar with brick and stone vaulting methods because they came from a part of the world where timber was scarce. The Catalan masons of today can still build their brick vaulting without reinforcing steel or wooden forms.'

Naturally this condition of 'Mediterraneanhood', not only in terms of its constructional

Cover designed by Joan Miró for José Luis Sert's *Gaudí*.

traditions but also of its light and landscape,[89] were factors that would leave a deep imprint on Gaudí, a fact that led him to declare: 'Let us think what it means to be Mediterranean. It means we are equidistant from the blinding light of the tropics and the northern lack of light that creates ghosts. We are brothers to the Italians; and this makes us more apt for creative (plastic) work.' This revealing remark strengthens our argument: through Gaudí, Sert could again take up his discourse on Mediterranean architecture, except that now it was not only presented as the basis for the first vanguard architecture, as was the case in the 1930s, but also as a model for post-war architecture. Furthermore, this architecture was executed by a Catalan who had hitherto been 'forgotten', as the authors of the book inform us in its opening pages, and whose roots were the same as those that Sert so proudly boasted.

It is therefore not surprising to find that what follows after this declaration of historical and geographical affiliation is an analysis of the terms 'form', 'colour', 'texture', 'lighting' and 'sculpture' as applied to Gaudí's buildings. Sert's conclusion is interesting because it was made at a time when architects were talking about integrating all the arts within architecture as a way to revise it and achieve a new monumentality: 'To build in the Greek manner was always one of Gaudí's ideals … It must have been to the qualities of Greek architecture in general, its sculptural expression, its use of colours, its scale in the Mediterranean landscape, that Gaudí was referring, more than to the details of the particular style … Perhaps it was the intuitive recognition of a need to balance his Gothic and oriental predilections with another structural discipline.'

Thus, based on the lesson offered by Gaudí, the Mediterranean again became the starting point from which new post-war architecture could branch out to find an optimistic continuity with the production of the 1930s. Moreover, Sert was also a good friend of Giedion, whose *Space, Time and Architecture*, with its praise of continuity, must have made him look back to his own culture as a focus for the work he was to execute.

In Europe during those years, Alberto Sartoris, whom Sert knew, was also undertaking the enterprise of recovering the Mediterranean, although he did so from a different point of view and with different protagonists. In 1948, his book, *Encyclopédie de l'architecture nouvelle: Ordre et climat méditerranéens*, whose subtitle clearly defined its contents, was published by Hoepli publishing house in Milan, although it was written in French.

Sartoris went even further back than Sert in his search to prove the supremacy of Mediterranean culture, a supremacy that he took for granted from the very outset of his work: 'Despite everything, Mediterranean functionalists possess a great part of the values of this civilization and the means to turn them into universal elements.' Sartoris was intent on affirming that the rationalist spark had originated in Italy, a Mediterranean country,[90] and his book would attempt an obvious historiographic manoeuvre: to dismantle the work written by Nikolaus Pevsner in 1936, *Pioneers of the Modern Movement: from William Morris to Walter Gropius*, in which the author had attempted to demonstrate that modern architecture originated in England and Germany.[91]

To accomplish this, Sartoris reviewed work ranging from that of the Comaschian masters to Lodolian rationalism, including Leonardo da Vinci, Filarete and Guarini, right up to Ledoux: these were the predecessors of modernity because they had been able to conceive architecture and cities with the strictest rationality and greatest functional and structural honesty, far removed from ornaments and decoration. This led Sartoris to affirm categorically: 'One therefore cannot speak of modern architecture without referring exclusively to the Mediterranean order and climate that have engendered it.'

Sartoris' contribution is interesting because it reveals that the Mediterranean had again been retrieved as a common cultural ground in the architectural scene of the post-war years; even more interesting and relevant, however, is the graphic documentary material employed by the Italian-Swiss architect. Among the many architectures shown, the main ones being Italian, followed by Le Corbusier, André Lurçat and Pierre Chareau, we find three buildings by Sert: the apartment buildings on the Carrer Muntaner and Rosselló, and the Casa Bloc.

Thus Sert, along with the French and Italians, was considered an authentic representative of this ideology even though his buildings were created before its formulation, which, as we have seen, Sert himself invented and developed in the pages of *A.C.*

In the late 1940s and early 1950s, both Sert and Sartoris, each using different mechanisms, were to legitimate the Mediterranean as the place from which to depart in search of new architectures. Such reflections encouraged Sert to take up architecture with renewed force, and he did so by accepting the project of building a studio for his friend Miró.

In 1947, while still dreaming about his large studio, Miró travelled to the United States to paint a mural for the Cincinnati Terrace Hotel, and there he met up with his friend architect, who was living and working in New York. Miró was facing the possibility that he had hoped for

poetry – and that already is much – but one must go towards big things of human and collective, almost anonymous, magnitude. You architects have the word … [Y]our mother is getting better.'[93] We can see a new path of communication opening up between architecture and the visual arts, an issue that we know was debated by the architects attending the Bridgwater Congress; the difference was that now this need was also being expressed by artists.

We find no reference to the painter's studio until 18 January 1954: 'The ideas that you gave me in your letter of 9 October seem very good ones, and will make the construction even more beautiful; I'd recommend that you keep in mind the climate of Mallorca, hot in the summer, and the great surface area of the studio, which is difficult to heat, especially taking into account the fact that I start working very early … We have been in Palma for a couple of

Joan Miró's studio, Palma de Mallorca, 1953–57, plans.

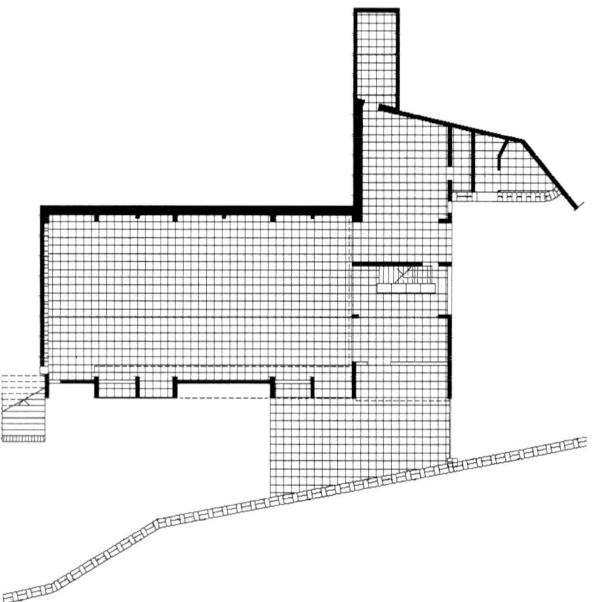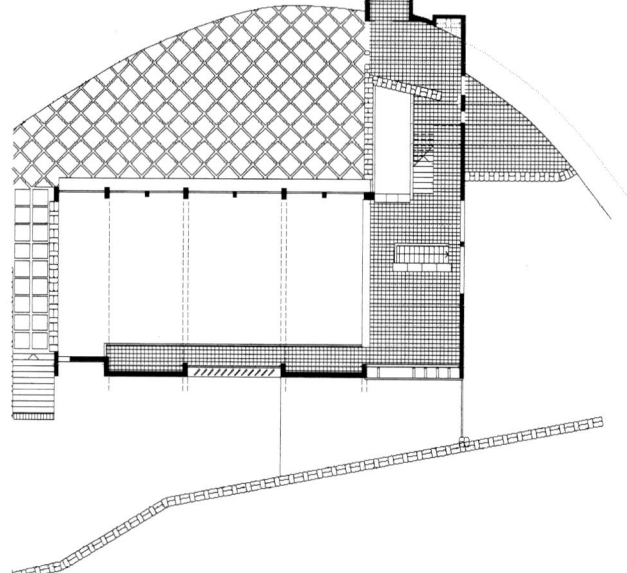

in 1938 – to reach the masses through large-scale works of art that would be exhibited in public places, a concern that he was still voicing in 1958: 'Mural art is the very opposite of solitary creation. While one must preserve one's personality, one must also commit it profoundly to the collective spirit of the work.'[92]

He also expressed this preoccupation to Sert, immediately after returning to Spain, in a letter of 19 November 1947, in which after telling him of his visits to Montroig, he added: 'Easel painting only serves to take a rest or to achieve

days and everyone is working very hard. Enric totally agrees with everything you say; you know how correct he is and he would not consider changing anything without first consulting it.'[94] These last two sentences do not fit chronologically with the other data. It seems that work was underway since the letter states that everyone was working hard, and suggests that the architect Enric Juncosa, Miró's brother-in-law, was supervising the construction work. Since the Miró couple was building a house as well as the artist's studio in the Mal-

246

SECCIO TRANSVERSAL EST

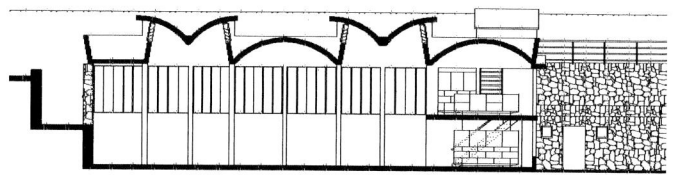

Joan Miró's studio, sections.

Joan Miró's studio, first sketch, 1953 (SC).

SECCIO LONGITUDINAL SUD

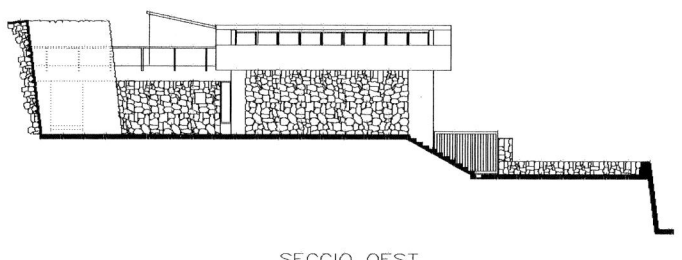

SECCIO OEST

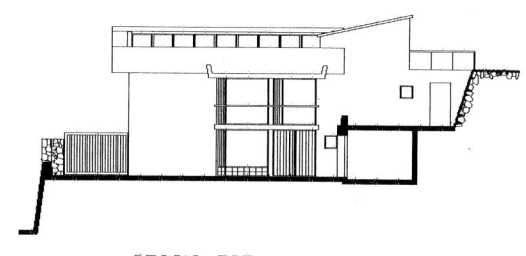

SECCIO EST

lorcan residential area of So N'Abrines, and Juncosa's plans for the house bear the date of January 1955, while the plans for building the studio – which were made in Harvard – are dated 4 January 1955, it is not clear which works were being carried out in January of the previous year. Miró, moreover, made reference to something that can be interpreted as revisions of previous drawings, which further reduces the possibility that the studio was being built, unless the work he was referring to was the levelling of the terrain for the studio, which had a considerable slope.

One thing seems clear at any rate: the space for art and the space for living were to be radically separated, and would need to be presented as belonging to two distinct worlds. Daily life would be manifested by an anonymous, vulgar architecture, whereas the place for art required special treatment, to be carried out by a state-of-the art architect with whose professional career Miró was extremely familiar.

Little clarification is afforded by other letters from 1954,[95] since work on the project proceeded very slowly. One from 25 November, however, does shed some light: 'We sent your letter to Enric, who says they are working on the layout and the foundations of the studio, for with the plans he now has he can get on with all of that, but he hopes that you will afterwards

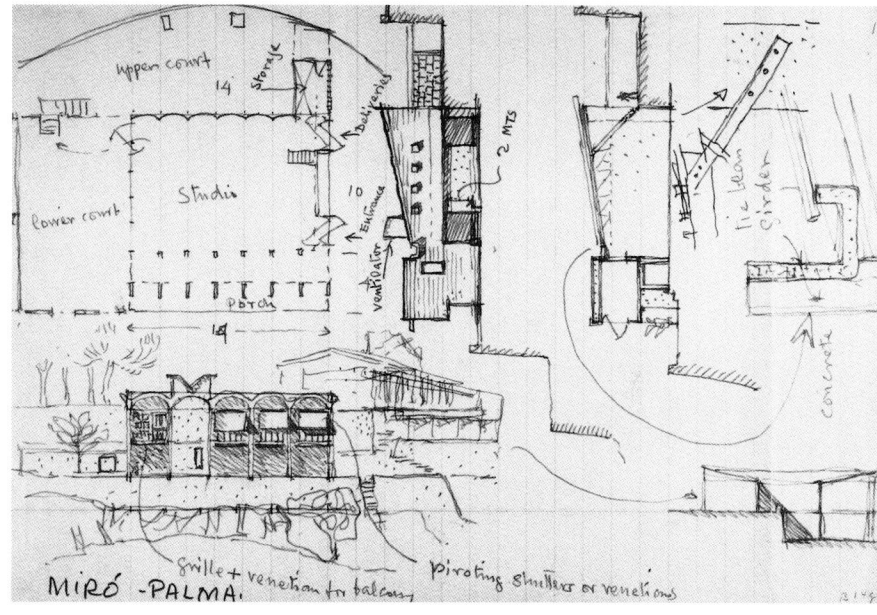

send him all the definitive plans.' The 'definitive plans', therefore, do not coincide with the beginning of construction work. Sert must have taken an especially long time to do them, given that at this time he was constantly travelling back and forth between Cambridge and New York to fulfil his professorial obligations and carry out his work at the TPA office;[96] meanwhile, work continued to advance, although presumably at a slow pace given the technology available at the time and the scarce volume of the commission. A letter of 1 April 1955 tells

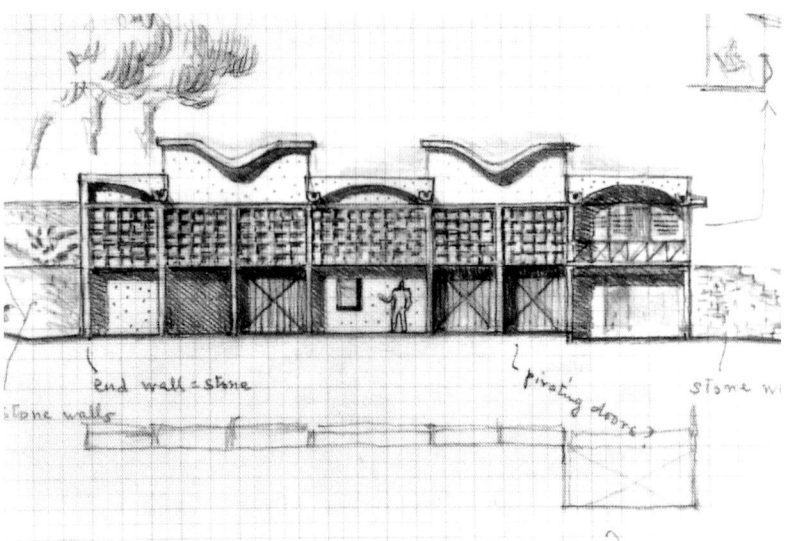

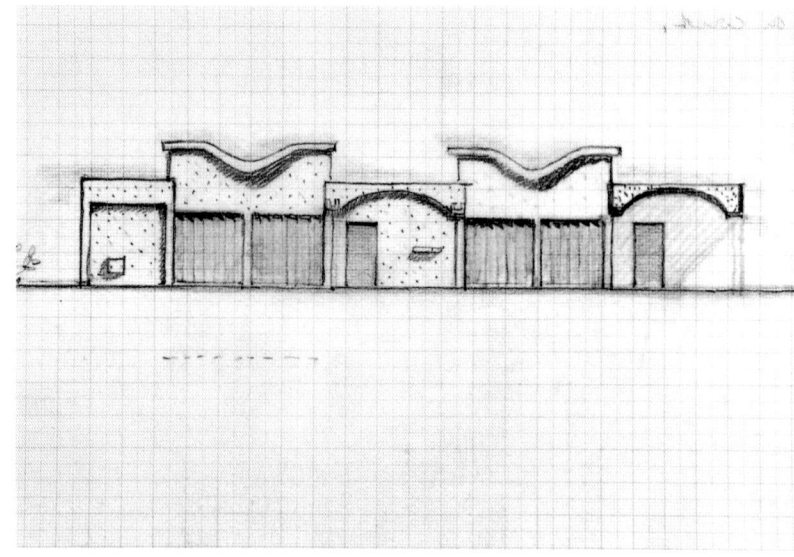

Joan Miró's studio, perspective, interior view and elevations (SC).

us: 'Work is proceeding but we have not yet got to the roof', which became easier to execute once Miró had received the model of the building in June 1955, so that the builders could visualize it. On 15 March 1956 the studio was almost finished, but in March 1957 they became aware that there were some inconvenient leaks. It was not until November 1957 that Miró's dream of 1938 was finally fulfilled and he was able to write to his friend: 'The studio is completely finished and it is *extraordinarily magnificent*, I can't wait to start working … I cannot start working until I have created the right atmosphere to do so.'[97]

Some documents about the project have been kept, and they allow us to trace its development, highlighting Sert's main interests during this period and helping to focus the debate on architecture at this time. In what seems to be a first study we already see an outline: a cubic form with a volume added to its top part suggests the desire to create a working space with very little communication with the exterior and yet with the best possible illumination, ensured by a skylight.

In the next drawing we become aware of the existence of a great empty space, which is adapted to the terrain on a stepped slope and which is covered with a series of vaults in the Catalan style, recalling the project executed by Sert in 1935 for the kindergarten in Viladecans. This second drawing is especially noteworthy because of its iconography: the vaults cover the space assigned to the mezzanine and present an enclosure walling that is extremely sunken-in when compared to the exterior limit of its piers, thus making patent, through the effect of shadows, its repeated form, which in no way coincides with the structural modules of the plan. These vaults were formal advertisements for Mediterranean culture, which the melancholic architect employed in order to affirm his sense of belonging within it, his right to work with these elements. In the lateral elevation we find that the full-height area was to be covered with a shed roof supported by tie beams, and with some surprise we note the presence of Marcel Breuer's architecture, which (as we will see in the following chapter) had been decisive in the project for Sert's Long Island house. Thus, not only did the melancholic Sert incorporate elements of the culture he had left behind, but he also incorporated what was new into his constantly fluctuating practice. The spatial variations of the interior were reflected in the formal external result, while two courts appeared on different levels (the lower one being fairly large) as did a storage room, about whose location Miró would express his doubts to the architect.

There are also various undated hand-drawn studies on plotting scale paper that formed the basis for the definitive plan, and Sert must have sent these from the US throughout most of 1954. In these, the Catalan vaults cover the entire space and have begun a metamorphosis that transforms them into exuberant forms while at the same time acting as skylights and vents. The mezzanine now coincides with the

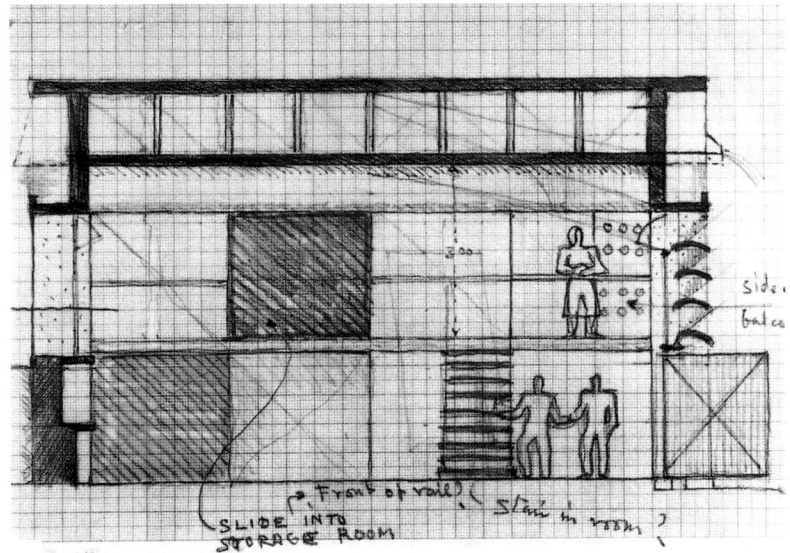

entrance, and the storage room has been moved to the side.

Even from the plan drawing it is evident that the building 'rejects' the exterior: the common walls are sealed while the plane of the facade moves away from the limits of the structure, seeking stable horizontal planes that serve to distance it from the topography; this is achieved through traditional stone walls or terraces. There is no sense of possible integration, just the yielding of certain laws to others.

In the drawings of the facades we see Sert's intention of showing the structural grid, which however, has disappeared in the exterior perspective. We also notice that the image of the

Joan Miró's studio, sections (SC).

Joan Miró's studio, view of the exterior.

Joan Miró's studio, view of the interior.

roof is used as a counterpoint to the 'formal' rigidity of the grid: both its shifting forms and its modulation, which changes at its extremes, seem to corroborate this. The solution of the ventilated double roof, which in the pavilion in Paris had simply aimed to fulfil a functional purpose without drawing attention to itself, here aspires to become the visual protagonist of form. Reinforced concrete shells provide a roof as well as reflected diffuse light. Arranged in a fan shape these shells are closed on their sides with what appears to be latticework and functions as a brise soleil. These shells also allow for cross-ventilation, while the larger ones trap the incoming light.

In the built version, the way in which these structural spaces were covered was varied in a much more complex way than that attempted in the Pomona buildings, and broke up the 'rigidity' of earlier buildings such as the Paris Pavilion and the Dispensary. Sert has explained that his use of the modulor's proportions directed and ordered the heterogeneous ensemble of materials employed: enamelled fired clay, ceramic latticework, thick wooden transoms of uneven modulation, wooden enclosures of red, yellow and blue. The relationship between the plane of the structure and the plane of the perimetral enclosure varies, producing contrasts of varying intensity in different parts of the building. The whole ensemble is completed by a spectacular girder, which supports the pressure, its silhouette modified by illumination from the skylights.

In the interior, the contrast of materials continues: exposed stone, varnished wood and the ceramic tiles on the floor are unified and dominated by an exquisite white concrete. It is a unity that in some way recalls those white volumes that were reproduced in *A.C.*, a recollection that the nostalgic architect uses to his advantage; we again see modern art alongside elements of popular tradition. This evocation of past experiences again draws attention to Sert's insidious melancholy, which intersects with the body of architectural theory that Sert had learned, developed, disseminated and debated at the CIAMs, his urban experiences in Latin America, and his lectures and writings produced between 1952 and 1955.

A central concern for Sert at the time was the patio or courtyard, as evidenced by three texts dedicated to this topic: 'The Rebirth of the Patio', 'Can Patios Make Cities?' and a third untitled text[98] that makes a series of points in favour of the use of this element both in architecture and in urban environments.

The patio had held this central place in Sert's ideas ever since his experiences in Barcelona and Paris, and he incorporated it on many occasions in his proposals for South American cities, and even in the first sketch of his plan for Miró's studio. After explaining the Asian, African and Mediterranean origins of the patio, Sert wrote: 'The "patio house" is basically an inward-looking house. The patio itself is a roofless room, one of a group of rooms, some of which are enclosed for protection from the elements, all of which are included within the arms of the encompassing walls, which extend to the boundary lines. The interior spaces, therefore, all enjoy a view onto controlled exterior spaces.' This was the beginning of a text conceived for a North American context, where buildings tend to look out towards the landscape, or towards the exterior of its garden cities, and which seem to be incompatible with the more introspective mentality represented by the patio.

Sert, insisted, clearly from a European point of view, on the advantages of the patio while at the same time expressing his familiar opposition to the garden-city: 'The "patio house" obviously combines admirably in series with others of its kind, uses land efficiently, and establishes individual advantages of self-control, privacy and economy through the use of the party wall.'

The advantages of the patio, however, were less clear in domestic architecture than in the other types of buildings listed by Sert in a disjointed inventory that aimed to prove not only the patio's connection with the Mediterranean, but also its universal presence: 'The patio as a core, one of the oldest plans (Egypt, Mesopotamia, Greece). Its use in temples, palaces and modest homes. The public square – a patio space. The patios scale and shape the cities of antiquity (Asia, Persia, etc. – Mediterranean, Precolumbian America). Apartment houses in Ostia. The patio in the monastery, the Cloisters (Carthusian monasteries). The City and the Cloister – Lima, etc. The university cities: Oxford, Cambridge, Salamanca, Lima, etc.: use of the patio. The patio in Northern climates.' Despite forming part of the universal tradition of architecture, he continues, the patio has disappeared from today's cities, in which we have lost our sense of privacy, the sights we are afforded are hateful, and the communication among people that was formerly fostered by public spaces that were in essence large patios, has died out: 'The idea of a city where all the land is a public park is not too attractive. It would be monotonous, and endless views discourage walking. A system of meandering pathways connecting differently shaped courts, and where parks of varied sizes occur only at certain points, is a more human and more civic kind of environment.' Thus, the patio is understood as a mechanism that shapes the city, which Sert illustrates with his urban proposals for South America, comparing them to nothing less than the mythical model of Radburn.[99]

The patio was not Sert's exclusive preoccupation; he was also interested in some other issues that were taking the limelight in architectural debates at the time. The issue of the integration of the visual arts, for example, which calls to mind the Paris experience and some key moments in the CIAM discussions, was repeatedly voiced. In a text of 1955 that bore this title,[100] we find: 'Very often architecture is called the "mother of the arts". I don't agree with this. The city is the real mother of the arts, for the arts as we know them were born in the city.' He went on to point out that in the last decades people had witnessed the divorce of the arts, acknowledging that this was a result of ruptures that had occurred in the nineteenth century. He believed that as a consequence neither modern architects nor painters and sculptors were prepared for reintegration because they were too caught up in trying to give preeminence to their particular art.

However, this had not always been the case: 'Many times in the past, walls were used to tell stories or historical facts, but many other times walls were animated because the artist and the architect felt that the wall came to life by treating it in a certain fashion … Architecture itself may become a piece of sculpture, and should have certain sculptural qualities of fullness in volume and form, and varying effects when the light of the sun changes.' To read these lines and to recall the treatment given to the facades of Miró's studio in Palma is a simultaneous process: we can now grasp more fully the reasons underlying their design.

These reasons go hand in hand with Sert's interest in proportions at this time, spurred by his reading of the two volumes of Le Corbusier's *Le Modulor*, which had come out in

251

1948 and 1952 respectively. On 1 September 1951, the Milan Triennial organized a Convegno internazionale sulle proporzioni nelle arti, and Sert was invited to give a lecture. As a consequence of being unable to participate in this meeting, Sert decided to organize a symposium on the same theme at MoMA, New York, on 11 March 1952.[101] In this meeting he gave a lecture in which he once again emphasized the nineteenth century's responsibility for letting questions of proportions fall into oblivion. However, thanks to the works of Matila Ghyka and Le Corbusier, this subject, an eternal theme from ancient Egyptian to Mayan architecture, was again being debated.

Remarking on its superior significance and its human foundation Sert commented: 'If a work of art, a picture, a building, a city, is related to man and to the world around him, its proportions should be related to those governing the structure of that world, so that by studying and knowing how to employ and use these proportions, our work will come closer to the works of nature and consequently closer to man himself.' The loss of unity between art and science was responsible for the greater introspection and hermeticism practised in each discipline by its followers. 'The Greek temples, the best cathedrals, etc., are products of team work. Of course, this joint work and the existence of certain rules and principles means a certain discipline in art but *I believe it would be useful to reestablish some discipline in this free-for-all art world of today.*'

After affirming that the so-called 'free forms' possess as great a numerical base as do 'geometric' forms – using the example of Gaudí's architecture or the latest proposals of engineers inspired by the world of nature to demonstrate the absolute lack of rigidity in any system of proportions – Sert sought to bring out the modernity of this system of controlling forms by the application of modular systems or window designs. Attention to proportions would ensure harmonious, unitarian and human-scale architectures, and would produce harmonious cities in which it would be a pleasure to live. The idealism and the utopia that had inspired so many of his project reports for South American cities was clearly still in force.

Moreover, the architecture he was advocat-

ing had to move away from the functionalist assumptions that had allowed it to 'erase' its near past, but without losing sight of them, an argument along the lines of Giedion's hypotheses of continuity. Functionalist assumptions, already universally accepted, were now to be revised, especially since by that time they were being routinely taught, falling into a new academicism in the schools of architecture: 'There are two kinds of modern architecture: the fashionable style that can only be a superficial new disguise of the old way of living, and the real and more profound new architecture that will take as a basis a different way of living that parallels the changes of the times.'[102] In this undertaking, it had become urgent to overcome the limitations and the strict laws of functionalism: 'After the house-cleaning of the '20s we have to recognize a need for a more complete architectural idiom, a richer architectural expression … We were all excited back in the '20s over a monstrosity called the "minimum house". We realize now how miserable it was to aim at such a goal and how inhuman to think in those terms.'

'Poetry is also a part of life!', he declared.[103] The direction he advocated was to seek a more humanized architectural expression, and to look – without imitating it – to the lesson taught by Baroque architecture, to the co-operation among the different disciplines, and to team work, to the use of natural materials, to the free use of colour, to the use of light to produce sculptural effects, and above all, to keeping in mind that: 'We are building for both the physical comfort and spiritual pleasure of people; that architecture is not and never can be an abstraction … The home is a place to enjoy life, and as defined by the dictionary, "One's fixed place of abode, peace and rest".' Reading this text makes one mentally return to Miró's studio in Palma: Sert builds what he believes in, verifying in his architecture that which he conceives theoretically.

Finally, at a time when our architect was foreseeing the end of his work as a city planner and was looking forward to renewing his architectural profession with certain guarantees thanks to the position he now held at Harvard, it is logical to find him reflecting on the relationships between architecture and city, a concern that would constitute one of his central areas of reflection during his years in Cambridge: 'Architecture is an activity that is 90 per cent urban or civic … There seems to be a general agreement on the desirability of improving the present-day physical surroundings … We cannot continue talking or thinking in terms of isolated buildings. We are aware that buildings, big or small, form part of their surroundings and are shaped or deformed by these surroundings.'[104]

After reviewing the degree of degradation present in the downtown areas of American cities due to an excessive interest in the decentralization of cities towards the suburbs, he emphasized many points developed in the CIAMs that could be applied to the US: 'Man's knowledge has taken shape in the heart of our cities, and it is difficult to imagine this great country, for example, without its big metropolitan centres. If we believe in the progress of our times and in the contribution that this progress may make to achieve an improved environment, we must also believe that these urban centres will be transformed and improved, and that they will not be left at the mercy of a process of growing decay.'

The centre of the city was to be the place in which the qualities of architecture and city planning were to converge and work together to create better surroundings: 'The physical planning of these centres is the most important common ground for city planners and architects, although it is still a no-man's-land.' We cannot help detecting in these lines the hope that he would be able to contribute to the design of the cities – Boston and Cambridge – that would occupy him until his death. Nevertheless, the first intervention he undertook in the city where he would live for the rest of his life clearly reveals a mistrustful attitude that announces the difficulty he would have in achieving his illusory hopes of intervening in the urban-architectural problems directly surrounding him. The closed shape of his house in Cambridge, rejecting all relationship with the city, is proof of this mistrust.

The drafting of the project for the house, located on 64 Quincy Street, began in June 1956, as can be deduced from some sketches in the Sert Collection bearing the date of the 14th of that month. By autumn – according to a letter written on 27 November by Moncha to someone called Joan who could either have been Prats or Miró – it seems that the first version of the house had greatly advanced: 'Josep Lluis is preparing the plans for the house we want to build in Cambridge; we have got the land from the University.'

Other plans of 13 April 1957, already done to scale, offer a first version of the house, which underwent some changes, as we can tell from the plans that were finished on 17 May. The definitive plan is dated 1 July 1957. Thus, conceiving and drawing his house took Sert a little more than a year.

The chief doubts that Sert manifested through the existing sketches all have a common nexus: the patio was there from the very beginning, and the whole process was geared around finding a way for this element to articulate the house, in which Sert and Moncha would live from the beginning of 1958.[105] In the end, instead of speaking of one patio we

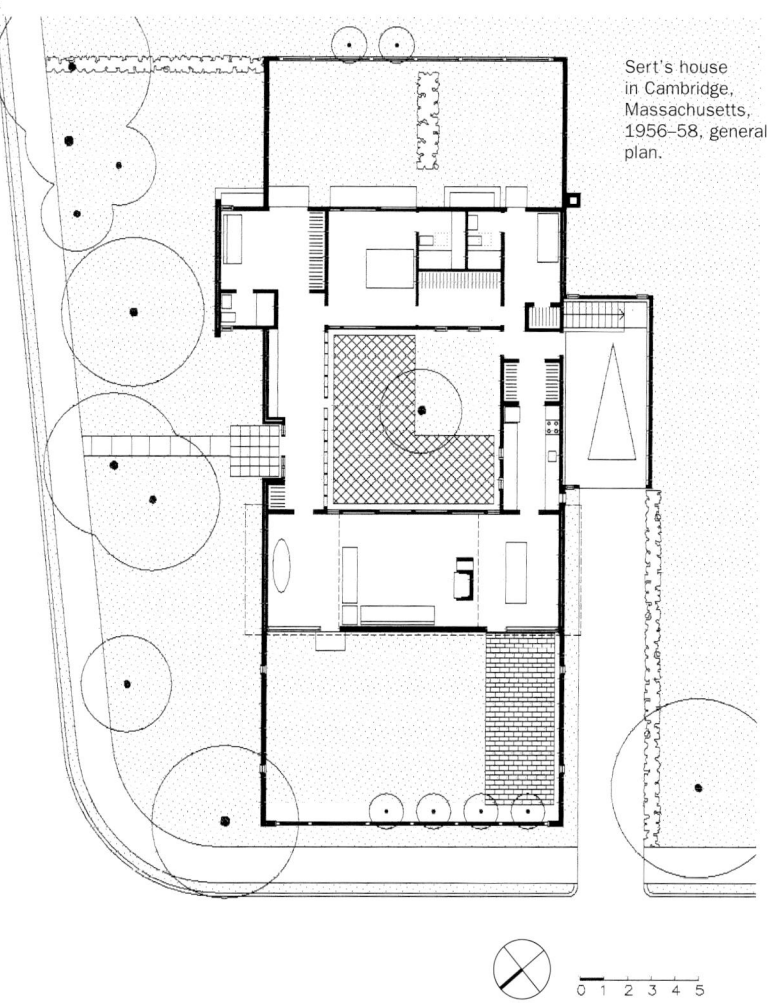

Sert's house in Cambridge, Massachusetts, 1956–58, general plan.

0 1 2 3 4 5

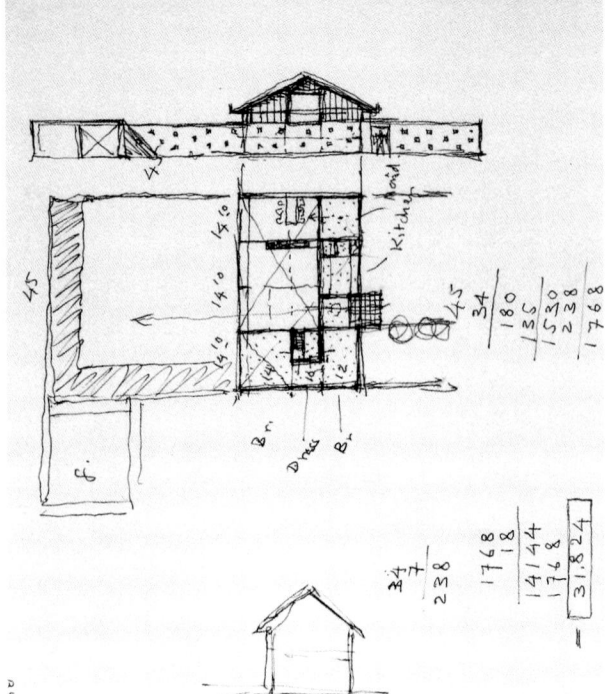

Sert's house,
first sketch, 1954
(SC).

enclosing walls out close to the hot line, better use is made of expensive land. Both indoor and outdoor living space is private and serene. Every room can have pleasant views regardless of what is beyond the walls.'[106]

In an interview held and published many years later, of which there is a copy in the Sert Collection, the architect said of his home: 'This is an introverted sort of house. The front of the house doesn't exist. There is no front facade. We are not sacrificing anything to keep in touch with the neighbours.' This was an introversion that had a fundamental reason: that of providing a 'showcase for his art collection'. The objective was to achieve the greatest amount of interior space in which to contemplate the works of art accumulated over time and the fetish objects from far-away cultures, which in the houses in El Garraf were lined up in special places allocated to them throughout the house. Paintings by Le Corbusier, Léger and Miró shared space with triptychs from the Late Middle Ages and entered into a dialogue with traditional earthenware, primitive idols and straw baskets. The central placing of the fireplace called to mind Breuer's house in New Canaan or his residence for the Clark family in Orange.

should speak of three, each with a specific function, both separating and connecting the diurnal and nocturnal areas of the house.

A magazine expressed its perception of the patio as follows: 'As close-in urban land becomes scarcer, more crowded and more expensive, more and more attention should be paid to the concepts of the Mediterranean court house. The reasons are simple. By pushing the

Sert's house,
sketches.

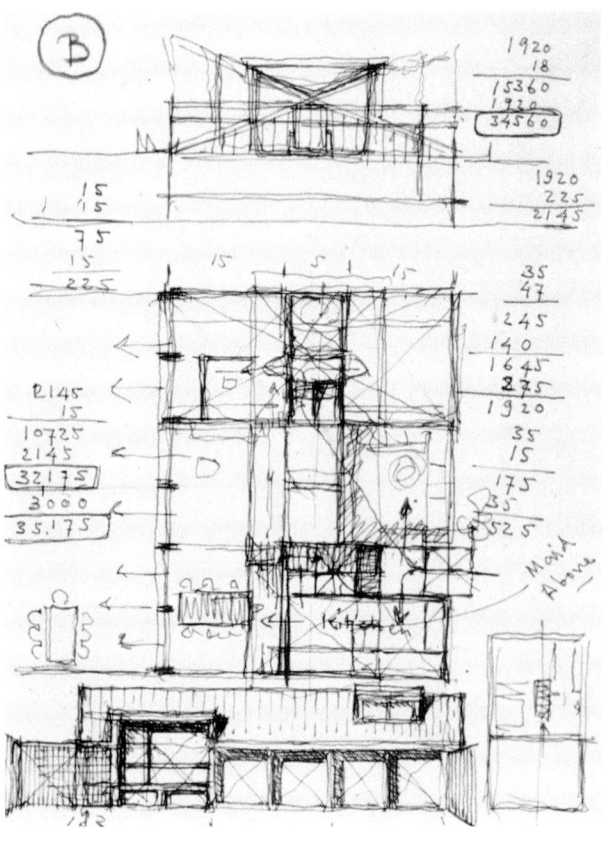

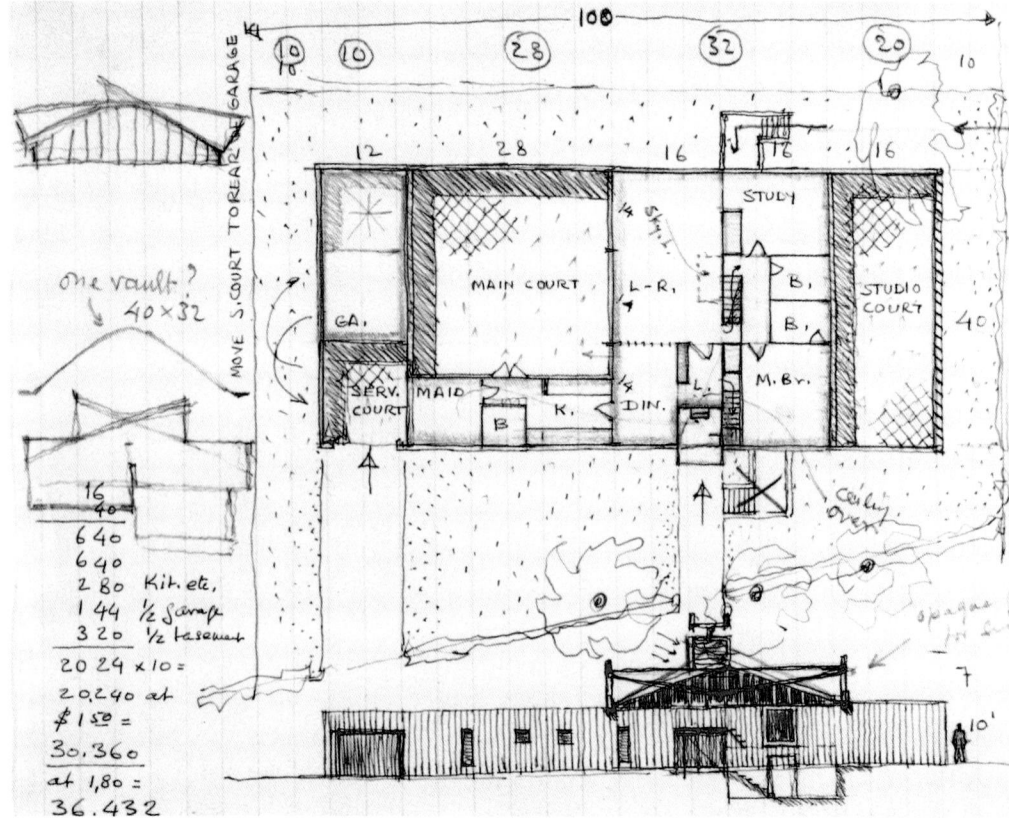

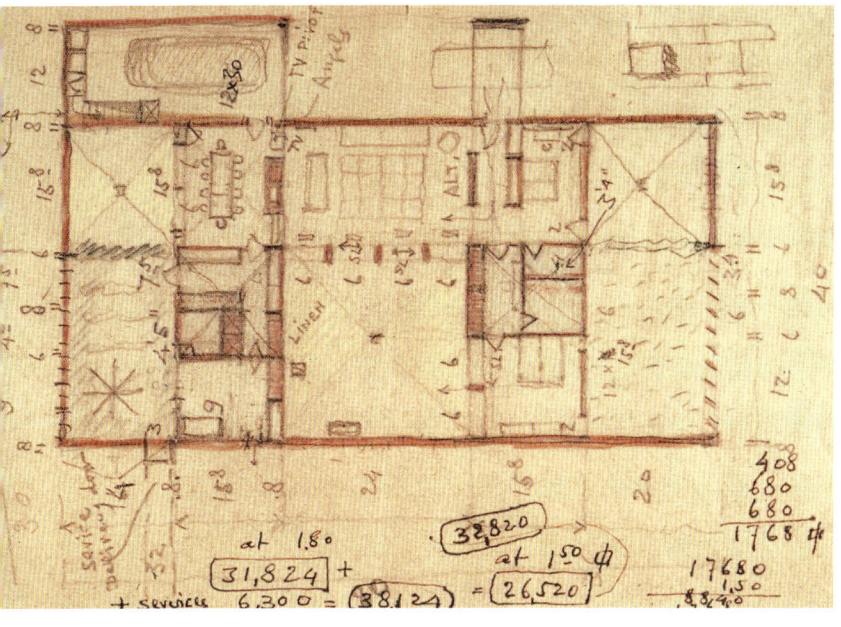

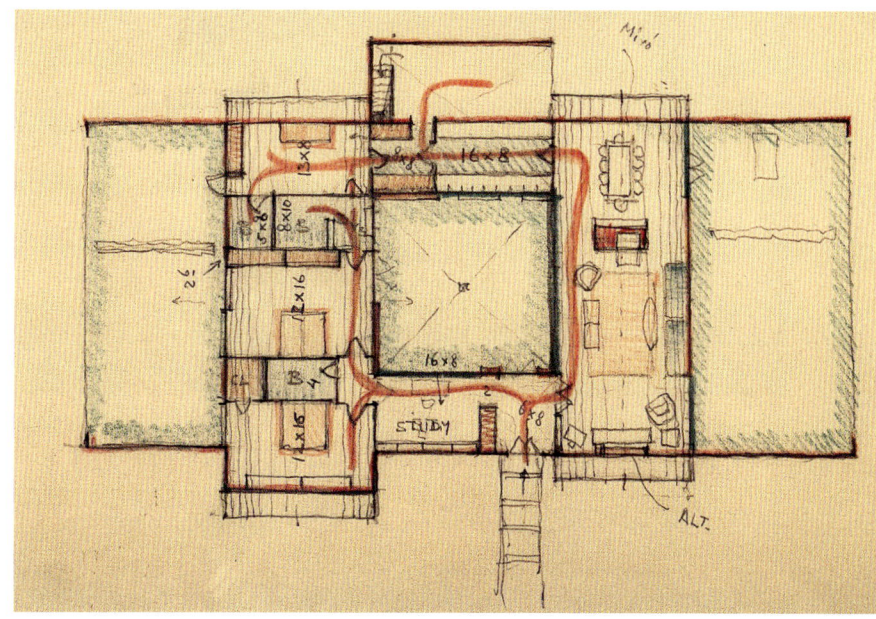

Sert's house, sketches.

Sert's house, facade on Francis Avenue; facade of a single-family dwelling, published

in *Architectural Record*, June 1951; private collection; entrance.

Sert's house,
views
of the patio.

A mobile by Calder and a mural by Constantino Nivola defined the boundaries of the house, whose fence was copied from one in an American magazine.[107] It is not the enclosing walls that delimit the space, but the works of these two renowned artists and friends of the architect, which make up a beginning and an end for this *promenade artistique*. The spectator could share the contemplation of these works of art with the owners of this art gallery-cum-house; a photograph shows a group of students sitting with their backs to the camera, looking at a medieval painting that Sert had placed in his living room, taking a moment of respite before continuing on their stroll through the house.

With this building, the exile would leave an imprint on the place that had welcomed him, and at the same time protect his own culture, painstakingly constructed, from the eyes of unwanted onlookers. In this sense, the mythological message of the Greek house remained intact. Hermes and Hestia, the gods who protected the Greek home and hearth, had deter-

Sert's house, the living room; view with medieval altarpiece and view facing the chimneybreast.

ones. Either way the legacy embodied by the house is twofold: on the one hand, it provides confirmation of the cultural superiority of the exile's place of origin, and on the other, a thorough combination of cultures from all countries and origins. Moreover, Sert's house, generous and exemplary at the same time, is a lesson in the sad reality of American garden cities: 'The patio house obviously combines admirably in series with others of its kind, uses land efficiently and establishes individual advantages of self-control, privacy and economy through the use of the party-wall.' Designing according to the proportions of the Modulor, responding to concerns about a building's impact on the city, combining architecture, painting and sculpture: we are again looking at an architecture that is the tangible embodiment of

mined its shape and its meanings centuries before: both open and closed, in contact with the sky, custodian and trader. Perhaps the role of this exile's architecture was to stage a re-encounter with his Mediterranean ancestors, or to preserve his own culture within foreign

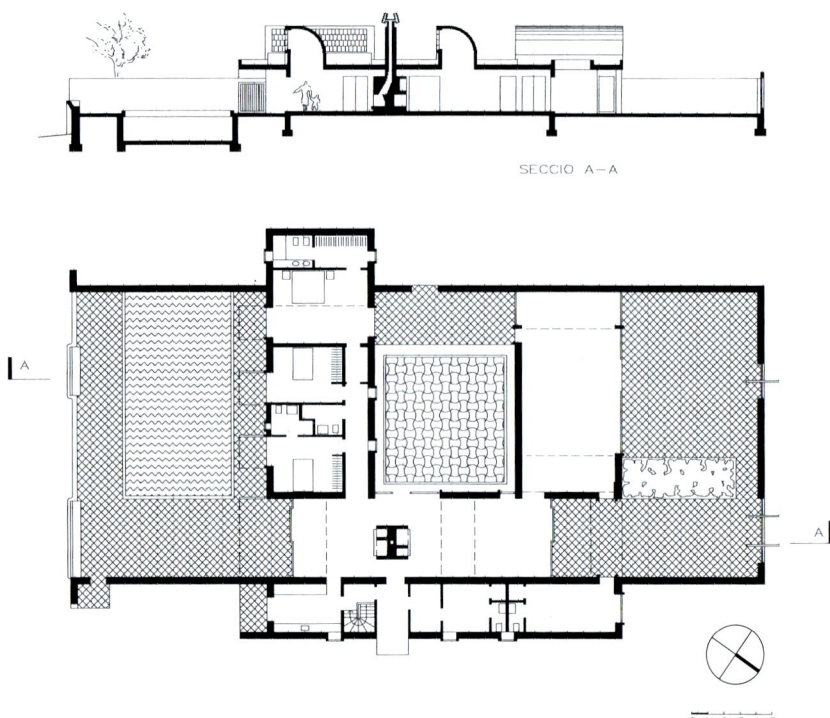

SECCIO A—A

0 1 2 3 4 5

Braque House,
Saint-Paul-de-
Vence, 1959–60,
section and plan
(SC).

Sertian thinking: 'There is a moment in life when one has to pull things together and I am doing that now.'[108]

There is too marked a similarity between Sert's house and his unbuilt project for the painter Georges Braque to warrant its analysis here, even though the design objectives are different.[109] Conceived and drawn, including a model, immediately after the architect's own house was completed between 1959 and 1960, this residence also reveals a succession of three patios among buildings destined for different activities. What is especially remarkable in the Braque house is the process of refining and polishing the roof of Miró's Palma studio, which is resolved with some skylights that Sert would repeat in future projects and which would end up becoming a trademark of his architecture.

Marguerite and Aimé Maeght were also seeking to gather works of art by different authors and to syncretize cultures from different latitudes in a museum for art in Saint-Paul-de-Vence, where Braque's house would have been. Grief-stricken by the death of their son Bernard of leukaemia in 1953, they took a trip to the United States following the advice of Fernand Léger, and visited the Barnes, Phillips and Guggenheim foundations in 1955. As Aimé Maeght put it in an interview for *Le Monde*

years later: 'I had six hectares of land on the hill, and there I had built my house. But when one of my sons died, I lost interest in everything. For the first time in my life, I let myself go. I can truly say that once again it was the painters who helped to get me back on my feet and gave me a direction to follow. Georges Braque persuaded me to undertake something that would help me overcome my grief: a place for modern art there where we were, amidst the thyme and rosemary … And Fernand Léger told me: "If you carry it out, I will bring you

Braque House,
sketches (SC).

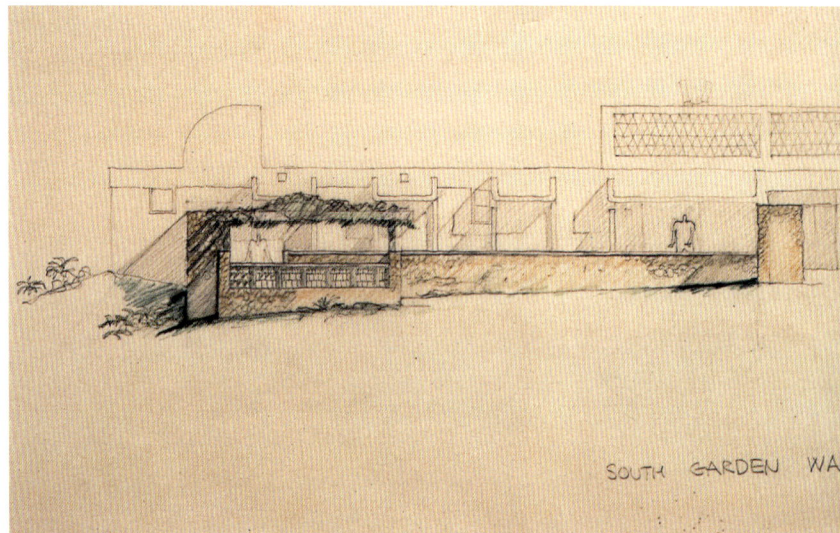

SOUTH GARDEN WAL

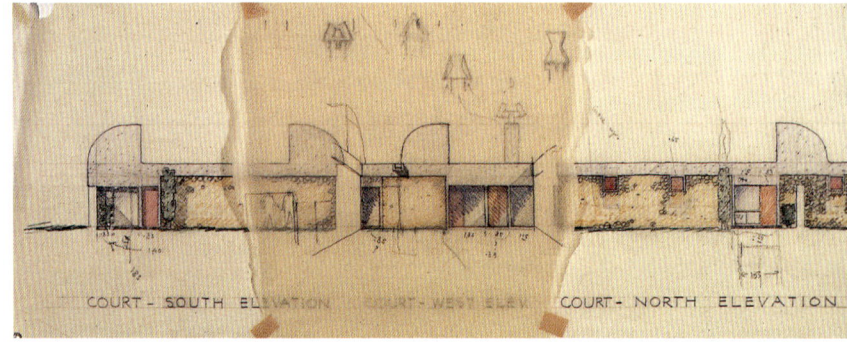

COURT - SOUTH ELEVATION   COURT - WEST ELEV   COURT - NORTH ELEVATION

WEST ELEVATION

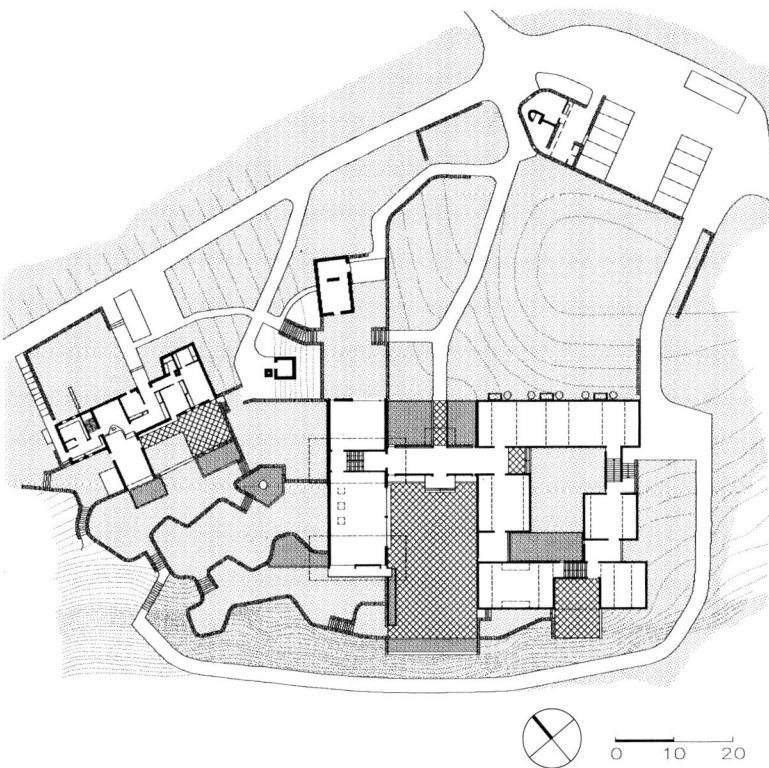

Maeght
Foundation,
Saint-Paul-
de-Vence,
1959–64/
1974–79, general
plan; insertion
in the landscape
(SC).

already in Saint-Paul, he added: 'I don't think it is necessary that I come during this first stage of siting and other technical matters.'[111]

The building was inaugurated on 24 July 1964, a time-span that reflects the painstaking care with which it was planned and built, as can be seen through Sert's correspondence, which affords further information on some of the stages of its creation. In a letter to Le Corbusier of 16 June 1959, which is housed in the Sert Collection, we read: 'I have to go to Saint Paul de Vence because Maeght has asked me to make the plans for a museum down there. I am working with Miró and other painters and sculptors. I've drawn up a preliminary design which has been accepted and I am working on developing the plans for the first phase.'

Through another letter addressed to Miró we learn that the model for the building was completed by 9 October 1959, and that the painter was working hard on the project. On 28 February 1962 Miró wrote to Sert: 'Afterwards we will work together in Saint Paul. Naturally you will have to be there, that is absolutely necessary … With team work and on site, enthusiasm and ideas will surge forth. Of course, it is a unique opportunity for us and it is worth making an all-out effort, working

my doodles. I will even paint the stones!'.[110]

When Maeght visited the States he met Sert at Harvard, and it seems he had seen Miró's studio in Palma. The first sure reference to their collaboration comes through a letter from Miró to the architect on 20 February 1957, in which, after mentioning that Sert was

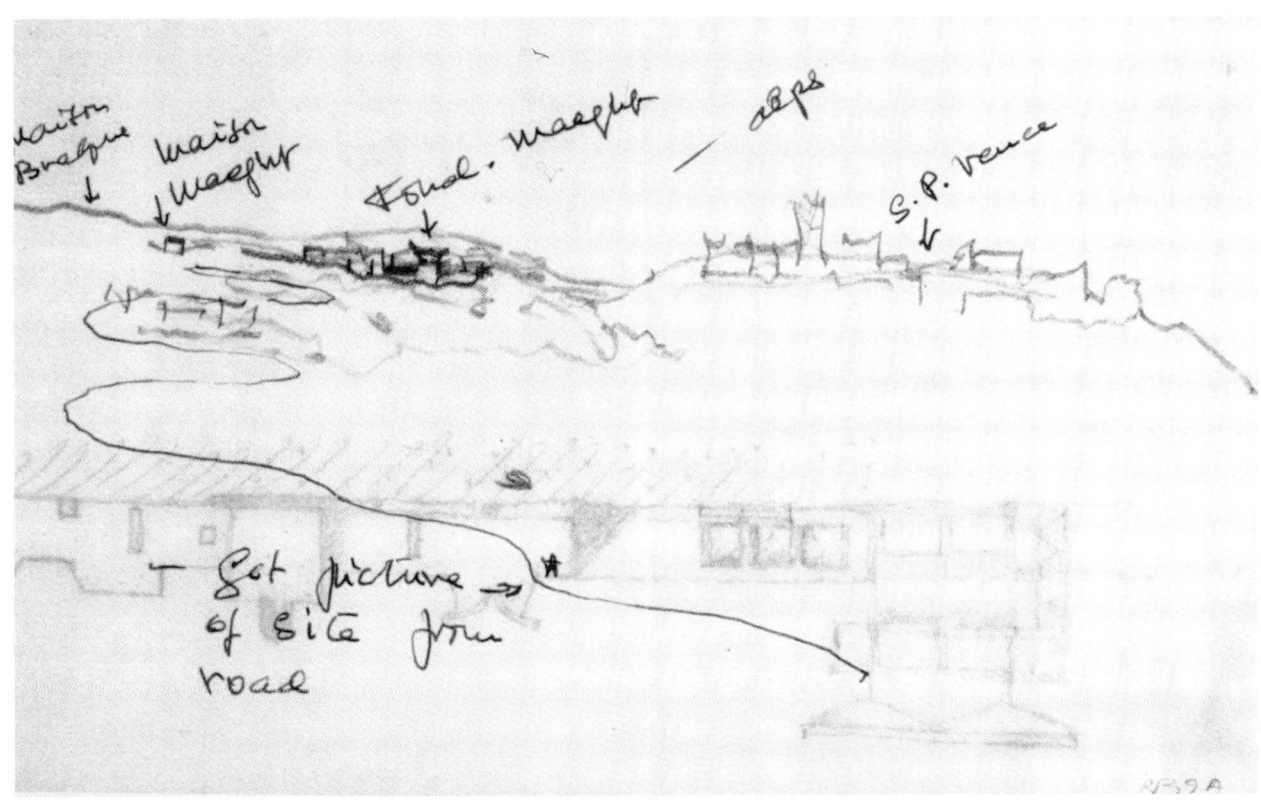

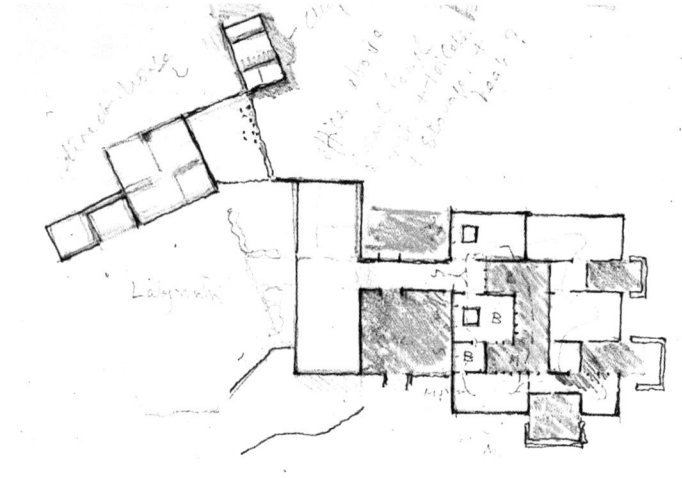

Fondation Maeght
1959 ?

without any conditions and with new, virgin conceptions.'

Thus, the architect collaborated with artists from the very beginning, an experience further enhanced by the idyllic Mediterranean setting. On this occasion the commission and the intellectual interest coincided in such an obvious way that one is immediately struck by Sert's good fortune: he was being handed a golden opportunity to achieve the most important intellectual synthesis of his life. He was to design a museum, a place in which the visual arts would be gathered, and where dialogue between the works would be inevitable. It is therefore not surprising that he approached the project on tiptoe, and that the earliest sketch found represents the territory shared by the neighbours of the future museum. The first thing to be done was to inscribe the building within the landscape using the rules that time had imposed on a local Mediterranean architecture without architects.

These rules are transmitted through the silhouette of the buildings in the town of Saint-Paul, which Sert took as his first reference and which would be a definitive element in the final shape of the Fondation Maeght. The next sketch seems to confirm this: a building with volumetric discontinuities in all directions seems the extension of the representation of Saint-Paul in the previous sketch. Naturally, the 'parti' of this model led to an isolated complex of buildings whose sense of unity is derived from the design of its layout and from the patio element, interpreted in different ways.

Thus the final result should be understood as an effort to reassemble the project after this initial dispersion, into two main buildings to which others could be added should the Foundation's needs increase over time. This idea of regrouping, however, seeks to dissipate itself through the treatment given to the topmost part of the buildings: the two great dominating forms of the *impluvia*, probably a Mediterranized recollection of Le Corbusier's building for the Governor's Palace in Chandigarh. Miró's *Pájaro de la Torre* or his *Gran Arco*, have the same aspiration: to make volatile the mass of the architecture, to allow it to take off from the ground in an ideal dematerialization both of itself – built with powerful stones from the area or with rustic bricks baked on firewood in the local factory of Clausones – and of the earth. The building must find its ultimate puri-

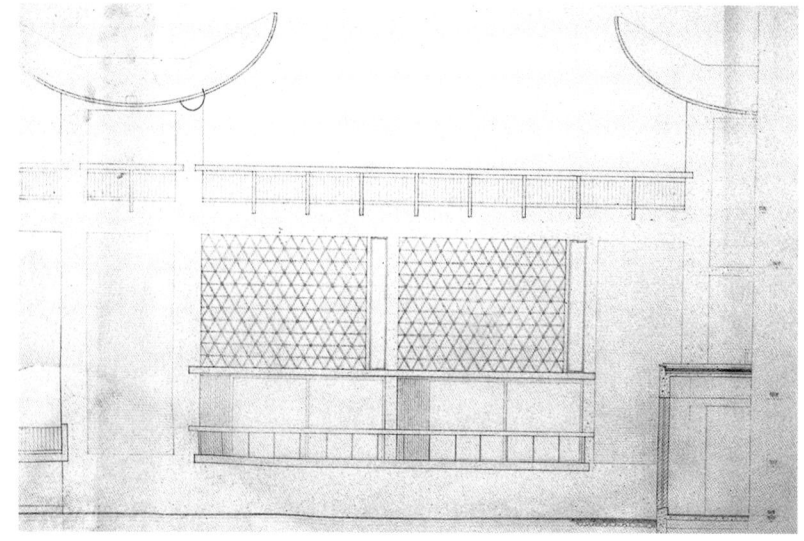

Maeght
Foundation,
a courtyard
and an exhibition
room.

ty in its fusion with the sky, just as it had since the earliest architecture, the *menhir*, in which man placed his trust due to its ability to elevate itself from the ground, reaching into the firmament that controlled his destiny, which had power over him, and which he did not understand but wished to appease. Once again the ancestors of form had been summoned by Sert

and his friends to rediscover their karmic debt, but this time the task was undertaken by many artists whose knowledge and power contributed to its fulfilment.

Sert's comment concerning the intrinsic value of bricks seems to confirm this: 'The brick, neither light nor dark, of a toasted, rosy hue varied by the fire, suits the tranquillity of the courtyards. Moreover, employed in rectangular surfaces between the pillars and beams of concrete, it sustains the reality of the wall by giving consistency to its surface, and body to its elevation.' Varying according to the intensity of the fire, the brick makes one aware of the patio's evocation of emotional stability. Within the concrete structures it increases the gravity of the wall that struggles to elevate itself.

The air freely circulating through nature and architecture; the water in the pools, the earth

Views of the
patio-terrace with
the sculptures
of Alberto
Giacometti.

261

Sert working on the Maeght Foundation project and chatting with Joan Miró and Pablo Picasso (SC).

represented by bricks and stones, the fire with which the artisan Artigas' ceramic pieces were made before Miró set them in the walls: the four elements make a primeval statement in this sanctuary of art. Tal-Coat, Arp, Kriche, Calder, Chagall, Hepworth, Chillida, Giacometti, Braque: all converge in Miró's labyrinth, next to which is the library, which could be interpreted as the final stage in this initiation into the magical world of art, after taking in the patios, the different materials used, and the continuing dialogue between the arts.

Modern architectural culture and its remote origins, which can be traced back to the Cretan palace of Knossos, seek a joyous encounter. Dedalus, the Minotaur and Ariadne again size each other up. It is not by chance that in 1957, the same year that he started to have frequent contact with Aimé Maeght, Sert participated in a movie by Hans Richter called *A Chess Sonata for Film*, which was filmed in Sert's Long Island house and featured other cast members such as Marcel Duchamp, Paul Lester, Frederick Kiesler, Jacqueline Matisse, Yves Tanguy, Richard Huelsenbeck, Max Ernst, Jean Cocteau and others. In the eighth improvisation, Sert, in the role of a bullfighter, lost against the bull and died, with Lester acting as arbiter within the surrealistic logic of the scene. Dedalus too, lost his life at the hands of the Minotaur because Ariadne did not get there in time to give him the spool of thread he needed to find his way through the labyrinth. In Saint-Paul-de-Vence things went

differently: Ariadne gave her knowledge without heeding the sacrifice involved, a knowledge that Dedalus, always holding her hand and without running any risks, ordered and built. The Minotaur was not around. Without an enemy to defeat, so much effort seems useless: the

Hans Richter, *A Chess Sonata for Film*, 1957.

ancestors cannot be exhausted in a gesture, they must continue to be present to emphasize human futility, witness its limited strength, and continue keeping vigil.

We are familiar by now with Miró's perseverance. It took him twenty years to make his dream come true, but just when it had become a reality, on 2 March 1958, he began to see another dream taking shape. In a letter to the architect, after having looked at the publication of some works by Sert in the magazines he had sent him, Miró wrote: 'All of your work looks wonderful. That makes my desire to work with you on a large-scale project even greater; I hope we will do so some day.'

The long-awaited day took more than ten years to arrive. We know this from their correspondence, housed in the Sert Collection, which was renewed on 1 October 1968, when Miró sent Sert a possible outline for the programme of the future Miró Foundation in Barcelona: 'I have been thinking in a very clear-headed way on everything we have pro-

jected doing in Barcelona. Before coming I'll look at the sites to see which one seems the most appropriate. They are very enthusiastic about the museum and this is what requires greatest reflection and study.'[112]

Miró then listed the elements that he wanted the programme to include. Concerning the copper sheets or the wooden or stone bases for exhibiting his graphic work, he said: 'They are elements which have to be taken into account to make lively halls for my engravings. Since it is impossible for everything to be exhibited at once, we must study how to exhibit in such a way as to be able to vary.' There was to be a library as well as a place for lectures and slide shows, concerts and theatre. Miró then commented on his own work: 'My painting is becoming mural both in its conception and size. Many of them are conceived as triptychs, which will have to be grouped together to enhance their meaning and increase the concentration of the spectator. Others are treated in a very detailed, precious way and are of a small

Miró Foundation, Barcelona, 1958, general plan.

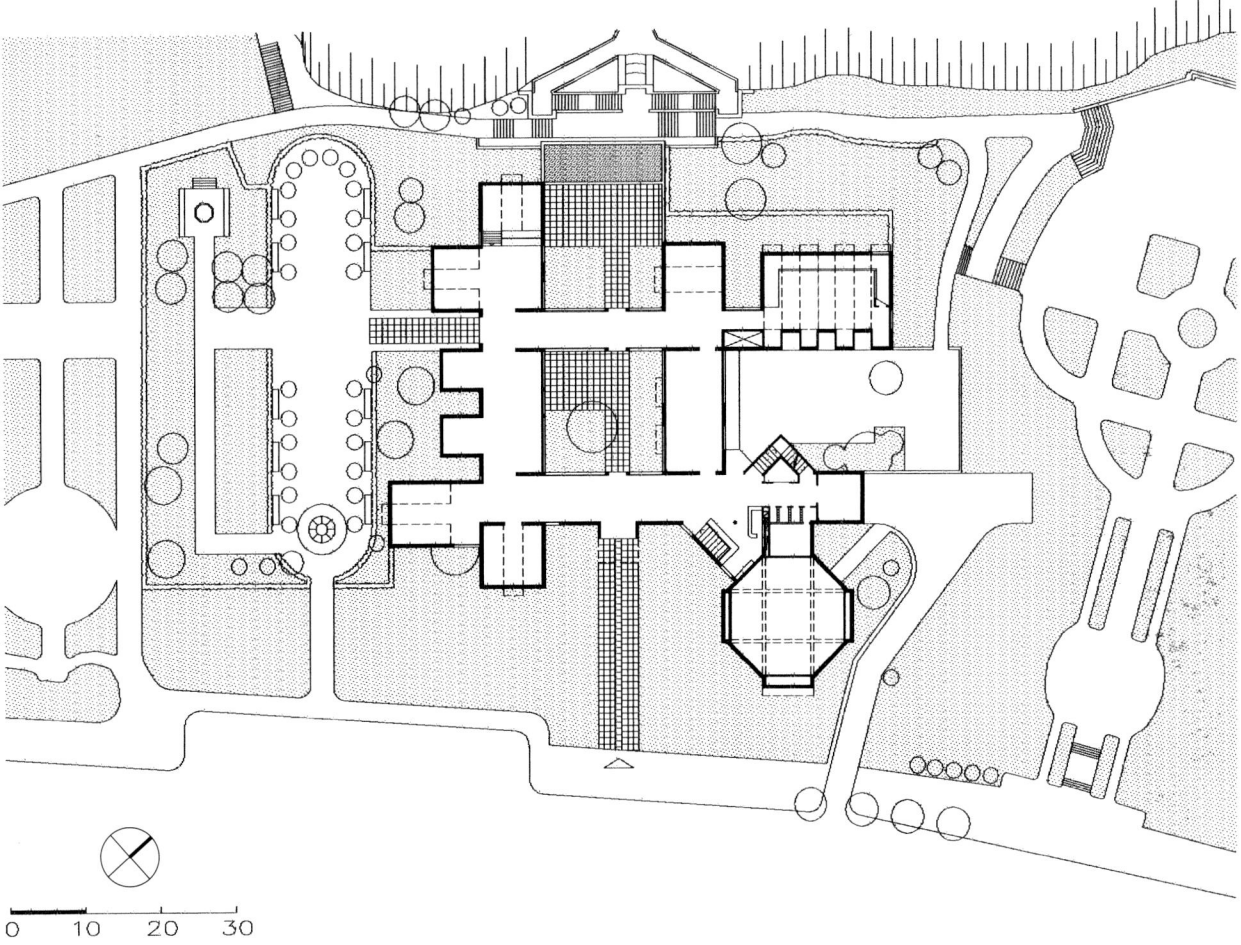

0   10   20   30

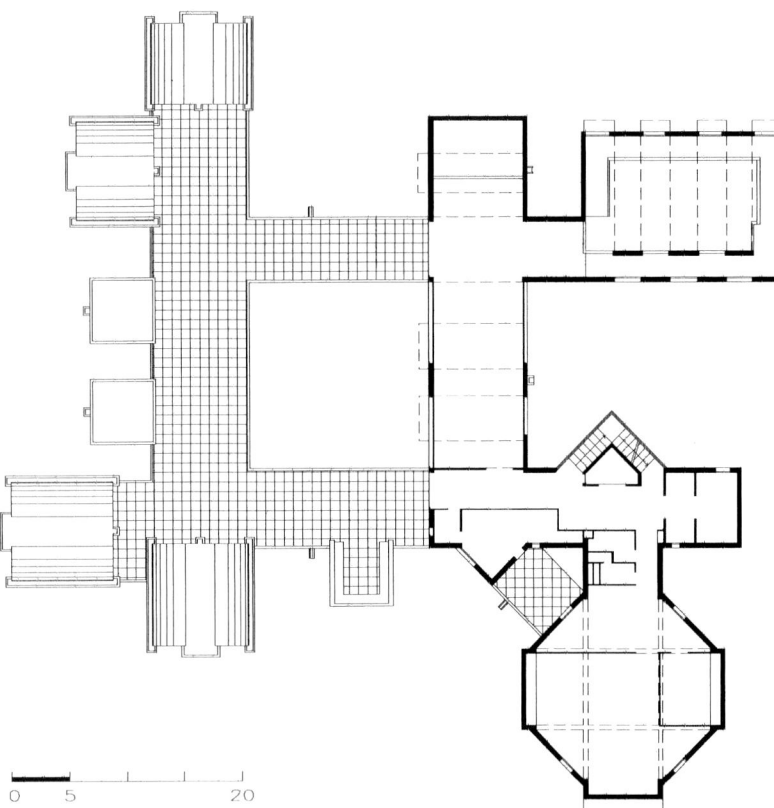

Miró Foundation, plan and sections.

size.' He also pointed out the need for 'a hall or showcases for mounted objects'. He recommended a visit 'to the Matisse museum set up by his sons in the environs of Nice, which could help you to come up with some good ideas.' He even foresaw the issue of future enlargement: 'Prats has also spoken to me about your idea of being able to enlarge the Museum depending on whether it got to be necessary; I think that is great, considering that none of us know how many more years we'll be working.' The recollection of the Saint-Paul-de-Vence experience probably pushed Miró to say: 'I think it would be good to consider places in which the architecture or the landscape require accompaniment: ceramic, mosaic, stained-glass windows or sculptures.'

Sert seems to have met his friend's desires very quickly through a first sketch of the building since in the next letter that Miró sent him on 27 November, we read: 'The suggestions you make for the future museum are fantastic, full of great possibilities of development.' Some time later, on 28 February 1970, the project had apparently greatly advanced, as Sert informed Miró: 'Regarding the definitive plans of the CEAC [Centre for the Study of Contemporary Art], as soon as we have the permit from the Town Council

we will start to work … [I]n a few months we could begin construction work, in six months' time at the very least.' Other news tell us that in July 1973 work was going ahead. The building was opened to the public on 10 June 1975.

If we look at some of the preliminary studies we can see that there was no hesitation as to what the project should look like: the overall idea was that of a fortress, a building that was closed and that had watchtowers oriented towards the exterior. From a courtyard, the complex was to overlook the city thanks to its privileged position.

The first sketches, drawn with a red marker, partially reveal this. In the next sketch, the patio is hermetically closed: now the building has become a monastery. Five sentinels, volumes that hold exhibition halls, with the skylights that had been Sert's trademark ever since the Braque house, stepped in groups of three and two respectively, guard the main entrance from the city. Likewise, in the rear part two towers accommodating the stairs and showing aggressive pointed finials, dramatized by the sloping terrain they face, are projected against the backdrop of Barcelona. From the initial timid opening with the open courtyard we have gone to a completely closed building. Moreover, a square-plan volume veered at a 45-degree angle acts as a watchtower to warn of possible dangers from afar.

We should ask ourselves what occasioned

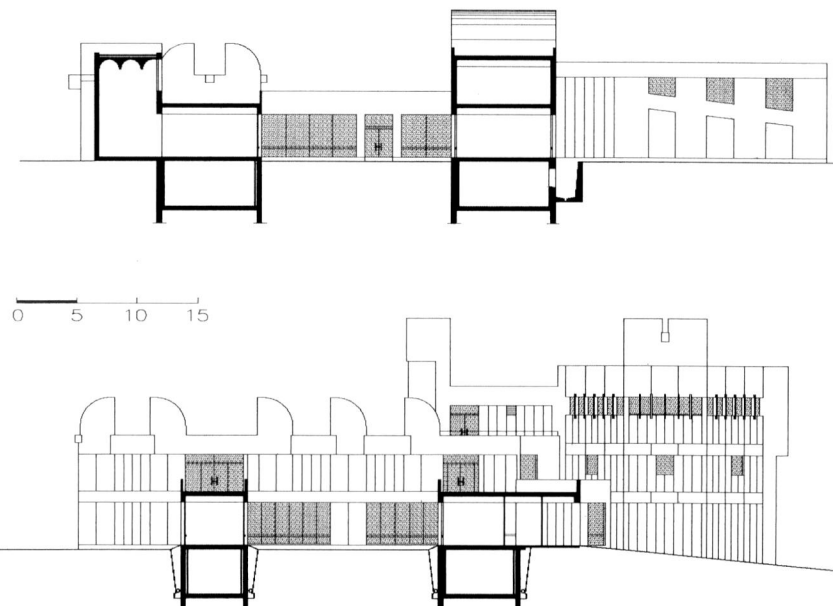

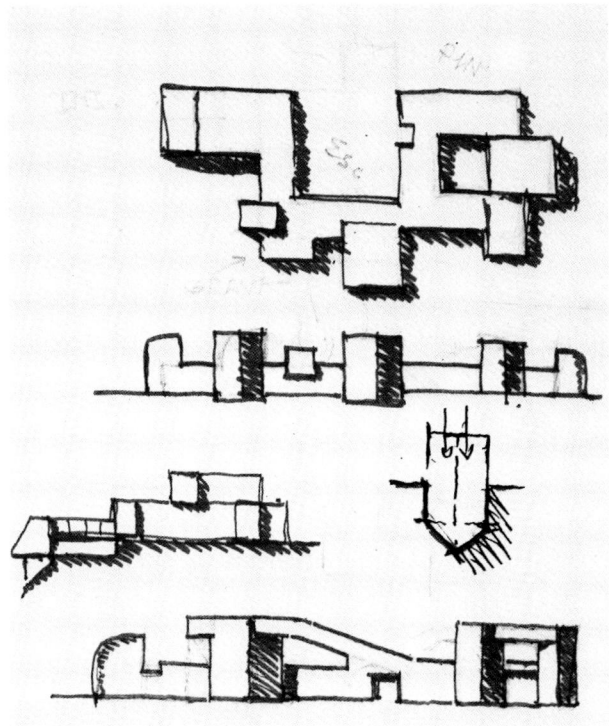

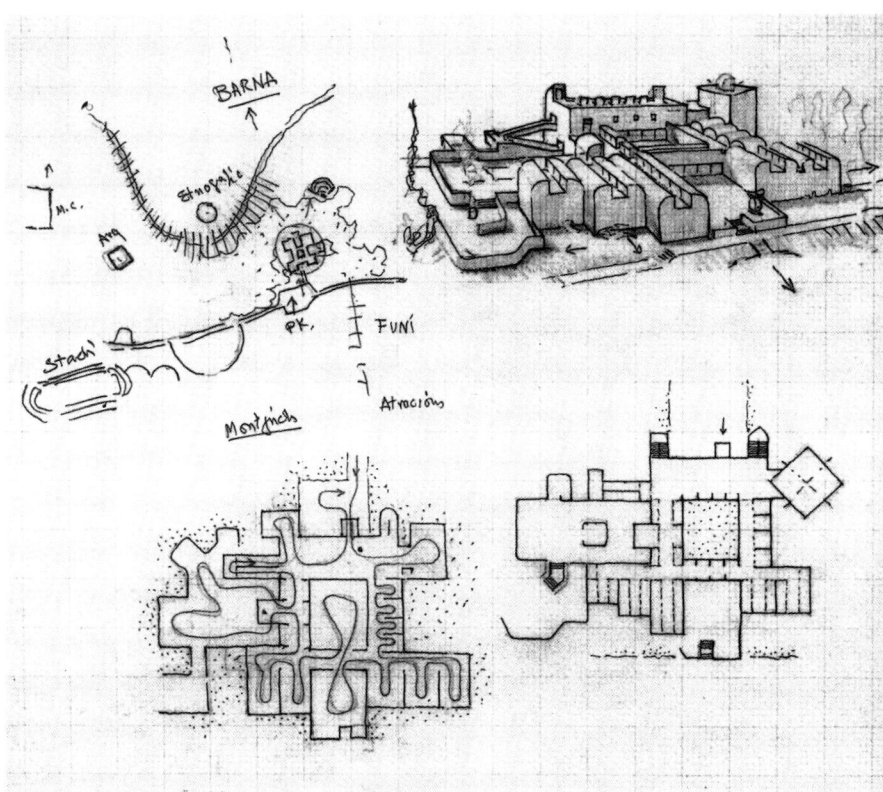

this seeming mistrust towards the city. The world of Sertian recollections can provide some initial answers to this question. The building, located on Montjuïc, overlooks the city that Sert had endeavoured to develop in a new way – surroundings for which he could feel little respect. The sad Barcelona, which its mayor José María de Porcioles had led to its most de-

Miró Foundation, sketches.

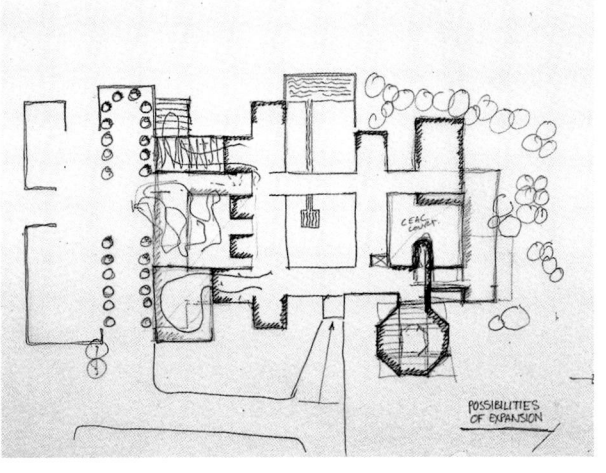

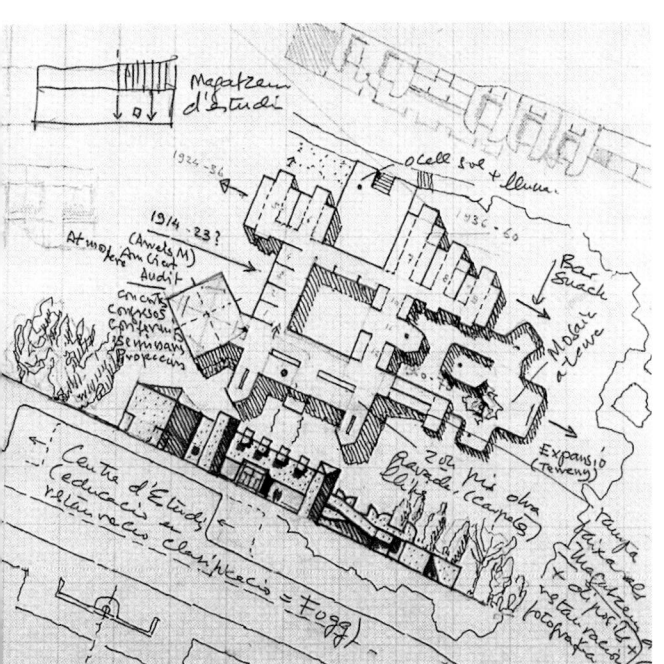

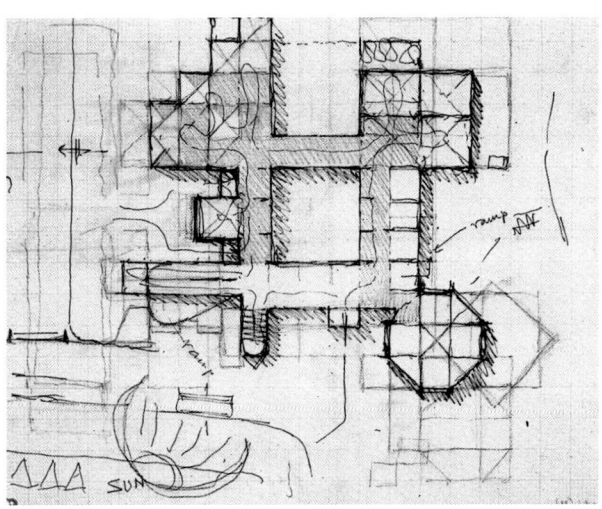

Miró Foundation, model of the complex (SC).

plorable state of urban degradation, could not be to the liking of Sert or any other sensitive person with a minimal capacity for analysis. The mountain that had housed the memorable International Exhibition of 1929, whose buildings were to disappear some time ago, continued exhibiting an architecture that Sert had hated as a young man and still hated now. As we know, in the year of its inaugural splendour our architect and his friends had demonstrated their opposition to it, so why not do so again?

The memory of the challenges posed by the Macià Plan and the continued presence of academicist architectures must have wounded Sert's cultural sensitivity. Moreover, we could allude to the country's political situation at a time when General Franco's Fascist regime was caving in, a period of especially cruel oppression, and by doing so we face another type of recollection. Now Sert's sense of melancholy could be manifested with greater feeling, mixed with rage. The shape of the monastery, a closed building that during certain periods in the Middle Ages represented and treasured the only possibility of culture, is a good starting point: guarding Miró's art from the city that now welcomed him was a way of demonstrating a historical rejection of the cultural poverty shown by the Barcelona of Franco's times. Making this rejection patent, Sert declared during the proclamation that opened the 1978 festivities in honour of Mercé, the patron saint of Barcelona: 'May the patron saint of the city free us from the subtle enslavement of the establishment, which has proven itself incapable

of using in an intelligent fashion that which nature has given us with so much generosity: sea, mountain and a privileged climate, for the benefit of all Barcelonians.'

Miró generously donated some of his work to the foundation and Sert built an appropriate building for it. The city offered the grounds for the museum on a propitious site, again sanctified during Franco's regime by the events held there during the International Eucharistic Congress of 1951.[113] Montjuïc, a location used for sports events and to house museums, was vindicated by progressive sectors of the population in the urban struggles that occurred towards the end of Franco's rule. It was a mountain that had won the affection of the masses of the city, who at the time had no other outdoor place in which to walk. The political leaders of the city were attempting an enterprise that Sert, at least initially, meant to foil: that of harbouring a modern building that would hold the work of a modern artist and that would be a centre for the study of modern art, but without making any historical amends to accomplish this.

In the letter of October 1968 that we mentioned previously, Miró wrote: 'Think about the citizen of tomorrow.' Perhaps he was not as radically sensitized as the architect. We cannot be sure that this advice softened Sert's project, but what is certain is that the final plan substantially differs from the second sketch. The obsession

Miró Foundation, exterior view.

Miró Foundation,
views
of the exterior.

with presenting a closed project has somehow diminished, although a number of other characteristics still remain. Now the central courtyard, surrounded by a succession of exhibition rooms laid out around it, which help organize the visitor's tour of Miró's work, opened itself to Barcelona through a second courtyard that looks towards the city. Nevertheless, this patio ends with a pool and a sculpture, or in other words, with a mirror on the ground, an abyss, thus making evident the reluctance to participate in the urban chaos of Barcelona, although the mechanism chosen is markedly poetic.

To the right of the main entrance an octagonal-plan tower accommodating the library, the auditorium and the administration office is what remains of the previous watchtower, except that this time it is on the main street,

which the Foundation faces. Bruno Zevi has defined the ancestral and Catalan origins of this form, tracing them back to the Monastery of Poblet and to Santa Maria del Mar.[114] These fundamental forms, inextricably linked to Catalan culture, speak of another type of resistance: that put up by Catalan culture against the determined attacks of Franco, which it had suffered since 1939.

Flanking the entrance, the semi-circular skylights, a reference to previous works, represent a defiance of the passing of time for an architect who had been forced to abandon his city for political reasons. In return he wished to reassert himself as the melancholic continuator of crucial elements that he had never forgotten.

Naturally this was not the right setting to offer an endless range of materials, textures and

Miró Foundation, views of the interior.

colours; this had come to an end with the Maeght Foundation, where everything was purity and harmony in a world suggesting memory, cosmos and landscape. Here the idea was to show an austerity born from a joyless reaction to history, biographical criteria and the suffering caused by the distance of the exile. The proposal of only one material – reinforced concrete, which acts as the enclosure walling and also has structural functions – is a way with which to bring out the hardness of this material as well as returning to the constructional 'transparency' that we saw in the facades of the Dispensary for Tuberculosis. It is also a way to demonstrate his command of the construction trade, a skill he had learned in the United States (in many buildings that we will analyze later). In other words, he wished to show that he was returning with a greater technological and expressive capacity and to offer them to the city in which he had taken his first professional steps.

The hermeticism of the Miró Foundation greatly contrasts with the very open plan of a building dedicated to a function that seems to require the opposite treatment: the Convent of Carmel de la Paix built in Mazille, France for the Carmelite order, and whose shape was conceived between 1968 and 1972, when Sert was still working on the his friend's museum.[115] Set in rural surroundings, it owes nothing to what surrounds it, and can therefore establish an unconditional rapport with the landscape – a mountain slope. Sert grouped the different functions of the compound and built volumes for

them, which he scattered on the mountainside, clearly indicating which element should overlook the rest. This function of watchtower was carried out by the church of the community, laid out in an octagonal-plan building (as was the case with the library of the Miró Foundation), which became a volume of considerable height, finished with Sert's trademark skylight (which he would also use in the roof of his studio, on the top floor of an office building in Cambridge).

Open versus closed – the excessive difference between these two plans and their voluntary typological subversion makes more patent the meaning of the Miró Foundation, although

Convent of Carmel de la Paix, Mazille, 1968, volumetric survey of the complex (SC).

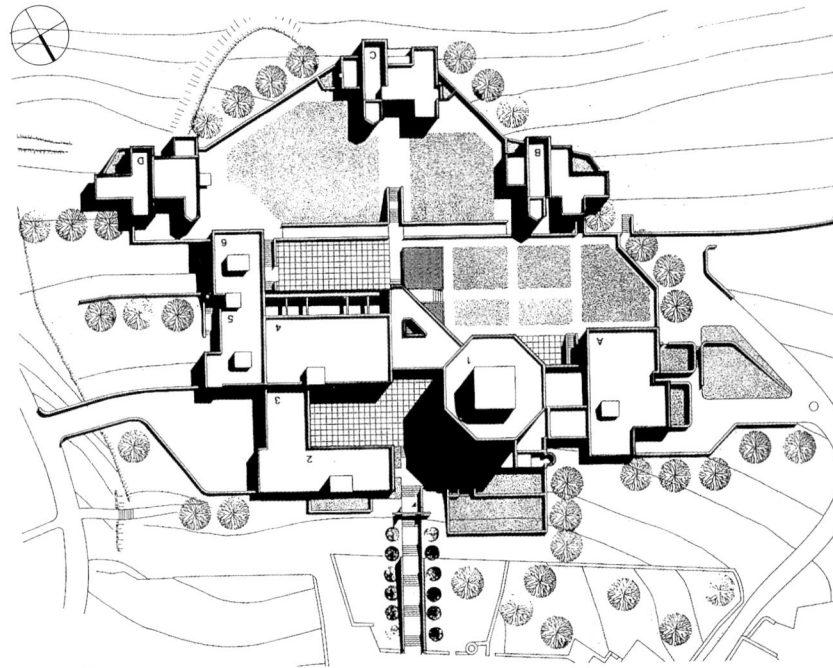

the interpretations expressed here are by no means exhaustive. In Sert's mind there were too many cross-references to the architectures he had known and conceived in the United States. We will have to wait until we review his work on the other side of the Atlantic to offer a conclusive interpretation of the project in Montjuïc.

[84] With a cover and jacket designed by Miró, it was published by Frederick A. Praeger, New York, and by Gerd Hatje, Stuttgart.

[85] Ibid., p. 173.

[86] SC C 2E.

[87] 'Skira saw the dummy some time ago and he proposed making an edition himself to Sert. Sert told him that he would have to get in contact with us to establish the conditions and the contract.' The letters that went back and forth between Sweeney and Sert during March 1950 reveal some details of the negotiations concerning the publication, as well as comments on Gaudí's assistant, Jujol, which were offered by the painter Salvador Dalí, whose hypotheses were included in the rough draft of the book. SC C 2E.

[88] Taken from a text by Antonio Pizza called 'En torno a Franco Purini y su arquitectura didáctica'. This is the introduction to Purini's work 'La arquitectura didáctica', *Arquitecturas*, no. 15, Murcia, 1984. Some of Pizza's reflections on melancholy and its distinctions from nostalgia and tragedy have been drawn upon in this text.

[89] 'It is likely that Gaudí's vision of form was also deeply conditioned by the clear light of the Mediterranean coast, which accentuates the three-dimensional values and sculptural quality of all objects it falls upon. The landscape, too, of Tarragona countryside, its red earth, the shadowed furrows of its ploughed fields, the vines and olive trees with sculptural, contoured trunks, the dark leaves of the carob trees, the terraced hillsides and rounded hilltops – all must have helped to develop his plastic sense of form and his love of colour, just as this same countryside was later to influence the painting of Gaudí's Catalan fellow and admirer, Joan Miró.' op. cit., p. 55. Sert also wrote another text on Gaudí's work: 'The Crypt of the Guell Colony Chapel', of which there is a typewritten copy in SC D9.

[90] On page 15 of Sartoris' book we read: 'Functional architecture's order and Mediterranean atmosphere can only be explained by the transmission of a generous injection of creative sap originating on the other side of the Alps, in Italy, and whose consequent intense ramifications from this transfusion have covered the world gradually, step by step, methodically, year after year.'
A good book that summarizes Sartoris' activity is Alberto Abriani and Jacques Gubler (eds.), *Novanta gioelli*, Mazzotta, Milan, 1992.

[91] An interpretation of Pevsner's manoeuvres regarding Morris and Gropius can be found in Mario Manieri Elia, 'Il complesso d'Enea. Nikolaus Pevsner e la storiografia della continuità', *Casabella*, no. 423, March 1977.

[92] Blanton, op. cit., p. 576.

[93] SC E 63. Sert and Lester Wiener participated, along with Hans Hofmann, in the exhibition 'The Muralist and the Modern Architect', held from 3 to 23 October 1950 at the Kootz Gallery of New York, 600 Madison Avenue. PLWA, Incoming Correspondence, Box 14.

[94] SC E 64. Miró's workshop in Mallorca has appeared in: *Aujourd'hui art et architecture*, no. 15, Paris, December 1957; *Cuadernos de Arquitectura y Urbanismo*, no. 33, Barcelona, 1958; *Architectural Record*, January 1958. The most extensive compilation of original documentary material including an interpretation of this work is found in *D'A Revista del COAB*, no. 5–6, Palma de Mallorca, 1990.

[95] In the one from 27 October 1954, along with condolences on the death of his mother, we read,: 'Also hoping to receive your letter with more details on the plans; these I have liked tremendously, we have also looked at them with Joan and we believe that I will have a wonderful workshop.' SC E 64. On 5 November Miró wrote: 'I have looked very carefully at the workshop plan on the terrain; I find it is very well designed and am looking forward to working in it. Enric has also seen it and has got a very clear idea of it, although he is worried about the solution of the vaults, he fears that being so thin and of cement they will not offer much insulation against the heat and cold. I am sure you must have foreseen that so you could give him some technical explanations. The possibility of seeing the workshop space and the paintings from the balcony seems an excellent idea. Looking at the plan I have not understood clearly whether that is also how one sees it when going inside the storage room. If that is so, and taking into account that there will be paintings that will be resting and that I will prefer not to see, and there will be dismantled frames and other materials, don't you think it would be better to place this part of the building in such a way as for me not to see inside it when I go down to work so I can concentrate my vision on the big workshop?'. SC E 64.

[96] Jaume Freixa maintains that the project for the Miró Workshop was carried out in a professional office that Sert opened in Cambridge in September 1954 on top of the garage of the house he rented on Brattle Street, where Zalewski, Bastlund, Maki and Howes worked. *D'A Revista del COAB*, no. 5–6, cit., pp. 46–47.

[97] SC E 65.

[98] The first and third texts mentioned, typewritten and housed in the Sert Collection, are also published in: *J.L. Sert y el Mediterráneo*, op. cit., pp. 220–22. The second, 'Can Patios Make Cities?' was published in *Architectural Forum*, no. 8, 1955.

[99] From 'Can Patios Make Cities?'.

[100] 'The Integration of the Visual Arts', SC D 73. It is a typewritten text with the following annotation: 'Cut version of Dean Sert's remarks made at the Symposium at Bennington College last May', 27 June 1955.

[101] José Luis Sert, 'De Divina Proportione', typewritten copy housed in Cambridge, SC D 56. In Sert's library there was a Spanish edition of Luca Pacioli's work by the Argentinean publishing house Losada, Buenos Aires, 1946.

[102] José Luis Sert, 'The Scope of Architecture'. This typewritten copy is the text of a lecture given by the architect at the Graduate School of Design on 17 March 1953, SC D 87. There is another text with similar content for a lecture given on 12 May 1953 at the Boston Society of Architects: 'The Human Factor in Architecture and City Planning', SC D 69.

[103] 'The Changing Philosophy of Modern Architecture', Sert's contribution to the AIA Symposium of 16 June 1954, SC D 54, partly published in *Architectural Record*, August 1954, p. 181.

[104] 'The Architect and the City', lecture given at the Detroit Institute of Arts on 17 November 1954, published by the Michigan Society of Architects, SC D 45.

[105] Some houses with patios that were built in the United States were published in American magazines of the 1950s. See *Architectural Forum*, October 1948, pp. 101–03 (house of the architect Ralph S. Twitchell assisted by Paul Rudolph); *Architectural Forum*, April 1950, pp. 168–71. In the two issues of *Architectural Forum* from May and July 1951 we find Pietro Belluschi's houses with patios. The house of the Eames couple in Santa Monica, which was published in the September 1950 issue of *Architectural Forum*, can also be considered a house with a patio.

[106] *House & Home*, October 1958, p. 87.

[107] See *Architectural Record*, June 1951, p. 162 and following pages.

[108] From an interview in the *Boston Globe*, of which there is a photocopy in the Cambridge archive. The articles in which Sert's Cambridge house appeared are: 'Cloistered Privacy on a Busy Street', *House & Home*, October 1958; 'La maison de J.LL. Sert', *L'Oeil*, no. 50, 1959; 'Una casa con patio', *Arquitectura*, Madrid, 1960, and 'Wohnhaus in Cambridge', *Baumeister*, no. 1, 1961.

[109] The documentary material on the house for Braque is kept in the Sert Collection, SC B 15a–15m.

[110] *La Fondation Marguerite et Aimé Maeght*, Maeght Editeur, 1993, p. 29. A sketchy biography of Aimé Maeght's personal life and professional career is found in this book. The plans of this building are kept in the Sert Collection, SC B 39b–39z.

[111] SC E 65.

[112] The correspondence between Sert and Miró on the Miró Foundation, Barcelona, are in the Sert Collection in Cambridge, SC E 68 and E 69. The building plans are in the same archive, SC B 18a–18z.

[113] Josep M. Rovira, *La Arquitectura Catalana de la Modernidad*, op. cit., pp. 222–45. We do not know why Sert refused to have a selection of his writings published in Barcelona. It may have been his strange love-hate relationship with the city; what is certain is that there are two letters in the Sert Collection from the architect Oriol Bohigas, one of 15 December 1964, and the other of 29 November of the following year, through which we become aware that Sert had not sent to Edicions 62 the texts which Bohigas had asked him for. SC E 10.

[114] Bruno Zevi, *Arquitectura de Sert en la Fundación Miró*, Polígrafa, Barcelona, 1977.

[115] The documentary material concerning the project for the Convent of Carmel de la Paix is found in the Sert Collection, SC B 24 zz.

Return to Ibiza

The 1950s marked the return to Ibiza of many of the survivors from the 1930s who yearned for the days gone by on the island. It was also the decade of the arrival of many newcomers who were attracted to the island by the stories that were circulating in intellectual spheres all over the world.[116]

Broner returned to Ibiza in February 1952, after undertaking a number of different jobs, including working with Richard Neutra in Los Angeles. He returned to the States in 1956 in order to retain his American citizenship, and after a sojourn in England, returned to the island in March 1959 and settled there permanently. He soon set up the Grupo Ibiza 59, along with other artists, to develop his aesthetic interests. The first projects of his re-encounter with the island date from the following year and are similar in outlook to his previous work, although we should not underrate the influence of his experiences in the US (this subject goes beyond the scope of this work, however).[117]

In 1958 Germán Rodríguez Arias also came back to the island from his exile in Chile, and never left it again, developing the rest of his professional work there until his death in 1987.[118]

We do not know exactly when Sert decided to return to Ibiza, but what is certain from his correspondence is that his visits to Catalonia became regular at the end of the 1950s. A date that is incontrovertible and that therefore helps to orient us is that of a plan for Sert's first house on the island, addressed to the stock company Inversiones Inmobiliaras, S.A. In the heading is the date 'May 1960'.

It might be helpful to consider the reasons that motivated the return to the island of its modern 'inventors'. The last years of the 1950s saw the revision of many of the ideas and enterprises of the so-called modern movement.

As president of CIAM, Sert himself had experienced the progressive alienation manifested by the younger generations (although this was more a vindication of a space of their own than anything else) concerning the postulates of the functional city, and had observed their unwillingness to write a Charter of Habitat, etc. If we add to this his condition of exile – a golden exile, for he had been both Dean and Chairman of the prestigious GSD in Cambridge since 1953 and moreover had a professional office with a considerable turnover of commissions – we get a clearer picture of the multiple facets that characterized his uprooting. After the disappearance of CIAM, Sert no longer enjoyed a prominent position in the international scene; he had worked on a series of projects for Latin American cities that had not turned out well, and the Town Planning Associates partnership that he, Lester Wiener and Paul Schulz had formed in the 1940s was liquidated in 1959.

The Mediterranean again summoned him, this time with no need for ideological manifestos, but rather as an echo calling for his presence, calling him back to his origins, requiring through demanding commissions that he come up with new answers.

Those who have attempted to provide plausible explanations for Broner's return have based their point of view on the interpretations offered by his companion Gisela, who recalled his obsession with what he termed 'going back to his roots': 'And in that Europe, Erwin used to explain to Gisela, there was the Mediterranean, from which sprang forth a whole new way of understanding life; and in that Mediterranean, there was a small island called Ibiza, in which, according to Gisela's recollections, Erwin always used to say that he had felt free for the first time in his life.'[119]

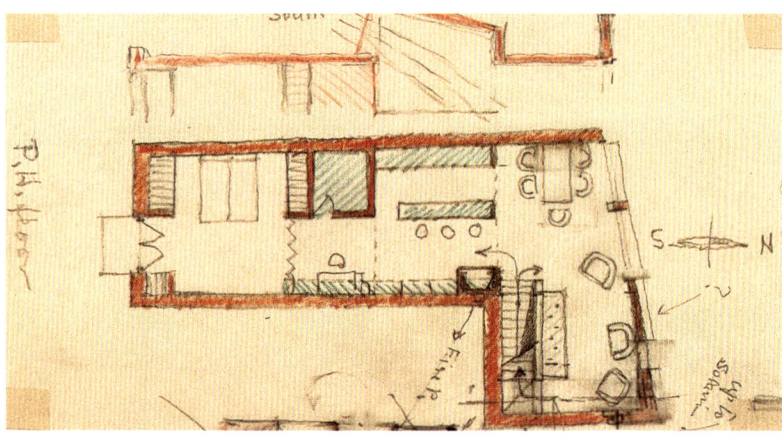

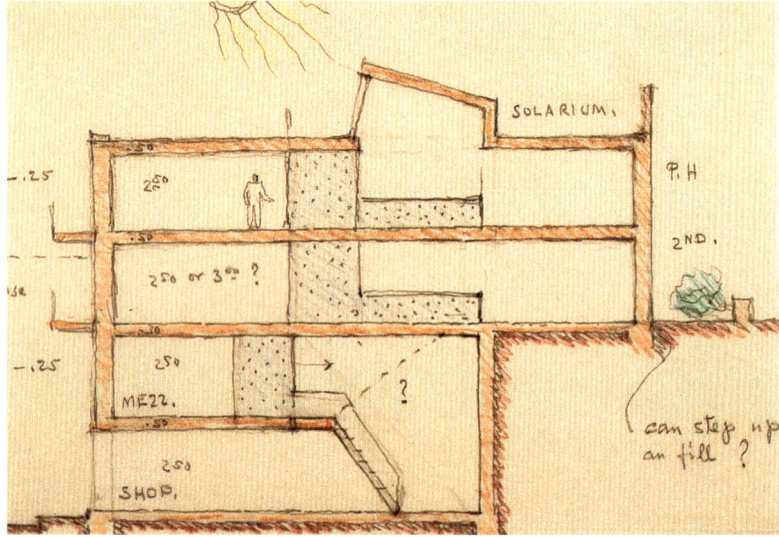

Sert's house
in Dalt Vila, Ibiza,
1960–61,
sketches of the
plan and section
(SC).

both places at the same time, and the possibility of a respite, in life and in death, after a career of ups and downs. When he was almost sixty years old, and despite the fact that his greatest American projects were still to come, Sert saw before him a horizon of rest in Ibiza.

In May 1960 he finished the design for his first residence in the oldest part of the capital, Dalt Vila. It was a small building between party walls, where he lived on the two upper floors above his friend, the carpenter Vicarías, whose home and workshop occupied the ground floor and the mezzanine. In the section of the building, as was also the case with the house in Cambridge, one observes the presence of a skylight whose illumination combines with the sunlight filtering in from the windows on the rear facade, which afford a view of the Mediterranean. In the corner of the flat roof, two false windows have been put in to frame the landscape, whose contemplation at the time must still have been a pleasure and from which one could see all the way to Punta Martinet. This was undoubtedly an observatory, a place from which to take off in search of new horizons.

In Ibiza, then, it was possible to feel liberated, especially for those who had been living in the States at the end of the 1950s. However, this freedom was annonced by the impending tourist boom, which had not yet begun, but was being annonced by the opening of the airport in 1958. Moreover, it was a freedom that one must view with mistrust considering the political situation of Spain under Franco at the time. It was not a freedom that implied collective values, but an illusion created by distancing oneself from the epicentre of power, which allowed artists to believe in the possibility of living in a pleasurable oasis that was isolated from the rest of the world.

Sert never liked the Spain of Franco, and would never have allowed himself any conciliatory gesture towards the regime. However, he liked even less the freezing winters of Cambridge, as is seen in numerous letters in the Sert Collection in which he expressed this aversion. Ibiza offered the possibility of fleeing from

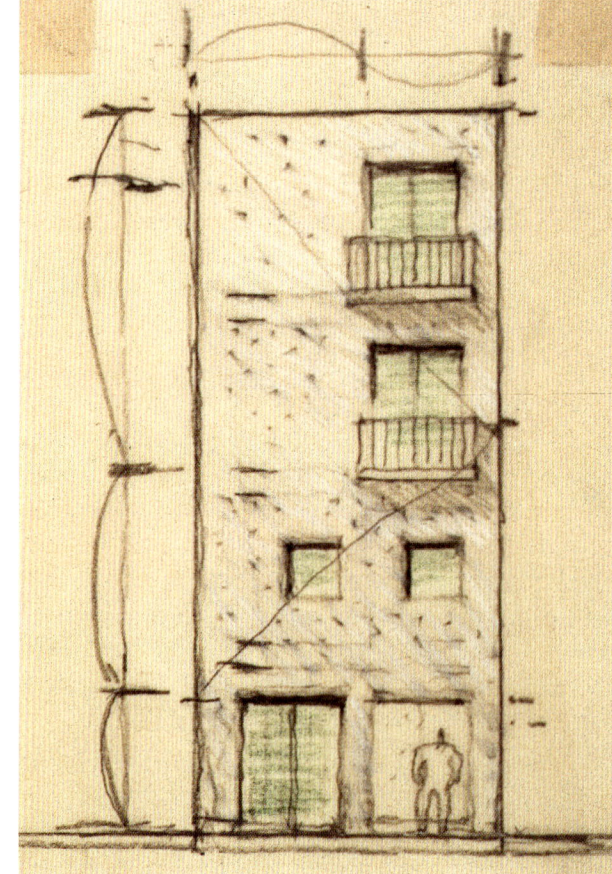

The house in Dalt
Vila, sketch
of the elevation
(SC).

modification or reform may be carried out without the approval of the housing development's board of directors, and without the necessary previous authorizations required by the administration.' Thus, the property developers controlled any building that could be constructed there. It is not surprising, therefore, that the majority of the buildings were designed by Sert and monitored by his faithful collaborators, Arias, Antoni Ferrán and Sixte Illescas.

The buildings had a controlled image clearly laid out in the guidelines in section D of the same statutes: 'Exteriors of Ibizan architecture only in white and ochre colours. Absence of artificial veneers of stone or similar materials. Prohibition of any type of railings that can be seen from the outside ... There will be no boundary walls marking the plots of land, only hedges without any artificial stakes being allowed for this purpose ... Individual TV antennas will not be allowed without previous authorization from the Directing Board ... The exterior of the buildings will be maintained with natural decorum.'

Sert's house in Dalt Vila, view of the exterior.

Cap Martinet, a steep promontory on which grew a few almond and carob trees, rises in front of the old city of Ibiza. From this vantage point one has the best view of the city, and thus it must have quickly become a coveted spot. In a letter from Moncha to Joan Prats of 9 October 1963, we come to understand this clearly: 'I am waiting for Germán's definitive plan to send you a copy of the housing development in Punta Martinet.'[120] This means that very shortly after arriving, and despite his only intermittent stays on the island due to his activities in the United States, Sert had almost finished drafting the proposal for the complex. The undated Statutes of Urbanización Can Pep Simó (Can Pep Simó Housing Development), set up by Sert with the active participation of his old friend Germán Rodríguez Arias, and with the fundamental financing of Joaquín Font Gorina, define its basic parameters. Among these, the most interesting are those that mention aspects of the complex's design. Article 17, section C, for example, states: 'For the sake of preserving the aesthetic unity of the housing development, no construction work,

Sert's house in Dalt Vila, views of the interior.

Can Pep Simó development, Ibiza, general plan.

0 10   50

1.	CASA JUTTA	1965
2.	CASA GOMIS	1967
3.	CASA ZAO WO KI	1967
4.	CASA VALLS	1968
5.	CASA J. LL. SERT	1968
6.	CASA F. SERT	1968
7.	APARTAMENTOS "ELS FUMERALS"	1970
8.	CASA DODANE (E. BRONER)	1971

In Chapter Two of the Regulating Ordinances of the Housing Development, which are also undated, they reiterate these aspects: 'On the exterior the architecture will be Ibizan and the exterior colours will be solely and exclusively white or ochre … No work may be carried out that may affect the building's exterior aspect, without the express authorization of the Property Development Company … (If such work were carried out without the Company's consent the Society then has the written authorization from that moment to gain access to the plot and carry out all the necessary works to return the building to its original aspect, and the owner of the plot will have to cover all expenses for the work carried out.)'

Despite the fact that we are dealing with what is conventionally understood to be a planned development, or a partial plan, we cannot say that its urban aspects are of any great relevance, aside from the emphasis on not using boundary walls or fences to define each separate property. The simple opening of roads in search of the best slope was the beginning of an 'illegal, amicable and common property development', which was initially set up by Rodríguez Arias and Manuel Font, and was afterwards carried out successfully by Joaquín Font.

Later, this group of friends became obsessed with 'building Ibizan architecture', reconstructing a doomed way of doing things. It was no longer a time of experimentation, but more of wisdom and retirement. It was if they were attempting to preserve a collector's item from catastrophe, to rescue valuable artefacts from oblivion and neglect, to keep alive an endangered memory. This was still a time of melancholy, although they resisted a reduction to pure nostalgia.

As we have seen, there were to be no fences in Can Pep Simó, just as there are none enclosing the country houses in the interior of the island. Terraces like those seen in the Ibizan fields were to be maintained. Moreover, the architecture was to be characteristic of Ibiza, with a formal and chromatic appearance that was markedly similar to the rest of the island. With this gesture the group was positioning itself midway between a defiant resistance of the encroaching tourist invasion that would destroy everything, and the risky task of trying to make time stand still – the risk being that they could be seen as anachronistic for insisting on maintaining a familiar style. These concessions to mimesis move away from the creation of a 'vanguard' architecture and make one think more of property developers at the end of their careers.

In the Europe of the 1960s there was much talk – especially in Spain due to the influence of *Casabella*, which had subtitled its heading with the word *Continuità* (Continuity) – about the importance of the environmental past. In the United States people had been aware for quite some time of the importance of taking the vernacular into account when conceiving an architecture in a given region. Europeans

Can Pep Simó development, view of the complex.

too had used the term 'organic' for some time as a way to free themselves of the 'rational'. These categories were effectively useless, or perhaps only useful to the less intelligent, but were nevertheless employed in the sense indicated in Bruno Zevi's text.[121] The situations in the two continents were not exactly the same, but they were similar. Sert, who was a pioneer in this field, as was demonstrated by the houses in El Garraf, was halfway between both continents.

In the debates, great emphasis had been placed on analyzing the conditions of the old historic city centres, and on the fundamental role of history. Thus, this old Europe was heading in the direction of rejecting the avant

garde, which was paradoxically termed 'historical'. After having lived through the internationalist 'malady' prior to the war, which had swept over the continent, Europe sought to recover the identities of its different countries, its autochthonous roots. As we have seen, it was a search that a group of architects back in the 1930s (despite their different intentions) had also discussed, based on their interest in the Mediterranean and its architectural production. Europe was struggling to recover its diversity, and it was certainly not the right moment for vanguards, at least not with regard to architecture.

Settling down in Ibiza in the 1960s must therefore have meant taking all of these considerations into account, and the architectures of Can Pep Simó demonstrate both these controversies and the will to explore the different possibilities afforded by this architectural project, such as those derived from painstaking work on the development of plans.

The first building of this planned development, which was to be Sert's own house and which belonged to Jutta van Seht, was finished in 1965 and set the general standard for the rest of the dwellings that the architect would plan

Can Pep Simó development, general plan.

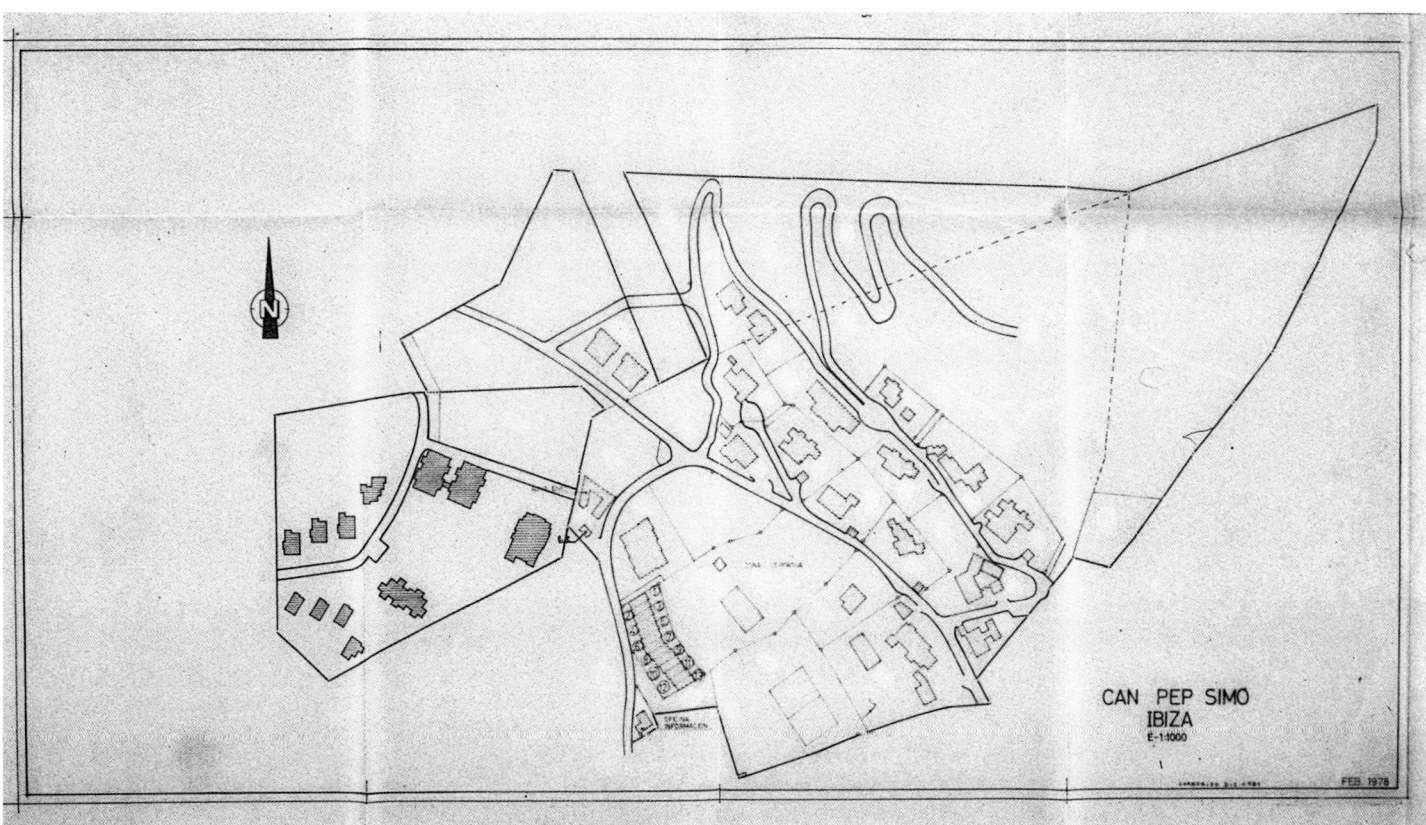

CAN PEP SIMO
IBIZA
E-1:1000

FEB. 1978

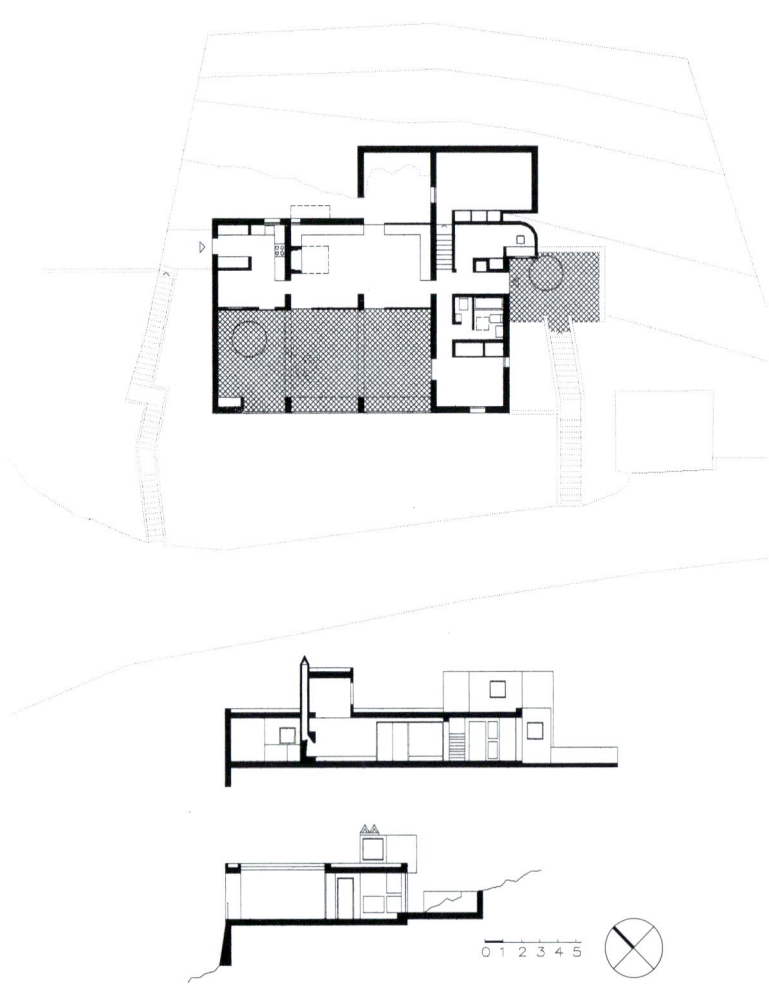

Can Pep Simó development, Jutta House, plan and sections.

hesive element departs from the original, ancestral patio, and though it originates from the housing programmes of the 1930s, it is now impossible to recognize it within this ideology because Sert has carried out an important typological transformation by giving it such generous dimensions.

This patio-terrace or terrace-patio, whichever one prefers, is an open element that allows one to enjoy the view and evokes a peaceful lifestyle, long restful evenings, conversations and parties among the friends who would live in the development and other like-minded people staying on the island. The adjacent dormitories, including bathrooms, close the terrace on the right and give cohesion to the programme.

Now, however, the abstract void of the 1930s is surrounded or trapped by more concrete matters: ochre colours delimited by a white strip along the building's borders, the rounded edges of the volume, the presence of thick intermediate columns where before there was only a fragile iron column, the whitewashed void of the windows, the stone base as a way of adapting the building to the slope, as seen in the Garraf houses (and a house in Punta Prima of 1935 that we have not examined). The building therefore has two ways of exhibiting itself: as something without shape, on the one hand, and as the manifestation of an excess of references to popular architectural forms from certain periods on the other. The past history of the ar-

Jutta House, view of the exterior.

from his studio in Cambridge. In the initial sketch we see the inevitable presence of the patio, highlighted by the drawing of a tree that seems out of proportion with the house. The patio occupied a border position, on one end of the project, and in fact is a terrace specially designed to resemble a patio.

In the final result things have taken a different turn. Recalling his first housing proposal for the island in the 1930s, a great void in the elevation that accommodates a generous terrace – covered by latticework to avoid excessive heat – placed between two volumes of the edifice, becomes the main protagonist of the building. The terrace has much greater depth than the one in Sert's first project. Here it gives unity to the organization of the house, as is the case in many popular Ibizan homes, and it allows one to dwell not on the exhibition of the youthful bodies of its inhabitants, but rather on the pleasurable life that older people can lead in its interior. Thus, this co-

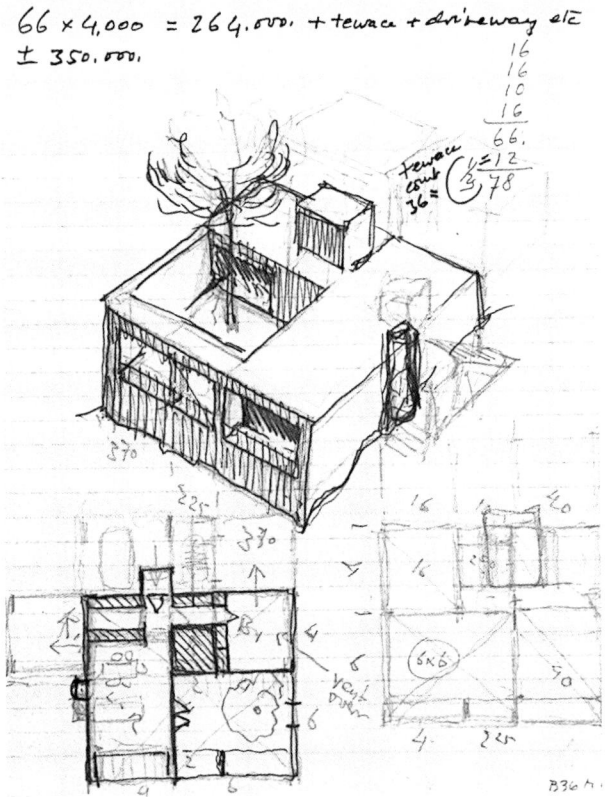

Jutta House,
sketch, preliminary
study (SC).

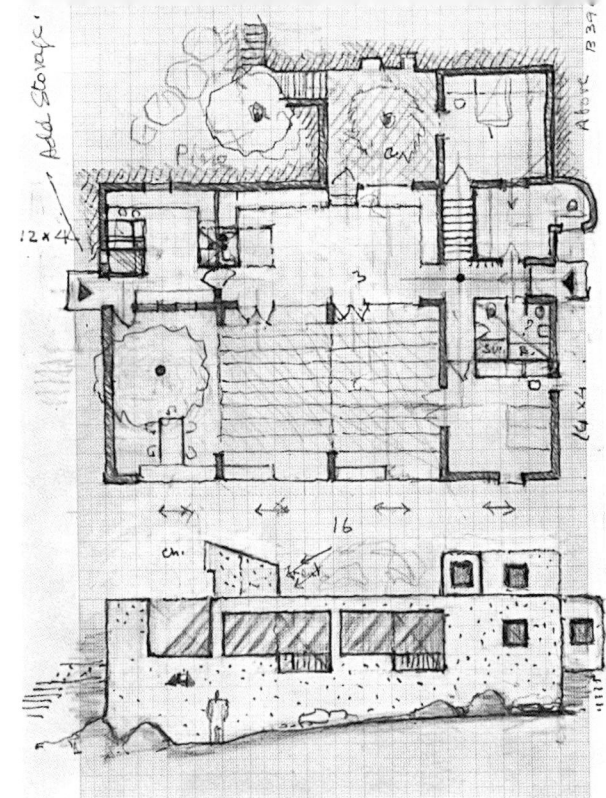

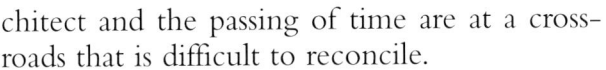

chitect and the passing of time are at a cross-roads that is difficult to reconcile.

This first house that Sert built when he returned to Ibiza was located in an area in which the tourist invasion had not yet destroyed the autochthonous. In the words of the architect himself: 'In contrast to other areas in which evolution has caused the capital to become a victim of speculation to limits unforeseen by any provision, Ibiza (until recently the only city on the island) has not been damaged. The houses that form the high part of the city, the harbour, as well as the houses near the seashore, all press against one another, and the marvellous ancient city walls, the only element of the whole island on a monumental scale, enclose the high part of the city, whose houses have similar dimensions to those seen scattered about the countryside.'[122]

At first, Sert wished to live sheltered from the passing of time, as if he could recover what he had contemplated in the 1930s, and he chose the old part of the city as his settling place. When he and other friends saw Punta Martinet, he perhaps thought that they would be able to preserve that natural area by turning it into a replica of Dalt Vila, with the equivalent of its rural dwellings; moreover, since it faced the old city, time could stand still there while so many other parts of the island were being dismembered.

A price had to be paid in order to flee from all of that. The avant-garde utopia of going back to one's roots no longer worked, and it was no longer possible to project onto the island's architecture the imaginary worlds that had been dreamt up in the 1930s. By the mid-1960s, Ibizan society, with the rise of tourism, was willing to exploit commercially that which had been encoded in the 1930s, and to foment its consumption without limit. The architects were wasting their breath in the many publications in which they spoke of the historical memory that the vanguards had tried to bury and was now necessary to reawaken.

Thus, for those who were not in favour of destroying nature and architecture, it was time to show that a new discourse was possible, in which the achievements of the 1930s could go hand in hand with popular forms: a void and some specific references, that mechanism we have seen in Sert's proposals, could perhaps constitute this integrating solution, in which no one way of doing things was imposed over another, and modernity was not surpassed by vulgar picturesqueness, accepting instead the fact that it had come to the end of its intellectual project and must form part of a new proposal.

Sert believed that the formal mechanism we have described was sufficiently open and flexible. Once the first house, which was to serve as an experiment, was finished he designed Casa

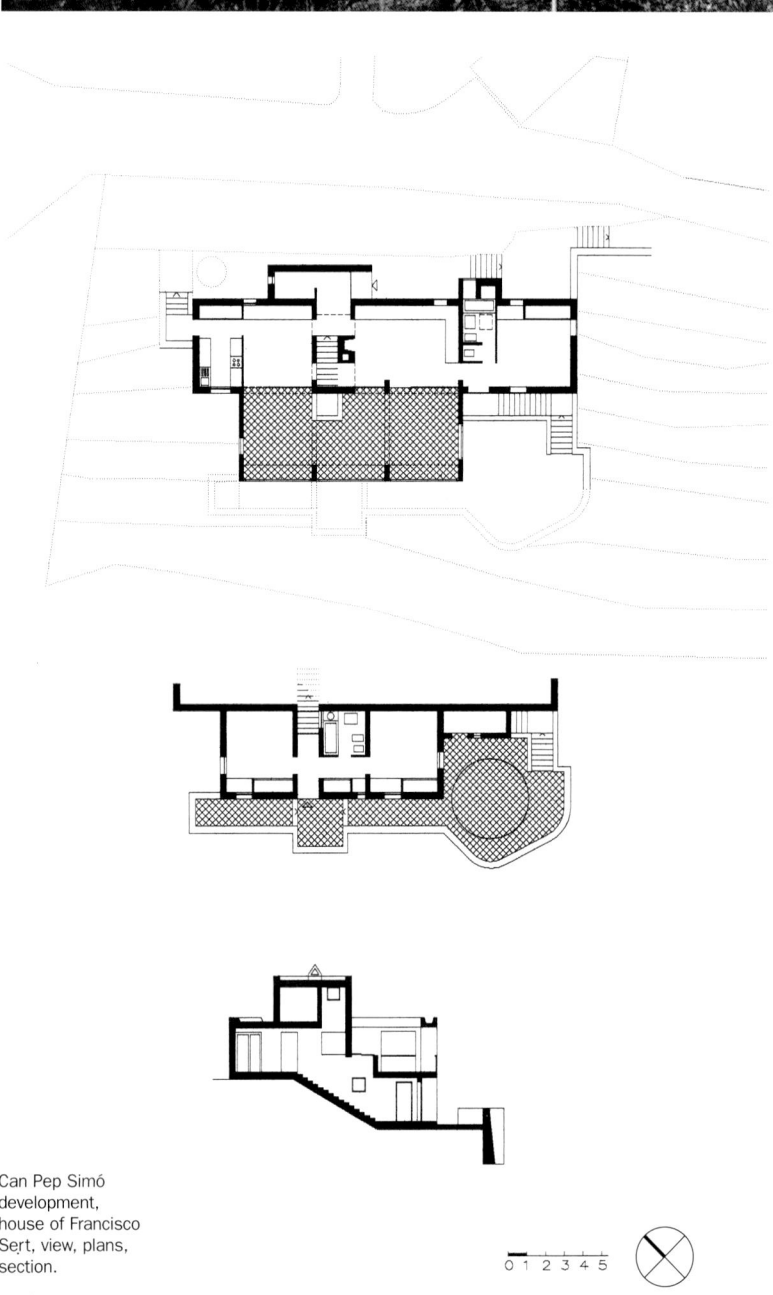

Can Pep Simó development, house of Francisco Sert, view, plans, section.

0 1 2 3 4 5

Gomis in 1966, and in 1967 executed the plans for the Casa Valls and for a residence that would later be bought by the artist Zao Wouki, who employed the architect himself to enlarge it in 1971. Sert also designed a house for his brother Francisco, in which he repeated his previous idea, adapting it to the different conditions of the sloping terrain and to the greater complexity of the programme.[123]

In Casa Gomis, the large terrace on one of its sides opens up to achieve better views, and an interior patio signals the access to the rooms located in the upper part of the plot of land. The patio becomes a natural extension of the living room and facilitates its cross-ventilation, while at the same time creating the effect of a room that organizes the ensemble of the house. Casa Valls, on the other hand, follows the outline of Casa Jutta, although with a greater surface area, also opening up the terrace on one of its ends. In Sert's brother's house the terrace is situated above the bedroom area and is unobstructed, although conveniently closed to ensure privacy without sacrificing any of the views. The materials and elements used are always the same, which confers a necessary unity to the ensemble of buildings, also ensured by the rounded edges of the volumes and the criterion used to resolve the question of the adaptation to the slope of the terrain.

Sert's own house, which he finished in 1969, after investing a long time on its construction, presents some variations that should be analyzed. Located on a corner plot of land, and having to adapt itself to a marked unevenness in the steepness of the slope, it emphasizes a composition based on free-standing volumes that form an open patio, at the edge of which we find a swimming pool. In this way, the guest rooms and the garage are superimposed to become the imagined door of the complex, something that strikingly recalls a statement made by Sert in 1967: 'A farmhouse is nothing more than a cluster of rooms that spring up with absolute freedom in a given spot.'[124] The terrace of Casa Sert is a volume superimposed on the rest of the loose volumes that make up the house, and is divided into two parts by means of a patio that signals one's arrival in the common area, in which a dining room and living room are laid out separately. They were al-

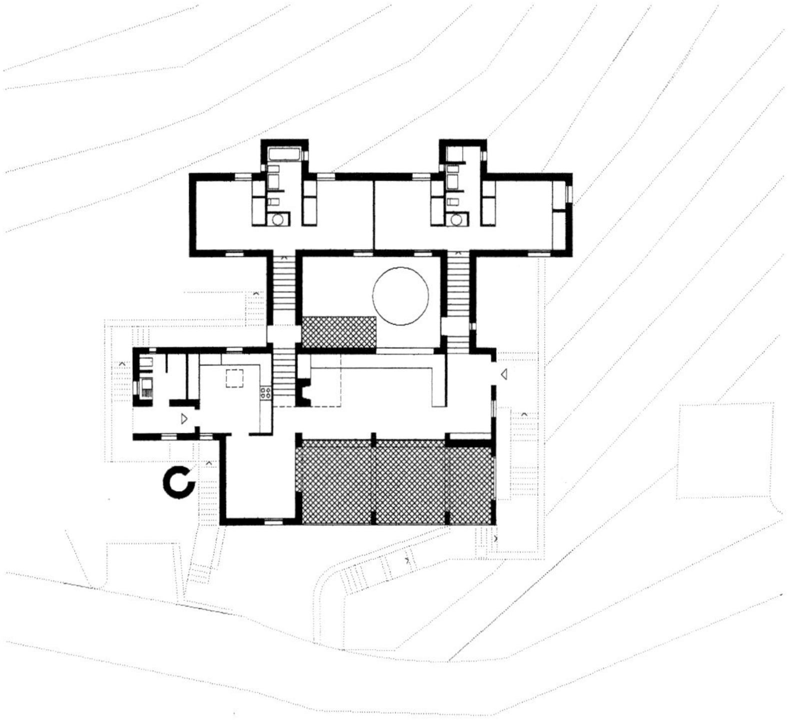

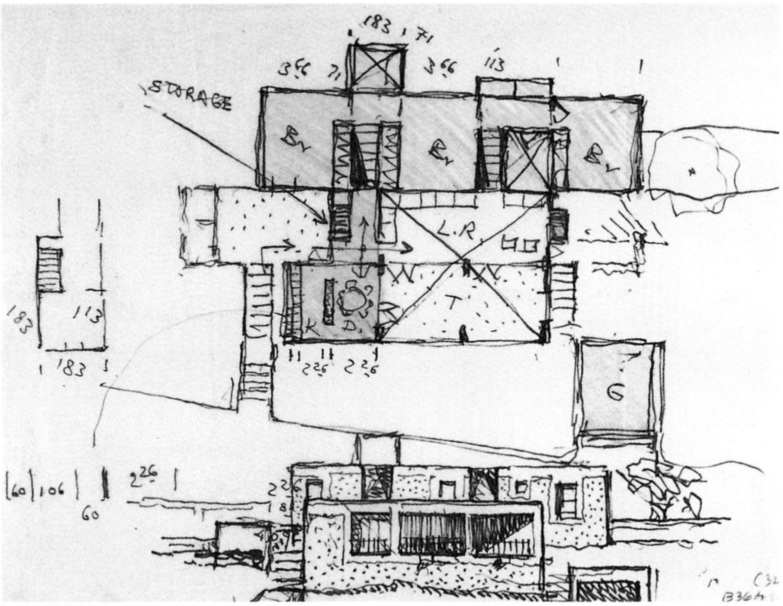

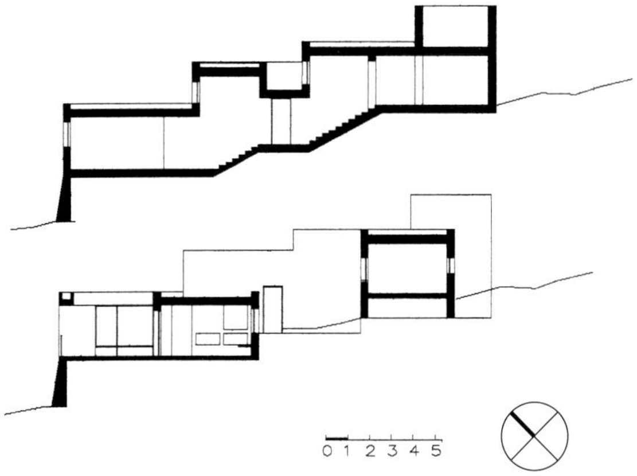

STORAGE

C

0 1 2 3 4 5

Can Pep Simó development, Casa Gomis, plan and sections, sketch (SC), perspective and picture of the exterior.

Can Pep Simó
development,
Casa Valls, plans,
exterior view,
and sketch (SC).

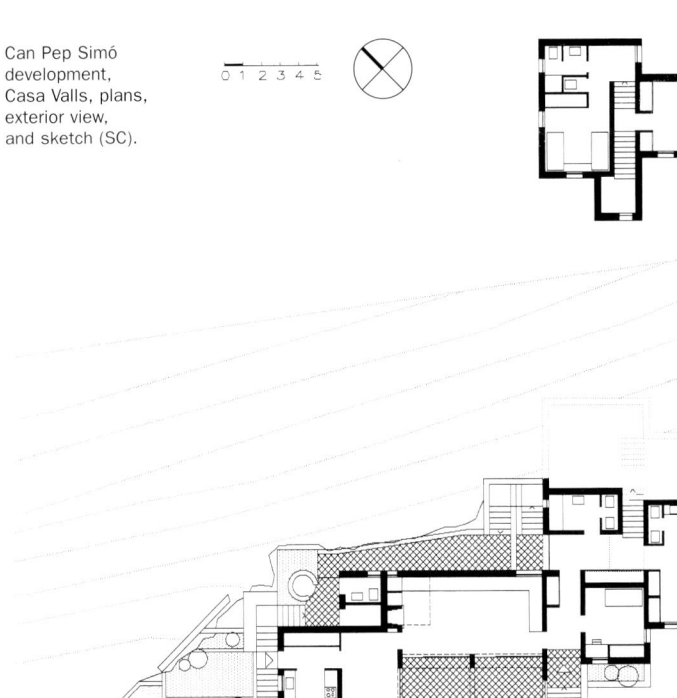

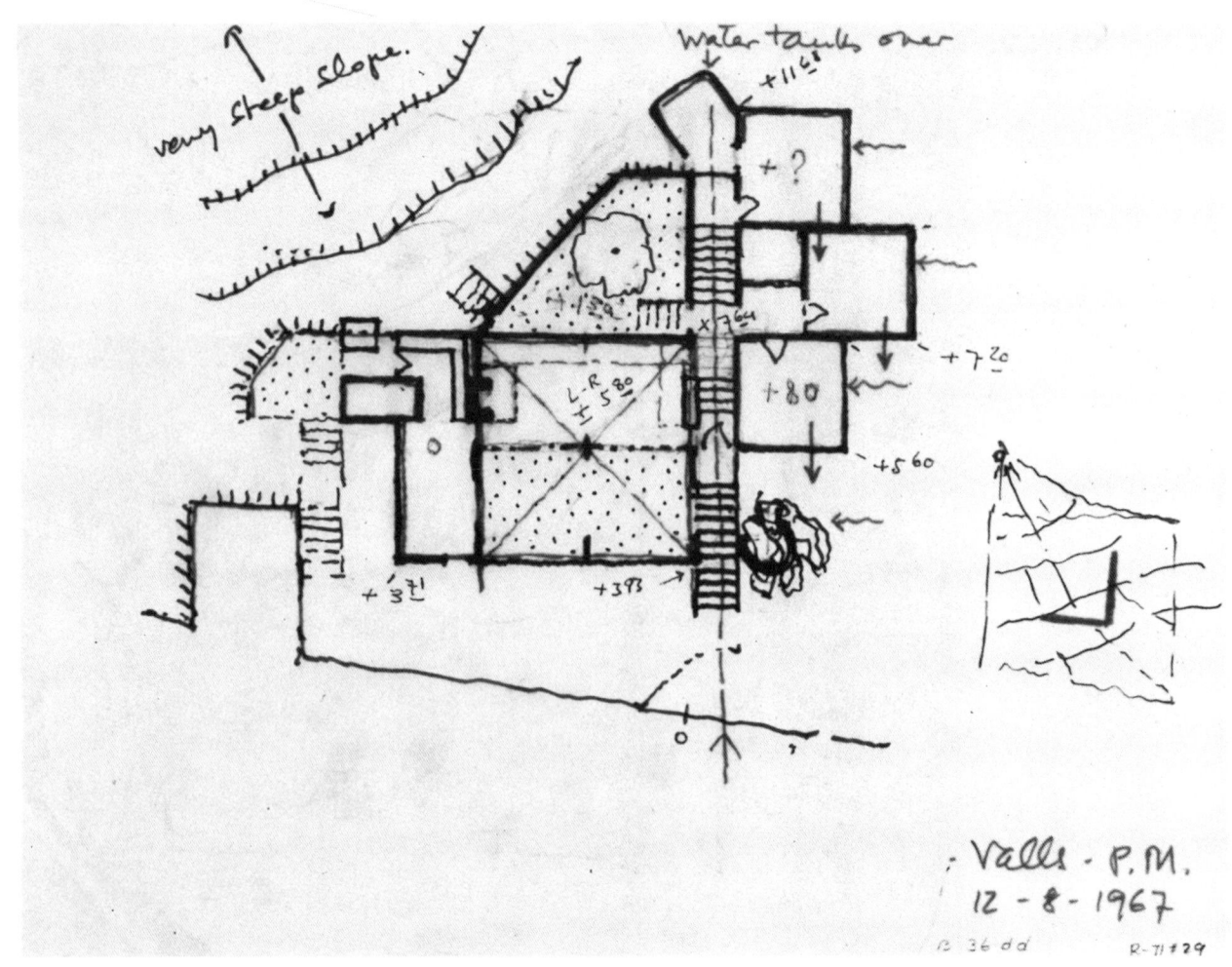

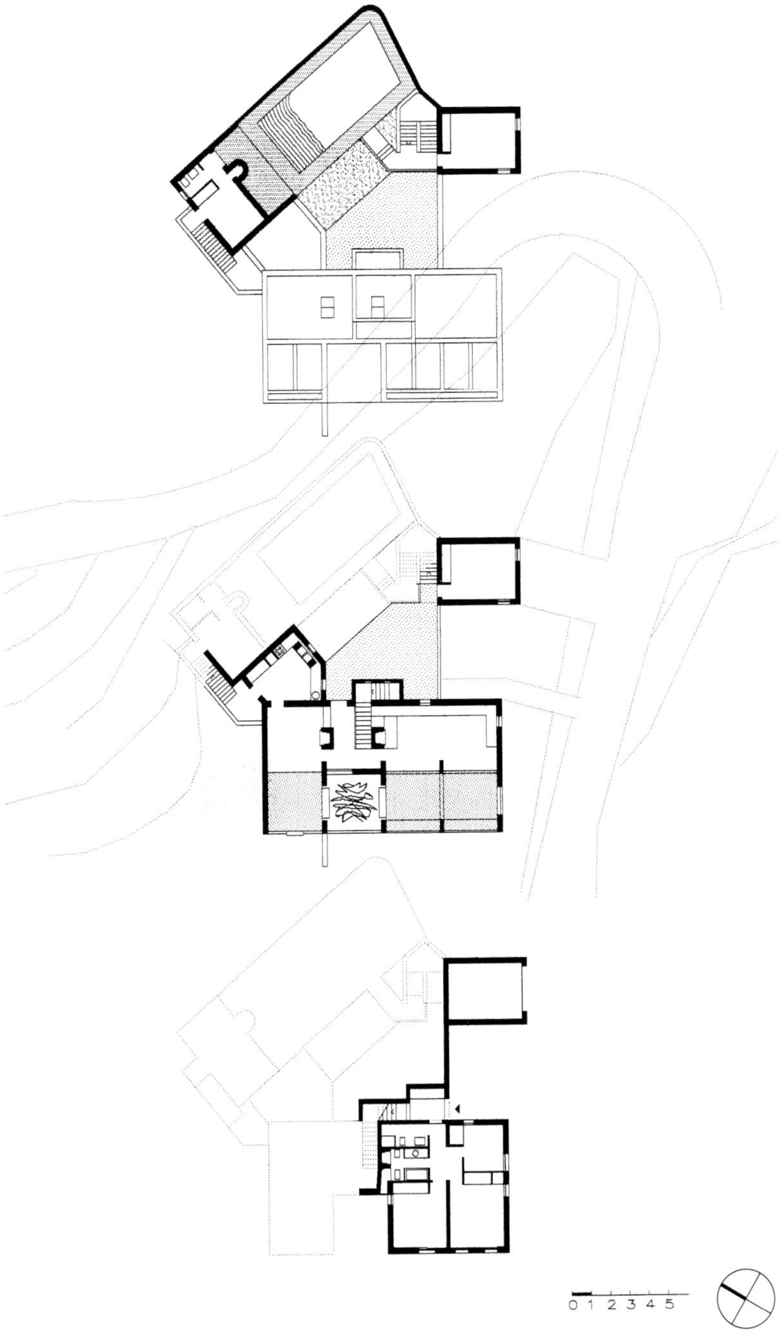

Can Pep Simó
development,
Casa Sert,
plans, exterior
and interior views.

0 1 2 3 4 5

so separated in the other buildings, this being a characteristic that originated in certain projects by Marcel Breuer and which we also see in Sert's house in Cambridge.

The functional clarity observed in all of the buildings comes from their organization and their destiny as holiday homes. The slope of the terrain provides the opportunity to develop the isolated expression of each one of the volumes that make up the ensemble, which links them to some aspects of the architectural tradition of the island. However, little observance here is paid to Hausmann's insistence on the human gesture to determine the construction of a building, where dynamite was used to build some parts of Sert's house,[125] a violent attack on nature that was necessary to achieve the desired results. In his letters Sert insisted that the house be 'pressed close to the ground', a difficult effect to achieve naturally, given the terrain.

Els Fumerals, the group of thirteen apartments that occupy the lower part of the planned development, in which Arias and Antoni Ferrán resided (and to which Huson Jackson, one of Sert's American associates, still travels to escape the cold of Massachusetts), use the mezzanine connected by stairs as a way to organize the interior space. They were planned at the end of 1969 and the construction was finished by 1971, according to the correspondence consulted. In the plan they are grouped together to form a stepped silhouette so as not to resemble a unitary block, and their layout is varied to avoid repetitive facades, fleeing from series in an attempt to seem unique, even though this is not the case.

Sert was proud of having been able to hold a dialogue and seek connections with rural Ibizan architecture through the use of sophisticated aspects of architectural discipline: 'In this development there is a common measure. In all of the dwellings we have used a system of measurement created by Le Corbusier which is called Modulor and which is based on the Golden Section. It is a system that serves to give things their correct proportions, and it is the repetition of elements (windows, for example) that gives them human scale, and that humanizes this architecture.'[126] All of this was taken into account in the project, of which Sert was one of the main property developers. Concerning their intention of transforming Cap Mar-

Can Pep Simó development, view of the complex.

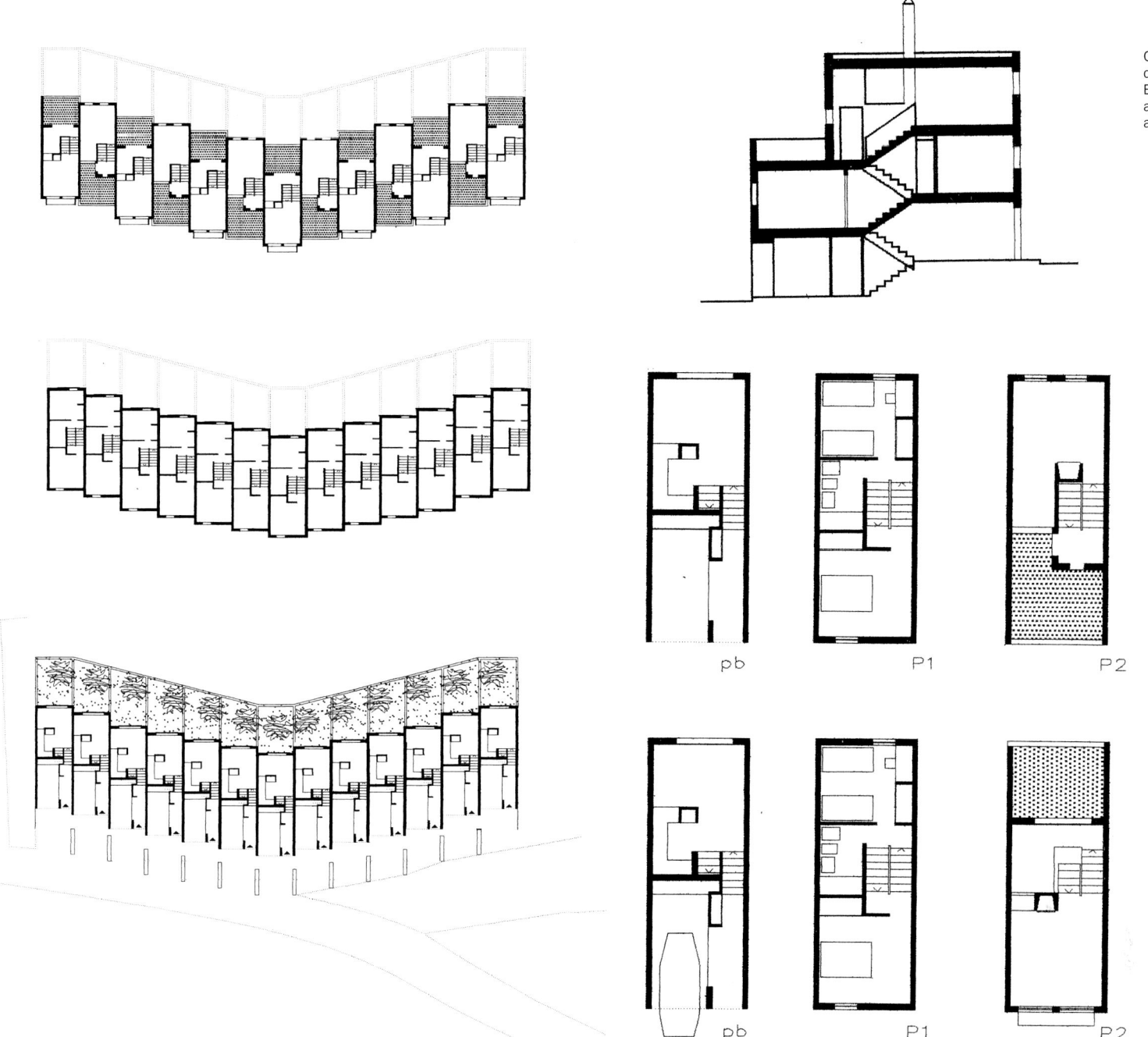

Can Pep Simó
development,
Els Fumerals
apartments, plans
and sections.

pb   P1   P2

pb   P1   P2

tinet into an oasis he stated: 'The only thing we have done in this housing development is to try to perpetuate a language, a system of forms that existed centuries before, and to adapt them to the uses and needs of men of today.'

This statement was made in 1973, when the degradation of the island had already taken place, as Sert himself lamented: 'The volume of construction in Ibiza surpasses by far the island's possibilities … there is too much construction, too many wide roads, too many cars. If this goes on, the end will be total paralysis, catastrophe.' Utopia has indeed become an impossible dream: Can Pep Simó had not been able to take on its exemplary role, but had been forced to become an impotent witness to what Sert so rightly called a 'catastrophe'.[127]

On 26 April 1982, shortly before he died, Sert gave a lecture for the symposium 'Creativitat Mediterrània', held in Sitges. In his speech, whose title is self-explanatory: 'Característiques constants en les arquitectures o urbanisme mediterrani' ('Consistent Characteristics in Mediterranean Architectures and Town Planning'), Sert emphasized certain topics with which we are now familiar, as well as discussing all architectures as if they originated from the one produced on the shores of the sea, which

Can Pep Simó
development,
Els Fumerals
apartments,
views, section.

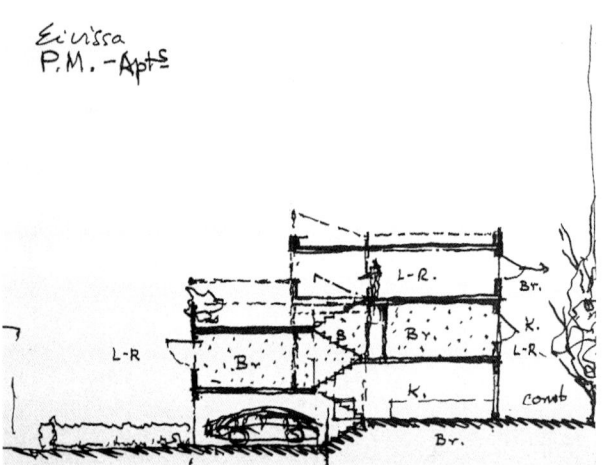

The tomb
of José Luis Sert
in the cemetery
of the village
of Jesús, Ibiza.

had always seduced him: 'One could say that architecture and urbanism make their first manifestations near the Latin sea, and are born in the great Mediterranean region. The Mediterranean is their cradle … The great monuments of art history find their most fruitful area and their greatest samples of creativity in the environs of the Latin sea, and if you take away from the history of architecture that which has been produced in the surroundings of this great region, you would find it to be greatly mutilated.'[128]

Sert, however, came to believe that there was no longer any solution for this: 'At present the Latin sea is importing incommensurate horrors that are out of scale and lacking in harmony, which come to us from a world alien to our own, a world dominated by profit and by the cult of a misinterpreted technology.' However, despite this harangue, he implored: 'You young architects, town planners, economists, politicians and citizens, generally aware of this, are the ones who must take on this great human-civic task of protecting what the past has bequeathed to us.' It was an understandable wish for someone who had not been capable of avoiding the catastrophe and for whom Mediterranean civilization was so important that he had determined that his ashes should rest eternally on the seashore of one of its islands.[129]

[116] For a better understanding and more information on the intellectuals and artists who began settling on the island during this period, see Mariano Planells, *Ibiza, la senda de los elefantes*, vol. I, Imprenta Soler, 1978; Rafael Pascuet, *Teorías de Ibiza*, La Gorgona, Ibiza, 1983; Mariano Planells, *La senda de los elefantes*, vol. II, Ediciones Obelisco, Barcelona, 1986.

[117] Diverse authors have detected changes in Broner's second sojourn in Ibiza. See Felix Julbe, *Una utopía realizable*, in *Erwin Broner*, op. cit., pp. 20–25. For a beginner's guide to Neutra's work in those years see Thomas Hines, *Richard Neutra and the Search for Modern Architecture*, University of California, 1982, pp. 193–222.

[118] Information forwarded by the architect Orlando González, who is writing a thesis on this architect within the framework of the Chair of History of Art and Architecture of the ETSAB.

[119] Broner, op. cit., p. 87.

[120] Sert trunk, AFJM, in the envelope Barcelona Accounts, Joan Prats, To go over.

[121] Bruno Zevi, *Storia dell'architettura moderna*, Einaudi, Turin, 1950.

[122] José Luis Sert, 'Ibiza', in *Ibiza fuerte y luminosa*, Polígrafa, Barcelona, 1967. Taken from *Arquitectura y espacio rural en Ibiza*, COAB, 1982, p. 156. Another book by the same publisher is worthy of mention for its images: Maria Lluisa Borràs, *Sert: Arquitectura mediterránea*, Barcelona, 1974.

[123] See letter to Antoni Ferrán of 11 December 1967. The letters referred to in this work also encompass the correspondence between Sert and Ferrán. They are of interest because they help to time the construction of the complex. They belong to Helena Bargas, the widow of Sert's construction foreman, whom we wish to thank for allowing us to consult them at will.

[124] Sert, *Ibiza fuerte y luminosa*, op. cit., p. 155.

[125] Letter to Antoni Ferrán, 21 March 1968.

[126] Speech given by José Luis Sert on the occasion of the exhibition of his work at the Museo de Arte Contemporáneo, Ibiza, on 25 May 1973. Included in *Arquitecturas en Ibiza*, COAB, Ibiza, 1983, p. 105.

[127] In a letter to Antoni Ferrán of 29 June 1974, we read: 'We'll be on the island the whole month of August and you can count on my doing everything I can to stop the destruction of Ibiza.' Despite all the pessimism, there were still voices that expressed a wish to preserve Ibiza in the excellent *Quaderns del TEHP*, of which several issues had already come out. More questionable, although well worth taking into account, are the proposals made by the architect Philippe Rotthier, which are compiled in *Maisons sur l'île d'Iibiza*, AAM éditions, Brussels, 1990.

[128] José Luis Sert, 'Característiques constants en les arquitectures i urbanisme mediterranis', lecture given on 26 April 1982, typewritten manuscript in SC E 24.

[129] The remains of José Luis Sert, along with those of his wife Ramona 'Moncha' Longas, are buried in the cemetery of the Ibizan town of Jesús, at the foot of the Punta Martinet development. Moncha died in Barcelona on 6 October 1985.

New York

In the *Architectural Record* of January 1941, Edwin Bergston, President of the AIA, had this to say concerning the role and duties of architects in those times of war: 'Architects must now prepare to assume their increased future responsibilities. They must combine exactness of technical knowledge and of costs, the competency and efficiency of business with their native ability in design ... Architects can truly become co-ordinating administrators on whom alone owners will depend for putting into practice their building projects.' The USA would not officially enter the war until the end of that year, conferring a premonitory character to Bergston's words, but his intuition did not fall on deaf ears: it was clear that something was going to happen, and architects would have to be prepared for it. In all likelihood, the Spanish citizen José Luis Sert López, who had arrived in the States on 26 June 1939 will have read this text during the many hours of enforced leisure that he enjoyed while living at the Hotel Van Renssealer of East 11th Street in New York. During this time Sert was receiving disheartening news from his own country concerning his chances of going back, for José María Ros Vila, the first President of the Official School of Architecture of Catalonia after the Civil War, had concluded his report on 'the actions of colleagues attached to our corporation' in August 1940. In this text, housed in the archives of this School, is an analysis of the trajectory of our architect: 'Sert López, José Luis. Fled abroad. Renowned career in Spain and abroad. Founder and spiritual leader of the GATCPAC. Communist record. Designed and directed the Pavilion of Communist Spain in Paris.' As a result of this report, a sentence was passed on 18 February 1942, by which Sert, along with his colleagues Rodríguez Arias and Rubió i Tudurí, were prohibited from carrying out professional work 'in all the national territory, its possessions and dependencies'.

Thus for Sert the only remaining alternative was to try to make a space for himself in the US in the only way open to him, given the information he had available and the amount of time on his hands: by writing the book that we have analyzed in previous pages, which he managed to get published in November 1942, and which turned out to be a necessary step in his acceptance in the intellectual circles of that nation and an essential requirement for his professional launch in Latin America.[1]

Sert set about seeking out professional contacts, aided by his reputation as one of the pillars of the CIAMs and by his friendships with Weissmann, Breuer, Papadaki and Gropius, which would allow him to be 'presented' within the intricate American professional and university market. As we know, he soon began working with Paul Lester Wiener, whose office was on West 42nd Street.[2]

José Luis Sert.

Sert's house in Locust Valley, Long Island, New York, 1949.

Roca jewellery shop, Barcelona, 1934.

The publication of the Roca jewellery shop in the *Architectural Record* of January 1937 probably also helped him to receive his first professional commission on American soil, which had to do with landscape gardening and the decoration of public halls and restaurants, which he signed on 31 August 1941, although we have been unable to find any evidence of the actual work he carried out.[3] Shortly afterwards, on 12 November 1941, the Regional Tribunal of Political Responsibilities of Spain also condemned him, due to his political affiliations, to 'the total loss of his possessions, the absolute and perpetual prohibition of holding any political or labour union post or any such position related to his profession, and forced exile more than two hundred kilometres away from Catalonia during a period of fifteen years.'[4] He therefore could not return to Barcelona, at least not in the near future, which must have increased his desire to stay in America, as well as pushing him to integrate himself into the American professional scene.

America's entry into the war may have added in some senses to this sombre outlook, but it also made matters easier for our architect since work picked up considerably in the office of the new associates, who by then numbered three due to the recent incorporation of Paul Schulz. These favourable circumstances were propitiated both by the state of war and by the personal contacts of Lester, who was married to Alma Morgenthau, daughter of Henry Mor-

genthau, the Secretary of the Treasury in President Roosevelt's administration. As we have seen, by 17 December 1940 Morgenthau had already taken steps to provide his son-in-law with a worthwhile job. As may be recalled, in a letter of this date addressed to Cordell Hull, Secretary of State, he offered the following recommendation: 'The reason I am writing to you is that I think he could be useful in the cultural field in the capacity of adviser in Architectural Planning for Latin America, or in the field of Art and Design.'[5]

It was at this point that the members of Town Planning Associates began establishing contacts with South American countries, a trajectory that we have examined at length in the first part of this book. Nevertheless, it is necessary to examine Lester's relationship with the American administration to introduce the issue of the specific commission that TPA received from the government, which was linked to the climate of war that took hold of the country at the end of 1941.

A fragment of the book *On Being an Architect*, written by the architect William Lescaze and published in 1942, also helps explain the war context: 'Between flights a plane must find shelter – hangar. A pilot must have rest – house, dormitory. A plane must be refuelled – oil depot. The depot must be replenished – trucks, moving on roads, transportation. The pilot may have been wounded – hospital. The plane may have to be repaired – factories where parts are made. The plane must be armed – arsenal where bombs are manufactured. Future pilots, future mechanics must be trained – vocational schools.'[6] Thus the war process required hangars, houses, dormitories, transportation, hospitals, factories, arsenals and training schools; it required planning, design and construction, specially conceived for these circumstances, and the more one reads of this work, the more evident it becomes that Lescaze was bent on proving that it was precisely these skills that architects possessed. The outbreak of war had given rise to new needs, and these had to be solved urgently by making use of a powerful industrial infrastructure and by seeking strategically viable sites. A new and fundamental motive – the motive of war, which necessarily calls for planning – was settling at the core of the American way of life, and this the United States would use in order to achieve objectives of another type.

Modern architecture would be called upon to come up with solutions to the diverse demands of war, and it was to do so in the name of some of the postulates that its creators had always upheld. When the MoMA exhibition on modern architecture was held in 1942, these concepts were summarized as: rationality, construction for the masses with prefabricated systems, planning – concepts that had to take on new meaning in the United States to become determining factors in ensuring a swift victory over the enemy. This exhibition took place ten years after the one set up by Philip Johnson, Henry-Russell Hitchcock and Alfred H. Barr between 10 February and 23 March 1932. Their catalogue is fundamental to understanding the public dissemination that led to the first contacts between the architecture of modern Europeans and American culture,[7] an issue that leads us to take a small detour to analyze various interpretations.

Deborah Frances Pokinski has carried out an analysis that highlights some of the conditions that facilitated the 'acceptance' of modern architecture in the United States, an architecture that was to be understood as a 'style' by American architects and the public at large. Her hypothesis is simple but enlightening: at that point in the US, adequate conditions had been created and the necessary seeds had been sown to make this circumstance possible. Pokinski reviews the visual categories to which Johnson and Hitchcock had reduced the architecture of modern Europeans so as to be able to interpret it as a style, although she does acknowledge the possibilities of its original social implications: 'In Europe the unadorned surface also implied the ethical choice of utilitarian construction and social commitment which led some European functionalists to deny their architecture any aesthetic association whatever',[8] something that was impossible to find in the US at that time: 'The aspects of social responsibility and aspirations inherent in European modernism, however, were never really appreciated or adopted in the United States.'[9]

Nevertheless, the US was in need of new aesthetics, and this spurred the authors of the 1932 catalogue to show great interest in the qualities of this new architecture that they defined as style, a style they considered to be 'real and fertile again'. This reduction would have shocked modern Europeans, who called it a 'movement', or simply 'architecture' or 'design', understandably in light of the aversion they felt towards academicism and the official doctrines of the schools of architecture, and in view of the negative connotations of a word that made them recall the decorative pastiches of much of the architecture they had been forced to endure. Thus 'The basic distinction between the American and the European conception of modern architecture is made clear by the different use of terms. The Europeans conceived of a radical transformation in the whole nature of architecture, including structure, materials, theory and design, which they called modern architecture after the new age it was seen to reflect. The Americans, on the other hand, first recognized and then began to cultivate a novel appearance in architecture which they called modernism or the modernistic style. The Europeans never called modern architecture a style; but the Americans always considered the radically changed look of architecture as a new style or styles.'[10]

Pokinski goes on to seek the conditions that made it possible for the work of Johnson and Hitchcock to succeed, a success that was evidently only available to a small milieu of people. She finds these conditions in isolated moments of modernity offered by American architectural culture of the 1920s and early 1930s, which began with the *Chicago Tribune* open tender of 1922, leading certain American architects to take an interest in some projects that presented forms from which all ornamentation had been stripped away.[11] Later, Pokinski quotes a text written by Lewis Mumford in 1924, which suggests that historicism was beginning to be perceived as a synonym for lack of creativity in America: 'What is called Renaissance architecture today has nothing to do with the original Renaissance movement; it is merely characteristic of our dreadful facility of imitation, and it expresses the willingness of even the architect in a machine age to accept a pattern for cheap reproduction instead of undergoing the abysmal labours of creative design.'

However, it was not until 1928 that it occurred to Mumford to take up the names of Sullivan, Root and Wright as the genuine standard bearers of American values, as 'new energies' worthy of being sources of inspiration for new architecture.[12] Nevertheless, his attitude concerning Europeans, who in his opinion held machines in too high esteem, was very clear: 'But they are still human beings, not dynamos or Diesel engines, and there must be something more.'

In 1929 two books were published that were crucial at the time, which Pokinski refers to extensively in her survey and reasonings: *The New World Architecture* by Sheldon Cheney and *Modern Architecture: Romanticism and Reintegration* by Henry-Russell Hitchcock.

Although his contribution did not have as much impact as the 1932 MoMA catalogue, Cheney anticipated its theme, deploring eclecticism and considering new architecture as a phenomenon that, though exclusively aesthetic, drank from many sources and had many possible manifestations. Like a good American, he ended his work by praising the skyscraper.[13] Not surprisingly, Hitchcock dealt with modern Europeans, although his main focus of interest was on the architects of commercial buildings in Chicago, with H.H. Richardson as the foremost amongst them: 'He included all of them within the New Tradition and for the first time presented a cogent interpretation of the "Chicago School" as a conspicuous and consequential

forerunner of modern architecture.'[14] Mumford's renowned *The Brown Decades*, is just a step away from this text: here, he attributes to Americans the invention of a new architecture.[15]

Pokinski ends her book (after mentioning several architectural works carried out for the Chicago World Fair of 1933) with some conclusions regarding the rise of modern architecture, possibly springing from the eclecticism to which Americans were so accustomed. This she backs up by drawing on the contributions of certain architects: 'It should be clear that by 1933 American architects had evolved a firm commitment to modernism in architecture and had been engaged for several years in a serious attempt to define a modern style. Moreover, by 1930 these endeavours had materialized into several important building designs, particularly the work of Raymond Hood in New York City and George Howe and William Lescaze in Philadelphia. These designs suggest that two distinct influences were at work in the development of American modernism at this time: the first and most pervasive was American skyscraper design, which had evolved out of the eclectic tradition of the past half century; the second was European avant-garde functionalism … Americans considered these several European styles as fodder for the interrupted process of creating a unique American style; toward this end, they continued to have faith in an eclectic process and therefore, they never intended to copy any one style directly.'[16]

William Lescaze, Williamsburg Houses, Brooklyn, 1934.

Oscar Stonorov and Alfred Kastner, Carl Mackey Homes, Philadelphia, 1934.

Vernon De Mars,
Yuba City,
California, 1940,
aerial view
and picture from
private collection.

Anatole Kopp offers a different reading of this subject, since his point of departure is based on considering modern architecture as a cause, not as a style. This opposition to the ideas of Johnson and Hitchcock leads him to trace other sources for the signs of modernity in the US: 'It is the great economic depression of 1929 that will upheave American politics and economy and that will mark the beginning of a new policy, which in turn will give birth to a new architecture and a new urbanism, originally and specifically American in certain aspects, and close to certain European orientations in others.'[17]

For Americans, the New Deal would mean state intervention in vast urban works and the relegation of private enterprise to a second term, which therefore meant that the logic of profit would be eliminated due to the modification of the relationship between the State and the market. It would also represent the need for careful national planning in a country that knew nothing about it[18] and the possibility of questioning American realities such as isolated individual houses and garden cities – which certainly held no interest for the representatives of European modernity – albeit timidly, due to a social demand that had not existed previously.[19]

In this way, 'Those who will want to promote a policy of social habitat in the United States will have to search for references in the interventions of the 1920s and 1930s in Eu-

Vernon De Mars,
Vallejo, 1942.

rope, due to the total absence of American precedents.'[20] One of the first people to work on this task was Catherine Bauer, director of the National Public Housing Conference, who dealt with the issue in her book *Modern Housing*, published in 1934. A fundamental text in the US in the 1930s, it attempted to learn from the European experiences it analyzed so as to elevate the conditions of American dwellings to the level of the technical and economic means available in the country.[21]

Of the fifty-one interventions, greatly varying in form, which were carried out by the Housing Division attached to the Public Works Administration, Kopp highlights two projects of 1934: the 'modern' work of William Lescaze for the Williamsburg Houses in Brooklyn, and a project for the Carl Mackey Residences in Philadelphia by Oscar Stonorov and Alfred Kastner.[22] After reviewing the well-known TVA work, Kopp goes on to analyze the trajectory of another institution that was highly important during that period: the Farm Security Administration, which organized fields for immigrant workers during the depression and which between 1936 and 1937 aided the construction of renowned projects by Vernon De Mars such as the Farm Community co-operative in Chandler, Arizona, and Yuba City and Woodville, both in California. Some time later, in 1942, De Mars would write: 'The range of activities covered by the FSA includes a medical and health-care programme, lodgings for different groups … elementary school and adult education programmes … The possibilities thus opened and the challenge offered to architecture to furnish the skeleton of these activities is evident … The central administration has concerned itself with the results and the goals to be achieved, and has not imposed either the details or the solutions.'[23]

Despite their scarce relevance given the size of the US, these projects contributed decisively to the rationalization of the use of interior spaces through a strict application of hygienic ordinances and regulations concerning the durability and quality of dwellings, partly borrowed from the experiences of modern architecture and not concerned with fulfilling speculative ends.

Pokinski and Kopp, each following very different routes, demonstrate the impact of modern architectural ideology in the US during the 1930s. Both from the point of view of form taken as style and from the ethical sense of European interventions in the 1920s and 1930s, the advantages of forming the modern are clear, as well as being an inevitable and natural way for American reality to proceed in the process of evolution it had been undergoing since the end of the nineteenth century. Paradoxically, the two texts have very similar endings, both affirming that the appointment of modern Europeans to the highest posts in the most reputed American universities resulted in the convergence of histories that had previously been running parallel.[24]

In his first speech in the US – published in block letters in the May 1937 issue of *Architectural Record* – Walter Gropius described the good will with which European architects were received in the country: 'I hope my appointment will be a further proof of the American ability to reconcile and amalgamate the most diverse types of people to create a new form of life of typically American stamp … My intention is not to introduce a, so to speak, cut and dried "Modern Style" from Europe, but rather to introduce a method of approach which allows one to tackle a problem according to its peculiar conditions … My ideas have often been interpreted as the peak of rationalization and mechanization. This gives a quite wrong picture of my endeavours. I have always emphasized that the other aspect, the satisfaction of the human soul, is just as important as the material, and that the intellectual achievement of a new spatial vision means more than structural economy and functional perfection.' It seems evident that the integration among different points of view was going to be easier than it had seemed in a country that met the necessary conditions and that moreover had opened its doors to newly arrived Europeans who wished to adopt the American way of life and work to improve it from their privileged posts in the work market.

Let us go back to the 1942 exhibition that we mentioned earlier. It was called 'What is Modern Architecture?', and was the first in a series dedicated to the modern arts. To find out exactly what new architecture was, the exhibition's curators came up with the idea of going all the way back to Vitruvius. After declaring that the modern architect must operate like a scientist, since he had to be able to approach problems with an analytical spirit, while testing and verifying its worth like a psychologist, so as to overcome, like an artist, the cold conception of a house as a machine to live in, they subjected some of those modern buildings to the Vitruvian triad. Concerning its utility, they cited the capacity of new architecture to come up with and optimize new uses by creating new typologies, and its ability to make the most of technology to better equip buildings. In the same way, they remarked on the importance given to location, considered a key element in the design of dwellings, as well as pointing out the need for large-scale planning so as to help maintain a healthy balance among regions. Both new structural systems of steel and concrete and new materials such as plywood and glass bricks were taken as effective guarantees of solidity. When speaking of beauty, they used well-known canons: absence of ornament, sincerity of materials, volume instead of mass, use of abstract forms and asymmetry. The catalogue then went on to present examples from the architectural work of leading European and American figures.[25]

Thus, new demands arising from the war were to be fulfilled by new architecture in a country that was beginning to have a huge need for it and which, as we have seen through Pokinski and Kopp, had moreover shown sufficient signs of being able to deal successfully with the problem. We can put forward a further example of this: in 1942, De Mars designed another vast group of community dwellings and buildings for several thousand workers near the dockyards of San Francisco Bay using plywood panels produced by a factory that had adapted the construction systems of the aircraft industry. These houses could be dismantled when they were no longer needed, and transported to other sites to avoid the creation of ghost towns once the war was over and the war industries stopped working.[26]

The war therefore decisively helped to bring the depression years to an end, and also ushered in the better times of the post-war period, which promised to fulfil the American dream of houses in the suburbs, modern kitchens and shopping centres. The massive building programme required to house the workers in the war industries, set up mostly on

the West Coast, made it necessary to sharpen both wits and technology to satisfy such a great demand for housing. Some figures may help illustrate this process: between 1940 and 1947 the populations of the states of California, Washington and Oregon increased by 40 per cent, and between 1940 and 1944, 500,000 people moved to the Los Angeles area. Prefabricated houses, therefore, were an absolute necessity, and architects and engineers devoted themselves to the task of fulfilling the commissions they were receiving, full of hope in that accelerated progress and acclaimed as heroes by the war propaganda. Among those who contributed to this great task were a number of avant-garde names: William W. Wurster, Walter Gropius, Marcel Breuer, George Howe, Louis I. Kahn, Richard Neutra and Frank Lloyd Wright.[27]

In 1941 the Quonset hut was designed at the Quonset Naval Air Station in Rhode Island – of which there would be more than 170,000 all over the world by 1946 – and at the same time Neutra designed Avion Village for the workers in the aircraft industry. From 1942 onwards a series of large-scale interventions followed one another in rapid succession, such as the creation of a new city in Vanport, Oregon, with 10,000 dwellings for the Kaiser dockyard workers and their families, and the creation of enterprises that produced mass housing using specially invented processes for this purpose, as

Walter Gropius and Marcel Breuer, Aluminum City Terrace, Pennsylvania, 1941–42.

Quonset Hut, at the Quonset Naval Air Station of Rhode Island, 1941.

Howe, Stonorov and Kahn, Carver Court housing in Coatesville, Pennsylvania.

was the case with Barrett and Hilp, who constructed 5,000 dwellings for the workers of the Portsmouth, Virginia shipyard at a rate of eighty houses a day by using the Homasote Company's Precision Built Jr. system.

Among all these projects, the ones that probably present the greatest formal interest are the Aluminum City Terrace built by Gropius and Breuer in New Kensington, Pennsylvania, and the Carver Court housing project of Howe, Stonorov and Kahn in Coatesville, also in Pennsylvania.

Although Lester, Sert and Schulz did not receive any large-scale commissions, they were nevertheless involved in these matters. Meanwhile, in the *Architectural Record* of July 1942, an article entitled 'Design for Democracy' stated: 'The first, immediate, urgent task in the Design for Democracy is to WIN THE WAR. Otherwise is a futility and nonsense … We must devote our energies to one of three spheres of activity, the one where each can do his part, for all are vital in the Design for Democracy: 1. Active military service. 2. War construction. 3. Planning for an America better fitted for the needs of an industrialized, civilized people.' A few days earlier, on 16 June, Lester had sent a letter to someone by the name of Dr Somary enquiring about the prices of some plywood panels, in which he wrote that they were working on a 'barrack complex which could be bought by the unit. Each unit is 20 × 30 feet.'[28] We can therefore assume that they were already designing what they would subsequently call Ratio Structures, a project for a multipurpose prefabricated modular system commissioned by the War Production Board.

In a letter enclosed with a copy of Sert's recently published *Can Our Cities Survive?* addressed to Oscar Niemeyer on 18 November of the same year, Lester explained the work in which he and Sert were engaged: 'Here in America, work is strictly reduced to Government constructions … I have been working with Sert on the problem of housing for workers of the war industry, and it is very interesting.'[29] The work must have been almost finished by November since they began to submit it for consideration by the War Department, pointing out its immense capacity to cover different functions; it also received its first criti-

cisms at this time. A letter from Lester to C.T. Wood of the War Department, reads: 'We demonstrated the model and layout for hospital units to Colonel Crandall and his staff of architectural draftsmen', but even though the Colonel apparently liked its spatial solution and flexibility, 'he said he was unable to intervene in all matters relating to construction and engineering.' After insisting that the design of Ratio Structures should be capable of conversion to fit multiple uses, and that it was very different from that used habitually by the army, he enumerated its possibilities: 'The Ratio Structure System would be of greatest benefit for hospital units, training schools, officers' quarters, war apartments, dormitories, recreation halls, warehouses, where construction must be rapid and inexpensive, but semi-permanent.'

Thereafter Sert and Lester would focus almost exclusively on the design of the idea, although Sert also devoted himself to teaching and lecturing at different universities thanks to the invitations he began receiving as a result of the publication of his book. They must have worked so hard that in January of 1943 Alvin Johnson suggested to Phillip N. Youtz, Chief of the Consumer Office of Production Research and Development, that he increase their monthly salary from $500 to $625. From March onward there was an incessant influx of letters and visits from official organs interested in the project, as well as attempts on A.F. Somary's part to commercialize the product, which by April had already been granted

Sert and Lester Wiener, Ratio Structures prefabricated modular system, 1942, sketch (SC).

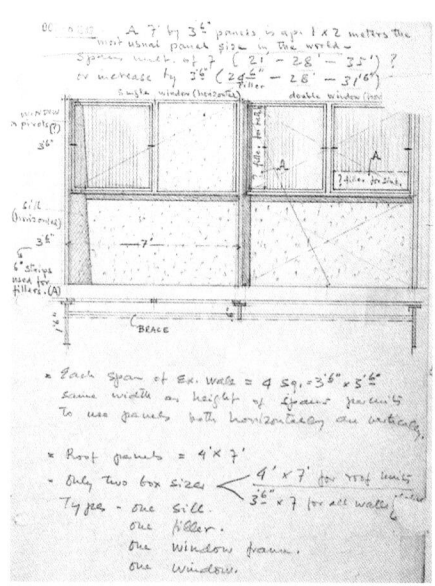

296

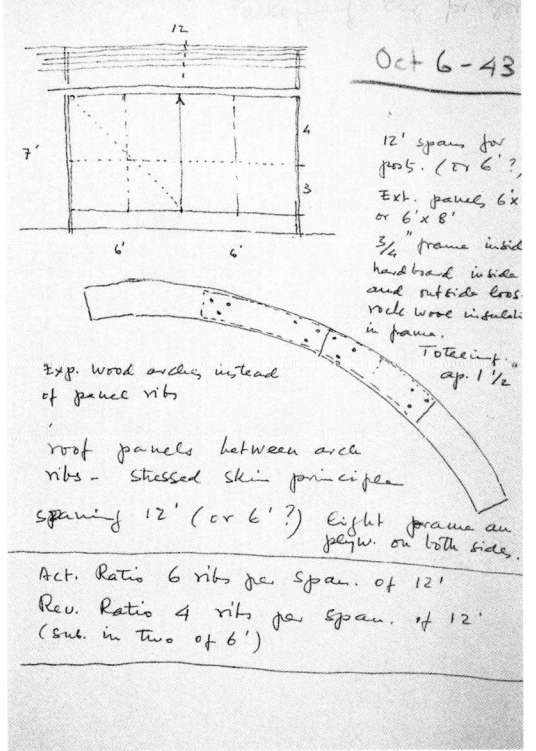
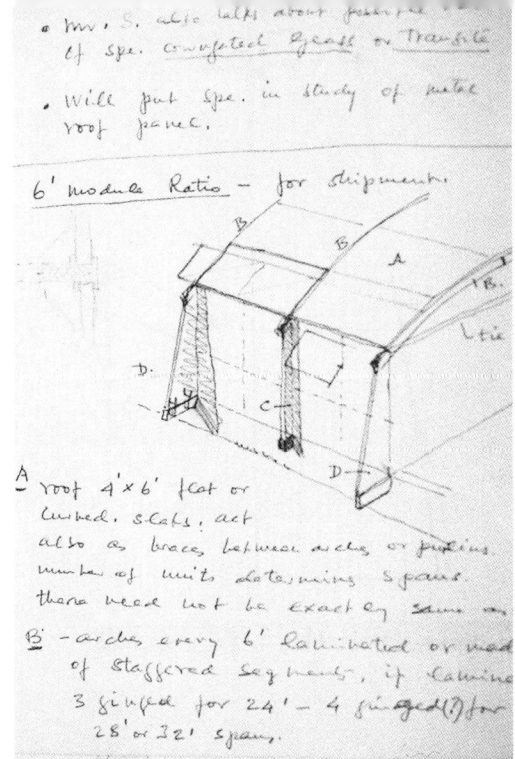
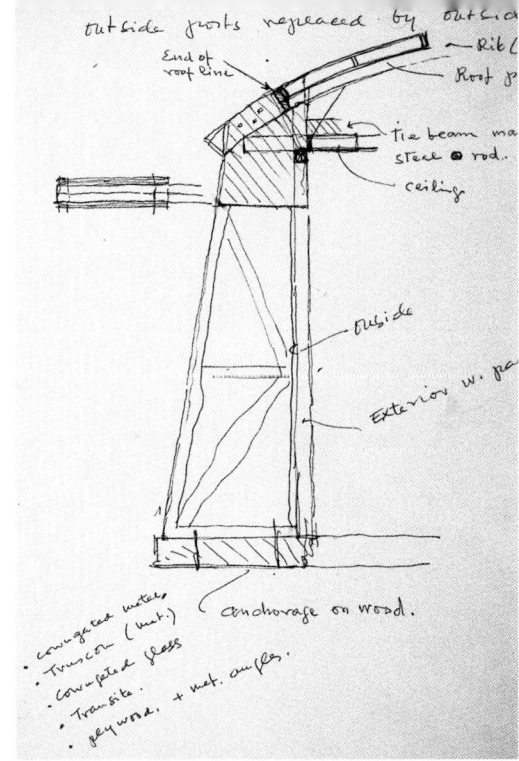

Ratio Structures, sketches (SC).

patent number 476.008. There were also many consultations with structural engineers, and we know through some dated sheets of manuscripts and sketches that in October 1943 Sert was reworking some important aspects of the design, especially those that had to do with the joints of the curved panels for the roof and the dimensions and detailing of the wall panels so as to reduce packaging and shipping costs.

A letter dated 25 October from Phillip N. Youtz, who had helped them in numerous matters concerning the viability of the project, leads us to gather that they were in the final stages of their work: 'I am glad that you are going ahead with the practical development of your building system, I think that it is very important that this be ready for the market at the earliest possible date.'

In December 1943 the project and its prototype construction were published in *Architectural Forum*. There we find a report on the supposed novelty it represented, as well as the first pictures of a module-type construction that had been put out to tender at the end of the previous year. The text lists various points of interest: the construction proceeds from the bottom upwards, while the walls are just a skin assembled independently from the structure, which is left exposed on the facade. Instead of a traditional double-pitch roof, a single curved roof was used, finished with standardized panels. The special design of the facade allowed for a great variety of combinations, while the con-

ception of the project made possible its adaptation to any use, as was shown in the architects' drawings. The structure, which could bridge spans of 20 and 32 feet, was made of wood, while the vertical and horizontal elements were attached to each other with metal cover plates, which allowed for substantial savings on iron and wood in relation to the maximum quotas allowed for wartime houses by the WPB.

In this project, Sert drew on some of the experiments with demountable wooden houses that he had developed in Barcelona in the 1930s, which had sprung from modern architecture's conceptual interest in the prefabrication of low-cost housing as a way to alleviate the acute housing shortage of that city during those years. He took up again the form (although not the structural essence) of the typically Catalan low vault, which he employed in several projects around that time. He was also able to make use of both the high level of technology and the new materials available to the American industry. The result, which can be gathered from the pictures, was something between a hangar of almost unlimited size and a series of houses of a somewhat Mediterranean appearance, which could be laid out to form interior courtyards, all depending on the combination of modules chosen. Independently of the site on which it was located, the project could be combined in various ways according to the requirements of the functions it was to fulfill.

Ratio Structures,
built element.

Ratio Structures,
flexibility
of the module
(SC).

However, despite the architects' efforts, the project failed to prosper. At the beginning of 1944 Sert promoted it throughout the US and some European countries in the hope of winning contracts. He and Lester even went so far as to register their patent in Canada, England and Sweden, but they did not generate any commissions. At the end of 1944, Benjamin W. Gelb asked them for permission to erect a standard module in Patterson, New York. Despite acclaim from the architectural profession, such as that ex-

pressed in the *Architectural Record* of September 1944,[30] one must bear in mind that the conditions of access to housing changed radically in the post-war period, so that the fall in the production of new houses was in no way linked to the design and quality of the project proposals.

Ratio Structures was one of the many victims of this new situation, which sprang from new economic and production conditions, changes in the criteria applied to the policy of granting mortgages, new zoning legislations opposed to modern design and the use of standardized systems, the resistance shown by construction unions, the banks' wariness with regard to financing experimental projects, and undoubtedly from the psychological misgivings of consumers, as set forth by Peter S. Reed. On 17 July 1945, a letter from Lester to someone named Alfred seems to signal the end of Ratio Structures, confirming that it was a lost battle: 'Ratio Structures … is suspending activities, awaiting the clarification of the material situation and the end of the war.'

Nevertheless, American architectural magazines from the end of the 1930s and throughout the 1940s gave widespread publicity to these wartime experiments, while at the same

Gropius'
house, Lincoln,
Massachusetts,
1938.

Gropius
and Breuer,
James Ford's
house, Lincoln,
Massachusetts,
1939.

time advocating the 'normalization' of these 'new' forms. In the July 1939 issue of *Architectural Forum* we find an article entitled 'Modern Houses in America' that corroborates this: 'The modern house today is no longer the frigid white symbol of a small cult, and in changing it has immeasurably broadened its appeal. Discussion of whether the modern is here to stay or not has become academic. It is here.' This introduction led on to the presentation of modern single-family dwellings from different American architects mixed in with those that Gropius had constructed in Lincoln.[31]

In the *Architectural Record* of March of 1940, we find James Ford's house by Breuer and Gropius, and in April of that same year *Architectural Forum* went so far as to compare a dwelling that developed a traditional scheme with the Hagerty house by Breuer and Gropius. The editor's note enclosed a comment that was symptomatic of events at the time and which seems to corroborate Pokinski's point of view: 'There is a distinct trend in house design today, clearly visible in any representative collection of new work. It shows, reasonably enough, a combination of old forms and new forms. It offers the possibility of an indigenous, workable and com-

pletely persuasive architecture for America … The question here, however, is not one of good or bad but rather of contrast: here is the composite symbol of an architecture in transition.'[32]

In June 1943 *Architectural Forum* published two houses by Walter Gropius, one in Lincoln and the other in Framingham, as well as Mies van der Rohe's project for a museum in Chicago, Charles Eames' Town Hall, and a hotel by Kahn and Stonorov. In the *Architectural Record* of May 1945 Joseph Hudnut wrote an article in which he expressed his interest in the impact of war-time architecture on future buildings. Significantly entitled 'The Post-Modern House', it reads: 'I am for every change in construction or equipment or organization which will promote comfort or security or economy in the modern house … I mean, in short, that search for expression which transforms the science of building into the art of architecture.' He then used the 1932 text of Johnson and Russell to explain the formal categories of architecture by Le Corbusier, Oud, Mies and Gropius, and advocated the possibility of conceiving architecture as a machine that would rationalize the house.[33]

Frank Lloyd Wright's project for the Guggenheim museum was published in the *Architectural Forum* of January 1946, and in the *Architectural Record* of May 1947 an article entitled 'Houses are for Humans' seemed to answer Hudnut's earlier text. The *Architectural Forum* of the same month defended the idea that Wright's houses were designed before the Ville Saboye and the Bauhaus building, and that their style, imported from Europe, 'has been modified by

Gropius
and Breuer,
Hagerty House,
Cohasset,
Massachusetts,
1938.

native influences'. It offered pictures of architectural examples going back to the first half of the nineteenth century that lent weight to the claim of a 'Contemporary American Architecture' that had resulted from these earlier manifestations. It is therefore clear that by 1947 there was a keen awareness of the existence of this new American architecture that had come about through the combination of an indigenous tradition and European vanguards, as well as the ever-present Wright, to whom *Architectural Forum* dedicated an issue in January 1948.[34]

At around this time the TPA office on West 42nd Street was busy with other assignments that required a great deal of attention; the many commissions they were receiving for the urban planning of Latin American cities not only involved much work but also many prolonged trips to that region. According to the contracts consulted, these projects must have been economically advantageous, and the benefits must have allowed Sert to start thinking about building his own house. In August 1946, after the architect's family had managed to get a visa for them to enter Spain, Sert travelled with Moncha to Barcelona to see his mother Genara López, who was seriously ill. When he returned to the United States on 15 November he initiated the slow administrative proceedings to register as an architect in the National Council of Architectural Registration Boards, a matter that would drag on until 19 August 1949.

By that time Sert was already involved in the planning of what would be his own house in Locust Valley, Long Island, New York. This is gathered from a letter from his friend the painter Joan Miró of 15 May 1948: 'First of all, let me congratulate you for the purchase of the house. I recall it clearly, as well as the setting, which is also marvellous; I can already promise you that I will visit you frequently there when I return to New York.' If we consider that Miró had been in the States from March until the beginning of November 1947, it is not difficult to work out the date of Sert's interest in setting up residence on Long Island.[35] Miró's letter also provides us with an interesting piece of information: Sert had bought an existing house in that area, a circumstance that has been heavily distorted by some publications, which insisted on giving a more romantic vision of the affair, claiming that the Catalan architect had converted an old barn into his home.[36]

In reality things were more complicated: Sert had in fact bought a large mansion, for which he lost no time in drawing up plans and, undoubtedly due to its elevated cost, dividing it in half and offering to sell one of the two parts to Fernando Teixidor and to Alma Morgenthau, Lester's wife. After this initial operation, Sert demolished one wing of the pre-existing house,

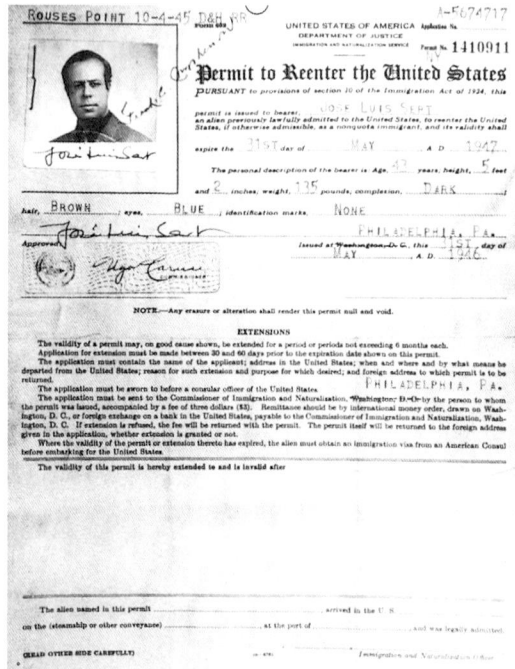
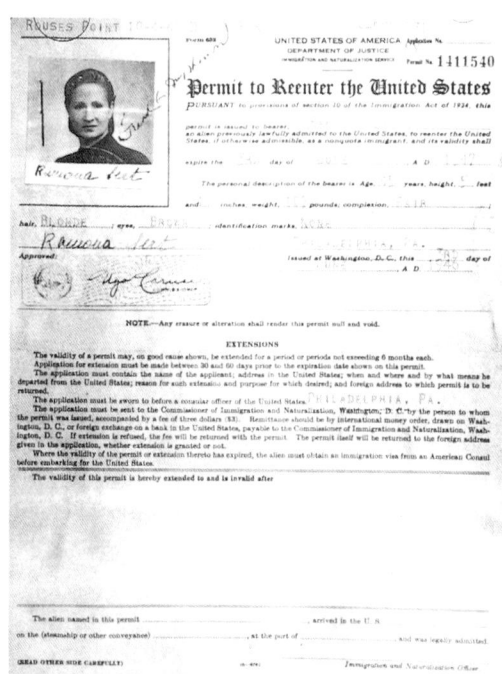

Permits to re-enter the United States for José Luis Sert and Ramona Longas.

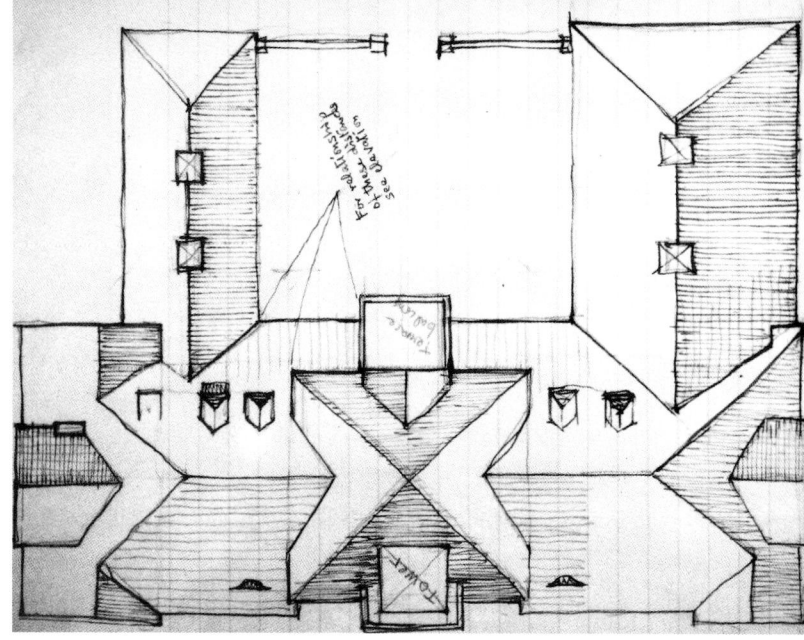

Sert's house
in Locust Valley,
Long Island,
New York,
1949, sketches
of the pre-existing
house (SC).

cleared out the remaining structure of the interior, and taking advantage of the great void space of the stable-cum-garage, and the addition of a new wing, he built what was to be his home until he moved to Cambridge in 1958.

Some blueprints found in his archive, dated 28 June 1949, indicate the date on which he must have completed the project. The building must have been ready by July 1950, for there is a letter of 2 August 1950 from *House & Garden* and another from *Progressive Architecture* of 24 August expressing their interest in publishing the house.

The final result, despite the more generous proportions and the greater complexity of its functions, was the development of some of the ideas that Sert had first carried out in the houses in the Garraf area, at least with regard to the floor plan. A large empty space houses the living room, while the kitchen and the architect's studio turn their backs on the bedrooms and the landscaped space connected to the surrounding countryside. The final volume presented itself as the union of two radically different bodies. The first maintained the form of a covered volume under a double-pitch roof, which pertains to the remaining structure of the old stable of the former house, container of the void space. The other was topped with a flat roof and laid out on two levels, and was resolved following the golden-section proportions, as Sert was fond of explaining.[37] This

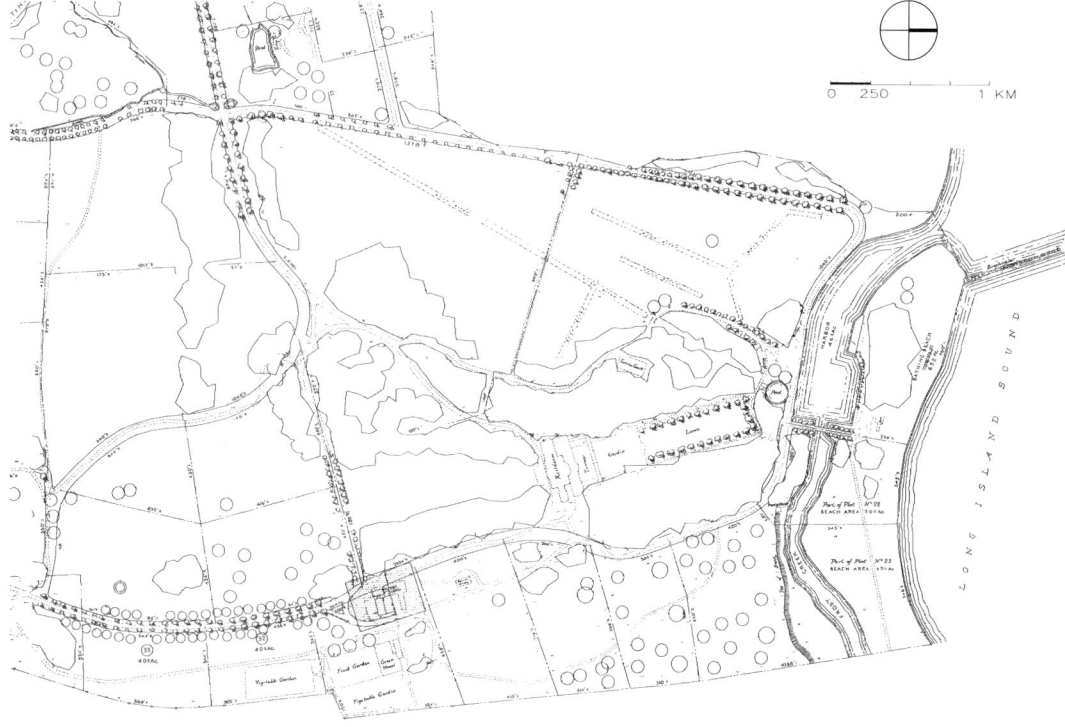

Sert's house
in Locust Valley,
plan of the area.

Sert's house
in Locust Valley,
plan and section.

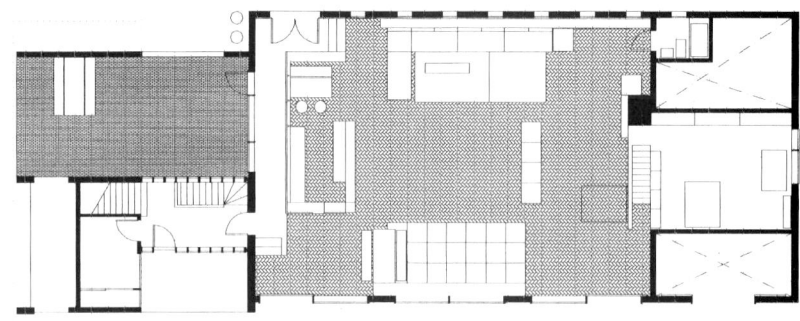

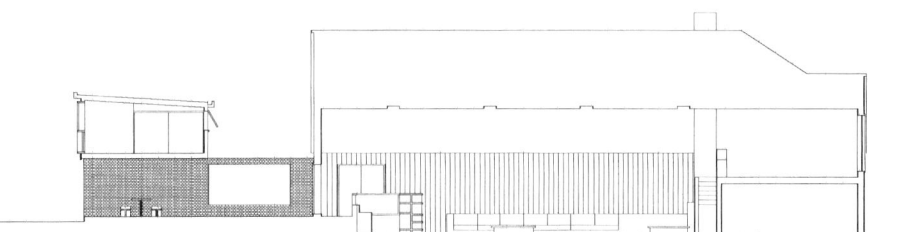

0 1 2 3 4 5

brings to mind certain earlier works by Marcel Breuer, such as the Chamberlain Cottages in Wayland from 1940 and the Cantilevered house of 1947 in New Canaan, or the Resor house by Mies van der Rohe, in that it was conceived as a compact box supported by walls that clearly separate it from the ground. However, in Sert's house these walls enclosed courtyards, entrances and secluded gardens, due to the fact that they were one storey high.

The outcome was one architecture in front of another. Were they engaged in a dialogue or a dispute? Integrated with or separated from each other? Making friends or falling out? Let us leave the answers and Sert's intentions for later. Peter Blake commented that this house was at a crossroads, just as its architect was, since Sert combined the work of the architect with that of a city planner, and that the house's great, excessive space (whose dimensions were always repeated by each successive publication)[38] was to be taken as something halfway between a living room and a civic centre. He also likened it to a plaza, borrowing the simile from a friend, a constructor by the name of Barbagallo. He quoted the comments of the humourist Saul Steinberg, a friend of Sert, who said that whenever he entered the house he always forgot to take off his hat because he had the feeling that he was still outdoors, and he would walk about with it on throughout his visit, greeting those he met by touching its brim. If

one views this space as a plaza, the Calder mobile represents a bell tower, the bench running along the wall a café, and the kitchen a City Hall. It was a plaza that was often visited by Calder, Le Corbusier, J.J. Sweeney, Miró, Nivola and the rest of the friends who surrounded Sert during the time he lived in New York.

To speak of a plaza in Blake's terms recalls the content of the CIAM held in Bergamo in 1949, with its talk of the heart of a city, in which Sert played a decisive role. Aside from one or two excesses to which Blake was prone, one issue in his description calls our attention: the interior of the 'community space' contained a great variety of works of art, a bold

Breuer
and Gropius,
Chamberlain
cottage
in Wayland,
Massachusetts,
1940.

Sert's house in Locust Valley, view of the exterior and interior.

combination of colours, and a special system of laying out the furniture that is certainly noteworthy. Additionally, the original pavement of that former garage, its tiles laid out in a kind of herring-bone design that included the drainage system in its pattern, was conserved by Sert.

In 1947, the year in which the project began to take shape, several significant events had occurred, both in the North American architectural context and in Sert's life, which were inevitably reflected in the building; it is worthwhile to explore these aspects to get a better understanding of the building. Between 5 and 6 March 1947 a symposium entitled Building for Modern Man (published in 1949) was held at Princeton, in which outstanding figures such as Walter Gropius, Konrad Wachsmann, Richard Neutra, Gyorgy Kepes, Joseph Hudnut, Sigfried Giedion, George Howe, William W. Wurster, Frank Lloyd Wright, Robert Moses and others took part, and which Sert must certainly have attended, as a letter to Sigfried Giedion seems to attest.

We cannot go into a lengthy analysis of each of the participants' contributions, and will therefore confine ourselves to mentioning some of the issues voiced there:[39] respect for the past; the need for a radical change in architectural training, in which visual education was considered to be essential; and an unshakeable commitment to recovering the aesthetic values of architecture as well as the need for architecture to contribute to the enrichment of human life. The conviction that industry should not be the master but the servant of architecture, and the need to rise to the challenge of the machine, was directly advocated by Gropius, who insisted that despite the fact that architecture might depend on prefabrication for economic reasons, prefabrication should be sufficiently flexible to solve individual needs. Likewise, post-war architecture was to take into consideration social, emotional and economic factors.

These terms distance us from the pragmatism of the war years, when needs were quite different; the stance of those championing abstract architecture associated with machine aesthetics and mass-production no longer made sense. The architecture that was being advocated was to recover its links with the past once the parenthesis of the war and the apogee of the vanguards

had come to an end, vanguards who were moreover European (which meant that they represented a continent that had been defeated or that had been incapable of avoiding the conflict, and whose leading figures had been forced to flee Paris and settle in New York).

An article by Lewis Mumford published on 11 October 1947 in *The New Yorker* unloosed widespread controversy. For the polemical American critic, something was in the air; new winds were beginning to blow through the world of architecture, borne out by the fact that critics such as Henry-Russell Hitchcock – who twenty years earlier had identified 'modern' architecture with Cubism in painting and with the general glorification of all that the mechanical and abstract stood for – were now advocating the personalism of Frank Lloyd Wright. Mumford wrote, evidently with biased simplification: 'Certainly Le Corbusier's dictum of the 1920s – that the modern house is a machine for living in – has become old hat.' For Mumford, it was time to focus on life, not on the machine, and he emphasized the fact that one of the inventors of the modern architects, Sigfried Giedion, along with Sert and Léger, had some years earlier championed the monumental and the symbolic.[40] He also reported that some of the younger architects were incorporating elements with an emotional charge, such as colour, texture, painting and sculpture. Mumford took the opportunity to affirm that various architects in the US had for some time been moving in this direction, and he coined the term Bay Region Style to differentiate buildings of this tendency from factories or museums.

The article prompted another symposium held at MoMA on the evening of 11 February 1948, in which Walter Gropius, Marcel Breuer, Peter Blake, Henry-Russell Hitchcock, Eero Saarinen, Alfred H. Barr and Gerhard Kallmann took part, with Lewis Mumford acting as moderator.[41] During the evening it became clear that Gropius was irritated by the term that Mumford was trying to institutionalize, an annoyance that he traced back to the 1932 exhibition, insisting that the 'international style' was neither international nor a style. He also pointed out that it encompassed a commitment to regionalism, and that Mumford's interested in it was belated given that the idea had been advocated by many modern architects twenty-five years earlier. Breuer attempted to relativize Mumford's term, seeking points of agreement between 'machinists' and 'regionalists', borrowing a Spanish bullfighting expression for the purpose: '*Sol y sombra*, as the Spanish say; sun and shadow, not sun or shadow.' Blake held the opinion that to speak of an industrial revolution in architecture was nonsensical,[42] considering the terms of the debate to be inflated.

In his closing speech, Mumford took a conciliatory step, declaring that he felt it would be more fruitful to speak about a continuous development of the modern in order to avoid these pitfalls. This was the situation that American architecture was experiencing at the time, attested to by many specialized publications in the States. Thus, it was no longer a question of clinging to categories that were as obvious as they were useless and sterile in that new scenario. The post-war period had no further use for an architectural rhetoric that produced manifestos and stock phrases, but was instead seeking for ways to learn and progress that involved drawing together skills, integrating disciplines, and promoting encounters between different facets of the arts. Some or all of these points, as well as aesthetic questions, were debated at Bridgwater during the meeting that ran from 7 to 14 September 1947, at which Sert was appointed president of CIAM, a post he would hold until the dissolution of the congresses.

The Hungarian Bauhaus member Marcel Breuer has repeatedly cropped up in our path, and we would do well to consider this figure now, for as we have seen, he was very useful to Sert, who employed and integrated many elements of his architecture into several of his own buildings.[43] William H. Jordy,[44] a classical author of North American architectural history, has suggested an even more powerful reason to look into this figure, labelling him 'the tamer of the modern', and as the essential bridge spanning two cultures that allows one to understand how American architecture drew closer to European forms. Jordy's hypothesis is different from those of Pokinski and Kopp, but equally clear in its concept, and it provides us

with an opportunity to increase the depth of our analysis. In the period in which the US was looking towards Europe, in the old continent there were already examples of integration between the machine and popular constructional tradition. This was something that, as we know, Sert had practised, and Jordy gives a further example by referring to the house that Le Corbusier built for Madame de Mandrot in Le Pradet, along with other of his dwellings: 'Between 1930 and 1935 … Le Corbusier built three vacation houses in which he subordinated the machine image to regional traditions of building in masonry and wood without compromising his own architectural ideals.'[45]

This concern with taking up regionalist values must have interested an America submerged in the New Deal: 'In the United States, the 1930s were a time especially congenial to the rediscovery of regional traditions and not in architecture alone. Domestic problems forced the country to turn inward on itself, where it remained focused until foreign events broke the isolation trance.'[46] As Jordy willingly points out, in 1934 Breuer had already given a lecture in which he expressed his admiration for popular architecture, and in which he declared: 'If we ask ourselves what is the source of the solid, unselfconscious beauty, the convincing quality and reasonableness of peasant work, we find that the explanation lies in its unconsciously and therefore genuinely traditional nature. A given region has only a few traditional crafts and uses a few definite colours … If one examines industrial standardization, one cannot fail to perceive that it is representative of an "art", of a traditional development which is the result of exploring the same problem over and over again. What has changed is our method: instead of family traditions and force of habit we employ scientific principles and logical analysis.'[47]

This naturally leads one from Le Corbusier's buildings to the Ganes Exhibition Pavilion in Bristol, built in 1936 by Breuer, where the masonry walls and the large glass surfaces became the exclusive visual protagonists of a project in which the presence of Mies is equally important in the configuration of the floor plan. Breuer's arrival in the US made it possible to count on an architect whose attitude allowed him to es-

Marcel Breuer,
Pavilion for the
Royal Show
in Bristol, 1936.

tablish a dialogue with a modernity transformed by its relationship to popular architecture, a work that both Breuer and Sert had taken upon themselves to explore in depth.

In this climate of debate, it is also worth taking note of an ambitious work by Sigfried Giedion, published in 1948 by the Oxford University Press, a key text in understanding a good part of post-war American architectural culture. This book, *Mechanization Takes Command: A Contribution to Anonymous History*, was the result of a prolonged analysis carried out by the Swiss historian over a number of years, starting with his first visit to the United States, and it was based on industrial catalogues and patents for American industrial products.[48] The author declared that the objective of the book was 'to describe the impact of a mechanized world on the human organism and feelings'.[49]

The point was to explain the impact of this world of machines within the context of American culture, which invited a comparison with what had occurred in Europe, written from the point of view of a European who had seen in the United States famous precedents for the modern. In this confrontation, which was in some ways already latent in *Space, Time and Architecture*, Giedion brought to the surface profound differences between the two cultures, always seen through the prism of an undisputed American superiority. The most important of these was a basic conceptual difference. Although it was not stated in this way, the examples that Giedion offered implied that whereas in Europe artists had interpreted the machine as a metaphoric cultural pretext, in the United States it was always viewed as something that helped to improve the living conditions of a people who even at the beginning of the nineteenth century were still conquering virgin territories.

To put it bluntly, while Le Corbusier was preaching that the house was a machine for living in, and nobody in Europe really knew what he was talking about, the Americans were actually living among machines that made their lives more comfortable and increased their leisure time, with the added bonus of producing lower housing costs. In Cincinnati, they had designed slaughterhouses that used a similar process to what would later be the assembly line; Oliver Evans had already built an automatic mill in the seventeenth century; and in 1871, Walter A. Wood had patented a reaper driven by a single man. Giedion reproduced designs of barber's and dentist's chairs propelled by simple mechanisms to facilitate the tasks of those working with them, and he also showed adjustable railway seats that were specially designed to achieve a high degree of comfort. The historian vindicated the idea of comfort as a decisive factor in the attainment of the democratic condition.

Household electrical appliances came next in a never-ending list that pointed out each chronological step in this progress: the washing

Cover of Sigfried
Giedion's
*Mechanization
Takes Command*,
1948.

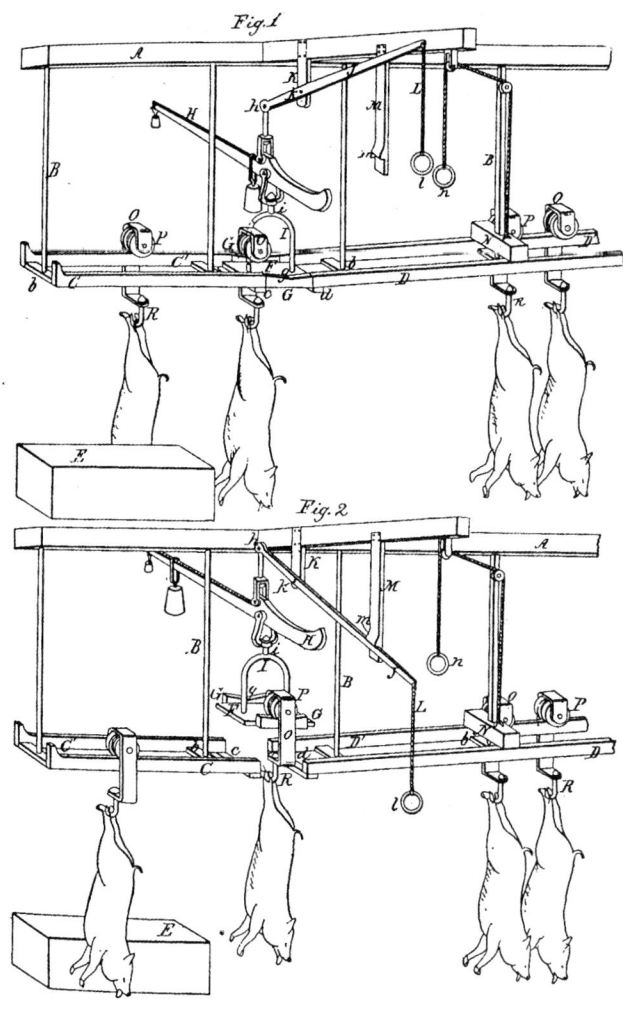

Automatic
assembly lines
and plan
and perspective
of bi-nuclear
houses illustrated
in *Mechanization
Takes Command*.

furniture from previous centuries, far removed from the uncomfortable monumentality of its European counterparts.[50]

This exhibition of superiority had a clear objective: to help convince US culture that the American architect must stop being 'a professional whose mission consisted in decorating the house, as a baker does with a cake',[51] so that he could again take up his position at the forefront of a mechanized world full of almost infinite

machine, the vacuum cleaner, the garbage-disposal unit, and other devices were upheld as the legacy of the American culture, which until then had not flaunted its modernity, but which in the triumphant post-war period became the standard bearer of a new world from which Europeans had much to learn.

The fundamental point of the work was the demonstration of the backwardness of the Old World in comparison with this unquestionable technological superiority in the United States, something that as we know had already been detected by Le Corbusier and Gropius. Now, however, at the end of the 1940s, it was a matter of using this superiority as a starting point to renew ideas and therefore to trivialize the contributions of Le Corbusier and Aalto did not seem problematic, showing the lack of sophistication of their furniture design in comparison to what the American industry had produced many years earlier, or demonstrating the functionalist convertibility of American

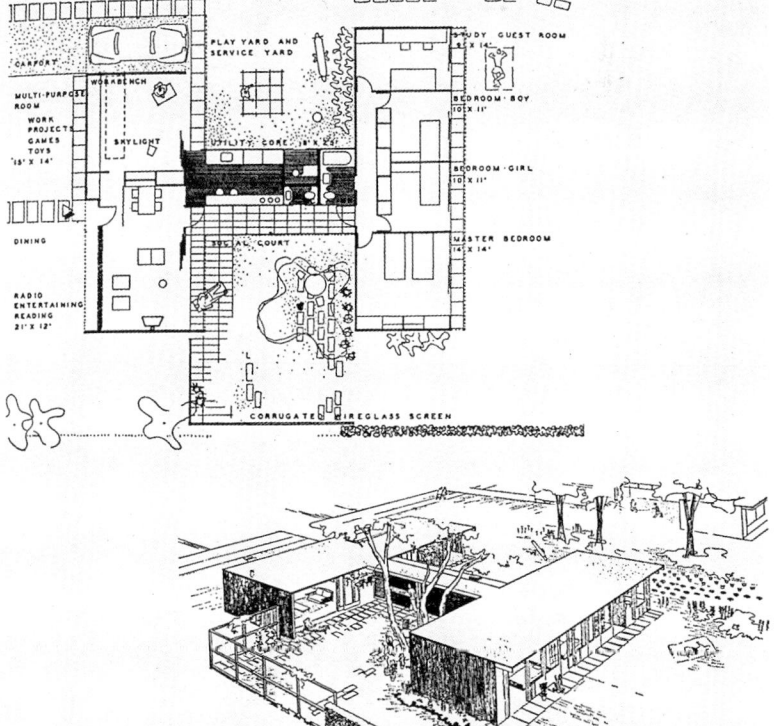

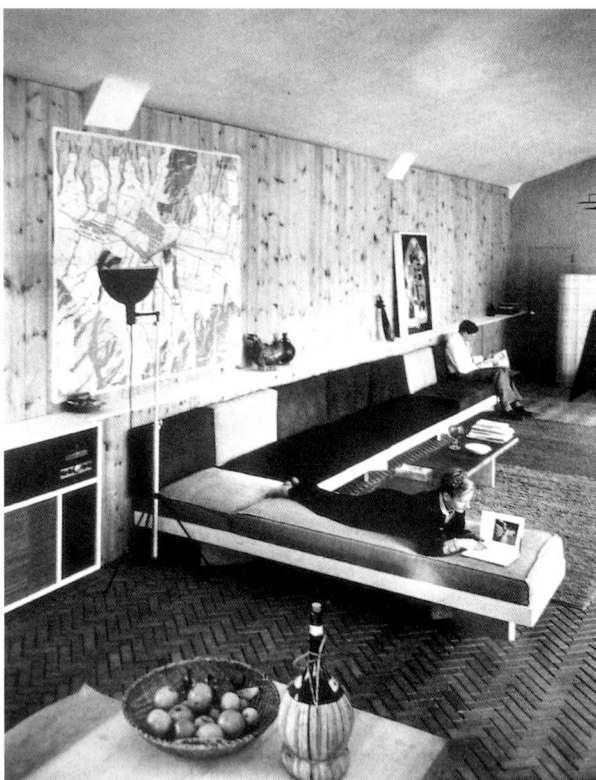

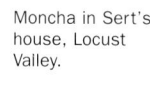

possibilities. These advances had already fostered the projects of Richard Buckminster Fuller at the end of the 1920s, whose results made it possible to assemble, with a considerable saving of money, the mechanical nucleus of the house, encompassing kitchen, bathroom, washing room, heating, electricity and plumbing as if they were the parts of a car. In this mechanized world it was also feasible to design a binuclear house in H-form, as the architects J. and H. Fletcher proved with their project in 1945 in which the diurnal and nocturnal areas were separated by a nucleus of services in which all the 'humid' rooms of the dwelling were clustered.[52]

The last pages of *Mechanization Takes Command* were explicit: 'Like the forces of nature, mechanization depends on man's capacity to make use of it and to protect himself against its inherent dangers. Moreover, since mechanization arose wholly out of man's mind, it is even more dangerous for him, because it is less easily controlled than nature's forces and it furthermore reacts in the senses and mind of its creator.'[53] The shadow of war and the widespread destruction it had caused, magnified by the lethal machines that had been employed in the conflict, motivated these words. The machine that before the war had seemed to

promise progress and well-being for all had shown another facet of its might. Now, once destruction had come to an end, Giedion advocated the idea that Americans were part of a country and a democracy capable of demonstrating the beneficial effects of mechanization if it were channelled towards human well-being. The European Marcel Breuer also considered a redefinition of mechanization to be necessary, so that the terms expounded on by Giedion could achieve a certain equilibrium: this equilibrium would be present in a great part of American domestic architecture of the 1940s, which would decisively take up the language of modernity to construct itself on the basis of the advanced technology of industrial production.[54]

Let us go back to Long Island, then, a binuclear house that asks to be understood as a great question mark, or as a long series of question marks, which become meaningful in relation not only to the architectural culture of the time, but also to the lives of its inhabitants. To split up and demolish a traditional house belongs to the realm of outdated ideas that scorn any building exhibiting ornamentation, convinced that the new message should be the only one to have a place in the world. For Sert to maintain a part of that house seems to indicate a somewhat guilty conscience about the intervention carried out there, as well as granting an opportunity to the commonplace aesthetics, run of the mill yet inherent to the country that had welcomed him. It also represented, on a more pragmatic level, considerable savings in the planning of the new house.

In the great interior void space, traditional and enclosed, Sert placed a set of avant-garde works of art and an array of brightly coloured hand-woven fabrics and rugs produced by Latin American Indians, whose handicrafts he had bought on his frequent trips to that continent; on the walls he hung some of his projects for its cities. This is a space to be lived in, in which these diverse cultural products mingle and converse with each other, representing Sert's interest in combining different aspects of the reality in which he lived, something he had already enjoyed doing in the 1930s in the Garraf houses, in which one saw avant-garde works alongside traditional Mediterranean ceramics and pottery. Now, however, in the architect's intimate cosmos it was possible to observe other fetishes: the plan for the city of Medellin presiding over his living room attested to the intellectual value of his knowledge, and to his capacity to offer order to the world.

Popular culture, rationalism American-style such as that propounded by Giedion, elite art and functionalist urbanism all coexisted in that American barn-stable, that mantle protecting so much complexity, that all-encompassing container, lord and master of the popular and the modern, ruler of the world, easing, through its will to integrate, the social and historical tension represented by all these things.

The ensemble is accompanied by furniture that is both uncomfortable and nearly invisible, also forcing its user practically to disappear since he or she must use it from a horizontal position. This constitutes a warning: nothing could be further removed than this from a happy integration into American tradition, in which the commodity was everything, as Giedion pointed out around this time. Here the items and the furniture are placed to be seen, to act as continual reminders of the other worlds to which the owners belong and to which they cling by exhibiting them to visi-

tors. Observing the floor plan, it is not difficult to perceive that its heteroclite universe is controlled from the two opposite ends of the space, the places in which the real activity of the house takes place: the kitchen and the architect's weekend studio. The domestic and the professional are the two poles that direct and supervise the interior space, a synthesis of so many and such different cultural worlds with which Sert had become familiar in his continuous travels, and in which no item could be used or displaced unless under the constantly watchful eye of Moncha or José Luis.

Domestic order and intellectual order went hand in hand in the daily life of the Sert couple, each with his or her own well-defined function in an equilibrium that they always maintained; this was the way to manage this vast space, in which there was no architectural passage nor visual accident that had not been first spotted by the owners themselves.

It is in the private zone that the true meaning of the house is enclosed: a lightweight box seems to float on top of brick walls that run parallel and stop short of the ends, with openings wherever needed. It is in this wooden volume that Sert and Moncha were finally able to share an intimate space of their own, after having married in secret, probably for family reasons, many years before in Paris (or after having married in Cuba due to other circumstances before entering the United States). This was their love nest, separated from the ground, brushing against the beautiful trees that surrounded the house, looking straight towards the future and the perfect natural setting with serenity, as Moncha did in one of the most widely published pictures of this building.

The contrast between the two volumes, the old and the new, is therefore complementary: sun and shadow, two sides of the same coin; neither friends nor antagonists, they simply seek to reflect the different nuances of night and day, work and sex, intellectual culture and daily life, private and public spheres, facets of a relationship that until then had been nomadic and which in that new period and space – just like modern architecture, which was still establishing itself in the US – had been able to settle down and take root.[55]

Johnson house,
1950.

[1] We are referring to *Can Our Cities Survive?*, published by Harvard University Press in 1942. In the first chapter we described the circumstances that led to the publication of this work, and we also analyzed its contents.

[2] In a handwritten letter from Le Corbusier to Sert of 5 May 1940, which is kept in the Sert Collection, we read: 'Deliver these words personally to Paul Lester Wiener, 33 West 42nd Street. You can talk to him about the CIAMs and he will tell you about our friends in Rio de Janeiro.' SC E 28.

Thus we can gather that Sert and Lester were introduced to each other thanks to the Swiss architect, whom Lester had probably met in Paris in 1937 since he was the author of the American Pavilion at the World's Fair held in the French city that year. It could also be that Sert and Lester met due to the same circumstances. A letter among Sert's papers of 25 August 1944, addressed by Lester to the Commissioner of Immigration and Naturalization declares: 'I have the pleasure of certifying the fact that I have known them [the Sert couple] since 1937 and that Mr Sert is a gentleman of a most noble character and of great validity for the architectural profession.' But since the ob-

jective of this letter was to achieve the legalization of the couple's situation in the United States, the date offered by Lester could have been manipulated.

Paul Lester Wiener was born in Leipzig in 1895 and studied in Berlin, Vienna and Paris. He arrived in the States in 1913, although he then returned to Europe, where he stayed until 1927. In 1937 he designed the American Pavilion at the Paris World's Fair, and in 1938 the interior of the Brazilian Pavilion for the New York World's Fair. In 1942 he founded TPA jointly with Schulz and Sert, and the firm continued to run until 1958. He died on 16 November 1967.

On Sert's activities in New York, see his recollections in John Peter, *The Oral History of Modern Architecture*, Harry Abrams, New York, 1994, pp. 253–55.

More information is also found in Joan Ockman, *The War Years in America: New York, New Monumentality*; various authors, *Sert. Arquitecte a Nova York*, exhibition catalogue, MACBA, Barcelona, April 1997.

In a typewritten text that will be quoted later entitled 'Meeting Places for the Arts', we find: 'So in New York we continued meeting in

"The Jumble Shop" in MacDougal Alley. Calder brought all newcomers from Europe there. Léger, Chagall, Breton, Tanguy, Lipchitz, Masson, etc. And the talks continued with dreams and plans for better days.'

[3] Sert Collection (SC), Correspondence, Folder E2. This is the contract signed by Sert and Weissmann with the company 'Real Estate Projects', which was directed by Dorothy Harvey and Gertrude Nervel. It also specified that the architects would give preference to commissions from Harvey and Nervel.

[4] Archive of the Superior Tribunal of Justice of Catalonia. In the report one can read the charges against Sert: 'He has a record as a leftist, despite belonging to the family of the Count of Sert, whose patriotic Spanish feelings are deeply rooted and whose sympathies lie with the National Cause to which he has lent valuable services. He was an activist in Izquierda Catalana (Catalan Left Wing), although he did not carry out any noteworthy activities, and he formed part of a group called Grupo de amigos de Rusia (Group of Friends of Russia), making propaganda.' The same report details the trial process with declarations for and against our architect. On 1 July 1944, thanks to

an appeal made by the Sert family to the National Tribunal of Political Responsibilities, the sentence was reduced for reasons that are not wholly clear, with an ambiguous wording that would be difficult to verify. Thus, the Tribunal of Appeals considered that: 'Perhaps because he belonged to a distinguished family with an ideology opposed to his, he was persecuted in the first period of the National Movement, going abroad … Receiving the commission to construct the Pavilion of Republican Spain for the Paris World's Fair, being in charge afterwards of its maintenance and demolition, remaining thereafter as an aggregate of the Tourist Office of the Reds, despite which it seems that shortly after the triumph of national arms, or shortly before this took place, he managed to get in touch with the national Embassy, acknowledging the possibility of lending some informational service.' For which reasons the sentence was reduced as follows: 'We sentence that … we must and do impose an economic sanction of seventy-five thousand pesetas, remaining in force the sanctions of disqualification and exile determined by the Regional Tribunal of Barcelona in its sentence, but for a term of ten years.'

The Spanish extreme right-wing still thought of Sert as a dangerous left-wing activist as late as the end of the 1960s. Thus, in issue no. 131 of *Fuerza Nueva* in July 1969, which carried information about an act in the United States to aid Spanish refugees, we read: 'And thus, among the riffraff, Reds and gangsters, figure José Luis Sert, Francisco García Lorca, Victoria Kent, Sánchez Albornoz, Salvador Madariaga and PABLO CASALS [in capitals in the original], the last two contributors to the *ABC* newspaper. Mr Tarín; Mr Director of TVE: I have called RIFFRAFF, REDS AND GANGSTERS all Spanish renegades and international "brigade men" who sign these summonings or who speak up to spread lies.'

There is a good summary of the US intervention in the Spanish Civil War in Michel E. Parrish, *Anxious Decades*, W.W. Norton, New York and London, 1992, pp. 452–55.

We have no information as to its origins, but in the July 1937 issue of *Architectural Record* we find an article entitled 'Professional News Here and Abroad', in which part of the manifesto of the Sindicat d'Arquitectes de Catalunya (Architects' Union of Catalonia) is reproduced. In the October issue of the same magazine an unsigned article was published, which was dedicated to the 1937 Paris World's Fair, along with the plans for the Pavilion of the Republic.

[5] Paul Lester Wiener Collection (PLWC), Box 14, Incoming Correspondence, 'US Department of State'.

[6] William Lescaze, *On Being an Architect*, New York, 1942, p. 270. Lescaze was born in Geneva in 1896. He had worked in Karl Moser's studio and had arrived in the US in 1926.

[7] Phillip Johnson and Henry Russell, *The International Style: Architecture since 1922*, Norton and Company, 1932. For detailed information on the secret workings to achieve what was an unexpected exhibition given the American architectural scene at the time see Terence Riley, *The International Style: Exhibition 15 and the Museum of Modern Art*, Rizzoli and Columbia Books, New York, 1992. Colin Rowe has carried out a critical appraisal of many of the intentions contained in the catalogue of the 1932 exhibition, and the circumstances surrounding Russell-Hitchcock's sojourn in Paris going back to September 1926. See Colin Rowe, *Henry-Russell Hitchcock* (1988), in Alexander Caragonne (ed.), *As I Was*

Saying: Recollections and Miscellaneous Essays, MIT, Cambridge, 1996, pp. 11–23.

The penchant for reducing architecture to style acquires almost comical nuances in Marcus Whiffen, *American Architectures since 1870. A Guide to the Styles*, MIT Press, 1969. Less known to the general public interested in architecture is the publication on Barr's trajectory by Alice Golfarb: *Alfred H. Barr Jr. Missionary for the Modern*, Contemporary Books, Chicago/New York, 1989.

[8] Deborah Frances Pokinski, *The Development of the American Modern Style*, UMI Research Press, Michigan, 1982–84, p. 11.

[9] Ibid., p. 12.

[10] Ibid., p. 52.

[11] 'Following the Tribune Competition in 1922, American architects began to take a greater interest in non-historical or original styles because these appeared to be more up-to-date when compared to Ionic columns or ribbed vaults. For the same reason, Americans began to give more attention to the unprecedented forms developing in Europe, although many of these appeared to have no decorative characteristics whatsoever … Among the modernistic styles, Americans usually included German and Dutch avant-garde architecture, the designs presented at the 1925 Paris Exposition, the work of the Viennese Secession, and the designs of Le Corbusier, who was particularly known through his architectural treatise, *Vers une Architecture*.' Ibid., p. 53.

[12] The text by Mumford chosen by Pokinski states: 'For a whole generation, from 1890 to 1920, the energies of American architecture worked under the surface … The energies that worked below ground so long are now erupting in a hundred unsuspected places; and once more the American architect has begun to attack the problem of design with the audacity and exuberance of a Root, a Sullivan, a Wright.'

[13] According to Cheney: 'I definitely state my belief: (1) that a new mode is established, constituting an architectural revolution more fundamental than any in seven centuries; (2) that the principles and methods underlying are nearer to universal than any that have previously governed art, and that, therefore, this is the beginning of a world trend, not merely a racial or national phase; and (3) that nothing is to be accomplished hereafter in the "historic" styles known to civilization will really matter … Honesty, openness, economy, brightness, direct thinking, faith in a new life, consideration of one's neighbours, these breathe in the very air of this experimental "development", projected consciously to give the dreamers of new worlds opportunity to crystallize their ideas in concrete and glass and metal … The skyscraper, then, is the building that symbolizes the times … Nor is the skyscraper only symbolically typical of today; nowhere else is architecture so perfectly expressive of the materials.' Quoted in Pokinski, op. cit., pp. 69–70.

[14] Ibid., p. 70.

[15] Mumford expresses himself forcefully with regard to this: 'The foundations of a new architecture had been laid … Between 1880 and 1895 the tasks and methods of modern architecture were clarified through the example of a group of American architects whose consistent and unified efforts in this line anticipated, by at least a decade, the earliest similar innovations in Europe … Modern architecture had its beginnings in this period.' In 1941 he would publish *The South in Architecture*, a compilation of four conferences. The third of these, 'The Regionalism of H.H. Richardson', would later be extremely successful when re-

published by Da Capo Press, New York, 1967. Apart from Mumford's most important books, two other works that offer his short writings are: Donald L. Miller, *The Lewis Mumford Reader*, University of Georgia Press, 1995; *From the Ground Up*, Harvest Books, New York, 1964, a selection of his articles in *The New Yorker* edited by Mumford himself. A recent biography of Mumford is Agatha C. and Thomas P. Hughes, *Lewis Mumford: Public Intellectual*, Oxford University Press, New York, 1990. A global perspective on Mumford is found in Rossella Cominotti and Giuliano Della Pergolla, *Lewis Mumford nella storia e nella critica*, Grafo, Brescia, 1992.

[16] Pokinski, op. cit., pp. 79–80. The points made by Pokinski are corroborated by the publication in 1934 of F.R.S. Yorke's book, *The Modern House*, which was a great publishing success and whose contents were expanded in successive editions. European and American dwellings share space in the pages of this book. Its author, an English architect, clarifies the cultural climate that we are examining here: 'We can no longer afford to build a house that makes bad use of space, or to employ ornamental devices to counteract weaknesses in basic design. Anything that is for use must be, above all else, efficient, and the design of the modern house is based on the principle of utility – it is fundamentally a thing for use.' Quoted in Lesley Jackson, *Contemporary Architecture and Interiors of the 1950s*, Phaidon Press, London, 1954, p. 12.

[17] Anatole Kopp, *Quand le moderne n'était pas un style mais une cause*, École nationale supérieure des Beaux Arts, Paris, 1988, p. 194.

[18] 'An important aspect of the new policy undertaken is that which has to do with the building sector and public works, which is based on the National Housing Act of 1934 established by the Federal Housing Administration (FHA), but it has even more to do with the creation of the Public Works Administration (PWA) set up by the national Industrial Recovery Act of 1933, key element of the new policy. The most important aspect of the PWA has been the impulse given to urban renovation through the elimination of slums and the direct construction of social housing by public authorities for the first time in the history of the United States.' Ibid., p. 196.

The foundation of the Housing Division, directed by the architect Henry Wright of the PWA, was an important step in the promotion of fifty-one urban renovation operations without criteria of economic profitability and with measures for hygiene, safety, comfort and communal facilities.

[19] In regard to this, see Francesco Dal Co, 'De los parques a la región. Ideología progresista y reforma de la ciudad americana', in *La ciudad americana*, Gustavo Gili, Barcelona, 1975, pp. 141–293.

[20] Kopp, op. cit., p. 205.

[21] There is a review of Bauer's book in the *Architectural Forum* of February 1935, p. 35. On Catherine Bauer, see 'Housing's White Knight', *Architectural Forum*, March 1946.

[22] Kopp, op. cit., pp. 214–17. Kopp speaks about the European origins of Stonorov and Kastner, the first of whom worked with André Lurçat. He also discusses the direct influences of Ernst May's experience on the work of these two architects in the Carl Mackey complex, considered the best American project for workers' housing by Catherine Bauer in *Modern Housing*.

[23] Vernon De Mars, 'Social Planning for Social Agriculture', *Task*, no. 2, February 1942. Quoted in Kopp, op. cit., p. 230.

[24] Regarding this topic of emigration, Pokinski writes: 'The Style gained even greater au-

311

thority and influence when several of its European masters arrived in this country in 1937. The presence of Walter Gropius and Mies van der Rohe was eventually manifest in actual buildings, but their most significant impact was made through their direct contact with scores of young architecture students at Harvard University and the Illinois Institute of Technology where the masters accepted teaching positions.'

In Kopp's version: 'Apart from minor works destined for their own use, such as Gropius' and Breuer's houses in Lincoln which aroused the admiration of the students at Harvard and the Massachusetts Institute of Technology located nearby but which went unnoticed by the users of architecture at large, the masters of the Bauhaus devoted themselves exclusively to the teaching of architecture until the end of the war … Neither Gropius at Harvard, nor Mies van der Rohe at the Illinois Institute of Technology nor Moholy-Nagy at the New Bauhaus of Chicago, nor Albers at the Black Mountain College did nothing else than initiate their students in the methods laid out in the Bauhaus. Nothing recalled the relatively communal life of the teaching and student groups, nor the attempts to respond to a real demand, nor the work carried out in common with the labour unions.'

Another symptom of this integration of modernity within the scope of American architectural culture is found in the competitions for single-family dwellings published by *Architectural Forum*. In the March 1935 issue of this magazine, we observe that in one of these competitions the architects Hays and Simpson won with a project for a house in Cleveland, and Neutra obtained second place in category D. On pp. 400–03, we are told that Neutra had won the award 'Better Houses in America' for the William Beard house in Altadena, California.

[25] See *What is Modern Architecture?*, The Museum of Modern Art, New York, 1942.

[26] For the most relevant constructions that were originated due to new war-time needs, see Donald Albrecht (ed.), *World War II and the American Dream: How Wartime Building Changed a Nation*, MIT Press, Cambridge, 1995.

[27] Peter S. Reed, 'Enlisting Modernism', in ibid. Here we are informed of both the ideological and social changes that brought about the needs that the war industries had to fulfil, and the most important commissions made to well-known architects for these vast housing interventions. Reed also compiles the critical appraisals of various architects, who review the quality of the buildings.

On the consequences and significance of the war on the US economy and the American mentality, indicated both through statistics and the ideological proclamations of politicians, see Oscar & Lilian Handlin, *Liberty and Equality: 1920–1994*, Harper Collins Publishers, New York, 1994, pp. 78–110.

All types of articles concerning the circumstances of the war began to appear, starting with the *Architectural Record* of January 1942: 'Building Needed for Civilian Health and Welfare in War-time Production Centres'; 'War Requirements Accelerate Progress in Design'. In March 1942: 'More and Faster – Now'. In the editorial page of the April issue, entitled: 'Clearer Perspective', we read: 'In clear perspective, we see beyond the dark foreground of immediate war necessities the sunnier form of the planning and the building that inevitably will follow and for which we must prepare.' In the May issue: 'Technical Teams for War Work'. In the June editorial

page, entitled 'Certainties and Uncertain Times', we find: 'The great need now is to prepare for this opportunity and responsibility by increasing our capacity for leadership through a clearer understanding of all that is involved.' In the July issue, the wording takes on political connotations, as in 'Design for Democracy', a fragment of which we have quoted, while at the same time the projects of the FPHA begin to appear: 'Duration Dormitories for Industrial War Workers'. The September 1942 editor's note is also indicative: 'They Plan for Democracy Now'. In it we read: 'Plans for the immediate future centre on production for winning the war. Nothing can be built that does not contribute to that effort. Materials are not available for any other purpose.'

The 1943 issues have a similar tone, whereas in the 1944 issues we witness an anticipated celebration of the victory of the Allies and an initial look ahead towards the future. Thus, for example, the editorial page of September 1944 bears the title 'Postwar Quantity and Quality', and the December issue offers an article entitled 'Products for Postwar Plans', while the May 1945 issue carries an article called 'Possibilities in Post-war Techniques'.

The *Architectural Forum* issue of May 1942 is dedicated to 'War Housing', and in the October issue we find a text of similar content to many of those we have mentioned: 'Building's Post-war Pattern'.

[28] PLWC, Box 12. All the letters quoted referring to the Ratio Structures project are in this box in the Oregon archive.

[29] Ibid.

[30] In it we read: 'The quantity of buildings needed is tremendous and is growing like a snowball rolling down the hill. But what of the quality? … We look for more logical designs, as well as more efforts of the imaginative to outdo their contemporaries in producing the unusual. We look for greater freedom from the conventions of modern stylists as well as from the conventions of journalists. We look for more "delight" in architectural design, more knowing use of colour, of expressive light and shade and shadow, of forms more carefully proportioned. We look for an architecture that has passed his belligerent, self-conscious adolescence, freed from self-imposed taboos, an architecture mature and efficient, honest and sincere, soul-satisfying as well as serviceable … We believe post-war architecture will stand qualitative as well as quantitative analysis!'.

[31] We cannot avoid mentioning the influence exerted by the single-family dwelling in Oslo built by Eyvind Moestue and Olelind Schistad in the design of Gropius' house in Lincoln. The former was published in the March 1936 issue of *Architectural Record*. This was a 'modern' house that must have interested Gropius because it was found in the midst of the many traditional buildings that dominated the pages of architectural magazines during those years, although we do find several buildings by Neutra and Lescaze.

The September 1936 issue of *Architectural Record* bears the eloquent title: 'The Architect in the Modern World: Education of the Architect', in which we find an interesting contribution by Joseph Hudnut, Dean of the GSD of Harvard at the time, who had addressed the same topic in the February 1935 issue of *Architectural Forum*. There are also articles by Mumford and Wright, and the Bauhaus experience is also mentioned along with Gropius' work.

That certain American magazines followed Gropius' work can be gleaned from the news published in *Architectural Record* of October

1936, in which we are told that the German architect had set up an association with Maxwell Fry. Two years earlier, in the May 1934 issue, we find an article by Giedion entitled 'What Should Be Done to Improve Architectural Education?', which recommends the 'appointment of architects of outstanding experience and technical ability as professors of the important schools of architecture. For example, would not an experienced educator and creative head such as Walter Gropius be very helpful for the reorganization of architectural schools of America?'.

[32] On the evening of 5 March 1940, an exhibition entitled 'VERSUS' was inaugurated at the Architectural League of New York. It exhibited traditional architectures versus modern ones. A thorough review of the exhibition can be found in *Architectural Forum*, April 1941, including this fragment of the commentary that Lewis Mumford published in *The New Yorker*: 'That there is still any debate about these matters in architectural circles is a sign of curious architectural innocence … On one floor are depicted the dead buildings that were built to resemble other dead buildings. On the upper floor a vivid array of fresh buildings, evolved freely out of the needs and tastes of our own day. One floor is a cemetery, the other is a delivery ward. How can they clash? How can there be any question of choice?'.

The first two issues of *Architectural Record* in 1941 are interesting, finding a sort of balance between the latest American architecture in which 'modern' architectures are combined with other traditional ones. In 'Old Siwash Builds', in *Architectural Forum*, July 1948 we find another charming comparison between modern and traditional architecture, through vignettes that compare the two and an imaginary history, written and illustrated by John Allcott, Director of the Department of Art of the North Carolina University.

[33] 'I shall not imagine for my future house a romantic owner, nor shall I justify this client's preferences as those foibles and aberrations usually referred to as "human nature". No, he shall be a modern owner, a post-modern owner, if such a thing is conceivable. Free from all sentimentality or fantasy or caprice, his vision, his tastes, his habits of thought shall be those most serviceable to a collective-industrial scheme of life; the world shall, if so it pleases him, appear as a system of casual sequences transformed each day by the cumulative miracles of science. Even so, he will claim for himself some inner experiences, free from outward control, unprofaned by the collective conscience. The opportunity, when all the world is socialized, mechanized and standardized, will yet be discoverable in the home.' *Architectural Record*, May 1945, p. 75.

[34] Another way of capturing the impact of modern architecture in the US in the 1940s is provided by the ironic cartoons that Alan Dunn published monthly in the *Architectural Record*.

[35] A description of the architecture of the existing houses in Long Island at the time, which resembled that of the one bought and renovated by Sert, is found in Harold Donaldson Eberlein, *Manor Houses & Historic Homes of Long Island and Staten Island*, Philadelphia, London, 1928.

[36] The habit of remodelling old barns as dwellings can be observed in some works published in *Architectural Forum*. For example, in the July 1947 issue we find the publication of one of these projects with the statement: 'A Connecticut barn is remodelled into a country house pleasantly free of affectation or

cliché.' In the August 1951 issue of the same magazine, Mary Mix Foley published an extensive report on different types and forms of 'The American Barn'. This concept, which recovered ancient and obsolete architectures, is likely to have confused the critics who insisted on speaking about the old, romantic barn remodelled as Sert's dwelling.
The Long Island house has been published in the following publications: *House and Garden*, February 1952, pp. 26–31; *Progressive Architecture*, August 1952, pp. 96–101; *House & Garden's Book of Building*, 1952, pp. 86–89; *Architectural Record*, August 1953; *Domus*, no. 275, November 1952, pp. 15–18; *Arquitectura*, Mexico, no. 41, March 1953, pp. 49–54; and Robert Winkler, *Architects' Home*, Zurich, 1955.
A piece of news from the daily *The Courier-Journal of Louisville*, published somewhat later, on 4 November 1956, and kept in the Sert Collection, clarifies certain points, explaining how Sert 'demolished the original two-storey house attached to the stable, and rebuilt on its foundations a new, breathtakingly modern wing … Many owners of such a vast barn as this would have been tempted to cut it up into many rooms, or install a second floor under the soaring roof. Not Sert. He capitalized on the spaciousness of the 52-foot-long room. At one end he designed a compact kitchen area, with nothing above shoulder height. At the opposite end, the barn was already arranged on two levels, with space for a garage underneath.'

[37] As reported in the previous chapter, on 1 October 1951 Carla Mazoli invited Sert to the Milan Triennale to participate in a 'Convegno internazionale sulle proporzioni nelle arti'. Sert was unable to attend, according to a letter he wrote on the 6th of the same month. Instead, he organized something along similar lines at MoMA, New York, centred on the Divine Proportion. The Congress was held on 1 March 1952, and Sert wrote a speech for it, which is in the Sert Collection.

[38] The measurements of the great space made up by the living-dining-kitchen-studio of Sert's house were 75 × 36 feet, with a height of 16 feet in the highest part, or 22.86 × 10.97 × 4.9 metres.

[39] It is published under the name of *Building for Modern Man: A Symposium*, ed. by Thomas H Creighton (ed.), Princeton, 1949.

[40] In the *Architectural Review* of April 1949, under the title 'Monumentalism, Symbolism and Style', we find the debate concerning the term 'monumentality'. Giedion's text 'The Need for a New Monumentality' was published in *New Architecture and City Planning*, New York, 1944, pp. 549–68. In its July 1943 issue, *Architectural Forum* reported on a debate in which Giedion had spoken about monumentality.
In 1943, Giedion, Sert and Léger had written 'Nine Points of Monumentality', which Giedion included in his 1958 book *Architecture, You and Me*, Harvard University Press, translated into English from *Architektur und Gemeinschaft. Tagebuch einer Entwicklung*, Hamburg, 1956.
In the November 1950 issue of *Architectural Forum*, we find a debate on monumentality in relation to the construction of the United Nations building in New York.

[41] The discussions and some writings that accompanied this debate are found in *The Museum of Modern Art Bulletin*, Spring 1948, vol. XV, no. 3, pp. 1–21.

[42] Blake's commentary is found in ibid. For a contextualization of the symposium, it may be useful to consult Peter Blake, *No Place Like Utopia*, W.W. Norton, New York, 1993, pp. 104–13.

[43] In 1949, Blake published *Marcel Breuer, Architect and Designer*, the catalogue of the MoMA exhibition of the same year. Shortly afterwards he was in charge of editing a book about Breuer: *Marcel Breuer: Sun and Shadow: the Philosophy of an Architect*, Dodd, Mead & Company, New York, 1955.
The house in Zurich by Marcel Breuer in collaboration with E. Roth appears in the October 1936 issue of *Architectural Record*, pp. 288–89.
American magazines of the 1940s habitually published Breuer's houses. Thus, for example, the architect's own house came out in *Architectural Record*, October 1948, and the Tompkins house appeared in *Architectural Record*, November 1947.

[44] William H. Jordy, *The Impact of European Modernism in the Mid-Twentieth Century*, Oxford University Press, 1972.

[45] Ibid., pp. 169–70.

[46] Ibid., p. 170. A similar hypothesis concerning American painting at this time is found in Erika Doss, *Benton, Pollock, and the Politics of Modernism: From Regionalism to Abstract Expression*, the University of Chicago Press, Chicago and London, 1991.
An extensive text that followed William's describes with greater perspective this period of encounters between US and European architectures, which especially clarifies Mumford's stance: Marcus Whiffen and Frederick Koeper, *American Architecture: 1607–1976*, MIT Press, 1981. On page 391 we find: 'José Luis Sert, a follower of Le Corbusier since the 1930s … supervised its construction [Carpenter Center]. In his own work for Harvard, married Student Housing and Holyoke Center, Sert remained loyal to Le Corbusier's philosophy, balancing a modular rationale with visual diversity and maintaining a high density of occupation.'
Due to the interest it shows in urbanism, another worthwhile text is Hélène Trocme, *Les Américains et Leur Architecture*, Aubier Montaigne, Paris, 1981.
For the particular focus given to the issue, centring on four competitions by North American university institutions, see James D. Kornwolf (ed.), *Modernism in America 1937–1941: A Catalogue and Exhibition of Four Architectural Competitions*, Virginia, 1985.
For the different opinions it compiles, see David De Loog, Helen Searing and Robert Stern, *American Architecture: Innovation and Tradition*, Rizzoli, New York, 1986.

[47] Jordy, op. cit., p. 189.

[48] On the circumstances surrounding the publication of this text, although with a debatable interpretation of the intentions of its author, see Sokratis Georgiadis, *Sigfried Giedion: An Intellectual Biography*, Edinburgh University Press, 1993, pp. 153–66.
More incisive, on the other hand, is the interpretation offered by Stanislav von Moos. See 'Sigfried Giedion ou la deuxième découverte de l'Amérique', in J. L. Cohen and H. Damisch, *Américanisme et Modernité*, Flammarion, Paris, 1993, pp. 239–48.

[49] Sigfried Giedion, *La mecanización toma el mando*, Spanish Edition, Gustavo Gili, Barcelona, 1978, p. 136. All the quotations are taken from this edition.

[50] Giedion compared the bascule chaise-longue designed by Le Corbusier and Charlotte Perriand in 1929 with the North American kangaroo sofa produced in Virginia around 1830. Leaving aside stylistic considerations, the latter is evidently much more comfortable, and more importantly, was produced almost a hundred years earlier (ibid., pp. 502–

05). He also compares Alvar Aalto's plywood chair of 1937 with one produced in the US in 1874 (pp. 509-10). Likewise, free-hovering seats bracketed to the frames by a single support were familiar to Americans, for they were employed in many seagoing vessels at the end of the nineteenth century and in reapers of the same period (pp. 505-07).

[51] Ibid., p. 602. We have only to consult the *Architectural Forum* of April 1948 (the year Giedion published his book) to corroborate the capacity for design and freedom in the conception of a plan displayed by American architects at the time, shown through forty single-family dwellings. In the May issue of this magazine were published forty commercial premises, in which we can also observe this capacity for modernity, aided by the great technological skills offered by the American industrial world.

[52] A building by Louis I. Kahn from this period echoes this model of a binuclear house. See *Architectural Forum*, September 1950. In the commentary about the building we read: 'A plan as clearly articulated as a machine.'
Another example of a binuclear house by the designer Thomas Wright is found in *Architectural Forum*, May 1950.

[53] Giedion, op. cit., p. 713.

[54] Jackson, op. cit., 1994.

[55] *Architectural Forum*, July 1950, features a single-family dwelling in Lattingtown, New York, in which Sert appears as architect-consultant; the exact degree of his responsibility in the planning and construction of the building is therefore unclear. It is a two-storey building in which the ground floor is made of fieldstone and the upper floor is a wooden box suspended over the marked socle constituted by the lower part of the building. It is a similar scheme to many of Breuer's houses and identical to the new part of the Long Island house. It also corresponds to the so-called Johnson House, of which no plans are kept in the Sert Collection, although there are some pictures. SC 45 E.

Cambridge, Massachusetts

In an interview with John Peter held in 1959, Sert admitted his initial lack of interest in devoting himself to teaching: 'At the beginning, I didn't want to go into the field of education at all because I had my own independent profession and I had been working freely all my life like that, but finally Gropius convinced me that it was important. I told Chancellor Conant of Harvard when he came to see me that I would like to orient the school and give it a certain approach to the problems of architecture and planning, but at the same time I would like to keep myself rather free to do my own work. I took the job on a part-time basis.'[56]

Gropius took upon himself the task of finding someone to substitute him at the Graduate School of Design,[57] writing on 20 November 1951 to the Italian E.N. Rogers and offering the post to him, while apparently doing the same with Sert, as witnessed by a letter to Reginald Isaacs on 4 December: 'I think I told you recently that I have been seeing José Sert and that I pressed him hard that he should think twice and accept if he should be asked to come to the GSD. On account of the large commissions for South America, he was very doubtful, but to my pleasure he has just written to me that he has decided to accept the job if it should be offered to him … I am completely positive towards Sert. He is forty-nine years old; a very mature wise man and with a very broad philosophy of his own.'[58]

When Sert arrived in Cambridge, he must have felt that he was again facing the phantoms that had always pursued him – that is to say, a city without rational planning and cluttered with buildings constructed according to historicist canons. He was to devote himself almost exclusively to his teaching tasks in the city, as his posts as Chairman and Dean did not give him much leeway to take on any work re-

lated to his own profession, especially if we take into account the amount of time he must have spent travelling between New York and Cambridge to finish his pending projects for the TPA office. Considering the negative recollections he had of his years as a student in the School of Architecture in Barcelona, the outlook was not particularly bright.

Gropius, who resigned from his academic post in October 1952, had once again relied on Sert to come to his aid, on this occasion with the objective of putting an end to the crisis provoked by his departure from the GSD, evidenced in the headline of a Harvard newspaper: 'Design … A School Without Direction. Needs Leadership and Funds To Regain Spirit, Stability.'[59] Thus the GSD needed a leader to pull it out of the tight spot in which it found itself, someone who could be as good a director as Gropius had been, in the opinion of the writer of the article: 'During the thirteen years he spent at the University, Walter Gropius became almost a spiritual leader of the Graduate School of Design. To the outside world he was the school; to much of the faculty, he, not Dean Joseph Hudnut, set the policy; and to the students, he was the ideal architect, the master mould into which they poured their talents. When Gropius resigned this fall, many felt the school had lost its heart.'[60]

The school was passing through an economic and organizational crisis. Despite the fact that since 1948, thanks to Hudnut's tenacity,[61] an initiative had begun to integrate the three departments that made it up – Landscape, City Planning and Architecture – after offering its first joint course for all of the disciplines,[62] confusion had set in.[63] This is why Gropius suggested a solution that needed to be carried out by his successor: 'I suggest to promote the closest integration of all departments of the School

Sert, Jackson and Gourley, Peabody Terrace, Harvard, Cambridge, Massachusetts, 1962–64.

315

of Design by placing it under one director as the responsible key man; this director to be simultaneously the Chairman of the Department of Architecture, since architecture is historically the mother of the art of design from which all the others have branched out.'[64]

Thus, Sert's work was cut out for him. The next step taken by Gropius from the wings was to advise our architect on the professors with whom he should surround himself, as well as counselling him on certain strategies that he should carry out in order to make a good initial impression on entering Harvard.[65]

Gropius' own arrival had meant a relative modification of the study programmes of the Bachelor's Degree of Architecture and the inclusion of Martin Wagner and Marcel Breuer within the team of professors. It also represented the introduction of three more courses: Contemporary Architecture, Housing and Design, while many of the drawing courses that had previously been taught were dropped.[66]

In the contents of the report for the 1944–45 academic year, we find some significant comments: 'Problems in the design of buildings form the core of the studies leading to the Bachelor Degree in Architecture … Around this central discipline are grouped a number of related courses, including courses in the techniques of construction and in professional practice.' Thus, once the student had passed through the three courses in the History of Architecture taught by Professor Conant, the rest of the study programme developed around this project.

Things continued to follow this course until the 1948–49 academic year, when the three departments were unified for the Freshman year, while Gropius and other faculty professors offered a year-long postgraduate course on Architectural Design and Planning. Gropius' course continued along similar lines, demonstrating his desire to make University students work on spatial and design problems, only this time in relation to a real commission that was to be built on the north campus of the University: the Harvard University Graduate Center, for which the German architect transcribed his programme so that it could be developed during the classes at the same time as he was working on it in his office.[67]

The sessions of critical appraisal that were held on Monday, Wednesday and Friday evenings were crucial to the final form of the building, which represented one of the first 'in-

Walter Gropius, Harvard University Graduate Center, Cambridge, Massachusetts, 1949.

terventions' of modern architecture into Harvard's historicist architecture, and although it cannot be proved, it seems to show Gropius' determination to establish a linear continuity – probably pedagogically sterile to the students – between the work in a professional office and the university classroom, an issue that also interested Sert to a certain degree.

With these precedents, backed up by the recollection of the debates on architectural education held in the Bridgwater CIAM of 1947, Sert made his initial declaration of objectives in October 1953 for a 'Graduate School of Environmental Design – City Planning, Architecture, Landscape Architecture' during his first course as Director. The need for a single GSD headquarters, instead of three buildings scattered across the campus, and the will to integrate efficiently the teachings of these departments under the overall concept of Environmental Design, are found in this proposal, whose subtitle was significant: 'Working for the creation of a physical environment that will satisfy man's emotional and material needs and stimulate his spiritual growth.'[68]

The idea was to design a school whose belief was that: 'Planning is the organization of the spiritual and material conditions of community life … Architecture and planning have a place in the social and economic sphere … There is today a new conception of architecture, liberated from the historical styles.' This model school was to see that 'city planning, architecture and landscape architecture be studied as part of the human habitat in the totality of environmental design', and in it the student 'should be able to gain personal experience and insight as to what our environment is and should be. He will then understand the need to design for better physical surroundings that will take man as their measure, both as an individual and as a member of the community.'[69]

This project for the school would offer its students a 'basic human approach to all professional problems', a unified student programme during the Freshman year, and the determination to work jointly with the rest of the students attending the school so that the three professions 'are concerned with the control of man's environment, and a knowledge of man's reactions to social and physical factors is necessary.'

This provided a more than ample basis for a plan by which he could carry out his intentions in the school of which, since July 1953, he had become both Dean and Chairman of the Department of Architecture. The idea was especially important for someone who declared at around this time: 'To talk about architectural education is to talk about architecture in general, architecture today and the activities of the architect. I don't think they can be separated very well; they really form one body.'[70] Therefore, if strong bonds existed between architecture and education, the objective would be to transmit to the students the latest in state-of-the-art architectural thinking, with which Sert was perfectly familiar given his direct involvement in the debates of the CIAMs and his own professional experience.

One of the issues that especially concerned him was the rapport between architecture, city and setting, and this would soon be borne out by his interventions in Cambridge: 'You are too young, but I know that we all know that the last fifty years have produced more changes in architecture, if you measure in terms of the past, than the previous five hundred. They have transformed our cities, and architecture today is more closely tied to the urban setting than it ever was before. None of our buildings really stand alone today. It is very rare when you will be asked to design a building that stands completely alone, unrelated to other buildings or to its environment. Thus, what we are doing today in architecture is mainly urban architecture by definition and by nature … All architectural schools should try to emphasize the relation of architecture to the improvement of our physical environment, an environment that would result in a better way of living.'[71]

His following words stressed something with which we are also familiar, namely the plastic component of architecture, thanks to the possibility of integrating the other visual arts, once the machine, strict functionalism and the objectivity of architectural issues had been relegated to a second place: 'The world of the architect, like that of the painter or sculptor, is basically a world of form, forms in space, the shaping of space, the relationship of colour, texture, light', something that would bring to the fore the 'plastic and emotional side of architecture. This means that you consider that the work you are doing has a certain quality that is above the purely functional or practical.'[72]

In another text written more or less at the same time and again dealing with this topic, after repeating his original points he added that it was necessary for faculties of architecture to incorporate courses of history: 'One of the problems we are faced with today is how to teach history courses to the architect. Many schools practically abolished these courses from their curricula when Beaux Arts methods of teaching were replaced by our modern programmes, and as a result there is a generation of young architects that lack the essential knowledge of our architectural heritage, and I have heard many young architects tell how bad they feel about this.'[73]

Sert must have been thinking about his collaborative project for Joan Miró's studio in Palma, and very shortly afterwards he began to put these ideas into practice in his teaching. In the register of the GSD professors in 1954, we find artists such as Constantino Nivola and Naum Gambo, and architects such as E.N. Rogers, as well as his friend, the architectural historian Sigfried Giedion. Moreover, in the curriculum for the Architecture study programme there were two new courses, one entitled 'Urban Design' and the other, probably conceived as a supporting course, called 'History of Urban Design'.[74] Nivola and Gabo appeared under the heading 'Instructors in Design', while Rogers was designated 'Visiting Professor of Architecture'. The first two were therefore in charge of increasing the sensibility of students regarding the rapport between the different visual arts, whereas the latter, director of the magazine *Casabella-Continuità*, was invited as one of the pioneer theorists on the relationships between architecture and its environment, known for his writings on environmental pre-existence, an issue that greatly interested Sert.

Giedion's presence was also essential, especially since at that point he was exploring far more distant architectural origins than he had in his work of 1941; indeed his investigations went all the way back to the Rome of Sixtus V. This allowed him to establish connections between ancient architectures from all over the world, and therefore made it easier for him to come up with examples in which monumentality, the integration of all arts into architecture, and the rapport between architecture and city could be directly observed by the students and understood as belonging to the discipline they were studying.

The correspondence between Giedion and Sert regarding the Swiss historian's visit to the University attests to the importance given to the history of architecture in the training of students. On 18 March 1954 Sert wrote a letter to Giedion, who was then in Baghdad, expressing his interest in having him come to the GSD, given that Kenneth Conant, the professor in charge of teaching the history classes, was going to take an eighteen-month sabbatical leave and would soon be retiring.[75] On 9 April Giedion answered: 'I would like, if possible, not to repeat … *Space, Time and Architecture*. I would like to outline a course out of the evolution of architecture … which gives the student a feeling for the working of the human spirit, the continuity and discontinuity of architectural development right from its earliest beginnings; this is the problem which has interested me for the last five years and the three months in Egypt and Mesopotamia gave me the courage to try [out] how a basic course of history should be organized for architects.'[76]

Moreover, Sert needed his friend to point the way forward for the future professor of architectural history of the GSD, since he was aware that Giedion would be unable to remain at Harvard, despite the fact that he would continue to invite him during the following years.[77] Giedion's concerns and advice can be gathered from their correspondence. On 27 April he wrote to Sert: 'In the one or the other way we will find, I guess, a solution as to how to give students of architecture a certain insight into the past so that they may know where they are standing. But as we all know it is not too easy to change the present way of giving courses, as if nothing had happened since 1900.'[78] He then went on to suggest the possibility of organizing joint seminars with an architect whose ideas would correspond to these issues, suggesting that Sert invite G.E. Kidder Smith or Eduard F. Sekler. However, to Giedion it was not simply a matter of teaching the history of architecture, but rather – tied in with other concepts that we have previously mentioned – of encouraging students to learn about art history: 'Maybe one should begin even now in collecting from different universities their opinions about the role of teaching art history in architectural education and to get proposals [regarding] what and how [it] should be taught.'[79]

Giedion stated all of this, shortly before he travelled to Harvard to give his seminar, with a certain scepticism, since in his opinion, students of architecture had inadequate previous training, a point of view that can be detected in a letter written in French to Sert on 6 August: 'They do not understand the ulterior significance of words such as the Eiffel Tower, Versailles, Pyramid, etc. They hear the word, but do not see the development that lives behind these words. The result: repetition of words and misunderstandings and stock phrases, which they repeat as if they were parrots.'[80] Some unanswered questions finally led Sert to ask him to specify the content of his programme for the coming term at GSD, which Giedion would visit as a teacher while developing his works on the origins of art and architecture that had by then become the centre of his investigations.[81]

Aside from his teaching concerns, Sert continued to show great interest in the professional work that he was able to pursue thanks to some commissions that arrived in his office, which was still in New York. In a letter from Paris of 3 September 1954 he informed Giedion: 'The new work that has turned up in my NY office obliges me, *helás!*, to change plans. I have given up Istanbul, hope to make it next summer. I am sorry we will not travel together, as I am leaving by plane next Monday.' What were these new projects that prevented Sert from travelling with his friend to Istanbul? One must have been the Havana Plan, of which we have previously spoken. We must also take into account his incursions into the design of American embassies that the US government was building all over the world. Sert carried out at least two projects of this nature, although not with the TPA office in New York but from his office in Cambridge with the collaboration of his future associates, Huson Jackson and Joseph Zalewsky, who were also pro-

fessors at the GSD. These commissions were offered directly to Sert, a state of affairs propitiated by a series of circumstances that should be elucidated.

The first of these has to do with the theories in which Americans had begun to believe, based on works written throughout 1951 by such authors as Pietro Belluschi, Henry-Russell Hitchcock, and Lewis Mumford, in which these Americans expressed opinions on architecture that coincided with those of their European counterparts, especially with the works written between 1945 and 1951 by Bruno Zevi, a great detractor against rationalist architecture and a passionate advocate of organicist ideals.

The first of these texts was written by the architect Pietro Belluschi (whom we will later find involved in defining the shape of the US embassies) when he was designated Dean of MIT. In it we can observe allusions to familiar themes: 'The ideals of a modern architect may then be very briefly summarized as follows: he must come to terms with his environment; only then can he hope to again become creative … as a lively interpreter of the new social order and as a prophet of his age.'[82] This architecture was to distance itself from functionalist rigidity and from objectivist banality to rediscover lost feelings and emotions, which Belluschi explained thus: 'Today we are more honest, more practical and quite functional, but it has been at the expense of grace and gentility. We have taken away many of the established forms, so cherished by our ancestors, and have replaced them with stark utilitarian ones, which give little nourishment to the senses. We have taken away from the man in the street all the stereotyped little ornament, cornices, cartouches and green fake shutters, but we have not been capable of giving him back the equivalent in emotional value.'

Hitchcock's contribution was more incisive, as is to be expected from someone who twenty years earlier had been deeply committed to the functionalist cause. Shortly after its preamble, the text anticipated what would follow: 'The work of many architects of distinction such as Frank Lloyd Wright, who make no bones about their opposition to the supposed tenets of an International Style, certainly belongs to modern architecture as much as does the work of Gropius and Le Corbusier.'[83] It seems clear that the hero of post-war architecture was to be Wright, just as Zevi had affirmed in Europe. In those days in which western Europe and America were merged together in one 'bloc', which had to confront with its democratic ideals what was taking place 'on the other side', the figure of the American architect and the preponderance of American architecture seemed to be the best bets with which to incarnate the Western architectural ideology of the future.

After retracting some of the programmatic points that had made up his work in 1932, and after criticizing Americans for having given too strict an interpretation to that contribution, Hitchcock continued his analysis by demonstrating through solid reasoning that Wright was at the origin of everything modern,[84] and went on to expound the flimsiness of European functionalist architecture by contrasting it with the supremacy of the buildings that had been produced in the US many years earlier.[85] The article concluded with praise for a European who had triumphed in the States by building an architecture far removed from functionalist orthodoxy. This European was Alvar Aalto, and his building was the students' residence for MIT of 1948, which had broken 'with the rigidities of the International Style', due to the 'expressive irregularity of the plan and a few rather minor details, such as the willful roughness of the brickwork and the excessive clumsiness of some of the membering.' Aalto's residence was an example of this new architecture, which had its unmistakable roots in the United States, to which homage was owed and supremacy granted.

A few months later, also in the *Architectural Record*, Mumford also contributed to this idea. His habitual aversion to the consequences that a mechanized universe might have on the world of architecture and cities now found fertile ground in which to sow its seed. According to him, modern architecture had 'crystallized at the moment that people realized that the older modes of symbolism no longer spoke to modern man; and that on the contrary, the new functions brought in by the machine had something special to say to him. Unfortunately, in the act of realizing these new truths, me-

chanical function has tended to absorb expression, or in more fanatical minds, to do away with the need for it. As a result, the architectural imagination has, within the last twenty years, become impoverished.'[86] The machine aesthetic, which had previously lorded it over architecture, was no longer well looked upon, for other branches of knowledge were now delving into the human condition, a condition that architecture was to interpret as far removed from the tenets of mechanized objectivity: 'Thanks to advances in biology, sociology, and psychology, we begin to understand the whole man; and it is high time for architects to demonstrate that understanding in other terms than economy, efficiency and abstract mechanical forms.'

The example upheld by Mumford was that of Wright's architecture, which having been subjected to 'arbitrary criticisms' in the 1920s, when it was compared to Le Corbusier's work, could now be considered a model for a future renovated and modern North American architecture. The rejection that Wright had suffered was based precisely on those attributes that were now vindicated: 'This disparagement was based on the very qualities that made Wright's architecture superior to the work of Le Corbusier school. In Wright's work, the subjective and symbolic elements were as important as the mechanical requirements'; in his buildings, in which 'the plan and the elevation were informed by the human ideals', nature was introduced in the interior and there was also 'the idea of horizontality as an expression of the prairie that led Wright to emphasize horizontal lines in his early regional houses.'

Thus at the beginning of the 1950s, three influential figures in the panorama of US architectural culture coincided in demanding this ideological shift in which the presence of the machine was substituted with other values that for the time being we will denominate 'human' and about which we can gather a number of elements from different sources. They also coincided in the notion that their culture could offer a solid existing basis from which to undertake the task, thanks to the figure of Wright, which provided historical consistency to their aspirations.

Sert knew quite well what the announced

change stood for; ever since the Garraf houses he had been practising a certain type of regionalism, and was continuing to develop the idea in his project for Miró's workshop, although with the nuances that we have seen. It was essential that this identification between organic architecture and democracy should not only be ideological but also political, since democracy was the political system proposed by the US to confront the Eastern bloc. After all, this architecture was to be a synthesis of the American values that had formed the basis of a tireless odyssey to conquer the West and which they now extrapolated to achieve the conquest of the world.

This nation had 'invented' democracy in the same city in which architectural history acknowledges that modern architecture had first been erected – Chicago. The former claim is corroborated by the words of Adlai E. Stevenson, presidential candidate of the Democrats, in whose welcoming speech on 16 July 1952, at the inauguration of the National Democratic Convention, we find: 'Here, my friends, on the prairies of Illinois and of the Middle West we can see a long way in all directions … You are very welcome here in the heartland of the nation. Indeed, we think that you were wise to come here … For it was in Chicago that the modern Democratic story began … It was here, my friends, in Chicago just twenty years ago this month that you nominated Franklin Roosevelt.'[87] We should not take this coincidence lightly.

Just a little over two years before, on 1 April 1950, Eleanor Roosevelt had addressed another passionate speech to the organization Americans for Democratic Action, from which we highlight: 'We live in a time when every single one of us must realize that what actually is important in a democracy is that sense of individual responsibility … [A]t present we need all the courage that our forefathers had and perhaps a little more because we have a job to do at home and a job to do in the world.'[88] If America believed it had to undertake this exemplary task in the world, the architectural image of its buildings there (that is, its embassies and consulates) had to match this importance.

Ron Robin has incisively analyzed the intentions behind the changes in the formal priorities of this operation throughout the twentieth century, and it is worth examining what occurred in the period after World War II, when a number of organizational changes were succeeding one another in the State Department: 'The quest for unambiguous political architecture abroad led to the dismantling of the interdepartmental Foreign Service Building Commission (FSBC) after World War II and the subsequent rehauling of the building procedures. By separating the architectural process from the inevitable crosscurrents of an interdepartmental agency, the State Department could now pursue its own agenda with no outside interference. A new internal division in the State Department, the Office of Foreign Building Operations (FBO), enjoyed almost complete autonomy in deciding upon relevant styles, as opposed to the mostly technical duties of State Department building officials during the reign of the FSBC.'[89]

This autonomy fostered the development of an initial programme in which the buildings representing the US were to appear as 'oases of American soil in foreign lands' and were to be viewed by the public at large as 'the only physical embodiment of our culture they are likely to see other than automobiles or refrigerators'. The first man responsible for managing this operation was Leland King, who in 1946 had designed the embassy in Lima in Spanish colonial style and who was now to impose other

Leland King, United States Embassy in Lima, 1946.

guidelines akin to the International Style as a mode of operation that was radically opposed to the Soviet policy of erecting buildings of historicist design. By choosing this path the US demonstrated its capacity to be up-to-date and to offer a modern image of its democratic credo, whereas the USSR evidenced a formal backwardness that corresponded to the scarce credibility of its Communist project.

According to Robin, the choice of the International Style was an answer to interests that ranged farther than the ideological contrast: 'The choice of boxlike embassies of clean glass and naked steel was influenced, too, by contemporary architectural theories derived from the Gestalt school of psychology', according to which human beings were deemed more capable of noticing and remembering simple, symmetrical forms than complex, asymmetrical ones. By showing an elementary quality, American embassies offered 'beauty through clarity … dignity without pomposity', as well as a 'sense of importance but not of overbearing officialdom'. Thus, these embassies, very similar to the simple office buildings in the US, which were to repeat themselves with little modification in all the countries that the Americans meant to control, were to be taken as the bearers of a message that was presented on the basis of an internationally valid (though possibly already outdated) modern credo – absence of ornament, modulation and new materials: 'The undecorated surfaces of these ahistorical structures, their simple shapes and deliberately conspicuous display of modern building materials, were the communal representations of a future-oriented society completely at ease with the new technologies, a society that would not repeat the mistakes of history.'[90] This apparently was what was transmitted by the embassies in Rio, Havana, Madrid and the consulates in Bremen and Le Havre.[91]

In 1953, however, this way of working began to be looked upon as 'not recommendable', and some members of the American Congress even criticized it for being unsuitable for the Cold War atmosphere, at the same time denouncing favouritism in the granting of commissions.[92] The similarity between the buildings of private business entities flooding American and European cities and public architecture was the first symptom that something had gone awry; moreover the reappraisal to which Western architects and critics had subjected the International Style also spoke of an intellectual atmosphere that would contribute to the downfall of King's ideas.

The situation was further aggravated by the fact that the new Secretary of State, John Foster Dulles, who held that embassies were 'the good fruits of our freedom', decided to take the affair into his own hands by giving his support to changing the form of these buildings so that, according to him, they would be more in keeping with the regionalist cultures of the places in which they were to be built.[93] This provoked the resignation of the FBO director Leland King, whose role was substituted by a new organization, the Architectural Advisory Panel (AAP), directly controlled by the State Department, and initially directed by Colonel Harry McBride. Most directly responsible for the AAP, however, was a group of architects whose ideas were far removed from any dependence on the International Style, and who were extremely capable of translating political symbols into effective architectural forms following the new guidelines set by Foster Dulles: Henry R. Shepley, from an important architects' office in Boston, Ralph T. Walker, President of the AIA, and Pietro Belluschi, Dean of MIT.

We do not know with any certainty what motivated Belluschi's appointment, but we can imagine any number of reasons, ranging from his particular way of interpreting the International Style to his ability to imagine other formal styles, something that was manifested in his work and in the text mentioned above, and to his prestigious University position. It was probably due to all these factors that Belluschi was charged with writing the requirements to be fulfilled in carrying out these commissions, which is borne out by a text in which he wrote: 'To the sensitive and imaginative designer [the FBO commission] will be an invitation to give serious study to local conditions of climate and site, to understand and sympathize with local customs and people, and to grasp the historical meaning of the particular environment in which the new building must be set. He will avoid being either bizarre or fashionable, yet he will not fear using new techniques or new materials should these constitute real advances in architectural thinking. It is hoped the selected architects will think of style not in its narrower meaning but as a quality to be imparted to the building, a quality reflecting deep understanding of conditions and people. His directness and freshness of approach will thus have a distinguishable American flavour.'[94] The selection of architects that would be called upon to design embassy buildings and consulates in this new stage – Neutra, Saarinen, Weese, Stubbins, Raymond, Yamasaki, and Kahn – were inevitably those who could synthesize this ideology.

One of those chosen was Sert, which was perhaps to be expected given that Belluschi knew him as a neighbour and as Dean, and had invited him to give lectures at MIT in the past.[95] Sert's work in Latin America, his struggles with the impositions of local conditions on architecture, as well as his extensive professional trajectory, must have been more than sufficient motive to encourage Belluschi to count on him; in all likelihood, the MIT Dean would have also been familiar with the Catalan architect's project for Miró's studio as well as the Garraf houses. In April 1955 the project courses that Sert directed at the GSD, along with Gourley and Coates, included the US Embassy in London, for which Sert had been invited to compete,[96] and in the same year, he drew the first sketches for the US Embassy in Baghdad, a project that sat in Sert's office for a long time before it was actually built.[97]

By proposing his students that work on the competition for the US Embassy in London, Sert gave himself the opportunity to think out loud about the project in front of a prepared audience, combining teaching with his profession as he had announced he was interested in doing when he entered the GSD. In this combination of disciplines, Sert laid out before his students all of the ideological aspects that surrounded the construction of these buildings, as is shown by a text underneath a heading written in capital letters in the programme script: 'ARCHITECTURAL POLICY'. Those registered on Sert's project course could read: 'The policy shall be to provide requisite and adequate facilities in an architectural style and form which is distinguished and will reflect

Eero Saarinen, United States Embassy in London, 1956.

credit on the United States, will create goodwill by intelligent appreciation, recognition and use of the architecture appropriate to the site and country.'

After a detailed description of Grosvenor Square, the setting in which the building was to be located, the text introduced a new consideration: 'Designers will be particularly interested in the long and rich history of the Square and surrounding London. The United States has had a substantial interest in that history, beginning with the residence on Grosvenor Square of John Adams, first American Minister to the Court of St. James in 1875.' The US presence in London therefore had a long-standing tradition, which had to be reaffirmed and put into practice while respecting the setting in which the new building would be inserted, a surrounding that the embassy would dominate: 'Its visual relationship to the other three sides as well as to the surrounding area of London is of utmost importance … This does not imply copying anything. The building should represent the United States at this time: it will form one side of Grosvenor Square and be of great importance in relation to London.'

Apart from issues regarding the programme's needs and other technical aspects, these must have been the instructions (drafted by the architect Robert McLaughlin, Dean of Princeton) received by the rest of the architectural teams summoned to the tender. Those participating in the competition were: Saarinen, who would be the winner, Edward D.

Stone, Yamasaki and Leincueber, Wurster, Bernardi & Emmons, Ernest J. Kump, Hugh Stubbins and Anderson Beckwith & Haible. In almost all the projects we observe the intention of interpreting the surroundings of Grosvenor Square through buildings that present, each in its own way, a ground floor acting as a socle, an intermediate volume and a finial. Some projected a facade of white Portland stone, which was also present in the surroundings. Saarinen considered it a matter of 'creating a lively facade with sufficient irregular surfaces so as to give a dramatic effect to the stone', keeping the stone frames floating over the rest of the structure, maintaining its autonomy, as we observe in the adjacent buildings, but without falling into the mistake of copying.

These characteristics, however, were a 'compromise' as to the real intentions behind the building, which were soon revealed: the figure of the golden eagle and its unmistakable meaning ended up lording it over the rest of the square, despite Saarinen's good intentions. Belluschi's manifestos were thus shown to be ineffective from the very first. R. Furneaux Jordin, a critic on *The Observer*, was radical in his attack: 'What then has gone wrong? The building falls between two stools – diplomatic delicacy and American status-seeking. Diplomatic immunity from building and planning regulations left the State Department free to build a mile-high skyscraper if it wished. Therefore it became coy and polite; it fell over backward in telling its architect to remember the Georgian scale of Grosvenor Square. Hence the false humility, the Georgian proportions and height …

Sert, Jackson and Gourley, project for the competition of the US Embassy in London, 1955 (SC).

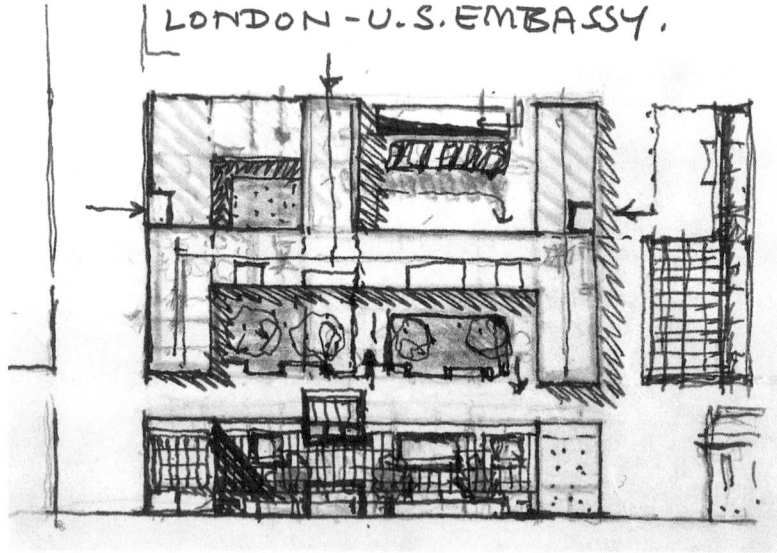

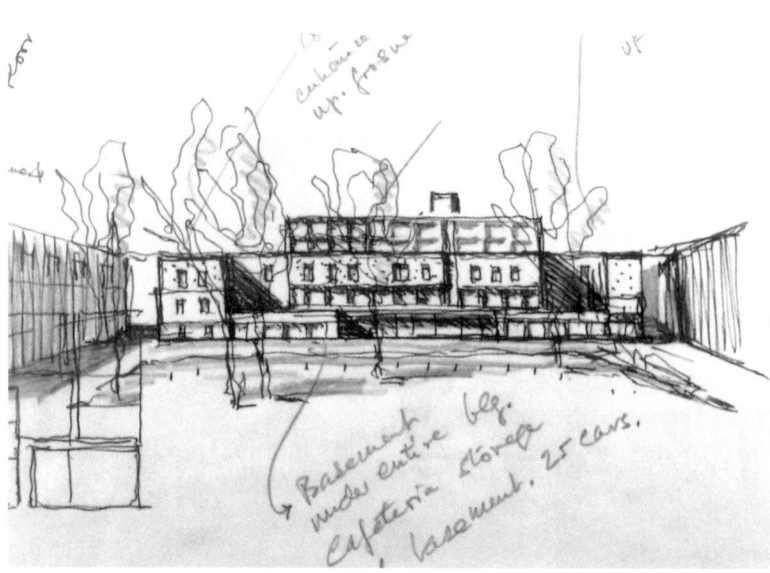

Hence the rather aggressive, staccato modelling of the facade, the perpetual gilding, the costume jewellery that overbedecks it all. The rather childish controversy over the xenophobic nature of the 35-foot golden eagle … is false. The eagle is consistent with the architecture, which in its turn is consistent with the tragedy of Americanism.'[98] Peter Smithson, another critic, was annoyed by the excessive monumentality of the building: 'There is a certain perplexity as to why America must have produced these buildings. We are also somewhat wary.'

Sert's proposal was clearly different from those of the other architects, although it presented an almost identical set of windows to those of Saarinen, as well as starting from a tripartite composition in elevation. Two end wings contained the information and consulate sections, while in the recessed central body he highlighted two volumes corresponding to the Ambassador's offices and an auditorium. These volumes did not define an axial symmetry and were of different sizes, 'destabilizing' the ensemble. The result was an excessively fragmented facade, conceived from inside to outside, exhibiting its intimacy without bashfulness, and introducing a *varietas* that evidently did not correspond to the imperial and sovereign power that the building inevitably had to show, despite Foster Dulles' declarations and Belluschi's good intentions. Sert's project was probably the most consistent with the architectural thinking of the

have laid out: 'The programme employs American architects to prepare designs that will utilize as fully as possible the resources of the respective countries. It is a programme of cultural exchange and mutual practical benefit. As a preliminary to each design, the State Department sends the architect to the country in question to examine the site, to learn local materials, resources and craftsmanship, and to gain an acquaintanceship with the culture, climate and people.'[100]

With these preliminaries, Sert justified the occupation of the plot of land and the language that would be employed in the complex. He set the buildings required by the programme in sequence one after the other, separated by courtyards with palm trees and water in a plot of land whose limits were Al Mansur Street and the

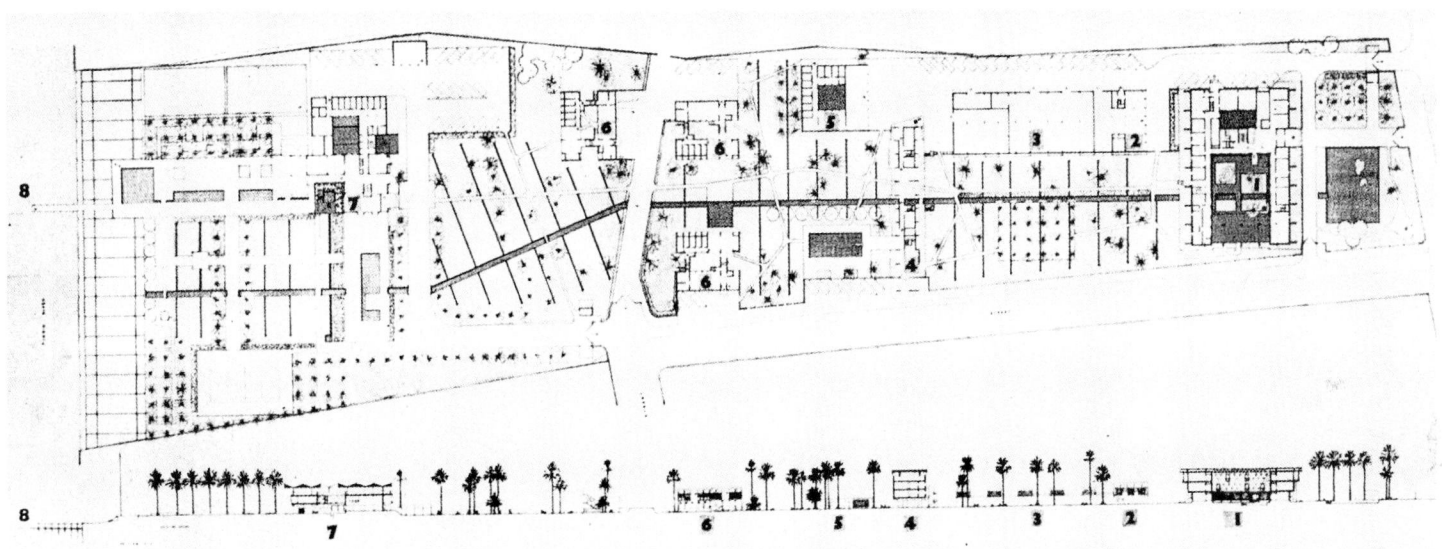

Sert, Jackson and Gourley, United States Embassy in Baghdad, 1955–61.

time, but it was the one that least understood the subliminal play of words employed by the North American State Department, and therefore it never stood a chance.

The main conditions for the project for the US Embassy in Baghdad were a more complex programme, a plot of land of excessively long dimensions bordering the Tigris River, and a climate of extremes. In the first lines of a version of the report attached to the project, Sert wrote: 'The architectural design of the new US Embassy in Baghdad was determined by the site, the sun, the river and the trees.'[99] In another version, the beginning was different, but consistent with the ideological context that we

Tigris River. Proceeding from the street one could thus observe a great pool in which the embassy would be reflected, which runs up to the formal entrance to the complex. An elongated building for services is placed perpendicular to it, in which the Staff Housing Building is situated orthogonally, forming a courtyard crossed by a canal of the river and landscaped with palm trees. Behind this building were located the three residences and the servants' building, which circumscribed another pair of courtyards in which the recreational and social activities of the staff members and their families were to be concentrated. A dyke separated these activities from the Ambassador's residence,

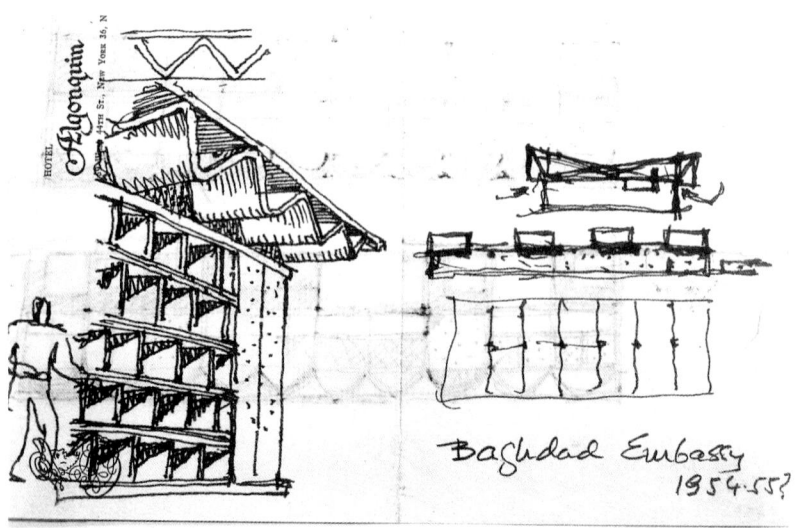

United States
Embassy
in Baghdad,
sketches
of the study.

which was located facing the river and two roomy landscaped terraces. Like a village surrounding an oasis, the scattered buildings were low in height so as not to show themselves as excessive volumes that would be alien to their setting and the city that housed them.

The water of the Tigris River was pumped into the canals that ran across the complex, lending unity to the whole and ensuring the irrigation of the vegetation in an extremely hot climate. In provision of this Sert designed special protection systems with ventilated roofs and latticework that made up the first walling, some distance behind which the woodwork structure was placed. Taking advantage of previous experiences in relation to extreme climates, such as the churches for Tumaco and Puerto Ordaz, or simply using visual references with which he had felt comfortable since his work on Miró's workshop in Palma, Sert offered a repertoire of diverse solutions to similar problems, revealing his intention of giving each aspect a personality of its own.

The Embassy building is situated towards the interior to achieve the necessary shade. Its facades show a concrete structure that is variously filled in with coloured ceramic tiles, latticework and woodwork painted in primary colours.

The residence buildings hold three apartments each and have an open ground floor. Ceramic latticework, placed in various ways following a strict modulation limited by a concrete structure, vary in depth depending on the height at which they are placed, which may be observed when analyzing the section. Here too

United States
Embassy
in Baghdad, view.

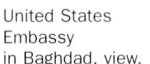

United States Embassy in Baghdad, view.

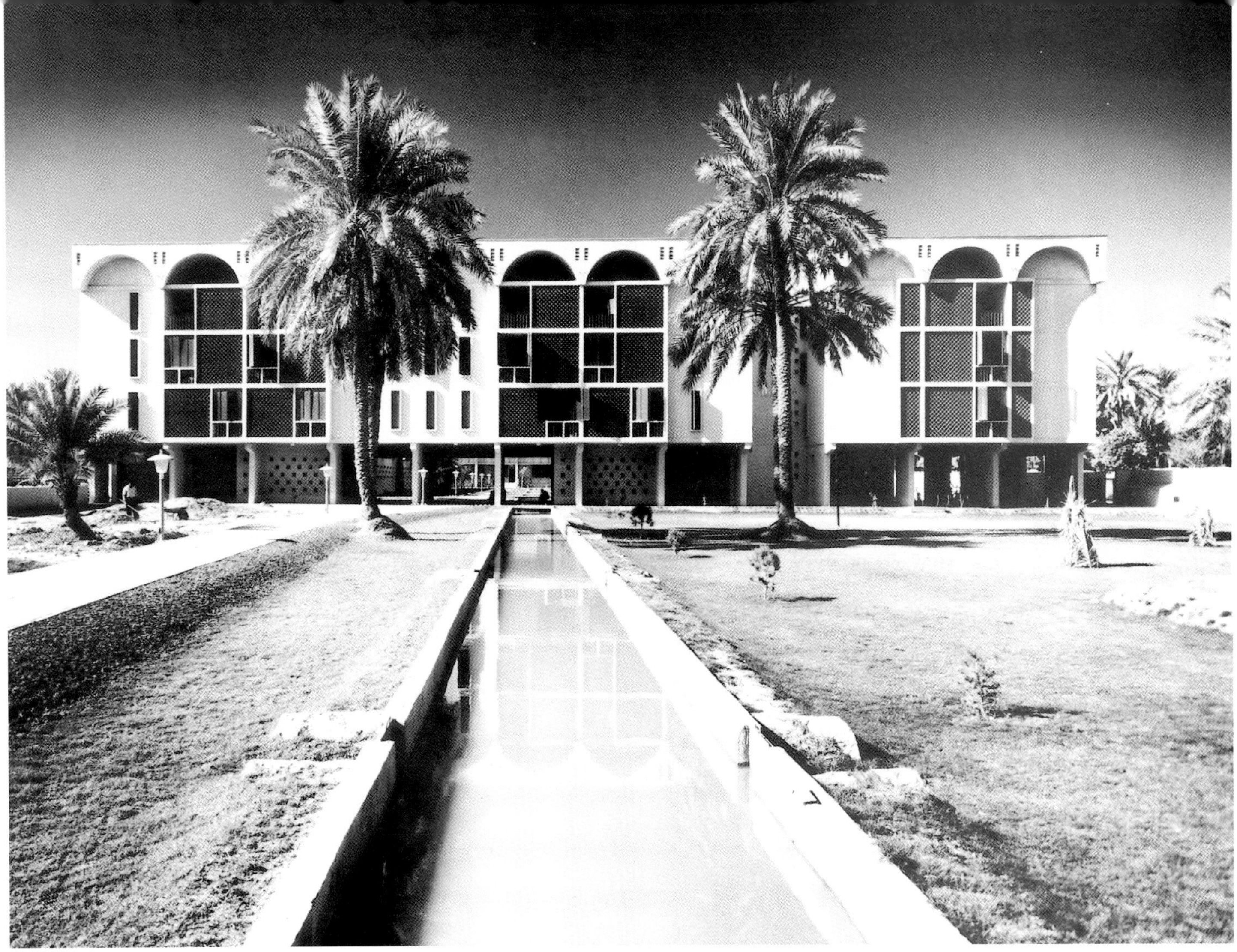

the roofs were ventilated, but topped by arches that completed the ensemble.

The Ambassador's residence, oriented by the river towards the old city, had a more complex programme due to the representative, diplomatic and domestic functions it was to house, and it was conceived as spaces at different heights that could be enlarged by means of sliding elements developed around a courtyard. The ventilated roof, designed as a concrete hyperbolic paraboloid parasol, recalls a tree-like structure engaged in a dialogue with the palm trees around it. The ceramic of the latticework wall and the painted woodwork of great dimensions allow the building to converse with the rest of the complex.

United States Embassy in Baghdad, views.

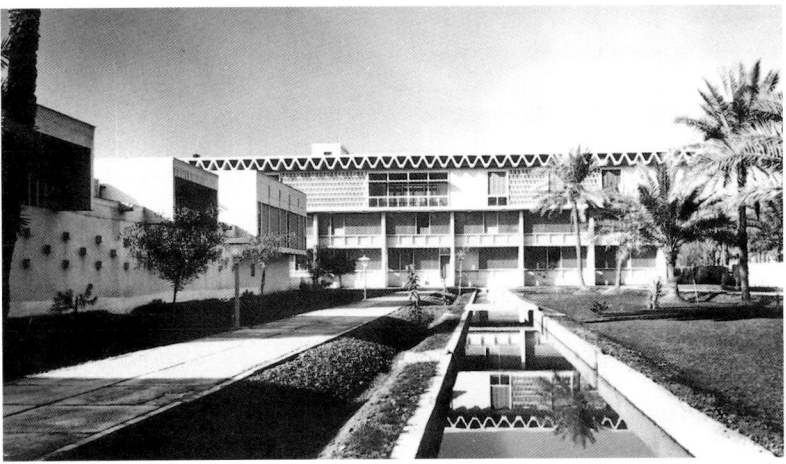

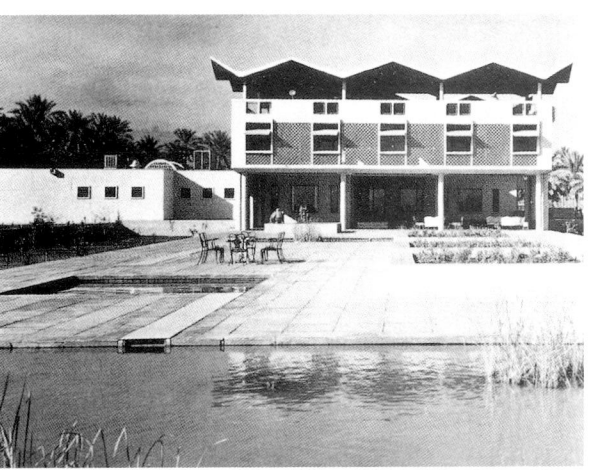

An obsessive *varietas* runs throughout the whole project, and yet we feel that we are facing a unitary complex. The capacity to alternate materials and elements is strictly calculated and dominated by the order imposed by the structure, something that the *Foreign Service Journal* of February 1959 interpreted correctly when stating that Sert's proposal meant to 'draw up plans that would reflect an artistic combination of Eastern and Western motifs … modern yet conservative.'[101]

The palace of President Batista in Havana must also have seemed a modern yet conservative project by Sert, who incorporated it into his town-planning project for the city. The chronology of this building coincides with that of the Baghdad project, and therefore shows a conceptual and formal parallelism that allows us to avoid repeating similar descriptions. Nevertheless, the 'good will' that the Americans wished to demonstrate by giving regional attributes to their embassies acquired another meaning in Havana. The roof of this building, with its concrete paraboloid

President Batista's Palace, perspective (SC).

shape, rivalled the great number of palm trees that surrounded it, seeking to establish an impossible continuity between nature and artifice – a continuity that was intended to make the power of the dictator of Cuba seem natural. This is the first time that we see Sert design a building based on comparisons with other historical architectures representative of absolute power, of which royal palaces abound. He was searching for redemption in history, a redemption that he could not find in the design of an excessive building for a military despot.[102]

During the many years in which he carried out his professional work in Cambridge, Sert would be working in a varied yet conservative setting, which was urbanistically disordered, and this forced him constantly to rethink the relationships between architecture and the city. In their book on the architecture of the Harvard campus, Brainbridge Bunting and Margaret Henderson have addressed this lack of order, viewing it as part of its charm.[103] In the opening pages, they speak of this chaos, a result of the continuous absence of planning, which impedes a vision of the whole. In these pages we read how many of the architects of the Beautiful City movement 'had tried and failed to introduce into Harvard Yard the ideal of axial symmetry and vista that so influenced other Beaux Arts university campuses', while the projects of Charles McKim for Columbia University or the extension of the University of Virginia became models to be followed in all of the US territory.

TPA (Town Planning Associates), Pilot Plan for Havana, 1955–58, President Batista's Palace, model.

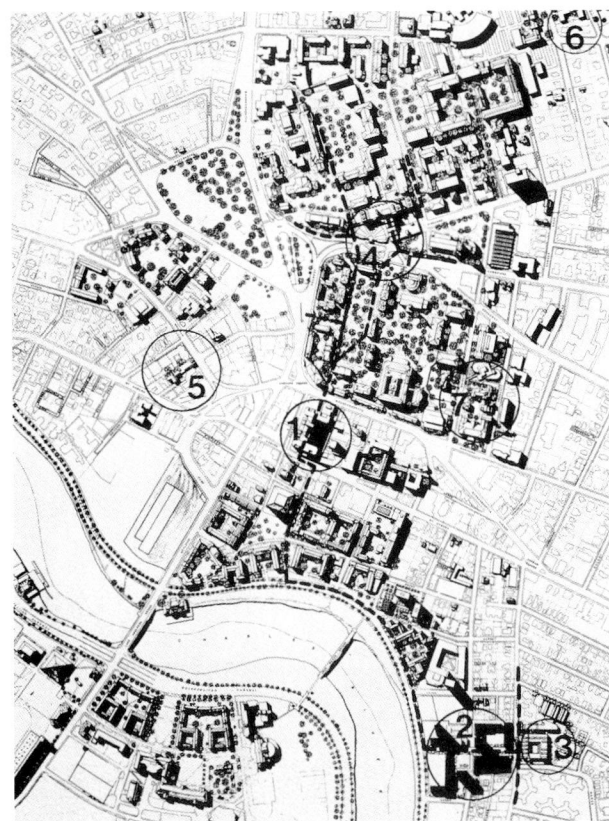

sual impact of Harvard derives more from that human scale that invites exploration than from heroic architecture.'[104] A stroll through Harvard's campus offers the possibility of observing without transition all possible stylistic reinterpretations: from a Greek to a Roman temple, from a Norman church to an Italian bell tower; all these different architectures parade before the eyes of the spectator, not giving him a chance to keep a clearly individualized recollection of any of them.

This variety is to a certain extent unified by the materials and scale of the buildings, which was achieved following different intervention processes dating back to 1869, when Charles W.

Hemenway
Gymnasium,
1878, and
Holyoke House,
1870, Harvard
Campus.

It was difficult to reorder Harvard, but it showed a characteristic that must have caught Sert's eye at the time: 'In contradistinction to the traditional American campus, Harvard's quality of design stems from its focus on deference: an architectural strength drawn from the totality of its buildings rather than from individual, assertive monuments. The successful vi-

Littauer Center,
Harvard Campus,
1937.

Eliot was designated president of the university and took it upon himself to turn it into a cosmopolitan institution. To him it little mattered what style was used to design the more than thirty-five buildings he had erected during his presidency, since it was enough that the buildings be solid and adequately located on the campus site. His successor, A. Lawrence Lowell, who was Dean of Harvard between 1909 and 1933, dealt with the growth of the campus towards the south and began to be aware of the need for planning and harmonizing this growth with that of Cambridge. He had a great interest in architecture, debating in depth the plans and the buildings with their architect, Charles A. Coolidge, who was responsible for almost all

Nathan Pusey, James Conant and Derek Bok, Deans of Harvard.

the works carried out during this period, usually following classicist tenets.[105]

Opportunities to enlarge the campus under James Bryant Conant, Dean between 1933 and 1953, were much scarcer due to the Depression and the war. Under him, however, modernity at last emerged, consequently leading to controversy[106] within the already babelish Harvard, on whose campus were erected modern buildings by Henry R. Shepley, Aalto, Gropius and Bulfinch and Abbott.

Nathan Pusey, Dean between 1953 and 1971, was indirectly responsible for the work that Sert and his associates developed at Harvard. Pusey obtained 72 million dollars for the

construction of buildings between 1953 and 1963, a considerable quantity if we compare it with the 23 million dollars allotted to Lowell for the 1923–33 decade. Bunting's explanations may be helpful in clearing up this issue: 'Like those earlier administrations, Harvard buildings erected under President Pusey have a recognizable character. Yet this architecture, although entirely contemporary, is by no means uniform. There is a new repertoire of building materials, and structures are generally of a larger scale than before. For the first time Harvard uses high-rise structures. There is also less of an overall order and plan in the placement of buildings than in Lowell's day. The reasons for such changes are not obscure. Open land was running out, and the school was encountering some opposition in attempts to acquire additional land. Building vertically was the only way to secure the space it needed. Increasing costs were another factor.'[107] Pusey commissioned projects from renowned architects, ordered old buildings to be remodelled, and undertook important installations and infrastructures, for he seemed to be very conscious of the need for the university to 'renew and change itself because the inner intellectual and spiritual Harvard is growing and changing all the time, and it has to find a new form, and do it today within the complexities created by this great urban area in which we live.'

Thus, aside from his concern with urban chaos, Sert had to deal with the introduction of high-rise buildings in a context occupied by constructions of scarce vertical dimension. As was his custom, he began by listing the problems that concerned him to his students, although in this case the motives for doing so were more evident, given that they were working on issues related to the urban design of a zone owned by the University. As a result, the programme of Projects II, which he taught along with Gourley, Horsbrugh, Isaaks and Sasaki, published on 11 October 1956, bore an unequivocal title: Redesign of South Harvard Square.[108] It divided the part of the city of Cambridge that went from Massachusetts Avenue to the Charles River and from Boylston Avenue to De Wolfe Street into three zones in which it seemed essential to remodel its shape so as to make possible the introduction of new uses.

The first sector – that which most interests us – since it held business and commercial activities was not to vary its activities, but it was to modify its shape: 'The actual offices and shops will be replaced by new structures making better use of space in buildings and between buildings, increasing the income-producing areas … It may be advisable to design some arcaded streets and porticos along Massachusetts Avenue. Pedestrian paths linking the campus area across Massachusetts Avenue with the dormitory section along the Charles River should be provided.'[109] It was the University's new demands that made it necessary to take into account this consideration: 'The demand for goods and services generated by the 16,000 students, faculty and staff of Harvard University, the demand for professional services from University-associated individuals, i.e. faculty members who carry on non-University associated practices, but who desire to locate near the University, space demands for University administrative staff and contract research.'[110] Sert was taking his first steps in understanding the zone in which shortly afterwards he would plan one of his best buildings, the Holyoke Center.

The course programme's content manifests concerns that may be considered a preparation for the round table on Urban Design that Sert organized at the GSD on 26 and 27 November 1956, a meeting held prior to the Congress on Urban Design that Sert meant to carry out at Harvard from 12 to 13 April 1957. In the typewritten report of the conclusions of this first round table we find certain aspects of interest concerning Sert's trajectory. In the introductory text, after reviewing the achievements of the previous generation regarding the city's needs, it concluded: 'While recognizing the many considerations involved, the group agreed that Urban Design should be primarily concerned with the visual aspects of the contemporary city: the area most neglected today, and of most concern to this group.'[111] Sert knew he could not raze Harvard to the ground and make new proposals, and was therefore aware that any intervention in the campus would have to take into account these formal and spatial considerations, in which the necessary question of the relationship between city and architecture would play a decisive role.

Thus it was a matter of re-urbanizing, of recovering the existing city and improving its living conditions: 'The need for re-urbanization as opposed to suburbanism was emphasized. It was felt by the group that a pseudo-country and pseudo-town existence had led to a waste of human energy and was denying us the pleasure of contrast.' It was a question of promoting the vitality of urban existence, which could be 'expressed in biological and psychological terms, but are far from realization in our actual environment', and of doing so through the instruments of urban design that could make the experience of the city comprehensible: 'In their present shapes, cities are not conducive to a truly urban and urbane way of life as they do not have comprehensible visual order on the scale of the individual human observer to compensate for the increasing incomprehensibility of their total environment. The group therefore considered that a re-vision and revitalization of "cities" was called for.' After stressing old aspirations such as the separation of motorized from pedestrians traffic and the need to define the use of open spaces, it concluded: 'The group considered that the introduction of coherence into our present urban chaos needs make no claim on new land: it was rather a process of shrinkage and more intense land use', a factor that designers, politicians and legislators were to take care of, but which depended most of all on those designing the projects 'to make sure that they serve as tools to implement a sound urban aesthetic.'

In a typewritten text, Sert explained how the Planning Office of Harvard was established in 1956, and how the university was understood as a city within two other cities, Boston and Cambridge, with its own urban problems: the high price of the ground given its scarcity, lack of parking space, excessive traffic, conflicts between pedestrians and motorized traffic, etc. The growth and congestion required a more intensive use of the land, since the university at that point could not purchase more. This forced a 'rearrangement of spaces in existing buildings and careful designing of spaces in new ones',[112] which 'required the use of some high-rise buildings in strategic points properly related to the environment and to the transportation facilities.'[113] The interest in separating the different types of circulation was again emphasized, and this was achieved by Sert at a problematic point in the campus when he dealt with the Science Center, hoping that his solution for the Holyoke Center of a covered walkway with businesses would provide an example.

In the following academic years, Sert would insist on the need for these concepts to abound both in the lectures and the worktables of the GSD students. Thus, in the 1957–58 year, he was professor of a course called 'Introduction to the Visual Arts' jointly with Chermayeff, Newton and Jacqueline Tyrwhitt. He developed his course on urban design with Giedion and Sasaki, giving it the clear title: 'The Human Scale', at the same time changing the title of the history courses to better represent his interests at the time.[114] His course 'Advanced Architectural Design', which he shared with Jackson, Sasaki and Ortega, was dedicated to studying the residential sector as part of the city, and in the text of the programme Sert's interest in the rapport between architecture and the city in the heart of Cambridge was again made patent, as this criterion formed part of his collaboration with the Town Council in order to plan the foreseeable future growth of the University: 'Lying between Massachusetts Avenue on the north, the Charles River on the south, De Wolfe Street on the west and Western Avenue on the east. This is an area of crowded wooden houses and tenements, largely obsolete, with a fairly large intrusion of industry. It has been designated by the Planning Board of Cambridge as an area for redevelopment.'[115]

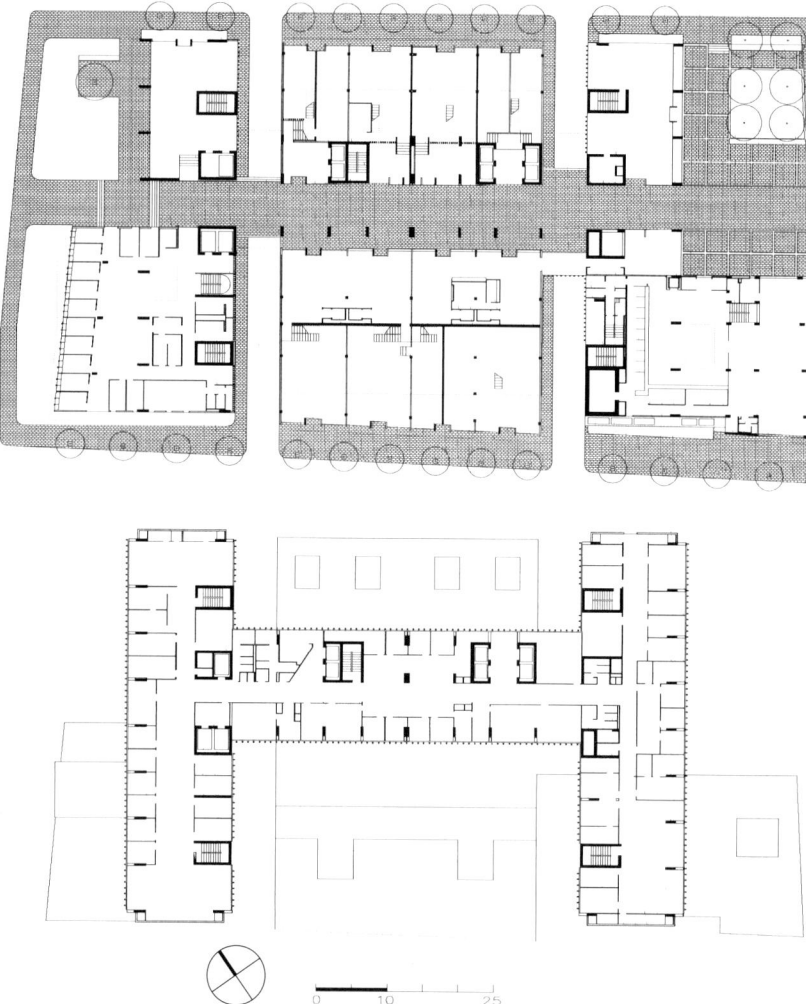

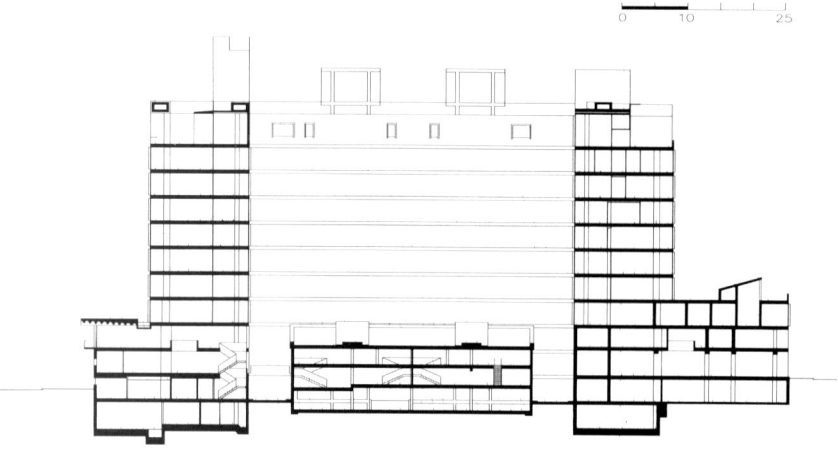

The programmes of the two following terms show a similar content. We are now in possession of sufficient information to be able to analyze the buildings that Sert designed in Cambridge for the University of Harvard: Holyoke Center (1958), Center for the Study of World Religions (1960), the Peabody Terrace (1962) and the Science Center (1968).

The Holyoke Center took its name from Holyoke House, a student residence with a facade facing Massachusetts Avenue, which was designed in 1870 by the architect Edward Harris within a campaign directed by Dean Eliot to promote this type of building; it was demolished to allow for the construction of the new building.[116]

Located on a sizeable plot of land with a facade on four streets, the new Holyoke attempted to come up with a building for the University that had to hold a complex programme of services for health, publications, planning, finances, administrative offices, parking, etc.[117]

Sert, Jackson and Gourley, Holyoke Center, Harvard University, Cambridge, 1958, plans and sections.

Since this was too extensive a programme for the plot, evidently the building would have to adopt a height that was not in accordance with the Cambridge setting. Given that Sert was so familiar with the location due to his teaching practice, we can imagine that the final design would not be indifferent to its setting. Thus, the main challenge the architect had to face in Holyoke was solving the excess of height while exercising urban responsibility.

Located between the south campus of Harvard, in which there were a great many student residences, and the Yard – that is to say, the heart of the University and the site of faculties and libraries – Holyoke was intended to facilitate communication between the two. Sert achieved this with a covered pedestrian walkway, 'an animated street', which on the ground-floor level joined Mount Auburn Street with Massachusetts Avenue. Thus, the longed-for separation between motorized traffic and pedestrian circulation was ensured, while at the same time im-

proving the organization of some of the multiple accesses to the building and lending greater presence to this interior street by placing shops on it. Faced with the problem of height, Sert employed diverse strategies: he set back the high bodies of the facades facing Massachusetts Avenue and Mount Auburn Street, avoiding alignment with the rest of the neighbouring buildings, and delivered the building to the sidewalk by means of the two low volumes flanking the tall H-shaped building. These in turn generated two urban spaces that acted as the entryway from the public pedestrian concourse to the building.[118]

The two high buildings are joined together by a transversal volume (giving it is H-shape), which functions as a type of urban courtyard due to its recessed position with respect to Dunster Street and Holyoke Street, to which it is also delivered through a low volume.

The attentive spectator will see various architectural perceptions at the same time in this

Holyoke Center,
Harvard, rear
facade.

formal strategies: a continuous gallery on the fourth floor; the alternation of randomly modulated glass and concrete panels; four volumes looking out onto Massachusetts Avenue and a rigorously modulated rhythm of solids and voids in Mount Auburn Street; separation of the planes of the facade so as not to imply any wish to emphasize the volume; the 'discontinuous' treatment of the facades of the headwalls, etc. As the architect liked to say: 'The varied fenestration in facades is an expression of the variety of uses of inside space.'[119]

The complexity of the building and its urban responsibility needed to be indicated somehow. Even the view from the banks of the Charles River allows one to see the dialogue between the church steeples of the South campus and the elevator tower of Holyoke, just as the finial of the facade on Mount Auburn Street floats lightly over the strict neo-Georgian buildings that Dean Eliot had erected. The academic play of window variations in the River Houses dissolves into the sky with its mischievous neighbours.[120]

Behind all great intellectual effort there is drama, and Sert made no effort to disguise this fact. Reinforced concrete predominates in his building, to which it owes its nickname of the 'growing grey dragon'; in other words, a material was employed that does not seek affection or friendship from its neighbours, which are mostly made of brick. Unlike Gropius, who wished to be kind to his surroundings, building the Graduate Center with traditional materials that were easily integrated with the 'Harvard

unitarian ensemble, which Sert emphasized through the varying design of the fenestration of the facade, seeking visual effects that would bring about a greater adaptation of the building to its surroundings. Michelozzo's lesson of varying the stone textures of the different storeys of the Medici palace to integrate it with the medieval constructional tradition has been taken up again here. The consideration of visual principles applying to an architecture that means to follow an objective or strictly functional tradition from the 1930s can continue to provide food for thought while producing varying results depending on the setting in which it is carried out.

Along these lines, Sert would give the impression of cutting the plane of the building's facades at certain points by employing diverse

Holyoke Center,
view of the Charles
River banks.

Charles Coolidge, Strauss and Lehman Halls.

Holyoke Center, integration with the traditional buildings of Cambridge.

spirit', Sert confronted face on the aggression that his building was likely to provoke.

The Holyoke Center is located in front of the Strauss and Lehman Halls, built at the end of the 1920s by the ubiquitous Charles Coolidge, and these buildings seemed to aim to protect the sacred Yard of Harvard and the conservative peace of the university from the continuing onslaught of traffic and overcrowding. Sert knew that his building would surpass the other buildings in height, despite the fact that the body of the Forbes Plaza, which houses the

bank of Holyoke, has three storeys – the same number of floors as the Strauss and Lehman buildings. However, this is only a numerical coincidence: in reality the three floors of Lehman Hall are equal to the first four floors of Sert's building. Above these, Sert inserted a strip of continuous glass, as if it were a gallery, cutting the facade of the building in two. This gesture showed both respect and a menacing attitude: the presence of the grey dragon will forever loom over the centenary Yard, guardian of Harvard's values.

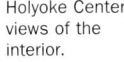

Holyoke Center, views of the interior.

The illusion of walking without the risk of being run over by a car lasts only as long as it takes the pedestrian to cross the covered street, despite the fact that it is aligned with the door that has given access to the Yard since 1857. Once the protection of the street contained in Holyoke has been abandoned, pedestrians have to keep their eyes open for the implacable traffic of Massachusetts Avenue with its deafening noise, its perils and its pollution.

The excessive volume of the building cannot hide the basic problem of lack of ground space, the evident cause of this excess, while the use of concrete announces technological and economic possibilities that suppress all nostalgia and longing for continuity. It is said that at Harvard many professors and students began to use Linden Street to avoid the presence of Holyoke.

In the interior of the building, Sert managed to differentiate between some of the settings he was to design by creating double spaces with different forms, personalizing the furniture and seeking, through the treatment of glass, spatial qualities that would distance it from a uniformizing idea.

Sert faced fewer responsibilities in the urban setting when he began to design a project for the Center for the Study of World Religions. It was set on a plot of ground that was somewhat distant from the campus and the idea was to come up with a residence for students of different religions, which would house twenty apartments, auditoriums, a chapel and services. The need for such a building arose from Dean Pusey's religious policy: 'Now in a time divided by politics and ravaged by messiahs of far right and left, Pusey turned to traditional faith as an antidote to cynicism … A much more publicized campaign to restore religion at Harvard gave Pusey a platform from which to display his liberal, pluralistic approach to the subject.'[121]

The idea was based on the University's 'projection' towards the world, an action paralleled by American expansionist policies, but in this case directed by the cultural and educational

Sert, Jackson and Gourley, Center for Study of World Religions, Harvard University, Cambridge, 1960, plans.

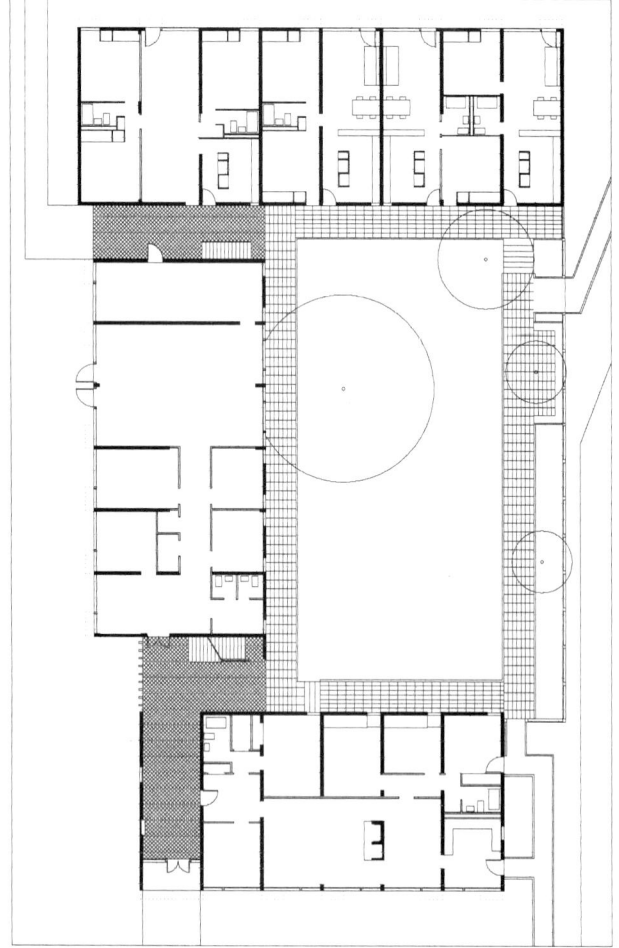
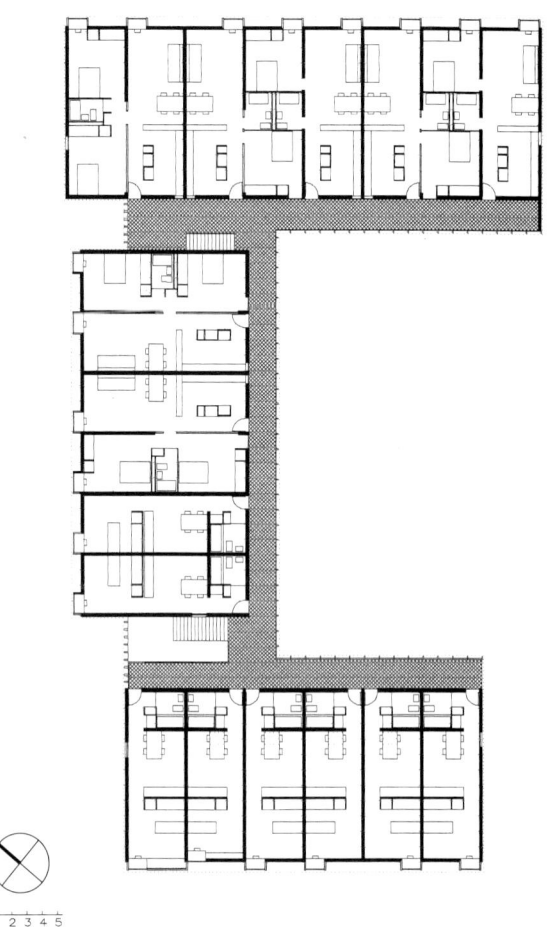

Center for Study
of World
Religions, views.

services that Harvard could provide: 'Harvard sent experts to staff management schools in Switzerland and Guatemala, to provide health services in poverty-stricken areas of the Third World, to raise awareness everywhere of environmental and nutritional urgencies. The divinity school has its Center for World Religions. Engineering and Applied Physics, in tandem with other specialists, advised India on how to control its rivers. The Development Advisory Service did what its name implies in Colombia and Korea, and the school of education signed a contract to supervise Nigeria's first comprehensive high school.'[122]

The study of all religions at Harvard is the distant mirror of this activity, which 'solves' all the world's problems through the knowledge and techniques emanating from the University: it is a well-known fact that since the time of Hadrian religious syncretism has been one of the mechanisms of an empire seeking long-lasting power. Around a courtyard open to the world, people of all beliefs were to be able to think about religion from the common universal basis that united all its different manifestations, and they were to exchange experiences and project new paths for the spiritual benefit and happiness of humankind. For this reason Sert designed a U-shaped courtyard onto which all the apartment-cells faced, connected on the first floor by a street hallway, while the chapel, in which any believer could meditate

or pray, was placed on the terrace of the building, separated from the rest and almost without light except that coming from the sky (until some unfortunate later reforms modified this).

Located, as we know from its closeness to Sert's own house, in a typical American suburb, the building gives little away in terms of having a different function from that of its neighbours, at least not when seen from the street. It is low in height and uses similar materials to those of its surroundings, brick and wood, always controlled by a structure and concrete finish that reconducted the variations that the architect wished to introduce. The impressive windows were emphasized on the facade, a formal strategy that represents the fruit of the inside-outside study that our architect was so fond of practising. The worktables are placed near the windows, so that the spiritual scholar may face away from daily actions such as eating or sleeping, only engaging in a dialogue with the air and the existing trees, which Sert decided to keep.[123]

As was becoming habitual, the course programme that Sert developed during the 1961–62 academic year gives us some idea of his further commissions. In a meeting of 16 October 1961 he proposed to his Urban Design students the development of a work on the banks of the Charles River, where he would create two of his most ambitious projects.[124] At the same time he stressed some familiar subjects in his writing of the general programme for the School of Architecture, whose title also rings a bell: 'Man and Environment'. In some ways this text constitutes a review of the past, as is suggested by the following words: 'During the last fifty years the results of a great revolution have become well established in architecture, and now the personal interpretations of these results open up many new roads, expressing different approaches and preferences. This is a healthy and normal consequence of a natural tendency in creative individuals to assert their own and differing personalities … One cannot neglect such conditions of architecture as site and climate, industrialization and mass production, the complexity of mechanical controls, the special qualities of new materials, and the totality of a city in which every building is related to many other buildings and spaces.'[125] Possibly in keeping with this feeling, that school year showed a marked emphasis on the teaching of history, which was reinforced by the addition of courses in Architectural Theory and Criticism, in which we find for the first time James Ackerman as professor since Giedion did not travel to Harvard that year.

To understand the relationship between architecture and the historical context based on singular selected examples, sometimes a group of buildings or urban ensembles, 'A thorough study of a selected number of significant examples is encouraged; these are placed in their historical context as fully as possible before being subjected to detailed formal analysis and comparison. Special emphasis is placed on the conceptions underlying the shaping of space in individual buildings and urban ensembles and on the problems of structure, construction and tectonics … Architectural theory and criticism are handled within the framework of the history courses and in advanced seminars.'[126] To proceed to a critical analysis based on theory seemed a good way to review and test all the work carried out during the last ten years.

We can also view it as a way of thinking out architectural problems that were on Sert's mind at the time and which now began to take on a different scale given their great dimensions. It is not by chance that the declarations made in the history programmes coincides with the objective of the only graduate course that Sert, along with Soltan and Zalewski, taught that year. The course dealt with designing buildings that were complex either because of their structure or because of their function: 'Advanced problems dealing with complex structure in a building of particular character such as a civic or religious building, or with building types which require special methods of approach resulting from our changing social, economic, and cultural conditions.'[127]

These buildings, which formed a complex unity given the amplitude and diversity of the programme, had to be somehow related both to each other and to the open spaces that connected them: 'During the second term, problems deal with the relationships of buildings to one another and to open spaces.' Thus, attention was focused on the surroundings of the Charles River and on the ensembles of single buildings. It seems evident that we are dealing with a preface to two complex projects that would reach Sert's worktable almost at the same time: the Peabody Terrace and the central campus of Boston University.

The first of these is the generic name – a homage to Reverend Francis Greenwood Peabody, professor of theology at Harvard between 1880 and 1902 – given to a residential complex of 500 apartments, 350 parking spaces, shops, nursery schools, auditoriums and other services for married students who until then had not enjoyed residences suited to their marital status. It was located in front of the Charles River on a plot of land marking the boundary between the city and the university campus. The dimension of the site and the complexity of the programme allowed Sert to project a highly dense complex set up as three towers, twenty-two storeys high, connected by a series of buildings of variable heights, which were on certain occasions stepped. These formed two great landscaped courtyards that were contained within the interior of the complex, and two courtyards open to the river on the facade looking east, which were for public use. This solution had appeared in some projects for civic centres in Latin America, which we saw in the first part of this work, but they had remained on paper; now they cropped up again.

Sert reproduced the idea of courtyards among low-rise buildings that abounded in

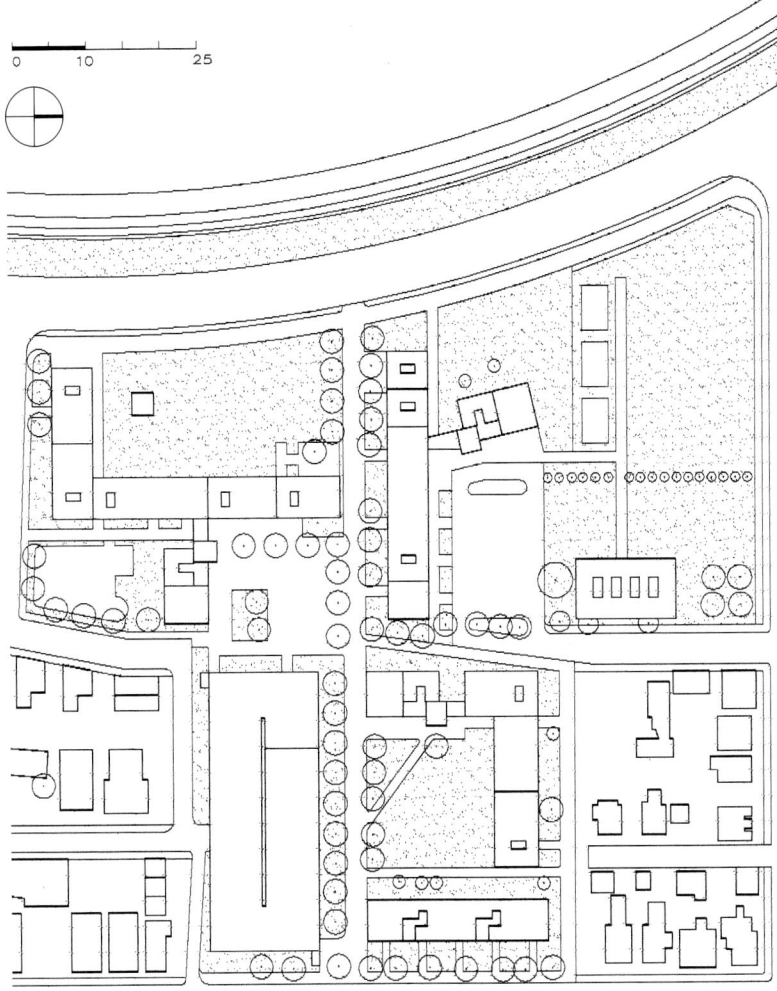

Peabody Terrace,
Harvard University,
Cambridge,
configuration
of the complex
and plans.

ment. They could continue shaping quadrangles as in the past. The high-rise building that could be of many different shapes determined by different uses and conditions should not break the high barrier or have a bulk which could overpower the lower ones and the quadrangle scale. Between Chicago and San Gimigniano there are many happy mediums.'[128]

A medieval image seems to be the initial reference for the Peabody Terrace. As if they were watchtowers, the high-rise buildings of the complex overlook university activities, guaranteeing its success and sheltering the chosen ones being trained there. The one closest to the river, which is also the one nearest to the university campus, is rotated in relation to the ensemble, thus ensuring the natural flow of knowledge by imitating nature, since its rotation corresponds to the curve of the meandering river. After this gesture, however, its twin sisters remain solid as rocks, ensuring through their orthogonal relationships with the rest of the complex the impenetrability of daily life into the ensemble.

Jonathan Hale has underlined the complex's problem of integrating itself with the life around it on the basis of some decisions of the plan as well as the evident social barriers existing between it and its neighbours: 'At Peabody Terrace, the urban design aspects of the scheme have had ambiguous results. While the sur-

Harvard. This allowed him to establish a transition between the adjacent modest wooden buildings and their new neighbour; his discourse on the human scale in architecture was being brought to life. These courtyards were connected by an interior street that was both public and pedestrian, which directly linked the bank of the Charles River with the urban grid of the city. The peaceful route through Harvard's courtyards has been rationalized using impeccable logic, and once again pedestrian and vehicle circulation has been successfully separated. A text by the architect helps us understand both general issues about the need for high-rise buildings in a place in which they did not formerly exist, and a previous outline to which the project is a response: 'What shape will Harvard have in the near future? If it has to make more intense use of land, we may see high and low buildings combine to make this possible. The low buildings should lodge the larger spaces and those requiring special treat-

339

rounding neighbourhood is not walled off, it isn't invited in either. The garage faces neighbouring residential blocks, providing a barrier to two of the courts; living rooms turn away from the city streets and adjacent houses … The University seems to be hostile to outsiders. The surrounding community (especially children) can use the open space, but some Peabody Terrace residents are still afraid. Vandalism takes place, though the degree to which it occurs may be exaggerated. The University reportedly removed seating in the lobby because neighbourhood kids used it, and campus police are said to have ordered children off the premises. Some tenants support this line and have suggested walling off the whole project.'[129]

To design the plan of the towers, Sert thought of using the Skip-Stop system, a mechanism that uses to maximum economic benefit the solution of the corridor-street by making it serve three dwellings at the same time, with a considerable saving on elevators and stairs, and which allows for privileged views and cross-ventilation in the majority of cases. A nearby precedent that our architect must have observed with a great deal of attention was the residential complex called Eastgate, an MIT neighbour that was also on the banks of the Charles River.[130] Through a combination of seventeen apartment types offered to the user, Sert sought to vary the design of the facades, so that the height of the buildings

Peabody Terrace, view from above.

W. Hopkins, C. Koch, V. de Mars, R. Rapson, Eastgate residential complex, Boston, 1950–51, section in perspective of the Skip-Stop system.

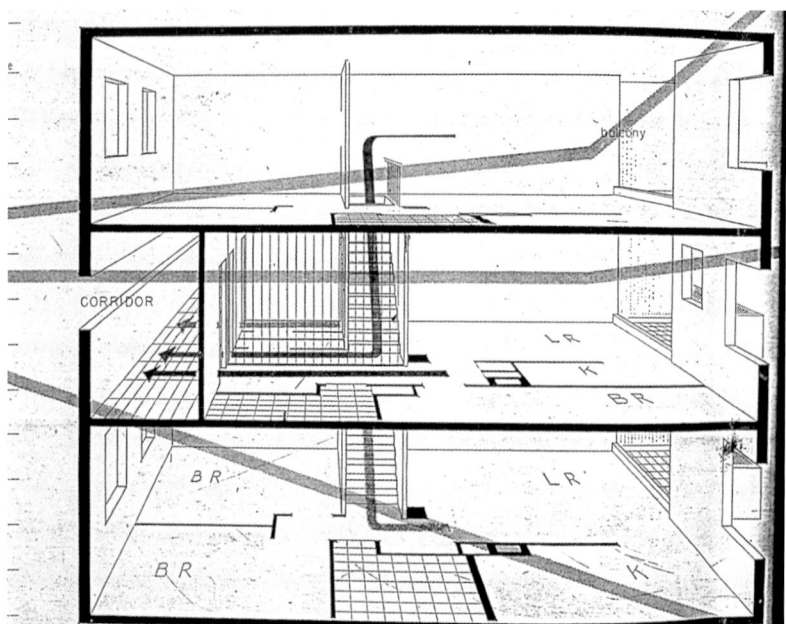

would not be perceived from the mechanical superimposition of the horizontal structures. Sert continued experimenting with visual effects, which – as he pointed out – he had learned from Miró and Léger. He provided certain points of the facades with overhanging galleries, which are terraces overlooking the river, closed in certain cases by wooden slats functioning as sunbreakers, rotating the floors located in the upper part of the building, and breaking the continuity of height of the concrete headwall; he also designed different types of windows, interrupted their alignment in height, and painted them different colours, placing the towers of the elevators on the corners, etc.[131]

The *varietas* of Holyoke here reached its apex and the effectiveness of this mechanism is evident in the result, a monument that, as Sert once said, he did not wish to be static. All of this was achieved by maintaining a rigorous vertical communication with the premises in which the services were located and a modulation of the openings and standardization of the walling elements to ensure a good economic result.

Peabody Terrace,
views.

341

Sert employed similar intellectual solutions for the Boston University campus, whose first sketches date back to 1959 and of which there was already a model in 1963.[132] The campus was to house the Boston University School of Law, a large library and a student centre. Three buildings of different characteristics were to be connected on a plot of land of reduced dimensions that was located between the busy Commonwealth Avenue and the Charles River. Lodged in the Wesleyan Building on Bronfield Street since its foundation in 1872, the BUSL had changed location several times until it was accommodated in the building on 11 Ashburton Place: 'In all these locations, the School of Law was kept in close proximity to the other colleges of Boston University, which for many years were centred on Beacon Hill. Even when this historic area became overcrowded, and later Boston University colleges were established in the vicinity of Copley Square, it was wisely decided that the ideal quarters for future lawyers were most certainly close to the legal capital of the community and state, at least until they could be integrated into an all-university community.'[133]

Boston University, view of the Charles River, sketch (SC).

Thus, the idea was to decisively integrate the law school within the university community, including it in a joint project with the generous services typical of a North American campus, and turning it into a major protagonist and representative of an institution that was nearly a hundred years old. In a passionate speech of 13 March 1942, Dean Marsh had pronounced: 'Great is our Law School, and justly renowned as are our neighbouring schools, yet I visualize a Law School of the future better than any school in existence today – a strong school which will bring a new approach to the problem of teaching law, and a fresh point of view on the law as a science.'[134]

Boston University, overall plan.

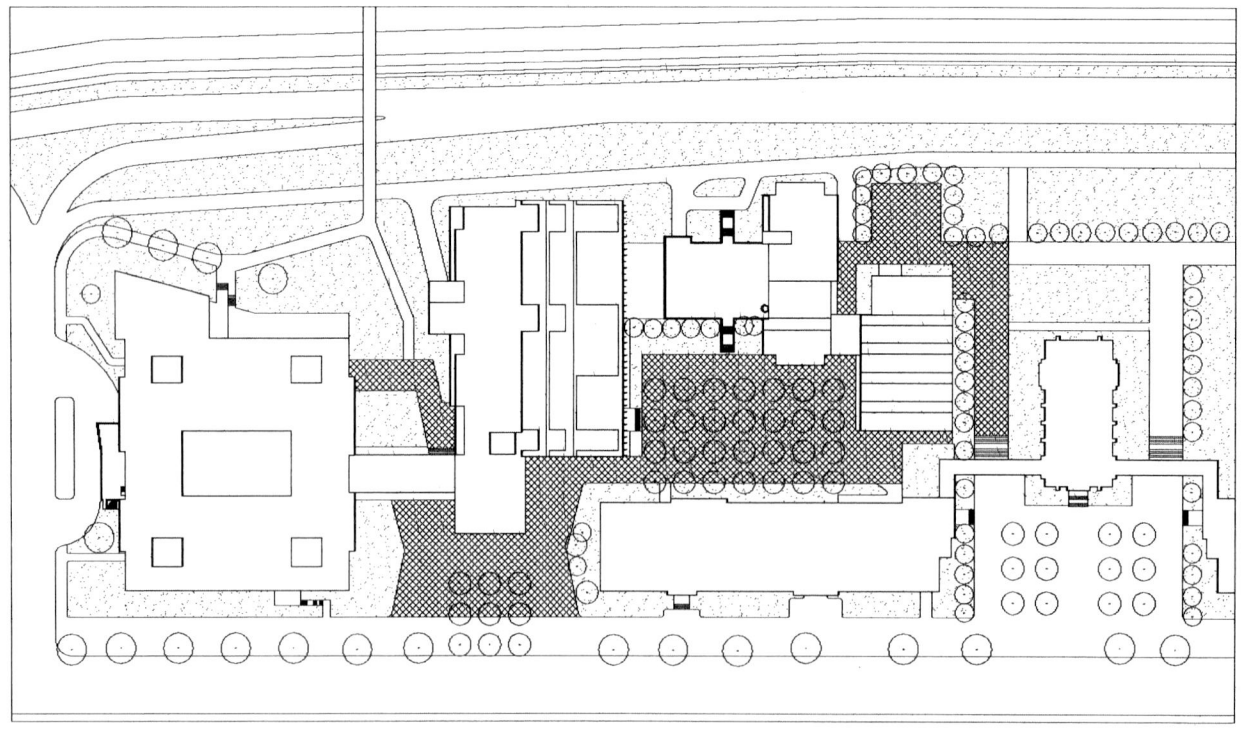

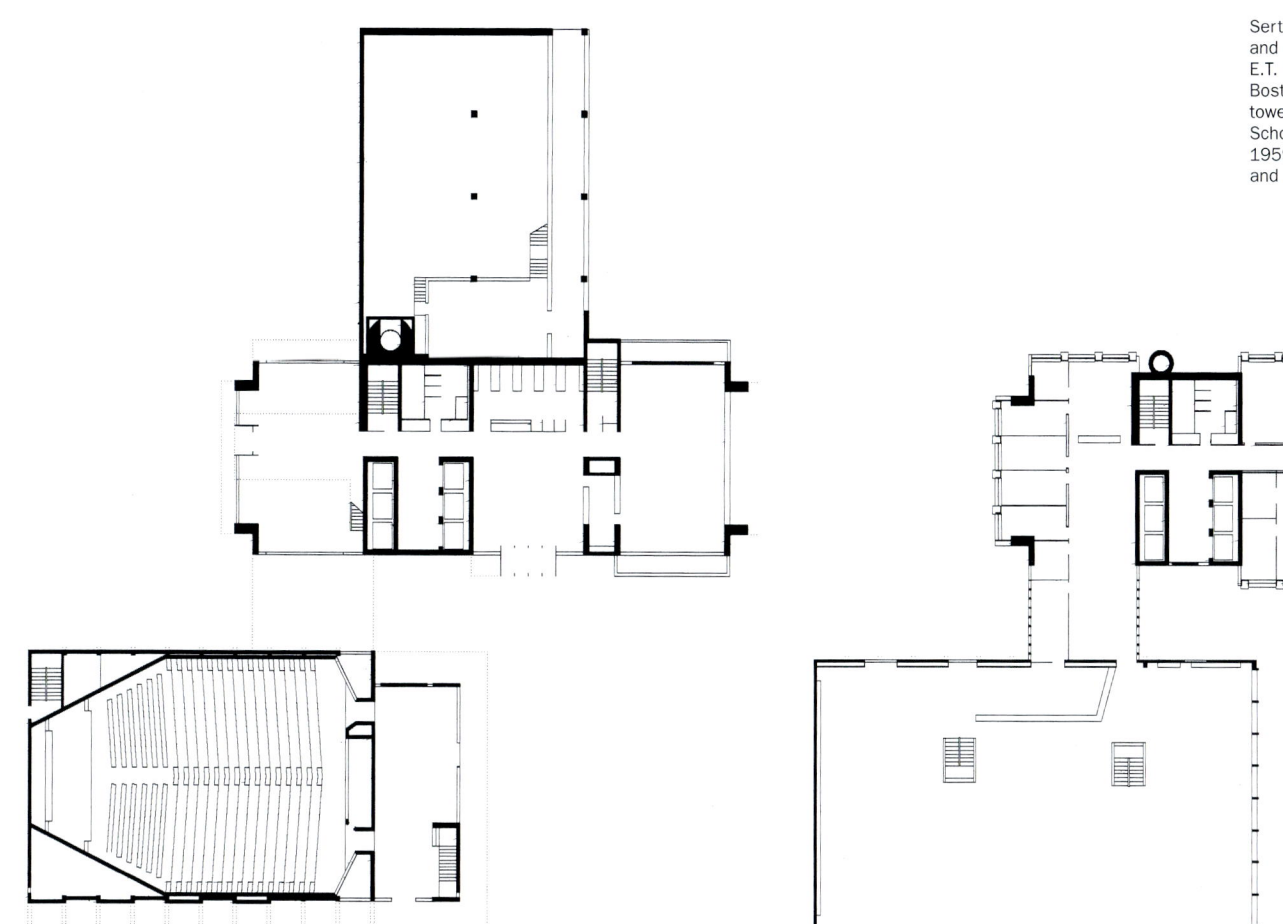

Sert, Jackson
and Gourley;
E.T. Steffian,
Boston University,
tower of the Law
School,
1959–66, plans
and views.

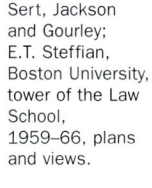

Sert, Jackson
and Gourley;
Hoyle, Doran
and Berry, Boston
University, Mugar
Library, 1959–66,
view and plans
of the second
and fourth floors.

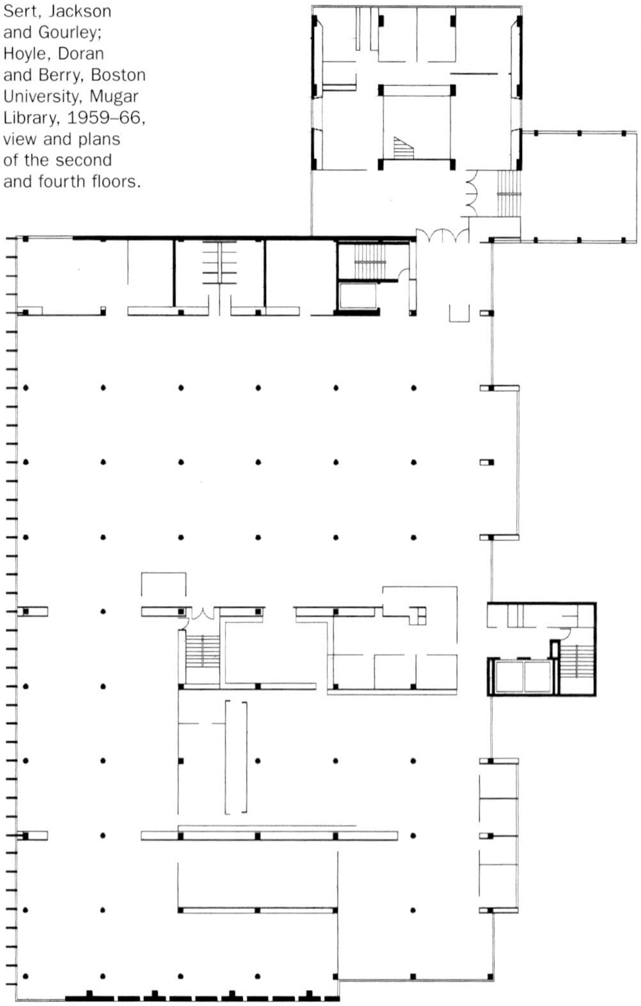

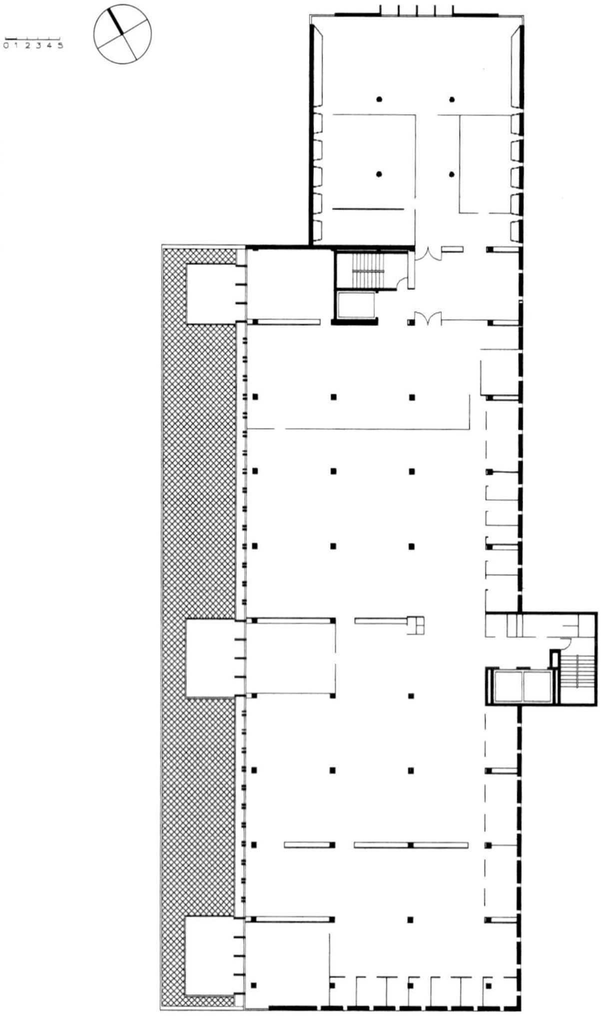

Marsh's dream would become a reality twenty years later, and the tower that was to hold his visions of a brighter future would be part of the complex that Sert designed.

When it became impossible for the university to remain at Copley Square any longer, and the BUSL still had its quarters in Ashburton Place, the academic authorities decided to move: 'When Copley Square, in its turn, made it impossible for the University Trustees to centralize the University in one geographical site there, the Charles River land plot near the Cottage Farms Bridge was purchased. Here, in September 1939 the University's first really new building constructed in modern architectural and functional form, was opened for the College of Business Administration. Since 1939, the campus centralization has continued, with new structures and the conversion of existing adjacent and nearby buildings … In the summer of 1960, the campus building at 308 Bay State Road, on the River, which is actually an administrative annex … housing the Placement Service, News Bureau, Scholarship and Loan Office, and the Alumni Association offices, will be razed to release ground for the new Law Center.'[135]

Sert, Jackson and Gourley; Hoyle, Doran and Berry, Boston University, Student Center, 1959–66, view.

Much was expected of the new BUSL building, both in solving the physical problems that its users had been facing in carrying out their work, and in providing an atmosphere in which professors and students could work and study together. The new BUSL headquarters were to have 'a library to house 200,000 volumes, a Moot Court Room, auditorium, a bar-

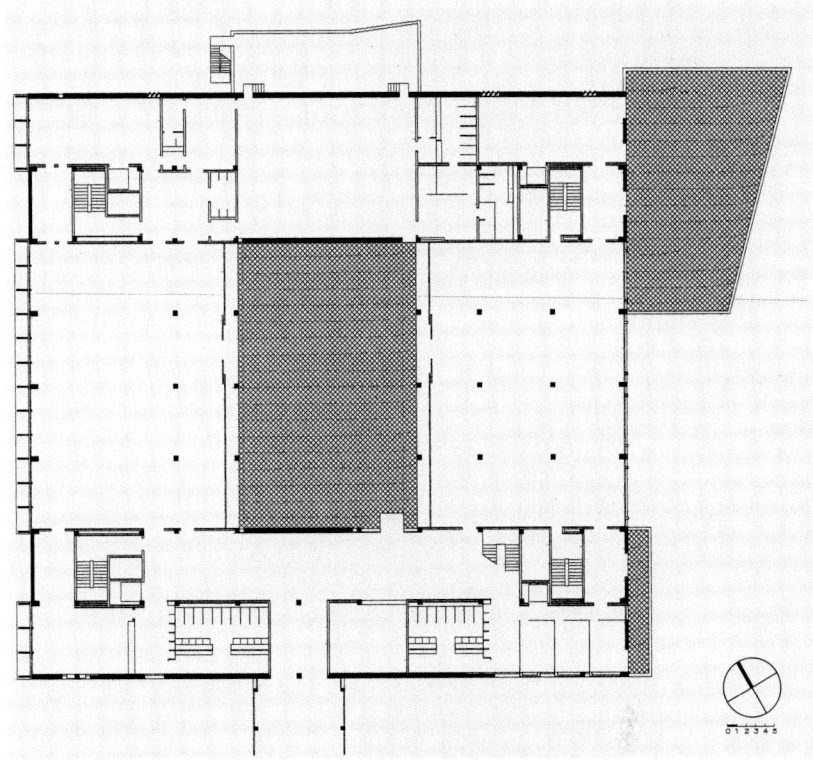

Student Center, plan.

rister's hall, student lounge, large lecture halls, small classrooms, Law Review suite, seminar rooms, student bar association room, faculty lounge, conference room, student research rooms, faculty offices and student carrells.' Sert made the most of this programmatic variety to continue working along the lines that interested him at the time.

The architect laid out a body of a low height that acted as an intermediary between the tower and the ground, and in this building he accommodated the auditorium and library, illuminated from above by the skylights derived from the Miró workshop, which had also been essayed in the Braque house and were soon to become a trademark of the architect. Connected by a covered bridge and yet not aligned with each other, the two buildings managed to integrate themselves with the low buildings of eclectic style that had been retained in the campus, and allowed a visual transition towards the wilful height of the tower. Sert continually altered the volume of the tower: he split the building in two parts in its vertical component at the height of the existing building, which also functioned as a barrier against the aggressive activity of Commonwealth Avenue;[136] he employed the mechanism of denying compactness to the volume already

345

used on the corners of the Holyoke Center; he also cut the plan in two parts joined by the vertical communications and the services, etc.

Seen from the Charles River, the faculty tower on the left is deposited on the ground by means of the 'intermediary' mentioned, and Sert would set up to the right of it a visually similar mechanism. The Mugar Library takes off from the Law School tower, and goes upwards in stepped form to reach the height of the student centre. Both buildings were completed with enormous towers that augmented their real dimensions and made this transition more effective. This formal strategy was underlined by a highly successful element: none of the facades of the four buildings are consigned to the ground, which causes a strong shadow line, making it impossible for them to be directly reflected in the river. This virtual image, which duplicates the lower part of the complex, always somewhat set back and therefore always in the shade, underlines the surface character of the buildings. All of this increases the unreal sensation of a complex that in fact has a very high constructional density. Once again the urban strategies that the architect had developed in Latin America have been used to full advantage.

The Law School tower was to form a complex with the Mugar Library and the Student Center, but it was to do so not only when viewed from afar. To achieve this on the scale of the user of the complex as well, Sert repeated the scheme of the landscaped courtyards among buildings that were typical in American university campuses, creating a sequence in which the size of the courtyards was determined by the height of the nearest building.

Sert was about to take on a great deal of work at precisely the time when the first signs of a crisis in his intellectual principles began to emerge. It was also a period of university crises, a reflection of the general unrest that the 1960s represented in the US. In that decade, our architect directed the works of the projects mentioned above and also drafted others that never came to fruition. One of these was a project for a business centre in Worcester, Massachusetts with a complex programme formed by hotels, warehouses, residential centre, parking lots, etc.; another was for the South Station business and

Sert, Jackson and Gourley, Business Management Center in Worcester, Massachusetts, model.

transportation centre located in Boston, which was to have a similar programme, and another project was that of Interama, the Latin American Cultural Center of Florida, a permanent fair exhibiting the economic and cultural products of Latin American countries. He would still have time to design the exquisite chapel for the renovated Boston Civic Center, which he conceived as a square central plan and a blind volume lit on the inside by light from above provided by strategically placed skylights. This project was similar to that proposed by the architect Barry Byrne for the Thomas More Chapel of the Catholic Student Center of the University of Iowa.[137]

Although Sert's office was having its heyday at the time, the same certainly did not apply to his beloved GSD. Since Sert is not listed as teaching any course during the 1962–63 year,[138] he must have left his teaching duties unattended, only taking care of the unending bureaucratic tasks that his post required of him, and he hardly took on any courses in the following years either, possibly due to his excessive workload at his office, or even because he was becoming aware of the exhaustion of the model that he had made a decisive contribution to implanting.

An analysis of the March 1965 issue of *Connection* magazine, a monographic issue on the crisis of the teaching model of the GSD with many contributions from varied sources, gives

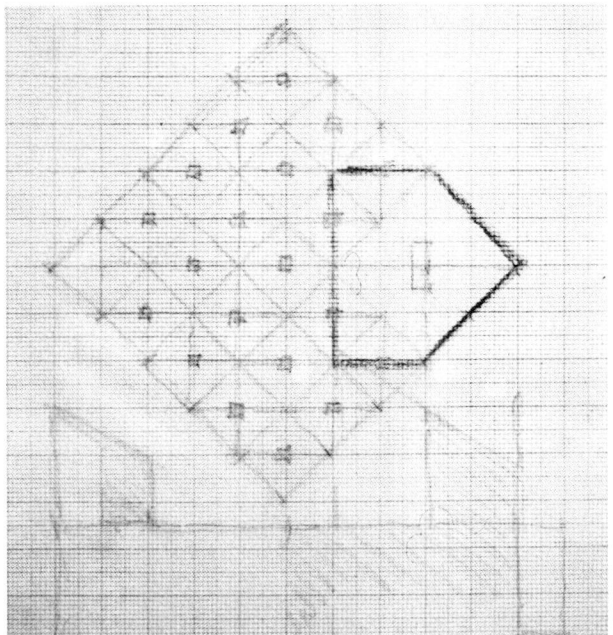

Chapel
for the Boston
Civic Center,
plan and model
(AJFM).

us some clues. The opening words of Perry Neubauer's article were explicit: 'In its fifth year of existence at the Graduate School of Design, the Urban Design Programme has made considerable progress in the formulation of educational objectives and a curriculum of study; but it has not fully realized one of the concepts on which it was based: the integration of the three design disciplines of architecture, landscape architecture, and city planning.'[139] Thus, after so much work, little progress had apparently been made with respect to the goals set out, and it seems that the good intentions of

Barry Byrne,
Thomas More
Chapel, Catholic
Student Center,
University
of Iowa, 1957,
plan published in
the *Architectural
Record*,
September 1957.

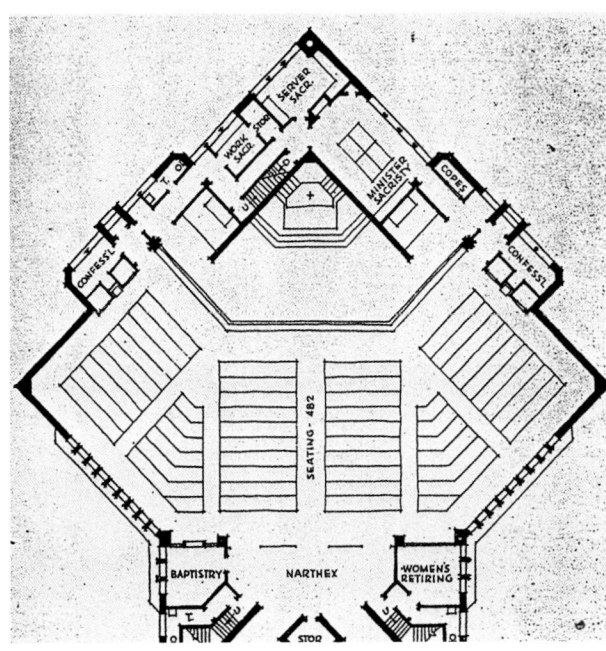

Sert and his colleagues had run aground on the inertia of so many years. Moreover, according to the same author, urban design had not won for itself the renown it needed as an autonomous discipline: 'Since the programme is relatively new and as yet is not widely known, the degree has undefined professional value at the moment; and urban design has not yet gained the respect of the design field as an autonomous discipline.' The text continued with a list of requirements to increase the time dedicated to this discipline as well as suggesting strategies for the improvement of the functioning of the courses, but the sensation of lack of identity nevertheless seemed to persist: 'To caricature the question, is an urban designer an overblown architect or an underdeveloped city planner? Along with this comes the question of whether the stringent course and presentation technique requirements of the programme do not preclude the success of students without an architectural background.'[140]

Roy Mann lamented the fact that their MIT neighbours were able to dedicate much more time to investigation: 'Harvard has conceded the initiative in research of urban phenomena to MIT … In other words, investigations into design criteria are out of sight and out of mind to students at the GSD. What is needed is the housing of design studios and research programmes of all departments under one roof.'[141] Mann also complained about the fact that little time was dedicated to urban design and he proposed that the issue be addressed from the earliest years of an architects career by designing a new study programme directed with more educational meaning instead of continuing with the dispersed project course teachings and the shocking lack of connection between the programmes of the different school terms. He concluded by calling for urgent renovation: 'The GSD has an excellent opportunity to establish a bold new pattern in urban design education. It should do so without delay and thus make a contribution of great importance to the development of the urban world.'[142]

The most radical article was that written by Charles Jencks, the key writer of the magazine. Jencks globalized the crisis of the educational model by identifying it with the crisis of the 1960s in the US: 'There have been strange noises heard at the GSD … The noises, deceptively harsh, really indicate that the student is alive and responding to the pressures of advanced specialized education … They are heard at other graduate schools, in other disciplines, other campuses … [P]erhaps the recent clamour at Berkeley is just a last explosive gurgle, an excited gasp of a dying animal, just as the amoeba is said to agitate excitedly before dissolving … This particular crisis is caused by disruptive outside forces; these forces, for instance the population increase, seem to demand a significant, almost radical (if one believes the polemicists "total" is the right word) change in the role and attitude of the designer.'[143] Jencks went on to declare that he detected a chasm opening between the disciplinary advances that post-war architects had introduced and the current situation: 'The designer cannot directly deal with the disruptive forces because they are outside his area of control, being the legitimate responsibility of the government. He must concern himself with architectural questions of scale, tectonics, expression, function, and manage his artistic responsibility rather than go beyond his depth into an area of social control.'

According to Jencks, an introductory course was needed to orient the student towards an in-depth debate on the different architectural tendencies. To achieve this, he proposed investigating the differences underlying the approach to architecture of Christopher Alexan-

der and Louis I. Kahn, for example, correctly placing technical courses within the study programme, and making an effort towards achieving collaboration between the different disciplines. He continued thus: 'One of the reasons for the crisis in architectural education is as mentioned the unclear relationship between art and technique or art and knowledge.'[144] These contradictions were to be solved within the GSD, a task that no one seemed willing to carry out, perhaps because of the disparity in wages received, or perhaps because it had become habitual to wish to unify education and professional practice: 'Because there is an unsophisticated educational system, there is an unclear delegation of authority and responsibility, an inequity in salary and teaching load. Because there is flexibility and inequity there is lack of dedication to the school from certain quarters. Because there is need for more common spirit and joint venture, there is a tendency to put the school second to professional practice. What can be done to break this cycle?'

We certainly do not observe any intention of breaking this cycle in Sert's article, significantly entitled 'Continuity and Change'. Written from the point of view of his status and interests as Dean of the GSD and as an architect whose career was in full swing, the article began by complaining about the lack of funds to promote new educational initiatives, while at the same time invoking the idealist spirit of Harvard, a premise that was undoubtedly out of place with regard to the debate being carried out at the time: 'This School is part of a great University whose main concern is not the sciences or the arts for their own sake, but as they contribute to man's progress, to greater knowledge resulting in better and happier living. Its ideal is not man's welfare alone, but the dignity of his spirit … We find in Harvard a humanistic background.'[145]

Sert stressed that the knowledge of human civilization was a fundamental element in an architect's training since architects were supposed to design to satisfy human needs, and it was therefore important that there should be continuity in this aspect. When he addressed concrete issues, he acknowledged the need to have the three design departments work more closely in collaboration with each other to provide students with a more complete education, and with respect to the changes happening in the world and its repercussions on teaching, he affirmed: 'There is no doubt the complexity of the problem of urban growth resulting from the world population explosion demands specially trained professionals who will receive an education that goes far beyond anything available today. The task is ambitious and difficult, but if we obtain the necessary financial assistance, our school is as well suited as any other for such an undertaking.'[146]

Sert also described the progress made, mentioning the courses taught by Sekler and Giedion as exemplary,[147] the advances accom-

Sert, Mies van der Rohe and Giedion.

plished in the teaching of structures, and the introduction of computers into the classrooms. He admitted that little attention was being paid to investigation, and proposed creating more seminars and discussion groups, as well as changing the summary corrections of the final school project for a monitoring of this project throughout the last year. Sert showed special interest in the construction of one sole building for the GSD, since he considered it essential to solve the problems of disciplinary interconnection that the school was facing; he in fact did manage to arrange for its construction to begin in 1967 with a project by the architects John Andrews and Anderson Baldwin.[148]

After once more reminding the public of the imminent need for funds to solve all these problems, he concluded, perhaps too proudly: 'The GSD should continue to develop its broad humanistic approach that provides the philosophical roots of its programmes of study. Through closer contact with other [Harvard] University schools and with the College, we can consolidate and enlarge what has been well started. Balance can be our motto, the balance that characterizes the University as a whole. We should develop the Harvard way, and let other schools find their own best answers to their problems.'[149]

Thus his was a proposal of continuity that called for the improvement of technical and functional deficiencies, but which did not alter the slow development of events. Sert was perhaps not aware that the cause of discontent was a reflection of the unrest that was in the air in North America during the mid-1960s, although he had apparently not lost the ability to protest. Proof of this is provided by a letter published in *The New York Times* on 10 May 1961, condemning the anti-Castro policy of President Kennedy, which was signed by a great many American intellectuals including Sert.[150] Additionally, in three undated typewritten sheets kept in the Sert Collection of the GSD, we find him amongst the Committee of One Hundred Architects and Planners for Peace who signed an article protesting against the war in southeast Asia.[151]

In the first version of another article by Sert, 'The GSD: New Trends, New Programs', it seems that there is greater commitment to understanding the changes floating in the atmosphere: 'To question and redefine the purpose and direction of professional education is now timely. For whom are we working and designing? What kind of "great society" is our goal? What does a "great society" mean to the majority of people?' Sert's placing of the term 'great society' in inverted commas indicates that he was quoting from elsewhere. It was in fact the title of a speech by President Lyndon B. Johnson, delivered at the University of Michigan on 22 May 1964, in which he promised aid to the poor, better medical assistance and funding for education.

In this speech Johnson acknowledged grave urban failings in many American cities, precisely those in which it was a priority to build a better society: 'In the remainder of this century urban population will double, city land will double, and we will have to build homes, highways and facilities equal to those built since this country was first settled … The catalogue of ills is long: there is decay of the centres and the despoiling of the suburbs … Our society will never be great until our cities are great. Today the frontier of imagination and innovation is inside those cities and not beyond its borders. New experiments are already going on. It will be the task of your generation to make the American city a place where future generations will come, not only to live but to live the good life.'[152]

Sert must have surely been interested in the President's speech. On the one hand there was the promise of funding for the educational system, although without any direct reference to Harvard, and on the other there was the official acknowledgment of many of the issues regarding the needs of American cities that Sert had been bringing to the fore ever since the publication of his first book in 1942. Critical of political power back in 1961, and eager to benefit from Johnson's internal policies in 1964, which demonstrated his own foresight, Sert was caught in the middle of a crisis of far greater scope.

Gerald Howard uses the term 'Politicization of Culture' to define part of this crisis: 'There was a deeper vein of radical disaffection with American life and with just this kind of thinking that would become progressively more widespread and bitter as the decade wore on and the "creative spark" between expectations and fulfillment widened to an unbridgeable gulf.'[153] This malaise can be traced within the radical writings of Paul Goodman, Wright Mills and Herbert Marcuse, nimble exponents of this unrest in their denouncement of the living conditions in American society at the beginning of the 1960s.[154] Threatened civil rights, racial discrimination and assassinations of the principal black leaders, Muslim separatism, more than forty million inhabitants living below the poverty threshold, student demonstrations etc.[155] amplified the discontent voiced by those most aware of America's discredited foreign policy: bent on the Vietnam war they had been defeated by the Russians in the space race and made fools by the missile crisis in Cuba.

Norman Mailer hailed John F. Kennedy as the saviour of the US, the hero who would redeem the country from the conformism that had characterized Eisenhower's presidency: 'One tried to construct a simple model. The thesis is after all not so mysterious; it would merely nudge the notion that a hero embodies his time and is not so very much better than his time, but he is larger than life and so is capable of giving direction to the time, able to encourage a nation to discover the deepest colours of its character',[156] a chimera that was dismantled by several bullets and the passing of time.

For Susan Sontag it was a matter of teaching people to feel a new sensitivity: 'In place of hermeneutics we need an erotics of art'. All of this was occurring in the days of pop art, happenings, living theater, and Merce Cunningham, in tune with the music of Milton Babbit and Morton Feldman and under the influence of paintings by Frank Stella and Marc Rothko. It was a time when it was possible to see such movies as *The Graduate*, *Easy Rider* and *Bonnie and Clyde*. In other words, it was a moment when the American public, according to Sontag, finally had to face the fact that it was being confronted by an art that could shake and modify sensations and consciences, an art that was to be taken as an extension of life.[157]

In the same year in which Sontag spoke in this vein, Robert Venturi published *Complexity and Contradiction in Architecture* (a book that Sert had in his library), in which the American architect offered a response, from within his discipline, to the challenges that Sontag and a sector of American architectural culture had launched in quest of a new sensitivity. This motivated Vincent Scully's slightly unfocused reasonings in the preface: 'It is a very American book, rigorously pluralistic and phenomenological in its method … It marks, in this way, a complete shift of emphasis and will annoy some of those who profess to follow Le Corbusier … But, as his Friend's Housing shows equally well, he is one of the very few architects whose thought parallels that of the pop painters – and probably the first architect to perceive the usefulness and meaning of their forms.'[158] Despite the fact that Scully aimed to point out the humanistic and at the same time functionalist origins of Venturi's thinking, and to bring to the fore Venturi's strong American roots, his intention of being the other side of the coin to Le Corbusier's *Vers une architecture*, Scully was portraying an approach that Sert could not and did not wish to incorporate into his own way of working. He neither felt at ease with the American architect's frivolity, nor was he inclined to look on the past with nostalgia, and he had never been in favour of cladding his buildings with direct references to historical architecture in search of characteristics that he could never successfully reach by this means.

In the opening sentences of his work, Venturi wrote: 'I like complexity and contradiction in architecture … I like elements which are hybrid rather than "pure", compromising rather than "clean", distorted rather than "straightforward", ambiguous rather than "articulated", perverse as well as impersonal, boring as well as "interesting", conventional rather than simple, vestigial as well as innovating, inconsistent and equivocal rather than direct and clear.'[159] It seems obvious that Venturi's preferences made possible another way of looking at architecture, a way that Sert had certainly not applied to his buildings in Cambridge, obstinately bent on understanding the relationships between architecture and the city, on fleeing from the staff aesthetics exhibited by Harvard architectures, still seeking the moral exemplar of an architecture that lent itself to 'setting right' the chaos that previous architectures had built and accumulated. Now, hybrid, distorted, perverse, equivocal, boring and conventional qualities had suddenly become privileged values in the architecture of the 1960s in the United States, where artists and art dealers had managed to place a box of soap in a museum, ironically if one recalls the fact that in the 1930s the word 'soapbox' had been employed by some Americans as a name for rationalist architecture.

The adjectives that Venturi used seem to transmit an impression of another way of looking at architecture after having taken a long stroll around the Harvard campus. One need only read the description of that experience written by Jehangir Mugaseth in that same year to see that it is so: 'Aesthetically the Harvard campus is a parcel of beauty packed in chaos, wrapped in contradictions, and surrounded by ambiguity. It is an area whose landscapings, open spaces, and small handsome buildings create the atmosphere students admire. It is also an area whose large, ugly buildings become landmarks by which people orient themselves … The quality of the architecture is very evident, and the contrasts created are blended quite successfully.'[160] It was an atmosphere that now, at the beginning of the 1960s, no longer permitted the perception of Harvard's architecture as something merely historicist or even as something pertaining to the most vulgar and ambiguous 'eclecticism', a criticism that the radicals in the 1930s would undoubtedly have proffered; instead, it promoted the acceptance of contrasts, the obliquity of paths, the perception of the conventional, the hybridity of forms, and the disarticulation of the yards as values worth vindicating in order to foster a change in the conception of architecture. For it was undoubtedly true that it had been living off theories and examples that had been forged in the 1940s and early 1950s.

Within this scenario, the Science Center building – which Sert began to design between November and December of 1968, some time before resigning from his post as Dean in June 1969 – symbolizes the will to hold on to the past as well as a shy attempt to grasp the new spirit of the times, a mission that was almost impossible.[161] Such a statement is authorized by the progression from the first sketches of the project to its final result. In fact, in one of these sketches we observe an initial intention to repeat tried and true schemes: four identical towers arose from a common base, which anchored them to the ground. In another, in which we can already observe two stepped volumes, the order introduced by the four towers was maintained, with the towers completing the complex and forcing the spectator to look upwards, distancing him or her from the coinciding perception of the neighbouring buildings. None of this, however, was carried out.

Located on the North campus of Harvard, the Science Center had to come up with solutions to a highly complex programme that was to accommodate the schools of Biology, Chemistry, Geology, Physics and Mathematics along with classrooms and seminar rooms. It

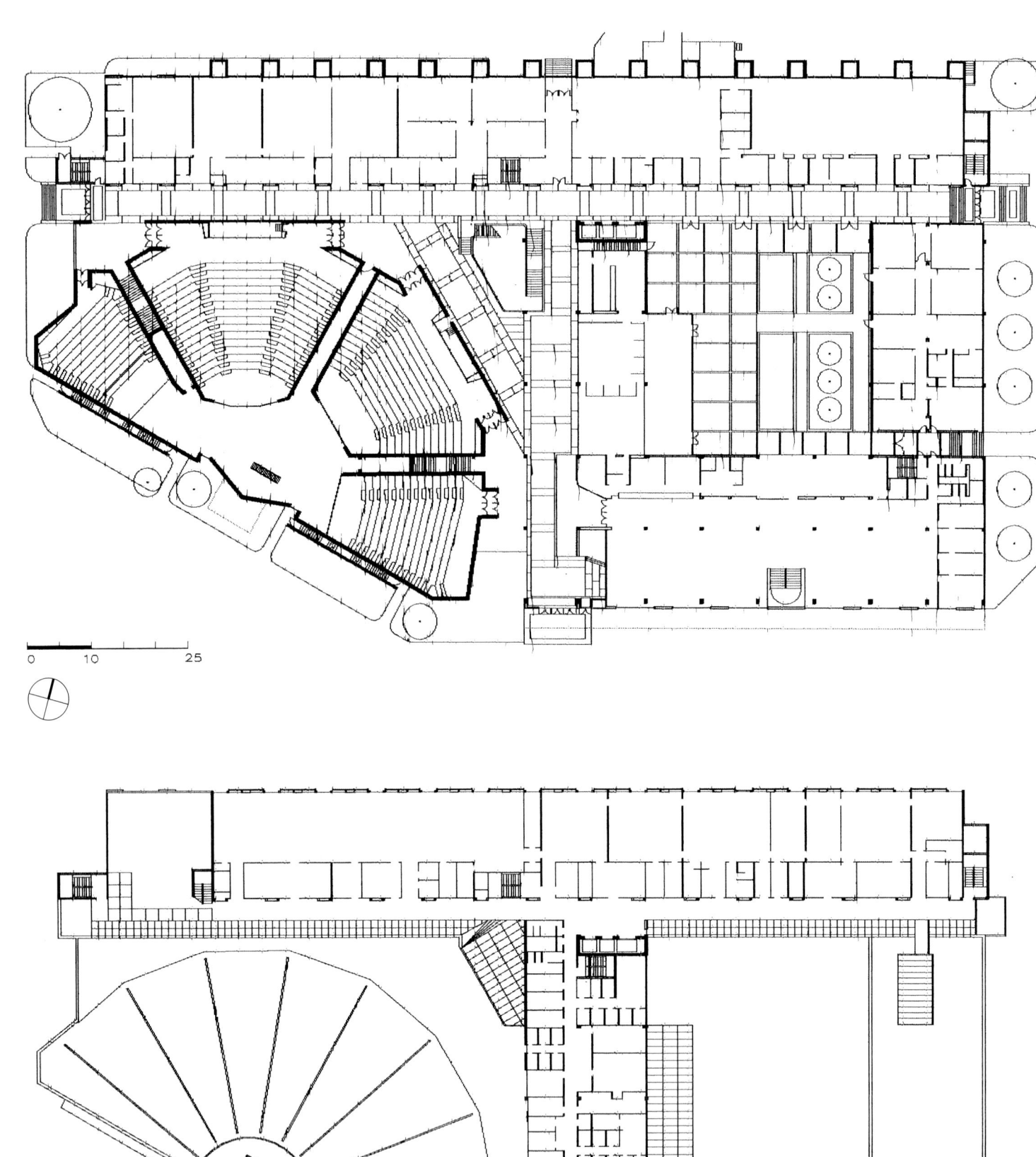

Sert, Jackson
and Associates,
Science Center,
Harvard,
Cambridge,
1968–75, plans.

0   10   25

Science Center, sections and views.

was also to house the air-conditioning installations of the north campus, a library, four auditoriums of different sizes and general administration services as well as a bar, etc: 'A micro-city rather than a building.'[162]

The site had been conveniently 'prepared' based on the planning intervention that Sert had proposed for Cambridge, sinking and covering Cambridge Street and eliminating its junction with Kirkland Street. In this way and with the purchase of additional terrain, Sert had at his disposal a sizeable plot of land that moreover faced the central Yard building thanks to the elimination of the crossing between pedestrian and traffic circulations. Thus, heading north from the Yard, the Science Center is the first building that meets the eye of the passerby, and it becomes a corridor passageway with a T shape that allows access to the different areas and services inside the building or to the different faculties, residences and museums established further north.

This way of working, with which by now we are familiar, attempted to design the building in such as way that the 'complexity' of its programme was visible on the exterior. However, instead of taking on the role of 'container' that Holyoke Center had played, the Sci-

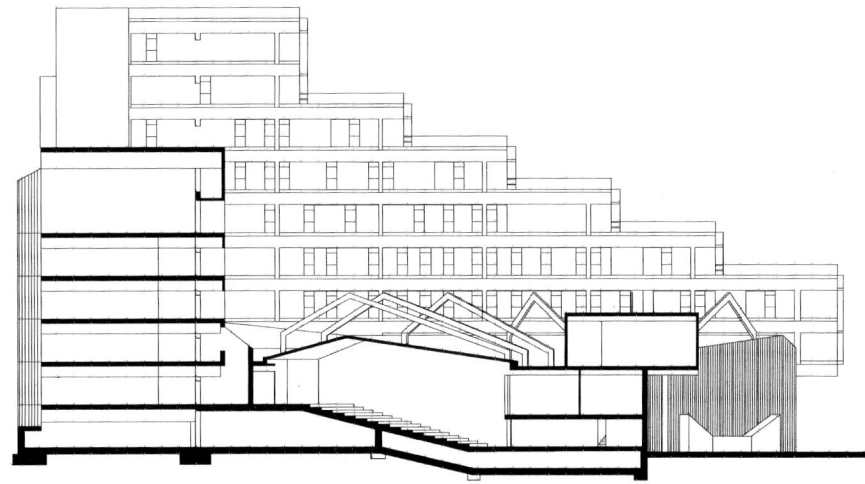

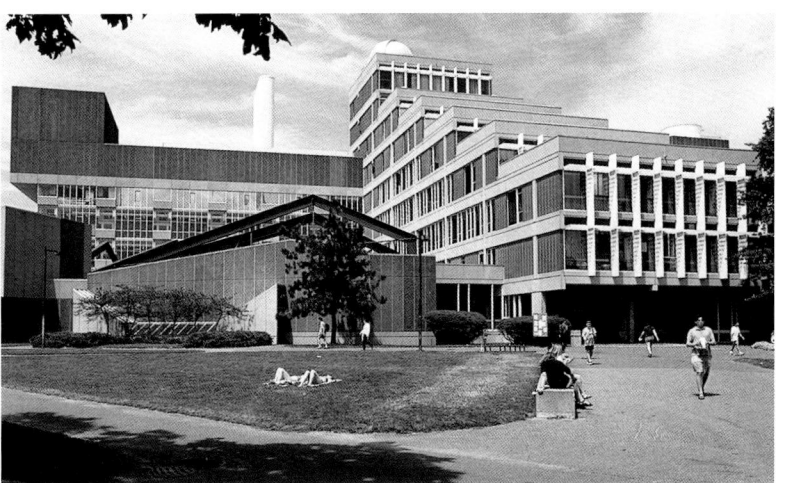

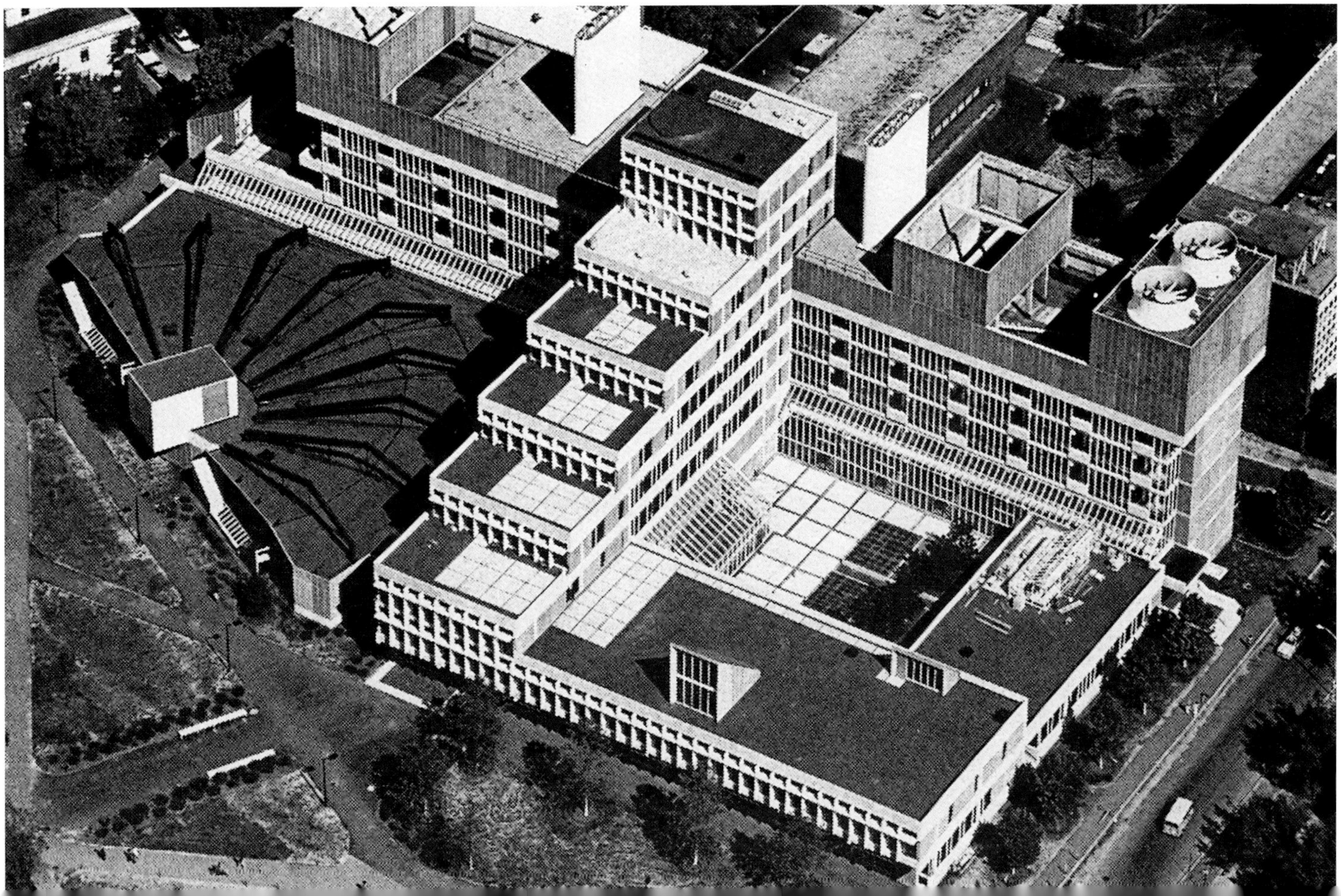

In comparison with the exemplary rotundity of the Holyoke Center, the fragmented form of the Science Center adds visual chaos to an already heterogeneous area of the campus. Adjacent to the Memorial Hall, one of Harvard's most emblematic buildings, constructed between 1866 and 1878 by Robert Ware and Henry van Brunt, and facing the neo-Georgian fire station by R. Clipston, the Science Center adds, with its play of volumes, to the babelish, perverse and insipid diversity that characterizes the discordant ensemble of buildings that make up the University of Harvard.

The price Sert paid to 'keep up with the times' was too high and he did not achieve the unity of the Holyoke Center, at least not in its 'main' facade, which is radically at odds with its rear facade, whose rotundity is as eloquent as its formal source of inspiration: the Richards Medical Research Laboratories by L. Kahn. Inside the Science Center we observe too many unresolved issues, ranging from the scale of the interior 'streets' to the point where they converge under the skylights that top them, from the location of the stairs and their design to the difficulty in finding the hierarchy of entrances to the different auditoriums, and even to the building itself. The bar's invasion of the courtyard prevents it from displaying its geometric clarity, and the library does not manage to enjoy its privileged view over this landscaped space. Even the location of Constantino Nivola's mural – which we know comes from another space – does not establish a good rapport with the prefabricated concrete beams that contemplate it: here art and architecture do not integrate, but instead seem to challenge and even flee from each other.

These were days of confusion, as an article by Sert seemed to announce on 13 April 1962: 'The confusion in the architectural profession is basically part of the general confusion. Can we expect clear directions in architecture after reading our newspapers and magazines? Events are driving us, as they drive politicians and economists, though by comparison with them we do not appear as such a "confused group". As a citizen, all the architect can do is fight for what he believes to be the right cause. If he is confused as a man, he will be confused as an architect, though the reverse is not entirely

ence Center scattered its diverse volumes and made patent the parts that made it up, based on an evident origin: the sunken volume of the lecture theatres that unabashedly dictated its structure, suspended from tensile cables forming a radial system of weather-resistant steel porticos. Designed in an impeccable semicircular shape, it faces straight towards the exit of the Yard and is aligned with its directrices. The semicircular shape becomes a rotula that solves the different urban alignments that converge in this plot of land. Away from this, two great parallel volumes of different height are joined together by a stepped building that Sert had employed in the Mugar Library, and an interior courtyard of considerable size. The constructed body that faces the Yard, similar to what Sert had done in the Boston project, seems to float, since its ground floor is set further back. On the one hand, the idea was to push back as far as possible the building's height for the people coming out of the Yard, and to accomplish this Sert resorted to the fragmentation of the complex; on the other hand, he attempted to reduce the sensation of heaviness of the total built volume by avoiding contact with the ground.

ferent. The last two buildings that Sert would design in Cambridge did not attempt to teach the lessons of urbanism to a setting that had already received all that Sert could possibly offer it. From now on, he would follow a policy of withdrawing within himself, something that we have already seen in the project for his house when he had his first encounter with an American suburb. We will observe a certain aristocratic gesture mingled with a tender disdain towards this explosive reality, for although by then he must certainly have been somewhat weary, he was nevertheless very sure of himself.

The Martin Luther King School, a project that he also began in 1968, is clearly a hermetic building, closed within itself, which exhibits

true, and he may still be a well-meaning, bad architect.'[163]

The outcome of the Science Center would lead Sert to rethink his position on finding ways to carry out a friendly compromise between architecture and the city, a problem that had deeply interested him for many years. In fact, it seems logical to speculate on the reasons for the Science building's T shape: in its stepped descent, it seems to aim to merge with the interior street of the Holyoke Center, and to close with this union the ensemble of architectures of the Yard; to enclose them or engulf them, to deny any capacity for disorder and eclecticism, in spite of Venturi's words. The towers of the Peabody Terrace watch over imaginary enemies, whereas in the 'interior' of the city, the only dialogue possible is the enclosed conversation between the Holyoke and Science Centers, which merge in an autistic embrace.

From that moment on, things would be dif-

in its almost blind facades yellow-tinted concrete walls with very wide joints. It was to develop a complex programme, for its sports field, auditorium and library were to be used by the lower-class neighbourhood in which it was located, just behind the Peabody Terrace. Adapting it to the geometrically irregular terrain, Sert placed the music hall and auditorium building in a central position so that it would be in charge of connecting the body that held the sports field, the gym and its services with the school building itself.

There was no intention of approaching its neighbour, designed by the same architect. The amiability of the Peabody Terrace found no answering echo. On the contrary, here Sert

Sert, Jackson and Associates, Martin Luther King School, Harvard, Cambridge, 1968–72, picture from private collection, general configuration, plan and view.

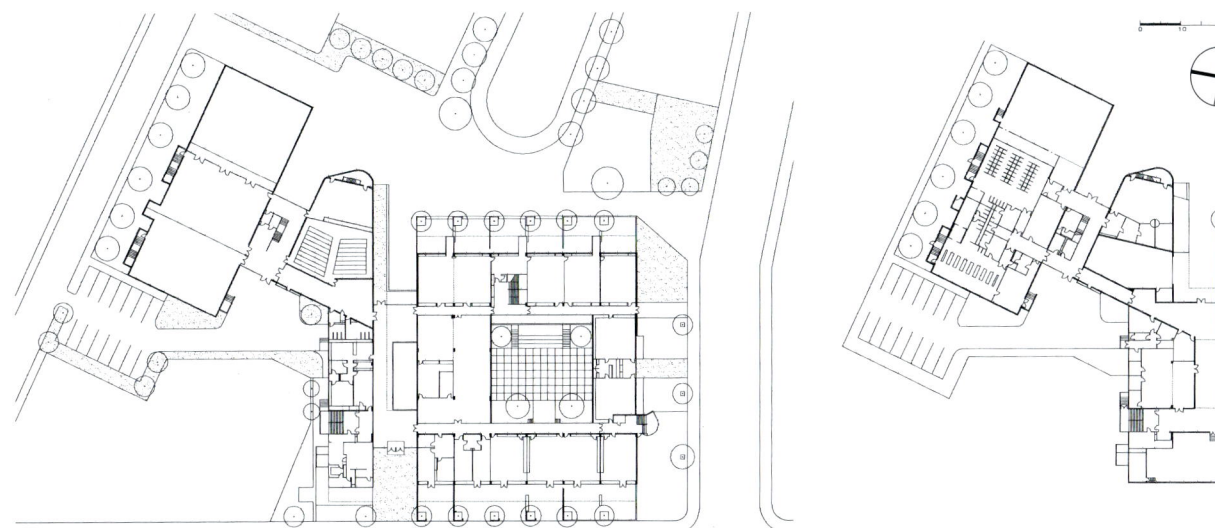

showed a preference for working on the special form of the plot of land as the best and most gratifying way to ensure the programme's resolution, which he now considered a better option than looking for unnecessary continuities between neighbours who had little or nothing to say to each other.

The school went on to emphasize this gesture of doing without its surroundings by closing itself around a courtyard, an element that Sert had widely used throughout his work. However, in this case it was not motivated by the climate or by cultural or biographical elements. Nor was it an educational matter, for the classrooms on the ground floor had individual exits facing the street or the rear part of the plot of land, forming a sort of alternative place in which the youngest pupils could have outdoor lessons. It was the entrance to the classrooms and the bar that faced the courtyard, thus reducing it to a simple element of lighting and access without any other intention. It was a void without a meaning to enhance it, without a spatial intention that could optimize the sense of this school architecture, originating in the firm decision to cut off all relationships with its setting.

On 44 Brattle Street, between 1970 and 1973, Sert designed a building for commercial premises and offices. Bordering the University campus limits the plot was located in a place of great commercial activity. Its small dimensions of facade were compensated for by its considerable depth. Sert designed a modulated glass facade that was repeated in height up to the fourth floor. Considerations as to the value of walling and vertical composition, which were strong points in Holyoke, have disappeared here. The access to the upper floors of the building was through an interior street, which also accommodated a restaurant. It was only an access, however, deprived of the values of Holyoke's 'animated street', both of whose sides had been attractive.

The excess of glass surfaces in the building either reflects the exterior or makes the interior transparent: the facade simply does not exist, an element that Sert had cultivated with so much affection in his previous projects in Cambridge. The objects on sale in the shops on the ground floor are multiplied by their reflec-

tions and become mute witnesses of the hustle and bustle outside on the street, a transitory place for passersby who are for the most part university people going to the two nearby cinemas or theatre halls. The activity of the staff working in the offices of the second, third and fourth floors increases the sensation of a building that rejects any sense of substance or of holding a discourse with the city.

A single point in the building, its fifth floor, has a concrete wall painted with similar colours to those used in the Science Center or the Martin Luther King School, and a few windows on this floor have varying dimensions for no apparent reason. It was on this storey that Sert set up along with Jackson and his other associates what would be his last professional office. A huge skylight, trademark of his professional work, overlooks Brattle Street, its silhouette looming over the urban panorama of Cambridge.

From all points of view unnecessary, the skylight looks outward from the highest point of the facade plane. This element, which Sert had so often employed, can only have one meaning:

Sert, Jackson and Associates, building on 44 Brattle Street, Cambridge, 1970–73, plans.

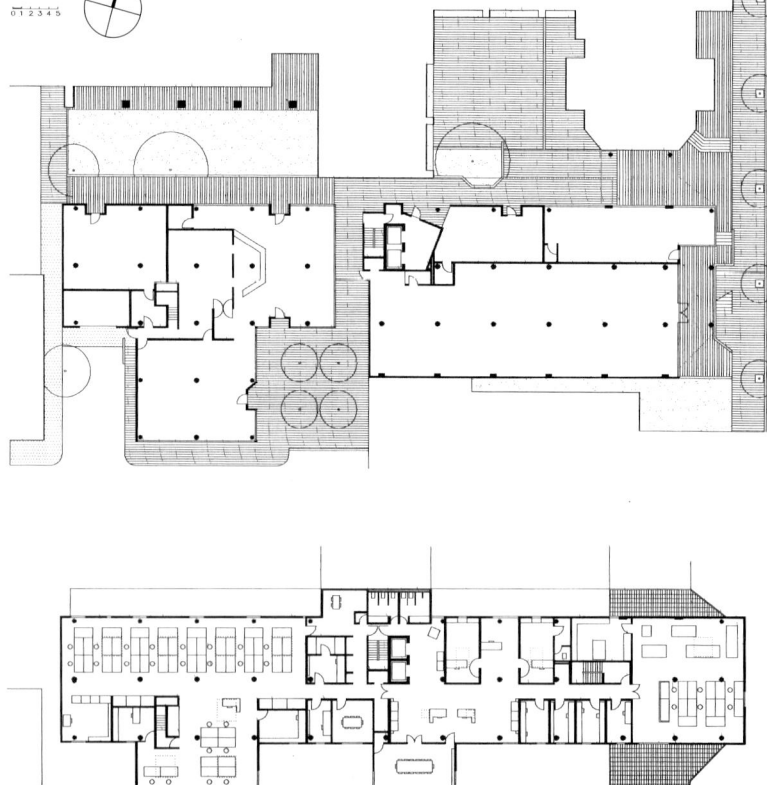

Building on 44
Brattle Street,
views.

to flaunt, with a form that belongs to him, the attitude (which we have observed in the Martin Luther King School) of having nothing to do with the city. From this vantage point, it was a matter of being above and beyond the city. So many years of struggle to improve the city had come to an end with few results. Sert seems to have been backing away from the boxing ring, although he made it clear that, despite being seventy-two, he would still be on the lookout.

Others would have to offer fresh ideas, new experiences and possibilities, but they would never escape the inquisitive eye of the skylight that Sert left floating over the city he had tried to set right in a courageous planning effort that Americans regarded as 'an apostolic contribution'. If we recall what Sert told Carles Soldevila in the issue of *D'Ací i D'Allà* that Sert edited in 1934, we are faced with a surprising coincidence.

[56] It is found in John Peter, op. cit., p. 258. In an interview which Daniel Giralt-Miracle held before 1968, we find similar reasonings concerning Gropius' interest in having Sert succeed him at Harvard's Graduate School of Design: 'After working in Central and South America I carried out several projects in the United States. While there, they requested, or more specifically Walter Gropius asked me, to take over his position at Harvard University in the School of Architecture, Urbanism and Landscaping … From then on I have continued my work around these regions, harmonizing it with my work as Dean at the University.' Typewritten copy, Miró Foundation archive, Sert chest.
Nevertheless, the interest shown by American university institutions in availing themselves of Sert's services before his incorporation at the GSD goes back much further, and we have detected it in the correspondence found in the Sert Collection. On 26 May 1943 Theodore Dreier of Black Mountain College wrote to

persuade him to give lessons the following year at that institution, and asked him to send a preliminary programme. In a letter from Albers, also from BMC of 31 January 1944, we read: 'I should like to have you here as a guest lecturer for a week or two for problems on planning and architecture which are important to artists and art teachers.'
A letter from Gropius to Sert of 17 April 1944 tells us that Sert had been unable to substitute for the German professor at GSD because of an overload of work.
On 22 March 1943 the University of Yale offered him a teaching post, an offer ratified on the 29th. On 17 February 1944 Yale repeated its request.
On 20 May 1946 Sert received a letter signed by Joseph Hudnut in which we read: 'The Graduate School of Design has accepted your suggested programme of lectures for the beginning of next term and would very much like you to get in contact with professor Gropius

early in September to further develop this programme together and make all the necessary preparation for this course.'
On 4 July 1946, Albers again asked him to go to BMC and on 11 August he was invited to the Carnegie Institute of Technology, Pittsburgh.
On 16 February 1950 MIT invited him to give some classes, and on 23 October GSD did likewise. On 15 October 1950 Gabriel Guevrekian invited him to Urbana, Illinois, an invitation that was again proffered on 23 January 1951.
Probably the most representative sign of this feeling was the interest shown by the young professors of MIT in having him become Dean of that institution when Wurster retired in January 1951. See Meredith L. Clausen, *Pietro Belluschi: Modern American Architect*, MIT Press, Cambridge, 1994, p. 200.
[57] A brief history of the GSD is found in the 'Official Register of Harvard University', vol. XXXIII, no. 34, June 27 1936, pp. 5–6. It is al-

so interesting to see what requirements for architectural studies were set by Harvard University at the time.

[58] Reginald Isaacs, *Gropius, An Illustrated Biography of the Creator of the Bauhaus*, Bulfinch Press, Boston, Toronto and London 1991, p. 267. The clashes between Gropius and Hudnut are explained, helping us to understand certain difficulties between the two men and how their careers at GSD came to an end, although this was not the main cause of their leaving.

[59] It was an article by Michael Maccoby published in *The Harvard Crimson* on 11 December 1952.

[60] Ibid., p. 3.

[61] Hudnut's intentions regarding education at GSD is found in the article 'Education and Architecture' published in the *Architectural Record* of October 1942.

[62] 'The planners, who alternated their training between Littauer and its social science courses and Hunt with its design courses, were to be the theorists who told the architects what was needed where and why. The landscape architects were concerned with the actual physical planning. What was needed for certain soils and rocks in both backyards, highways and large factories. And the architects, with the information and programmes of the other two were to do the actual construction designs. The purpose of the integrated programme was to acquaint each group with the problems of the other.' Ibid., p. 4.

[63] 'Today at the school, all agree that the three are inseparable, but some feel the programme is bogged down. Students in architecture say the planners do nothing but gather facts. They are not designers in any sense. The architectural faculty accuses planning of throwing screws into the joint student programmes, of failing to provide the planning in advance for the creation of model towns and projects. On the other hand, the planners feel the architects have never made themselves clear. The planners don't know what the architects really want.' Ibid.

[64] Ibid.

[65] The correspondence between Sert and Gropius, while the former was still residing in New York, is especially relevant between the months of February and April 1953, the period of circumstances mentioned. Thus, in a letter of 2 February, Gropius wrote to him: 'After I left you last Tuesday it came to my mind that we did not discuss one candidate who may be of particular importance, Charles Eames … He should be splendid for basic design and research … Eames, Serge, Pei and/or Rudolph would be the strongest team I can think of. Thinking again about it, I am inclined … to mention to you Reginald Isaacs … He is a very able experienced planner, a courageous social fighter, has unusually strong working capacity … During my last year in Harvard he was teaching there for three months and got the students going full blast.' SC E6. In another letter of 6 March he insisted on giving Isaacs a contract, and advised Sert: 'Be sure that I wouldn't have suggested Reg Isaacs to you if I were not sure that he understands our line of thinking and the necessity to get Planning in Harvard more towards the physical design than towards administration … I talked to Bogner about the memorandum, and his remarks tell me that you have to be careful that Hudnut doesn't put you before accomplished facts with which you are not in agreement.' SC E6.

On 30 March Gropius again insisted on his candidates and mentioned Reicheck, Raymond, Ralph Rapson, Harry Weese, Alexander Cochran, Robert Little and Ambrose Richardson.

On 24 April he gave Sert advice on the budget he had prepared for the GSD, such as how to save money by eliminating a course that could be absorbed within others, as well as how to avoid making enemies in the departments: 'The other point of criticism of the present budget is that I definitely think the expenditures for Landscaping and Planning should be reversed. I am sure it is part of Wheaton's and Hudnut's acting to almost abolish the Planning Department and leave too much of the Landscaping in. The restricted funds in both Departments cover only one Chair each, so you are perfectly free to distribute the means available more in favour of Planning than of Landscape Architecture.' The missive ended with a detail that puts us closer to the date on which Sert must have begun to taken over his post: 'Neither Bogner nor I think it is necessary that you be here before the 29th of April. We might check up before you have your final talk with Reynolds when you come.' SC E6.

[66] See 'Official Register of Harvard University', vol. XXXVI, no. 35, 1939–40, 29 June 1939.

[67] See GSD, 'Design Problems', H 261, vol. I.

[68] See GSD, 'Design Problems', H 261, vol. II. The new headquarters of the GSD, the Gund Hall, would be built by the architects John Andrews and Anderson Baldwin between 1967 and 1969.

[69] Ibid.

[70] 'On Architectural Education', SC D 47, typewritten text. This is a lecture given by Sert at a university whose name we have not been able to determine, and the exact date of the lecture is also unknown, although he must have given it shortly before accepting his position as Dean at Harvard. This can be deduced from the opening words of the lecture: 'I would like to begin by saying that there are many people better qualified than myself to talk about this subject, but the Student Council asked me if I wanted to talk about this, and after doubting for a while, I said, "Why not, let's try"'. An undated text that seems to respond to these preoccupations between project and university education would be 'The Design Process', a copy of which is kept in the Sert Collection, SC D 10.

The written account by the Japanese architect Fumihiko Maki, who studied and worked with Sert, corroborates this feeling and provides varied information on Sert's first professional steps in Cambridge. See Fumihiko Maki, 'J.L. Sert: His Beginning Years at Harvard', *Process Architecture*, no. 34, December 1982, pp. 12–15.

[71] 'On Architectural Education', op. cit., p. 4.

[72] Ibid., pp. 4, 7.

Sert wrote a text on the issue we are dealing with explaining his ample personal experience: 'Meeting Places for the Arts', SC D 78. It is an undated text but was written after the construction of the Maeght Foundation, judging by the references it contains. We find some scattered antecedents to this preoccupation with finding a rapport between architecture and the rest of the visual arts in some American magazines. See 'Art Forms in Architecture: To Be or Not To Be?', *Architectural Record*, May 1940, pp. 80–85.

[73] José Luis Sert, 'The Philosophy of Architectural Education', handwritten lecture, 195–?, SC D 106. In a text of 30 June 1967, written for the Boston Society of Architects' Centennial Volume, Sert advocated a synthesis between architectural thinking and university education. SC D3.

[74] 'Official Register of Harvard University', vol. LI, no. 11, 19 May 1954, p. 4. To become aware of Sert's changing interests one needs only review the contents of his 'Urban Design' course, where one can see the transformation of his ideas about the parts of the city, which at that point could no longer be encompassed by the four previous functions: 'Civic Design deals with the measure and scale – groups of buildings, open areas, roads, and their relationship – and effect of the different functions of the city on the design of: (1) residential sectors (community units); (2) parks and open areas; (3) social services and sector cores; (4) industrial, commercial and business sectors, supply and storage centres; (5) the heart of the city; (6) transportation network.'

[75] ASG 43–K–1954–3–18.

[76] ASG 43–K–4–9(6)–1/2.

[77] See ASG43–K–1955–4–2–1/2. 43–K–1957 –11–20(6). 43–K–1955–6–17–1/2.

[78] ASG 43–K–1954–4–27(6)–1/2. Sert must have been interested in the contents of the letter, because shortly afterwards, on 11 May 1954, he wrote to Giedion: 'I have just received the confirmation of your appointment for the history courses which you are expected to teach here this fall. The courses will begin on Monday 27 September, and will last until the Christmas recess, which starts on Sunday 19 December. Although I expect to see you this summer, when we can talk about these matters personally, I should appreciate it if you could be in Cambridge a few days ahead of time this fall, so that we could have the necessary time to discuss all of these matters in detail before we start to work.' ASG 43–K–1954–5–11.

[79] ASG 43–K–1954–5–21(G)–1/2.

In another letter that Sert sent to him from the Hotel Mediterraneo in Rome on 8 December 1954, we read: 'We have spent many hours talking about what should be done in a good school, *here is our chance*. I share your doubts, some of them at least, but we have to try it without conveying it to the students and faculty …' ASG 43–K–1954–8–12.

[80] ASG 43–K–1954–8–6(G)–1/4.

A letter from Giedion to Sert of February 1957 told of his arrival in New York on the 27th, where he would undertake a seminar called 'Town Planning in the Renaissance'. 43–K–1957–2–20. On 5 December of the same year, he wrote to Sekler to propose some seminars to be held at the GSD. 43–K–1957–5–12. On 3 January 1959, in a handwritten letter to Sert, Giedion informed him of the proposals that he intended to carry out the following semester: 'The problem of small communities. The problem of a middle and also a larger city. The problem of a square.' 43–K–1959–1–3.

[81] In a letter sent on 3 September 1954 from Paris, he urged him to be specific: 'Please bring notes about this preparatory work with you to Cambridge. The outline for the working programme *must be precise*, so that other groups understand it … Please write immediately to Cambridge and let me know what you prefer to do.' ASG 43–K–1954–9–3. Giedion's new interests are reflected in *The Beginnings of Art* and *The Beginnings of Architecture*, published in 1962, which are made up of texts from lectures he gave in the US in 1957 and of which he informed Sert in an aforementioned letter of 2 April 1955. To frame them within the ensemble of Giedion's work, see Sokratis Georgiadis, *Sigfried Giedion: An Intellectual Biography*, Edinburgh University Press, 1993, pp. 153–94.

[82] Pietro Belluschi, 'Architecture and Society', *Architectural Record*, February 1951.

[83] Henry-Russell Hitchcock, 'The International Style Twenty Years After', *Architectural Record*, August 1951.

[84] Some of the fragments of Hitchcock's text that insist on this point of view are as follows:

'Modern architecture in the 1950s should have room again for a range of effects as diverse, if not as divergent, as Victor Horta's Maison du Peuple in Brussels of 1897, an early modern building largely of metal and glass that is too often forgotten now, and Wright's River Forest Golf Club (first built in 1898), of ordinary wooden frame construction, in which most of the concepts of his now "classic" prairie houses of the next decade were already almost fully mature'; 'Wright's Yahara Boat Club, of 1902, in Madison, Wisconsin, prefigured, a decade before Cubism reached maturity, most of the plastic innovations that contact with abstract painting and sculpture were to suggest, some fifteen years later, to the young European architects who initiated the International Style.'

[85] To emphasize his point of view, when it is a matter of speaking about expression in the facade of a structure, he states: 'The particular relationship of skeleton and shell which we then considered most characteristic of the International Style can best be illustrated, paradoxically, by the plan of a building that has never been accepted as representative of the style, Perret's church at Le Raincy, of 1923. An early example of this, by one of the recognized leaders of the International Style, is illustrated in the plan of Le Corbusier's de Mandrot House of 1931. It has too often been forgotten – and apparently by us when writing in 1931 – that long before Raymond Hood's day the Bayard or Conduit Building, of 1897, in New York, by Louis Sullivan, or better still his Gage Building, of the next year, at 18 South Michigan Avenue in Chicago, illustrated more clearly than Hood's skyscrapers, then newly completed, the proper architectural expression of steel-skeleton construction in the external cladding of a tall edifice.'

[86] Lewis Mumford, 'Function and Expression in Architecture', Architectural Record, November 1951.

[87] Adlai Stevenson, welcoming speech to the Democratic National Convention, 16 July 1952, in James Andrews and David Zarefsky, Contemporary American Voices: Significant Speeches in American History, Longman, New York, 1992, pp. 36–38.

[88] Eleanor Roosevelt, 'Address to the Americans for Democratic Action', 1 April 1950, in ibid., pp. 23–26.

[89] Ron Robin, Enclaves of America: The Rhetoric of American Political Architecture Abroad, 1900–1965, Princeton University Press, 1992, p. 140. After the editing of the text of this book, an extensive study by Jane C. Loeffler was published on the theme of the USA Embassies. See: Jane C. Loeffler, The Architecture of Diplomacy, Princeton Architectural Press, 1998.

[90] Ibid., p. 145.

[91] The US embassies and consulates were widely published in architectural magazines of the time. Among them: Architectural Forum, March 1953 and March 1954; Architectural Record, May 1955 and October 1955. For more bibliographical information, see the works of Robin and Clausen.

[92] Too many commissions ended up in Gordon Bunshaft's hands of the SOM firm, a fact made even more evident by the repetition of forms apparent in the US embassies at the beginning of the 1950s. Clausen, op. cit., p. 219.

[93] See Robin, op. cit., p. 148. Foster Dulles was very sensitive to the image that US diplomacy was to offer abroad. See Jeff Broadwater, Eisenhower and the Anti-Communist Crusade, University of North Carolina Press, Chapel Hill, 1992, pp. 112–36. The reasons for the negative way in which the US was viewed are well covered in 'American Morality and Nuclear Diplomacy', speech delivered at Wilson College on 27 October 1961 by Clare Boothe, who was US Ambassador in Italy under the Eisenhower Administration. See Andrews and Zarefsky, op. cit., pp. 55–63.

[94] Clausen, op. cit., p. 221. Shortly afterwards, in the Architectural Record of December 1955, Belluschi published a heated defence of regionalist ideals: The Meaning of Regionalism, probably influenced by Giedion's text 'The State of Contemporary Architecture – The Regional Approach', which appeared in the Architectural Record of January 1954. The issue of regionalism had been analyzed by the art critic Clement Greenberg in an article published in Commentary under the title 'The Plight of Our Culture'. See Clement Greenberg, The Collected Essays and Criticism, vol. 3, University of Chicago Press, 1993, pp. 122–52. Richard Neutra was a forerunner in the use of the term 'regionalism'. See Architectural Forum, February 1934, p. 22.

[95] Belluschi invited Sert to MIT on 26 November 1952, although it is not clear whether Sert gave any classes or lectures there, for on 5 December he wrote a letter saying he could not commit himself to any specific date. SC E 5.

[96] GSD, 'Design Problems', H 261, vol. II. The texts cited are taken from this typewritten copy.

[97] To follow up the chronology of the US Embassy project in Baghdad, see SC Folder B 19 – Folder B 19 U. The first sketches are from 1955 and the last plans consulted are dated March 1961.

[98] Taken from Architectural Forum, March 1961.

[99] SC B 19 C, typewritten copy dated 25 January 1961. It seems to be a report written for a publication.

[100] SC B 19 C, undated typewritten copy.

[101] Robin, op. cit., p. 162.

[102] A version of the plans for the Palace of Batista is found in the folder that contains the Havana Plan, kept in the Sert trunk in the Miró Foundation. The preliminary sketches and photographs of the model are in SC B 70a–70n.

[103] Bainbridge Bunting and Margaret Henderson, Harvard: An Architectural History, Harvard University Press, 1985. To understand the development and interests of the University, see Samuel Eliot Morison, Three Centuries of Harvard, Harvard University Press, 1964; Richard Norton Smith, The Harvard Century: The Making of a University to a Nation, Simon & Schuster, New York, 1986.

[104] Bunting and Henderson, op. cit., p. VI.

[105] Ibid., pp. 150–210.

[106] The Allston Burr Lecture Hall and the Graduate Center were two buildings that were greatly attacked by some architects. R. Clipson Sturgis, for example, who designed the fire station of the University in 1950 in front of Memorial Hall following a neo-Georgian style, wrote: 'Time Magazine of 15 September published a cut of brutally ugly buildings designed by Gropius for Harvard and actually had the temerity to say "the buildings are true to an old Harvard tradition from Colonial to Bullfinch Federal, to Victorian Gothic, to nineteenth-century Romanesque; Harvard has moved with the tides of architecture"; these new buildings show not a gleam of interest in Harvard's past nor any sense of value or beauty … It is an inexpressibly sad day for the architecture of Harvard when such unsightly buildings … become part of the Harvard group … No possible stretch of the imagination can see any sign of beauty in these structures. There is no excuse for such absolute disregard of Harvard's traditional right to have buildings that are at once functional, and above all, beautiful.' Bunting and Henderson, op. cit., p. 228.

[107] Bunting and Henderson, ibid., p. 231.

[108] Some publications and texts of the years prior to Sert's arrival at Harvard already manifest the interest awoken by the planning of University precincts and the will to follow canons of modern architecture in the US. See Joseph Hudnut, 'On Form in the Universities', Architectural Record, December 1947; 'Toward Modern Architecture in the Campus', editorial page of Architectural Record, October 1950; 'Oklahoma City Goes Modern', Architectural Forum, September 1945.
On 13 April 1971 Sert gave a lecture in which he showed the rapport between the Thomas Jefferson campus project and the need for measure in an environment. See 'Measure and Environment', SC D 77.
The programme of the cited course is found in GSD, 'Design Problems', H 261, vol. III.
Somewhat later, and with greater perspective regarding the ensemble, Sert would write: 'The new highway system around the Charles River is part of the Boston Metropolitan area plan of radial roads and inner and outer belts. The University will soon occupy the centre of a well-defined urban sector. It is a City within a city, having its own police force, and with the addition of the expressways establishing a wall around it, it will become a sort of Principality of Monaco! Harvard has developed through the 300 years of its existence a plan without planning. It has a particular scale and character, a great variety of spaces, quadrangles defined by buildings of many different types. These in many cases seem to happily co-exist together. Like all urban campuses, it is faced today with the problems of lack of land and increasing parking and traffic problems. The high price of land around the campus, and the fact that University land and buildings are tax free, makes a low-density development impossible.' See J.L. Sert, 'Changing Views on the Urban Environment', RIBA Journal, May 1963, pp. 191–92.

[109] GSD, H 261, vol. III, p. 1.

[110] Ibid., p. 4.

[111] Graduate School of Design, Harvard University, Cambridge, Massachusetts. 'Summary of Notes Prepared at the URBAN DESIGN Round Table Conference', 26 and 27 November 1956. Typewritten copy, GSD, p. 2. The quotations that follow are from the same document. Sert wrote the 'Introductory Notes' for the congress on Urban Design that was to be held at the GSD between 12 and 13 April 1957.
A typewritten copy of these is found in SC D 93, jointly with the Congress programme, in which other participants apart from Sert included Neutra, Bakema, Chermayeff, Gyorgy Kepes and Kevin Lynch. The Sert Collection contains an undated typewritten text entitled 'The Architect and the City', a speech given at the Wayne State University during the 'Leo Franklin Memorial Lecture Series on the City'. It approached diverse problems of the city, among which was the rapport between the city and architecture. SC D 46. We find a shorter article with the same title published in the Michigan Society of Architects, February 1955. SC D 45.

[112] 'Physical Planning and Harvard University', SC D 81. There is another text by Sert, also undated, that is connected to the previous one: 'Open Spaces and Pedestrian Paths in the University', SC D 13. Likewise, in Folder B 95 of the SC we find some plans on urbanist ideas, along with a text, which Sert meant to develop in Harvard. The ensemble of documents bears no date, but it must have been around the end of the 1960s or beginning of the 1970s becau-

se in these plans we see a drawing of the Science Center.

The contract between Sert and Harvard University dealing with issues relative to the planning of this institution was signed on 5 November 1956. On 4 February 1957 Sert received a fee of $2,500 for his work. SC A 2.

[113] Ibid.

[114] During this term, the title of the history course was changed to 'Space, Structure and Urban Design in the Middle Ages through the Eighteenth Century', and taught by Professor Sekler. The next one was called 'The Evolution of Space in Architecture: Modern Times', and was taught by Giedion and Sekler. GSD Official Register of Harvard University, vol. LIV, August 1957, no. 18.

[115] GSD, Design Problems, H 261, vol. III.

On 5 February 1958 Sert wrote a letter to John Curry, City Manager of Cambridge, in which he informed him of his intention of resigning as Chairman of the Cambridge Planning Board due to his excessive workload. SC E 7. Harry Curry's answer on 10 March reads: 'I wish you to know that it is with very deep regret that I accept your resignation from these positions. During your tenure on the Planning Board you have been an inspiration, personally and professionally, to everybody who has had contact with you … You have been most understanding of the overall problems connected with planning and have been most practical in attempting to solve them. To you I give an especial credit for the comprehensive City Plan now nearing completion. Also, your advice concerning the meshing of planning with our Urban Renewal Program has been most valuable to me.' SC E 7.

[116] A description of the Holyoke House is found in Bunting and Henderson, op. cit., p. 69. Some issues concerning the conception of the project are manifested by the architect himself in RIBA Journal, op. cit., p. 192.

[117] For a description of the controversial reactions and successive criticisms that the Holyoke Center provoked among the student body, see Roy F. Knight, 'The Holyoke Center: A Few Comments', Connection, Autumn 1966, pp. 4–8.

[118] In an interview granted to Jeanne M. Davern (and published in the Architectural Record of May 1981), when Sert was awarded the gold medal of the AIA, he declared, regarding the excessive height of the buildings and their rapport with the city: 'A tall building is in many ways an example of a lot of the possibilities of modern technology. But even buildings of that type are incomplete as modern buildings. When the skyscraper gets down to sidewalk level, it doesn't work; it's just the old sidewalk, the old structure of the city. The infrastructure of the city hasn't changed at all. So we are putting modern elements on old plans, and relationships grow spontaneously like mushrooms. I think there will be an increasing reaction against some of the things that are happening in cities.'

[119] See AIA Journal, May 1977, p. 55. In a previous text, Sert wrote: 'The varied fenestration in facades is an expression of the variety of uses of inside space, small and large, meeting rooms, draughting rooms, filing and many different hospital uses in the Health Center floors from examination rooms, to labs, hospital wards, etc. The use of translucent walls has greatly helped to give each room its appropriate view and lighting. Bright colour accents enliven the vast grey concrete surfaces. I have learned something about this from my friends Fernand Léger and Joan Miró.' RIBA Journal, op. cit., p. 192. On the idea of variety in the ar-

chitecture of this period, see Charles Jencks, 'Variety and Architecture', Connection, no. 6, May 1964, pp. 22–30.

[120] In Bunting and Henderson we read: 'Holyoke Center's greatest success is the care with which it relates to and enhances its environment. Forbes Plaza on Massachusetts Avenue, with its benches and shade trees, is a refuge of just the right size to relieve the crowded, narrow sidewalks and automobile-clogged streets of Harvard Square. The I-shaped mass of the upper floors allows ample light and air to penetrate the narrow side streets and keeps the building from looking heavy or overbearing. The grass mall on Mount Auburn Street is also pleasant but less vital to the environment. All in all, Holyoke Center is a brilliant planning device, the first step in Sert's concept of linking the three Harvard Yards.' Op. cit., p. 235.

[121] Norton Smith, op. cit., p. 203. In the following pages Pusey's strategies to deal with religious issues at the University are explained, as well as his clashes with McCarthy, who was convinced that Harvard was a nest of Communists. 'Within days of his election, Pusey had launched a major fund drive for the moribund divinity school. Once a flourishing academy, the school now had only three professors, a handful of part-time instructors, and a dreary, outdated preoccupation with the sort of methodological scholarship popular in nineteenth-century Germany. It had virtually no constituency outside the old Unitarian precincts of Back Bay and Beacon Hill. Impressed after spending a weekend with Pusey in New York, John D. Rockefeller Jr. donated a million dollars toward revitalizing the place.'

[122] Ibid., pp. 218–19.

[123] There is a typewritten copy of the building's programme. See SC B 30 E.

[124] GSD Design Problems, H 261, vol. X, Typewritten. GSD.

[125] GSD General programme for the 1961–62 term, p. A–1. Typewritten copy kept in the GSD.

[126] Ibid., p. A–6.

[127] Ibid., pp. A–11. In a letter of November 1961 Sert told Giedion of his fatigue due to the excess of work that his position at the GSD had forced him to take on, and consulted him about a possible substitute who would take over his tasks as Chairman: 'Life in Cambridge is much too busy for my liking and enjoyment, but I still have to continue to carry the same load until I find somebody who can be appointed to the Department of Architecture and assume some responsibilities I have been carrying alone for the past nine years. If you have any ideas about who the man should be, please let me know … Unfortunately, I do not think Soltan will be able to stay with us. He was my best candidate for the position. I will have to make a decision in the coming months.' ASG 43–K–1961–11–14.

Sert enjoyed a deep friendship with Jerzy Soltan, who finally substituted him as Chairman of the GSD. The letter he wrote to him on 8 November 1965 about Pierre Jeanneret's illness and the disastrous state in which Le Corbusier's materials had been left after his death is particularly moving and attests to this affirmation. SC E 10.

[128] Sert, 'Physical Planning and Harvard University', op. cit., p. 4, SC D 81. Information about Reverend Francis Greenwood Peabody, founder of the Harvard Department of Social Ethics, and his activity at Harvard is found in Morrison, op. cit., pp. 366–67 and 376–77. Also in Norton Smith, op. cit., p. 50.

[129] Jonathan Hale, 'Ten Years Past at Peabody Terrace', Progressive Architecture, October 1974,

p. 74. Hale includes an analysis of the difficulties in establishing communication between the users of the building: he deplores the lack of common spaces, complains about the dimensions of the communal laundry room installed at the top of the towers, of the Skip-Stop mechanism, which does not promote communication among the users, etc. Peabody Terrace is also published in The Boston Sunday Globe, 21 March 1965.

[130] This was a complex of dwellings for MIT students built at the end of the 1940s. The architects in charge were William Hoskins, Carl Koch, Robert Woods, Vernon De Mars and Ralph Rapson. It is published in the Architectural Review of May 1951.

[131] A commentary on the Peabody Terrace is found in Charles Jencks, 'Harvard Architecture', Connection, December 1964.

[132] A picture of the model can be seen in RIBA Journal, op. cit., p. 193.

[133] Eleanor Rust Collier, 'The Boston University School of Law', typewritten copy, p. 7. There is a photocopy in the BUSL library.

[134] Ibid., p. 21.

[135] Ibid., p. 47.

[136] Sert insisted on orienting the complex to face the river: 'The existing campus buildings were conceived when Commonwealth Avenue was supposed to be the "front side", and nearby Charles River was ignored. Now the river has become much more alive – it is a vast central space that brings three universities and old Boston, with its State house on the Hill and its Back Bay development, visually together. Its banks see fast-moving cars, playgrounds and boat races giving the river life and interest. Commonwealth Avenue in this particular area has decayed – it is unsightly and congested, though it may improve with the new expressway … In designing these campus buildings, we advised the University to reverse its plans and turn its front to the Charles River. Our proposal was, to our surprise, accepted, and everything started from this premise.' RIBA Journal, op. cit., p. 192.

[137] It is published in Architectural Review, September 1947, p. 93.

[138] See 'Official Register of Harvard University GSD', September 1962.

[139] Perry Neubauer, 'Educating the Urban Designer', Connection, March 1965, p. 62.

[140] Ibid., p. 63.

[141] Roy Mann, 'Needed: A New Urban Design Curriculum', Connection, March 1965, p. 65.

[142] Ibid., p. 67.

[143] Charles Jencks, 'No Revolutions, Please', Connection, March 1965, p. 20.

[144] Ibid., p. 25.

[145] José Luis Sert, 'Continuity and Change', Connection, March 1965, p. 7.

[146] Ibid., p. 8.

[147] 'In the past years, some changes were started without any outside help, e.g., the courses in history and theory given under Professor Eduard Sekler, who jointly with Professor Sigfried Giedion, established a new approach to the teaching in this field. These courses range from introductory instruction in the visual arts and environmental criticism given to undergraduates, to the advanced seminar on the Shaping of Urban Space given to the candidates for the Master in Urban Design. These history courses are not archaeologically oriented as they were frequently in the past, but are focused on our problems of today; using morphological approach they relate the past to the present and give standards of judgement.' Ibid., p. 9.

Nevertheless, agreement between Sert, Giedion and Sekler regarding the idea of organizing common seminars with the participation of the students from the GSD and the Visual Arts Center was much more difficult to reach than Sert would lead us to believe, due to dissent between the latter two. See letter from Giedion to Sert, 6 March 1963, SC E 8; Letter from Sert to Giedion, 23 May 1963, ASG 43–K–1963–5–23; Letter from Sert to Giedion, 25 September 1963, ASG 43–K–1963–9–25; Letter from Sert to Giedion, 10 October 1963, ASG 43–K–1963–10–10; Letter from Sert to Giedion, 14 November 1963, ASG 43–K–1963–11–14. On 17 December he informed him of the dates of the lectures to be given at Harvard, ASG 43–K–1963–12–17. Letter from Martin Meyerson to Giedion, 27 May 1963, SC E 8. Letter from Giedion to Meyerson, 7 June 1963, SC E 8. Letter from Giedion to Sert, 22 November 1963, SC E 8. Handwritten letter from Giedion to Sert, 29 December 1963, announcing what seminars he wanted to teach, ASG 43–K–1963–12–29.

[148] 'As part of its fund-raising efforts, the Graduate School of Design is considering a new physical plant where the revised curricula could find the necessary facilities. The new building requires more than double the area of our present buildings to allow for the projected growth of the existing programmes and to provide for the new workshops, the audio-visual work, television link-ups with WGBH-TV (which will permit controlled channel television in classrooms) and ample space for the library, now working in impossible, congested conditions. It will also include a special section for fellows engaged in advanced study and research.' Ibid., p. 10. A commentary on the new building of the GSD, the so-called Gund Hall, is found in Bunting and Henderson, op. cit., pp. 237–39.

[149] Sert, ibid., p. 10. On 2 March 1966, shortly after this publication appeared, Sert gave a lengthy lecture at the GSD in which he insisted on these points in a more systematic and ample way. See 'The Graduate School of Design: New Trends, New Programs'. A typewritten copy is kept in SC D 61.

There is an undated first version of this text in the GSD files, which is somewhat different although it is also typewritten and bears the same title.

Sert was also undergoing certain difficulties at the GSD. The students were complaining about his lack of dedication to his teaching tasks, as is gathered from a letter of 12 January 1966: 'The most disappointing thing is that we have seen very little of Sert. He appeared once to introduce the Urban Design Seminar, twice for the last half hour of minor juries, not at all for the final jury and once informally for half an hour in the studio. This is rather a pity considering that he has probably more to offer than anybody else in the school.' SC E 11. A letter from Sert to Gropius of 27 January 1966, written in a bitter tone, confirms this malaise.

[150] 'An Open Letter to President Kennedy', New York Times, 10 May 1961. We find, among other signatures, those of Isaacs, Chermayeff, Chomsky, Leary, Lynch, Marcuse and Mumford.

[151] In the text we read: 'The Committee of the One Hundred Architects and Planners for Peace is composed of established members of the profession from all parts of the United States who have come together to express to the Congress and Administration our shared opposition to the policies of our national government in the continuing war in Indochina and in the resultant neglect of critical social and domestic issues. We are particularly alarmed by the expanding United States military involvement in Southeast Asia, the increasing empha-

sis of our economy upon war-related production, and the growing polarization of American opinion and repression of dissent … We urge the Congress and Administration to achieve a prompt and complete withdrawal from Southeast Asia and an immediate commitment of a large share of our national resources to the problems of our social and physical environment. Toward this goal we commit our time and energies to assist in the formulation of new programmes to build for a better future in peace.' SC E 19.

[152] Lyndon B. Johnson, 'The Great Society', in Andrews and Zarefsky, op. cit., pp. 171–74.

A contextualization of this term introduced by President Johnson in American political life is found in Oscar and Lilian Handlin, op. cit., pp. 151–97.

[153] Gerald Howard, The Sixties: Art, Politics and Media of Our Most Explosive Decade, Marlowe Company, New York, 1995, p. 32.

[154] The works chosen to manifest this crisis were Paul Goodman, Growing Up Absurd (1960); Wright Mills, Politics and People (1963); Herbert Marcuse, One Dimensional Man (1964).

[155] Fernanda Pivano, L'altra America negli anni sessanta, Officina Edizioni, Rome, 1971.

[156] Norman Mailer, 'Superman Comes to the Market', November 1960, in Howard, op. cit., p. 162.

[157] Susan Sontag, Against Interpretation, Farrar, Straus & Giroux, New York 1966.

[158] Vincent Scully, introduction to Robert Venturi's book, Complexity and Contradiction in Architecture, MoMA, 1966, pp. 11–16.

The main critic of the texts by Venturi and Scully was Manfredo Tafuri. In his book Teorías e Historia de la Arquitectura, we read: 'Venturi has many occasions in which to make precise observations on the structures of complex architectural organisms, revealing their less evident cultural matrixes. What we criticize on the one hand is the lack of historification of architectural ambiguity, which thus becomes a category lacking a priori meanings that are not generic; and on the other hand, the conclusion of his analysis, which even justifies personal figurative choices through historiographical destruction and the confusion between analysis and methods of projection … [W]e cannot comprehend how a serious and penetrating scholar like Vincent Scully has been able to write in his introduction that Robert Venturi's book is the most noteworthy cultural event within architectural debate since Le Corbusier's Vers une architecture.' Teorías e Historia de la arquitectura, Editorial Laia, Barcelona, 1972, p. 271.

Another text by Tafuri is relevant and important to an understanding of the consequences of what he terms Venturi's 'nostalgic narration' in American architecture at the beginning of the 1970s, markedly influencing architects who would later become renowned. See 'Les cendres de Jefferson', L'Architecture d'Aujourd'Hui, no. 186, August–September 1976, pp. 53–58.

[159] Venturi, op. cit., p. 22.

[160] Jehangir Ugaseth, 'The Image of Harvard', Connection, summer 1966, p. 14.

[161] It is not only the shape of the Science Center that leads us to speak in these terms, but also a text written by Sert in the same year. In the opening lines of the last programme that Sert wrote for the GSD, we read: 'We live in an era of swift and dramatic changes that deeply affect man's relation to his environment.' To face these times, Sert suggested: 'A basic role is given to the understanding of human behaviour in its individual and collective forms. As studies in these areas gain greater relevance for the designer, the assimilation of approaches from physiology, medicine, psychology, anthropology and

sociology become necessary.' GSD files, programme for the 1968–69 academic year.

In the last letter he addressed to Giedion, on 14 March 1968, we read: 'This coming year will be my last at the GSD and I am trying to settle matters at the school as well as possible before my departure. All other matters in this country are in a very bad state. The Vietnam monstrosity gets worse every day and the racial situation promises a rather troublesome summer. We all hope that change of Government will come soon.' ASG 43–K–1968–3–14.

[162] The Science Center was thus defined by Mildred F. Schmertz in her critical article, published in the Architectural Record of March 1974. It is a way of understanding the architecture-city rapport that is already present in the treatises of Alberti and Palladio, and which was taken up again in some debates of the CIAMs in the 1930s.

The three big buildings that Sert erected in Harvard are published in Architecture of the United States. vol.I. New England and the Mid-Atlantic States, Anchor Press, Garden City, New York 1981, pp. 270–76; Eva Jacob, New Architecture and New England, De Cordoba Museum, Lincoln, Massachusetts, 1974, pp. 102-06.

The Science Center was published in: New American Architecture: Fifty-Plus Notable Buildings Selected by the American Institute of Architects and the Editors of the AIA Journal, May 1974, pp. 170–71. This book also published the Miró Foundation, pp. 164–69. Sert described the Science Center building in what seems to have been the speech for the inaugural session of the edifice. See SC D 86.

[163] 'The Expanding Frontiers of Architecture', typewritten text of Sert's lecture at the Loeb Theater, SC D 58.

Homecomings: New York, Barcelona

Edward J. Logue's visit to the Peabody Terrace made such a positive impression on him that it brought about the greatest flow of commissions that Sert had ever received during his professional career. Logue had been director of the Boston Redevelopment Authority when Sert was consulted on certain urbanist problems in the city,[164] and he was now Executive Manager of the New York Urban Development Corporation,[165] an institution created as one more facet in President Nixon's policy to confront the need for reform in the United States.

On 8 August 1969 Nixon made a speech in which he made clear his intentions to bring about reform, the title of which was 'Welfare Reform'. In it we find a programme of general actions that began by acknowledging the following: 'We face an urban crisis, a social crisis – and at the same time, a crisis of confidence in the capacity of government to do its job.'[166] Of the President's four-point programme for reform, the fourth is of special relevance, since it attempted to de-centralize American bureaucracy to grant greater administrative facilities to the States: 'and fourth, a start on the sharing of Federal tax revenues with the States.' Nixon admitted that this would be one of the means to avoid the decay that many States and their cities were facing as a consequence of Roosevelt's welfare: 'Our States and cities find themselves sinking in a welfare quagmire, as caseloads increase, as costs escalate, and as the welfare system stagnates enterprise and perpetuates dependency. What began on a small scale in the Depression '30s has become a huge monster in the prosperous '60s. And the tragedy is not only that it is bringing States and cities to the brink of financial disaster, but also that it is failing to meet the elementary human, social and financial needs of the poor.'

Leaving demagogical aspects aside, the attempt to make taxes revert to the States was a way of constructing a new federalism that granted a relative economic autonomy proportional to its contribution to the country's coffers, and this was also beneficial for the cities most in need of funds, the victims of the previous economic practices: 'In recent years, we all have concentrated a great deal of attention on what we commonly call "crisis of the cities". These proposals I have made are addressed in part to that, but they are focused much more broadly.'[167] We observed before that the victory of the Russians in the space race had been one of the catalysts that had unloosed the crisis in the 1960s;[168] now, on the eve of the 1970s, and with his reforms ready to be executed, Nixon could not let the opportunity go by without mentioning in his speech the US victory in space, a metaphor of their longed-for triumph. After speaking about his trip around many countries of the world, he said: 'In all of them, however, I found that one event had caught the imagination of the people and lifted their spirits almost beyond measure: the trip of Apollo 11 to the moon and back. On that historic day, when the astronauts set foot on the moon, the spirit of Apollo truly swept through this world.'[169]

New York was the most visible embodiment of the crisis that Nixon hoped to remedy: 'Like every urban state, New York has been fighting a losing battle against decay. Its slums are spreading faster than its rate of new construction. Its old commercial cores can no longer compete with suburban shopping centres and are corroding ... Urban renewal at best has been an inadequate tool, trying to drain the flood of blight with an eyedropper, and at worst a quagmire, replacing neighbourhoods with vacant lots and promises ... Since it takes

Sert, Jackson and Associates, Riverview residential complex, Yonkers, New York, 1972–74.

365

on average thirteen years to complete an urban
renewal project in New York City and eight
years upstate, it would take New York at its present pace about 350 years to eliminate its
slums.'[170] This urban decay had affected all
spheres of daily life and its repercussions were
already being felt: 'New York City abandoned
the liberal policies of the 1960s; low transportation fares, excellent free schooling, and
well-paid, uncorrupted municipal workers. In
the 1970s one million of its eight million residents abandoned it, as the city slipped into
bankruptcy and services deteriorated. Omi-
nously, neighbourhood life disintegrated when
districts turned into quarters for lodging, not
living.'[171]

Given these conditions, it is not surprising
that Rockefeller, then Governor of the State,
insisted on the need to confront the crisis, and
the first step in doing so was to hire Logue,
who proposed the creation of a new state corporation, 'with vast powers which would allow
it to condemn property, to plan new structures
or even new cities, to build them if no one else
would, to own them and lease or manage
them, to receive tax exemptions and if need be,
to ignore local zoning and building codes.'[172]
Such arrogance made it unlikely that matters
would improve, and Logue's proposals fell on
the deaf ears of journalists, businessmen and

legislators. Nevertheless, on 9 April 1968 the
bill was approved and after a year and a half, the
Urban Development Corporation had become
a legal entity.[173]

By the end of the first year, the UDC had
agreements with eleven cities and had lined up
projects whose budgets exceeded the total sum
of 600 million dollars. The most ambitious was
undoubtedly that of developing what was still
called Welfare Island, a very large plot of land
in New York in the middle of the East River
between Manhattan and Queens, which had a
long history of problems before John V. Lindsay,
Mayor of the city since 1966, made it the
topmost priority in his urban policy agenda.

The first documents found by historians
concerning this area refer to it as Blackwell Island. It had belonged to New York ever since
its owners Robert and Mary Blackwell had
sold it to the city for 30,000 dollars on 9 July
1828. In that same year the city had begun to
build a jail there: 'This move was the first of
many during the subsequent one hundred
years as more and more of the City of New
York's social services found homes on the island. In fact, the island was eventually to become known as "Welfare Island"',[174] a name
that would not become official until 1914.
Thus, the island began to be filled with the institutions that the city preferred to keep away

Sert, Jackson
and Associates,
housing on
Roosevelt Island,
New York,
1970–76, plan
of the complex
and aerial view.

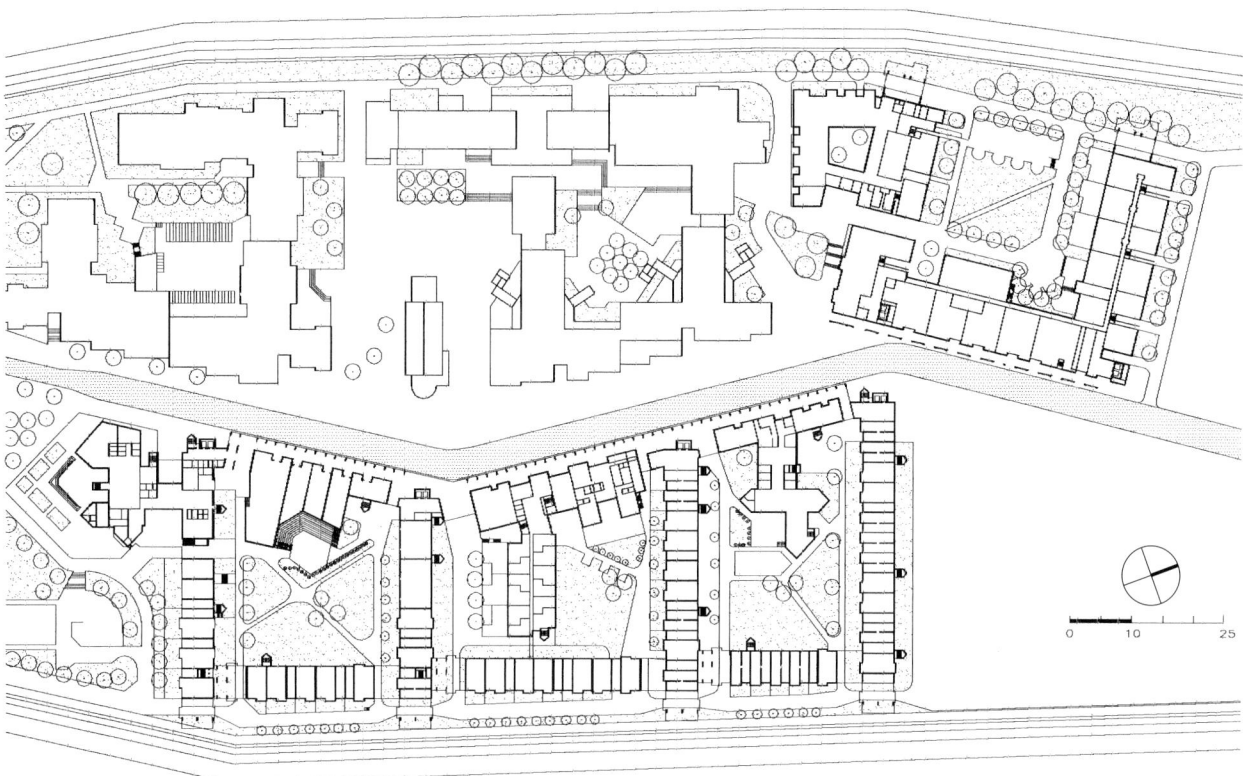

from its streets: an insane asylum, built between 1835 and 1848, a poorhouse called the
Alms House, built in 1840, the Island Hospital,
erected in 1856, and the Smallpox and Charity Hospitals were the first buildings that occupied this land before the Church of the Good
Shepherd was built in 1892. Other hospital infrastructures were built later, such as the
Strecker Memorial Laboratory, after which the
enlargement and modification of the existing
buildings were carried out at the beginning of
the twentieth century.

In the 1930s the prison was moved over to

Riker's Island and a new hospital took its place;
this building, along with three others built
some years before – the Central Neurological
Hospital (1909), the Reception Hospital
(1916), and the Cancer Institute (1923) – constituted over a number of years the functional
destiny of the island.

Welfare Island began to decline in the 1950s
due to the closure of several of the buildings
mentioned above, despite the fact that it still
maintained two hospitals for chronically hand-
icapped people, the Goldwater Hospital in the
south, and the Coler Hospital in the north,
along with the Fair Department Training
School. Nevertheless, this land was always coveted by the city, which put forward some proposals at different times, building an amuse-
ment park there, or turning it into a public
park, building a cemetery on its grounds for
those currently buried in Brooklyn and
Queens, creating an Egyptian art museum, a
nuclear plant, or even turning it into the headquarters for buildings annexed to the United
Nations.[175]

In February 1968 Mayor Lindsay established
the Welfare Island Planning and Development
Committee, made up of twenty-two members,
all of whom were influential New Yorkers. The

President was the banker Benno C. Schmidt, managing partner of the investment company J.H. Whitney & Co. The municipality was represented by Donald Elliott, President of the Planning Commission, Bernard Bucove of the Health Department, August Hecksher of the Parks Services, and Jason Nathan of the Housing and Development Administration. Other public figures such as Vincent Astor, William Bernbach, Ralph Bunche, Marcia Davenport and James Linnen were also included. The list was completed by two familiar names: Philip Johnson and Edward J. Logue.

A year later the committee had written a 141-page report in which it defined its priorities concerning the island, the most noteworthy of which were: the maintenance of the two hospitals with an ambulatory, the construction of a public park, scrapyard infrastructures, subway station, and a sufficient number of dwellings to justify a community with the necessary services and elements to ensure its survival.[176] In March 1969 Philip Johnson and John Burgee were assigned to set up a general plan for the island, and they handed in this document on 9 October of the same year, while organizing an exhibition at MoMA to make their plan known to the city; the need for this can be deduced from the title given to the exhibition: 'The Island Nobody Knows'.

The project consisted of formalizing the text written by the committee and implementing it within the geography of the island, as well as designing its initial zoning. The existing hospital zone (formed by the Smallpox Hospital, the Strecker Laboratory, the City Hospital and the Goldwater Hospital) was maintained in the south zone of the island. A wide green belt area separated it from the first large plot of land destined for housing, which in its turn, if one moves northwards (the direction we have chosen to navigate the proposal of Johnson and Burgee), bordered on another park on which the Blackwell House had been kept and restored, and which led the way to a second concentration of dwellings where Sert was to build his projects. Further north was a communal parking lot; Johnson dreamed of a place without cars, a type of 'rationalized French village, where lodgings could be quite dense, but right on whose outskirts one found oneself directly

in the countryside. Instead of fragmenting the ensemble, it is better to separate the parks from the city to render it more compact. We architects hope that this project will constitute a model that demonstrates how one can also make a city within a city.'[177] The parking lot was adjacent to a firefighter training school, on the verge of another park, which separated this building from the Bird S. Coler Hospital located on the northern tip of the island. This itinerary along the perimeter of the island allows one to contemplate the river and the city, and attempts, apart from providing a recreational aspect to the ensemble, to unify the planned territory.

In the zone destined for dwellings, Johnson and Burgee designed a central porticoed thoroughfare, Main Street. Going away from it towards the river they laid out open U-shaped city blocks. These blocks were formed by stepped buildings that went from being thirteen storeys high on this street to only six storeys when they reached the promenade along the river. Main Street was designed on a curve to increase the picturesque quality to which Johnson had made reference earlier, a strategy with a long architectural tradition, for we see it mentioned in Alberti's work *De re aedificatoria*.[178] This stance was far removed from some declarations that Le Corbusier had made concerning this question, thus further showing its rejection of certain urbanist conventions from functionalist days.[179]

The references included in the catalogue of the exhibition evoke characters and circumstances far removed from the Functional City. In it one could read how the project meant to enhance the fact that the island had 'some of the most charming tree-lined, paved and bench-equipped promenades west of the river Seine … The most spectacular views east or west of anywhere: panoramic views of Manhattan that remind you of Feininger's photographs; perspectives of a high-flying bridge that recall Piranesi's drawings; glimpses of docks and of industrial plants that look like Charles Sheeler's paintings at their most dramatic.'[180] When the authors described other imagined aspects of the project, they cast them under the same rosy light, so that the neuralgic centre of the ensemble, which was to be a covered glass gallery, was compared with the Galleria Vittorio Emanuele in Milan, or the staircase descending to the East River was likened to that which went down to the Ganges River in Benares.

Equipped with a 'minitransit system', Main Street was to be a mainly pedestrian road to which private cars would not have access, finally making it possible to fulfill the dream of separating pedestrians from cars; on this occasion certain rationalist aspirations were considered acceptable. Concerning this issue, Johnson pointed out: 'This is not a multi-level town. I'm too close to Jane Jacobs for two levels. In every two-level town that I have been in, one level is good and one isn't. In Montreal, all the action is down below; nobody walks in that square. You might just as well put a roof over it. In Hartford, nobody goes up to that second level.'[181]

This plan needed a managing company capable of carrying it out: the New York State Urban Development Corporation under Edward Logue's direction, a corporation that, as we know, had authorization to disregard existing local zoning and building ordinances if they were not considered opportune or profitable.[182] Logue distributed the work of developing the Johnson and Burgee plan amongst different architectural firms in Boston and New York, which resulted in the alteration of certain aspects of the project, a fact that provoked differences of opinion between the manager and the architects.[183]

Sert's office was asked to take care of designing two apartment complexes whose names were taken from their geographical orientation: Eastwood, facing Queens, and Westview, facing Manhattan. The first sketches are from November 1970, and the buildings were finished in 1976, three years after the island's name had been changed to Roosevelt Island, thanks to the Mayor's proposal.[184]

The apartment and services complex of Eastwood held 1,003 low-cost and medium-cost dwellings in which approximately 4,000 people of the following economic status were to live: 'At Eastwood, senior citizens with minimum incomes of $7,000 and maximum incomes of $13,500 pay $191 per month, heat, gas and electricity included, for a studio apartment. The studios are reserved for the elderly

0 1 2 3 4 5

Eastwood residential complex, Roosevelt Island, plans of the apartments.

only, and there are 139 of these units. One-bedroom apartments are available to the elderly and to young couples with income between $10,500 and $13,500 who pay a monthly rent of $281. Of these, 145 units are for the elderly and 195 for young couples. 266 two-bedroom apartments are available to persons with incomes of $14,000 to $22,000 depending on family size and the rent is $359 per month. 189 three-bedroom units rent for $395 per month and go to couples earning $15,000 to $23,000, again depending on family size. To get one of the 69 four-bedroom units a couple must have at least three children and an income ranging from $16,000 to $26,000. For this unit they must pay $421 per month ($764 is the fair market monthly rent for an equivalent apartment in New York City).'[185]

Social motives, therefore, determined the fate of these apartments, whose rents competed favourably in the real estate market of the city thanks to the density proposed in the Johnson and Burgee plan. The stepped profile that Sert adopted in his project was already included in the general plan, and we can consider that its shape formed part of the modern tradition that had begun with some proposals by Mallet-Stevens, had also appeared in certain projects by Loos, and were employed by Sert himself for the Science Center and for the library of Boston University. The shape would not be exactly as Johnson and Burgee had conceived it, since it would go up to a height of twenty-two storeys. Sert also proposed that the three blocks that made up the complex should have a closed form that could hold landscaped courtyards in its interior. These would conserve many of the existing trees, and he also built service buildings – a school, shops, diners for elderly people, meeting halls, etc. – inside these courtyards. Sert moreover allowed direct access to the river by laying out paved streets perpendicular to Main Street that went from there to the water.

For cost and safety reasons, the terraces generated by the stepped form would not be for public use as Sert had intended, but became linear blocks that organized the access to the dwellings based on the Skip-Stop system that we saw in the Peabody Terrace, the building complex that had so impressed Logue. Sert used a window running lengthwise in the corridor, which was repeated every three storeys, and thus cut the excessive vertical dimension of the buildings. At the same time he pushed forward the volumes of the living rooms to break the continuity of the walling surface. The great horizontal component of these windows *en longueur* achieves a balance with the powerful vertical lines of the elevator towers, treated with a concrete of a different mixture and colour and placed at the end of each corridor. The composition is altered depending on the programme it accommodates, and on the varied offer of the apartments previously mentioned. Their distribution is based on an impeccable mechanism of modular addition and subtraction, conceived in relation to the green spaces and the programme they are to hold; thus, for example, the larger apartments, which were to be inhabited by families with several

Eastwood residential complex, view.

children, were placed on the lower floors of the complex. This became a design resource that helped to escape from the possible mechanical repetition of the elements that would constitute the facades.

The final perception is of small compositional units scattered in an apparently haphazard way every three floors. It is thus a complex that exhibits a hermetic composition in which the Corbusian Modulor system is ever-present. The complex stands defiant, with its stepped towers pushed back in relation to the big city from which it seems to defend itself rather than engaging in a dialogue. Aware that it was located in a very privileged place, that its dwelling offer was more qualified than that of its city counterparts, and that the setting around it afforded maximum contact with green spaces and the river, Sert exaggerated this 'difference' in its favour, and at the same time allowed it to fulfill the dream that the members of the first CIAMs had been awaiting for so many years: the chance to disregard ordinances and ground property, to work with a manager who was on their side, and to imagine a better way of living.[186] Only by ignoring reality can one construct ideology.

After more than forty years of struggle, Sert was finally able to carry out that conception of architecture for the city made up of high-rise linear buildings that promoted high occupational density and hygienic cross-ventilation. It made possible the communal recreational spaces that we saw drawn and explained in the Brussels CIAM. The buildings on Main Street that were twenty-two storeys high were sheltered by other buildings orthogonal to them that were only seven storeys high, recalling Sert's endeavour to avoid anchoring to the ground buildings with enormous vertical dimension without an intermediary.

This intention was completed by the design of a 1,000-foot-long porch on Main Street, which gives access to the shops that were quickly installed on Roosevelt Island, an element that we also saw in many Civic Center projects for Latin America but which never got past planning stage. Here was an architect who had grown old but was finally building part of what he had always dreamed of, a dream that he had always put forward in precarious conditions. If in 1933 only a ship was able to shelter the champions of a possible Functional City, now it was a long island, a stranded ship, on which it had become possible to build a fragment of that reality. However, it will always remain a manifesto facing New York, the metropolis par excellence, which would at most play the role of curious and condescending spectator of so much accumulated intellectual energy.

Roosevelt Island, portico on Main Street.

Conditions would vary to a certain degree in the adjacent complex of Westview. Here the idea was to build 360 apartments for people with higher incomes, which seemed a good enough reason to organize them without having to go up and down the uncomfortable stairs of the Skip-Stop system. The city-block plan respected the Johnson and Burgee project, remaining open and looking towards Manhattan, and included a school and swimming pool. The stepped buildings were composed along similar lines to those in Eastwood, although the height was greater than that foreseen in the general plan, and Sert introduced variations to illuminate and ventilate the long horizontal corridors that in the majority of cases run between two dwellings, eliminating cross-ventilation and double views.

After Sert's intervention, the ideal section of Main Street, with its double-staggered effect oriented towards Manhattan and Queens, strikes one as a place that goes back and forth from the city, surrendering to it while at the same time defending itself from it. The white towers of the elevators and the play of battlement shadows created by the volumes introduced into the facade make one think of a fortified complex or citadel. By creating its own

Westview residential complex, Roosevelt Island, apartment plans.

0 1 2 3 4 5

surroundings in the street with porches, and by exhibiting peaceful gardens and the riverbank promenade, Roosevelt Island also becomes an example of harmonious coexistence among dwellers of different social classes – an oasis, which, as we know, is surrounded by desert. It is a necessary place for strollers to recover their strength, a place where architecture shows both its limitations and its capacity to make us aware of all that must happen so that it can exist; from here on, other illusions, other proposals, must surge forth in the continuous drive forward towards better situations.

Sert and his associates received two more commissions from the NYSUDC directed by Logue: the East Hills complex in Ithaca, and the Riverview complex located in the municipality of Yonkers, both in the state of New York. In the first of these, where the office in

Westview residential complex, views.

which he started working from August 1969 was located, Sert also designed the plan using almost totally closed city blocks that formed great interior courtyards, and he resorted to a variant of the Skip-Stop system, with apartments of different surfaces and distributions.

Although the facades did not go beyond their realization as sketches and models, we can see in them compositional mechanisms belonging to the tower of the Law School of Boston University and to the Peabody Terrace. Breaking the corners and seeking volumetric compartmentalizing effects to diminish the height of the dwelling towers, as well as resorting to the well-known mechanism of connecting high buildings with lower ones to create two effective levels of perception, Sert exercised his self-confidence, corroborating already trodden paths.

In Riverview, which was a project that had begun in 1972 and which was carried out in two stages, the idea was to come up with 798 apartments and services for people with low incomes. The plot of land occupied by six city blocks covered 7.8 acres, and was located in the shabby centre of the municipality of Yonkers.

Initially concerned with the relationship between the complex and its not very hospitable setting, Sert carried out a study to set up in the best possible way for the linear blocks to compose the project. He introduced an interior pedestrian street, which crossed the complex and joined it to the civic centre of the town, but here his good intentions to seek a fruitful rapport between his design and the municipality ended.

He went on to completely close the complex around the existing school, which came to

Riverview residential complex, Yonkers, New York, apartment plans.

0 1 2 3 4 5

Riverview
residential
complex, views.

374

occupy the physical centre of the ensemble but without meaning to integrate the rest of the buildings. This hermetism was repeated in the courtyards of varying sizes, which were closed by different volumetric plays that evoke the optical illusion of finding oneself in many different places at the same time. The comments of the journalist of the *Architectural Record* prefigured some of the observations above: 'These courtyards provide a sense of place for the community, are interesting to look at from the apartments and corridors which face them and provide an oasis from the noise and confusion of the adjacent streets.'[187]

The city was noise and confusion from which it was necessary to defend oneself, this time with an answering disdain. Sert built replicas of his previous experiences in a sort of premeditated will towards disorder: the high buildings meet with others of lower height, while the staggered buildings mingle without apparent logic. Whereas on Roosevelt Island the volumetric meaning corresponded to clear landscaping and formal and visual criteria, here the task of describing them seems difficult if not impossible, but we can attempt it at least in one example. The facade on Riverdale Avenue is formed from south to north by staggered buildings that go down from sixteen storeys to five. The void of the accessway to the complex, a low building of the same height as the lowest part of the former, defines a possible entrance, a building of huge vertical dimensions – twenty storeys high – and a linear staggered one descending from seven to four storeys, which acts as the high building's intermediary with the ground.

The city's chaos could not be solved by a good-will message from architecture, that impotent redeemer of urban ills, if it was to act on its own, nor by creating unreal paradises on the outskirts. Sert exhibited this harsh reality and left hanging possible solutions, forcibly evoking past days when he and his colleagues had become aware of the absolute need for a global approach to thinking about our surroundings, and had even endeavoured to fulfil this requirement. The Riverview residential complex – with its plan also based on the Skip-Stop system, its apartments essaying possibilities and variants that are deduced from the L-shaped

staircase and the interrupted planes of the facade, based on increasingly more sophisticated compositional mechanisms – represents the total surrender of the architect who had struggled so hard in a task that had borne so few of the results he had sought to achieve.

Sert's weariness coincided with the renovating intentions of the Institute for Architecture and Urban Studies (IAUS), which was established with financial assistance from private foundations and MoMA's sponsorship, and which was set up by a group of young architects from Princeton: Michael Graves, Peter Eisenman, Anthony Vidler, Kenneth Frampton and Anthony Eardley, who were soon joined by Emilio Ambasz, Mario Gandelsonas and Diana

Agrest. They received contracts to develop their investigations with the US Department of Housing, the National Institute of Mental Health and with the UDC itself. In 1973 they presented the result of their investigations at MoMA in an exhibition entitled 'A Second Chance for Housing: Low-Rise Alternatives'.

The core of the IAUS was responsible for the publication that same year of the first issue of *Oppositions: A Journal for Ideas and Criticism in Architecture*, which is fundamental to understand the complexity of the American scenario at the time. *Oppositions* wilfully distanced itself

Riverview residential complex, view.

from other publications on architecture by proposing critical analysis and reflection as the central focus of its work. In its first editorial note, which was signed by Eisenman, Frampton and Gandelsonas, we read: 'It is our joint belief that truly creative work depends upon such an extension of consciousness. To this end, *OPPOSITIONS* will orient itself towards the process of critical assessment and re-assessment … *OPPOSITIONS* will address itself to the evolution of new models for a theory of architecture.'[188]

Today we know that they offered more than they were able to give, but the format of *Oppositions*, almost square and with soft orange covers, that evoked magazines from the 1930s such as *Das Neue Frankfurt* or *ABC* in its second period, must have made Sert's eyes shine. His age and his long professional career probably allowed him to feel a strange melancholy in the fact that magazines were again providing the motor for reflections on architecture. However, in contrast to the capacity for pro-

posals and interventions that the original magazine model provided, this vehicle was irreversibly trapped into being simply a reference to those days of such tremendous change.

The idea of going back to Barcelona, as we have seen, provoked feelings that were exactly opposite to these, for the melancholy in this case arose from unsettled accounts. Possibly due to this, the site plan for the Les Escales Park residential complex in that city, which was included in the first proposal and whose earliest date indicates 9 December 1966 (although its first stage was completed in 1973), is also a totally hermetic proposal. Sert got rid of it as quickly as possible when problems arose with the real estate agents on the project. Located in a large plot of land in the high part of the city, it holds luxury apartments, most of which were set up as duplexes.[189]

Here the city was neither noise nor confusion, but a privileged place, secluded, peaceful and surrounded by the green of hundred-year-old trees. Sert's answer is too similar to Riverview for the analogies to go unperceived. The urbanist plan of the complex bears a striking resemblance to the American one: the initial density was also high, and the part of the project that Sert came up with shows a volumetric composition of similar characteristics to those of the complex in Yonkers. Riverview's continuous window of access to the dwellings provided by the low-cost Skip-Stop system is transformed in Les Escales Park into the one-level apartment, so that the composition of the facade plane became an acknowledged problem.[190]

Other differences are to be found in the finishes, which here were of much better quality: concrete, artificial stone, vitreous ceramic, roller blinds, small concrete vaults. Some of these changes to the skin are fragile reminiscences of the Mediterranean, although they are probably the weakest elements, as is the case with the neomodernist finials of the chimneys (which are not Sert's, but those of a detached assistant, in charge of the execution of the project). In Sert's opinion, the opulent suburban neighbourhood of Barcelona was just as uninhabitable as was the old centre of Yonkers. The city was still sick, and an extra dab of make-up was not going to conceal it. Barcelona, that city-en-

Cover of *Oppositions*, no. 3.

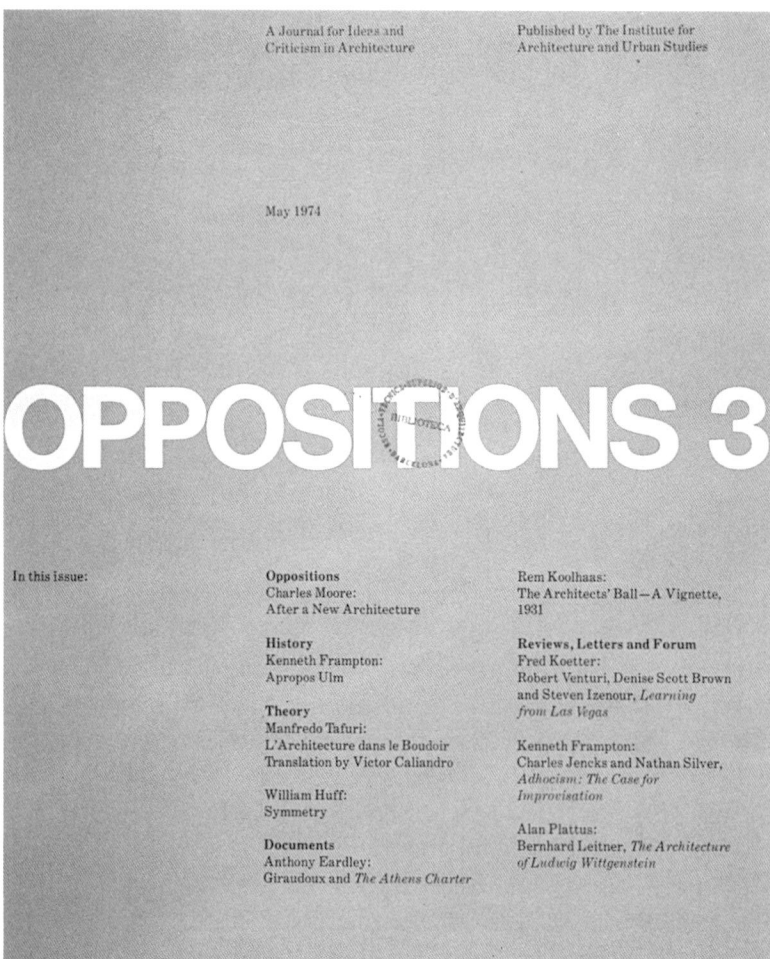

A Journal for Ideas and Criticism in Architecture

Published by The Institute for Architecture and Urban Studies

May 1974

OPPOSITIONS 3

In this issue:

Oppositions
Charles Moore:
After a New Architecture

History
Kenneth Frampton:
Apropos Ulm

Theory
Manfredo Tafuri:
L'Architecture dans le Boudoir
Translation by Victor Caliandro

William Huff:
Symmetry

Documents
Anthony Eardley:
Giraudoux and *The Athens Charter*

Rem Koolhaas:
The Architects' Ball—A Vignette, 1931

Reviews, Letters and Forum
Fred Koetter:
Robert Venturi, Denise Scott Brown and Steven Izenour, *Learning from Las Vegas*

Kenneth Frampton:
Charles Jencks and Nathan Silver, *Adhocism: The Case for Improvisation*

Alan Plattus:
Bernhard Leitner, *The Architecture of Ludwig Wittgenstein*

Sert, Jackson and Associates, Les Escales Park residential complex, Barcelona, 1966–73, sketches (SC) and main facade.

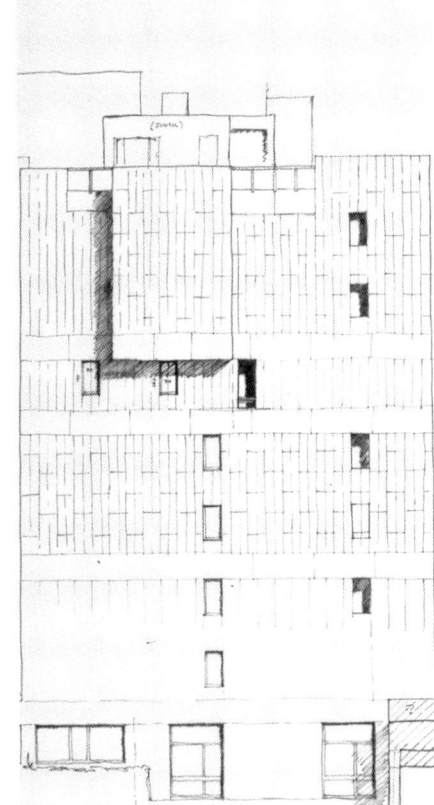

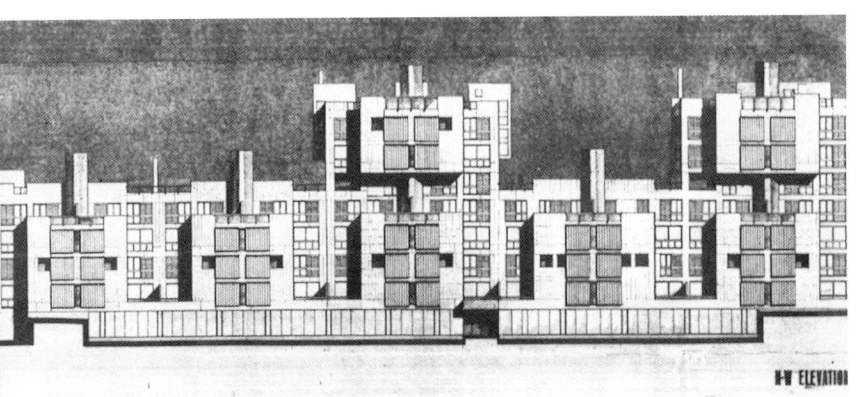

sign of new urban ideas back in the 1930s, had been an urbanistically diseased city for too many years, spanning from the Civil War to the mandate of Mayor Porcioles, during which time the speculation and laissez-faire attitude in favour of the most blatant interests of capital had been rampant in the city, without the implementation of adequate planning to take into account the collective values that its inhabitants deserved.[191]

Thus, despite the differences between the immediate surroundings of this complex and that of Yonkers, the need to put up a defence prevailed all the same. The main facade of Les Escales shows an almost blind foreground of artificial stone with wide discontinuous joints and sun-breaker enclosure wallings and with vertical recesses evoking the merlons of a fortress. To enter the building one must go down a sloping ramp surrounded by concrete walls that form an enclosure for the ancient trees, cross a bridge over a moat, as if it were a medieval castle, and reach a dark, empty and cold foyer made of concrete with mirrored walls that reflect what has previously been contemplated, so that there are no doubts as to the designer's intentions. The thickset forest brings

to mind the entrance to a castle that draws itself away from the city.

At the rear end of the building, where the dwellings face the garden, sun and swimming pool, Sert maintained the presence of a raw structure clad with artificial white stone. In its repetitive and abstract image it is possible to accommodate all variations, and the play of solids and voids achieved is further dramatized by the Mediterranean light that falls upon the ensemble, something that we have already observed in Miró's studio in Palma. In this way the initial structure is emphasized, which is transformed into the second basic element of the architecture, completed by a luxuriant and effective *toit-jardin* similar to those found in some areas of the Peabody Terrace. A wall facing the city, a porticoed structure in the interior – based on archaic elements of architecture, the wall and portico, and on their eternal present, as Giedion liked to tell in his last writings – the architect now began to attempt to separate architecture from the city, a task that he would only manage to outline.

On 21 June 1976 the President of the Caja de Ahorros Provincial of Barcelona wrote to Sert to request from him what would be the

Les Escales Park
residential
complex, housing
typologies
and views
of the rear facade,
main corridor,
vestibule,
and double-height
terrace
of an apartment.

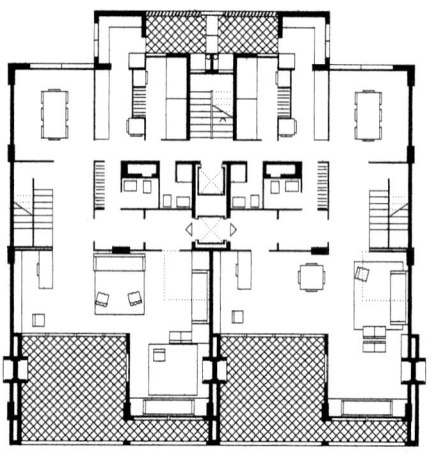

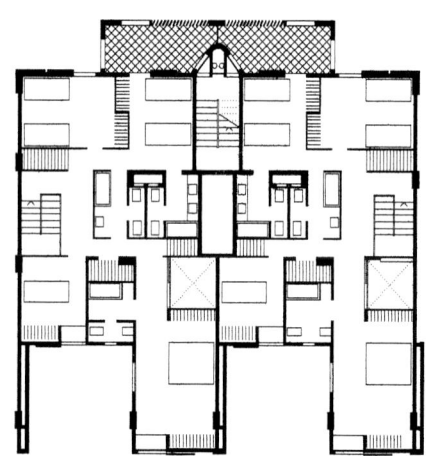

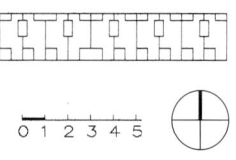

0 1 2 3 4 5

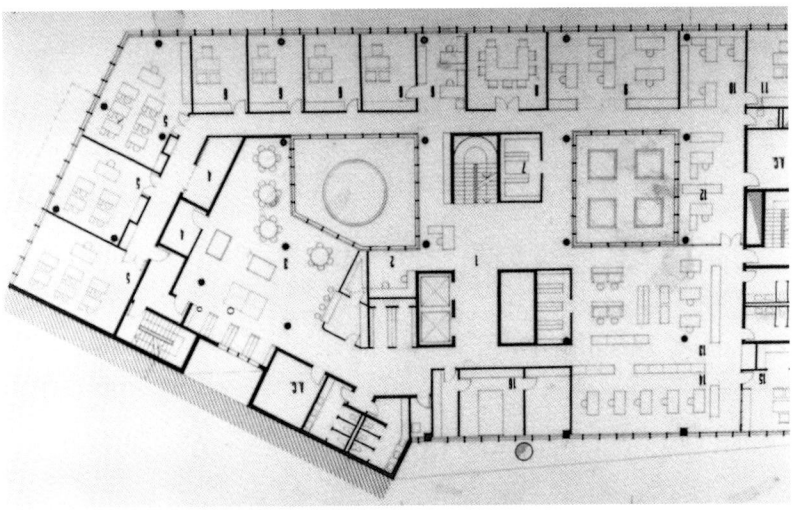

Building on the Diagonal-Tuset intersection, Barcelona, 1976, plan.

last commission he would undertake in Barcelona: a building for offices, an auditorium, an assembly hall and exhibition halls that was to be located on the junction between Avinguda Diagonal and Carrer Tuset. The letter went on to add: 'I would like that this building bring prestige to the city and to our savings bank by offering to Catalonia a House of Culture, modern and capable of developing all types of artistic and cultural activities.'[192] Sert, already with a shaky pulse, underlined the last five words of the text in the letter, more interested in thinking about these activities than about anodyne bureaux and offices.

Despite his efforts, the commission never went beyond the preliminary design, but in it we can identify certain noteworthy aspects, especially the forceful presence of three great voids in the facades, which generate a trio of landscaped courtyards faced by different rooms of the building. Sert took up again the system of concrete transoms that he had tried out in Holyoke to design the woodwork for the glass surface of the offices. He also placed some of the most representative functions of the cultural dimension of the building in its upper part, which allowed him to lay out the last floor with almost no openings so that it comes to be identified as its finial, a technique that he had already employed in Brattle Street, and whose resemblance to the latter was surely not accidental. There the blind finial lit by a skylight had been his office, whereas here it was the auditorium and exhibition halls, located behind what were almost certainly to have been concrete walls.

Sert was saying farewell to Cambridge with the haughty aristocratic gesture of someone who aspires to transcend, from the heights of his office with its blind walls, a reality that he has been unable to change. In the last building he designed for Barcelona, other blind walls, which were to contain the cultural rooms, expressed his farewell to his native city. The professional practice of architecture, and cultural values – albeit mediated by a banking entity far removed from the transformations that culture had promised in the vanguard years – were identified in a last meaningful gasp.

On 10 May 1977 Sert drafted the list of contents and introduction to a book that he would not have time to finish and which was to be called *Balanced Habitat*, a work that should be understood as a last will and testament,[193] and whose introduction entitled 'Why this book?', reminds us of the enormous failings still demonstrated by our cities, despite so much effort: 'The federal government and the

Building on the Diagonal-Tuset intersection, elevation and sections.

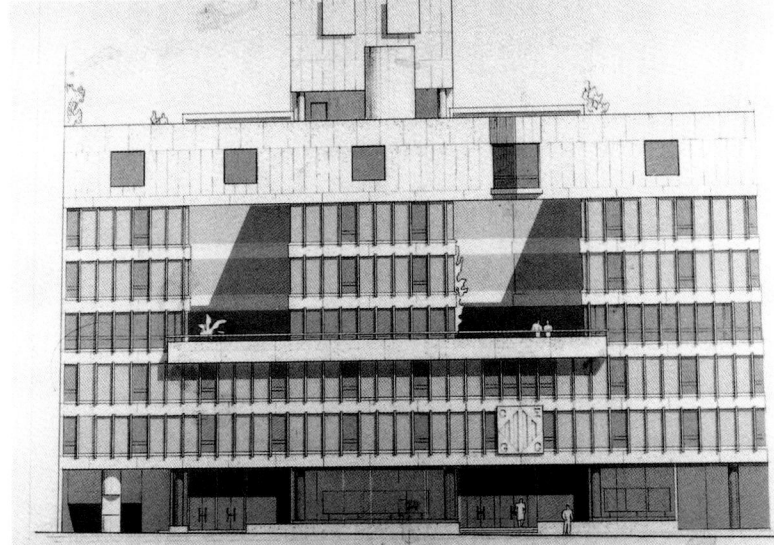

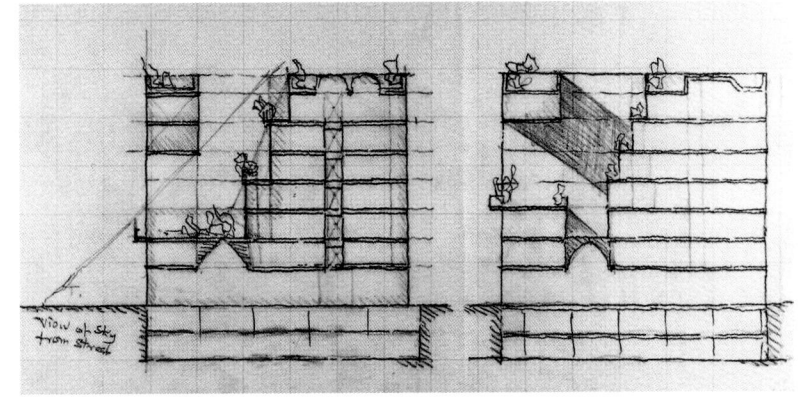

local governments seem incapable of undertaking corrective measures to stop the increasing decay of the cities, and the people are being consistently told that such measures are beyond the means of city, state or federal government … There is not enough courage to get to the roots of the causes that have produced the actual state of decay. There is a deep conviction that nothing efficient can be done. This results not only in not taking any measures but in continuing to allow and tolerate the process of decay and confusion.'

A feeling of pessimism invaded the architect who had struggled so hard to improve conditions for human life in the city and who observed with desolation how much effort had been expended with so little success. This pessimism pervades his last projects, which showed themselves unwilling to collaborate with the city. By then cities were more congested and scattered than before, but we are no longer in the 1930s, and Sert acknowledged that the book 'does not attempt to outline remedies for all these ills as a whole'. Instead it would only try to 'clarify and define the conditions that could and should govern the closer environment of families in our cities.'

Thus, at the end of his life, Sert no longer felt capable of approaching the urban problem in all of its complexity, and resigned himself to this functional reductionism: 'So, this text will be limited in scope and will only examine conditions from the human side of the viewpoint.' Nevertheless, the introduction ended by mentioning the contents of the CIAMs. This was a last reminder that all that was to follow in the book, despite its bias, sprang from the contemplation of the city in which only the correct location of all its functions would ensure the wholesome operation of the ensemble. It was also intended to show that what had been laid out was in keeping with the times of rationalist utopia at a moment, the end of the 1970s, when this ideology was not highly regarded.[194]

Angela Giral, who was librarian at the Frances Loeb Library of the GSD, visited Sert at the Quiron Clinic in Barcelona on 14 March 1983, the day before he died of cancer. We are informed of this last and moving meeting by the *HGDS News*: 'His room was bare, but he did not want any paintings or posters on the wall. He kept murmuring the word "yellow", that he wanted yellow. So, at lunchtime, I went and bought him a huge bouquet of yellow flowers. I gave them to him saying that if I had my own choice I would have bought him purple, the colour that distinguished the Spanish Republican flag (red, yellow and purple) from the monarchy's flag (red, yellow and red). He smiled at me and then replied: "The new flag of hope will be *roja, roja, roja* (red, red, red)" which I took to be a reference to the Republicans who were known as *los rojos*, the Reds.'

This sounds tremendously utopian, especially since it was uttered in the climate of terrible crisis hanging over left-wing activists in Catalonia in 1983, just a few months after an attempted coup d'état by a brainless member of the Civil Guard. But it is nevertheless proper for someone who, despite his many contradictions, never wanted to give up on so many ideals that even today have never been achieved.

[164] From the author's interview with H. Jackson in Cambridge on 20 July 1995. Corroboration of Sert's opinion on Boston can be found in 'Can Boston Survive? The Sert Solution', interview in the *Boston Globe*, 31 August 1969, SC D 41.

[165] 'Edward J. Logue, who has perhaps the best reputation in the nation as an urban administrator dedicated to getting a job done. Logue was then a part-time professor of public administration in Boston and a constant renewal consultant and critic. Following an overwhelming rejection by voters in his 1967 bid for the Boston mayoralty, Logue built his national reputation while rebuilding New Haven and Boston.' Samuel Kaplan, 'Bridging the Gap from Rhetoric to Reality: The New York State Urban Development Corporation', *Architectural Forum*, November 1969, p. 70.

[166] Richard Nixon, 'Welfare Reform', in Andrews and Zarefsky, op. cit., p. 188.

[167] Ibid., p. 192.

[168] See Handlin, op. cit., p. 173.

[169] Nixon, op. cit., p. 193.

[170] Handlin, op. cit., p. 270.

[171] Kaplan, op. cit.

[172] Ibid., p. 71. According to this author, Logue advised beginning this operation with 5 million dollars: '$3.5 million in "first instance" appropriations to cover planning and project costs prior to permanent financing, and a bond authorization of $1 billion!' Logue also proposed the creation of two subsidiary institutions: the Corporation for Urban Development and Research, which was to deal with planning and initiating projects, and an Urban Development Guarantee Fund in charge of solving problems regarding mortgage financing in the project areas.

[173] Through Kaplan's text we are able to find out more about the UDC, such as the problems that began to surface immediately after its constitution: 'But as the studies are bound and articulated, and the minutes of the last meeting typed and reviewed, it has become evident to observers and some staff members that the UDC is having problems bridging the gap from rhetoric to reality, particularly its promise

to provide low- and moderate-income housing, the UDC's most important objective, according to Logue. Though it can plan, build and manage any form of housing, it cannot finance subsidized housing, other than to provide short-term construction loans. For low-income housing, it must turn to the local housing authorities and work through their channels to the federal government, acting as any other turn-key developer, hat and plans in hand. To achieve moderate-income housing, it must act as a package developer on behalf of a local nonprofit sponsor in applying for FHA mortgages, an increasingly difficult road to travel.' The work of the UDC was essentially to be that of management: 'the UDC will almost always have to work through the local renewal agency in developing inner city sites for subsidized housing' as well as creating projects 'with its experienced staff to process papers for local renewal agencies and to move the projects through bureaucracy; with the resources to build the projects, win them and manage or lease them; and with the option to ignore local building or zoning codes, the UDC is, in fact, a super-developer.' There are diverse articles on the result of the UDC experiment and its failure: William Marlin, 'After the Pitfall: UDC Dusts off the Debris of Default', *Architectural Record*, October 1975, pp. 121–24; Charles Hoyt, 'Crisis in Housing', *Architectural Record*, October 1975, pp. 107–10; Sharon Lee Ryder, 'UDC Financial Woes a Political Ploy?', *Progressive Architecture*, April 1975, pp. 32–38; Marie Christine Gagneux, 'Derrière le miroir', *Architecture d'Aujourd'Hui*, August–September 1976, pp. 2–3.

[174] David A. Rogan, 'The rehabilitation of the Roosevelt Island Ruins, New York City', typewritten thesis for the Master of Science in Historic Preservation, Graduate School of Architecture and Planning, Columbia University, 1986, p. 4.

[175] Two other works are of interest for several reasons, especially for the information and the proposals for conservation they provide regarding the existing architectures present on Roosevelt Island, some of which proposals were carried out: Elizabeth Ann Frosch, 'The Abandoned Structures of Roosevelt Island, New York, and Their Place Among the Ruins of America', Columbia University, 1985, typewritten copy; Giorgio Cavaglieri, 'Protection of Landmark Buildings: Welfare Island, New York City', Columbia University, March 1970, typewritten copy.

[176] 'Report of the Welfare Island Planning and Development Committee, submitted to John V. Lindsay, Mayor, City of New York', February 1969, typewritten copy kept at Columbia University.

[177] Quoted in Diana Agrest and Alessandra Latour, 'Roosevelt Island Housing Competition', *Architecture d'Aujourd'hui*, no. 186, August–September 1976, p. 22. In reality it is a translation of an opinion expressed by Johnson, which appears in a text by Richard Rogin called 'New Town on a New York Island', *City*, May–June 1971.

[178] 'Within the city, they must not form straight lines, but rather bend in wide curves, as the meandering of a river, curving on one side and on the other. In this way, first of all, the road seems to be longer, and one will have the impression that the city is bigger; secondly, because this is of extreme utility, be it to beauty, to practical convenience, or to the needs of specific moments. And it is not at all an insignificant thing that the paths slowly, step by step, lead one to new perspectives of buildings; that the access to the facade of each building is exhibited in the middle of the road; and that the same width be what makes it useful, whereas an excessive length

would end up being disagreeable and unhealthful.' Leon Battista Alberti, *L'Architettura*, Edizioni Polifilo, Milan, 1966, p. 306.

[179] In *Urbanisme*, Le Corbusier wrote: 'Man walks straight because there is a goal; he knows where he is heading. He has decided to go somewhere and he walks straight to it. The ass zigzags, muses a bit, his brain empty and distracted, he zigzags to avoid big stones, to avoid the slope, to search for shade; he commits himself as little as possible.' Editions Crès, Paris, 1924, p. 5.

[180] The quotations used by Johnson for the catalogue of the MoMA exhibition are taken from Stern, Mellis and Fishman, *New York 1960*, The Monacelli Press, New York, 1995, p. 645.

[181] John S. Margolies, 'New Town for New York City', *Architectural Forum*, October 1969, p. 40.

[182] The New York State's Urban Development Corporation promoted, along with the projects to be undertaken on Welfare Island, diverse interventions in the State of New York. See Robert Jensen, *Architectural Record*, April 1971, pp. 124–29.

[183] Stern, Mellis and Fishman, op. cit., pp. 645–46. The result of this work was also the subject of an exhibition at MoMA, inaugurated on 6 October 1970 under the title 'Another Chance for the Cities'.

[184] In 1974, shortly before his death, the architect Louis I. Kahn designed two versions of a monument to Roosevelt for the south end of the island that was never built. Stern, Mellis and Fishman, op. cit., pp. 646–47.

[185] 'Eastwood, Roosevelt Island, New York City', in *Architectural Record*, August 1976, pp. 102–04. It is a useful article because it reproduces some of the technical characteristics of the complex, such as the type of structure, cost of the operation, densities, etc.

[186] Between pages 98 and 105 of the *Architectural Record* of December 1973 we find an article that analyzes some of the sociological variants of Sert's intervention. In *New York* magazine of 8 November 1976, an article signed by Priscilla Tucker and entitled 'Roosevelt Island: A New Deal for Living' gathered the jubilant accounts of those who had the opportunity to live in the new dwellings on the island. In a news article in *The New York Times* of 24 July 1975 written by Joseph Fried we read all sorts of favourable comments from the residents of the new island, whether they were to live in Sert's projects or in those by other architects.
In 1974, Sert chaired the jury of a competition for a new community of 18,000 inhabitants to be located on Roosevelt Island, and wrote jointly with the other jury members the requirements to be fulfilled. A copy of the pamphlet of the competition with these requirements, as well as abundant information about the island is found in the Sert trunk in the Miró Foundation, Barcelona. Some magazines published the results of the competition, among them: *L'Architecture d'Aujourd'Hui*, no. 186, op. cit., pp. 25–41; *Architectural Record*, January 1975; *Progressive Architecture*, July 1975, pp. 58–63; *Architectural Record*, October 1975, pp. 107–20; *Architectural Design*, November 1975, pp. 693–96.
The final destiny of Roosevelt Island and of its development manager, Logue, can be found in Stern, Mellis and Fishman, op. cit., pp. 655–59.

[187] *Architectural Record*, August 1976, op. cit., p. 108.

[188] The editorial pages of both the second and fourth issue of *Oppositions* are equally important to fully grasp the goals and intentions of this magazine. A contextualized criticism of the ideals of *Oppositions* is found in Brace Taylor, Brian, 'Self-Service Skyline', *L'Architecture d'Aujourd'Hui*, no. 186, op. cit., pp. 42–46.

Manfredo Tafuri, 'Les bijoux indiscrets', introduction to *Five NY Architects*, Officina Edizioni, Rome, 1976.

[189] The project was commissioned by José María Figueras, a Catalan manufacturer and real estate developer who had a house near Sert's in the old part of the city. They met there through Robert Gardner, a North American anthropologist who was a resident of Cambridge and a friend of both, and this circumstance fostered the commission. The correspondence between Sert and Figueras is kept by the daughter of the latter, the architect Virginia Figueras, whom I wish to thank for all the facilities given to me in their consultation. The correspondence between the client and the architect began on 14 January 1966 and continued until 12 May of the same year, at which point it was possible to specify the scope of the commission. Diverse problems with the Committee of Urbanism of Barcelona delayed the final approval of the Partial Plan of the complex – handed in at the beginning of April 1969 – until February 1970.

[190] An interesting critical commentary on the Les Escales project is found in David Ferrer, 'Roda el món i torna al Born', *Arquitecturas Bis*, no. 6, Barcelona, March 1975.

[191] A critical appraisal of the status of Barcelonian urbanism during the period in which Sert was working on the Les Escales project (a time of great social, political and urban vindication in the city) can be found in: 'La Gran Barcelona', *Revista CAU*, Colegio Oficial de Aparejadores y Arquitectos Técnicos de Cataluña, no. 10, November–December 1971; 'La Barcelona de Porcioles', *Revista CAU*, no. 21, September–October 1973; 'El fet urbà a Barcelona', *Revista CAU*, no. 22, November–December 1973.

[192] The typewritten original of the letter is found in the Sert trunk, Miró Foundation, Barcelona.

[193] We can also observe a certain pessimistic tone in a text by Sert written that same year and presented as a lecture at the VI Congreso Interamericano de Vivienda (VI Inter-American Congress of Housing): 'Experiencia en el planeamiento y desarrollo de ciudades' ('Experience in City Planning and Development').

[194] The rest of the contents of the book were split up as follows: 'Part I. Generating Principles A. The Dwelling Unit and the Quality of Life B. Grouping of Units C. The "Skip-Stop System" D. Shaping the Buildings E. Shaping Spaces with Buildings. Part II. A. Married Student Dormitories B. Roosevelt Island C. Yonkers Phases I and II. Part III. The Continuing Search.'
On 1 November 1977 Sert gave a lecture at the Robert B. Church Memorial of the University of Tennessee, which had a similar title to that of the book he was planning to write: 'Balance in Human Habitat'. SC D 52.
Towards the end of his life Sert gave various lectures in which he liked to review and broadcast the most important professional and ideological steps of his life. See 'Achieving Livability in Human Settlements: A Challenge for the 80s', SC D 44; 'AIA Speech', 20 May 1981, SC D 43; speech delivered on the occasion of his being awarded the gold medal of the French government on 18 March 1976, typewritten in French, SC D 42.

381

Appendices

Bibliography

Julio Garnica

The following bibliography is divided into two parts. The first concerns the published writings of J.L. Sert: books, essays, articles and the texts of lectures and interviews. The second comprises writings on Sert and his work published by specialists, critics and devotees of architecture: books, essays, monographic issues, articles in magazines and newspapers. To make this part easier to consult, the various references to a single work by the architect have been grouped at the end of the bibliography.

It is my hope that this bibliography will serve as a means of reconstructing, together and without haste, the way that Sert felt about life, how he imagined the world and proposed his architecture; and that all the material gathered will help readers to understand who Sert was and what he did, as well as, reading between the lines, what he was not and never did. (J. G.)

SERT'S WORKS

Books and essays

Can our cities survive? An ABC of urban problems: their analysis, their solutions, based on the proposals formulated by the C.I.A.M. International Congresses for Modern Architecture, The Harvard University Press, Cambridge, Massachusetts, 1942; H. Milford, Oxford University Press, London 1942; Generalitat de Catalunya, Departament de Política Territorial i Obres Públiques, Barcelona 1983.
'The human scale in city planning', in Paul Zucker (ed.), *New Architecture and City Planning: a Symposium*, Philosophical Library, New York, 1944, pp. 394–413.
'From architecture to city planning', in Stamo Papadaki (ed.), *Le Corbusier, architect, painter, writer*, Macmillan Company, New York, 1948, pp. 82–86.

VIII CIAM: The heart of the city: towards the humanisation of urban life (with E. N. Rogers and J. Tyrwhitt), Lund Humphries, London, 1952; Pellegrini and Cudahy, New York, 1952; Hoepli, Milan and Barcelona, 1954; Cientifico Médica, Barcelona, 1961.
'Nine points on monumentality' (with S. Giedion e F. Léger), in *Architektur und Gemeinschaft*, Rohwolt, Hamburg, 1956, pp. 40–42. Also published in J. Ockmann, *Architecture Culture 1943–1968, A documentary anthology*, Rizzoli, New York, 1993, pp. 29–30; in *The Harvard Architecture Review*, IV, spring 1984, pp. 62–63, and in *Sert: arquitecte a Nova York*, Museu d'Art Contemporani de Barcelona, Actar, Barcelona, 1997, pp. 14–15.
'The shape of our cities' (with J. Tyrwhitt), Fund for Adult Education, United Nations Seminar on Regional Planning, Tokyo, 1958, in *Contemporary Architecture of the World*, Editorial Committee, Contemporary Architecture of the World, Shokokusha Publishing Co., Tokyo, 1961, pp. 101–13.
Plan piloto de la Habana: directivas generales, diseños preliminares, soluciones tipo (with P.L. Wiener, P. Schulz), Junta Nacional de Planificación, Habana 1959.
Antoni Gaudí (with J.J. Sweeney), Frederick A. Praeger, New York, 1960, 1970; Verlag Gerd Hatje, Stuttgart, 1960; The Architectural Press, London, 1960.
Ibiza, fuerte y luminosa (with J. Gomis and J. Prats Vallès), La Polígrafa, Barcelona, 1967.
'The rebirth of the patio', in Knud Bast-lund, *José Luís Sert: Architecture, City Planning, Urban design*, Les Editions d'Architecture, Artemis, Zurich, New York and Washington, 1967, pp. 134–39; Thames and Hudson, London, 1967; 'The impact of popular architecture', ibid., pp. 150–51; 'The integration of the visual arts', ibid.,

pp. 168–69; 'On windows and walls', ibid., pp. 192–95. See also 'Inédito, 1954: Patio, intriguing word ...' and 'The rebirth of the patio', in *J. Ll. Sert i la Mediterrània*, Col.legi d'Arquitectes, Barcelona 1997, pp. 220–21 and pp. 221–22.
Cripta de la colonia Güell de A. Gaudí (with J. Gomis and J. Prats Vallès), La Polígrafa, Barcelona 1969, 1972.
'Introduction', in Jorge Arango, *The urbanisation of the Earth*, Beacon Press, Boston 1970, pp. XI–XIV.
'Edward Waldo Forbes, City Planner', in *Edward Waldo Forbes, yankee visionary*, Fogg Museum, Cambridge 1971, pp. 47–48.
'Introduction', in Le Corbusier, *The Athens Charter*, Grossman, New York 1973, pp. VII–X.
'Alexander Calder', in Jean Lipman, *Calder's Universe*, Whitney Museum, New York 1976.
'Sculptures in Architecture', in *Miró: Sculpture*, Pierre Matisse Gallery, New York 1976.
'Preface', in Eduard Sekler, *Le Corbusier at work*, Harvard University Press, Cambridge 1978, pp. VII–IX.
'Victoria del Guernica', in *Guernica-Legudo Picasso*, Museo del Prado, Madrid 1981, pp. 24–30.
'Un centre per a l'encontre de les arts', in Manuel Duran, Albert Porqueres-Mayo, Josep Roca-Pons (ed.), *Actes del segon col.loqui d'Estudis Catalans a Nord-Amèrica. Yale, 1979*, Biblioteca Abad Oliba, Publicacions de l'Abadia de Montserrat 1982, pp. 27–32.

Magazine articles

1930

'La position de Le Corbusier et Jeanneret dans l'évolution architecturale d'aujourd'hui. Espagne, J. Ll. Sert, architecte à Barcelone, président de Gatepac', in *L'Architecture d'Aujourd'hui*, October 1934, pp. 11–12.
'Arquitectura sense "estil" i sense

"arquitecte"', in *D'Ací i D'Allà*, Christmas special issue edited by J. Ll. Sert and J. Prats, winter 1934. Republished as 'Antologia de textos. Arquitectura sense "estil" i sense "arquitecte"', in Félix Julbe, Rafael García Pascuet, *Arquitectura y espacio rural en Ibiza*, Publicación de la Delegación en Ibiza y Formentera del Colegio de Arquitectos de Baleares, 4/5, La Gaya Ciencia, Ibiza 1982.
'La Arquitectura popular mediterránea', in *A.C.*, 18, II quarter 1935, p. 15; also in *J. Ll. Sert i la Mediterrània*, Col.legi d'Arquitectes de Catalunya, Barcelona 1997, pp. 216–17.
'Poblaciones mediterráneas', in *A.C.*, 18, II quarter 1935, pp. 28–29; anche in *J. Ll. Sert i la Mediterrània*, Col.legi d'Arquitectes de Catalunya, Barcelona 1997, p. 216.
'Raices mediterráneas de la arquitectura moderna', in *A.C.*, 18, II quarter 1935, pp. 31–32; also in *J. Ll. Sert i la Mediterrània*, Col.legi d'Arquitectes de Catalunya, Barcelona 1997, pp. 217–18.
'Casas de fin de semana' (with J. Torres), in *Nuestra Arquitectura*, 82, May 1936, pp. 202–07.
'Rapport núm 2 al V C.I.A.M.', in *Cuadernos de Arquitectura y Urbanismo*, 90, July–August 1972, pp. 44–47.

1940

'Arched roof structure gives convertibility' (with P.L. Wiener and P. Schulz), in *Architectural Record*, November 1943, p. 66.
'Brazil builds a new city: Cidade dos Motores' (with P.L. Wiener), in *Progressive Architecture*, vol. 27, 9, September 1946, pp. 52–75.
'To the Editor' (with M. Breuer, S. Chermayeff, S. Giedion, W. Gropius, E. Kaufman), in *The Architectural Review*, February 1947, pp. 74–76.
'La cité des moteurs' (with P.L. Wiener and P. Schulz), in *L'Archi-*

tecture d'Aujourd'hui, 13–14, September 1947, pp. 99–119.

1950
'Urbanisme en Amérique Latine. Medellín, Tumaco, Chimbote, Lima' (with P.L. Wiener), in *L'Architecture d'Aujourd'hui*, 33, December 1950–gennaio 1951, pp. 1–55.
'How to combine architecture, painting and sculpture', in *Interiors*, vol. 110, 10, May 1951, pp. 101–05.
'Can patios make cities?' (with P.L. Wiener), in *Architectural Forum*, August 1953, pp. 124–31.
'A Church for Puerto Ordaz', in *Liturgical Arts*, vol. 21, 4, August 1953, pp. 112–18.
'Letter to the schoolmaster re activities and policy of C.I.A.M.', in *Progressive Architecture*, vol. 34, 10, October 1953, pp. 176–80.
'Brief comment on C.I.A.M.', in *L'Architecture d'Aujourd'hui*, 113–14, April–May 1964, p. 37.
'Complicated and delicate', in *Progressive Architecture*, vol. 35, 5, May 1954, p. 22.
'Introduzione a Gaudí', in *Casabella Continuità*, 202, August–September 1954, pp. 48–56.
'Architecture and the Visual Arts', in *Harvard Foundation for Advanced Study and Research. Newsletter*, 31 December 1954, pp. 6–8.
'Gaudí: visionnaire et précurseur', in *L'Œil*, 2, 15 February 1955, pp. 26–35. Published as 'Gaudí from nature to geometry', in Bernier (ed.), *The selective eye*, Reynal, New York 1955.
'Comments on Harvard School of Design's Times Square Problem', in *Architectural Forum*, vol. 103, 2, August 1955, p. 112
'Unité de voisinage de Pomona à Maracaibo' (with P.L. Wiener), in *L'Architecture d'Aujourd'hui*, vol. 27, 67–68, October 1956, pp. 98–101.
'Art or building', in *Progressive Architecture*, vol. 38, 3, March 1957, p. 13.

'The work of Town Planning Associates in Latin America, 1945–56. Bogotá, Orinoco, Puerto Ordaz, Ciudad Piar, Pomona, Quinta Palatino, Isla de Pinos (with P. L. Wiener)', in *Architectural Design*, vol. 27, 6, June 1957, pp. 190–213.
'Les plans régulateurs de Medellin et Bogotá', in *L'Architecture d'Aujourd'hui*, 80, October–November 1958, pp. 73–75.
'A comment on life and work of Frank Lloyd Wright', in *Architectural Forum*, vol. 110, 5, May 1959, p. 113.
'In response to article "The new sensualism"' (Letter to the editor), in *Progressive Architecture*, vol. 40, 11, November 1959, p. 51.

1960
'La Havane' (with P.L. Wiener), in *L'Architecture d'Aujourd'hui*, 88, February–March 1960, pp. 62–71.
'More jazz. Letter to the Editor', in *Architectural Forum*, vol. 113, 5, November 1960, p. 228.
'What became of CIAM?' (with W. Gropius, Le Corbusier, S. Giedion), in *Architectural Design*, gennaio 1961, p. 5. Also published in *The Architectural Review*, 769, March 1961, p. 154.
'An open letter to President Kennedy' (with one hundred and fifty intellectuals), in *The New York Times*, 10 May 1961.
'Windows and Walls: an approach to design', in *Architectural Record*, 5, May 1962, pp. 132–33.
'A Lively and Human City', in *Boston Sunday Globe Magazine*, 15 March 1964, pp. 12–13.
'Brief comment on C.I.A.M.', in *L'Architecture d'Aujourd'hui*, 113–14, April–May 1964, p. 37.
'Continuity and change', in *Connection*, March 1965, pp. 7–10.
'Il n'y construisit qu'un institut', in *Le Figaro Littéraire*, 1011, 2–8 September 1965, p. 6. Also published as 'Remembering Le Corbusier: what

we have lost', in *A.I.A. Journal*, vol. 44, 5, November 1965, pp. 31–33.
'Témoignages pour Le Corbusier', in *L'Architecture d'Aujourd'hui*, 122, September–November 1965, p.VII.
'Le Corbusier the Educator', in *Progressive Architecture*, October 1965, p. 237.
'Le Corbusier and the Younger Generation', in *H.G.S.D.A. Newsletter*, 1, November 1965, pp. 1–4.
'Le Corbusier', in *Connection*, winter 1966, p. 18.
'Educating the architect', in Marvin E. Goody, *The Boston Society of Architects: the first hundred years*, BSA, Boston 1967, pp. 109–11.
'Paul Lester Wiener', in *L'Architecture d'Aujourd'hui*, 135, December 1967–gennaio 1968, p.VII.
'Pierre Jeanneret', in *L'Architecture d'Aujourd'hui* 136, February–March 1968, p. XII.
'Hommage à Sigfried Giedion', in *H.G.S.D.A. Newsletter*, 3, June 1968, p. 10. Also in *Institut für Geschichte und Theorie der Architektur, Schriftenreihe*, vol. 13, 1971.

1970
'Joan Miró, catalitzador de la joventut', in *Miró 80*, Col.legi d'Arquitectes, Palma de Mallorca, November 1973–January 1974, pp. 2–3.
'Apuntes sobre el auditorio "Manuel de Falla"', in *Bellas Artes*, 61, III quarter 1978, p. 9.

1980
'Below the Alhambra: Manuel de Falla Centre, Granada; architects José García de Paredes with José M. Vinuela' (with F.Woods), in *The Architectural Review*, vol. 167, 997, March 1980, pp. 138–43.
'Josep Torres Clavé i el G.A.T.C.P.A.C.', in *Cuadernos de Arquitectura y Urbanismo*, 140, 1980, pp. 22–25.
'Marcel Breuer: obituaries', in *A.I.A. Journal*, 9, August 1981, p. 12.
'A key to understanding Le Cor-

busier', in *A.I.A. Journal*, 11, September 1981, pp. 67–69.
'Design process', in *Process: Architecture*, 34, December 1982, pp. 7–11.
'Apuntes autobiográficos', in *Q. Revista del Consejo Superior de los Colegios de Arquitectos de España*, 66, April 1983.
'En la mort d'en Josep Lluís Sert. Carta inèdita de Josep Lluís Sert a Josep Muntañola, 6 de juny de 1967', in *Gaseta*, 2, October 1983, p. 3.

Talks

'L'esdevenidor urbanístic de Barcelona', Barcelona, Ateneu Barcelonés, published in *Arquitectura i Urbanisme*, June 1934, pp. 28–29.
'Quina orientació cal que prengui l'arquitectura contemporània a Catalunya? Josep Lluís Sert', Barcelona, January 1935, Escola Superior d'Arquitectura de Barcelona, published in *A.C.*, 16, IV quarter 1934, pp. 43–44, and in *Arquitectura i Urbanisme*, 5, March 1935, p. 25.
'The scope of the architect', Harvard, 15 March 1953, Graduate School of Design, published in *Architect & Building News*, 9 April 1953, p. 419.
'Human factor in architecture and city planning', Boston, 12 May 1953, Boston Society of Architects, published as 'El factor humano en la arquitectura y el urbanismo' in *Cuadernos de Arquitectura y Urbanismo*, 93, November–December 1972, pp. 18–19.
'The changing philosophy of modern architecture', Boston, 16 June 1954, A.I.A. annual meeting, published as an extract in *Architectural Record*, vol. 116, 2, August 1954, p. 181.
'The architect and the city', Detroit, 17 November 1954, Detroit Institute of Arts, published in *Monthly Bulletin. Michigan Society of Architects*, February 1955, pp. 21–23; published as an extract in

Architectural Forum, April 1955, p. 147 and as 'El arquitecto y la ciudad' in *Cuadernos de Arquitectura y Urbanismo*, 93, November–December 1972, pp. 19–20.

'The architect and the city', Detroit, 5 March 1956, Leo M. Franklin Memorial, Wayne State University, published in Warren Dunham (ed.), *The City in Mid-Century*, Wayne State University Press, Detroit 1957, pp. 13–27. See also 'The human factor in urban design', Sert Collection D71, 1956, published as 'El factor humano en el diseño urbano', in *Cuadernos de Arquitectura y Urbanismo*, 93, November–December 1972, pp. 20–21.

'The institution as a generator of urban form', Harvard, April 1961, closing speech of the Fifth Conference on Urbanism of the Graduate School of Design, published in *H.G.S.D.A. Newsletter*, 1961, pp. 55–57.

'Le Corbusier and the image of a man', Columbia, 26 April 1961, Columbia University, published in *Four great makers of modern architecture*, Columbia University, School of Architecture, 1961, pp. 172–76.

'Changing views on the urban environment', London, 14 February 1963, Royal Institute of British Architecs, published in *R.I.B.A. Journal*, vol. 70, 5, May 1963, pp. 188–94, and as 'Opiniones cambiantes sobre el entorno urbano' in *Cuadernos de Arquitectura y Urbanismo*, 93, November–December 1972, p. 44.

'Sert en Ibiza', Ibiza, 25 May 1973, a tribute to Sert, Museu d'Art Contemporani, Eivissa, published in *Arquitecturas en Ibiza*, Publicación de la Delegación en Ibiza y Formentera del Colegio de Arquitectos de Baleares, 6/7/8, Ibiza 1983, pp. 104–06.

'Cómo estimular la creatividad arquitectónica', Madrid, 8 May 1975, XII U.I.A. Congress, Escuela Politécnica de Madrid, published as an extract in *Arquitectura*, 00, April–May 1975, and in *Arquitectura*, 303, III quarter 1995, pp. 57–59.

'Un encuentro en Santiago', Santiago de Compostela, May 1975, published in *Arquitectura*, 303, III quarter 1995, pp. 35–43.

'Pregó de la mercé', Barcelona, 21 September 1978, Ajuntament de Barcelona, published as an extract in *La Vanguardia*, 22 September 1978, p. 20, and in *Diari de Barcelona*, 22 September 1978, p. 16.

'A la recerca d'un equilibri urbà', Barcelona, 26 February 1981 on occasion of the UPC award of the honoris causa degree, Càtedra Gaudí, published as 'En busca de un equilibrio urbano' in *CAU*, 75, November 1981, pp. 38–41.

'On architecture', Minneapolis, 20 May 1981, A.I.A. annual meeting, on occasione of the Gold Medal award, published as 'Consideraciones sobre arquitectura' in *On Diseño*, issue titled *J. Ll. Sert*, 29, 1981, pp. 72–75.

'Característiques constants en les arquitectures i urbanisme mediterranis', Sitges, 26 April 1982, Palacio de Congresos, symposium Creativitat Mediterrània, published in *J. Ll. Sert i la Mediterrània*, Col.legi d'Arquitectes de Catalunya, Barcelona 1997, pp. 223–25.

Interviews and debates

'Conversa entre Sixte Illescas, Joan Prats, Germán Rodríguez Arias, Josep Lluís Sert i Raimon Torres, mantinguda a Eivissa el setembre de 1968, amb la presència de Mercè Torres i Montxa Sert', in *Cuadernos de Arquitectura y Urbanismo*, 140, 1980, pp. 5–21.

Davern, Jeanne M., 'A.I.A. Gold Medallist, 1981. Josep Lluís Sert. Interview by Jeanne M. Davern', in *Architectural Record*, 6, May 1981, pp. 96–101.

Ed., 'Que penseu de l'arquitectura moderna?', in *Mirador*, 65, 10 April 1930.

Ed., 'Can Boston survive? The Sert solution', in *Boston Sunday Globe Magazine*, 31 August 1969, pp. 11–16.

Ed., 'L'avantguarda lúcida. Una conversa amb Josep Lluís Sert', in *Quaderns d'Arquitectura i Urbanisme*, 152, May–June 1982, pp. 74–77.

Muñoz, Jordi, 'Conversación con: Josep Lluís Sert', in *On Diseño*, 29, 1981, pp. 55–58.

Murray, Peter, 'A certain feeling', in *Building Design*, 23 May 1975.

Peter, John, 'José Luis Sert', in *The oral history of modern architecture*, Harry N. Abrams, New York 1994, pp. 246–59.

Porcel, Baltasar, 'Josep Lluís Sert o la preocupació urbanística', in *Serra d'Or*, 6, June 1967, pp. 48(488)–55(495).

WORKS ABOUT SERT

Books and essays

A.C. Avantguardes a Catalunya 1906–1939, Olimpiada Cultural, Fundació Caixa de Catalunya, Barcelona, 1992.

Arquitectura del Movimiento Moderno. Registro Do.co.mo.mo Ibérico 1925–1965, Fundación Mies van der Rohe, Barcelona, 1996.

Arxiu Històric COAC, *Fons G.A.T.C.P.A.C. Catàleg*, Col. legi d'Arquitectes de Catalunya, Barcelona, 1996.

Bastlund, Knud, *José Luis Sert: Architecture, City planning, Urban design*, Les Editions d'Architecture, Artemis, Zurich, New York and Washington, 1967; Thames and Hudson, London, 1967.

Bohigas, Oriol, *Arquitectura Española de la Segunda República*, Tusquets Editor, Barcelona, 1970.

Bohigas, Oriol, *Arquitectura i urbanisme durant la República*, Dopesa Dos, Barcelona, 1970.

Bohigas, Oriol, 'Josep Lluís Sert', in *Once arquitectos*, La Gaya Ciencia, Barcelona, 1976, pp. 189–206.

Borràs, María Lluïsa, *Sert, Arquitectura Mediterránea*, Ediciones Polígrafa, Barcelona, 1974.

Boston Society of Architects, *Architecture Boston*, Barre Publishing, Massachusetts, 1976.

Daniels, Mary F., *The Josep Lluís Sert Collection: a descriptive inventory of the archival holdings in the Frances Loeb Library, Harvard University Graduate School of Design*, Frances Loeb Library, Cambridge, Massachusetts, 1990.

Fargas i Falp, Josep Maria, *Llibertat i arquitectura*, Reial Acadèmia Catalana de Belles Arts de Sant Jordi, Barcelona, 1996.

Flores, Carlos, *Arquitectura Española Contemporánea*, Aguilar, Madrid, 1961, 1989.

Freixa, Jaume, *Josep Ll. Sert. Estudio Paperback*, Ed. Gustavo Gili, Barcelona, 1975.

Fullaondo, Juan Daniel and María Teresa Muñoz, *Historia de la Arquitectura Española*, Kain Editorial, Madrid, 1994.

G.A.T.E.P.A.C., *A.C./G.A.T.E.P.A.C 1931–1937 (Números 1–25)*, Ed. Gustavo Gili, Barcelona, 1975.

Hernández, F. Xavier, Mercé Tatjer and Mercé Vidal, *Passat i present de Barcelona: materials per a l'estudi del medi urbà*, vol. III, Publicacions Universitat de Barcelona, Barcelona, 1991.

Hernández-Cros, J. Emili, Gabriel Mora and Xavier Pouplana, *Arquitectura de Barcelona*, Col.legi d'Arquitectes de Barcelona, Barcelona, 1990.

Heyer, Paul, *Architects on architecture: new directions in America*, Waljer, New York, 1966; George O. Mc Leod, Toronto, 1966.

J. Ll. Sert i la Mediterrània, Col.legi d'Arquitectes de Catalunya, Barcelona, 1997.

Josep Lluís Sert. Arquitectura i disseny urbà. Treball en equip, Fundació Joan Miró, Centre d'estudis d'Art Contemporani, Barcelona, 1979; Ministerio de Cultura, Madrid, 1978.

Lement, Marie-José, *L'architecture fonctionelle: le projet de José-Luis Sert pour l'Ecole des Beaux-Arts de Besançon pose la question*, Les Belles Lettres, Paris, 1982 (dissertation).

Mackay, David, *Els utòpics moderns: la recerca de la identitat en el futur*, in *L'Arquitectura Moderna a Barcelona (1854–1939)*, Edicions 62, Barcelona, 1989, pp. 93–113; Anglo-Catalan Society, Sheffield, 1985.

Mannino, Edgardo and Ignacio Paricio, *J. Ll. Sert: Construcción y Arquitectura*, Ed. Gustavo Gili, Barcelona, 1983.

Pizza, Antonio, *Guía de la Arquitectura Moderna en Barcelona (1929–1936)*, Ed. del Serbal, Barcelona, 1996.

Rovira, Josep Maria, '"Can our cities survive?" Un texto de Josep Lluís Sert. Lectura desde intercambios epistolares', in *La tradición moderna*, COAC, Girona, 1996, pp. 111–13.

Rovira, Josep Maria, 'Le Corbusier y Josep Lluís Sert: momentos de una amistad', in José Lahuerta (ed.), *Le Corbusier y España*, Centre de Cultura Contemporània de Barcelona, Barcelona, 1997, pp. 95–99.

Sert: arquitecte a Nova York, Museu d'Art Contemporani de Barcelona, Actar, Barcelona, 1997.

Monographic issues

'Sert: Obras y proyectos 1929–1973', *Cuadernos de Arquitectura y Urbanismo*, 93, November–December 1972, pp. 1–44 (ed. by Emili Donato and Jaume Freixa; includes texts of four talks by Sert and presentation of thirty works).

'Sert', *Destino*, 1859, 19 May 1973, pp. 33–46 (articles by Oriol Bohigas, Maria Lluïsa Borràs, Jaume Freixa and Alexandre Cirici); also in *Temas de Arquitectura y Urbanismo*, 167, May 1973, pp. 3–17.

'Número especial: Arquitectura, J. Ll. Sert', *On Diseño*, 29, 1981, pp. 6–75 (article by Jaume Freixa, interview with J. Muñoz, text of a conference and presentation of nine works).

'Josep Lluís Sert: his work and ways', *Process: Architecture*, 34, December 1982, pp. 4–167 (articles by Josep Lluís Sert, Fumihiko Maki and Robert Campbell and presentation of twenty-five works).

'Homenatge a Josep Lluís Sert', *Boletín de la Comisión de Cultura del Colegio de Arquitectos de Galicia*, 13, April 1983, pp. 1–16.

'Josep Lluís Sert', *Q. Revista del Consejo Superior de los Colegios de Arquitectos de España*, 66, April 1983, pp. 18–56.

Magazine articles

Baldellou, Miguel Angel, 'Desarraigo y encuentro. Las arquitecturas del exilio', in *Arquitectura*, 303, 1995, pp. 16–19.

Barbey, Gilles, 'José Luís Sert 1902–1983', in *Werk, Bauen + Wohnen*, vol. 70/37, 6, June 1983, p. 18.

Barbey, Gilles, 'José Luís Sert (1902–1983)', in *Archithese*, vol. 13, 4, July–August 1983, pp. 69–70.

Bayón, Mariano, 'José Luís Sert (1902–1983). Un arquitecto para el futuro', in *Lápiz*, 6, May 1983, pp. 68–70.

Bohigas, Oriol, 'Josep Lluís Sert. Persistir i criticar', in *Serra d'Or*, 284, May 1983, pp. 13–15; also published as 'Perseverare e criticare. Oriol Bohigas ricorda J. L. Sert', in *Casabella*, vol. 47, 493, July–August 1983, pp. 30–31.

Bonet Castellana, Antonio, Antonio Fernández-Alba and Josep Corredor-Matheos, 'Josep Lluís Sert. El racionalismo mediterráneo', in *Arte y Cemento*, 1351, April 1983, pp. 46–68.

Boix, José, 'José Luís Sert', in *Cúpula*, 265, November 1983, pp. 655–60.

Borràs, Maria Lluissa, 'Homenaje a J. Ll. Sert en Canarias', in *Destino*, 1795, 26 February 1972, p. 42.

Cabrero, Félix, 'La llegada de los viejos y de los nuevos maestros: J. L. Sert, L. Krier', in *Temas de Arquitectura y Urbanismo*, 226, April 1979, pp. 9–16.

Campbell, Robert, 'Homage to a Catalonian. A personal view of A.I.A. Gold Medalist Josep Lluís Sert', in *A.I.A. Journal*, 2, February 1981, pp. 50–53.

Campbell, Robert, 'Josep Lluís Sert noted architect, Harvard dean', in *H.G.S.D. News*, vol. 11, 4, March–April 1983, p. 2.

Canty, Donald, 'The Universities: Tall new symbols of their significance', in *Architectural Forum*, 6, vol. 120, June 1964, pp. 114–23.

Català-Roca, Francesc, 'Archivo en blanco y negro: crónica gráfica de tres generaciones', in *Arquitectura Viva*, 12, May–June 1990, pp. 33–35.

Costa, Xavier, 'Un moderne à New York', in *L'Architecture d'Aujourd'hui*, 310, April 1997, p. 12.

Dean, Andrea O., 'The urbane and varied buildings of Sert, Jackson & Associates', in *A.I.A. Journal*, 6, vol. 66, May 1977, pp. 50–57.

Doménech i Girbau, Lluís, 'Situació de Josep Lluís Sert arquitecte', in *Serra d'Or*, 168, September 1973, pp. 25(577)–28(580).

Ed., 'Viviendas de alquiler en la c. Rosellón, Barcelona', in *A.C.*, 2, II quarter 1931, pp. 18–21.

Ed., 'Proyecto de urbanización de la Diagonal de Barcelona', in *A.C.*, 4, IV quarter 1931, pp. 22–27.

Ed., 'Estudio con vivienda en la cala S. Vicente', in *A.C.*, 6, II quarter 1932, p. 25.

Ed., 'Arquitectura Moderna. Ultima planta d'una casa de lloguer', in *D'Ací i D'Allà*, vol. XXI, 169, June 1932.

Ed., 'Casa Galobart – Barcelona. Vivienda para dos familias', in *A.C.*, 8, IV quarter 1932, pp. 18–20.

Ed., 'Despacho del Arq. J. Luis Sert – Barcelona', in *A.C.*, 8, IV quarter 1932, p. 30.

Ed., 'Neues Bauen in Spanien', in *Wasmuths Monatshefte für Bau-kunst*, vol. 16, 1932, pp. 85–88.

Ed., 'Proyecto de grupo escolar en la Avenida de Bogatell – Barcelona', in *A.C.*, 10, II quarter 1933, pp. 18–20.

Ed., 'Escuela Elemental en Palausolitar (Barcelona)', in *A.C.*, 10, II quarter 1933, p. 23.

Ed., 'Barcelona – Estudio de J. Luis Sert, arquitecto', in *A.C.*, 19, III quarter 1935, p. 23.

Ed., 'Vivienda en la azotea de una casa en el Ensanche de Barcelona', in *A.C.*, 19, III quarter 1935, pp. 43–44.

Ed., 'Local para la "Unión de Cooperadores de Gavà"', in *A.C.*, 23–24, III–IV quarter 1936, p. 19.

Ed., 'Hotel for Curaçao, N.W.I.', in *Interiors*, vol. 106, September 1946, pp. 76–81.

Ed., 'Consideraciones generales sobre el plan de Tumaco elaborado por el Departamento de Edificios Nacionales del Ministerio de Obras Públicas', in *Proa*, 2, September 1946, pp. 12–19.

Ed., 'A remodeled dairy building on a Long Island pond by Architect Jose Sert has the colorful elegance of a Mondrian in Architecture', in *Architectural Forum*, vol. 93, 1, July 1950, pp. 96–98.

Ed., 'Five civic centers in South America. Puerto Ordaz and Ciudad Piar, Venezuela', in *Architectural Record*, vol. 114, 2, August 1953, pp. 121–36.

Ed., 'Architekturphilosophie im Wandel', in *Der Aufbau*, vol. 10, 2–3, February–March 1955, pp. 66–67.

Ed., 'Parasols of Sert', in *The Architectural Review*, vol. 123, 736, May 1958, p. 295.

Ed., 'José Luis Sert', in *Der Aufbau*, vol. 13, June 1958, pp. 234–36.

Ed., 'Nouveau bâtiment de l'Université de Harvard à Cambridge. Holyoke Center. Diverses réalisations aux Etats-Unis et à l'étranger', in *L'Architecture d'Aujourd'hui*, 113–14, April–May 1964, pp. 106–09.

Ed., 'Six houses from abroad', in *Architectural Record*, vol. 139, 1, January 1966, pp. 149–54 (152).

Ed., 'I.N.T.E.R.A.M.A. exposition hailed as "full-scale experiment in urban design". The Special Projection Theater "Area"', in *Architectural Record*, vol. 141, 3, March 1967, pp. 40–44 (41).

Ed., 'Great builders of the 1960's. José Luis Sert', in *J. A. The Japan Architect*, vol. 45, 7–165 July 1970, pp. 55–78 (74).

Ed., 'Carmel de la Paix "Cluny"', in *L'Architecture d'Aujourd'hui*, 156, June–July 1971, p. XXXVIII.

Ed., 'Distinción francesa para J. Luís Sert', in *Gazeta del Arte*, 48, 30 September 1975, p. 19.

Ed., 'Happy birthday, José Luis Sert', in *H.G.S.D. News*, vol. 6, 1, October 1977, pp. 1–2.

Ed., 'Arquitectura y urbanismo de Josep Lluís Sert, en la Fundación Joan Miró', in *On*, 1, marzo 1979, p. 44.

Ed., 'Sert named A.I.A.'s 42nd Gold Medalist', in *A.I.A. Journal*, vol. 70, 1, January 1981, pp. 13–20.

Ed., 'The A.I.A. presents 1981 Gold Medal to Josep Lluis Sert', in *Architectural Record*, vol. 169, 1, January 1981, p. 35.

Ed., 'Sert ha muerto (1902–1983)', in *Arquitectura*, 240, vol. 64, 240, January–February 1983, p. 8.

Ed., 'Sert ha muerto', in *Boletín del Colegio Oficial de Arquitectos de Asturias*, 105, March 1983.

Ed., 'Josep Lluis Sert dies aged 79', in *Building Design*, 634, 25 March 1983, p. 5.

Ed., 'È morto José Luís Sert', in *L'Architettura cronache e storia*, vol. 29, 7 (333), July 1983, p. 489.

Ferrer, David, 'Las últimas obras de J. Ll. Sert en Barcelona. Roda el món i torna al Born', in *Arquitectura Bis*, 6, March 1975, pp. 2–6.

Flores, Carlos, 'Un arquitecto en un libro: José Luís Sert', in *Hogar y Arquitectura*, 74, January–February 1968, pp. 65–76.

Furió, Vicenç, 'Josep Lluís Sert', in *El Ciervo*, 387–88, May–June 1983, p. 35.

Garcés Feliu, Eugenio, 'Josep Lluís Sert en la hora de su muerte', in *Arq*, 8, November 1983, pp. 22–26.

Gelabert, Daniel, 'Un arquitecte català als Estats Units: Josep Lluís Sert', in *Serra d'Or*, 7, July 1965, pp. 29(525)–33(529).

Gifreda, Màrius, 'Quatres artistes de viatge', in *Mirador*, Barcelona, 30 July 1930.

Giralt-Miracle, Daniel, 'Josep Lluís Sert, el G.A.T.C.P.A.C. y Barcelona (1)', in *Destino*, Barcelona, 30 February 1971.

Giralt-Miracle, Daniel, 'Josep Lluís Sert y su obra de Barcelona al mundo (2)', in *Destino*, Barcelona, 6 March 1971.

Gueguen, Pierre, 'Jose Luís Sert, urbaniste et plasticien', in *Art et Architecture d'Aujourd'hui*, 15, December 1957, pp. 47–65.

Hernández-Cros, J. Emili, 'Cronología de la obra de los socios directores del G.A.T.C.P.A.C.', in *Cuadernos de Arquitectura y Urbanismo*, 94, January–February 1973, pp. 30–54.

Hernández-Cros, J. Emili, J.C. Theilacker and J.F. Chico, 'Cuatro proyectos no realizados. 1. J. Lluís Sert: Parvulario en Viladecans (1935). 2. J. Lluís Sert: Escuelas Graduadas en Martorell (1935). 3. J. Lluís Sert – J. Torres Clavé: Hospital para tuberculosos en Barcelona (1936). 4. J. Lluís Sert – J.B. Subirana – J. Torres Clavé: C.U.I. (1934)', in *Cuadernos de Arquitectura y Urbanismo*, 94, January–February 1973, pp. 24–27.

Herrera, José Maria, 'Josep Lluís Sert: la profundidat poética de la casa', in *Reüll*, 2, March–June 1983, pp. 1–2.

Holroyd, Jeoffrey, 'The scope of the architect', in *Architect & Building News*, 9 April 1953, p. 419.

Mackay, David, 'Noticiario. ¿Cómo se trata a nuestra arquitectura?', in *Cuadernos de Arquitectura y Urbanismo*, 42, IV quarter 1960, p. 48.

Moltke, Willo von, 'Josep Lluís Sert. 1902–1983', in *Progressive Architecture*, vol. 64, 6, June 1983, p. 27.

Monaco, Antonello, 'Sert e Barcellona', in *Domus*, 732, November 1991, pp. XI–XVI.

Monegal, Ferran, 'Sobre Sert', in *Destino*, 1912, May 1974, p. 51.

Monteys, Xavier, 'Una actitud de modernidad', in *2C Construcción de la Ciudad*, 15–16, May 1980, pp. 58–61; the article is completed by Ed., 'Hospital en el valle de Hébron', pp. 54–57.

Mumford, Eric, 'C.I.A.M. Urbanism after the Athens Charter', in *Planning Perspectives*, vol. 7, 4, October 1992, pp. 391–417.

Pernas Galí, Francesc, 'Sert o no Sert?', in *Batik*, 48, March 1979, pp. 8–9.

Ribalta, Mariona and Francesc Roca, 'Bibliografía del G.A.T.C.P.A.C., Nota sobre la bibliografía del G.A.T.C.P.A.C, Notas críticas a una bibliografía sumaria del G.A.T.C.P.A.C y de su época', in *Cuadernos de Arquitectura y Urbanismo*, 90, July–August 1972, pp. 48–50, 50, 51.

Rovira, Josep Maria, 'Architecture and ideology in Catalonia', 1901–1951, in *A.A. Files*, 14, spring 1987, pp. 62–68.

Rubert, Maria, 'Cinco esquemas de ciudad funcionalista: los planes de Josep Lluís Sert en América Latina', in *Arquitecturas Bis*, 49, March 1985, pp. 8–12.

Sartoris, Alberto, 'Homenaje a José Luís Sert', in *Arquitectura*, 137, May 1970, pp. 49–53.

Sartoris, Alberto, 'Recuerdo a José Luís Sert', in *Arquitectura*, 156, December 1971, pp. 29–32.

Sartoris, Alberto, 'Memoràndum para el conocimento de José Luís Sert', in *Cimal*, 15, September 1982, pp. 9–12.

Soubriet, Teresa, 'Sert, una arquitectura viva', in *Bellas Artes*, 60, II quarter 1978, pp. 25–30.

Torres Clavé, Josep, 'Carta d'en Torres Clavé a en Sert', in *Cuadernos de Arquitectura y Urbanismo*, 140, 1980, pp. 44–45.

Vélez, Antonio, 'Una ventana indiscreta sobre el Racionalismo. Comentarios al libro *J. Ll. Sert. Construcción y Arquitectura* de E. Mannino e I. Paricio', in *Croquis*, 9–10, May–June 1983, pp. 46–49.

Victorino Alvárez, Fernando, 'José Luís Sert 1902–1983', in *Summa*, 187, May 1983, pp. 18–19.

Zabalbeascoa, Anatxu, 'Sert en Nueva York: la modernidad humanizada', in *Arquitectura Viva*, 53, March–April 1997, pp. 70–72.

Newspaper articles

Baltasar, Basilio, 'Joan Miró ha perdido a su gran amigo', in *El País. Artes*, 19 March 1983, p. 4.

Bassegoda Nonell, Joan, 'Un arquitecto universal', in *La Vanguardia*, 18 March 1983, p. 6.

Bonet Castellana, Antoni, 'Sert en Cataluña, antes de su exilio', in *La Vanguardia*, 16 marzo 1983, p. 19.

Bohigas, Oriol, 'La interpretación crítica de la tradición', in *La Vanguardia*, Dijous, 17 March 1983, p. 45.

Corea, Mario, 'La etapa americana: un habitat merjor', in *La Vanguardia*, Dijous, 17 March 1983, p. 45.

Donato, Emili, 'Notas para una historia del racionalismo arquitectónico español', in *Diario de Barcelona. Extra*, 13 June 1969, pp. 17–18.

Duplàs, Cristina, 'J. Ll. Sert ...', in *Avui*, 5 January 1982, p. 29.

Ed., 'Sert, Ainaud de Lasarte y Alicia de la Rocha recibieron la Medalla de Oro de Bellas Artes', in *La Vanguardia*, 29 June 1982, p. 11.

Ed., 'José Luis Sert falleciò anoche', in *La Vanguardia*, 16 March 1983, p. 16.

Ed., 'Morí l'arquitecte de la Fundació Miró de Montjuïc. L'arquitectura mundial perd Sert', in *Avui*, 17 March 1983, p. 31.

Ed., 'Sert adiós', in *La Vanguardia*, 17 March 1983, pp. 38, 44–45.

Ed., 'Barcelona despidió a Sert en Sta. Maria del Mar', in *La Vanguardia*, 19 March 1983, p. 31.

Gelabert, Daniel, 'José Luis Sert. Arquitecto y urbanista', in *Diario de Barcelona. Extra*, 13 June 1969, pp. 13–15.

Giralt-Miracle, Daniel, 'L'escultor, Catalunya i el món', in *Avui*, Dijous, 17 March 1983, p. 34.

Mateo, Josep Lluís, 'El joven Sert', in *La Vanguardia*, Dijous, 17 March 1983, p. 45.

Miravitlles, Jaume, 'El petit-gran home, Josep Lluís Sert', in *La Vanguardia*, 3 May 1983, p. 49.

Moragas i Gallissà, Antoni de, 'Una gran aventura del moviment artístic', in *Avui*, Dijous, 17 March 1983, p. 32.

Moragas i Gallissà, Antoni de, 'Fe en el progreso', in *La Vanguardia*, Dijous, 17 March 1983, p. 45.

Oliveras Sanitier, Jordi, 'Un capítulo sobresaliente de nuestra vanguardia', in *El País. Artes*, 19 March 1983.

Parcerisas, Pilar, 'El seu llegat a Barcelona', in *Avui*, 17 March 1983, p. 33.

Permanyer, Lluís, 'Fins ara, Sert', in *La Vanguardia*, 17 March 1983, p. 44.

Puig, Arnau, 'La recerca d'una arquitectura catalana', in *Avui*, 17

March 1983, pp. 31–32.

Pujol, Jordi, 'Va manifestar la fe en el nostre poble', in *Avui*, 17 March 1983, p. 32.

Solà-Morales, Ignasi de, 'El corazón de la ciudad', in *La Vanguardia*, 17 March 1983, p. 45.

Uberquoi, Marie-Claire, 'Tres figures de l'arquitectura contemporània eivissenca', in *Avui. Art*, 13 October 1983, p. IV.

WRITINGS ON SERT'S WORKS

Hotel on a Beach
Benet, Rafael, 'Hotel en una platja. Salutació a Le Corbusier', in *La Gaseta de les Arts*, 1, June 1928, pp. 16–17.

Ed., 'Arquitectura mediterránea. Proyecto de hotel en la playa', in *Arquitectura*, 114, October 1928, pp. 319–21.

Summer Resort Town in Levante
Ed., 'La nova arquitectura a Catalunya', in *La Gaseta de les Arts*, 9, May 1929, pp. 111–18.

Ed., 'Casas de verano para la costa levantina', in *Arquitectura*, 122, July 1929, p. 278.

Ed., 'Pueblo de veraneo en la costa de Levante', in *A.C.*, 7, III quarter 1932, p. 42.

Gifreda, Márius, 'Els arquitectes joves', in *Mirador*, 13, 25 April; 14, 2 May; 15, 9 May 1929.

Sacs, Joan, 'Arquitectura nova. Exposició de projectes arquitectònics', in *Mirador*, 13, 25 April 1929.

Apartment Building on Carrer Muntaner
Ed., 'Viviendas de alquiler en la calle Muntaner', in *A.C.*, 4, IV quarter 1931, pp. 16–19.

Moneo, Rafael, 'Si te dicen que caí ...', in *Arquitecturas Bis*, 6, March 1975, pp. 10–11.

Pérez i Sánchez, Miquel, *El*

G.A.T.C.P.A.C. Casa al carrer Muntaner 1930–1931, Biblioteca ETSAB, 1981.

Roqueta, Santiago, 'Visita n° 7: Casa al carrer Muntaner 342', in Miquel Pérez i Sánchez (ed.), *Vint-i-cinc anys d'arquitectura barcelonina 1914–1938. Cicle de visites 1981*, COAC, Barcelona, 1981, pp. 195–217.

Casa Duclós
Isac, Ángel, 'Vanguardia al margen, Andalucía años treinta', in *3ZU*, 4, June 1995, pp. 34–35.

'La obra olvidada: Casa Duclós en Sevilla, 1930', in *Hogar y Arquitectura*, 76, May–June 1968, pp. 57–64.

'Veinte obras del Movimiento Moderno en Andalucía', in *PH Boletín del Instituto Andaluz del Patrimonio Histórico*, 15, 1996.

Casa Bloc
Carol, Màrius, 'La Generalitat está dispuesta a financiar la restauración de la Casa Bloc, de Sert', in *El País*, 19 March 1983, p. 15.

Cia, Blanca, 'La Generalitat invierte 417 millones en la rehabilitació de la Casa Bloc de Sant Andreu', *El País. Cataluña*, 27 June 1998, p. 4.

Leroy, Aline, 'Le rivincite del moderno', in *Area*, 7, September 1991, pp. 32–39.

Ed., 'Grupo de viviendas obreras en Barcelona', in *A.C.*, 11, III quarter 1933, pp. 22–26.

Ed., 'Casa Bloc', in *2C Construcción de la Ciudad*, 15–16, May 1980, pp. 48–53.

Ed., 'Casa Bloc, Barcelona, 1934–1936', in *A&V. Arquitectura y Vivienda*, 56, November–December 1995, pp. 46–47.

Mackay, David, 'Noticiario. ¿Cómo se trata a nuestra arquitectura?', in *A&V. Arquitectura y vivienda*, 11, 1987, pp. 20–23.

Permanyer, Lluís, 'La Casa Bloc de Sert se degrada en Sant Andreu', in *La Vanguardia*, 2 June 1991, p. 44.

Postico i Soler, Núria and Rosa Maria Murtra i Bellpuig, 'Un nou paissatge urbà: la Casa Bloc', in *Revista Catalana de Geografia*, 0, May 1985, pp. 22–30.

Tarragó, Salvador, 'Reivindicació de la Casa Bloc', in *Cuadernos de Arquitectura y Urbanismo*, 140, 1980, pp. 41–43.

Torres Clavé, Josep, 'La transformació del concepte de l'estatge', in *Nova Ibèria*, 2, February 1937; Idem, in *Cuadernos de Arquitectura y Urbanismo*, 90, July–August 1972, p. 41.

City of Leisure and Vacations
Donato, Emili, 'Cronología (y bibliografia) del proyecto de la C.R.V.', in *Cuadernos de Arquitectura y Urbanismo*, 94, January–February 1973, p. 20; Idem, in *Ciudad y Territorio*, January–March 1971, p. 4.

Ed., 'La casa para el fin de semana (Week-end), La ciudad de reposo que necesita Barcelona', in *A.C.*, 7, III quarter 1932, pp. 18–23, 24–31.

Ed., 'Dos tipos de vivienda mínima para la playa', in *A.C.*, 8, IV quarter 1932, pp. 21–22.

Ed., 'Expansión de la ciudad de reposo de Barcelona', in *A.C.*, 13, I quarter, 1934, pp. 23–28.

Ed., 'Strandproject voor de stad. Barcelona', in *De 8 en Opbouw*, 12, 9 June 1934, pp. 97–98.

G.A.T.C.P.A.C., 'Ha estat constituida la Ciutat de Repòs i de Vacances..., Elementos del proyecto de la Ciutat de Repòs i de Vacances, Breve estudio económico', in *Cuadernos de Arquitectura y Urbanismo*, 94, January–February 1973, pp. 7–13, 14–19, 21–22.

G.A.T.E.P.A.C., 'Ingezonden door de katelaansche Afd. van de Groep G.A.T.E.P.A.C.', in *De 8 en Opbouw*, 12, 9 June 1934, pp. 99–100.

Roca, Francesc, 'Noticia de la Cooperativa de la Ciutat de Repòs i de Vacances', in *Cuadernos de Arquitectura y Urbanismo*, 94, 1973, p. 23.

Sambricio, Carlos, 'La Ciutat de

Repòs, variaciones sobre un tema', in *A&V. Arquitectura y Vivienda*, 11, 1987, pp. 16–19.

Torres Clavé, Josep, 'Els nou procediments de l'urbanisme actual', in *Higia. Revista d'higiene i divulgació sanitària*; Idem, in *Cuadernos de Arquitectura y Urbanismo*, 94, January–February 1973, p. 6.

Macià Plan

Candilis, Georges, 'Problème d'une ville: Barcelone', in *L'Architecture d'Aujourd'hui*, 88, February–March 1960, pp. 58–61.

Ed., 'Urbanización de la Barcelona futura', in *A.C.*, 1, I quarter 1931, pp. 20–21.

Ed., 'Ensayo de un típo mínimo de viviendas obreras, Grupo de viviendas obreras', in *A.C.*, 11, III quarter 1933, pp. 19–21, 21–26.

Ed., 'Notas previas a un estudio urbanístico sobre Barcelona, Barcelona. Esquemas para el proyecto de conjunto, Estudio de viviendas mínimas para Barcelona. Arquitectos: Le Corbusier y Pierre Jeanneret', in *A.C.* 13, I quarter 1934, pp. 14–20, 21–23, 29–31.

G.A.T.C.P.A.C., 'Copia de la instancia presentada por el G.A.T.C.P.A.C. al Ayuntamiento (1933), La urbanització de la Barcelona futura', in *Cuadernos de Arquitectura y Urbanismo*, 90, July–August 1972, pp. 37, 38–40; Idem, in «Mirador», Barcelona, May 1932.

Marzà, Fernando, *Le Corbusier i Barcelona*, Fundació Caixa de Catalunya, Barcelona 1988.

Roca, Francesc, 'El G.A.T.C.P.A.C. y la crisis urbana de lo años 30', in *Cuadernos de Arquitectura y Urbanismo*, 90, July–August 1972, pp. 18–23.

Roca, Francesc, *El Pla Macià*, La Magrana, Barcelona, 1977.

Tarragó, Salvador, 'El "Pla Macià" o la "Nova Barcelona" (1931–1938)', in *Cuadernos de Arquitectura y Urbanismo*, 90, July–August 1972, pp. 24–36.

Tarragó, Salvador, 'El Plan Macià, síntesis del trabajo del G.A.T.C.P.A.C. para Barcelona', in *2C Construcción de la Ciudad*, 15–16, May 1980, pp. 68–85.

Roca Jewellery Shop

Ed., 'Joyería Roca. Barcelona', in *A.C.*, n.14, II quarter 1934, pp. 14–17.

Ed., 'Josep Lluís Sert (de G.A.T.C.P.A.C.). Joieria a Barcelona, 1933', in *D'Ací i D'Allà*, winter 1934.

Ed., 'Roca Jewellery', in *Architectural Record*, June 1937.

Mateo, Josep Lluís, 'Barcelona 1934. Una obra de interiorismo de Josep Lluís Sert', in *JRJ. Revista de joyería, arte y cultura*, January 1988, pp. 44–51.

Weekend Houses in El Garraf

Ed., 'Pequeñas casas para "fin de semana"', in *A.C.*, 19, III quarter 1935, pp. 33–42.

Ed., 'Casas para fin de semana en España', in *Revista de Arquitectura*, 30, July 1945, pp. 276–82.

Central Dispensary for Tubercolosis

Corea, Mario and Francisco Gallardo-Bravo, 'Arquitectura sobre arquitectura', in *On Diseño*, 161, March 1995, pp. 152–53.

Corea, Mario, Francisco Gallardo-Bravo and Edgardo Mannino, 'Aprendiendo de J. LL. Sert', in *Diseño Interior*, 23, March 1993, pp. 62–63.

Corea, Mario, Francisco Gallardo-Bravo and Edgardo Mannino, 'Rehabilitación del Dispensario Central Antituberculoso de Barcelona', in *On Diseño*, 161, 1995, pp. 172–79.

Ed., 'El Dispensario Antituberculoso de la calle Torres Amat 1934–38', in *Cuadernos de Arquitectura y Urbanismo*, 40, II quarter 1960, pp. 6(270)–11(275).

Ed., 'Sanar a un sanatorio', in *Revista Técnica de la Construcción*, 20, January 1984, pp. 56–60.

Ed., 'Dispensary for Tuberculosi, Barcelona', in *A+U. Architecture and Urbanism*, 7 (166), July 1984, pp. 90–97.

Ed., 'Equipments. Dispensaire de Sert à Barcelone', in *Le Moniteur Architecture AMC*, 42–43, June–July 1993, p. 66–69.

Fort, Josep Maria, 'El Dispensario Antituberculoso de Sert. Recuperación de un ejemplo paradigmático de la modernidad catalana: Mario Corea, Edgardo Mannino y Francisco Gallardo', in *Diseño Interior*, 23, March 1993, pp. 64–75.

Frampton, Kenneth, 'The antitubercolosis Center of Barcelona', in *On Diseño*, 161, March 1995, pp. 180–81.

Grupo 2C, 'Dispensario Central Antitubercoloso', in *2C Construcción de la Ciudad*, 15–16, 1980, pp. 62–67.

Leroy, Aline, 'Le rivincite del moderno', in *Area*, n.7, September 1991, pp. 32–39.

Leroy, Aline, 'Luogo del risanamento. Restauro e progetto', in *Area*, 16, December 1993, pp. 34–41.

Pizza, Antonio, *Dispensario antituberculoso de Barcelona, 1933–1937*, Colegio de Arquitectos de Almería, Almería, 1993.

Tarragó, Salvador, 'Visita n° 8. Dispensari antituberculós', in Miquel Pérez i Sánchez, *Vint-i-cinc anys d'arquitectura barcelonina 1914–1938. Cicle de visites 1981*, COAC, Barcelona, 1981, pp. 218–45.

Torres, Raimon, 'Dispensario Central Antituberculoso. Notas sobre una restauración', in *Arquitectura*, 303, III quarter 1995, pp. 85–90.

Pavilion of the Spanish Republic at the Paris World's Fair, 1937

Art contra la guerra. Entorn del Pavelló Espanyol a L'Exposició Internacional de París de 1937, Ajuntament de Barcelona, Àrea de Cultura, Publicacions, Barcelona, 1986.

Blanton Freedberg, Catherine, *The Spanish Pavilion at the Paris World's Fair*, Garland, New York and London, 1986.

Busquets, Jordi, 'La "joya" de la República: Barcelona reconstruye el Pabellón que representó a España en la Exposición de 1937 en París', in *El País*, 17 May 1991, p. 42.

Ed., 'Le Pavillon de l'Espagne. Architects: Luis Lacasa e J.L. Sert', in *L'Architecture d'Aujourdhui*, 8, August 1937, pp. 22–23.

Ed., 'The Spanish Pavillion at the Paris exhibition; architects, J.L. Sert & L. La casa, French consultant, M. Abella', in *Architect & Building News*, 151, August 1937, pp. 193–95.

Ed., 'Spanish Pavilion. J.L. Sert & L. A. Casa, Architects, Pavilion Floor Plans Paris Fair 1937', in *Architectural Record*, vol. 82, 4, October 1937, p. 91.

Ed., 'Le Pavillon de l'Espagne à l'Exposition, 1937', in *Cahiers d'Art*, 8–10, 1937, pp. 283–89.

Ed., 'El Ministerio de Cultura intenta reconstruir el pabellón español de la Exposición Universal de París en 1937', in *El País*, 2 January 1986.

'El Pabellón de la República Española en la Exposición Internacional de París en 1937', in *España. Vanguardia artística y realidad social 1936–1976*, Ed. Gustavo Gili, Barcelona, 1976.

Espada, Arcadi, 'El Pabellón de la República se abrirá sin el Rey ni el «Guernica», contra el deseo de sus promotores', in *El País*, 8 July 1992, p. 21.

Espinet, Miquel, Antoni Ubach and J. Maria Hernández-León, *Reconstrucción del pabellón español en la Exposición Universal de París de 1937*, in *On Diseño*, 140, 1993, pp. 106–19.

Espinet, Miquel and Antoni Ubach, 'Modernes vergegenwärtig. Du moderne remis en mémoire', in

Werk, Bauen + Wohnen, 12, December 1993, pp. 22–35.

Martín, Fernando, *El Pabellón Español en la Exposición Universal de París en 1937*, Servicio de Publicaciones de la Universidad de Sevilla, Sevilla, 1983.

Muñoz, Alfonso, 'Lo efímero permanente. El pabellón de 1937: de París a Barcelona', in *Arquitectura Viva*, 25, July–August 1992, pp. 42–45.

Pabellón Español: Exposición Internacional de París 1937, Ministerio de Cultura, Dirección General de Bellas Artes y Archivos: Centro de Arte Reina Sofía, Madrid, 1987.

Pérez Escolano, Victor, 'Los planos del Pabellón español en la Exposición de 1937 de París', in *Jano*, 62, December 1978, pp. 32–37.

Permanyer, Lluís, 'Reconstruir en Barcelona aquel mítico pabellón del "Guernica"', in *La Vanguardia*, Dimarts, 21 June 1988.

Rovira, Josep Maria, 'D'un roig encés ...', in *DiVersa. Revista Universitaria de Arte y Arquitectura*, 2, November 1994, pp. 24–25.

Sainz, Jorge, 'Reconstruir un mito: el pabellón de 1937, de París a Barcelona', in *Arquitectura Viva*, 21, November–December 1991, pp. 49–51.

Villamor, Miguel, 'El modelo infográfico del pabellón. Su viva imagen', in *Arquitectura Viva*, 25, July–August, 1992, pp. 46–47.

Ratio Structures

Ed., 'Prefabrication: Ratio Structures', in *Architectural Forum*, vol. 79, 6, December 1943, pp. 83–88.

U.S. War Production Board Office of Production Research and Development, *Modern designs for prefabricated and desmountable buildings*, War Production Board, Washington, 1944.

Cidade dos Motores

Ed., 'Une cité nouvelle au Brésil: Cidade dos Motores', in *Techniques et Architecture*, vol. 6, 7–8, 1946, pp. 363–69.

Ed., 'Cidade dos motores', Brasil, in *Pencil Points*, vol. 27, September 1946, pp. 52–73.

Ed., 'Brasil edifica una nueva ciudad', in *Revista de Arquitectura*, vol. 31, October 1946, pp. 387–408.

Le Corbusier, 'La Cidade dos Motores', in *L'Architecture d'Aujourd'hui*, 13–14, September 1947.

Two Cities. Planning in North and South America, Museum of Modern Art, New York, June 1947.

Sert's House in Locust Valley, Long Island

Ed., 'Recipe for remodelling... a two-part house (Long Island, N. Y.)', in *House and Garden*, 101, January 1952, pp. 26–31.

Ed., 'Studio-house; Locust Valley, New York', in *Progressive Architecture*, 33, August 1952, pp. 95–101.

Ed., 'La casa di campagna di un architetto', in *Domus*, 275, November 1952, pp. 15–18.

Ed., 'Casa-Estudio en Locust Valley, N. Y.', in *Arquitectura México*, 41, March 1953, pp. 49–54.

Ed., 'La maison d'un architecte à New York', in *L'Architecture d'Aujoud'hui*, 49, October 1953, pp. 47–49.

Ed., 'Casa Sert en Locust Valley', in *Arquitecturas Bis*, 44, July 1983, pp. 30–31.

Winkler, Robert, 'Jose L. Sert', in *Architects' Homes*, Verlag Girsberger, Zurich, 1955, pp. 196–99.

Joan Miró's Studio

Ed., 'L'atelier du peintre Miró à Palma de Mayorque', in *Art et Architecture d'Aujourd'hui*, 15, December 1957, pp. 44–49.

Ed., 'José Luis Sert. Studio for Joan Miró, Mallorca', in *Architectural Record*, January 1958, pp. 138–40.

Ed., 'Taller del pintor Miró en Palma de Mallorca', in *Cuadernos de Arquitectura y Urbanismo*, 33, III quarter 1958, pp. 29–31.

García Herrera, Adela, 'De Harvard a Son Abrines: Miró, Sert y Moneo en Palma', in *Arquitectura Viva*, 27, November–December 1992, pp. 68–69.

Pons, Josep, '*Revista d'Art* estudia com Sert va construir el taller de Joan Miró a Mallorca', in *Avui*, 17 January 1991.

Ruthven, Malise, 'Miró on Majorca: remembering the artist at his studio designed by José Luis Sert', in *Architectural Digest*, vol. 49, 1, January 1992, pp. 30, 32–35.

'Taller per a Joan Miró', in *D'A*, 5–6, November 1990, COAB monographies.

United States Embassy, London

Ed., 'U.S. Embassy for London', in *Architectural Forum*, April 1956, pp. 138–45 (143).

Shear, John Knox, 'Competition for U.S. Chancery Building, London', in *Architectural Record*, vol. 119, 4, April 1956, p. 220.

United States Embassy, Baghdad

Alexandrian, Sarane, 'L'ambassade des USA à Bagdad', in *L'Œil*, 110, February 1964, pp. 26–31.

Ed., 'USA abroad', in *Architectural Forum*, vol. 107, 6, December 1957, pp. 114–23.

Ed., 'Ambassade américaine à Bagdad, Irak', in *Aujord'hui Art et Architecture*, 15, December 1957, pp. 50–57.

Ed., 'American Embassy at Baghdad', in *Architectural Record*, January 1958, pp. 126–33.

Ed., 'New work of Sert, Jackson and Gourley. United States Embassy, Baghdad', in *Architectural Record*, vol. 131, 5, May 1962, pp. 140–46.

Ed., 'Ambasciata degli Stati Uniti a Bagdad', in *Casabella Continuità*, 267, September 1962, pp. 16–23.

Havana Pilot Plan

Ed., 'Palais Présidentiel, La Havane', in *Aujourd'hui Art et Architecture*, 15,

December 1957, pp. 60–65.

Ed., 'Presidential Palace of Cuba, Havana', in *Architectural Record*, 1, January 1958, pp. 134–37.

Maribona, Armando, 'Dependen de la planificación el bienestar y riqueza de los pueblos', in *Arquitectura*, vol. 21, October 1953, pp. 428–29.

Sert's House in Cambridge

Donato, Emili, 'In memoriam. La casa de Josep Lluís Sert en Harvard', in *Arquitectura*, 241, March–April 1983, pp. 10–12.

Ed., 'Cloistered privacy in a busy street', in *House&Home*, October 1958, p. 87.

Ed., 'La maison de J. L. Sert', in *L'Œil*, 50, February 1959, pp. 40–45.

Ed., 'Habitation de l'architecte José Lluís Sert à Cambridge, Massachusetts', in *L'Architecture d'Aujourdhui*, 86, October–November 1959, pp. 2–3.

Ed., 'Vivienda en Cambridge', in *Revista Informes de la Construcción*, 121, May 1960, pp. 161–78.

Ed., 'Una casa con patio', in *Arquitectura*, n. 20, August 1960, pp. 7–13.

Ed., 'Wohnhaus in Cambridge /USA', in *Baumeister*, 1, January 1961, pp. 1–2.

Ed., 'Profeta en su tierra. La Casa Sert de Cambridge en Bellaterra. Arquitecto: Jaume Freixa', in *A&V. Arquitectura y Vivienda*, 11, 1987, pp. 58–61.

Freixa, Jaume, 'La reinvención del patio por Josep Lluís Sert', in *DPA Documents de Projectes d'Arquitectura. Patio y casa*, 13, December 1997, pp. 36–45.

Gourley, Ronald, 'A synthesis for good living', in *Architectural Record*, vol. 125, n. 6, May 1959, pp. 67–75.

Oshima, Ken Tadashi, 'The modern house in the postwar period. 2. Rural urbanity. The Sert house', in *A&U. Architecture and Urbanism*, 2 (318), March 1997, pp. 122–25.

Peter, John, 'A city house with perfect privacy', in *Look Magazine*, vol. 23, 2, 9 June 1959, pp. 58–62.

Holyoke Center, Harvard University

Canty, Donald, 'Harvard completes a course in urban design', in *Architectural Forum*, vol. 126, 1, January–February 1967, pp. 64–77.

Ed., 'Four current projects in the News. Harvard square development, Cambridge, Mass.', in *Architectural Record*, vol. 123, 7, July 1958, p. 149.

Ed., 'New work of Sert, Jackson and Gourley. Holyoke Center: Design in relation to site', in *Architectural Record*, vol. 131, 5, May 1962, pp. 134–37.

Ed., 'Holyoke Center: Uffici e centro medico per la Harvard University, Cambridge, Massachusetts', in *Casabella Continuità*, 267, September 1962, pp. 4–9.

Ed., 'Evaluation: "Gray elephant" in Harvard Square: Holyoke Center, most successful of the university's first generation highrises', in *A.I.A. Journal*, 1, January 1979, pp. 48–51.

Harvard University Planning Office, *Harvard University. 1960: an inventory for planning*, Harvard University, Cambridge, Massachusetts, 1960.

Knight, Roy, 'The Holyoke Center: a few comments', in *Connections*, Tardor, 1966, pp. 4–8.

Boston University Campus

Anderson, Stanford, 'Universities High-Rise on the Charles River', in John Donat (ed.), *World Architecture 3*, Studio Vista, London, 1966, pp. 58–62.

Ed., 'Integrated campus for Boston University's Landlocked Site', in *Architectural Record*, vol. 135, 5, May 1964, pp. 161–70.

Ed., 'Nouveaux bâtiments de l'Université de Boston', in *L'Architecture d'Aujourdhui*, 122, September–November 1965, pp. 36–39.

Ed., 'Universität Boston/USA', in *Baumeister*, 64, April 1967, pp. 424–29.

George Sherman Union University Student Center:
Dunhill, Priscilia G., 'The George Sherman Union', in *Interiors*, vol. 124, 1, August 1964, pp. 81–83.

Mugar Library:
Ed., 'Terraces on the Charles', in *Architectural Forum*, vol. 124, 3, April 1966, pp. 48–49.

Ed., 'A major library fullfills the master plan for Boston University's Central Campus', in *Architectural Record*, vol. 143, 1, January 1968, pp. 125–28.

Raymond, Betty, 'In Boston: Hans Kriek's Furniture and interiors for Boston University's Mugar Library. Seats for learning', in *Interiors*, vol. 126, 9, April 1967, pp. 140–43.

Central campus: Law and Education Tower, Pappas Law Library, Auditorium:
Anderson, Stanford, 'Law and education tower, Boston', in John Donat (ed.), *World Architecture 3*, Studio Vista, London, 1966, pp. 62–67.

Ed., 'José Luís Sert's Tower for Boston University', in *Interiors*, vol. 124, 5, December 1964, pp. 72–73.

Ed., 'University Campus, Boston', in *Architectural Design*, vol. XXXV, 8, August 1965, pp. 383–88.

Marguerite and Aimé Maeght Foundation, Museum of Contemporary Art

Allen, Gerald, 'Museums. A portfolio of designs for display. Addition to the galleries of the Marguerite and Aimé Maeght Foundation St-Paul-de-Vence. A "meeting place for the Arts" grows', in *Architectural Record*, 10, October 1974, pp. 102–03.

Birksted, Jan, 'Sert's hilltop sanctuary for art in the South of France', in *Architects' Journal*, vol. 203, 15, 18 April 1966, pp. 28–29.

Ed., 'Three Museums. Modern art on the French Riviera', in *Architectural Forum*, vol. 120, 3, March 1964, pp. 98–103.

Ed., 'Fondation Maeght', in *Architect & Building News*, 226, July 1964, pp. 111–16.

Ed., 'La Fondation Maeght à Saint-Paul de Vence, France', in *L'Architecture d'Aujourd'hui*, 117, November 1964, pp. 82–85.

Ed., 'Neu Centre Artistique a Riviera', in *Realités*, vol. 243, April 1965, pp. 478–80.

Ed., 'Galerie Maeght, St. Paul-de-Vence, Südfrankreich', in *Deutsche Bauzeitung*, vol. 70, 6, June 1965, pp. 478–80.

Ed., 'Museumserweiterungen – Imitation als Architektursprache', in *Baumeister*, 11, November 1990, pp. 44–47.

Joly, Pierre, 'Saint-Paul de Vence – Fondation Maeght', in *Techniques et Architecture*, serie 26, 1, October 1965, pp. 88–92.

Maldiney, Henri, *Philosophie et de l'architecture par Bruno Queysanne. La fondation Maeght St-Paul-de-Vence par Henry Maldiney*, Ecole d'Architecture de Grenoble, Grenoble, 4 February 1985.

Netter, Maria, 'Die "Fondation Marguerite et Aimé Maeght" in St.-Paul-de-Vence (Alpes Maritimes)', in *Werk*, vol. 52, 6, June 1965, pp. 208–11.

Center for the Study of World Religions, Harvard University

Ed., 'New work of Sert, Jackson and Gourley. World Religions Center, Harvard University', in *Architectural Record*, vol. 131, 5, May 1962, pp. 138–39.

Ed., 'Centro per lo studio delle religioni. Harvard University. Cambridge, Mass.', in *Casabella Continuità*, 267, September 1962, pp. 10–11.

Ed., 'Centre d'études des religions. Université d'Harvard. Etats Unis', in *L'Architecture d'Aujourdhui*, 125, April–May 1966, pp. 98–99.

Office Building for the New England Gas and Electric Association

Ed., 'Skip-Stops on Module', in *Architectural Forum*, vol. 116, January 1962, pp. 72–75.

Ed., 'Uffici per la NEGEA Corporation, Cambridge, Massachusetts', in *Casabella Continuità*, 267, September 1962, pp. 12–15.

Ed., 'Office building for NEGEA Corporation, Cambridge, USA', in *Architectural Design*, vol. XXXIV, 4, April 1964, p. 181.

Francis Greenwood Peabody Terrace, Married Student Apartments, Harvard University

Anderson, Stanford, 'Sert's concept of living', in *Architectural Design*, vol. XXXV, 8, August 1965, p. 376.

Anderson, Stanford, 'Married students' dormitory, Harvard', in John Donat (ed.), *World Architecture 3*, Studio Vista, London, 1966, pp. 68–71.

Dixon, John Morris, 'Yesterday's paradigm, today's problem. Sert's 1960s embodiment of housing ideals has become a 1990s challenge for the firm of Bruner/Cott', in *Progressive Architecture*, vol. 75, 6, June 1994, pp. 100–07.

Ed., 'Harvard married students apartments', in *Architectural Record*, vol. 134, 3, September 1963, pp. 208–09.

Ed., 'Married students residence completed at Harvard', in *Architectural Record*, November 1964, pp. 12–13.

Ed., 'Harvard's new married students housing', in *Progressive Architecture*, December 1964, pp. 122–33.

Ed., 'Université d'Harvard. Résidence d'étudiants mariés', in *L'Architecture d'Aujourdhui*, 120, April–May 1965, pp. 82–84.

Ed., 'The 1965 A.I.A. Awards. Sert, Jackson & Gourley', in *A.I.A. Journal*, vol. 44, 1, July 1965, pp. 23–46 (26–27).

Ed., 'Married students housing, Harvard', in *Architectural Design*, vol. XXXV, 8, August 1965, pp. 377–82.

Ed., 'Wohnhäuser für Studenten, Harvard University, Cambridge/

USA', in *Deutsche Bauzeitung*, 70, September 1965, pp. 747–50.

Ed., 'Harvard's new married students housing', in *Kenchiku Bunka*, 20:229, November 1965, pp. 101–08.

Ed., 'Unità residenziale per studenti', in *Casabella*, 300, December 1965, pp. 62–69.

Ed., 'Studentenwohnheim für Ehepaare, Harvard Universität in Cambridge, Massachusetts', in *Baumeister*, 63, March 1966, pp. 261–68.

Giedion, Sigfried, 'New ventures in university buildings (Le Corbusier, Sert)', in *Zodiac*, 16, July 1966, pp. 24–34.

Hale, Jonathan, 'Ten years past at Peabody Terrace', in *Progressive Architecture*, October 1974, pp. 72–77.

Tzonis, Alexander, Liane Lefaivre and Richard Diamod, 'Francis Green-wood Peabody Terrace', in *Architecture in North America since 1960*, Thames and Hudson, London, 1995, pp. 100–01.

Can Pep Simó Development
Julbe, Félix and Rafael García Pascuet, 'Josep Lluís Sert. Urbanización en Cap Martinet', in *Arquitecturas en Ibiza*, Publicación de la Delegación en Ibiza y Formentera del Colegio de Arquitectos de Baleares, 6–7–8, Ibiza, 1983, pp. 79–166.

Rovira, Josep Maria, *Urbanización en Punta Martinet, Ibiza, 1966–1971*, Colegio de Arquitectos de Almería, Almería, 1996.

Torres, Elías, 'Urbanización Can Pep Simó', in *Guía de Arquitectura de Ibiza y Formentera: islas Pitiusas*, La Gaya Ciencia, COAC, Barcelona, 1981, pp. 113–15.

Villagómez Llobet, Marià, 'Forma i color en l'arquitectura eivissenca de Josep Lluís Sert', in *Lluc*, 596, November 1970, pp. 20–21.

University of Guelph
Dubois, Macy, 'Towards a new prose architecture', in *The Canadian Architect*, vol. 13, November 1968, pp. 33–34.

Ed., 'Ausbau der Universität Guelph/Kanada', in *Bauwelt* 35, 26 August 1968, pp. 1092–95.

Ed., 'Art and Library Buildings, University of Guelph, Ontario', in *The Canadian Architect*, vol. 13, November 1968, pp. 31–47.

Ed., 'Designing for growth: The metamorphosis of a rural campus into a university town', in *Architectural Record*, vol. 151, 5, May 1972, pp. 89–98.

Joan Miró Foundation
Bartolomé, José Luis, 'Análisis de la Fundación Joan Miró de Barcelona', in *Jano*, 30, September 1975, p. 51.

Benet, Amèlia, 'Josep Lluís Sert i la Fundació Miró', in *Tretzevents*, annata 38, 587, 1990, pp. 8–9.

Cirici, Alexandre, 'La Fundació Joan Miró obre les portes', in *Serra d'Or*, 15 June 1975, pp. 79–82.

Denti, Giovanni, 'Fondazione Miró. Armonie fuori tendenza', in *Costruire*, 103, December 1991.

Denti, Giovanni and Amedeo Zilioli, *Josep Lluís Sert. La Fondazione Miró di Barcellona*, Momenti di Architettura Moderna, Alinea, Firenze, 1992.

Ed., 'Fundación Joan Miró de Barcelona', in *Jano*, 30, September 1975, pp. 50–65.

Ed., 'Fondation Juan Miro. Parc Montjuich. Barcelone, Espagne', in *Architecture*, 396, April 1976, pp. 24–25.

Ed., 'Centre d'Etudes d'Art Contemporain, Barcelone. Architecte: José-Luis Sert', in *L'Architecture d'Aujour-d'hui*, 185, May–June 1976, p. XXVIII.

Ed., 'Centre for the study of contemporary art – Joan Miró Foundation, Montjuic Park, Barcelona, Spain 1975', in *A+U. Architecture and Urbanism*, 85, December 1977, pp. 25–32.

Ed., 'Conversación con Francesc Vicens', in *On Diseño*, 3, May 1979, pp. 44–48.

Ed., 'Fundació Miró. Creix l'edifici de Josep Lluís Sert', in *Barcelona Metropolis Mediterrània*, 5, July–September 1987, pp. 165–66.

Ed., 'Museumserweiterungen. Imitation als Architektursprache', in *Baumeister*, vol. 87, 11, November 1990, pp. 44–47.

Ferrer, David, 'Las últimas obras de J. LL. Sert en Barcelona. Roda el mòn i torna al Born', in *Arquitecturas Bis*, 6, March 1975, pp. 2, 7–9.

Garín Llombart and V. Felipe, 'Testimonio de un encuentro', in *Cimal*, 17, November 1982, pp. 9–10.

Joly, Pierre, 'Miró & Sert à Barcelone', in *L'Œil*, 242, September 1975, pp. 34–37.

Mackay, David, 'Sert for Miró', in *The Architectural Review*, 953, July 1976, pp. 34–36.

Malet, Rosa Maria, 'Dinàmica i arquitectura a la Fundació Joan Miró', in *Barcelona Metròpolis Mediterránea*, 7, spring 1988, pp. 6–7.

Minola de Gallotti, Marianna, 'Centro-studi di arte contemporanea "Fundación Joan Miró" nel parco de Montjuich, Barcellona', in *L'Architettura cronache e storia*, 241, November 1975, pp. 400–05.

Miró Rufà, Josep Maria, 'Fundació Joan Miró. Centre d'Estudis d'Art Contemporani', in *Cuadernos de Arquitectura y Urbanismo*, 107, March 1975, pp. 40–50.

Montaner, Josep Maria, 'Más Sert para Miró. Un museo que crece', in *Arquitectura Viva*, 1, June 1988, pp. 18–20.

Olmo, Santiago B., 'El sueño de un artista', in *Lápiz*, 91, February 1993, pp. 52–55.

Osman, Mary E., 'An art center around a luminescent core: The Joan Miró Foundation – Center for Studies of Contemporary Art, Barcelona, Spain; architects: Sert, Jackson and Associates', in *A.I.A. Journal*, vol. 68, 6, May 1979, pp. 164–69.

Penrose, Roland, 'A Study Centre of Contemporary Art', in *The Architectural Review*, 953, July 1976, pp. 37–43.

Schmertz, Mildred F., 'Homage to Catalonia: a contemporary art Museum in Barcelona by Sert, Jackson & Associates', in *Architectural Record*, 3, March 1977, pp. 85–92.

Sert, Josep Lluís, 'La Fondation Joan Miró. Centre pour l'étude de l'art contemporain à Barcelone', in *Museum*, vol. XXXI, 4, 1979, pp. 246–53.

Zevi, Bruno, *Arquitectura de Sert a la Fundació Miró*, Polígrafa, Barcelona, 1976; Barcelona S.A., Barcelona, 1977.

Science Center, Harvard University, Cambridge
Ed., 'Science Center is precast for fast assembly', in *Architectural Record*, vol. 151, 2, February 1972, pp. 129–32.

Ed., 'Harvard urbanizzata', in *L'Architettura cronache e storia*, 228, October 1974, pp. 388–89.

Ed., 'Harvard Science Center', in *A+U. Architecture and Urbanism*, 54, June 1975, pp. 97–106.

Osman, Mary E., 'A science center that is also a "street": Undergraduate Science Center, Harvard University, Cambridge, Massachusetts', in *A.I.A. Journal*, vol. 68, 6, May 1979, pp. 170–71.

Schmertz, Mildred F., 'High density design for undergraduate science at land-starved Harvard', in *Architectural Record*, March 1974, pp. 111–18.

Spring, Bernard P., 'Evaluation: well used "pathway": Josep Lluis Sert's Harvard Undergraduate Science Center', in *Architecture A.I.A.*, vol. 74, 4, April 1985, pp. 88–93.

Housing on Roosevelt Island
Agrest, Diana, Latour, Alessandra,

'Roosevelt Island housing compétition', in *L'Architecture d'Aujourd'hui*, 186, August–September 1976, pp. 22–35 (25–27).

Ed., 'Roosevelt Island', in *Architectural Record*, vol. 154, 7, December 1973, pp. 98–99.

Ed., 'Eastwood, Roosevelt Island, New York City', in *Architectural Record*, 8, August 1976, pp. 102–08.

Ed., 'Selearchitettura: Sert sulla Roosevelt Island', in *L'Architettura cronache e storia*, 10, February 1977, pp. 582–83.

Krog, Steven R., 'Evaluation: the fabric of Roosevelt Island', in *A.I.A. Journal*, vol. 68, 5, May 1979, pp. 38–47.

Stern, Robert A. M., Thomas Mellis and David Fishman, 'Roosevelt Island', in *New York 1960. Architecture and Urbanism between the Second World War and the Bicentennial*, The Monacelli Press Inc., New York, 1960, 1995, p. 645.

Riverview Residential Complex, Yonkers, New York

Ed., 'New concrete forming techniques tried for multi-story housing. The speed of cycling the forms is directly related to the repetition and tipicality of the structural volumes', in *Architectural Record*, vol. 159, 4, October 1973, pp. 162–63.

Ed., 'Riverview Yonkers, N.Y.', in *Architectural Record*, 8, August 1976, pp. 108–09.

Rosenthal, Steve, 'Housing from the '70s: what we did right, what we did wrong', in *Architectural Record*, vol. 182, 4, April 1994, pp. 22–25.

Casa Blajot

Ed., 'Una casa del arquitecto Sert', in *TG Revista de las Artes Decorativas*, 3, March 1983, pp. 22–27.

Macià i Bigorra, Teresa, 'Sert redescobert. Una obra desconeguda de l'arquitecte i una altra restaurada per ell, a Arenys del Mar', in *El País*, 30 November 1989, Quadern, p. 8.

Chronology of Works

1928
Hotel on a Beach (competition project), *with J. Torres, J.B. Subirana*

1928–29
Summer Resort Town in Levante (project), *with J. Torres, J. B. Subirana*
Apartment Building on Carrer Roselló 36, Barcelona

1929–31
Apartment Buildings in Carrer Muntaner 342-348, Barcelona

1929–30
Casa Duclós, Carrer Ceán Bermúdez 5, Seville

1930
Casa Galobart, Travessera de Dalt 102, Barcelona (destroyed)

1931–36
Casa Bloc, Avinguda Torres i Bages 91-105 e 107, Barcelona

1931–35
City of Leisure and Vacations, Viladecans-Gavà-Castelldefels, Barcelona (project), *with GATCPAC*

1932–35
Macià Plan, Barcelona (project), *with GATCPAC, Le Corbusier*

1932
School Development in Avinguda Bogatell, Barcelona (project)

1934
Roca Jewellery Shop, Paseo de Gràcia 18, Barcelona

1935
Weekend Houses in El Garraf, Garraf Coast, Barcelona (modified and destroyed), *with J. Torres*

1933–37
Central Dispensary for Tuberculosis, Passatge de Sant Bernat 10, Car-

rer Torres Amat s.n., Barcelona, *with J. Torres, J.B. Subirana*, (restored in 1992 by M. Corea, F. Gallardo Bravo, E. Mannino)

1937
Pavilion of the Spanish Republic at the Paris World's Fair, *with L. Lacasa* (rebuilt in 1992 by M. Espinet, A. Ubach, J. M. Hernández-Leon, in Avinguda Cardenal Vidal i Barraquer, Carrer Jorge Manrique, Barcelona)

1943–45
Ratio Structures, *with P.L. Wiener, P. Schulz*

1943–47
Cidade dos Motores, Brazil (project), *TPA (Town Planning Associates: J.L. Sert, P.L. Wiener, P. Schulz); Otto da Rocha*

1946–48
Chimbote Pilot Plan, Peru (project), *TPA (Town Planning Associates: J.L. Sert, P.L. Wiener, P. Schulz)*

1947
Lima Pilot Plan, Peru (project), *TPA (Town Planning Associates: J.L. Sert, P.L. Wiener, P. Schulz)*

1948–49
Tumaco Pilot Plan, Colombia (project), *TPA (Town Planning Associates: J.L. Sert, P.L. Wiener, P. Schulz); G. Samper, E. Mejía, H. Vieco, A. Pradilla, L. Amorocho, F. Martínez, E. Burbano*

1948–52
Medellin Pilot Plan, Colombia (project), *TPA (Town Planning Associates: J.L. Sert, P.L. Wiener, P. Schulz); Le Corbusier*

1949–50
Cali Pilot Plan, Colombia (project), *TPA (Town Planning Associates: J.L. Sert, P.L. Wiener, P. Schulz)*

1949–53
Bogotá Pilot Plan, Colombia (project), *TPA (Town Planning Associates: J.L. Sert, P.L. Wiener, P. Schulz); Le Corbusier, H. Ritter*

1949
Sert's House in Locust Valley, Long Island, New York

1951–53
Plan for Ciudad Piar, Orinoco Valley, Venezuela, *TPA (Town Planning Associates: J.L. Sert, P.L. Wiener, P. Schulz); Carlos Guinand Baldo, Moisés Benacerraf*
Church and Civic Centre, Puerto Ordaz, Venezuela, *TPA (Town Planning Associates: J.L. Sert, P.L. Wiener, P. Schulz)*

1952–53
Apartment Buildings at Pomona, Maracaibo, Venezuela, *TPA (Town Planning Associates: J.L. Sert, P.L. Wiener, P. Schulz); Carlos Guinand Baldo, Moisés Benacerraf*

1953–57
Joan Miró's Studio, Camí de Son Abrines, Palma de Mallorca, *with E. Juncosa*

1955
United States Embassy, Grosvenor Square, London (competition project), *Sert, Jackson and Gourley*

1955–61
United States Embassy, Baghdad, *Sert, Jackson and Gourley*

1955–58
Havana Pilot Plan, Cuba, *TPA (Town Planning Associates: J.L. Sert, P.L. Wiener, P. Schulz); Seelye, Stevenson, Value, Knecht*

1956–58
Sert's house, 64 Francis Avenue, Cambridge, Massachusetts

1958–65
Holyoke Center, Harvard University, 1350 Massachusetts Avenue, Cambridge, Massachusetts, *Sert, Jackson and Gourley*

1959–66
Boston University Campus, Commonwealth Avenue, Boston, Massachusetts: George Sherman Union Student Centre, *Sert, Jackson and Gourley; Hoyle, Doran and Berry*; Mugar Library, *Sert, Jackson and Gourley; Hoyle, Doran and Berry*; Central Campus, Law and Education Tower, Pappas Law Library, Auditorium, *Sert, Jackson and Gourley; E. T. Steffian*

1959–60
Georges Braque House, Saint-Paul-de-Vence, Alpes Maritimes (project)

1959–64/1974–79
Marguerite e Aimé Maeght Foundation, Saint-Paul-de-Vence, Alpes Maritimes

1960
Center for the Study of World Religions, Harvard University, Francis Avenue, Cambridge, Massachusetts, *Sert, Jackson and Gourley*

1960–61
Sert's house, Carrer Muralla 12–13, Dalt Vila, Ibiza

1961
Office building for the New England Gas and Electric Association (NEGEA), 130 Austin Street, Cambridge, Massachusetts, *Sert, Jackson and Gourley*

1962–64
Francis Greenwood Peabody Terrace, Married Student Apartments, Harvard University, 900 Memorial Drive, Cambridge, Massachusetts, *Sert, Jackson and Gourley*

1963–71

Can Pep Simó Development, Cap Martinet, Santa Eulàlia del Riu, Ibiza, *J.L. Sert (general plan), E. Broner, S. Illescas, G. Rodríguez Arias, J.L. Sert (works)*

1966–73

Les Escales Park, Barcelona, *Sert, Jackson and Associates; Anglada, Gelabert, Ribas*

1967–68

University of Guelph, Ontario, *Hancock, Little, Calvert, Associates; Sert, Jackson and Associates*

1968–72

Convent of Carmel de la Paix, Mazille, Saône-et-Loire (project)

1968–75

Study Centre for Contemporary Art, Joan Miró Foundation, Avenida Miramar s.n., Barcelona, *Sert, Jackson and Associates; J. Freixa; Anglada, Gelabert, Ribas* (enlarged by J. Freixa in 1987–88)

Science Center, Harvard University, 1 Oxford Street, Cambridge, Massachusetts, *Sert, Jackson and Associates*

1968–72

Martin Luther King School, Putnam Avenue-Magee Street, Cambridge, Massachusetts, *Sert, Jackson and Associates*

1970–73

Office Building on 44 Brattle Street, Cambridge, Massachusetts, *Sert, Jackson and Associates*

1970–76

Housing on Roosevelt Island, 510-580 Main Street (East Side), 595-625 Main Street (West Side), Roosevelt Island, New York, *Sert, Jackson and Associates*

1972–74

Riverview Residential Complex, Riverdale Avenue, Yonkers, *Sert, Jackson and Associates*

1978-79

Casa Blajot, Premià de Dalt, Barcelona

Index of Names

The photographic material published in this volume has been kindly provided by:
Jaume Freixa Archives, Fundació Joan Miró, Barcelona
The Paul Lester Wiener Collection, BX 55. Division of Special Collections and University Archives, University of Oregon Library System, Eugene, Oregon
Sigfried Giedion Archives, ETH, Zurich
Fondation Le Corbusier, Paris; Sert Collection, Cambridge, Massachusetts
Josep M. Rovira Archive
Daniel Rovira Archive

Holders of rights to any unidentified photographs are invited to bring the matter to the attention of the publishers